# Rendezvous with Ada 95

*Second Edition*

# Rendezvous with Ada 95

**Second Edition**

## David Naiditch

**John Wiley & Sons, Inc.**

New York • Chichester • Brisbane • Totonto • Singapore

Publisher: Katherine Schowalter
Senior Editor: Diane D. Cerra
Managing Editor: Robert S. Aronds
Editorial Production & Design: Publishers' Design and Production Services, Inc.

*Library of Congress Cataloging-in-Publication Data:*

Naiditch, David.
    Rendezvous with Ada 95 / David Naiditch. — 2nd ed.
        p.    cm.
    Rev. ed. of: Rendezvous with Ada. c1989.
    Includes index.
    ISBN 0-471-01276-9 (paper : acid-free paper)
    1. Ada (Computer program language)    I. Naiditch, David.
Rendezvous with Ada.    II. Title.
QA76.73.A35N35    1995
005.13'3—dc20                                                          94-32049
                                                                                  CIP

Printed in the United States of America
10  9  8  7  6  5  4  3  2  1

*To my parents, Sam and Hannah Naiditch, and my wife's parents,
Al and Shirley Wittenberg*

# Contents

# Acknowledgments

I would like to thank my wife, Jacqueline Naiditch, who was the Technical Editor for this book. Jacqueline did extensive rewriting and consulting with me to ensure clarity and conciseness.

I would also like to thank Mike Assennato, who reviewed the text for technical accuracy and completeness.

# Introduction

In the early 1970s, there was a full-blown software crisis. Department of Defense (DOD) funds were being rapidly drained by exorbitant software costs. In 1973, software costs constituted $3 billion of the $7.5 billion spent by the DOD on computer systems. These costs were primarily caused by a plethora of programming languages and the "primitive" nature of these languages.

The huge number of languages—more than 450—was created by the military, defense agencies, and system project offices, which kept spawning new languages from existing ones in order to meet project requirements. With numerous languages came numerous problems. For instance, languages were largely incompatible; they could not easily "talk" to each other. Another problem with numerous languages was that software was not portable: it could not be easily transported to different computers or projects. Similarly, software engineers could not transfer their skills across a broad spectrum of projects; rather, they had to become highly specialized. The many languages also resulted in minimal software being available for each language, as well as restricted competition in the maintenance and enhancement phases of projects. Competition was restricted because a competitor had to bear the initial investment—including support software and programmer training—already made by the developer of a language.

In addition to the overabundance of computer languages, the existing languages were inadequate because they were primitive—they did not support modern software engineering principles. Thus, code was difficult to maintain because it was hard to read and understand. The code lacked clear structure and contained low-level details that would have been hidden by a more modern language. The failure to support modern software engineering principles also resulted in software that was hard to reuse, because units of code were so interdependent. Modules often could not be extracted and used in different programs. This interdependency also made it difficult to modify code without introducing unwelcome side effects.

All of the problems mentioned were especially severe in embedded systems. An embedded system is one in which a computer is part of a larger system, such as computerized radar used in aircraft. Embedded systems are typically complex real-time systems that contain many lines of code, are long lived, and are continually being modified. Because of the size, complexity, life span, and volatility of these systems, they were responsible for 56% of DOD software costs in 1973. Interestingly, most of this money was spent on maintaining embedded system software after it was written, not on its original development.

The software crisis, then, included problems such as software being excessively expensive, not portable, difficult to maintain, and not reusable. All of these problems were exacerbated in embedded systems. Clearly, something had to be done to help address this crisis. The "something" was Ada.

In this chapter, we explore the development of the Ada programming language, both in its original Ada 83 form and in its updated Ada 95 form. We then examine a sample Ada program that illustrates the basic features of Ada. The chapter ends with a brief discussion of the language features introduced by Ada 83, followed by those features introduced by Ada 95.

## DEVELOPMENT OF ADA 83

In 1975, the DOD acted to reverse the trend of proliferating computer languages. Instead of hundreds of languages, only one computer language would be used. To determine which language would become the new standard, a requirements document was written for a high-level language appropriate for embedded computer systems.

The requirements document was sent to interested civilians and military personnel. These people reviewed the document and sent their comments to the joint-service High Order Language Working Group (HOLWG), which had been organized to write the requirements document.

As the requirements document was evaluated by members of the software community, it went through many revisions. When the requirements document became relatively well-established, it was used as the basis for an international design competition. There were 15 bidders who entered the competition. The winner of the competition was Cii-Honeywell Bull.

In 1979, the winning language was named Ada. Note that this name is not an acronym. The acronym ADA stands for the American Dental Association or the Americans with Disabilities Act. Rather, this new language was named in honor of Ada, the Countess of Lovelace and daughter of the famous poet, Lord Byron. Ada Lovelace lived in the early 1800s, was a mathematician, and is often given the honor of being considered the first computer "programmer." Her programs were written for a computer designed by Charles Babbage. The computer, called the Analytical Engine, was never built because the technology was not sophisticated enough to manufacture gears and levers of the required precision. Development of such a computer had to await the age of electronics, about 100 years after Ada developed her computer programs.

The language now had a name but was still called Preliminary Ada. Before being standardized, Ada went through an extremely rigorous test and evaluation phase, again unprecedented by any other language. Approximately 80 teams of programmers reviewed the language and suggested changes. In October 1979, a workshop was held, with presentations and discussions. The resulting 900 comments were analyzed by a company contracted by the DOD and by a group of language experts called the "distinguished reviewers." As always, comments were solicited from people in diverse fields: academia, industry, DOD, and consulting firms. Finally, in February 1983, Ada was published as a standard: ANSI/MIL-STD-1815A. The number 1815 was selected since this is the year that Ada Lovelace was born.

Ada 83 offers many advantages over other programming languages. For instance, since Ada is defined in great detail, and since no subsets or supersets are allowed, Ada source code may be ported between different Ada compiler systems, with minimal changes. In addition to code portability, people portability is enhanced. Programmers can move from project to project without having to learn new languages.

As we have seen, Ada 83 was primarily developed for large embedded systems. To lower development and maintenance costs, Ada provides features for making code more maintainable and reusable. For reliability, Ada provides many compile-time and runtime checks. Since embedded systems often run on multiprocessor systems, Ada supports concurrent programming. Since such systems often need to communicate with the environment in which they are embedded, Ada supports low-level programming features. Finally, to manage the complexity of such systems, Ada supports sound software engineering principles.

For maintainability, Ada emphasizes the ease of reading code over the ease of writing code. As we previously mentioned, it costs more to maintain code over many years than it does to originally develop the code. Therefore, even though more keystrokes may be required to enter an Ada program, the extra effort is well worth it if the program reads better. Code that is easy to read is easy to understand and hence easy to maintain.

Besides maintainability, software reusability is another way of bringing down software costs. Why develop and test new software components when such components already exist that have been tested on previous projects? Ada, therefore, provides features such as generics (to be discussed later) that can be employed to make software very flexible and general purpose, allowing it to serve the needs of many different clients.

Besides maintainability and reusability, Ada emphasizes reliability, by catching as many errors as possible at compile time and the rest at runtime. Reliability is critical when people's lives depend on the software working properly. For example, a program monitoring a heart patient or nuclear power plant must operate day and night without error. An unexpected event, such as the illegal mathematical operation of dividing by zero, cannot cause the program to abort without warning. Instead, the program must intercept the error, take corrective action, and continue normal processing. Ada provides such support through its exception-handling mechanism.

Another requirement of Ada is to support concurrent programming. Even back in 1983 when Ada was first adopted, computer scientists realized computers would be developed that contain more and more processors. For the software to fully exploit multiple processors, chunks of code need to be allocated to each processor, to be run in parallel. In Ada, such chunks of code are called tasks. Ada is one of the few languages that defines tasks.

Ada also supports low-level programming, which is needed for applications such as embedded software that must communicate with the "outside world." The outside world may be the underlying hardware, a peripheral device such as a printer or disk drive, or even code written in other languages. To communicate with the outside world, Ada provides low-level features to get down to the bit and byte level. Specifically, Ada supports access to machine instructions, hardware interrupts, addresses, and so on.

Finally, developing large complex programs requires a highly disciplined approach to software engineering. Ada helps manage the complexity and improve the maintainability of software by supporting sound software engineering principles. Software engineering principles include modularity, strong typing, data abstraction, and information hiding.

Modularity means that a program can be written as many separately compiled modules. This makes code much easier to understand and maintain than if the program had been written as one monolithic structure. For example, when a module is modified and recompiled, typically few, if any, other modules need to be recompiled. However, if the program is written as one monolithic structure, then any change, no matter how minor, requires the recompilation of the entire program. Also, when code is broken down into modules, these modules can easily be farmed out to programmers working on the same project.

Although modules are separately compiled, they are not independently compiled. To reduce errors, the Ada compilation system makes sure that the modules properly interface with each other and that a change to one module does not render other modules obsolete.

Finally, Ada clearly separates a module's interface from its implementation. This separation encourages programmers to keep the interconnections between modules simple and well-defined.

The principle of strong typing mandates that every object belong to a type and have a clearly defined set of values and operations. (An object is a variable or constant that can hold a value.) The compiler reduces coding errors by preventing objects of different types from inadvertently being compared or assigned to one another. The compiler also prevents an operation from being applied to an object of the wrong type. In Ada, type checking is performed at compile time, both within and across modules.

Information hiding helps enforce data abstraction. Data abstraction enables the programmer to extract essential properties of an item while ignoring irrelevant details. These irrelevant details can be made inaccessible by hiding them. Thus, reliability is improved, because coding strategies cannot be based on these hidden details.

## DEVELOPMENT OF ADA 95

**Ada 95 ▶** Although Ada is a very good language for most applications, much has been learned since it was introduced in 1983. Since 1983, new software methodologies, such as object-oriented programming, have become popular. Ada 83 is often said to be object based but not fully object oriented because it lacks some of the essential ingredients of object-oriented programming. Missing functionality has also been identified. For example, Ada 83 fails to provide pointers that can point to declared objects, functions, and procedures. Furthermore, a few problem areas of Ada 83 have been discovered. For example, in Ada 83, the contract model for generics can be breached, and private types are too private for code reusers.

The goal of Ada 95 is to fix the problems with Ada 83, to generalize and simplify Ada 83 features that are unreasonably restrictive or complex, and to provide enhancements that will satisfy the special needs of many different application domains. The goal is to do all this without negatively impacting the existing Ada community, without compromising software reliability and long-term maintainability, and without degrading performance. To minimize impact, emphasis was given to upward compatibility between Ada 83 and Ada 95. As a result, most Ada 83 code can be compiled with little or no modification on Ada 95 compilers. Also to minimize impact, solutions to Ada 83 problems are provided by extending or generalizing existing Ada features rather than inventing radically new features.

Many of Ada's new features add flexibility to the language and eliminate unnecessary restrictions. Such new features, however, were carefully scrutinized to make sure that software reliability and long-term maintainability were not compromised. For example, pointers can now point to regularly declared objects, which they could not do in Ada 83. The implementation of this new feature, however, includes checks to guarantee that the object does not cease to exist while it is still being pointed to. If this were to be allowed, the pointer would be left pointing to some "garbage" value. Such "dangling pointers" are a main cause of errors in other, less reliable languages.

The new language features were also scrutinized to make sure that they would not significantly slow down execution speed or result in significantly larger executable modules. Furthermore, new features were designed so that any space or time overhead would only be incurred when the feature was used. Code not using the new feature would not be penalized.

To verify that Ada 95 meets the preceding goals, three teams were established, each consisting of a user and an implementor. Users were represented by companies experienced in developing Ada code. To get a broad sampling of users, companies were selected that developed software for different kinds of applications. The implementors were represented by different Ada compiler vendors interested in developing Ada 95 compilers. These user/implementor teams verified that Ada 95 features could be implemented efficiently and could be of significant benefit to software developers.

The decision to revise Ada was made in 1988. The first step in the revision process was to identify the new Ada requirements. The Ada user community submitted numerous revision requests. These requests were categorized and evaluated. A final set of 41 requirements was developed from the revision requests. Requirements that were incompletely understood or whose solutions were uncertain became "study topics." There were 22 study topics. The goal was to satisfy all important requirements and as many study topics as possible. Unresolved study topics were shelved, to be examined sometime in the next century when Ada may again be updated.

After the new Ada requirements were identified, changes to the Ada language were defined to satisfy these requirements. Intermetrics (one of the finalists for Ada 83) was awarded the contract to modify the Ada language to accommodate the new requirements.

Ada 95 was developed by searching for deep-rooted needs underlying the numerous revision requests. No attempt was made to provide a special new language feature for each identified need. Rather, a limited number of features was designed to be used in combination to satisfy many needs.

Whereas many of the requirements and study topics for Ada 95 were of general user interest, some were of specialized interest. A requirement of general interest is programming by extension, which allows new features to be added to existing software without impacting the existing software or its clients. Another such requirement is the support for an international character set, or support for programming paradigms such as object-oriented programming. Topics of specialized interest include parallel or distributed processing and support for outputting formatted monetary information with properly aligned currency symbols and numeric fields.

A dilemma was soon reached in the development process. Requiring all Ada 95 compilers to meet all the specialized requirements would make these compilers too expensive and large. On the other hand, allowing compilers to implement customized extensions to the Ada language would result in the proliferation of uncontrolled supersets of Ada, destroying Ada's portability and standardization. After much debate, a solution to the dilemma was reached: specialized-needs annexes. These annexes are additions to the core language catering to particular kinds of programming applications. Validated Ada compilers must implement the core Ada language in its entirety. The annexes are optional, but, when provided, must be separately validated. To be validated, an annex must be fully implemented. (An implementation may provide additional capabilities in an annex, as long as the capabilities specified by the annex are all met.)

Although annexes are language "extensions," they can only extend the Ada language in ways that Ada has always allowed: by providing new packages, pragmas, attributes, and capacity and performance constraints. Annexes are not allowed to introduce new keywords or to deviate from the core part of the Ada language. As it turns out, many annex features have been provided in nonstandard ways by Ada 83 implementations. Ada 95 standardizes these features.

Areas covered by the annexes are systems programming, real-time systems, distributed systems, information systems, numerics, and safety and security. The systems programming annex is primarily for programmers needing low-level programming features in order to develop software such as operating systems and linkers. The real-time annex is primarily for defense and aerospace projects that deal with embedded systems such as computer-controlled radars on satellites, planes, and ships. The distributed systems annex is primarily for applications that distribute Ada programs across loosely coupled processors. The information systems annex is primarily for business applications that require features such as decimal-scaled numbers needed for performing monetary calculations, and formatted output with properly placed currency symbols. The numerics annex is primarily for programmers performing intensive mathematical calculations for scientific and engineering applications. The safety and security annex is designed for programmers using Ada in safety-critical applications, such as the control of a nuclear power plant or for systems that have classified components that must be protected from unauthorized users.

In summary, annexes provide standardized language features needed by programmers of specialized applications but without forcing these features to be implemented for programmers who do not need them. Ada 95 enhancements to the core language are thus restricted to those that can be of general benefit to the Ada community.

Despite these annexes, many new features were added to the core language. As a result, Ada 95 is more complex than Ada 83, although some of the features of Ada 83 have been simplified. The added complexity, however, is more than compensated for by the increased flexibility and power of Ada 95.

Those wishing to transition from Ada 83 to Ada 95 will find that most of their Ada 83 code will compile with Ada 95 compilers without any modification. Modifications that are needed will tend to be trivial. Those currently writing Ada 83 code, who expect to transition to Ada 95 in the future, may wish to impose coding restrictions to make the eventual transition as easy as possible. Such coding restrictions can be extracted from Appendix A of the *Ada 95 Rationale* document. This appendix provides detailed coverage of all the upward compatibility issues.

Although Ada 95 is very upwardly compatible, to fully exploit the new Ada features, Ada 83 code must be significantly modified, and Ada 83 programmers must be retrained. For example, adding object-oriented features requires major design modifications and requires that programmers understand object-oriented methodology.

Let us now give a brief overview of Ada. When learning a large, complex language such as Ada, there is a risk of initially focusing too much on the details and not seeing the overall structure of the language. Since this chapter is an overview, concepts and features of the language are introduced that will not be fully explored until later in the book. Read this chapter, then, without expecting to fully understand everything; concentrate on getting a feel for the Ada language.

## A SAMPLE PROGRAM

Let us begin the overview by examining an Ada program that, despite its simplicity, illustrates many important features of Ada. These features include control structures, the context specification, procedures, packages, generic instantiation, input/output operations, the Ada.Text_IO package, overloading, default parameter values, and the Ada library:

```
with Ada.Text_IO; use Ada.Text_IO;   -- context specification
     -- equivalent to with Text_IO; use Text_IO
procedure Totem_Pole is    -- procedure specification
                           -- (excluding the keyword is)
     -- declarative part
     Totems : Integer := 1;
     package Int_IO is new Integer_IO (Integer);
     use Int_IO;

begin

     -- statement part
     Put_Line ("How many faces in the Totem Pole?");
     Get (Totems);

     New_Line;     -- advances 1 line on screen
     Put ("Here is a Totem Pole with "); -- outputs a string
     Put (Totems);    -- outputs an integer
     Put (" faces:");    -- outputs a string
     New_Line (2);

     for Faces in 1..Totems loop    -- for loop
        Put_Line ("\\\\\\\\\");
        Put_Line ("|(*) | (*)|");
        Put_Line ("|    o    |");
        Put_Line ("_____/");
     end loop;

end Totem_Pole;
```

If you have access to an Ada compiler, try compiling and running this program. A sample run of the program follows:

```
How many faces in the Totem Pole?
> 3

Here is a Totem Pole with  3 faces:


\\\\\\\\
|(*)|(*)|
|   o   |
_____/
\\\\\\\\
|(*)|(*)|
|   o   |
_____/
```

```
\ \ \ \ \ \ \ \
| ( * ) | ( * ) |
|    o     |
_____/
```

The user is first prompted for the number of faces to be placed in the totem pole. The user's response is entered after the prompt, >. In this sample run, the user enters the number 3. The user is then informed that a totem pole consisting of 3 faces follows, and the totem pole is output.

We will begin our discussion of this program with a few general comments. We will then explain the program line by line. When you look at the code, the first thing you might notice is that words are written two different ways: in lowercase bold letters and in "mixed-case" (uppercase and lowercase) letters.

The words in lowercase bold letters, called keywords, are those that have special meaning in the Ada language. These words are printed in boldface letters to help flag them out to the reader. The keywords used in our example are **with, use, procedure, is, package, new, begin, for, in, loop,** and **end.** For a complete list of keywords, see Chapter 2.

Words that appear in mixed-case letters are identifiers (names) of items such as variables, constants, types, procedures, and packages. Mixed-case letters are also used in strings and comments. Strings consist of text that appears within double quotes. Comments consist of text that follows two hyphens.

This use of uppercase, lowercase, and boldface letters follows the conventions used in the *Ada 95 Reference Manual*. As far as Ada is concerned, uppercase letters are indistinguishable from lowercase letters. However, as far as humans are concerned, uppercase letters are easily distinguished from lowercase letters, and choosing one versus the other can greatly affect the readability of code. For readability, the first character of each word should be uppercase; the other characters should be lowercase. If the identifier consists of multiple words such as `Totem_Pole`, separate the words with an underscore. Of course, if the word is an acronym, then use all uppercase letters.

In the sample program, you may have also noticed the use of semicolons. Unlike languages such as Pascal where the semicolon is used as a separator, in Ada the semicolon is used as a terminator. Every complete Ada statement must end with a semicolon. This does not mean that every line of code ends with a semicolon. The following line of code does not end with a semicolon because it is not a complete statement:

```
for Faces in 1..Totems loop
```

This **for** loop statement is not complete because it does not end with the keyword **loop.** Rather, it ends with the keywords **end loop** several lines later in the code. The terminating semicolon therefore appears after **end loop.**

Statements like this **for** loop not only may extend through many lines of code; they may contain other statements within them. In our example, the **for** loop statement extends through six lines of code and contains four `Put_Line` statements.

The `Put_Line` statements embedded within the **for** loop are indented several spaces to the right. Even though the Ada compiler does not care how you indent your code, people who read your code do care. When embedded statements are indented, the structure of the code can easily be seen.

The layout of Ada programs, then, has an impact on how easily code can be read. This layout can vary, depending on the programmer. Again, this book closely follows the layout style presented in the *Ada 95 Reference Manual*. It is recommended that you follow a similar style. However, as just mentioned, the Ada compiler is not concerned about indentation of code or other matters of layout. The compiler even accepts the following unsightly layout:

```
-- acceptable to compilers but not to humans
with Ada.Text_IO; use Ada.Text_IO; procedure Totem_Pole is
Totems : Integer := 1; package Int_IO is new Integer_IO
(Integer); use Int_IO; begin Put_Line -- etc.
```

## Line-by-Line Analysis of Program

Let us now examine the preceding program, `Totem_Pole`, one line at a time. The first line of this program consists of two statements, which form the context specification. These statements contain the keywords **with** and **use**:

```
with Ada.Text_IO; use Ada.Text_IO; -- context specification
```

These two statements are often placed on the same line because they are frequently used together. A context specification defines the context or environment in which an Ada program exists. Context specifications play a key role in Ada. We will therefore return to this topic after we finish our line-by-line discussion of this program.

The two hyphens that appear after the context specification denote the beginning of a comment. The comment extends to the end of the line. Comments are ignored by the compiler; they are provided for the benefit of humans who read the code.

The next line in the program begins with the keyword **procedure**. In Ada, the main program is almost always a procedure. Other program units making up a program may also be procedures. Following the keyword **procedure** is a user-supplied procedure name. In this case, the procedure name is `Totem_Pole`. In Ada, a name can be of any length (as long as it fits on a single line) and can consist of uppercase and lowercase letters and embedded underscores. The procedure name is followed by the keyword **is**. A semicolon is not placed after **is**. Even though **is** appears at the end of a line of code, it does not terminate this procedure. The procedure terminates with the last line of the program:

```
end Totem_Pole;
```

In this last line, the procedure name, `Totem_Pole`, is placed between the keyword **end** and the semicolon. Repeating the procedure name at the end of a procedure is optional but highly recommended because it makes code easier to read and understand. If the procedure name is supplied, then the compiler will check to make sure that the name is correct.

The keyword **procedure,** followed by the procedure name, is known as the procedure specification. The procedure specification defines this unit of code as a procedure with the name `Totem_Pole`. The remainder of the code is known as the procedure body. The body contains the implementation of the procedure and has two parts: the declarative part and the executable statement part. The declarative part lies between the keywords **is** and **begin**. The executable statement part lies between the keywords **begin** and **end**. In the declarative part, items such as types, variables, and constants are declared. In the executable statement part, processing is performed. At runtime (as the program is executing), declarations are elaborated and executable statements are executed. The elaboration of declarations brings objects into existence, and the execution of statements manipulates or processes objects. An object is a variable (or constant) that contains a value of a specific type.

In the `Totem_Pole` example, the first declaration defines a variable, `Totems`, to be of type `Integer`:

```
Totems: Integer := 1;
```

A variable is an object that can assume different values as the program executes. An initial value may be given to a variable when it is declared. The symbol, :=, assigns the value on the right of the symbol to the variable on the left. In this example, `Totems` is given the initial integer value of 1. An integer is a whole number that has no decimal point.

The next declaration in `Totem_Pole` is an instantiation of the generic package `Integer_IO`:

```
package Int_IO is new Integer_IO (Integer);
```

Such an instantiation of the `Integer_IO` package is required whenever integers need to be input or output. The `Integer_IO` package is a generic unit, which means that it serves as a template from which actual packages are created. The effect of this instantiation is to create an "instance" of the `Integer_IO` package, called `Int_IO`. Once created, the `Int_IO` package can be used to input or output integers. Thus, even the simplest of programs often requires generic packages. However, the topic of generic packages is advanced and cannot be fully explained until Chapter 8.

The next line of code in `Totem_Pole` makes the package `Int_IO` directly visible (directly available) to the programmer:

```
use Int_IO;
```

The **use** clause will be discussed later in this chapter.

Now that we have covered all the declarations in `Totem_Pole`, we will discuss the executable statements of this procedure. Before we do so, note that the order in which declarations and executable statements are placed in a program is critical. Declarations are elaborated, and statements are executed, in the order listed in the code. As a consequence, an object must be declared before the point in the code where it is used. In our example, this requirement is satisfied since the variable Totems is declared before it is used in the **for** loop.

Now let us consider the first seven executable statements in the example. These are procedure invocations or procedure calls. These statements call other procedures that exist outside the main procedure Totem_Pole. To invoke (call) another procedure means to activate it. Unlike some computer languages, however, no keyword **call** is used.

The first of these seven procedure calls prompts users of the program to enter the number of faces that they wish to appear on the totem pole:

```
Put_Line ("How many faces in the Totem Pole?");
```

This procedure call is a Put_Line statement. A Put_Line statement outputs a string to the standard output device, which we will assume is a video screen, and then automatically advances to the next line. As previously mentioned, a string consists of text within quotes. The text appears on the screen exactly as written because, within strings, Ada distinguishes between uppercase and lowercase letters.

The next procedure call is a Get statement:

```
Get (Totems);
```

A Get statement gets input from the user as the program is running and assigns it to the variable placed in parentheses. If the user of our program, for example, enters the integer 3, then the value of the variable Totems will be set to 3. Even though Totems is initialized to 1 when it is declared, because it is a variable, this initial value may be replaced with a new value. Initializing Totems to 1, therefore, serves no purpose in this program; it is only done for illustrative purposes.

Ada is a strongly typed language. Objects belonging to different types may not mix. In our example, since Totems is declared to be an integer variable, it can only be assigned integer values. If the user enters a value that cannot be interpreted as an integer, then a type mismatch is reported and the program aborts.

The next executable statement is the following procedure call:

```
New_Line;
```

When this procedure is called, the program advances to the next line on the screen.

The next three statements output a message explaining that a totem pole follows with the number of faces previously specified by the user:

```
Put ("Here is a Totem Pole with ");     -- outputs a string
Put (Totems);                           -- outputs an integer
Put (" faces:");                        -- outputs a string
```

The first and third of these `Put` statements output strings. The second `Put` statement, however, outputs the value of `Totems`. `Totems` does not appear in quotes since we are not outputting the name `"Totems"` but rather the value of the variable called `Totems`. The same procedure, `Put`, thus appears to be capable of outputting both strings and integer values. But this is not the case. We are actually invoking two different `Put` procedures, one that outputs strings, the other that outputs integer values. Two different procedures with the same name are said to be overloaded.

A question that naturally arises is, how does the compiler know which overloaded version of the `Put` procedure is being invoked? The answer is, by examining the item that is being output. If the output item is a string, the compiler selects the `Put` procedure that outputs strings. If the item is an integer, the compiler selects the `Put` procedure that outputs integers. Other languages besides Ada support overloading. What is unusual about Ada, however, is that the programmer can do the overloading. That is, the programmer may assign the same name to different procedures. As we shall show in Chapter 6, a programmer may even overload operators such as + or > !

Returning to the `Put` statements in the code, even though three separate `Put` statements are used, only one line of output is displayed on the screen. Unlike the `Put_Line` statement, these `Put` statements do not advance to the next line after outputting data to the screen. Three separate `Put` statements must be used because a `Put` statement can only output a single value. A statement such as the following is illegal:

```
Put ("Here is a Totem Pole with ", Totems, " faces:");
   -- illegal
```

A statement is said to be illegal if it contains an error that must be caught by the Ada compiler at compile time.

After the third `Put` statement, another call to `New_Line` is made. Whereas `New_Line` was first called without any parameter (a value in parentheses following the procedure name), this time it is called with a parameter value of 2. Whenever `New_Line` is invoked without a parameter, the default of 1 is assumed, and the program advances 1 line on the screen. If `New_Line` is called with a parameter, such as 2, then this value overrides the default of 1, and 2 lines are advanced. Most other programming languages do not support default parameter values.

The next statement is a control structure called a **for** loop, which is like the **for** loop of Pascal and the **DO** loop of FORTRAN. A **for** loop is used to repeatedly execute a group of statements. Within this **for** loop are four `Put_Line` statements, which output a "face" by printing the special symbols inside the quotes.

Let us examine the **for** loop more closely. Following the keyword **for** is the user-supplied name of the loop counter (loop index). In our example, the loop counter is named `Faces`. The loop counter steps through (i.e., gets assigned, in turn) each value in the range `1..Totems`, which appears after the keyword **in**. Since `Totems` was assigned the value 3, the range becomes `1..3` (1 to 3). For each value assigned to the loop counter–first 1, then 2, then 3–the group of statements within the loop is executed. Thus, three faces are output on the totem pole, one for each time through the loop.

The astute reader may have noticed that the loop counter, Faces, is used without ever having been explicitly declared. This seems to violate the rule that objects must be declared before they can be used. In general, this rule is true. However, loop counters are not explicitly declared. Rather, the compiler infers their type from the range of values that the counters assume. For instance, by examining the range 1..Totems, the compiler can determine that Faces is an object that can assume integer values from 1 to Totems. (More details about the **for** loop will be given in Chapter 3.) After the **for** loop is exited, the program ends.

## With Clause

Now that we have gone over the code line by line, let us consider some issues that have been sidestepped. Throughout our program, such procedures as Put and Put_Line are called. But where do these procedures exist? The answer can be found by reconsidering the first clause in our context specification:

```
with Ada.Text_IO;
```

This specification makes the resources of the Ada.Text_IO package, which comes with every Ada compiler, available to the Totem_Pole program. Among these resources are the procedures called by the Totem_Pole program to perform input and output (I/O) operations. Put and Put_Line are therefore not keywords that are built into the Ada language to allow us to perform I/O. Rather, these are procedures that need to be imported from an external package. Without the **with** clause, the compiler would complain that it could not find these procedures. Package Ada.Text_IO also contains the generic package Integer_IO that is needed for inputting or outputting integer values.

In general, packages are used to bundle together related resources. These resources can include items such as procedures, functions, and other packages; and declarations of types, variables, and constants. Packages such as Ada.Text_IO are supplied with every Ada compiler. Packages may also be written by programmers. In either case, the resources of these packages can easily be made available by employing a **with** clause and optionally a **use** clause.

**Ada 95 ▶**    The dot within the name Ada.Text_IO indicates that package Text_IO is a child of the package Ada. Package Ada contains many child packages besides Text_IO. A child package acts as though it were nested inside the tail end of its parent package. However, child packages, just like their parent, are separately compiled program units (library units).

As stated in the comments of procedure Totem_Pole, Ada.Text_IO can simply be referenced as Text_IO. Normally, one must provide the full extended name. However, through the use of a renaming mechanism (to be discussed later in this book), Ada defines Text_IO to be an alternative name for Ada.Text_IO. This was done for upward compatibility between Ada 83 and Ada 95. Ada 83 does not support child packages, so Text_IO is referenced without the Ada prefix.

The `Ada.Text_IO` package, as well as other library units that can be accessed by the **with** clause, is contained in the Ada library. Although our sample program is very short, Ada was designed with embedded systems in mind. The software for embedded systems typically consists of many thousands of lines of code. Such large Ada programs may consist of many different library units. To manage all these units (a job nasty enough to give any software configuration manager conniptions), an Ada library is provided. The Ada library contains information about each library unit. This information is used to check that library units are referenced correctly by other library units. Whenever a library unit such as `Ada.Text_IO` is mentioned in a **with** clause, the Ada library is searched and, if found, this unit is made available. A check is made that the `Ada.Text_IO` package contains all the procedures, such as `Put`, that are used within the program `Totem_Pole`. In addition, a check is made that these procedures are properly used–that they are called with the correct number and types of parameters.

## Use Clause

Whereas the **with** clause makes the resources of the `Ada.Text_IO` package available to the program, the **use** clause makes these resources directly visible. By directly visible, we mean that a resource, such as a procedure, can be called simply by using its name, such as `New_Line` and `Put_Line`. If we omit the **use** clause, these procedures can only be called by placing the name `Ada.Text_IO` (or just `Text_IO`) before the procedure name, as follows: `Ada.Text_IO.New_Line`, `Ada.Text_IO.Put_Line`, or `Ada.Text_IO.Put`. This "dot notation" tells the compiler from which library package to import the procedure.

Not all of the procedures in `Totem_Pole` come from the `Ada.Text_IO` package. Procedures such as `Get` and `Put`, which handle input and output of integer values, come from the `Int_IO` package. The resources of this package are not made available through a **with** clause, like the resources of the `Text_IO` package. Rather, these resources are made available when the `Int_IO` package is created by generically instantiating the `Integer_IO` package contained within the `Text_IO` package.

As with the `Text_IO` package, a **use** clause is needed to make the resources of the `Int_IO` package directly visible. Without this **use** clause, the procedures provided by this package can only be called using dot notation, as follows: `Int_IO.Get` and `Int_IO.Put`.

The procedure `Int_IO.Put` must be used when outputting integer values, whereas `Ada.Text_IO.Put` must be used when outputting strings. Thus, without the **use** clauses, the three lines in our program that inform the user about the Totem Pole would appear as follows:

```
Ada.Text_IO.Put ("Here is Totem Pole with"); -- Put from Ada.Text_IO
Int_IO.Put (Totems);                          -- Put from Int_IO
Ada.Text_IO.Put (" faces:");                   -- Put from Ada.Text_IO
```

Recall from our discussion on overloading that there are two procedures with the name `Put`, one for outputting strings, the other for outputting integer values. As we have just seen, these two procedures are contained in different packages. The `Put` procedure that outputs strings is imported from the `Ada.Text_IO` package. The `Put` procedure that outputs integer values is imported from the `Int_IO` package that is created by instantiating the `Integer_IO` package.

As we have seen, all the input and output procedures are either defined in `Ada.Text_IO` or in the package `Int_IO`. But where is type `Integer` defined? Since types such as `Integer` are basic to Ada programs, they are placed in a special package called `Standard`. Package `Standard` is unique because, although it cannot be mentioned in a **with** or **use** clause, its resources are always available. Programmers can therefore always access predefined types such as `Integer` from anywhere in their code.

Our sample program has been used to guide us through a number of Ada topics. The main topics covered have been **for** loops, the **with** and **use** clauses, procedures, generics, input/output, the Ada library, overloaded procedures, and packages. The next two sections provide an overview of important Ada features not shown or not sufficiently covered in the sample program. The first section deals with features provided in Ada 83. The second section deals with features introduced by Ada 95.

## FEATURES INTRODUCED BY ADA 83

Ada 83 supports control structures, arrays and records, subprograms, access types, types, attributes, packages, generics, exceptions, tasking, and low-level programming. Each of these features will be briefly covered, in turn.

### Control Structures

Ada supports a variety of control structures: the **if** statement, the **case** statement, the **goto** statement, and three kinds of loop statements. Control structures control the program's path of execution. Instead of sequentially executing one statement after another, control structures allow code to be executed along different paths. For instance, an **if** statement or **case** statement selects one group of statements to execute instead of alternative groups. The **goto** statement jumps over a section of code and continues execution elsewhere. In Ada, the **goto** statement is rarely necessary and should be avoided.

A loop is used to repeatedly execute a group of statements. There are three varieties of loops: the simple loop, which loops forever (unless another statement causes the loop to be exited); the **while** loop, which keeps looping while a certain condition is satisfied; and the **for** loop, which loops each time its loop counter advances to the next value. We have already seen an example of the **for** loop in the `Totem_Pole` program.

Ada does not support the **repeat until** loop that is supported by other languages such as Pascal. In Ada, however, an equivalent control structure is easily created using the **exit** statement. The **exit** statement exits from a loop when a specified condition is met.

## Arrays and Records

Both arrays and records have components. Individual components can be referenced, or the entire set of components may be referenced and manipulated as a whole. In the case of an array, components are selected by placing an index value in parentheses. For example, an array called `Seat_Taken` might contain index values from 1 to 200 representing seats in a auditorium numbered from 1 to 200. The value of a component of `Seat_Taken` is `True` or `False`, depending on whether or not the specified seat is occupied. If, for instance, the 10th seat is occupied, then `Seat_Taken(10)` is set to `True`, else it is set to `False`. Thus, `Seat_Taken` is a 200 component array of `True/False` (`Boolean`) values. Each component of `Seat_Taken` may be referenced individually by specifying an index value. Alternatively, the entire set of `Boolean` values may be referenced as a whole, using the identifier `Seat_Taken` (without specifying an index value).

Although arrays and records are to be found in most modern high-level languages, Ada adds a few new twists. For example, in a single assignment statement, an array or record may be given an entire set of component values. Perhaps even more surprising is that in Ada, arrays belonging to the same type may differ in size, and records belonging to the same type may have different components.

## Subprograms

Subprograms come in two varieties: procedures and functions. In the sample program, `Totem_Pole`, we have seen calls to procedures `Put`, `Put_Line`, `Get`, and `New_Line`. In addition, the `Totem_Pole` program is itself a procedure. There is nothing about a main program which, by itself, distinguishes it from other procedures. We have not yet seen any examples of functions. The main difference between a procedure and a function is that a procedure is invoked as a statement and returns values (if any) through its parameters:

```
Circle_Area (Area, 1.0); -- procedure
```

The value 1.0 is passed to the procedure, `Circle_Area`, which calculates the area of a circle and returns the result through the parameter, `Area`.

A function is invoked as an expression and returns a single value through the function name. Consider, for example, the following function call:

```
Area := Circle_Area (1.0); -- function
```

The function, `Circle_Area`, appears on the right side of the assignment operator because it is an expression that yields a result. This function calculates the area of a circle with a radius of 1.0. The result is returned through the function identifier `Circle_Area`. This result is then assigned to the variable `Area`.

## Access Types

Many modern languages provide pointers that are used to point to objects. Ada has its own version of pointers called access values (values of access types), which designate (point to) objects. Due to Ada's strong typing, however, pointers may only point to objects of a specified type. Thus, a character pointer may only point to characters, and an integer pointer may only point to integers.

## Types

In Ada, every object belongs to some type. Ada provides a variety of predefined types. For instance, there are integer types, floating point types, `Boolean` types, and character types. In addition, a programmer is allowed to create new types. For example, a programmer can create a type called `Fabric` consisting of the different fabrics:

```
type Fabric is (Wool, Silk, Mohair, Terylene, Linen, Angora,
     Cashmere, Tweed, Dacron, Cotton, Polyester);
```

Types such as `Fabric` are called "enumeration" types since their values–`Wool`, `Silk`, `Mohair`, and so on–are enumerated within parentheses. These values are to be thought of as actual values of type `Fabric`, not as integers or strings. Just as 7 is a integer value, `Wool` is a Fabric value.

## Attributes

Ada supports many predefined attributes. Attributes yield various characteristics of items. In other languages, programmers often have to search through code or documents to find these characteristics. For example, in most computer languages, if one wants to know the largest (or last) value of a specific type, `T`, one must read the compiler's reference manual. In Ada, however, this attribute of `T` can be referenced from within one's Ada program by writing `T'Last`. Thus, in the previous enumeration type, `Fabric`, the expression `Fabric'Last` yields `Polyester` since this is the last value listed. Similarly, `Integer'Last` yields the largest value of type Integer. On a 16-bit machine, this expression often yields the value 32,767; on other machines, this value will probably be different. By using attributes like `Integer'Last`, code is made more general and portable, and the use of "magic numbers" such as 32,767 may be avoided.

## Packages

As previously mentioned, a package (which is typically a separate "top-level" compilation unit) bundles together related resources. Packages usually consist of two parts: a specification and a body. The specification contains interface information that is available to the users of the package. This information includes everything users need to know in order to use the resources of the package. The package body, however, contains the underlying implementation of the resources defined in the corresponding package specification. The contents of the package body are unavailable to users of the package. Users of a package do not need to know how the resources of a package are implemented any more than the users of a radio need to know how radio waves are propagated, received, and converted into sound. Since the code that implements the resources is hidden, users of a package cannot abuse or corrupt this code or base their design on irrelevant details contained in this code.

## Generics

One of the most unusual features of Ada is generic units. Generic units serve as templates from which procedures, functions, and packages can be created. We have already seen, in our sample program, how an instance of the `Integer_IO` package is created by a method known as generic instantiation. By using generic units, code duplication can be greatly reduced because, from a given template, many copies can be created that only differ in specific ways. For instance, a generic package can be written that sorts objects. The code within this package that does the sorting need only be written once. From this generic package, many copies (instances) can be created that only differ in the types of objects that can be sorted. Thus, the generic sort package can be used to create packages that sort integers, strings, characters, and so on. Without generics, each type of item to be sorted would require that another version of the sort package be written.

Generics are also essential for code reuse. Instead of designing code from scratch every time a new program is written, money can be saved and reliability increased by reusing previously written and tested software components. To be reusable, these components must be very flexible and general purpose. Generics are excellent candidates for code reuse. For example, the generic sort package just discussed is far more flexible than a sort package only allowing one kind of type to be sorted. Depending on how the generic sort package is instantiated, different packages can be created to sort any kind of data one wishes.

## Exceptions

As anyone with even a modicum of programming experience can attest, large programs, even those that have been successfully running for years, may encounter an error or an exceptional condition. In such situations, different responses are required, depending on the kind of exceptional condition that is encountered. At one extreme, a condition arises that is fatal, and the program is required to halt as soon as possible. At the other extreme, the condition is simple to rectify, and processing continues after perhaps a friendly warning message is issued.

Ada provides a special mechanism for handling errors or other exceptional conditions that occur at runtime. Such exceptional runtime conditions are called exceptions, and the mechanism for handling these exceptions is called the exception handler. Exception handlers intercept exceptions, identify the type of exception that was raised, and then follow a specified course of action depending on the nature of the exception.

Exceptions are identified with either predefined names or user-defined names. Predefined exceptions, such as `Constraint_Error`, are automatically raised whenever a value such as an array index goes out of range. This should be welcome news to programmers of most other languages. Instead of spending hours attempting to debug a program where data is being clobbered by a wayward array index, Ada will announce the error as soon as it is encountered.

In addition to predefined exceptions, programmers may define their own exceptions. The programmer names the exception and then explicitly raises this exception, by name, whenever warranted.

## Tasking

In certain applications, various activities need to be performed during the same period of time. In Ada, each activity can be concurrently executed by a unit of code known as a task. Tasks may be used to model events in the real world that occur at the same time. Tasks may also be used to increase execution speed, especially when the computer has multiple processors.

Tasks may meet each other and exchange information. Such a meeting of tasks is called a rendezvous. As we shall see in Chapter 15, tasking is one of the more innovative features of Ada.

## Low-Level Programming

Since Ada was designed with embedded systems in mind, Ada supports low-level programming. Low-level programming means getting down to the "bare silicon" of the machine. This means dealing with bits and bytes, hardware interrupts, machine specific instructions, addresses, and so on.

In Ada, low-level programming can be performed without jumping into low-level assembly language, and without giving up Ada's high-level abstractions.

## FEATURES INTRODUCED BY ADA 95

**Ada 95 ▶** All of the previously described features are included in Ada 95. In addition, Ada 95 has introduced the following features: hierarchical libraries, programming by extension, classwide programming, and protected objects. Note that throughout this book, new features added by Ada 95 are indicated with the Ada 95 icon placed in the margin. This book can, therefore, be used by Ada 83 programmers with little interest in Ada 95 and by Ada 95 programmers who already know Ada 83. (Of course, this beginning text is also appropriate for programmers who know neither Ada 83 nor Ada 95.)

## Hierarchical Libraries

Ada 95's hierarchical libraries overcome the "flat" structure of Ada 83's libraries. In a hierarchical library structure, packages can have child units. The child units can either be packages, functions, or procedures. Child units can be attached to an existing parent unit without affecting the parent or the parent's clients. This brings us to the next important feature introduced by Ada 95: programming by extension.

### Programming by Extension

Programming by extension allows new features to be added to existing software without impacting the existing software of its clients. Specifically, extensions to the existing software can be made without requiring the existing software to be modified or even recompiled. Since the existing software is left completely untouched, it should not even need to be retested, except in conjunction with the added extensions. Also, clients of the existing software need not even be aware that extensions have been added, as long as they do need these extensions.

Programming by extension is extremely important for large software systems. This is because such systems are typically developed incrementally over the course of many years, instead of being developed all at once.

### Classwide Programming

Classwide programming allows one to abstract away the differences between a class of related types and to deal with the common properties of the types. A class of types is all ultimately derived from the same ancestor type. This ancestor must be a special kind of type called a "tagged" type. As we shall see in Chapter 13, classwide programming is one of the ingredients of object-oriented programming.

### Protected Objects

Protected objects provide an efficient and safe means for concurrently executing tasks to share data. The data is hidden and can only be accessed through "protected" calls. The protected calls only allow mutually exclusive access to the data. In other words, only one task at a time can update the data. This prevents the data from being corrupted by being simultaneously updated by more than one task. Unlike tasks, protected objects are very efficient and can therefore be freely used in time-critical applications.

Now that we have an overview of the Ada language, we are ready to delve into the details. The next chapter, therefore, covers the basics of Ada.

---

## EXERCISES

1. What problems constituted the software crisis?

2. How was Ada developed?

3. What are some of the advantages of Ada over other programming languages?

4. Describe three modern software engineering principles supported by Ada.

5. What is an embedded system, and what are its characteristics?

**6a.** Modify the `Totem_Pole` program to output the integer numbers from 1 to the value of `Totems`.

**6b.** Try outputting the values of `Faces` after the **for** loop (after keywords **end loop**). Can you explain the problem?

**6c.** What happens if you try to declare the loop counter `Faces`?

**6d.** What happens when the `Totem_Pole` program is executed with a request to output 0 faces? What about a request to output a negative number of faces?

7. Give an example of an application where Ada tasks might be used.

8. Give an example of an application where low-level programming might be used.

9. Compare the general features of Ada with those of any other high-level language with which you are familiar (e.g., Pascal, FORTRAN, C).

# 2

# Basics of Ada

The last chapter provided an overview of the Ada language. This chapter focuses on the details of the language. The chapter begins with a discussion of the basic components of Ada programs, called lexical elements. Lexical elements are keywords, identifiers, delimiters, literals, and comments. We will then explore scalar types, which are the integer, floating point, and user-defined enumeration types; character types; and Boolean types. Next, we will cover subtypes and some of the commonly used attributes. Derived types are then covered, which are types derived from existing types. A discussion of type conversion then follows. We conclude the chapter with a discussion of the order of operations, which covers arithmetic, relational, and logical operations.

## LEXICAL ELEMENTS

Lexical elements, the basic language components of Ada programs, are keywords, identifiers, delimiters, literals, and comments.

## Keywords

Reserved keywords (in Ada, all keywords are reserved) have special meaning in the Ada language. Throughout this book, keywords are written in lowercase bold letters to help flag them out to the reader. This convention follows the *Ada 95 Reference Manual*. Ada has 69 keywords, all of which are listed below:

| | | |
|---|---|---|
| **abort** | **abs** | **abstract*** |
| **accept** | **access** | **aliased*** |
| **all** | **and** | **array** |
| **at** | **begin** | **body** |

| | | |
|---|---|---|
| case | constant | declare |
| delay | delta | digits |
| do | else | elsif |
| end | entry | exception |
| exit | for | function |
| generic | goto | if |
| in | is | limited |
| loop | mod | new |
| not | null | of |
| or | others | out |
| package | pragma | private |
| procedure | protected* | raise |
| range | record | rem |
| renames | requeue* | return |
| reverse | select | separate |
| subtype | tagged* | task |
| terminate | then | type |
| until* | use | when |
| while | with | xor |

**Ada 95 ▶**   The six keywords that are marked with an asterisk are newly introduced in Ada 95. Perhaps the most common reason for Ada 83 code to fail to compile with an Ada 95 compiler is that one or more of these six keywords are being used as identifiers. Identifiers cannot have the same name as a keyword, so the names of such identifiers must change.

## Identifiers

Ada identifiers are names that identify various items, such as variables, constants, procedures, and functions. The following are examples of Ada identifiers:

```
Age
Number_Of_Near_Misses
P23
```

Identifiers should be descriptive and easy to interpret. For instance, avoid identifiers such as `Recnum` and instead write `Record_Number`.

There are seven rules to follow when constructing Ada identifiers:

1. Identifiers can only contain letters, numbers, and underscores.
2. Identifiers can be of any length, as long as the entire identifier appears within a single line.
3. In identifiers, Ada does not distinguish between upper- and lowercase letters.
4. Identifiers cannot have the same name as keywords.
5. Identifiers must begin with a letter.
6. Identifiers cannot have underscores at the beginning, end, or side by side.
7. Underscores in identifiers are significant.

Rule 1 states that identifiers can only contain letters, numbers, and underscores. This means that special symbols, such as * or &, cannot appear in an identifier. The following identifiers are therefore illegal:

```
Spin-Off                 -- illegal symbol: -
Brightness&Sunshine      -- illegal symbol: &
Mobius Strip             -- illegal embedded blank
```

**Ada 95** ▶ However, letters may have diacritical marks that are used in the languages of western Europe:

```
Straße          -- OK
Möbius_Strip    -- OK
```

Rule 2 states that identifiers can be of any length, as long as the entire identifier appears within a single line. The following identifier is therefore legal:

```
This_Is_A_Very_Long_Identifier
```

Rule 3 states that in identifiers, Ada does not distinguish between upper- and lowercase letters. In this book, identifiers are written in "mixed-case" letters for readability and for contrast with keywords, which are written in bold lowercase letters. Specifically, identifiers in this book use uppercase for the first letter of every word (including words separated by underscores) and lowercase for all other letters. For identifiers that are acronyms, all uppercase is used, for readability. As far as the Ada compiler is concerned, the following four identifiers are the same:

```
CONTINUE   -- these four identifiers are considered
Continue   -- to be the same
continue
CoNtInUe
```

Rule 4 states that identifiers cannot have the same name as keywords. (A complete list of keywords is given in the previous section.) A keyword, such as **procedure**, has a predefined meaning and cannot be redefined by the programmer. Thus, a syntax error will occur if an attempt is made to use an identifier name such as `Procedure`, `Begin`, or `Loop`. However, the name of a keyword can appear as *part* of an identifier:

```
Rem           -- illegal identifier; Rem is a reserved word
Remarkable    -- OK
```

Rule 5 states that identifiers must begin with a letter. The following identifier is therefore illegal:

```
2_By_4     -- illegal; begins with a number
```

Rule 6 states that identifiers cannot have underscores at the beginning, end, or side by side. The following identifiers are therefore illegal:

```
_Etc       -- illegal; leading underscore
A_B__C     -- illegal; two underscores between B and C
Continue_  -- illegal; trailing underscore
```

Rule 7 states that underscores in identifiers are significant. The following three identifiers are therefore considered to be distinct:

```
One_And_A_Two    -- each of these identifiers is distinct
One_AndA_Two
OneAndATwo
```

## Delimiters

Delimiters are symbols that have special meaning within Ada. These symbols are used, for instance, as operators and statement terminators. There are single delimiters, which consist of only one symbol, and double delimiters, which consist of two symbols:

### Single Delimiters:

| | |
|---|---|
| + | Addition or positive |
| – | Subtraction or negative |
| * | Multiplication |
| / | Division |
| = | Equality |
| < | Less than |
| > | Greater than |
| & | Catenator |
| \| | Vertical bar (or selector) |
| ; | Terminator |
| # | Based literal bracket |
| ( | Left parenthesis |
| ) | Right parenthesis |
| . | Dot |
| : | Separates object from its type |
| " | Double quote |
| ' | Single quote or tick mark |

### Double Delimiters:

| | |
|---|---|
| ** | Exponentiation |
| /= | Inequality |
| <= | Less than or equal |
| >= | Greater than or equal |
| := | Assignment |
| <> | Box |
| => | Arrow |
| << | Left label bracket |

>>   Right label bracket
..   Double dot for range

The preceding lists only give a basic idea of how these delimiters are used. Detailed descriptions will be given as the delimiters are introduced in this book.

One of these delimiters, however, deserves special consideration in this chapter because it is so frequently encountered. This is the assignment operator, :=. We have seen this operator used in the `Totem_Pole` program in Chapter 1:

```
Totems: Integer := 1;
```

When `Totems` is declared as an integer variable, it is assigned a default value of 1.

In addition to appearing in declarations, the assignment operator may appear in assignment statements:

```
Totems := 8;
```

In this assignment statement, `Totems` is assigned the value of 8.

The value to the right of the assignment operator may also be an expression:

```
Totems := 5 + 4 - 3;
```

The expression, 5 + 4 − 3, is evaluated to 6. The result, 6, is then placed in the variable `Totems`. Any previous value `Totems` may have had is replaced by this new value.

## Literals

A literal is a particular value of a type that is explicitly written and not represented by an identifier. In this section, we will discuss integer literals, such as 7; real literals, such as 7.2; character literals, such as 'c'; string literals, such as "Ada"; and `Boolean` literals, such as True.

Let us begin by considering integer literals. Integer literals are whole numbers that do not contain a decimal point:

```
21, 0, 187
```

Large integer literals, such as 5737639019, can be difficult to read if they are not separated into groups of numbers. Normally, we would write such large integers using commas: 5,737,639,019. However, in Ada, commas cannot be embedded within an integer literal. Underscores, though, are allowed. Unlike the underscores in identifiers, underscores in integer literals have no significance; they are ignored by the compiler. These underscores are only used to make numbers easier for humans to read. Therefore, the previous integer literal might be written as 5_737_639_019. Underscores can appear anywhere within an integer literal except at the beginning, end, or side by side.

In addition to underscores, integer literals may use scientific notation (also known as exponential notation), as follows:

```
2E3,   12E+15
```

The E, which can be written in upper- or lowercase, means "times ten to the power of." Thus 2E3 means 2 times 10 to the power of 3, or $2 \times 10^3$, which evaluates to 2000. Note that, in effect, the exponent to the right of the E indicates how many zeros follow the integer to the left of the E. Thus, 12E+15 is simply 12 followed by 15 zeros. The optional plus sign is used to explicitly state that the exponent 15 is a positive number. When the plus sign is omitted, the compiler assumes that a positive exponent is intended. An integer literal cannot have a negative exponent, since this would cloud the distinction between integer literals and real literals.

```
20E-1  -- Illegal
```

Not only can integer literals be written using scientific notation; they can be written in bases other than base 10. In everyday life, we use base 10 numbers, which are composed of the ten digits 0, 1, 2, 3, 4, 5, 6, 7, 8, and 9. Base 10 integers are written as a sequence of these digits. The place value of a digit is determined by its position in the sequence. Thus, in the number 2754, the rightmost digit, 4, is in the ones position, and the place value increases by a factor of 10 as one advances from right to left. The 5 is in the tens position, 7 is in the hundreds position, and 2 is in the thousands position.

There is nothing special about base 10 numbers. We write numbers in base 10 probably because we are equipped with a counting device consisting of 10 "digits" that we always carry with us, namely, our fingers. If we ever meet an intelligent extraterrestrial who has 12 digits, chances are that this creature will use base 12 numbers. Ada is designed to accommodate extraterrestrials possessing from 2 to 16 digits. In other words, integer literals can be written in any base from 2 to 16. For computer scientists, the most commonly used bases (besides base 10) are bases 2, 8, and 16. This is not because computer scientists have a different number of fingers from the rest of humanity, but because digital computers operate in base 2, and base 2 numbers are conveniently represented in base 8 or base 16.

Based numbers should be familiar to you from a mathematics class or an introductory computer class. The following explanation of based literals is therefore meant as a review.

Base 2 numbers, called binary numbers, are composed of the two digits 0 and 1. Base 2 integers are written as a sequence of these digits. In the binary number 1101, the rightmost digit is in the ones position, and the place value increases by a factor of 2 as one advances from right to left. The 0 is in the twos position, the 1 to the left of the 0 is in the fours position, and the leftmost 1 is in the eights position.

Base 8 numbers, called octal numbers, are composed of the eight digits 0, 1, 2, 3, 4, 5, 6, and 7. Base 8 integers are written as a sequence of these digits. In the octal number 1247, the rightmost digit, 7, is in the ones position, and the place value increases by a factor of 8 as one advances from right to left. The 4 is in the eights position, the 2 is in the 64s position, and the 1 is in the 512s position.

Base 16 numbers, called hexadecimal numbers, are composed of the 16 digits 0, 1, 2, 3, 4, 5, 6, 7, 8, 9, A, B, C, D, E, and F. Note that since there are only 10 digits in our number system, letters are used to represent the other 6 digits: A is 10, B is 11, C is 12, and so on. Base 16 integers are written as a sequence of these digits. In the hexadecimal number 3A4F, the rightmost digit, F, is in the ones position, and the place value increases by a factor of 16 as one advances from right to left. The 4 is in the 16s position, the A is in the 256s position, and the 3 is in the 4096s position.

In Ada, a based literal is enclosed within the pound sign (sharp sign) symbols, #, and is preceded by the number that indicates the base. The binary number 1101, for example, is written as 2#1101#. The octal number 1247 is written as 8#1247#. The hexadecimal number ADA is written as 16#ADA#.

Based literals can be written using scientific notation, such as 2#11#E3. But be careful. Because this is a binary number, the E3 does not mean $10^3$ but $2^3$. In the hexadecimal number 16#BEEF#E2, the E2 means $16^2$.

This concludes our discussion of integer literals. Now let us consider real literals. Real literals have a decimal point (fractional part):

```
3.5, 0.0, 127.021
```

Real literals must have a digit on each side of the decimal point. The literal .5, for example, is illegal; it must be written as 0.5.

Just as integer literals can use underscores, so can real literals. Thus, 4129345.01 can be written as 4_129_345.01. (An underscore, however, cannot be placed beside the decimal point. Therefore, 4_129_345_.01 is illegal.) Also, like integer literals, real literals can use scientific notation. Thus, 1.2345E3 means $1.2345 \times 10^3$, which evaluates to 1234.5. Note that, in effect, the exponent to the right of the E indicates how many places the decimal point is shifted to the right. Unlike integer literals, real literals can have negative exponents. When an exponent is negative, a left shift is required instead of a right shift.

Just as integer literals can be written as based literals, so can real literals can be written as based literals. Note that in base 10, the place values decrease by a factor of 10 from left to right. In the base 10 number 0.754, for example, 0 is in the ones position, 7 is in the tenths position, 5 is in the hundredths position, and 4 is in the thousandths position.

Similarly, for real binary literals, the place values decrease by a factor of 2 from left to right. For instance, in the binary number 0.101, the 1 to the right of the radix point is in the one-halves position, the 0 to the right of this 1 is in the one-fourths position, and the rightmost 1 is in the one-eighths position. The term radix point is used instead of decimal point because, strictly speaking, decimal point implies a decimal (base 10) number. In Ada, the binary number 0.101 is written as 2#0.101#. Octal and hexadecimal real literals are handled similarly.

As with integer based literals, real based literals can be written using scientific notation, such as 2#11.0111#E3. Again, be careful. The E3 means $2^3$, not $10^3$.

This based literal may therefore be written without the scientific notation by shifting the radix point three places to the right: `2#11011.1#`.

Now that we have discussed integer and real literals, let us consider character literals. Character literals consist of individual characters, placed within a pair of single quotes, as follows:

**Ada 95 ▶**     `'A',      'a',       '*',       '8',       'Å',       '+'`

As shown, character literals include uppercase letters, lowercase letters, letters with diacritical marks, special symbols, and numerals written as text. (Although Ada is case insensitive, it does distinguish between upper- and lowercase character literals.) Note that the character literal `'8'` is not the same as the integer literal 8. The character literal `'8'`, unlike the integer literal 8, cannot be used in arithmetic calculations.

Whereas character literals are single characters that are placed within a pair of single quotes, string literals consist of a sequence of printable characters that are placed within a pair of double quotes:

```
                 "This is a string literal!"
Ada 95 ▶         "The 'β' in Straße is weird"
```

In string literals, as with character literals, upper- and lowercase letters are distinguished from one another.

Let us consider one more kind of literal: `Boolean` literals. `Boolean` literals consist of the values `False` and `True`. These values should not be thought of as strings. `False` and `True` are explicit `Boolean` values, just as 7 is an explicit integer value.

## Comments

In Ada and other programming languages, comments are placed within code to describe its purpose, use, and implementation. Comments are also used at the beginning of a unit of code to give header information, such as the name of the programmer, the date the code was last modified, the version number of the code, and the name of the project. Comments are provided for human readers and are ignored by compilers.

In Ada, comments are line oriented; they begin with two hyphens (--) and extend to the end of the line. Text consisting of any printable characters or symbols may follow the hyphens:

```
-- comments may take up a full line
-- or several lines
X := 2#1010#; -- comments may be placed after code
y := -- even the placement of this comment is OK
    100;
```

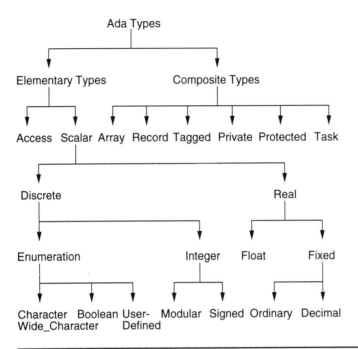

**Figure 2.1**  Classification of types.

## SCALAR TYPES

In Ada, every object belongs to a type. (An object is an entity such as a variable or constant that can take on values.) Similarly to the way a `collie` belongs to type `Dog` and `plum` belongs to type `Fruit`, the literal `'A'` belongs to type `Character`, and the literal `False` belongs to type `Boolean`. Furthermore, each type in Ada is characterized, not just by a set of values, but by operations that can apply to these values. Operations that apply to type `Dog`, for instance, could include such activities as walking the dog, feeding the dog, washing the dog, playing with the dog, or disciplining the dog. In Ada, types come in as many bewildering varieties as the life forms that inhabit the dense jungles of the Amazon. And just when you think you have encountered every variety, a new and even more exotic one greets you. The classification of types is depicted in Figure 2.1. Refer to this figure when reading the following discussion.  The figure clarifies how all the different types fit together.

**Ada 95 ▶**    Types in Ada are divided into two main groups: elementary types and composite types. Elementary types include access types and scalar types. As we will see in Chapter 11, access types are used to declare pointers to variables, constants, or subprograms. Scalar types are types that do not have any internal components or structure.

Unlike elementary types, composite types do have an internal structure. All composite types, except for array types, can include a parameter called a discriminant. Discriminants will be discussed later in this book. Composite types include the array, record, tagged, private, protected, and task types. Array and record types will be covered in Chapters 4 and 5, respectively. Tagged types are used in object-oriented programming in order to build classes. These types will be covered in Chapter 13. Private types are used to hide the internal structure of a type and to limit the kinds of operations that can be performed on objects of that type. Private types will be explored in Chapter 7. Protected and task types are used in code that can run concurrently. These types will be covered in Chapter 15.

Scalar elementary types are discussed in this chapter because they are basic to Ada and are frequently used in Ada programs. The other types previously mentioned are more specialized and thus will be covered in later chapters.

Scalar elementary types consist of discrete types and real types. A discrete type is composed of objects that have immediate successors and predecessors. A real type is composed of numbers that, from a mathematical perspective, form a continuum and have no immediate successors or predecessors. (However, as we shall see later, real numbers, as they are stored within the computer, have successors and predecessors.)

As shown in Figure 2.1, discrete types come in two varieties: integer types and enumeration types. Integer types are numbers that have no fractional part. In Ada, integer types can either be signed or modular. Signed integer types have a "sign bit" to accommodate negative values. Modular integer types are always treated as zero or positive values and have a "wraparound" feature that will be described in Chapter 12. Enumeration types are types that are defined by explicitly enumerating their values. For example, the enumeration type `Boolean` is defined by the list of values `False` and `True`. Enumeration types consist of user-defined enumeration types, as well as the predefined enumeration types: `Character`, `Wide_Character`, and `Boolean`.

Real types are used to represent continuously varying quantities that arise from measuring physical processes or from mathematical computation. Unlike integer quantities, not all real quantities can be exactly represented in a computer. We must therefore cope with the inevitable "round-off" errors.

Figure 2.1 shows that real types come in two varieties: float and fixed. Float numbers are real numbers whose decimal point is not fixed at a particular location but is free to move around. Thus, these numbers are known as floating point numbers. Fixed numbers are real numbers whose decimal point is fixed at a particular location. Thus, these numbers are known as fixed point numbers.

Scalar types are either predefined or user defined. The predefined scalar types are defined in the package called `Standard`, which is included with every Ada compiler. These predefined types are `Integer`; `Float`; `Character`; `Wide_Character`; `Boolean`; and a special fixed point type, `Duration`. (Fixed point types will be discussed in Chapter 12.) Package `Standard` is unique because, although it cannot be mentioned in a **with** or **use** clause, its resources are always available. Programmers can therefore always access these predefined types from anywhere in their code.

In the following subsections, we will discuss various scalar types. We will first discuss the two numeric types: `Integer` and `Float`. We will then describe user-defined enumeration types, followed by the predefined enumeration types: `Character`, `Wide_Character`, and `Boolean`. Fixed point types, which must be defined by the programmer, will not be discussed until Chapter 12.

## Integer Type

This section covers integer variables, integer constants, and integer expressions. We will first discuss integer variables and constants. An integer variable is an identifier that can assume different integer values during the execution of a program. An integer constant is an identifier with a value that cannot change during the execution of the program. As the following example shows, integer variables and integer constants can be declared using the predefined type `Integer`:

```
declare
   -- declarative part
   Number_Of_Near_Misses: Integer;
   A, B, C: Integer;
   Sum: Integer := 0;
   First_Score, Second_Score: Integer := 25;
   Total_Score: Integer := First_Score + Second_Score;
   Dozen: constant Integer := 12;
begin
   -- executable statement part
   null;     -- at least one executable statement is needed;
             -- the null statement satisfies this requirement
end;
```

Before discussing these integer variables and constants, let us briefly explain the structure of the code. There are two parts to this code: the declarative part and the executable statement part, which we will refer to as the statement part. The declarative part contains declarations, which are placed between the keywords **declare** and **begin**. The statement part contains one or more executable statements, which are placed between the keywords **begin** and **end**. At least one executable statement is required, even if it is only the "do-nothing" **null** statement. This entire structure is called a block, or block statement, and will be covered in detail in Chapter 6. Blocks will be used in many examples because they are the simplest Ada constructs that contain a declarative part and a statement part.

At runtime, statements are executed, and declarations are elaborated. When a statement is executed, some action is performed; when a declaration is elaborated, the declared object is created by allocating the required computer resources.

The first declaration in the preceding code defines the object, `Number_Of_Near_Misses`, to be an integer variable. Note that the word "variable" does not appear in the code. No initial value is assigned to this variable, and in Ada, no default value is given. If a value is not assigned to this variable before it is read, then an error results that may or may not be caught by the compiler.

The second declaration defines the objects `A`, `B`, and `C` to be integer variables. Once again, no initial values are assigned.

The third declaration defines the object Sum to be an integer variable and uses the assignment operator, :=, to initialize Sum to 0. Since Sum is an integer variable, it can only be initialized to an integer value, such as 0. Attempting to initialize Sum to, for instance, a real value, will result in an error at compile time. Also, note that since Sum is a variable, its initial value of 0 can later be overridden.

The fourth declaration defines the objects First_Score and Second_Score to be integer variables. With a single assignment operator, both of these integer variables are initialized to 25. Initializing more than one variable at a time is only allowed in declarations, not in assignment statements such as the following:

```
A, B := 5; -- illegal
```

The fifth declaration defines the object Total_Score to be an integer variable and initializes this variable to First_Score plus Second_Score. This can be done since First_Score and Second_Score have already been declared and initialized to 25. Total_Score is thus initialized to 50.

The last declaration defines the object Dozen to be an integer constant with the value of 12. Since Dozen is declared to be a constant, it must be given an initial value. (In Chapter 7, we will see an exception to this rule.) By making Dozen a constant, if an attempt is made to alter its value, the compiler will report an error.

As a rule, avoid the use of numeric literals, except when their meaning is obvious. The meaning of literals such as 0 and 1 is often obvious, but rarely is the meaning of literals such as 770 obvious. Replace literals such as 770 with constants whose name clearly conveys their meaning. For example, if 770 represents the speed of sound, introduce a constant called Speed_Of_Sound that is initialized to 770. Once the constant is declared, all references to the speed of sound should be made through the constant name.

Besides making code more readable, constants help make code more maintainable. Multiple occurrences of the same value can be modified by just changing the declaration of the constant. For example, if a constant Speed_Limit needs to be changed from 55 to 65, then only its initialization needs modifying. However, if the literal 55 is used throughout the code, then every occurrence must be changed to 65. This is an error-prone and time-consuming process.

So far in this section, we have discussed integer variables and integer constants. In the previous section, we discussed integer literals. Next we will consider integer expressions, in which operations on these integer variables, constants, and literals are performed. An integer expression is an expression that, no matter how complex, always resolves to a single integer result. Integer expressions may contain the following arithmetic operators:

| | |
|---|---|
| + | Addition, positive |
| − | Subtraction, negative |
| * | Multiplication |
| / | Division (with truncation) |
| ** | Exponentiation |
| **mod** | Modulus |

**rem**        Remainder
**abs**        Absolute value

The following code demonstrates how these operators can be used in integer expressions:

```
with Ada.Text_IO; use Ada.Text_IO;
procedure Integer_Expressions is

    package Int_IO is new Integer_IO (Integer);
    use Int_IO;
    A, B: Integer := 7;
    C: Integer := 2;
    D: constant Integer := -1;

begin -- Integer_Expressions

    Put (3 + C);                -- outputs 5
    Put (+A);                   -- outputs 7
    Put (A - C);                -- outputs 5
    Put (-A);                   -- outputs -7
    Put (3 * D);                -- outputs -3
    Put (7 / 4);                -- outputs 1
    Put (2 ** 5);               -- outputs 32
    Put (17 rem 9);             -- outputs 8
    Put (17 mod 9);             -- outputs 8
    Put (abs D);                -- outputs 1
    Put (2#1011# + 8#12#);      -- outputs 21

end Integer_Expressions;
```

Note that the operators + and – can be used in two different ways. As unary operators (operators that operate on a single object), + indicates that an integer is positive, and – indicates that an integer is negative. As binary operators (operators that operate on two objects), + adds one integer to another, and – subtracts one integer from another.

There are a few pitfalls to avoid when writing integer expressions. Be careful when dividing integers. The fractional part of the result, if there is one, is discarded. For instance, 7/4 is 1, since the fractional part, 0.75, is discarded. Also avoid placing two arithmetic operators side by side. The integer expression 2 * – 4, for instance, is illegal (will not compile) because the two operators, * and –, are placed next to each other. In such cases, parentheses are required: 2 * (-4). In addition, be careful when using exponents. Ada standards forbid the use of a negative exponent with an integer number. For example, 2**(-3) will result in a runtime error. Also, when using exponents, remember that any number with an exponent of 0 yields 1; even 0**0 yields 1.

The remainder operator, **rem**, and the modulus operator, **mod**, are very similar to each other. Both these operators give the remainder of integer division. The integer expressions 5 **rem** 3 and 5 **mod** 3, for example, both yield the value 2, because 2 is the remainder when 5 is divided by 3. The operators **rem** and **mod** yield the same result except when one operand (the object being operated on) is a positive integer and the other operand is a negative integer. In such cases, **rem** and **mod** yield different results, as shown in the following chart. Note that **mod** yields a result that has the same sign as its right operand, and **rem** yields a result that has the same sign as its left operand.

| $J$ | $K$ | $J$ **mod** $K$ | $J$ **rem** $K$ |
|:---:|:---:|:---:|:---:|
| −5 | −5 | 0 | 0 |
| −4 | −5 | −4 | −4 |
| −3 | −5 | −3 | −3 |
| −2 | −5 | −2 | −2 |
| −1 | −5 | −1 | −1 |
| 0 | −5 | 0 | 0 |
| 1 | −5 | −4 | 1 |
| 2 | −5 | −3 | 2 |
| 3 | −5 | −2 | 3 |
| 4 | −5 | −1 | 4 |
| 5 | −5 | 0 | 0 |
| −5 | 5 | 0 | 0 |
| −4 | 5 | 1 | −4 |
| −3 | 5 | 2 | −3 |
| −2 | 5 | 3 | −2 |
| −1 | 5 | 4 | −1 |
| 0 | 5 | 0 | 0 |
| 1 | 5 | 1 | 1 |
| 2 | 5 | 2 | 2 |
| 3 | 5 | 3 | 3 |
| 4 | 5 | 4 | 4 |
| 5 | 5 | 0 | 0 |

The **abs** operator returns the absolute value of a number. The absolute value of an integer is the magnitude of the integer, which is positive, regardless of whether the integer itself is positive or negative. Thus, **abs** 3 and **abs** (-3) both yield the value of 3.

The last Put statement of the program Integer_Expression adds the binary integer 2#1011# to the octal integer 8#12#. The result is output as a decimal number. (In Chapter 14, we will see how to output numeric values in other bases.)

## Floating Point Type

As shown in Figure 2.1, there are two types of real numbers: float (floating point) numbers and fixed (fixed point) numbers. This chapter only discusses floating point numbers. Fixed point numbers will be discussed in Chapter 12.

As the following code illustrates, objects can be declared to be floating point variables and constants by using the predefined type Float:

```
declare
    X, Y, Z: Float;
    Inches: Float := 8_532.19;
    Yards: Float := Inches / 36.0;
    Pi: constant Float := 3.1415927;
begin
    null;
end;
```

In this code, the first declaration defines the objects X, Y, and Z to be floating point variables. The second declaration defines the object Inches to be a floating point variable and initializes it to 8_532.19. The third declaration converts the value of Inches into yards and uses the result to initialize the variable Yards. The last declaration defines the object Pi to be a floating point constant with the value of 3.1415927. Since Pi is a constant, its value cannot be changed.

So far in this section, we have discussed variables and constants. In the previous section, we discussed real literals. Next we will consider real expressions (expressions that yield a real result), in which operations on these real literals, variables, and constants are performed.

Real expressions may contain the following arithmetic operators: +, −, *, /, **, and **abs**. These operators were already covered when we discussed integer operations, but a few differences should be noted. For instance, when division is performed on real numbers, the fractional part of the result is not truncated, as with integer division. Thus, 14.0 / 5.0 yields 2.8, not 2. Also, unlike integers, real numbers may have a negative exponent. For example, 4.0 ** (-2) yields the real number 0.0625. However, neither integers nor real numbers may have a real exponent. For example, the cubed root of 5.0 cannot be obtained using a real exponent of 0.33333:

```
5.0 ** 0.33333    -- illegal unless one uses the ** operator
                  -- defined in Ada.Numerics.Elementary_Functions
```

**Ada 95 ▶** If this capability is needed, however, use the exponentiation operator (**) provided in the predefined package Ada.Numerics.Elementary_Functions. Package

`Elementary_Functions` is a child of package `Numerics`, which is a child of package `Ada`. To access the exponentiation operator, apply the **with** clause and the **use** clause to the full expanded name. (Special steps covered in Chapter 7 need to be taken if the **use** clause is not employed.) This special version of the exponentiation operator raises a real value of type `Float` to a real power. Package `Ada.Numerics.Elementary_Functions` includes many other operations on values of type `Float`, including log functions, a square root function, trigonometric functions such as `Sin` and `Cos` (in both cyclic and regular forms), and hyperbolic functions such as `Sinh` and `Cosh`. Programmers needing these functions should read about this package in the *Ada 95 Reference Manual*. For those programmers needing random number generation, Ada supplies the package `Ada.Numerics.Float_Random`. Finally, the optional Numerics Annex defines child packages of `Ada.Numerics` for manipulating complex numbers.

Returning to the predefined real operators, note that **mod** and **rem** are not available for floating point values, only for integer values. The **abs** operator, however, is available for floating point values as well as integer values.

## User-Defined Enumeration Types

An enumeration type is defined by enumerating the values that belong to the type. Some enumeration types are predefined and reside in the package `Standard`. Enumeration types may also be defined by the user (programmer). We will begin our discussion with user-defined enumeration types.

Suppose that a program developed for a psychiatric institute needs a type that consists of the different kinds of personalities. Such a type may be declared as follows:

```
type   Personality is (Loving, Cute, Loathsome, Obnoxious,
       Bland, Volatile, Fun_To_Pinch);
```

The enumeration type `Personality` is defined by enumerating the values that belong to the type: `Loving`, `Cute`, `Loathsome`, and so on. These values are placed in parentheses. Each value is not a string but an enumeration literal. For instance, the literal, `Cute`, is an explicit value of type `Personality`, just as the literal, 7, is an explicit value of type `Integer`.

Ada enforces the data abstraction of enumeration literals by treating them as read-only values, by limiting the kinds of operations that can apply to them, and by making sure that they can only mix with objects of the same type. Thus, the compiler does not allow `Loathsome` to be assigned to `Loving` or `Loving` to be used in a mathematical expression such as `2 * Loving + 1`. (The operations that are defined for enumeration literals will be discussed in the section of this chapter on `Boolean` expressions.)

In addition to enumeration literals such as `Loving`, enumeration types can also contain characters. The following type contains characters that make up Roman numerals:

```
type Roman_Numerals is ('I', 'V', 'X', 'L', 'C', 'D', 'M');
```

Note that each character is placed in a single quote. Enumeration literals can also contain a mixture of character literals and regular literals:

```
type Grades is ('A', 'B', 'C', 'D', Pass, Fail, Noncredit );
```

Once an enumeration type such as type Personality is defined, variables and constants of this type can be declared. This is done in the same manner that variables and constants of integer and real types are declared:

```
Typical_Personality: Personality := Bland;
My_Type_Of_Person: constant Personality := Fun_To_Pinch;
```

The first declaration defines the object Typical_Personality to be a variable of type Personality that is initialized to Bland. The second declaration defines the object My_Type_Of_Person to be a constant of type Personality that is initialized to Fun_To_Pinch.

The order in which enumeration literals are listed is significant. The compiler assumes that enumeration literals are listed in ascending order, from left to right. This topic will be discussed when we cover Boolean expressions later in this chapter.

In addition to user-defined enumeration types, package Standard contains three predefined enumeration types: types Character, Wide_Character, and Boolean. We will cover these types in the next two sections of this chapter.

## Character Types

**Ada 95 ▶** Ada provides two versions of character types: Character and Wide_Character. These types support international and graphic characters. Type Character has 256 values, corresponding to the International Standards Organization (ISO) 8-bit 8859-1 character set. Some of these characters are control characters that cannot be printed. Control characters function as line feeds, carriage returns, line terminators, page terminators, and so on. The set of printable characters included in ISO 8859-1 are called Latin_1 Characters of type Latin_1 include uppercase and lowercase letters with diacritical marks such as 'Å' and 'å' and graphic characters such as '£' and '§'. Type Wide_Character has 65,536 values, corresponding to the ISO 16-bit 10646 Basic Multilingual Plane (BMP) character set. The first 256 values of type Wide_Character correspond to the 256 values of type Character. [In Ada 83, type Character has 128 values, corresponding to the American Standard Code for Information Interchange (ASCII) character set. No other character sets are provided. The first 128 values of Ada 95's type Character correspond to the 128 values of Ada 83's type Character.]

Type Character is defined in the package Standard, as follows:

```
type Character is
    (nul,...,'1',...,'9',...,'A',...,'Z',...,'a',...,'z',...,'ÿ');
```

Only a few of the 256 characters are shown in the preceding type declaration.

Note that printable character literals appear within a pair of single quotes.

(Pairs of double quotes are used for string literals.) The character denoted by *nul* is an unprintable character.

Character variables and constants can be declared as follows:

```
First_Initial, Last_Initial: Character;
Key: Character := 'A';
Star: constant Wide_Character := '*';
Period: constant Character := '.';
Single_Quote: constant Character := ''';
Copyright: constant Character := '©';
Infinity: constant Wide_Character := '∞';
Sigma: constant Wide_Character := 'Σ';
```

The first declaration defines the objects `First_Initial` and `Last_Initial` to be character variables. The second declaration defines the object `Key` to be a character variable and initializes it to an uppercase A. The third declaration defines `Star` to be a constant of type `Wide_Character` and initializes it to the asterisk. The fourth, fifth, and sixth declarations define the objects `Period`, `Single_Quote`, and `Copyright` to be character constants and initialize them to a period, single quote, and copyright symbol. The last two declarations define constants of type `Wide_Character` and initialize them to symbols for infinity and sigma. These two symbols are included in type `Wide_Character`, but not in type `Character`.

Programmers needing to manipulate characters should examine package `Ada.Characters` described in the *Ada 95 Reference Manual*. This package enables one to query whether a given character is a control character, a graphic character, a letter, a lowercase letter, an uppercase letter, a digit, a hexadecimal digit, and so on. Functions are also provided to convert characters to uppercase or lowercase.

Recall that Ada identifiers can only contain letters, numbers, and underscores. The only letters allowed are those contained in type `Character`. Letters of type `Wide_Character`, however, are allowed to appear in character and string literals. And there are no restrictions on what characters may appear in comments.

## Boolean Type

The `Boolean` type is defined in the package `Standard` as follows:

```
type Boolean is (False, True);
```

The `Boolean` type, then, is just a predefined enumeration type that contains two values (`Boolean` literals): `False` and `True`.

Boolean variables and constants can be declared as follows:

```
Politically_Correct: Boolean;
Male_Chauvinist_Pig: Boolean := True;
T: constant Boolean := True;   -- T is another name for True
F: constant Boolean := False;  -- F is another name for False
```

The first declaration defines `Politically_Correct` to be a `Boolean` variable. The second declaration defines `Male_Chauvinist_Pig` to be a `Boolean` variable and initializes it to `True`. The third and fourth declarations define `T` and `F` to be `Boolean` constants and initialize them to `True` and `False`, respectively. Once these `Boolean` constants `T` and `F` are declared, they can be used in place of the `Boolean` literals `True` and `False`.

Now that we have discussed `Boolean` variables, constants, and literals, let us discuss `Boolean` expressions. `Boolean` expressions are expressions that yield a `Boolean` result. Even though the expression yields a `Boolean` result, the expression may contain operations on objects that belong to non-`Boolean` types, such as integer, floating point, or character types.

`Boolean` expressions may use the following relational operators: <, >, <=, >=, =, /=. These operators, which are defined in the section of this chapter on delimiters, can be used to compare operands belonging to any of the scalar types. Consider, for example, the following program:

```
with Ada.Text_IO; use Ada.Text_IO;
procedure Relational_Operators is
    package Boolean_IO is new Enumeration_IO (Boolean);
    use Boolean_IO;
    type Dialectic is (Thesis, Antithesis, Synthesis);
    First_Step: constant Dialectic := Thesis;
    Dozen: constant Integer := 12;
    Highest_Grade: Character := 'B';
begin -- Relational_Operators
    Put ( 3 /= 5 );                 -- outputs TRUE
    New_Line;
    Put ( 8.1 < 1.1 + 1.2 );        -- outputs FALSE
    New_Line;
    Put ( True > False );           -- outputs TRUE
    New_Line;
    Put (Dozen = 6 * 2);            -- outputs TRUE
    New_Line;
    Put ( Thesis <= Synthesis );    -- outputs TRUE
    New_Line;
    Put ( First_Step = Thesis );    -- outputs TRUE
    New_Line;
    Put ( 'C' >= 'P' );             -- outputs FALSE
    New_Line;
    Put ( Highest_Grade = 'A' );    -- outputs FALSE
end Relational_Operators;
```

No matter what type of objects these relational operators are comparing, the result is a `Boolean` value of either `True` or `False`. Note that `False` < `True` and that `Thesis` < `Synthesis`. This is due to the order in which these enumeration literals are listed in their type declarations. As already mentioned, the compiler assumes that enumeration literals are listed in ascending order, from left to right. For example, False < True because, in the package Standard, type Boolean is defined with False preceding True.

In addition to relational operators, Boolean expressions may use logical operators. Whereas relational operators can operate on operands of any scalar type, logical operators can operate only on Boolean operands. Logical operators include **and**, **or**, **xor**, **not**, and the special "short-circuit" forms **and then** and **or else**. All of these operators are binary operators except for **not**, which is a unary operator. The behavior of these logical operators, excluding the short-circuit forms, is shown in the following "truth table" (Table 2.1).

As shown in this truth table, the **and** operator returns the value True only if both operands are True; otherwise, the value False is returned. The **or** operator returns the value False only if both operands are False; otherwise, the value True is returned. The **xor** operator is called the *exclusive or*. This operator returns the value True if the operands have opposite values, that is, if one of the operands is True and the other is False; otherwise, the value False is returned.

Two different forms of *or* are used in the English language as well as in computer science. Whereas in computer science, these two forms—*or* and *exclusive or*—are distinguished by two different operators (**or** and **xor**), in the English language, these two forms are both indicated by the word *or*. Consider the following sentence: "To be admitted to this university, you need a GPA greater than 3.0 or a SAT score greater than 600." Obviously, a person is not denied admission if he or she has both a GPA greater than 3.0 and an SAT score greater than 600. This sentence, therefore, uses the nonexclusive *or*. The following sentence, however, uses the *exclusive or*. "Charles will either rendezvous with Ada or attend a poetry reading with Lord Byron." The *exclusive or* is used because Charles will engage in one of these activities *or* the other but not both. Note the use of the word "*either*," which, in conjunction with *or*, indicates that an *exclusive or* is being used.

**Table 2.1**   Truth Table

| A | B | A **and** B | A **or** B | A **xor** B | **not** A |
|---|---|---|---|---|---|
| True | True | True | True | False | False |
| True | False | False | True | True | False |
| False | True | False | True | True | True |
| False | False | False | False | False | True |

The **not** operator is a unary operator that returns a value that is opposite its operand: **not** True is False and **not** False is True.

The following program demonstrates how the logical operators can be used in Boolean expressions:

```
with Ada.Text_IO; use Ada.Text_IO;
procedure Logical_Operators is
    package Boolean_IO is new Enumeration_IO (Boolean);
    use Boolean_IO;
    type Output_Device is (Disk, Printer, Screen);
    Default_Output: constant Output_Device := Screen;
begin -- Logical_Operators
    Put ( True or False );                          -- outputs TRUE
    New_Line;
    Put ( 2 < 5 and 2 + 3 = 5 );                    -- outputs TRUE
    New_Line;
    Put ( True xor True );                          -- outputs FALSE
    New_Line;
    Put ( not True);                                -- outputs FALSE
    New_Line;
    Put ( not ( Default_Output = Printer) );        -- outputs TRUE
    New_Line;
    Put ( Disk < Screen and 'P' < 'B' );            -- outputs FALSE
    New_Line;
    Put ( True xor ( 3.2 /= 1.1 and 1+1 /= 3) );  -- outputs FALSE
end Logical_Operators;
```

The logical operators **and** and **or** (as well as **xor**) always evaluate both operands, although in an order unspecified by the Ada language:

```
-- assume X and Y are Boolean operands
X and Y    -- always evaluates both X and Y
X or Y     -- always evaluates both X and Y
```

Ada provides variations of the **and** and **or** operators: the short-circuit forms **and then** and **or else**. Whenever possible, these forms short circuit the evaluation process by only evaluating the first operand, not the second operand.

Consider the following expression that uses the short-circuit **and then**:

```
X and then Y -- evaluates Y only if X is True
```

The Boolean operand X is evaluated first. The second operand, Y, is only evaluated if X is True. When X is False, there is no need to evaluate Y, because the entire expression is False regardless of the value of Y. By using the short-circuit form **and then**, processing time may be saved when the second operand is some complex Boolean expression because the second operand is not evaluated unless necessary. More important, the short- circuit **and then** may result in safer code. The following expression uses the standard **and** operator:

```
A /= 0 and B / A > C    -- runtime error when A = 0
```

The problem with this expression is that, when A = 0, an illegal mathematical operation is performed: dividing a number, B, by zero. When this happens, the compiler raises a runtime error.

To avoid the risk of dividing a number by zero, we can use the short-circuit form **and then**:

```
A /= 0 and then B / A > C    -- evaluates B / A > C
                             -- only if A /= 0
```

In this example, B/A > C is only evaluated when A /= 0.

Ada also has the short-circuit form **or else**:

```
X or else Y      -- evaluates Y only if X is False
```

The Boolean operand X is evaluated first. The second operand, Y, is only evaluated if X is False. When X is True, there is no need to evaluate Y, because the entire expression is True regardless of the value of Y.

In addition to using the operators just discussed, a Boolean expression may use the keyword **in** to perform a membership test. A membership test determines whether an object falls within a particular range. Consider the following membership test:

```
Number in 1..5
```

Assume that Number is an integer variable or constant. This Boolean expression is True if the value of Number is in the range 1 to 5; otherwise, this Boolean expression is False. Note that Number must belong to the same type as the specified range.

Membership tests provide a concise notation. Without using the membership test, we would have to write

```
Number = 1 or Number = 2 or Number = 3 or Number = 4 or
Number = 5
```

or an expression such as

```
Number >= 1 and Number <= 5
```

There is a variation of the membership test, which uses the keyword **not**. For instance, to determine whether Number is *not* in the range 1 to 5, we could write

```
Number not in 1..5
```

In this case, the Boolean expression yields the value True if Number is less than 1 or greater than 5; otherwise, it yields the value False. Note that this form of the membership test provides an alternative to the logically equivalent but less readable expression:

```
not (Number in 1..5) -- less readable than using not in
```

Membership tests can be applied not only to integer values, but to real values, and as we shall see in later chapters, to many other types as well.

## SUBTYPES

A subtype consists of a subset of values of a type. A subtype does not define a new type but defines a constraint upon an existing type.

When an object does not need to assume all the values of a type, a subtype should be introduced. For example, a variable should rarely be declared as type `Integer`, because a variable rarely needs to assume all the integer values. By using subtypes to restrict the range of values that an object can legitimately assume, errors that might be difficult for programmers to detect are raised at runtime as constraint errors. A constraint error is raised whenever an object is given a value that is out of range. Furthermore, by allowing the Ada compilation system to detect constraint errors, the programmer does not need to make his or her own explicit range checks.

In the following subtype, `Persons_Age` is constrained (restricted) to numbers of type `Float` from `0.0` to `120.0`:

```
subtype Persons_Age is Float range 0.0 .. 120.0;
    -- age in years
```

To declare a subtype, the keyword **subtype** is followed by a user-supplied subtype name. This name is then followed by the keyword **is** and the name of the subtype's base type (the type on which the subtype is based). This base type is then followed by an optional constraint, consisting of the keyword **range** followed by a range constraint. In the previous example, constraining the range from `0.0` to `120.0` makes sense if we are measuring a person's age in years.

Given the subtype `Persons_Age`, we can then declare objects of this subtype:

```
Age: Persons_Age;
Drinking_Age: constant Persons_Age := 21.0;
```

In the first declaration, `Age` is defined as a variable that belongs to the subtype `Persons_Age`. Therefore, `Age` is restricted to floating point values in the range of `0.0` to `120.0`. If an attempt is made to assign a value to `Age` that is outside of this range, then a constraint error is raised:

```
Age := 121.0;    -- constraint error is raised;
                 -- 121.0 is out of bounds
```

The second declaration declares `Drinking_Age` to be a constant of subtype `Persons_Age` and initializes it to 21.0.

Since range constraints are optional, a subtype may be declared that has the same range of values as its base type:

```
subtype Logical is Boolean;
```

In this case, `Logical` is simply another name for type `Boolean`.

Let us consider a few more examples:

```
subtype Hours_In_Day is Integer range 0 .. 23;
subtype Uppercase is Character range 'A' .. 'Z';
Hour: Hours_In_Day;
Upper: Uppercase;
```

In the first declaration, `Hours_In_Day` is defined to be a subtype of `Integer` from 0 to 23. In the second declaration, `Uppercase` is defined to be a subtype of `Character` from `'A'` to `'Z'`.

There are two forms of subtypes: explicit subtypes and implicit subtypes. Explicit subtypes have names; implicit subtypes do not have names. In the previous declarations, the variables `Hour` and `Upper` belong to the explicit subtypes `Hours_In_Day` and `Uppercase`, respectively. We could declare `Hour` and `Upper` to belong to implicit subtypes, which do not have names:

```
Hour: Integer range 0 .. 23;
Upper: Character range 'A' .. 'Z';
```

Once again, the variable `Hour` is constrained to integer values from 0 to 23, and the variable `Upper` is constrained to character values from `'A'` to `'Z'`.

Since explicit subtypes, unlike implicit subtypes, have names, explicit subtypes can be used to reflect our hierarchical view of the world. Light, for example, is part of the electromagnetic spectrum that includes visible light as well as "invisible" light–infrared and ultraviolet light. This hierarchical relationship between these parts of the electromagnetic spectrum is reflected in the following declarations:

```
type   Electromagnetic_Spectrum is
   (  Radio, Television, Microwave, Infrared, Red, Orange, Yellow,
      Green, Blue, Indigo, Violet, Ultraviolet, X_Rays, Gamma_Rays);
         -- listed from longest to shortest wavelength

subtype Light is Electromagnetic_Spectrum
   range Infrared .. Ultraviolet;

subtype Visible_Light is Light range Red..Violet;
   -- subtype of a subtype
```

Note that `Visible_Light` is a subtype of `Light`, which is a subtype of the enumeration type `Electromagnetic_Spectrum`.

The names of explicit subtypes may also be used to represent ranges, resulting in code that is more concise and general. Consider, for instance, the following explicit subtype:

```
subtype Digit is Integer range 0 .. 9;
```

Once this subtype is declared, the identifier `Digit` may be used to represent the range `0..9`. For example, the following two membership tests are logically equivalent:

```
Number in 0..9    -- these two membership tests are equivalent
Number in Digit   -- Digit represents the range 0..9
```

As a second example, consider the range `0..9` used in a **for** loop:

```
for Number in 0..9 loop...
```

Once again, we can represent this range with the name of the subtype:

```
for Number in Digit loop...
```

We will continue this discussion of alternate ways to represent ranges in Chapter 3 on control structures.

Ada is a strongly typed language. Objects of different types cannot be assigned or compared to one another and cannot appear in the same expression. The illegal mixing of types is shown in the following code:

```
declare

    type Mesozoic_Era is (Triassic, Jurassic, Cretaceous);
    type Cenozoic_Era is (Tertiary, Quaternary);
    Age_Of_Archaeopteryx: Mesozoic_Era := Jurassic;
    Age_Of_Neanderthal: Cenozoic_Era := Quaternary;

begin

    if (Age_Of_Archaeopteryx < Age_Of_Neanderthal) and
        -- error; mixed types
        (Age_Of_Archaeopteryx not in Cenozoic_Era) then
        -- error; mixed types
        Age_Of_Neanderthal := Age_Of_Archaeopteryx;
        -- error; mixed types
    end if;

end;
```

Since the variables `Age_Of_Archaeopteryx` and `Age_Of_Neanderthal` belong to different types, they cannot be compared or assigned to one another. The membership test is also illegal since the member being tested belongs to a different type than the range represented by the identifier `Cenozoic_Era`.

Whereas objects of different types cannot mix, objects of a subtype can mix with objects of its base type. Furthermore, objects of different subtypes can mix if these subtypes are descended from the same base type. This is as expected since, as mentioned previously, subtypes do not define new types. Consider, for instance, the following code:

```ada
declare

    type Geologic_Period is (Cambrian, Ordovician, Silurian,
        Devonian, Carboniferous, Permian, Triassic, Jurassic,
        Cretaceous, Tertiary, Quaternary);

    subtype Paleozoic_Era is Geologic_Period range
        Cambrian..Permian;

    subtype Mesozoic_Era is Geologic_Period range
        Triassic..Cretaceous;

    subtype Cenozoic_Era is Geologic_Period range
        Tertiary..Quaternary;

    Age_Of_Tyrannosaurus: Mesozoic_Era := Cretaceous;
    Age_Of_Trilobite: Paleozoic_Era := Cambrian;
    Age_Of_Mastodon, Age_Of_Homo_Sapien: Geologic_Period;

begin

    if (Age_Of_Tyrannosaurus in Cenozoic_Era) or
            (Age_Of_Trilobite < Age_Of_Tyrannosaurus) then
        Age_Of_Mastodon := Quatenary;
        Age_Of_Homo_Sapien := Age_Of_Mastodon;
    end if;

end;
```

Since all the subtypes are descended from a common base type, `Geologic_Period`, there is no problem of type mismatches. Also, since a subtype does not introduce a new type, operations such as <, which are allowed for objects of type `Geologic_Period`, are also allowed for objects that belong to any of the subtypes of `Geologic_Period`.

In addition to the user-defined subtypes just discussed, there are explicit pre-defined subtypes. Two of these subtypes, `Positive` and `Natural`, are defined as follows:

```ada
subtype Positive is Integer range 1 .. Integer'Last;
subtype Natural is Integer range 0 .. Integer'Last;
```

These subtypes are defined in the package `Standard` and are therefore always available for use. Note that the upper bounds of these subtypes are

Integer'Last. The 'Last is called an attribute, and when appended to a type such as Integer, returns the largest value of that type. Thus, Integer'Last yields the largest value of type Integer. As we will see in the next section, Ada provides many useful attributes.

## ATTRIBUTES

Attributes are characteristics of an entity, such as an object, a type, or a subprogram. For example, every Ada compiler has a largest value of type Integer. This value is an attribute of the Integer type. In most computer languages, attributes must be looked up in a manual or must be found by examining code. In Ada, however, attributes are available within the language. In other words, the code can directly reference attributes. We shall discuss 11 useful attributes that are frequently applied to scalar types: P'First, P'Last, P'Pos, P'Val, P'Succ, P'Pred, P'Image, P'Value, P'Base, P'Max, and P'Min. (Attributes Max and Min are new to Ada 95; attributes Succ, Pred, Image, Value, and Base have new capabilities.) In all of these attributes, P stands for a type or subtype, which is followed by a tick mark, ', and the name of the attribute. With the exception of P'First, P'Last, and P'Base, all of these attributes require parameters. In addition, all of them apply to real and discrete types, except for Pos and Val, which only apply to discrete types. To see how these attributes work, consider the following program:

**Ada 95** ▶

```ada
with Ada.Text_IO; use Ada;
procedure Attributes is

    type Solar_System is (Mercury, Venus, Earth, Mars, Jupiter,
        Saturn, Uranus, Neptune, Pluto);
    subtype Inner_Planets is Solar_System range Mercury..Mars;
    subtype Outer_Planets is Solar_System range Jupiter..Pluto;
    subtype Gas_Giants is Outer_Planets range Jupiter..Neptune;

    Dozen: constant Integer := 12;
    Pi: constant Float := 3.14159_26535;
    Our_Planet: constant Solar_System := Earth;
    Red_Planet: constant String := "Mars";

    package Bool_IO is new Text_IO.Enumeration_IO (Boolean);
    package Planets_IO is new Text_IO.Enumeration_IO (Solar_System);
    package Real_IO is new Text_IO.Float_IO (Float);
    package Int_IO is new Text_IO.Integer_IO (Integer);

begin -- attributes

    -- attributes First and Last
    Int_IO.Put (Integer'First);          -- outputs the
    Text_IO.New_Line;                    -- smallest integer
```

```
Int_IO.Put (Integer'Last);                -- outputs the largest
Text_IO.New_Line;                         -- Integer value
Real_IO.Put (Float'Last);                 -- outputs the largest
Text_IO.New_Line;                         -- Float value
Bool_IO.Put (Boolean'First);              -- outputs FALSE
Text_IO.New_Line;
Bool_IO.Put (Boolean'Last);               -- outputs TRUE
Text_IO.New_Line;
Planets_IO.Put (Solar_System'First);      -- outputs MERCURY
Text_IO.New_Line;
Planets_IO.Put (Outer_Planets'First);     -- outputs JUPITER
Text_IO.New_Line;
Planets_IO.Put (Outer_Planets'Last);      -- outputs PLUTO
Text_IO.New_Line;
Planets_IO.Put (Inner_Planets'Last);      -- outputs MARS
Text_IO.New_Line;
Planets_IO.Put (Gas_Giants'Last);         --outputs NEPTUNE
Text_IO.New_Line;

-- attributes Succ and Pred
Int_IO.Put (Integer'Pred(0));       -- outputs -1
Text_IO.New_Line;
Int_IO.Put (Integer'Succ(Dozen));   -- outputs 13
Text_IO.New_Line;
Planets_IO.Put (Solar_System'Succ(Earth));         -- outputs
Text_IO.New_Line;                                  -- MARS
Planets_IO.Put (Solar_System'Pred(Our_Planet));    -- outputs
Text_IO.New_Line;                                  -- VENUS
Real_IO.Put (Float'Succ(1.0));    -- outputs the machine value
Text_IO.New_Line;                 -- immediately following 1.0
Real_IO.Put ( Float'Pred (Pi) );  -- outputs the machine value
Text_IO.New_Line;                 -- immediately preceding Pi

-- attributes Image and Value
Text_IO.Put (Boolean'Image(False));  -- outputs FALSE
Text_IO.New_Line;                    -- (the string)
Text_IO.Put (Solar_System'Image(Our_Planet));   -- outputs EARTH
Text_IO.New_Line;                               -- (the string)
Text_IO.Put (Integer'Image(31));     -- outputs " 31"
Text_IO.New_Line;                    -- (the string)
Text_IO.Put (Integer'Image(-5));     -- outputs "-5"
Text_IO.New_Line;                    -- (the string)
Text_IO.Put (Integer'Image(Dozen));  -- outputs " 12"
Text_IO.New_Line;                    -- (the string)
Text_IO.Put (Float'Image(72.31));    -- outputs the string
Text_IO.New_Line;                    -- " 7.2310000000E+01"
Text_IO.Put (Float'Image(Pi));       -- outputs the string
Text_IO.New_Line;                    -- " 3.1415926535E+00"
Int_IO.Put (Integer'Value("31"));    -- outputs 31
Text_IO.New_Line;                    -- (the integer)
```

```
Real_IO.Put (Float'Value("72.31"));    -- outputs the number
Text_IO.New_Line;                      -- 7.2310000000E+01
Bool_IO.Put (Boolean'Value("False"));-- outputs FALSE
Text_IO.New_Line;                      -- (Boolean literal)
Planets_IO.Put (Solar_System'Value(Red_Planet));    -- outputs
Text_IO.New_Line;                                   -- MARS

-- attributes Pos and Val
Int_IO.Put (Solar_System'Pos(Mercury));  -- outputs 0
Text_IO.New_Line;
Planets_IO.Put (Solar_System'Val(0));    -- outputs MERCURY
Text_IO.New_Line;
Int_IO.Put (Integer'Pos(-7));            -- outputs -7
Text_IO.New_Line;

-- attributes Min and Max
Planets_IO.Put (Solar_System'Min(Mars, Our_Planet));-- outputs
Text_IO.New_Line;                                   -- EARTH
Int_IO.Put (Integer'Max(-3, Dozen));                -- outputs
Text_IO.New_Line;                                   -- 12
Real_IO.Put (Float'Max (Pi, 921.0));     -- outputs
Text_IO.New_Line;                        -- 9.2100000000E+02

-- attribute Base
Planets_IO.Put (Outer_Planets'Base'First);   -- outputs MERCURY
Text_IO.New_Line;
Planets_IO.Put (Gas_Giants'Base'Last);       --outputs PLUTO
Text_IO.New_Line;

-- The following code does NOT raise a constraint error
-- Succ, Pred, Pos, and Val always apply to their base type
-- Solar_System
Planets_IO.Put (Inner_Planets'Succ(Jupiter));   -- outputs
Text_IO.New_Line;                               -- SATURN
Planets_IO.Put (Outer_Planets'Pred(Our_Planet));-- outputs
Text_IO.New_Line;                               -- VENUS
Int_IO.Put (Outer_Planets'Pos(Our_Planet));     -- outputs 2
Text_IO.New_Line;
Planets_IO.Put (Inner_Planets'Val(8));          -- outputs
Text_IO.New_Line;                               -- PLUTO
Planets_IO.Put (Outer_Planets'Val(3));          -- outputs
Text_IO.New_Line;                               -- MARS
    end Attributes;
```

**Ada 95 ▶** The context clause, **use** Ada, enables items within Ada . Text_IO to be referenced without the Ada prefix. For example, the New_Line procedure within Text_IO can be referenced as Text_IO.New_Line instead of Ada.Text_IO.New_Line. However, as mentioned in Chapter 1, through a renaming mechanism to be discussed later in this book, items within Text_IO can referenced without the Ada prefix even when the **use** Ada clause is omitted.

The first 10 statements of procedure `Attributes` demonstrate the use of attributes `First` and `Last`. The attribute `First` yields the smallest value of the indicated type or subtype, while `Last` yields the largest value. Thus, `Integer'First` yields the smallest value of type `Integer` available on a particular Ada compiler. `Integer'Last` yields the largest value of type `Integer` available on a particular compiler. On a standard 16-bit machine, `Integer'First` might be equal to –32,768, and `Integer'Last` might be equal to 32,767. Similarly, `Float'Last` yields the largest value of type `Float` available on a particular compiler. Since type `Boolean` lists `False` before `True`, `Boolean'First` yields `False`, and `Boolean'Last` yields `True`. Similarly, consider the ordering of the planets listed in type `Solar_System` and its subtypes `Inner_Planets`, `Outer_Planets`, and `Gas_Giants`. `Solar_System'First` yields `Mercury`, `Outer_Planets'First` yields `Jupiter`, `Outer_Planets'Last` yields `Pluto`, `Inner_Planets'Last` yields `Mars`, and `Gas_Giants'Last` yields `Neptune`.

The attributes `Succ` and `Pred` yield the value of a SUCCessor and PREDecessor, respectively. Thus, `Integer'Pred(0)` yields the predecessor of 0, which is –1, and since the constant `Dozen` has a value of 12, `Integer'Succ(Dozen)` yields the successor of 12, which is 13. Similarly, `Solar_System'Succ(Earth)` yields `Mars`, and since the constant `Our_Planet` has a value of `Earth`, `Solar_System'Pred(Our_Planet)` yields `Venus`. The compiler knows that `Venus` comes just before `Earth`, which comes just before `Mars`, not because the compiler is equipped with a basic understanding of astronomy, but because of the order in which the planets are listed in the enumeration type `Solar_System`.

**Ada 95 ▶** From a mathematical perspective, real numbers form a continuum and do not have successors or predecessors. Between any two real numbers, no matter how close in value, there is an infinite number of other real numbers. However, unlike the ideal world of mathematics, a computer exists in a physical word using processors with limited memory storage. On a computer, only a finite number of real numbers can be exactly represented. These are called "machine numbers." When the attributes `Succ` or `Pred` apply to a floating point type, they respectively return the next higher or lower machine number. Thus, `Float'Succ(1.0)` yields the machine number immediately above 1.0. (That is, the value that exceeds 1.0 by the smallest amount that is exactly representable on the computer.) Since `Pi` has the value `3.1415926535`, `Float'Pred(Pi)` yields the machine number immediately below `3.1415926535`.

The `Image` attribute converts an object of type `P` to a string representation. When the object is an enumeration value, the characters within the string appear in uppercase. Thus, `Boolean'Image (False)` yields the string `"FALSE"`, and since the value of `Our_Planet` is `Earth`, `Solar_System'Image(Our_Planet)` yields the string `"EARTH"`. When the `Image` attribute is applied to a numeric value, a blank or minus sign always appears to the left of the string representation of the number, depending on whether the number is positive or negative. Thus, `Integer'Image(31)` yields `" 31"`, `Integer'Image(-5)` yields `"-5"`, and since

**Ada 95 ▶** the value of `Dozen` is 12, `Integer'Image(Dozen)` yields `" 12"`. When the `Image` attribute is applied to a floating point value, the string representation of the number always appears in scientific notation with a leading blank or negative sign, a single digit to the left of the decimal point, the remaining digits to the right of the decimal point, an implementation dependent number of trailing zeros, and a signed two digit exponent value following the E. Thus, `Float'Image(72.31)` yields `" 7.2310000000E+01"`, and since the value of `Pi` is `3.1415926535`, `Float'Image(Pi)` yields `" 3.1415926535E+00"`.

The `Value` attribute performs the opposite operation as the `Image` attribute: `P'Value` converts a string to a literal of type `P`. Thus, `Integer'Value("31")`

**Ada 95 ▶** yields the integer literal `31`, `Float'Value("72.31")` yields the real literal `7.2310000000E+01`, `Boolean'Value("False")` yields the Boolean literal `FALSE`, and since the value of the string constant `Red_Planet` is `"Mars"`, `Solar_System'Value(Red_Planet)` yields the literal `MARS`.

When the `Value` attribute is used, the compiler verifies that the string is convertible to a value of the specified type. For example, `Boolean'Value("Yes")` is illegal since `"Yes"` does not match either `True` or `False`.

**Ada 95 ▶** In addition to the attributes `Image` and `Value`, Ada also supports `Wide_String` versions of these attributes: `Wide_Image` and `Wide_Value`. Whereas objects of type `String` contain a sequence of values of type `Character`, objects of type `Wide_String` contain a sequence of values of type `Wide_Character`. To output values of type `Wide_Character` or `Wide_String`, one must reference package `Ada.Wide_Text_IO` in a **with** clause. Package `Ada.Wide_Text_IO` contains `Put` procedures for outputting `Wide_Characters` and `Wide_Strings`.

Attributes `Pos` and `Val` perform opposite operations. The attribute `P'Pos` yields the POSition of an object in type `P`, whereas `P'Val` yields the VALue of an object of type `P` at the specified position. (Do not confuse the attributes `Value` and `Val`; they are different.) Whereas the other attributes we have covered apply to any scalar type, `Pos` and `Val` only apply to discrete types.

The first value of an enumeration type occupies position `0`; the second value, position `1`; the third value, position `2`; and so on. For instance, within the type `Solar_System` defined previously, the position of the planets `Mercury`, `Venus`, `Earth`, and `Mars` are 0, 1, 2, and 3, respectively. (These position numbers do not necessarily coincide with the way that enumeration literals are internally mapped to numbers within the computer.) Thus, `Solar_System'Pos (Mercury)` yields `0`, because `Mercury` is the first literal listed in the declaration of the enumeration type `Solar_System`. Conversely, `Solar_System'Val(0)` yields `Mercury`, because `Mercury` is the value at position 0.

With integers, the position starts with `Integer'First`, not 0. Therefore, `Integer'Pos (-7) = -7`. In general, for all integers N, `Integer'Pos (N) = N`.

**Ada 95 ▶** The attributes `Min` and `Max` return, respectively, the smaller or larger of two scalar values. So `Solar_System'Min(Mars, Our_Planet)` returns `Earth`, `Integer'Max(-3, Dozen)` returns 12, and `Float'Max (Pi, 921.0)` returns `9.2100000000E+02`.

The attribute `Base` refers to a subtype's base type, that is, the type obtained by removing all range constraints. For example, `Outer_Planets'Base'First` is the same as `Solar_System'First`, since the base type of `Outer_Planets` is `Solar_System`. Thus, `Outer_Planets'Base'First` yields `Mercury`, and `Gas_Giants'Base'Last` yields `Pluto`.

**Ada 95 ▶**    As an aside, the `Base` attribute can be used anywhere in the code to specify the range of a base type. For example, the membership test

```
Our_Planet in Outer_Planets    -- yields False
```

evaluates to `False`, but when the `Base` attribute is applied, it evaluates to `True`:

```
Our_Planet in Outer_Planets'Base -- yields True
      -- same as: Our_Planet in Solar_System
```

When using the attributes `Pred` and `Succ`, be careful not to go out of bounds. In other words, if `Pred` is used with the first value of a type or `Succ` with the last value of a type, a constraint error is raised. There is no "wraparound" feature that automatically brings us from one end of the enumerated list to the other. For example, `Solar_System'Succ(Pluto)` generates a constraint error. Since `Pluto` is the last planet in the solar system, it has no successor. However, as illustrated in the last section of procedure `Attributes`, no constraint error is raised when `Succ` yields a result that resides outside the range of the specified subtype. For example, `Inner_Planets'Succ(Jupiter)` yields `Saturn`, and no constraint error is raised even though both `Jupiter` and `Saturn` lie outside the range of `Inner_Planets`. Similarly, `Outer_Planets'Pred(Our_Planet)` yields `Venus`, even though both `Our_Planet` and `Venus` lie outside the range of `Outer_Planets`. No constraint error is raised in either case because `Succ` and `Pred` actually apply to the base type `Solar_System`.

In the same manner as attributes `Succ` and `Pred`, the attributes `Pos` and `Val` do not apply to a subtype, but to the subtype's base type. Thus, `Outer_Planets'Pos(Our_Planet)` yields `2`, even though `Our_Planet` has the value `Earth`, which is outside the range of `Outer_Planets`. Also, the result of `2` refers to position `2` in the base type `Solar_System`. Similarly, `Inner_Planets'Val(8)` yields `Pluto`, even though `Pluto` is outside the range of `Inner_Planets`. The parameter `8` refers to position `8` in the base type `Solar_System`. Finally, `Outer_Planets'Val(3)` yields `Mars`, even though `Mars` is outside the range of `Outer_Planets`. The parameter `3` refers to position `3` in the base type `Solar_System`.

## DERIVED TYPES

A derived type creates a new type from an existing "parent type":

```
type Percent is new Integer range 0 .. 100; -- derived type
```

Derived type declarations resemble subtype declarations:

```
subtype Percent is Integer range 0 .. 100;  -- subtype
```

Syntactically, these type declarations differ in only two ways. First, derived type declarations begin with the keyword **type**; subtype declarations begin with the keyword **subtype**. Second, derived type declarations, unlike subtype declarations, contain the keyword **new**.

Despite the similar appearance between subtype and derived type declarations, there are important differences. First, recall that a subtype does not introduce a new type but merely places an optional constraint on the values of its base type. A derived type, however, creates a new type from an existing parent type. (Note the terminology: a subtype is based on a base type, but a derived type is derived from a parent type.) Second, since a subtype does not introduce a new type, objects of a subtype may mix with objects of its base type. Furthermore, objects of different subtypes created from the same base type may mix. Since a derived type introduces a new type, objects of a derived type may *not* mix with objects of its parent type. Furthermore, objects of different derived types may not mix, even when they are created from the same parent type.

So why are derived types needed? Why should, for example, two types be distinct when they are both implemented as integer types? After all, integer types have integer values and integer operations, so why should we introduce more than one integer type? To answer this, consider the following code that defines four integer derived types, `Miles_Per_Hour`, `Items_In_Stock`, `Population`, and `Card_Count`:

```
declare
    type Miles_Per_Hour is new Integer range 0..100;
    type Items_In_Stock is new Integer range 0..100;
    type Population is new Integer range 0..2_000_000_000;
        -- assumes Integer'Last >= 2000000000
    type Card_Count is new Integer range 0..52;
    Speed: Miles_Per_Hour := 65;
    Number_Of_Widgets: Items_In_Stock := 5;
    Population_Of_Toowoomba: Population := 58_000;
    Cards_Taken: Card_Count := 25;
begin
    -- these "logic" errors are caught at compile time
    Number_Of_Widgets := Speed;         -- illegal; type mismatch
    Speed := Population_Of_Toowoomba; -- illegal; type mismatch
    Cards_Taken := Number_Of_Widgets; -- illegal; type mismatch
end;
```

Even though the variables `Speed`, `Number_Of_Widgets`, `Population_Of_Toowoomba`, and `Cards_Taken` belong to integer types, they are logically distinct. The variable `Speed` takes values that represent the speed of travel expressed in miles per hour, `Number_Of_Widgets` takes values that represent the number of items in stock, `Population_Of_Toowoomba` takes values that represent the number of people inhabiting Toowoomba, and `Cards_Taken` takes values that represent the number of cards taken from a deck of 52 cards. By declaring these variables to be of different types, the code becomes more reliable. Reliability is enhanced since the compiler will generate an error at compile time if one of these variables is mistakenly compared or assigned to another of these variables. Thus, the preceding code will not compile because there is a type mismatch when an attempt is made to assign any of these variables to any of the other variables.

In the preceding examples, the derived types have range constraints. Range constraints, however, are optional. As the following declarations show, derived types may be declared with or without range constraints:

```
-- without range constraints
type New_Integer is new Integer;
type New_Real is new Float;
type Itsy_Bitsy_Integer is new Short_Integer;
type Real_Large is new Long_Float;

-- with range constraints
type One_To_Five is new Integer range 1 .. 5;
type Zero_To_Five is new Float range 0.0 .. 5.0;
```

In the first declaration, the derived type New_Integer is defined to be a new integer type that has the same range of values as its parent type, Integer. Although New_Integer is a "copy" of Integer, objects of these two types may not mix. The second declaration defines the derived type New_Real to be a copy of its parent type Float. The third declaration defines the derived type Itsy_Bitsy_Integer to be a copy of its parent type Short_Integer, and the fourth declaration defines the type Real_Large to be a copy of the predefined type Long_Float. Types Short_Integer and Long_Float, together with Long_Integer and Short_Float, are optional types that your Ada compiler may or may not provide. If provided, they are located in package Standard, together with the required types Integer and Float. Type Short_Integer covers a smaller range of values than type Integer; Long_Integer covers a greater range of values. Although types Short_Integer, Integer, and Long_Integer are integer types, they are distinct types and hence are not type compatible. Thus, objects of these different integer types cannot mix. In addition to these distinct integer types, many implementations of package Standard include the optional types Short_Float and Long_Float. Again, objects of these different types cannot mix with one another or with objects of type Float. The fifth declaration contains a range constraint: type One_To_Five is defined as an integer type constrained to the values from 1 to 5. Finally, the sixth declaration defines the type Zero_To_Five to be a floating point type constrained to the values from 0.0 to 5.0.

The lower and upper bounds of derived types must be static (determined at compile time), so that the compiler can choose an appropriate representation for the values of the new type. This is different from subtypes, whose upper and lower bounds can be calculated dynamically:

```
Upper_Bounds: Integer := 2 ** 15 - 1;
subtype Disk_Address is Integer range 0..Upper_Bounds;    -- OK
type Video_Address is new Integer range 0..Upper_Bounds;
   --illegal; bounds must be static
```

So far we have seen derived types derived from predefined numeric types such as `Integer` and `Float`. Derived types may also be derived from user-defined types and types that are nonnumeric:

```
type Color is (White, Tan, Beige, Gray);
type Stove_Color is new Color range White..Beige;
   -- derived from parent type Color
type Refrigerator_Color is new Color;
   -- derived from parent type Color
```

Both `Stove_Color` and `Refrigerator_Color` are derived from the parent type `Color`, which is a user-defined enumeration type. By creating these derived types, the programmer maintains the distinction between stove color and refrigerator color; the color of a stove cannot inadvertently be compared with or assigned to the color of a refrigerator.

## TYPE CONVERSION

Although Ada does not allow objects of different types to mix, this ban can often be circumvented, when necessary, by using type conversion. (An excessive number of type conversions usually indicates that derived types were defined that should have been subtypes of a common base type.) To convert an object from one type to another, use the name of the target type (or subtype) as a conversion operator. For example, if you wish to convert an integer variable $N$ to type `Float`, write `Float(N)`. The following code illustrates the ways type conversion can and cannot be used:

```
declare
   -- user defined types
   type New_Integer is new Integer range 0..100;
   type Enumeration is (Alpha, Beta, Gamma);
   type New_Enumeration is new Enumeration range Alpha..Beta;

   -- variables
   Nat: Natural := 22;
   Int: Integer := 7;
   Flt: Float := 3.8;
   Bool: Boolean := False;
   Char: Character := 'A';
   Short_Int: Short_Integer := 2;
   Long_Flt: Long_Float := 2.2;
   New_Int: New_Integer := 5;
   Enum: Enumeration := Alpha;
   New_Enum: New_Enumeration := Beta;

begin
   -- type conversions allow assignments to be made
   Nat := Natural (Long_Flt);          -- assigns 2
   Int := Integer (Flt);               -- assigns 4 (rounds)
```

```
      Int := Integer (Float'Truncation(Flt));     -- assigns 3
      Int := Integer (Float'Rounding(Flt));        -- assigns 4
      Flt := Float (Short_Int);              -- assigns 2.0
      Short_Int := Short_Integer (Nat);      -- assigns 22
      Long_Flt := Long_Float (Flt);          -- assigns 3.8
      New_Int := New_Integer (Int);          -- assigns 7
      New_Enum := New_Enumeration (Enum);  -- assigns Alpha


      -- illegal assignments
      Int := Integer (Bool);                 -- illegal
      Int := Integer (Char);                 -- illegal
         -- if the numeric code for Char is desired, replace with
         -- Int := Character'Pos(Char);
      Char := Character (Int);               -- illegal
         -- if character with the numeric code of Int is desired,
         -- replace with
         -- Char := Character'Val(Int);
   end;
```

The first statement converts Long_Flt (a variable of type Long_Float) to the subtype Natural and then assigns the result to Nat (a variable of subtype Natural). In this case, the name of the predefined Integer subtype Natural is being used to perform the type conversion. The second statement converts a Flt (a variable of type Float) to the type Integer. Note that when Flt is converted to an integer value, Flt's value of 3.8 is rounded to 4, not truncated to 3. [If the real number is midway between two integer values, then rounding is always away from 0. Thus, Integer(3.5) yields 4, and Integer (-1.5) yields -2.] As the next two assignments in the preceding code illustrate, rounding or truncation can be controlled with the attributes Rounding and Trunction. The next four assignments use the type names Float, Short_Integer, long_Float, and New_Integer as type conversion operators.

**Ada 95 ▶**

The next assignment statement converts Enum (a variable of type Enumeration) to New_Enumeration (a type derived from Enumeration). An object of a derived type can always be converted to the parent type or vice versa. In addition, objects of derived types can be converted to other derived types, as long as these types are ultimately derived from the same parent type. For nonnumeric types such as Enumeration and New_Enumeration, these are the only cases where type conversion is allowed. As the remaining statements in the previous code illustrate, type conversion is disallowed between nonnumeric types that are not derivatives of one another. Thus, neither a Boolean value nor a Character value can be converted to type Integer. Similarly, the last statement in the code shows that an Integer value cannot be converted to type Character. If such conversions are absolutely necessesary, Unchecked_Conversion must be employed (see Chapter 16). However, as mentioned in the preceding code comments, if the purpose of converting a character value to an integer is to obtain the character's numeric code, this can be accomplished using the Pos attribute: Character'Pos(Char). Conversely, if the purpose of converting an integer to a character is to obtain the character with the specified numeric code, this can be accomplished using the `Val` attribute: `Character'Val(Int)`.

## ORDER OF OPERATIONS

In this section, we will first discuss the internal hierarchy of arithmetic, relational, and logical operations. We will then consider how these three kinds of operations are ordered in relation to each other.

In Figure 2.2, the arithmetic operators are listed in order of precedence, from top to bottom. Operations on the same level are performed from left to right.

Consider the following expression:

```
-2 ** 5 + 2 * 3 ** 2
```

According to Figure 2.2, exponentiation is performed first, followed by multiplication, followed by negation (making a number negative), followed by addition. The preceding expression is thus evaluated as if parentheses were used as follows:

```
(- (2 ** 5)) + (2 * (3 ** 2))
```

This expression evaluates to $-14$.

Note from Figure 2.2 that **mod** and **rem** have a higher precedence than negation. This is not what one might expect. Thus, the following two expressions yield different results:

```
-A mod B       -- WARNING: these two expressions yield
(-A) mod B     -- different results
```

Since negation is applied after **mod**, $-A$ **mod** $B$ is equivalent to

```
-(A mod B).
```

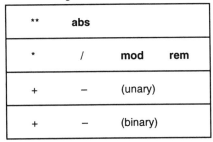

Highest Precedence

| ** | abs | | |
|----|-----|-----|-----|
| * | / | mod | rem |
| + | − | (unary) | |
| + | − | (binary) | |

Lowest Precedence

**Figure 2.2**   Hierarchy of arithmetic operators.

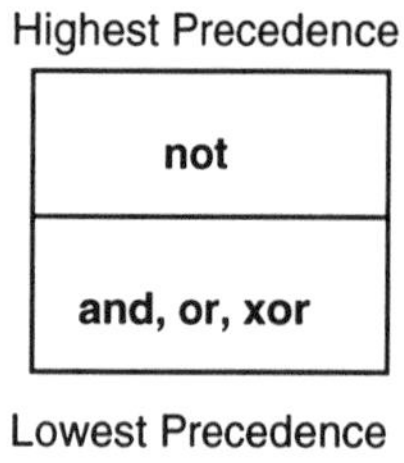

Highest Precedence

| not |
| --- |
| and, or, xor |

Lowest Precedence

---

**Figure 2.3**   Hierarchy of logical operators.

It is recommended that parentheses be used whenever the order of operations is not obvious, as in the preceding code. Fewer errors will be made, and those reading the code will have an easier time understanding it. Parentheses, of course, *must* be used when the precedence of the operations needs to be overridden.

Let us now consider the order of logical operators, shown in Figure 2.3. The logical operator **not** takes precedence over **and, or,** and **xor**, which are all on the same level. Consider the following compound expression, where P and Q are Boolean operands:

```
not P and Q   -- not takes precedence
```

Since **not**  P is evaluated first, this expression is equivalent to the following:

```
(not P) and Q
```

Unlike the arithmetic operators, even though the operators **and, or,** and **xor** are on the same level, order between these operators is undefined and must be provided by using parentheses. For instance, the following expression is illegal:

```
P and Q or R      -- illegal; must use parentheses
```

However, parentheses are not required when the same operator is used multiple times:

```
P and Q and R     -- legal; evaluated from left to right
```

In such cases, the expression is evaluated from left to right.

Unlike arithmetic and logical operators, the relational operators are all on the same level:

```
<, >, <=, >=, =, /=
```

The order of these operators is undefined and must be provided by using parentheses:

```
False < 7 < 9     -- illegal; must use parentheses
False < (7 < 9)   -- OK; evaluates to True
```

Be careful to avoid mixing types when using several relational operators in the same expression. In the preceding example, for instance, the following use of parentheses is illegal:

```
(False < 7) < 9  -- illegal, mixed types
                 -- False is Boolean, 7 is integer
```

The next expression also illegally mixes `Boolean` and integer types:

```
(3 < 5) < 9      -- illegal, mixed types;
                 -- (3 < 5) is Boolean, 9 is integer
```

When arithmetic, logical, and relational operations are used in the same expression, the hierarchy shown in Figure 2.4 applies. Arithmetic operations have the highest precedence, and binary logical operators have the lowest precedence. By limiting the logical operators to binary operators, we are excluding the unary logical operator **not**. The operator **not** does not fit into this hierarchy since it has the highest precedence level, along with the arithmetic operators ** and **abs**.

Let us consider an example of an expression that uses arithmetic and relational operators, and a logical operator:

```
1 + 2 > 0 and 3 - 2 = 1
```

As shown in Figure 2.4, the arithmetic operations, + and –, are performed first. The relational operations, > and  =, are then performed. Finally, the logical **and** operation is performed. The preceding expression is thus evaluated as if it contained these parentheses:

```
( ( 1 + 2 ) > 0 ) and ( ( 3 - 2 ) = 1 )
```

This expression evaluates to `True`.

This chapter has introduced basic features of Ada such as `Boolean` expressions, subtypes, and attributes. However, this chapter has not examined how these

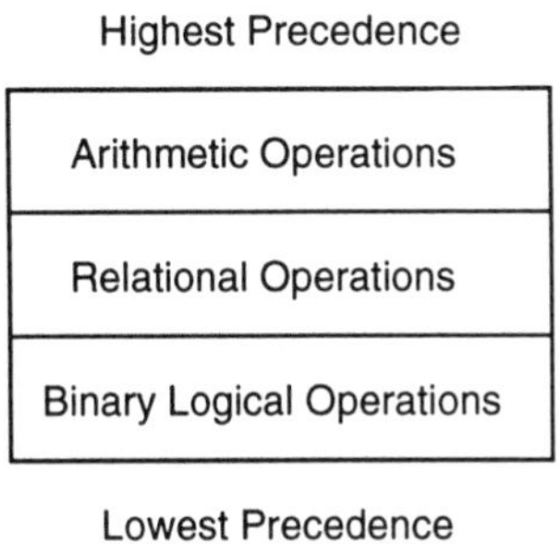

Highest Precedence

| Arithmetic Operations |
| Relational Operations |
| Binary Logical Operations |

Lowest Precedence

**Figure 2.4**  Hierarchy of operations.

basic features are used. The `Boolean` expressions introduced in this chapter are frequently used in **if** statements and **while** loops. Subtype names and certain attributes are frequently used to represent discrete ranges in **for** loops and **case** statements. Constructs such as **if** statements, **case** statements, **while** loops, and **for** loops are known as control structures. Control structures are the topic of the next chapter.

## EXERCISES

1. Which five of the following identifiers are illegal?

   | | | | | | |
   |---|---|---|---|---|---|
   | **a.** | 9W | **b.** | W9 | **c.** | Yes&No |
   | **d.** | Tucker_Taft | **e.** | _Go_ | **f.** | Begin |
   | **g.** | And_So_On_ | **h.** | Smörgåsbord | | |

2. Evaluate each of the following expressions. Note that these expressions may be of type `Integer`, `Float`, `Boolean`, or `Character`. If the expression results in an error, then give the reason(s) for the error. (Hint: there are five errors.)

   **a.** `16#1#E3 = 1_000`
   **b.** `13#BAD# = 2002`
   **c.** `2#111_101_001# = 8#751#`
   **d.** `2#1101_0011_1000# = 16#D38#`
   **e.** `12#10# = 11#11#`
   **f.** `15#BAD# = 14#D66#`
   **g.** `-1 + 3 * 2 ** 2 - 1`
   **h.** `-11 + 5 ** 2 - 5`
   **i.** `7.0 ** 2 + 9.1 * 3.5 ** 3`
   **j.** `0 ** 0`
   **k.** `abs ( (8#5.0#e-1) - (5.0 / 8.0) ) < 0.001`
   **l.** `'A' < 'B' and 1 < 2 or False`
   **m.** `2#1010# = 10 and 8#10# < 10 and 16#10# = 16`
   **n.** `not True or False`
   **o.** `0 < (5 and 2)`
   **p.** `(3 > 2) or else False`
   **q.** `-2 mod (-9) = -2 rem (-9)`
   **r.** `(-2) mod (-9) = (-2) rem (-9)`
   **s.** `5.0 rem 2.5`
   **t.** `Integer (3.6)`
   **u.** `.5 <= Float (1)`
   **v.** `Float (5 / 3) = Float (5) / Float (3)`
   **w.** `Character'Val (Character'Pos ('X'))`
   **x.** `Float'Succ (2.0)`
   **y.** `Boolean'Last = True`
   **z.** `Boolean'Image (True) = "True"`

3. Evaluate each of the following expressions. If the expression results in an error, then give the reason(s) for the error. (Hint: there is one error.)

Assumed Declarations:
```
type Music is (Classical, Jazz, Blues, Bluegrass, Klezmer);
subtype Background_Music is Music range Classical..Jazz;
```
a. (Klezmer < Jazz) **xor** (Jazz < Classical)
b. Music'Pos (Classical)
c. Music'Succ (Klezmer)
d. Music'Val (1)
e. Background_Music'Value ("Classical")
f. Music'First
g. Background_Music'Last
h. Background_Music'First = Music'First
i. Background_Music'Image (Jazz)
j. Music'Last = Klezmer
k. Background_Music'Pos (Jazz)
l. Blues **not in** Background_Music
m. Music'Succ (Blues) = Music'Val (Music'Pos (Blues) + 1)

4. Evaluate each of the following expressions. Note that these expressions may be of type Integer, Float, or Boolean. If the expression results in an error, then give the reason(s) for the error. (Hint: there are five errors.)

Assumed Declarations:
```
Int : Integer := 5;
Const : constant Integer := -10;
Flt: Float := 2;
Char: Character := 'A';
Yes: constant Boolean := True;
```
a. 6 + Int
b. -Int
c. Int / 3 = 1
d. **abs** Const
e. Int **rem** 4
f. (Int + 2#111#) < 16#E#
g. (Char < 'D') **and** Yes
h. Yes > False
i. Yes **xor** (**not** Yes)
j. Char **in** 'A' .. 'Z'
k. Int **not in** 1 .. 4
l. Flt **not in** 1.0 .. 4.0
m. Int ** (-1)
n. Int ** Flt
o. Flt ** Const
p. Int = 1_000.0

   **q.**  `Int * -CONST`
   **r.**  `Int > 1 and Const > (-2)`
   **s.**  `Int < Const < 10`
   **t.**  `True > (Int = Const)`

5. Which three of the following assignment statements will not compile?

```
declare
   Int: Integer := 5;
   Pos: Positive := 6;
   Flt: Float := 8.7;
   Neg: Integer := -5;
   Char: Character := 'P';
begin
   Int := Flt;
   Flt := 5;
   Int := Integer (Flt);
   Flt := Float (5);
   Flt := Float (Pos);
   Int := Pos;
   Char := Character (Int);
   Pos := Neg + Pos;
end;
```

6. Which one of the following integer literals does not equal 16?

   **a.**  `8#20#`
   **b.**  `8#2#E1`
   **c.**  `16#10#`
   **d.**  `2#10000#`
   **e.**  `2#1#E4`
   **f.**  `9#17#`
   **g.**  `3#121#`
   **h.**  `5#30#`

7. Explain why it is often better to use attributes rather than just the particular literal values. For instance, why is it often better to write `Solar_System'Last` instead of `Pluto`?

8. Write a program to calculate and output the area and the volume of a sphere whose radius, equals 72.52. Label each answer. Use the following formulas:

AREA $= 4 \pi$ Radius$^2$
VOLUME $= 4 / 3 \pi$ Radius$^3$
      where $\pi \approx 3.14159$

9. Let  X $= 12.6$
       Y $= 2.9$
       Z $= 1.5$

Write a program that calculates and outputs the values of the following expressions:

$$\frac{2X - 5Y}{2Z} \qquad \frac{Z + Y}{X - 1} \qquad \frac{Z}{2} - 2X^3$$

$$X^3 - 2.4X^2 + 3X - 1$$

Explain what happens when the value of Z is 0.0 or the value of X is 1.0.

10. Rewrite the expression

```
A /= 0 and then B / A > C
```

replacing the **and then** with an **or else**. Make sure that the new expression is logically equivalent to the original expression and that it also avoids the possibility of dividing B by A when A is 0.

# 3

# Control Structures

The kinds of Ada statements presented thus far are executed sequentially. There is only one "path" through the code. Control structures provide alternative paths. A control structure might execute one group of statements instead of another group of statements, or execute a group of statements multiple times, or jump over a group of statements and resume execution elsewhere in the code. In all of these instances, instead of always following a single path through the code, alternative paths may be selected.

In this chapter, we will examine four types of control structures: the **if** statement, the **case** statement, **loop** statements, and the **goto** statement. (In Chapter 15, we will discuss special control structures that apply to tasks.)

## THE IF STATEMENT

The **if** statement in Ada is very similar to the **if** statements of other languages. The **if** statement selects, at most, one group of statements to execute based on the value of one or more corresponding Boolean expressions. (Recall from Chapter 2 that a Boolean expression is an expression that yields the value of True or False.)

The **if** statement comes in several variations. In its simplest form, the **if** statement starts with the keyword **if**, which is followed by a Boolean expression, the keyword **then**, and one or more executable statements. The **if** statement terminates with the keywords **end if**. Note the necessary space between the **end** and the **if**:

```
if Boolean Expression then
    statements
end if;
```

A simple example of an **if** statement follows:

```
if Mood = Somber then
    Put_Line ("Read Dostoevski");
    Put_Line ("Listen to Mahler");
end if;
```

This example is not a complete, compilable Ada program, and we are assuming that certain declarations and assignments have been made. For instance, we are assuming that the variable, Mood, belongs to a user-defined enumeration type that includes various emotional states such as Somber. (Recall that a user-defined enumeration type is a type whose values are enumerated by the programmer. See Chapter 2 for a more detailed explanation.) However, this assumption should be evident. By using fragments of code such as the preceding example, it is easy to focus on the relevant aspects of the code and not to get sidetracked. Therefore, code fragments are presented throughout this book, but complete programs are frequently presented to reinforce the reader's understanding of the overall structure of Ada programs.

Let us return to the preceding example. The Boolean expression, Mood = Somber, is evaluated and resolves to either True or False, depending on whether one's mood is somber. If one's mood is somber, then the computer outputs "Read Dostoevski" and "Listen to Mahler" and proceeds to the statement (not shown) following the **end if**. If one's mood is not somber, then no action is taken, and the line of code following the **end if** is executed.

The **if** statement may include an **else** clause. The general form of this type of **if** statement is

```
if Boolean Expression then
    statements
else
    statements
end if;
```

An example of an **if** statement with an **else** clause follows:

```
if Art = Abstract or Art = Nonobjective then
    Put_Line ("Whine and complain");
    Put_Line ("Leave room");
else
    Put_Line ("Stay and enjoy");
end if;
```

In this example, if the art is abstract or nonobjective, the computer outputs "Whine and complain" and "Leave room." If the art is not abstract or nonobjective, then the statements between the **else** and the **end if** are executed, and the computer outputs "Stay and enjoy." Note that the **else** clause always guarantees that a group of statements in the **if** statement will be executed (but never more than one group).

The **if** statement may also include an **elsif** clause. The general form of this type of **if** statement is

```
if Boolean Expression then
   statements
elsif Boolean Expression then
   statements
elsif Boolean Expression then
   statements
       . . .
elsif Boolean Expression then
   statements
else       -- optional
   statements
end if;
```

The three dots are not part of the code, but indicate to the reader that any number of **elsif** clauses may be used. Note that the keyword **elsif** does not contain an e between the s and the i. Note also that **elsif** clauses may be used without the **else** clause. However, if an **else** clause is used, there can be only one, and it must be placed at the end of the **if** statement.

When an **if** statement has multiple Boolean expressions, each expression is evaluated in order, one after another, until either one evaluates to True, or all are evaluated and yield False. If one evaluates to True, then its corresponding group of statements is executed and the **if** statement is exited. If all expressions evaluate to False, then no group of statements is executed unless there is an **else** clause to execute. Thus, even though an **if** statement can contain many groups of statements, at most, only one group can be selected to execute.

A complete Ada program containing an **if** statement that uses the **elsif** clause follows:

```
with Ada.Text_IO;  use Ada.Text_IO;
procedure Daily_Activity is

   type Days_Of_Week is (Monday, Tuesday, Wednesday, Thursday,
      Friday, Saturday, Sunday);
   subtype Days_Off is Days_Of_Week range Saturday .. Sunday;
   Day: Days_Of_Week;
   package Days_IO is new Enumeration_IO (Days_Of_Week);
   use Days_IO;

begin  -- Daily_Activity

   Put_Line ("What day is it? (Fully type out the name.)");
   Get (Day);

   if Day = Friday then
      Put_Line ("Call in sick");
```

```
                    Put_Line ("Play computer games");
                elsif Day in Days_Off then
                    Put_Line ("Sleep");
                else
                    Put_Line ("Go to work");
                end if;

        end Daily_Activity;
```

There are three possible paths through this program. Each path results in a different group of statements being executed. One path results in the execution of the statements:

```
    Put_Line ("Call in sick");
    Put_Line ("Play computer games");
```

A second path results in the execution of the single statement:

```
    Put_Line ("Sleep");
```

A third path results in the execution of the single statement:

```
    Put_Line ("Go to work");
```

Consider, for instance, the following sample run of this program, which takes the first path through the **if** statement. The user's response follows the prompt, >:

```
    What day is it? (Fully type out the name of the day.)
    >Friday
    Call in sick
    Play computer games
```

When the user enters `Friday`, then only the two statements between **then** and **elsif** are executed: `Put_Line ("Call in sick")` and `Put_Line ("Play computer games")`. After these two statements are executed, the **if** statement is exited and the program ends.

Here is another sample run of this program, which takes the second path through the **if** statement:

```
    What day is it? (Fully type out the name of the day.)
    >SATURDAY
    Sleep
```

When the user enters `Saturday`, then only the statement between **then** and **else** is executed: `Put_Line ("Sleep")`. After this statement is executed, the **if** statement is exited and the program ends. Note that we are using the membership test described in Chapter 2 to test whether the value of Day, in this case, `Saturday`, is a day off: Day **in** Days_Off. The range `Saturday` to `Sunday` is represented by the subtype name `Days_Off`. There are other ways to represent ranges. The following four alternatives are logically equivalent:

```
if Day in Saturday..Sunday then...
if Day in Days_Of_Week range Saturday..Sunday then...
if Day in Days_Off'First..Days_Off'Last then...
if Day in Days_Off'Range then...
```

**Ada 95** ▶

The first alternative uses the range `Saturday..Sunday`. The Ada compiler knows that this range of values is taken from the base type `Days_Of_Week`.

The second alternative specifies the range: `Days_Of_Week` **range** `Saturday..Sunday`. This alternative is the same as the first alternative, except that the values used in the lower and upper bounds of the range, `Saturday` and `Sunday`, are explicitly indicated as belonging to the type `Days_Of_Week`. It is rarely necessary to indicate explicitly the type or subtype, except in ambiguous situations, which will be discussed later in this chapter. However, some programmers prefer this second form of range to the first form, because it clarifies the code by documenting the type or subtype of the range.

The third alternative uses the attributes `First` and `Last`. Recall that, when applied to a type or subtype, the attributes `First` and `Last`, respectively, yield the lower and upper bounds of the type or subtype. `Days_Off'First` is the same as `Saturday`, and `Days_Off'Last` is the same as `Sunday`. The range `Days_Off'First..Days_Off'Last` thus yields the range `Saturday..Sunday`.

**Ada 95** ▶ The fourth alternative uses the `Range` attribute. (Do not confuse the attribute `Range` with the keyword **range**.) `Days_Off'Range` is equivalent to `Days_Off'First..Days_Off'Last`. (In Ada 83, the `range` attribute could not be applied to scalar types, but only to array objects and certain array types.) Note that writing `Days_Off` (as shown in procedure `Daily_Activity`) or `Days_Off'Range` amounts to the same thing.

The advantage of the last two alternatives (and the one shown in `Daily_Activity`) over the first two alternatives is that the code is easier to modify: when changes are made in one part of the code, additional changes do not have to be made in another part of the code. For instance, assume that we decide to change the days listed in the subtype `Days_Off`. If we add `Friday`, then our new subtype appears as follows:

```
subtype Days_Off is Days_Of_Week range Friday..Sunday;
```

If we use either of the first two alternatives to represent a range of values, then we have to search throughout our code and change all ranges of the form `Saturday..Sunday` to `Friday..Sunday`. However, if we use the last two alternatives (or the one used in `Daily_Activity`), no changes are necessary. `Days_Off'First` automatically refers to `Friday`, and `Days_Off` or `Days_Off'Range` automatically refers to the new range `Friday..Sunday`.

There is a third path that can be followed in the preceding example, program `Daily_Activity`. If the user enters a day from `Monday` to `Thursday`, then the statement in the **else** part of the code is executed. This is demonstrated in the following sample run:

```
What day is it? (Fully type out the name of the day.)
>WEDNESDAY
Go to work
```

So far, we have only examined the **if** statement used by the program `Daily_Activity`. Now let us briefly examine the rest of the code. In the declarative part of `Daily_Activity`, which is the part of the code between the keywords **is** and **begin**, the enumeration type `Days_Of_Week` is defined, as well as the subtype `Days_Off`. The subtype `Days_Off` is defined as a subrange of values, `Saturday` to `Sunday`, of the base type `Days_Of_Week`. As we have seen, one of the advantages of subtypes is that the subtype name can be used to concisely represent a range of values.

The declarative part of the program `Daily_Activity` also contains a generic instantiation:

```
package Days_IO is new Enumeration_IO (Days_Of_Week);
```

This generic instantiation of the `Enumeration_IO` package, which will not be fully explained until the chapter on generics (Chapter 8), is needed to perform input or output on objects of the enumeration type `Days_Of_Week`. In this program, we need this instantiation because the user interactively inputs the value for `Day`, which belongs to the type `Days_Of_Week`. In general, whenever nontextual information (information that does not consist of strings or characters) needs to be input or output, a generic instantiation must be performed. The following generic instantiations are needed for various kinds of input/output:

```
package Int_IO is new Ada.Text_IO.Integer_IO (Integer);
   -- needed when Integer input or output is performed

package Real_IO is new Ada.Text_IO.Float_IO (Float);
   -- needed when Float input or output is performed

package Boolean_IO is new Ada.Text_IO.Enumeration_IO (Boolean);
   -- needed when Boolean input or output is performed
```

The names `Int_IO`, `Real_IO`, and `Boolean_IO` are user-defined names. The names `Integer_IO`, `Float_IO`, and `Enumeration_IO`, however, are not user-defined names. These are the names of the generic packages that are contained in the `Ada.Text_IO` package that comes with every Ada compiler. Because these generic packages are contained in the `Ada.Text_IO` package, the program that instantiates these packages must mention `Ada.Text_IO` in its **with** clause and optionally in a **use** clause.

We have seen how the program `Daily_Activity` uses the **elsif** clause. When possible, use the **elsif** clause instead of **else if**. Unlike the **elsif clause**, **else if** places an **if** statement inside the **else** clause of another **if** statement, as follows:

```
if Julius_Squeezer = Boa_Constrictor then
    Put ("Feed it a plump rabbit");
else
    if Julius_Squeezer = Rat_Snake then
        Put ("Feed it a live mouse");
    else
        if Julius_Squeezer = King_Snake then
            Put ("Feed it a lizard");
        else
            Put ("No information on this snake");
        end if;
    end if;
end if;
```

There is nothing illegal about this code, but it is hard to read with all the nested **if** statements and the final cascade of **end if**s. Note that the indentation reflects the structure of the code. In addition to being hard to read, the structure of the code might be misleading because it seems to imply that Julius_Squeezer is more likely to be a Boa Constrictor than a Rat Snake or a King Snake. This may or may not be the case.

The following code is logically equivalent to the preceding code (it produces the same results) but is improved by use of the **elsif** clause instead of **else if**:

```
if Julius_Squeezer = Boa_Constrictor then
    Put ("Feed it a plump rabbit");
elsif Julius_Squeezer = Rat_Snake then
    Put ("Feed it a live mouse");
elsif Julius_Squeezer = King_Snake then
    Put ("Feed it a lizard");
else
    Put ("No information on this snake");
end if;
```

This second version of the code is easier to read and understand than the first version. Unlike the first version, the structure of the code is not misleading. We can see from the two versions that style is very important when writing code.

Consider another example of poor coding style:

```
if Temperature > Melting_Point then
    Danger := True;
else
    Danger := False;
end if;
    ...
```

```
if Danger = True then
    Put ("Sound the alarm!");
end if;
```

This coding style is poor because it does not fully take advantage of the fact that a `Boolean` variable is itself either `True` or `False`. As a result, the code is unnecessarily wordy and awkward. Consider the following logically equivalent alternative that, to use Daniel C. Dennett's phrase, is a "cure for the common code":

```
Danger := Temperature > Melting_Point;
        . . .
if Danger then
    Put ("Sound the alarm!");
end if;
```

The first line of this code replaces the entire five-line **if** statement of the first version. The `Boolean` variable, `Danger`, is assigned the result of the `Boolean` expression, `Temperature > Melting_Point`. For instance, if the temperature is greater than the melting point, then the expression `Temperature > Melting_Point` is `True`, and the `Boolean` variable, `Danger`, is assigned the value of `True`.

The **if** statement of the new, improved version of code replaces the last **if** statement of the original version. Instead of testing whether there is danger by stating

```
if Danger = True then...
```

we simply write

```
if Danger then...
```

Because `Danger` is a `Boolean` variable, we can directly use it in place of the `Boolean` expression, `Danger = True`. The expression "if danger..." is simpler and sounds more Englishlike than the expression "if danger = true..."

Let us consider one more coding style issue, shown by the following nested **if** statements:

```
if A /= 0 then
    if B/A > C then
        -- statements
    end if;
end if;
```

To make this code easier to read, it is tempting to replace the nested **if** statements with a single **if** statement that combines the two `Boolean` expressions. But be careful. Note that the outer **if** statement checks to make sure that A is not 0 before allowing the nested **if** statement to divide B by A. Without this check, we risk dividing B by 0, thereby raising a constraint error at runtime. To combine the two **if** statements while preserving the logic, use the short-circuit logical operator **and then** instead of **and**:

```
if A /= 0 and then B/A > C then
   -- statements
end if;
```

As with the nested **if** statement, this short-circuit form guards against dividing B by 0. As explained in Chapter 2, the expression A /= 0 is evaluated first. If this expression is True, then the next expression, B/A > C, is evaluated. However, if the first expression is False (A = 0), then the second expression is not evaluated, and we avoid dividing by zero.

## THE CASE STATEMENT

The **case** statement is similar to the **if** statement because it selects, at most, one group of statements to execute. However, the **case** statement differs from the **if** statement because it uses a single **case** expression rather than one or more Boolean expressions. A **case** expression yields a value that belongs to a discrete type.

When possible, **if** statements should be written as **case** statements. In order to compare **if** statements and **case** statements, consider this example of an **if** statement that outputs names for flocks of various kinds of birds. (These are actual names and are not fabricated by the author.)

```
if Flock_Of_Birds = Larks then
   Put ("An exaltation of larks");
elsif Flock_Of_Birds = Peacocks then
   Put ("An ostentation of peacocks");
elsif Flock_Of_Birds = Crows then
   Put ("A murder of crows");
elsif Flock_Of_Birds = Geese then
   Put ("A gaggle of geese");
elsif Flock_Of_Birds = Sparrows then
   Put ("A host of sparrows");
elsif Flock_Of_Birds = Magpies then
   Put ("A tiding of magpies");
elsif Flock_Of_Birds = Pheasants then
   Put ("A bouquet of pheasants");
elsif Flock_Of_Birds = Owls then
   Put ("A parliament of owls");
elsif Flock_Of_Birds = Starlings then
   Put ("A murmuration of starlings");
elsif Flock_Of_Birds = Partridges then
   Put ("A covey of partridges");
elsif Flock_Of_Birds = Nightingales then
   Put ("A watch of nightingales");
```

```
   elsif Flock_Of_Birds = Woodpeckers then
      Put ("A descent of woodpeckers");
   elsif Flock_Of_Birds = Storks then
      Put ("A mustering of storks");
   elsif Flock_Of_Birds = Herons then
      Put ("A siege of herons");
   elsif Flock_Of_Birds = Finches then
      Put ("A charm of finches");
   elsif Flock_Of_Birds = Turtledoves then
      Put ("A pitying of turtledoves");
   elsif Flock_Of_Birds = Chickens then
      Put ("A peep of chickens");
   elsif Flock_Of_Birds = Turkeys then
      Put ("A rafter of turkeys");
   elsif Flock_Of_Birds = Swallows then
      Put ("A flight of swallows");
   elsif Flock_Of_Birds = Ravens then
      Put ("An unkindness of ravens");
   elsif Flock_Of_Birds = Ducks then
      Put ("A paddling of ducks");
   elsif Flock_Of_Birds = Hawks then
      Put ("A cast of hawks");
   elsif Flock_Of_Birds = Doves then
      Put ("A dule of doves");
   elsif Flock_Of_Birds = Woodcocks then
      Put ("A fall of woodcocks");
   elsif Flock_Of_Birds = Snipes then
      Put ("A walk of snipes");
   elsif Flock_Of_Birds = Rooks then
      Put ("A building of rooks");
   elsif Flock_Of_Birds = Plovers then
      Put ("A congregation of plovers");
   elsif Flock_Of_Birds = Lapwings then
      Put ("A deceit of lapwings");
   else
      Put ("Just a flock of birds");
   end if;
```

Note the 28 `Boolean` expressions. In each instance, we are testing whether the same variable, `Flock_Of_Birds`, is equal to one of 28 values: `Larks`, `Peacocks`, `Crows`, and so on. When a single variable, such as `Flock_Of_Birds`, is being tested in every `Boolean` expression, Ada provides a special control structure known as the **case** statement. If we rewrite the preceding code using the **case** statement, we obtain the following result:

```
case Flock_Of_Birds is
   when Larks          => Put ("An exaltation of larks");
   when Peacocks       => Put ("An ostentation of peacocks");
```

```
      when Crows          => Put ("A murder of crows");
      when Geese          => Put ("A gaggle of geese");
      when Sparrows       => Put ("A host of sparrows");
      when Magpies        => Put ("A tiding of magpies");
      when Pheasants      => Put ("A bouquet of pheasants");
      when Owls           => Put ("A parliament of owls");
      when Starlings      => Put ("A murmuration of starlings");
      when Partridges     => Put ("A covey of partridges");
      when Nightingales   => Put ("A watch of nightingales");
      when Woodpeckers    => Put ("A descent of woodpeckers");
      when Storks         => Put ("A mustering of storks");
      when Herons         => Put ("A siege of herons");
      when Finches        => Put ("A charm of finches");
      when Turtledoves    => Put ("A pitying of turtledoves");
      when Chickens       => Put ("A peep of chickens");
      when Turkeys        => Put ("A rafter of turkeys");
      when Swallows       => Put ("A flight of swallows");
      when Ravens         => Put ("An unkindness of ravens");
      when Ducks          => Put ("A paddling of ducks");
      when Hawks          => Put ("A cast of hawks");
      when Doves          => Put ("A dule of doves");
      when Woodcocks      => Put ("A fall of woodcocks");
      when Snipes         => Put ("A walk of snipes");
      when Rooks          => Put ("A building of rooks");
      when Plovers        => Put ("A congregation of plovers");
      when Lapwings       => Put ("A deceit of lapwings");
      when others         => Put ("Just a flock of birds");
   end case;
```

The **case** statement begins with the keyword **case**. The keyword is followed by a **case** expression, which is the variable Flock_Of_Birds in the example. (Usually the **case** expression just consists of a single variable.) The **case** expression is followed by the keyword **is**, which is followed by one or more **when** clauses. The value of the **case** expression determines which **when** clause is executed. For instance, if Flock_Of_Birds equals Peacocks, then the computer outputs "An ostentation of peacocks." The arrow, =>, separates the choice (Larks, Peacocks, etc.) from the statements to be executed for that choice. (As we will see in later chapters, Ada uses the arrow => in other contexts besides the **case** statement in order to associate pairs of items.) Any number of statements may be placed into a single **when** clause. Just place these statements before the next appearance of the keyword **when**.

The **when others** clause works similarly to the **else** clause in the **if** statement. In the preceding example, if the flock of birds is not one of the choices explicitly covered in a **when** clause, then the **when others** clause is selected, and the statement "Just a flock of birds" is output.

The keywords **end case** must be used to terminate the **case** statement. These two keywords must be separated by one or more blanks.

The general form of a **case** statement, then, is:

```
case case expression is
   when choices  => statements
   when choices  => statements
      ...
   when choices  => statements
end case;
```

Before we examine the rules governing **case** statements, let us consider a complete Ada program that uses the **case** statement:

```
with Ada.Text_IO;  use Ada.Text_IO;
procedure Classification_Of_Elements is

    type Atomic_Number_Type is new Integer range 1 .. 105;
    Atomic_Number: Atomic_Number_Type;
    package Int_IO is new Integer_IO (Atomic_Number_Type);
    use Int_IO;

begin  -- Classification_Of_Elements

    Put_Line ("Enter the atomic number of an element, ");
    Put_Line ("from 1 to 105");
    Get (Atomic_Number);
    New_Line;
    Put ("The element with atomic number ");
    Put (Atomic_Number);
    Put (" belongs to the group: ");

    case Atomic_Number is
       when 1                          =>
          Put ("Hydrogen");
       when 2 | 10 | 18 | 36 | 54 | 86  =>
          Put ("Noble Gas");
       when 3 | 11 | 19 | 37 | 55 | 87  =>
          Put ("Alkali Metal");
       when 4 | 12 | 20 | 38 | 56 | 88  =>
          Put ("Alkaline Earth Metal");
       when 5 | 13 | 31 | 49 | 81       =>
          Put ("Aluminum Family");
       when 6 | 14 | 32 | 50 | 82       =>
          Put ("Carbon Family");
       when 7 | 15 | 33 | 51 | 83       =>
          Put ("Nitrogen Family");
       when 8 | 16 | 34 | 52 | 84       =>
          Put ("Chalcogen");
       when 9 | 17 | 35 | 53 | 85       =>
          Put ("Halogen");
       when 58 .. 71                    =>
          Put ("Rare Earth");
```

```
        when 90 .. 103                     =>
            Put ("Actinide");
        when others                        =>
            Put ("Transition Metal");
    end case;
    New_Line;

end Classification_Of_Elements;
```

This **case** statement uses numeric literals (1, 2, 3, 4, etc.) for the **case** statement choices. The vertical bar, |, sometimes called a selector operator, is used to handle multiple choices within the same **when** clause. For instance, when the atomic number is 2, 10, 18, 36, 54, or 86, then this **case** statement outputs "Noble Gas," and so on. Consider the following sample run:

```
Enter the atomic number of an element, from 1 to 105
>17
The element with atomic number 17 belongs to the group:
Halogen
```

Note that the **when** clauses that are the second and third from the end of the **case** statement express choices using the discrete ranges 58..71 and 90..103. Also note that, because all the atomic numbers from 1 to 105 are not explicitly covered, we must use the **when others** clause at the end of the **case** statement to cover atomic numbers from 21 to 30, 39 to 48, 57, 72 to 80, 89, and 104 to 105.

Now that we have seen a complete program that uses the **case** statement, let us consider the rules that apply to **case** statements:

1. The **case** expression must be of a discrete type.
2. Every possible value of the **case** expression must be covered in one and only one **when** clause.
3. If the **when others** clause is used, it must appear as a single choice at the end of the **case** statement.
4. Choices in a **when** clause must be static.

Rule 1 states that the **case** expression must be of a discrete type. That is, it must yield a value that belongs to an integer type, a Boolean type, a character type, or a user-defined enumeration type. The following code has a **case** expression, Radiation, that is of type Light. This code follows Rule 1 because Light is a user-defined enumeration type.

```
declare

    type Light is (Infrared, Red, Orange, Yellow, Green, Blue,
        Indigo, Violet, Ultraviolet);
    subtype Visible_Light is Light range Red..Violet;
    Radiation: Light := Red;
```

```
begin

    case Radiation is
        when Infrared =>
            Put_Line ("Detect as heat");
        when Red .. Violet =>
            Put_Line ("Detect with eyes");
        when Ultraviolet =>
            Put_Line ("Detect as sunburn");
    end case;

end;
```

Note that within the second **when** clause, a choice is expressed using the discrete range Red..Violet. Other forms of discrete ranges are also permitted within the **when** clause. This **when** clause could be replaced by:

```
when Visible_Light'First.. Visible_Light'Last =>
    Put_Line ("Detect with eyes");
```

or

```
when Visible_Light => Put_Line ("Detect with eyes");
```

or

**Ada 95 ▶**
```
when Visible_Light'Range => Put_Line ("Detect with eyes");
```

Also note that a **when others** clause is not needed, because all the different kinds of light are covered.

The next example is illegal according to Rule 1, because the **case** expression, Age, is not discrete but is a real number belonging to the type Float:

```
declare
    subtype Age_Type is Float range 0.0..19.0;
    Age : Age_Type := 13.0;
begin
    case Age is -- illegal
        -- Age does not belong to a discrete type
        when 0.0..12.0 => Put ("Child");
        when others => Put ("Teeny-Bopper");
    end case;
end;
```

Rule 2 states that every possible value of the **case** expression must be covered in one and only one **when** clause. This rule can be violated in two different ways: a value of a **case** expression can exist that is not covered by a **when** clause, or a **case** value can exist that is covered by more than one **when** clause. The following code violates Rule 2 in the first way:

```
declare
    Response : Character;
begin
    Get (Response);
    case Response is  -- illegal
        when 'Y' | 'y' => Put_Line ("You are being positive");
        when 'N' | 'n' => Put_Line ("You are being negative");
    end case;
end;
```

This code is illegal because it does not account for all possible values of Response. Because the variable Response is declared to be of type Character, it can assume any character value, not just uppercase and lowercase Y and N. One method for correcting this code is to declare the variable Response to be of some type, such as:

```
type Response_Type is ('Y', 'y', 'N', 'n');
```

Another method for correcting this code is to use the **when others** clause to handle all inappropriate responses, as follows:

```
when others => Put_Line ("Your response is not recognized");
```

If no action needs to be taken after the preceding **when others** clause, then use the **null** statement, as follows:

```
when others => null;
```

The **null** statement is a do-nothing statement that is used as a place holder when no action is needed. This statement is used because, to enhance readability, Ada syntax requires that some statement be placed after the =>.

Although the **when others** clause corrects the preceding code, its use is often discouraged. Instead, programmers are encouraged to explicitly cover all values of the **case** expression. Thus, code becomes more reliable because the programmer will be immediately notified if any value of the **case** expression has not been covered. (Other languages supporting the **case** statement typically bypass it without any warning when a value is encountered that the **case** statement does not handle.)

The **when others** clause should also be avoided when it does not handle all new values that could reasonably be added to the discrete type. Thus, in the previous Classification_Of_Elements example, suppose that we extend the Atomic_Number_Type to include some values beyond 105. Are all elements with these high atomic numbers transition metals? If not, then the **when others** clause must not handle them, and the **case** statement must be updated to explicitly cover these new values. The danger is that it is easy to forget to update the **case** statement and, with the presence of the **when others** clause, the compiler will not generate any errors.

To illustrate the second way that Rule 2 can be violated, consider the following code:

```
declare
    Response : Character;
begin
    Get (Response);
    case Response is  -- illegal
        when 'Y' | 'y' | 'N' | 'n' => Put_Line ("Legal entry");
        when 'Y' | 'y' => Put_Line ("You are being positive");
        when 'N' | 'n' => Put_Line ("You are being negative");
        when others => null;
    end case;
end;
```

This code is illegal because the values 'Y', 'y', 'N', and 'n' are each covered by more than one **when** clause.

Since every possible value of the **case** expression must be covered in one and only one **when** clause, the order in which the clauses are arranged has no effect on program execution. In this respect, the **case** statement differs from the **if** statement. Unless the Boolean expressions of an **if** statement are mutually exclusive so that no more than one expression can ever be True, order can make a difference. For example, the following **if** statement must test grades in the order of 'F' to 'A':

```
if Score < 60 then      -- order makes a difference
    Grade := 'F';
elsif Score < 70 then
    Grade := 'D';
elsif Score < 80 then
    Grade := 'C';
elsif Score < 90 then
    Grade := 'B';
else
    Grade := 'A';
end if;
```

As a **case** statement, however, the order of the **when** clauses makes no difference:

```
case Score is          -- order makes no difference
    when 90..100 =>
        Grade := 'A';
    when 80..89 =>
        Grade := 'B';
    when 70..79 =>
        Grade := 'C';
```

```
      when 60..69 =>
          Grade := 'D';
      when others =>
          Grade := 'F';
  end case;
```

Rule 3 for **case** statements is that if the **when others** clause is used, it must appear as a single choice at the end of the **case** statement. Thus, the following **when others** clause is illegal because it is joined with the choice 'A':

```
  when 'A' | others => null; -- illegal
```

Rule 4 states that the choices in a **when** clause must be static: they must be determined at compilation time and not at runtime. The reason for this rule is that at compilation time, the compiler must check that every value of the case expression is covered in one and only one **when** clause (Rule 2). As we have seen, this check makes code more reliable because, in the absence of the **when others** clause, programmers will be immediately notified if they forget to cover any value of the case expression.

The following **case** statement violates Rule 4:

```
declare
    subtype Test_Value is Integer range 1 .. 100;
    Value: Test_Value := 10;
    Max: Integer := 15;
begin
    case Value is
        when 1..Max => Put_Line ("In range");
            -- illegal; Max is not static
        when others => Put_Line ("Out of range");
    end case;
end;
```

This **case** statement violates Rule 4 because Max is a variable whose value can change while the program is running; the value of the choice 1..Max is not static.

We can solve our problem by declaring Max to be a constant that is initialized to a static value:

```
declare
    subtype Test_Value is Integer range 1 .. 100;
    Value: Test_Value := 10;
    Max: constant Integer := 15;
        -- Max must initialized to a static expression
begin
    case Value is
        when 1..Max => Put_Line ("In range");    --  OK
        when others  => Put_Line ("Out of range");
    end case;
end;
```

It is not enough that `Max` be a constant. `Max` must also be initialized to a static value, such as the literal 15. This requirement may seem unnecessary because constants are typically perceived as static values. In Ada, however, making an object a constant only guarantees that its value cannot change. Although unusual, a constant can be initialized to a value that is calculated at runtime.

```
Get (Max_Value);
declare
    subtype Test_Value is Integer range 1 .. 100;
    Value: Test_Value := 10;
    Max: constant Integer := Max_Value;
begin
    case Value is
        when 1.. Max => Put_Line ("In range");   -- illegal;
            -- Max isn't static
        when others => Put_Line ("Out of range");
    end case;
end;
```

As the preceding code illustrates, Rule 4 is violated because, even though `Max` is a constant, its value must be determined at runtime. Its value must be determined at runtime since the value of `Max` is interactively input by the user when the program is running, so the compiler cannot possibly know in advance what value `Max` will be given.

## LOOP STATEMENTS

Whereas the **if** statement and the **case** statement select which group of statements to execute, the **loop** statement selects the number of times a group of statements is executed.

Ada has three forms of loop statements: the simple **loop**, the **while** loop, and the **for** loop. The similarities and differences between these loop statements can be seen below:

<u>Simple **Loop**</u>

```
loop   -- loop forever
    statements
end loop;
```

<u>**While** Loop</u>

```
While Boolean expression   loop
    statements
    -- loop until the Boolean expression becomes false
end loop;
```

<u>**For** Loop</u>

```
for loop counter  in discrete range   loop
    statements
end loop;
```

Note that the **while** loop and **for** loop statements contain the simple **loop** structure within them (**loop** ... **end loop**). Also note that all loops terminate with the keywords **end loop** and never with **end for** or **end while**.

## The Simple Loop

The most basic form of the loop statement is the simple **loop**. This form begins with the keyword **loop** and terminates with the keywords **end loop**. Without a special statement inside the **loop** such as an **exit** statement, the **loop** continuously executes whatever statements are inside of it. Such infinite loops can be useful. For instance, a 24-hour automated teller machine infinitely loops, forever seeking customer requests to withdraw cash, pay bills, deposit checks, or transfer funds.

The usual way to exit an infinite **loop** is to use the **exit** statement:

```
loop
    -- executable statements
    if A = 0 then
        exit;
    end if;
    -- executable statements
end loop;
```

One or more **exit** statements may be placed anywhere within the loop. In the preceding example, the loop is exited whenever A = 0. (We are assuming, of course, that some of the executable statements within this loop are modifying the value of A; otherwise, this **exit** statement would be pointless.) The preceding **if** statement that tests whether the loop should be exited has an alternative form that is more concise:

```
exit when A = 0;
```

Additional information on the **exit** statement will be presented in the subsection on the **for** loop.

Consider the following program that uses the simple **loop** and an **exit** statement:

```
with Ada.Text_IO;   use Ada.Text_IO;
procedure Abuse_The_User is

    Had_Enough: Boolean;
    package Boolean_IO is new Enumeration_IO (Boolean);
    use Boolean_IO;

begin   -- Abuse_The_User

    loop
        Put_Line ("Had enough?   Answer true or false");
        Get (Had_Enough);
        exit when Had_Enough;
    end loop;
```

```
            Put_Line ("OK");
      end Abuse_The_User;
```

## The While Loop

The following program uses the **while** loop and is logically equivalent to the preceding program that uses the simple **loop** with an **exit** statement:

```
with Ada.Text_IO;   use Ada.Text_IO;
procedure Abuse_The_User is

    Had_Enough: Boolean := False;
    package Boolean_IO is new Enumeration_IO (Boolean);
    use Boolean_IO;

begin   -- Abuse_The_User

    while not Had_Enough loop
       Put_Line ("Had enough?  Answer true or false");
       Get (Had_Enough);
    end loop;

    Put_Line ("OK");
end Abuse_The_User;
```

As you can see, the logic is more straightforward in the **while** loop than in the
simple **loop**, because the **while** loop is more descriptive of the action taking place.
Also, there is no special **exit** construct embedded within the loop, so the loop is
more concise. As the following sample run illustrates, the phrase "Had enough?
answer true or false" keeps being output to the screen until the fed-up user
enters "true" (or enters an illegal value that causes the program to terminate):

```
Had enough?  Answer true or false
>False
Had enough?  Answer true or false
>False
Had enough?  Answer true or false
>False
Had enough?  Answer true or false
>True
OK
```

The following is another example of a complete Ada program that uses the
**while** loop:

```
with Ada.Text_IO;   use Ada.Text_IO;
procedure Series_Of_Numbers is
```

```
package Int_IO is new Integer_IO (Integer);
Number: Positive;

function Even (N: Positive) return Boolean is
begin
   return N rem 2 = 0;
end Even;

begin -- Series of Numbers

Put_Line ("Enter a positive integer");
Int_IO.Get (Number);
New_Line;
Int_IO.Put (Number);
New_Line;

while Number /= 1 loop

   if Even (Number) then
      Number := Number / 2;
   else   -- Odd
      Number := 3 * Number + 1;
   end if;

   Int_IO.Put (Number);
   New_Line;

end loop;

end Series_Of_Numbers;
```

This program prompts the user for a positive number, outputs this number, and then outputs a sequence of numbers that is created within the **while** loop of this program. This **while** loop keeps executing until the number 1 is reached. The **if** statement within this **while** loop uses the Even function (to be discussed shortly) to check whether Number is even. If Number is even, then the value of Number is replaced by Number/2, else Number is replaced by 3 * Number + 1. The updated value of Number is then output.

For instance, let us assume that the user enters the number 7. Because 7 is odd, the next number generated is 7 * 3 + 1, or 22. The number 22 is even, so the next number generated is 22/2, or 11. Because 11 is odd, the next number generated is 11 * 3 + 1, or 34, and so on. The final series of numbers generated is:

```
7   22   11   34   17   52   26   13   40   20   10   5   16   8
4    2    1
```

Thus, starting with 7, it takes 16 steps to finally reach 1. The number of steps required is not a simple function of the size of the number. Some large numbers, such as 341, take few steps, while some small numbers, such as 27, take many steps (see Exercise 13).

This program continues looping until the number 1 is reached. But what guarantees that 1 will eventually be reached? Were we just lucky in this exercise? No. Computers have worked this problem, known as Ullam's Conjecture, with many different numbers. Without exception, the number 1 is eventually reached. However, no one has yet been able to prove mathematically that the number 1 will always be reached. For our purposes, though, we should feel confident that this **while** loop will eventually terminate.

A few features are introduced in the preceding example that we have not previously encountered. One such feature is a function called `Even`, which is written within the declarative part of the main procedure, `Series_Of_Numbers`. Once this function is declared, the remainder of the code can access it. The function `Even` is invoked (activated) in the following **if** clause, taken from the preceding example:

```
if Even (Number) then...
```

When `Even` is invoked, the value of `Number` is passed to the "formal" parameter `N`. The function `Even` then returns the result of the `Boolean` expression `N` **rem** `2 = 0`. If `N` is an even number, then this expression is `True` because there is no remainder when `N` is divided by 2. Thus, when the function is invoked, it returns a `Boolean` value `True` if its parameter, `N`, is even, but `False` if `N` is odd. (We will cover functions in detail in Chapter 6.)

As we have seen, the number of iterations through a **while** loop is determined by the `Boolean` expression at the beginning of the loop. Some languages, such as Pascal, have a special construct (often called a **repeat until** loop) for situations where the `Boolean` expression comes at the end of the loop. Ada does not have any special loop structures to handle this situation, but such a structure can be created by placing an **exit when** as the last statement in a loop. (See, for example, the previous procedure, `Abuse_The_User`, which uses the simple **loop**.)

## The For Loop

One of the most useful constructs introduced by FORTRAN in the mid-1950s was the **DO** loop. Since then, practically every programming language has supplied a similar construct. In Ada (as well as Pascal and BASIC), this loop is known as a **for** loop. **For** loops are used when the number of iterations through the loop is known in advance or can be determined by the compiler during runtime, before the **for** loop is entered. Conversely, **while** loops keep looping until some condition is met; the actual number of iterations may be unknown until the loop actually terminates, if it ever does terminate.

The **for** loop used in Ada is more abstract than the **DO** loop in FORTRAN. Whereas the **DO** loop can only loop over a range of numbers, the **for** loop can loop over any discrete range. A discrete range can be a range of integers or a range of enumeration values, including character and `Boolean` values.

The following complete Ada program uses a **for** loop to loop through the values of the user-defined enumeration type `Countdown`:

```
with Ada.Text_IO; use Ada;
procedure Launch is

    type Countdown is (Ten, Nine, Eight, Seven, Six, Five, Four,
        Three, Two, One, Blastoff);
    package Countdown_IO is new Text_IO.Enumeration_IO
        (Countdown);

begin  -- Blastoff

    for Counter in Countdown loop
        Countdown_IO.Put (Counter);
        Text_IO.New_Line;
        delay 1.0; -- wait at least 1 second
    end loop;

end Launch;
```

The loop counter, Counter, is not explicitly declared. Its type is implicitly determined from the type of its discrete range, Ten..Blastoff. (If one were to explicitly declare Counter, a new variable would be introduced that is distinct from the **for** loop counter.) Counter "steps" through the enumeration values from Ten to Blastoff. Since there are 11 values in the enumeration type Countdown, this loop cycles 11 times. Each time through the loop, a successive enumeration value of type Countdown is output, and the **delay** statement delays the action at least 1 second. The final output generated by this program appears as follows:

```
TEN
NINE
EIGHT
SEVEN
SIX
FIVE
FOUR
THREE
TWO
ONE
BLASTOFF
```

This example uses the **for** loop:

```
for Counter in Countdown loop...
```

Within this **for** loop, the discrete range is expressed by using the type name Countdown. Other ways of expressing the range are shown in the following **for** loops, which are logically equivalent to the preceding **for** loop:

```
for Counter in Ten..Blastoff loop...
for Counter in Countdown range Ten..Blastoff loop...
```

```
for Counter in Countdown'First..Countdown'Last loop...
for Counter in Countdown'Range loop...
```

In greater detail, here is what happens in procedure `Launch`. `Counter` is initially assigned the first value, `Ten`, of the discrete range represented by the type name `Countdown`. The program outputs this value to the screen and advances to the next line, and the **delay** statement delays execution at least 1 second. Note the value placed after the keyword **delay** is a real number that requests the number of seconds that the program is to delay execution. The **for** loop counter, `Counter`, is then assigned the next value of the range, which is `Nine`. Again, the program outputs this value to the screen and advances to the next line, and the **delay** statement delays execution at least 1 second. This looping continues until the loop counter, `Counter`, is finally assigned its last value, `Blastoff`. After `Blastoff` is output to the screen, the program advances to the next line and delays execution 1 second. The **for** loop is then exited, and the program terminates.

Even though a delay of 1 second is requested, the actual delay could be longer. The time expressed is a minimum time since the computer may be engaged in other activities such as running another program when the specified delay expires. In other words, even though the procedure, `Launch`, becomes eligible to resume execution after delaying 1 second, the computer may have other work to attend to before it can get back to this idle procedure. Further discussion of timing issues will be covered in Chapter 15 on concurrent programming, so let us return to our discussion of the **for** loop.

Now that the structure of **for** loops is understood, let us consider some rules that apply to **for** loops.

1.  The loop counter is not explicitly declared.
2.  The loop counter's range is tested at the beginning of the loop, not at the end of the loop.
3.  Inside the loop, the loop counter may be used but not altered.
4.  The loop counter's discrete range may be dynamic.
5.  The discrete range of the loop is evaluated before the **for** loop is first executed.
6.  The loop counter only exists within the loop.
7.  Within the loop, the loop counter hides identifiers that exist outside the loop and have the same name as the loop counter.
8.  **For** loops may only loop over a discrete range.
9.  **For** loops may step through the discrete range in reverse order.

Rule 1 states that the loop counter is not explicitly declared. The Ada compiler infers the loop counter's type from the upper and lower bounds of its discrete range:

```
for N in 1..3 loop...
```

In this clause, the compiler infers that the loop counter N is of type `Integer` in the range from 1 to 3.

It may seem peculiar that the **for** loop counter is an exception to the Ada rule that all identifiers must be explicitly declared. Why should **for** loops be an exception to this rule? The answer has to do with the software engineering principle of localization. According to this principle, identifiers, including the **for** loop counter, should only be available within the region of code where they need to be referenced. By following this principle of localization, code is simplified, and programmers do not need to worry about inadvertently referencing variables beyond their proper scope. In the case of **for** loops, Ada implicitly declares the loop counter because this restricts the counter to the region of code within the loop. This restriction is desirable because **for** loop counters are typically only referenced within the loop. In unusual cases where a **for** loop counter's value must be available beyond the loop, just assign the counter to a previously declared variable.

Rule 2 states that the loop counter's range is tested at the beginning of the loop, not at the end of the loop:

```
-- Rule 2
for Value in 5..1 loop      -- this is "dead" code
    Put ("This sentence will never appear");
end loop;
```

In this **loop** statement, the counter's range, 5..1, is tested at the beginning of the loop. Because the initial value, 5, is greater than 1, the statements within the loop are not executed. Control passes to the statement following the loop (not shown in example). By the way, since the upper and lower bounds of the loop are known at compile time to be 5 and 1, the compiler can determine that this **for** loop is "dead code." A good optimizing compiler will not generate any executable machine code for such dead code.

Rule 3 states that inside the loop, the loop counter may be used but not altered. Therefore, the following example is illegal:

```
-- Rule 3
for Do_Not_Change_Me in 1..5 loop
    Do_Not_Change_Me := 1;  -- illegal; can't modify value
end loop;
```

During each iteration through the loop, the loop counter is treated like a constant insofar as its value can be read but not modified.

Rule 4 states that the loop counter's discrete range may be dynamic. That is, the range of the loop may be determined at runtime rather than at compilation time, as follows:

```
-- Rule 4
Get (Upper_Bounds);
for Limit in 1..Upper_Bounds loop -- OK; dynamic range
    ...
end loop;
```

The value for `Upper_Bounds` cannot be known until runtime, which is when the `Get` statement obtains the value input from the terminal. When Rule 4 states that the loop counter's discrete range may be dynamic, it does not mean that the bounds can be changed from *within* the loop. For instance, the following example, though legal, does not do what the programmer may have intended: to go through the loop 100 times.

```
-- Rule 5
Limit := 3;
for Index in 1..Limit loop -- will only loop 3 times
    Limit := 100;
end loop;
```

The behavior of this loop is explained by Rule 5.

Rule 5 states that the discrete range of the loop is evaluated before the **for** loop is first executed. Therefore, in the preceding example, the value of the variable `Limit` is established when the loop is first entered and is never reevaluated. Thus, when the value of `Limit` is set to 100 within the loop, the **for** loop still loops only three times. (Of course, when the loop is exited, the value of `Limit` is 100 and not 3.)

Rule 6 states that the loop counter only exists within the loop. Therefore, the following code is illegal, because `X` does not exist after the loop is exited. In other words, `X` is undefined. (We are assuming that a different variable `X` is not declared above this loop.)

```
-- Rule 6
for X in 1..5 loop
    -- executable statements
end loop;
X := X - 1; -- illegal unless a different integer X is declared
            -- before the loop
```

Rule 7 states that within the loop, the loop counter hides identifiers that exist outside the loop and have the same name as the loop counter. This allows a programmer to freely choose a suitable name for a **for** loop counter without worrying about unintended clashes with identifiers declared elsewhere in the program. In the following example, a variable `N` is declared in procedure `P`, and an `N` is used as a loop counter:

```
-- Rule 7
with Ada.Text_IO; use Ada.Text_IO;
procedure P is
    package Int_IO is new Integer_IO (Integer);
    package Real_IO is new Float_IO (Float);
    use Int_IO, Real_IO;
    N: Float := 4.8;
begin
    -- the N of procedure P is visible here
    for N in 1..5 loop
```

```
                    -- the loop counter N hides the N declared in procedure P
                    Put (N);
                    Put (P.N);
            end loop;
            -- the N of procedure P is visible here
       end P;
```

As shown in this example, within the loop, the loop counter N hides the outer N declared in procedure P. Within the loop, however, the outer N can be referenced by using the dot notation: P.N.

A loop counter may also hide outer loop counters that have the same name:

```
-- Rule 7
for N in 1..5 loop
    -- the integers N are visible here
    for N in Monday .. Friday loop    -- Inner loop's N hides
                                      -- the outer loop's N
        -- the days N is visible here
    end loop;
    -- the integers N is visible here
end loop;
```

Note that both the inner and outer **for** loops use a loop counter named N. In such situations, within the inner **for** loop, the N of the inner loop hides the N of the outer loop. In other words, if N is accessed within the inner loop, then the N that is the inner loop counter is accessed, not the N that is the outer loop counter.

But what if, within the inner loop, we want to access the N of the outer loop? To do this, we assign a name to the outer loop. The name, which can be any valid Ada identifier, can then be used to reference hidden loop counters like the outer N. For instance, we can identify the outer loop as Outer_Loop by placing

```
Outer_Loop:
```

before the keyword **for**. The name Outer_Loop must also be placed at the end of the loop, after the keywords **end loop**. When a name, such as Outer_Loop, is given to the outer loop, then the outer loop counter, N, can be accessed within the inner loop through the use of dot notation: Outer_Loop.N. The following example shows how this is accomplished:

```
Outer_Loop :
for N in 1..5 loop
    for N in Monday..Friday loop
        Put (N);                -- outputs the day N
        Put (Outer_Loop.N);     -- outputs the integer N
    end loop;
end loop Outer_Loop;
```

This example assumes that the appropriate instantiations of the Integer_IO package and the Enumeration_IO package have been made.

Remember the reason that we have to go through all this trouble to access the loop counter of the outer loop from within the inner loop: both loops use the same loop counter name. If each loop used a different name for its loop counter, there would be no such problem.

Loop names can be given to any kind of loop, not just the **for** loop. Also, loop names have other uses besides accessing hidden identifiers. Loop names can also be used in conjunction with the **exit** statement to exit from various levels of nested loops. Normally, we exit the loop in which the **exit** statement lies. However, by using loop names, we can exit an outer loop from within an inner loop. In the following example, the **exit** statement lies in the inner loop; however, it is the outer loop that is exited:

```
Outer_Loop :
for J in 1..M loop

    . . .
    for K in 1..N loop

        . . .
        exit Outer_Loop when A = 0;

        . . .
    end loop;
    . . .
end loop Outer_Loop;
-- the exit statement passes control here
```

Note that the loop name is used by the **exit** statement to specify which loop to exit. **Exit** statements can use loop names to exit any type of loop: the simple **loop**, the **while** loop, or the **for** loop.

Rule 8 states that **for** loops may only loop over a discrete range. A range is discrete if its values belong to a discrete type. Thus, we cannot loop over real numbers:

```
-- Rule 8
for N in 0.0 .. 9.0 loop -- this is illegal
    ...
end loop;
```

The following example, however, is legal since it loops over the discrete range of Boolean values:

```
for Logical in Boolean loop    -- OK
    -- This code will loop twice
end loop;
```

Recall from Chapter 2 that the package Standard defines the Boolean type so that False precedes True:

```
type Boolean is (False, True);
```

Therefore, in the preceding **for** loop, the loop counter, Logical, has the value of False the first time through the loop and has the value of True the second time through the loop.

The following complete program uses nested **for** loops that loop over the Boolean type:

```
with Ada.Text_IO; use Ada.Text_IO;
procedure Truth_Table is
   P, Q: Boolean;
   package Boolean_IO is new Enumeration_IO (Boolean);
   use Boolean_IO;
begin
   Put ("    P          Q             P or Q        ");
   Put ("P xor Q       P and Q");
   New_Line (2);
   for P in Boolean loop
      for Q in Boolean loop
         Put (P, 6);
         Put (Q, 9);
         Put (P or Q, 11);
         Put (P xor Q, 11);
         Put (P and Q, 5);
         New_Line;
      end loop;
   end loop;
end Truth_Table;
```

This program outputs the following "truth table":

| P | Q | P or Q | P xor Q | P and Q |
|---|---|--------|---------|---------|
| FALSE | FALSE | FALSE | FALSE | FALSE |
| FALSE | TRUE | TRUE | TRUE | FALSE |
| TRUE | FALSE | TRUE | TRUE | FALSE |
| TRUE | TRUE | TRUE | FALSE | TRUE |

The second parameter that appears in the Put statements in the inner **for** loop is used to format the output so that the True and False values are aligned in columns. This parameter specifies the width of the output field. Note that the Boolean values are left justified with blank spaces appearing on the right. (When the width is not specified, then the minimum field width is used without any blank spaces.) Formatted input/output will be discussed in detail in Chapter 14.

Rule 9 states that **for** loops may step through the discrete range in reverse order. This form of **for** loops uses the keyword **reverse**:

```
-- Rule 9
for N in reverse 1..5 loop -- loops backwards: 5, 4, 3, 2, 1
   ...
end loop;
```

Even though the range is traversed from 5 to 1, the discrete range is still written as 1..5. The range 5..1 is a null range, even if the keyword **reverse** is added. The rationale for listing the range of values in a reversed **for** loop in increasing order is so that this ordering can work for both forward and reversed loops. For example, when looping through the integer range 0..120, the same range expression can be used regardless of the direction the loop advances:

```
subtype Persons_Age is Integer range 0 .. 120;
for Age in Persons_Age loop ...            -- loops 0..120
for Age in reverse Persons_Age loop ...    -- loops 120..0
```

Had the reversed loop required that Persons_Age be represented from 120 to 0, then the subtype, Persons_Age, could not be used. In fact, no subtype could be used, since integer subtype ranges can only be expressed in ascending order.

Unlike languages such as FORTRAN and BASIC, in Ada there are no step values that can be used in **for** loops. That is, there are no special forms of the **for** loop that permit us to step though the range, selecting every other value, or every third value, and so on.

Let us now consider a problem that occurs when the compiler cannot determine the loop counter's type by examining the loop counter's discrete range. Consider, for example, these two enumeration types:

```
type Philosopher is (Plato, Wittgenstein, Pythagoras, Locke,
    Descartes, Hume, Berkeley, Leibniz, Pascal);

type Mathematician is (Euclid, Pythagoras, Leibniz, Riemann,
    Lobatchewsky, Pascal, Gauss, Descartes);
```

Because many great philosophers were also great mathematicians, enumeration literals with the same name appear in both the preceding enumeration types. Such enumeration literals are said to be "overloaded." This overloading can lead to ambiguity, as in the following **for** loop clause:

```
for Great_Thinker in Pythagoras..Descartes loop   -- ambiguous
```

Because the upper and lower bounds of the range Pythagoras .. Descartes consist of literals that belong to both type Philosopher and type Mathematician, the compiler has no way of knowing which type to loop through. To solve this problem, we can qualify one or both of the literals forming the bounds of the discrete range:

```
for Great_Thinker in Philosopher'(Pythagoras)..Descartes loop
    -- qualification makes this unambiguous
```

In this case, only Pythagoras is qualified, but this is sufficient to resolve the ambiguity. (Descartes could also be qualified, but this is not necessary.) The qualifier explicitly states the type to which the value belongs. The qualifier consists of the name of the type, followed by a tick mark, ', followed by the value enclosed in parentheses.

Another way of solving this problem of ambiguity is to explicitly state the type to which the discrete range belongs:

```
for Great_Thinker in Philosopher range Pythagoras..Descartes loop
   -- explicitly stating the type makes this unambiguous
```

Note that the following **for** loop clause is not ambiguous.

```
for Great_Thinker in Plato..Descartes loop -- unambiguous
```

Although `Descartes` is overloaded, `Plato` is not overloaded. Since `Plato` is of type `Philosopher`, the compiler knows to loop over the values of that type.

An interesting situation occurs when integer literals (or literal expressions such as –1) are used to specify the loop counter's upper and lower bounds. Qualifying the literals may seem necessary since the compiler has no way of knowing whether the loop counter should belong to type `Integer`, `Short_Integer`, `Long_Integer`, or some other integer type. (Types `Short_Integer` and `Long_Integer` are optional types briefly discussed in Chapter 2.) For example, what integer type should the counter `Index` belong to?

```
for Index in -1 .. 9 loop... -- Index treated as type Integer
```

Instead of forcing –1 or 9 to be qualified, Ada assumes that `Index` belongs to the most common of integer types, type `Integer`. Thus, qualification is not required unless one wants the loop counter to belong to an integer type other than `Integer`. For instance, qualification makes the loop counter of the following **for** loop belong to type `Short_Integer`:

```
for Index in Short_Integer'(-1) .. 9 loop...
   -- Index belongs to type Short_Integer
```

**Ada 95 ▶** (In Ada 83, a language quirk required a loop range such as `-1..9` to be qualified, but not a range such as `1..9`. This quirk has been removed in Ada 95.)

## THE GOTO STATEMENT

The **goto** statement often results in unstructured code that is difficult to understand and maintain. Why, then, does a modern, structured language like Ada have the **goto** statement? Primarily because the **goto** statement is useful when translating programs, written in other languages that rely on the **goto,** into Ada. For instance, it would be very difficult to write an automatic FORTRAN-to-Ada translator program if Ada did not have the **goto** statement. However, when we write Ada code that has not been translated from another language, the **goto** statement can be avoided by using other Ada statements, such as the **exit** statement.

In the following example, a **goto** statement is used to jump to a point further down the code. A **goto** statement can also be used to jump to a prior point in the code:

```
goto The_Head_Of_The_Class;
   .
   .
   .
<< The_Head_Of_The_Class >>
```

When the **goto** statement is reached, the program branches to the label that is bracketed with << and >>. (Quality assurance personnel who attend code walk-throughs may have had a hand in making the Ada label so conspicuous.) The label name, `The_Head_Of_The_Class`, is directly used without declaring it as a **goto** label in the declarative part of the code.

In Ada, there are certain restrictions on the use of the **goto** statement. For instance, we cannot jump into an **if** statement, a **case** statement, a **loop** statement, or a block statement. We cannot jump into or out of a subprogram. We cannot jump from the declarative part of a block statement to its executable part, or vice versa. Neither can we jump between different groups of statements within an **if** statement or a **case** statement. The following code illustrates an illegal use of a **goto** statement:

```
if You_Tried_It then
   if You_Like_It then
      Put_Line ("Enjoy it");
      goto Continue;    -- this is illegal
   else
      Put_Line ("Go knock it");
   end if;
else
   << Continue >>  -- cannot jump into an else clause
   Put_Line ("Don't knock it");
end if;
```

Since Ada does not allow the **goto** to be used in the extremely objectionable ways described above, **goto**'s in Ada are less harmful than **goto**'s in languages that allow them to be used without any restrictions. Nevertheless, the **goto** makes code more difficult to understand. The problem is not so much knowing where a **goto** is going, because a **goto** can only have a single label. The problem is how to determine from where a label is reached. Since many **goto**'s can lead to the same label, the particular path that leads to the label can be difficult to determine. Even this problem, however, is not usually as bad in Ada as it often is in other languages. In the following code, for instance, the **goto** label <<Try_Again>> can only be reached from within the executable statement part of the block:

```
declare
   Done: Boolean := False;
```

```
begin
    <<Try_Again>>               -- This label can only be gotten to
                                -- from within this block
    while not Done loop
        ...
        if Network_Is_Busy then
            goto Try_Again;
        end if;
        ...
    end loop;
end;
```

The reason `<<Try_Again>>` can only be reached within the executable statement part of the block is because Ada does not allow

```
goto Try_Again;
```

to appear anywhere else. It is illegal to jump into the executable statement part of a block from the declarative part of the block or from outside the block.

In this chapter, we have discussed the **if** statement, the **case** statement, the **loop** statements, and the **goto** statement. In the next chapter, we will discuss a composite data type known as an array.

## EXERCISES

1. Which one of the following is true about **case** statements?
   a. The **when others** clause may appear anywhere in the **case** statement.
   b. The **case** expression may belong to any scalar type.
   c. Any **case** statement can be rewritten in a straightforward manner as an **if** statement.
   d. A value of a **case** expression may be covered by two or more **when** clauses.
   e. Any **if** statement can be rewritten in a straightforward manner as a **case** statement.
   f. The **if** statement without an **else** clause is like the **case** statement without an **others** clause in that the order in which the clauses are arranged has no effect.

2. Which one of the following is false about the **for** loop counter:
   a. Within the loop, it can be referenced but not changed.
   b. It does not exist outside the loop.
   c. If it is an Integer type, then it cannot be incremented by values other than 1.
   d. Its type must be explicitly declared.

3. Translate the following **if** statements into **case** statements:

   a.  ```
       if Goal = Doctor then
           Major := Any_Science;
       elsif Goal = Accountant then
           Major := Business;
       elsif Goal = Lawyer then
           Major := Anything;
       else
           Major := Undefined;
       end if;
       ```
   b.  ```
       if Month in April..June then
           Put_Line ("Do spring cleaning");
       elsif Month = January or Month = November then
           Put_Line ("Go skiing");
       elsif Month = July then
           Put_Line ("Go to Caribbean");
       else
           Put_Line ("Go to work");
       end if;
       ```

4. Translate the following **case** statements into **if** statements:

   a.  ```
       case Traffic_Signal is
           when Red     => Put_Line ("Stop");
           when Yellow  => Put_Line ("Speed_Up");
           when Green   => Put_Line ("Go");
       end case;
       ```
   b.  ```
       case Antagonist is
           when Me =>
               Put_Line ("I am firm");
           when You =>
               Put_Line ("You are stubborn");
           when others =>
               Put_Line ("He or she is pig headed");
       end case;
       ```
   c.  ```
       case Month is
           when January | March | November =>
               Put_Line ("Buy");
           when May | June..August =>
               Put_Line ("Sell");
           when others =>
               Put_Line ("Do nothing");
       end case;
       ```

5. Improve the following code by eliminating the numeric literals:
   ```
   declare
       type IQ is range 50 .. 180;
       subtype Genius is IQ range 140..IQ'Last;
       Ability: IQ;
   begin
       ...
       if Ability in 140..180 then ...
   ```
   ```

```
    for Intelligence in 140..180 loop ...

    case Ability is
        when 140..180 => ...

end;
```

6. State whether the following code segment is correct. If incorrect, explain what is wrong.

```
-- assume Text_IO is visible
declare
    type Days_Of_Week is (Monday, Tuesday, Wednesday,
        Thursday, Friday, Saturday, Sunday);
    package Days_IO is new Text_IO.Enumeration_IO (Days_Of_Week);
    use Days_IO;
    Day : Days_Of_Week;
begin
    Get (Day);
    case Day is
        when Monday .. Thursday => Put_Line ("Go to work.");
        when Friday => Put_Line ("Call in sick.");
    end case;
end;
```

7. Modify the **procedure** Daily_Activity, shown in this chapter, so that the days off are from Saturday to Monday.

8. Consider the following declarations:

```
type Destination is (France, Yellowstone, Las_Vegas);
subtype Long_Vacation is Integer range 21..70; -- days
subtype Average_Vacation is Integer range 7..20;  -- days
subtype Short_Vacation is Integer range 1..6;  -- days
```

Write a program that prompts the user for the length of his or her vacation and then uses a **case** statement to determine where the person should take the vacation. The program should select France, Yellowstone, or Las Vegas, depending on whether the vacation is long, average, or short, respectively. Use the names of the subtypes—Long_Vacation, Average_Vacation, and Short_Vacation—to express the discrete ranges within the **case** statement.

9. What values will the following program output? Is the X that is explicitly declared as an integer variable the same as the X used as a **for** loop counter?

```
with Ada.Text_IO; use Ada.Text_IO;
procedure P is
    X: Integer := -1;
    Sum: Integer := 0;
    package Int_IO is new Integer_IO (Integer);
    use Int_IO;
begin
    for X in 1..5 loop
        Sum := Sum + X;
```

```
        Put (Sum);
        New_Line;
    end loop;
    Put (X);
    New_Line;
    Put (Sum);
end P;
```

10. Rewrite the following program using a **while** loop instead of a **for** loop. Then rewrite the program using a simple loop with an **exit** statement.

```
with Ada.Text_IO;   use Ada.Text_IO;
procedure Strange_Claims is
    type Things_To_Be_Skeptical_Of is (Lock_Ness_Monster,
        UFOs, ESP, Bigfoot, Clairvoyance, Bermuda_Triangle,
        Dowsing, Ghosts, Palmistry, Astrology, Channeling,
        Psychic_Surgery);
    package Phenomenon_IO is new
        Enumeration_IO (Things_To_Be_Skeptical_Of);
    use Phenomenon_IO;
begin
    Put ("The following are things to be skeptical of:");
    New_Line;
    for Phenomenon in Things_To_Be_Skeptical_Of loop
        Put (Phenomenon);
        New_Line;
    end loop;
end Strange_Claims;
```

11. Write a timer program that, every second, outputs the number of hours, minutes, and seconds that have elapsed since the program started executing. Use nested **for** loops and the **delay** statement.

12. Find the errors in this code:

```
declare
    subtype One_To_Seven is Integer range 1..7;
begin
    for Index in One_To_Seven loop;
        Index := Index + 1;
    end for;
    Index := Index - 1; -- Index that is loop counter
end;
```

13. Modify the program Series_Of_Numbers in the **while** loop section of this chapter to output the number of steps taken to reach the number 1. Starting with the number 341, how many steps does it take to reach 1? Starting with the number 27, how many steps does it take to reach 1?

14. Simplify the following control structures:

```
a.  if not Empty then
        Empty := True;    -- assume this is all that is in
                          -- this if statement
    end if;
```

b.  ```
    loop
        if not Found then
            Continue_Search;
        else
            exit;
        end if;
    end loop;
    ```
c.  ```
    case Value is
        when A =>
            P;
        when B =>
            P;
            Q;
            return;
        when C =>
            P;
            R;
            return;
        when D =>
            P;
            S;
            return;
        when E =>
            P;
            return;
        when others =>
            P;
            return;
    end case;
    S;
    return;
    ```

**15.** Rewrite the following code so that all the **goto** statements are removed:

a.  ```
    loop
        ...
        loop
            if Error then
                goto Continue;
            end if;
            ...
        end loop;
        ...
    end loop;
    <<Continue>>
    ```
b.  ```
    if Sunny then
        goto Beach;
    end if;

    << Movie >>

    Watch_Movie;
    ```

```
    if Raining then
        goto Movie;
    end if;

    goto Home;

    << Beach >>

    if Windy then
        Fly_Kite;
    else
        Swim;
    end if;

    Eat;
    goto Movie;

    << Home >>
c.  << Weight_Clinic >>
    if Fat then
        Diet;
        goto Weight_Clinic;
    else
        goto Pig_Out;
    end if;

    << Try_Again >>

    if Thin then
        goto Pig_Out;
    else
        goto Exit_Program;
    end if;

    << Pig_Out >>

    Eat;
    goto Try_Again;

    << Exit_Program >>
```

16. Write a program that outputs the daily deposit and the total amount of money in a piggy bank each day a deposit is made. Assume that 30 consecutive daily deposits are made and that the size of the deposit doubles each day: one cent the first day, two cents the second day, four cents the third day, and so on, for 30 days.

17. Write a program that converts and outputs the temperatures from 0 to 10 degrees Centigrade (Celsius) to Fahrenheit and Kelvin in increments of 1 degree. Use the formulas:

```
Fahrenheit = 1.8 * Centigrade + 32
Kelvin = Centigrade + 273.15
```

In these formulas, is the use of numeric literals 1.8, 32, and 273.15 justified or should constants be used?

18. Write a program that finds and outputs the maximum and minimum values of Y, where

    $Y = -2X^2 + 4X - 2$, for $-2 \le X \le 2$.

    Test all values of X in this range in increments of 0.1.

19. Write a program that calculates and outputs the sum of all the odd integers from 1 to 199 that are not divisible by 7, 9, or 13.

20. Assume that the Boolean expressions within an **if** statement have different probabilities of being true. If execution speed is of utmost importance, how should the sections of this **if** statement be ordered?

21. Polar types are types with two values. Polar types are sometimes overused and should be replaced with type Boolean. Replace the polar types in the following code with type Boolean:

```
declare
    type Search_Status_Type is (Found, Not_Found);
    type Job_Status_Type is (Done, Not_Done);
    type On_Off is range 0 .. 1;
    Search_Status: Search_Status_Type;
    Job_Status: Job_Status_Type;
    Switch_State: On_Off;
begin
    . . .
    if Search_Status = Found then ...
        . . .
    if Job_Status = Not_Done then ...
        . . .
    if Switch_State = 0 then ...
        . . .
end;
```

22. Write a program that awakens each night at midnight and outputs "It's midnight." You will need to examine the predefined package Calendar to figure out what services are needed.

23. Write an Ada program that interactively prompts the user for a Roman numeral. The user indicates the end of the Roman numeral by entering a blank. Have the program calculate and output the value of the Roman numeral. Also have the program output an error message if an invalid character is entered. (You may also wish to check that the Roman numerals are entered in a proper order.)

24. Which of the following uses of the **goto** statement are illegal?

```
a.  <<Start_Over>>
    for Attempts in 1 .. N loop
        Make_Call;
        if Disconnect then
            goto Start_Over;
        end if;
    end loop;
b.  case Traffic_Signal is
        when Red =>
            Stop;
        when Yellow =>
            Speed_Up;
            goto Continue;
        when Green =>
            <<Continue>>
            Go;
    end case;
c.  if N = 100 then
        goto Execute;
    end if;
        . . .
    while N > 0 loop
        <<Execute>>
        . . .
    end loop;
d.  goto X;
        . . .
    declare
        A: Integer;
    begin
        <<X>>
        A := A + 1;
        . . .
    end;
e.  procedure Main is
        function Even (N: Integer) return Boolean is
        begin
            if N < 1 then
                goto Escape;
            else
                return N rem 2 = 0;
            end if;
        end Even;
    begin -- Main
        <<Escape>>
        . . .
    end Main;
```

# 4

# Arrays

**A**n array is an object that consists of multiple components, each belonging to the same type. An entire array is referenced with a single identifier. An individual component of the array is referenced with the array identifier, followed by an index value placed in parentheses. Consider, for example, an array called `Rainfall`, which represents the number of inches of rain for each month of the year. To reference a component of this array, we must supply an index value. Let the index assume the values `January` to `December`. Thus, the array component `Rainfall` (`April`) represents the amount of rain for the month of April. If there are 75 inches of rain in April, we can assign this value to the array component, just as we can assign a value to a regular variable:

```
Rainfall (April) := 75;
```

The array named `Rainfall` is a one-dimensional array because it is a list (row) of items. Only one index is needed to select an item in this list. A two-dimensional array can be thought of as a table or matrix. To reference an object in this table, two indexes are needed. The first index specifies the row (horizontal list) in which the item appears; the second index specifies the column (vertical list) in which the item appears. For example, a second index can be added to the `Rainfall` array to represent years. Thus, the array component `Rainfall` (`January, 1989`) represents the amount of rain during the month of January 1989.

A three-dimensional array can be thought of as pages of tables. To reference an item in a three-dimensional array, one needs three indexes. The first index specifies the row in which the item appears, the second index specifies the column in which the item appears, and the third index specifies the "page" on which the item appears. For example, a third index can be added to the previous `Rainfall` array to represent locations. Thus, the array component `Rainfall` (`January, 1989, Los_Angeles`) represents the amount of rain that fell in Los Angeles during January 1989. Arrays of dimensions greater than three are possible but infrequently used. Be careful: as you increase the number of dimensions, computer memory is quickly consumed to store all of these additional array components. For example, a three-dimensional array whose dimensions are 100 by 100 by 100 consists of $100^3$ or one million components.

The following topics are included in this chapter: one-dimensional arrays, multidimensional arrays, anonymous arrays, dynamic arrays, unconstrained array types, strings, `Boolean` vectors, array of arrays, array attributes, and operations on arrays.

## ONE-DIMENSIONAL ARRAYS

Let us consider how a one-dimensional array can be used. Suppose that a data structure is needed to store the various daily specials offered by a diner. Assume that the diner is open from Wednesday through Saturday and that a single daily special is provided on each of these days:

| Day | Special |
| --- | --- |
| Wednesday | Spam |
| Thursday | Burger |
| Friday | Meat Loaf |
| Saturday | Hot Dog |

Without arrays, this information could be stored using multiple variables:

```
Wed_Special      := Spam;
Thurs_Special    := Burger;
Fri_Special      := Meat_Loaf;
Sat_Special      := Hot_Dog;
```

Such unstructured data is error prone and awkward to manipulate, especially if the number of variables proliferates into the hundreds. By using a one-dimensional array, however, these related variables may be grouped together under the same name, for instance, `Special`. `Special`, then, is the name of the array, and `Wed` through `Sat` are its index values. A particular array component may be selected by using the name `Special`, followed by an index value—`Wed`, `Thurs`, `Fri`, or `Sat`—enclosed in parentheses. Thus, `Special (Wed)`, `Special (Thurs)`, `Special(Fri)`, and `Special(Sat)` represent the daily specials for Wednesday through Saturday, respectively.

Before an array can be used, it must be declared (defined). The following code declares the `Special` array:

```
type Food is (Burger, Hot_Dog, Spam, Meat_Loaf);
type Days_Open is (Wed, Thurs, Fri, Sat);
```

```
type Daily_Special is array (Days_Open) of Food;
Special: Daily_Special;
```

The first line declares the enumeration type Food, which contains the possible delicacies that can served as daily specials. The second line declares the enumeration type Days_Open, which lists the days that the diner is open for business. The third line declares the array type Daily_Special. Array type declarations have this form:

```
type array name is array (index specification ) of type;
```

In our example, the keyword **type** is followed by the name of the array type, Daily_Special, then the keywords **is array**, and the array index specification, enclosed in parentheses. The index specification defines a discrete range of possible values that the index can assume. In this example, the index specification consists of the type name Days_Open. This type name is used to represent the discrete range Wed..Sat. This method of representing discrete ranges was presented in Chapter 3 when we used discrete ranges in **for** loops and **case** statements.

The index specification is followed by the keyword **of**, which is followed by the type to which every component of the array belongs. In our example, every component belongs to type Food. The fourth line declares the variable Special to be an array of type Daily_Special. Since the components of Special belong to type Food, Special may be described as a Food array.

An array, then, is a composite object consisting of components, each belonging to the same type. Ada places no restrictions on the component type. Thus, a component type may be any scalar type, such as Integer, Float, Boolean, and Character; or a user-defined enumeration type, such as type Food. As we will see in the "Array of Arrays" section of this chapter, and in the next chapter, a component type can even be a composite type. The result is an array of arrays or an array of records.

Once the array Special is declared, values can be assigned to its components just like any variable of type Food:

```
Special (Wed)     := Spam;
Special (Thurs)   := Burger;
Special (Fri)     := Meat_Loaf;
Special (Sat)     := Hot_Dog;
```

Note again that each individual component of an array is referenced by the array name followed by an index value in the range Wed..Sat, which is placed in parentheses. (This index may be a literal, a constant, a variable, or an expression.)

The components of an array can be of any type; however, index values must belong to a discrete type. In our example, the index type, Days_Open, is a user-defined enumeration type.

Another example of an array follows:

```
type Beans is (Lima, Lentil, Garbanzo, Pinto, Kidney, Black,
    Soy, Mung, Jelly);
```

```
type Count_Type is array (Beans range Pinto..Jelly) of Natural;
Bean_Count: Count_Type;
```

In this example, `Bean_Count` is an array of natural numbers. (Recall that `Natural` is defined in the package `Standard` as an integer subtype whose range is from 0 to `Integer'Last`.) The index is constrained to values in the range of `Pinto` to `Jelly`; `Lima`, `Lentil`, and `Garbanzo` are excluded from this range:

```
Bean_Count (Soy)    := 181;
Bean_Count (Jelly)  := -5; -- error, component value out of
                           -- bounds
Bean_Count (Lentil) := 24; -- error, index out of bounds
```

Note that the second and third statements have errors as a result of values going out of bounds. The Ada compilation system will catch these mistakes at runtime and raise a constraint error. (A warning may also be generated at compile time.) This should be good news to, for example, FORTRAN programmers. Practically every FORTRAN programmer has, at one time or another, written code where an array index accidentally goes out of bounds. Standard FORTRAN does not catch this error, either at compilation time or at runtime. Therefore, programmers sometimes spend days debugging a program before catching this error. The philosophy behind Ada is to have the compiler detect as many errors as possible, thus reducing the time spent debugging code.

As we have seen, an array may be initialized by separately assigning a value to each of its components. In situations where every component of the array needs to be assigned the same value, the **for** loop may be used:

```
for Day in Days_Open loop
    Special (Day) := Spam; -- special for every day is spam
end loop;
```

Ada offers yet another alternative to array initialization. An entire array may be initialized by assigning it an array aggregate:

```
Special := (Spam, Spam, Spam, Spam);
    -- special for every day is spam
```

An array aggregate can be thought of as a complete array value, that is, a particular set of values for an entire array. Note that by initializing an array to an aggregate, different values may just as easily be assigned to each array component:

```
Special := (Spam, Meat_Loaf, Hot_Dog, Burger);
    -- positional notation
```

Each value in the aggregate is assigned to the array component in the corresponding position. The first value in the aggregate, `Spam`, is assigned to the first component, `Special (Wed)`; the second value in the aggregate, `Meat_Loaf`, is assigned to the second component, `Special (Thurs)`; and so on. The aggregate must be complete: it must assign a value to every component of the array. Incomplete aggregates are illegal.

Aggregates can be written using two different notations: named notation and positional notation. There is one restriction: the two types of notation cannot be mixed in one aggregate. The preceding example uses positional notation: each value in the aggregate is assigned to the array component in the corresponding position. The following example uses named notation:

```
Special := ( Wed => Spam,        Thurs  => Meat_Loaf,
             Fri => Hot_Dog,      Sat    => Burger );
                    -- named notation
```

In named notation, the name of the index value to the left of the arrow is associated with the value to the right of the arrow. In the example, `Spam` is assigned to the array component with the index value `Wed`, `Meat_Loaf` is assigned to the array component with the index value `Thurs`, and so on.

Named notation has two advantages over positional notation. First, named notation clearly documents which values are assigned to which array components. For instance, at a glance, one can see that spam is the daily special for Wednesday, and hot dogs, for Friday. Second, the order of items in the aggregate does not matter. Thus, ordering errors are avoided. The preceding aggregate could therefore be written in this equivalent form:

```
Special := ( Sat => Burger,    Wed    => Spam,
             Fri => Hot_Dog,   Thurs  => Meat_Loaf);
```

Array aggregates may use the **others** keyword to assign a value to array components that are not explicitly given a value. (Recall that the **others** keyword functions similarly in **case** statements.) Every component of the array `Special` may be assigned the same value, `Spam`, as follows:

```
Special := (others => Spam); -- special for every day is spam
```

The following example uses named notation to assign `Burger` to `Special (Wed)` and `Meat_Loaf` to `Special (Sat)`. All other array components are assigned the value `Spam`, as indicated by the keyword **others**:

```
Special := (Wed => Burger, Sat => Meat_Loaf, others => Spam);
   -- Wednesday special is burger
   -- Saturday special is meat loaf
   -- For all other days, the special is spam
```

**Ada 95** ▶ In Ada 83, aggregates using named notation with a **when others** clause must be qualified. In the next example, `Burger` is assigned to `Special(Wed)`, and `Meat_Loaf` is assigned to `Special (Thurs)`, by positional notation. All other array components are assigned to the value `Spam`:

```
Special := (Burger, Meat_Loaf, others => Spam);
   -- Wednesday special is burger;
   -- Thursday special is meat loaf
   -- For all other days, the special is spam
```

This is the only case where positional and named notation can be mixed in array aggregates. In other words, in mixed notation, only the named item **others** is allowed, and it must be placed at the end of the aggregate. The following mixed notation is therefore illegal:

```
Special := (Burger, Meat_Loaf, Fri => Spam, Sat => Spam);
   -- illegal; cannot mix positional and named notation
```

The keyword **others**, if used, must always appear at the end of the aggregate, even when named notation is used:

```
Special := (others => Spam, Wed => Burger);
   -- illegal; others must be last item
```

Recall that in Chapter 3, the vertical bar is used in **case** statements to select various choices. The vertical bar may also be used within an array aggregate, as follows:

```
Special := (Thurs | Sat => Burger, others => Spam);
   -- on Thursday or Saturday, special is burger
   -- for other days, the special is spam
```

In this statement, if the day is Thursday or Saturday, then the special is Burger; otherwise, the special is Spam.

The vertical bar cannot be used to combine an index value with the keyword **others**:

```
Special := (Wed | others => Burger);
   -- illegal; others cannot be combined with index values
```

The vertical bar is particularly useful when the index values (such as Thurs and Sat) are not contiguous. When the index values are contiguous, a discrete range may be used:

```
Special := ( Thurs..Sat => Burger, others => Spam);
   -- from Thursday to Saturday, special is burger
   -- for other days, special is spam
```

In this example, burgers are the daily special for all days from Thursday to Saturday. For all remaining days—in this case, Wednesday—the special is spam.

A discrete range can cover the entire range of index values:

```
Special := (Wed..Sat => Spam);
```

or

```
Special := (Days_Open => Spam); -- special for every day is spam
```

In this example, the value of every component of the `Special` array is set to `Spam`.

The selector, the discrete range, and the keyword **others** can, of course, all be used in a single aggregate:

```
Special := (Wed | Fri .. Sat => Meat_Loaf, others => Spam);
        -- special for Wednesday, or for Friday to Saturday is meat
        -- loaf
        -- for other days, special is spam
```

In this example, meat loaf is the daily special on Wednesday and on Friday through Saturday. Spam is the daily special on the remaining day, Thursday.

So far, our examples have only shown array aggregates with static values such as `Spam` and `Meat_Loaf`. Aggregate elements can also consist of dynamic values:

```
Default := Spam;
Special := ( Wed    => Burger,
             Sat    => Meat_Loaf,
             others => Default );
```

Note that the value of `Default` is dynamic since its value is not known until runtime.

In Ada, objects may be initialized when they are declared. Arrays are no exception, as shown in the `Dietary_Status` array in the following program:

```
with Ada.Text_IO; use Ada.Text_IO;
procedure You_Are_What_You_Eat is
    type Edible_Things is (Apple, Orange, Cake, Ice_Cream,
          Burger, Fries);
    type Food_Category is (Fattening, Nonfattening);
    type Food_Array is array (Edible_Things) of Food_Category;
    package Food_IO is new Enumeration_IO (Edible_Things);
    package Int_IO is new Integer_IO (Integer);
    use Food_IO, Int_IO;

    Dietary_Status: constant Food_Array :=  -- constant array
              ( Apple     => Nonfattening,
                Orange    => Nonfattening,
                Cake      => Fattening,
                Ice_Cream => Fattening,
                Burger    => Fattening,
                Fries     => Fattening );

    Morsel: Edible_Things;
    Number_Of_Sins: Natural := 0;
begin
    for Sample in 1..50 loop
        Put_Line ("What are you about to eat?");
        Get (Morsel);
```

```
        New_Line;
        if Dietary_Status (Morsel) = Fattening then
            Put_Line ("Remove from your mouth immediately!");
            Number_Of_Sins := Number_Of_Sins + 1;
        else
            Put_Line ("Good for you");
        end if;
    end loop;

    Put ("Number of times sinned is ");
    Put (Number_Of_Sins);
    New_Line;

    if Number_Of_Sins < 9 then
        Put_Line ("You did well");
    else
        Put_Line ("Failed again fatty");
    end if;
end You_Are_What_You_Eat;
```

After this user-unfriendly program finds out what morsel of food is about to be consumed, the "look-up" table, which is the constant array `Dietary_Status`, is used to check whether this particular morsel is fattening or nonfattening. (Since `Dietary_Status` is a constant array, it must be initialized when it is declared, and its value cannot be changed.) If the morsel is fattening, then the message "`Remove from your mouth immediately!`" is output, and the counter `Number_Of_Sins` is incremented by 1. If the morsel is nonfattening, then the message "`Good for you!`" is output. The program loops (prompts the user for the morsel and outputs the appropriate message) 50 times. When the program is done looping, it outputs the number of times that the person sinned. If this number is less than 9, then the message "`You did well`" appears; otherwise, "`Failed again fatty`" is output. Constant arrays such as `Dietary_Status` are useful for looking up information that cannot change.

## MULTIDIMENSIONAL ARRAYS

Let us modify our diner example so that three daily specials are served each day: one for breakfast, one for lunch, and one for dinner. Because breakfast is served, let us also add eggs to the list of possible specials:

|           | Breakfast | Lunch   | Dinner    |
|-----------|-----------|---------|-----------|
| Wednesday | Spam      | Hot Dog | Meat Loaf |
| Thursday  | Eggs      | Spam    | Hot Dog   |
| Friday    | Spam      | Spam    | Burger    |
| Saturday  | Spam      | Burger  | Meat Loaf |

To look up a particular special in the previous one-dimensional array example, all you have to know is the day of the week. Hence, an array with only one index, a one-dimensional array, is required. In this example, to look up a particular special, you have to know the day of the week and the meal. Hence, an array with two indexes, a two-dimensional array, is needed.

The following declarations result in the definition of a two-dimensional array, `Special`, which can be used to store the daily special for each meal of each day that the diner is open:

```
type Food is (Burger, Hot_Dog, Spam, Meat_Loaf, Eggs);
type Days_Open is (Wed, Thurs, Fri, Sat);
type Meal_Type is (Breakfast, Lunch, Dinner);
type Daily_Special is array (Days_Open, Meal_Type) of Food;
Special: Daily_Special;
```

As can be seen, a two-dimensional array has two indexes; in this case, these indexes are of different types. The index for the first dimension is of type `Days_Open` and has the range `Wed..Sat`. The index for the second dimension is of type `Meal_Type` and has the range `Breakfast..Dinner`. The first index specifies the rows of the table. There is a Wednesday row of specials, a Thursday row of specials, and so on. The second index specifies the columns of the table. There is the breakfast column, the lunch column, and the dinner column. Thus, each component of the array, such as `Special (Wed, Dinner)`, is referenced by two index values and belongs to the type `Food`.

Unlike one-dimensional array initialization, which can use a single **for** loop, two-dimensional array initialization requires nested **for** loops. Each loop ranges over the values of a different index:

```
for Day in Days_Open loop          -- rows
   for Meal in Meal_Type loop      -- columns
      Special (Day, Meal) := Spam;
   end loop;
end loop;
```

As with one-dimensional arrays, two-dimensional arrays can be initialized to an aggregate, either when the array is declared or by using an assignment statement later on. Each of the following assignments initialize every component of the array to `Spam`:

```
Special := (Wed..Sat => (Breakfast..Dinner => Spam) );
```

or

```
Special := (Days_Open => (Meal_Type => Spam) );
```

or

```
Special := (others => (others => Spam) );
```

Note that the range specified in the outer aggregate denotes the row values (`Wed..Sat`), and the range specified in the inner aggregate denotes the column values (`Breakfast..Dinner`).

The aggregate may use either positional or named notation for each of its dimensions. For a two-dimensional array, there are four consistent combinations possible for writing the aggregate. (There are other possible combinations if one inconsistently changes, for instance, between named and positional notation for each row of an array.) The four consistent combinations are as follows:

1. Positional notation for the rows and the columns.
2. Named notation for the rows and positional notation for the columns.
3. Positional notation for the rows and named notation for the columns.
4. Named notation for the rows and the columns.

Combination 1 uses positional notation for the rows (`Days_Open`) and the columns (`Meal_Type`). In the following aggregate, each row represents the specials for a particular day (Wed, Thurs, Fri, and Sat), and each column represents the meals (breakfast, lunch, and dinner):

```
Special :=
     (  (  Spam,   Hot_Dog,   Meat_Loaf),
        (  Eggs,   Spam,      Hot_Dog),
        (  Spam,   Spam,      Burger),
        (  Spam,   Burger,    Meat_Loaf) );
```

With Combination 1, it is difficult to see which special applies to which day and to which meal.

Combination 2 uses named notation for the rows (`Days_Open`) and positional notation for the columns (`Meal_Type`). This aggregate is easier to read than the Combination 1 aggregate. However, it is still not very clear which meal is for breakfast, lunch, or dinner:

```
Special :=
     (  Wed    => (Spam, Hot_Dog,  Meat_Loaf),
        Thurs  => (Eggs, Spam,     Hot_Dog),
        Fri    => (Spam, Spam,     Burger),
        Sat    => (Spam, Burger,   Meat_Loaf) );
```

Combination 3 uses positional notation for the rows (`Days_Open`) and named notation for the columns (`Meal_Type`). To make the code more readable, the meals for a given day are listed vertically instead of horizontally. In this combination, it is difficult to see which breakfast, lunch, or dinner special applies to which day:

```
Special :=    (        (  Breakfast => Spam,
                          Lunch     => Hot_Dog,
                          Dinner    => Meat_Loaf ),
                       (  Breakfast => Eggs,
```

```
                         Lunch      => Spam,
                         Dinner     => Hot_Dog ),
                  (   Breakfast =>   Spam,
                      Lunch      =>  Spam,
                      Dinner     =>  Burger ),
                  (   Breakfast =>   Spam,
                      Lunch      =>  Burger,
                      Dinner     =>  Meat_Loaf) );
```

Combination 4 uses named notation for both the rows (Days_Open) and the columns (Meal_Type). Once again, to make the code more readable, the meals for a given day are listed vertically instead of horizontally. This aggregate is easier to read than the preceding aggregates, because all values of the two indexes are clearly labeled. For instance, at a glance, we can see that hot dog is the Thursday dinner special:

```
Special :=
    (   Wed     => (  Breakfast => Spam,
                      Lunch      => Hot_Dog,
                      Dinner     => Meat_Loaf ),
        Thurs   => (  Breakfast => Eggs,
                      Lunch      => Spam,
                      Dinner     => Hot_Dog ),
        Fri     => (  Breakfast => Spam,
                      Lunch      => Spam,
                      Dinner     => Burger ),
        Sat     => (  Breakfast => Spam,
                      Lunch      => Burger,
                      Dinner     => Meat_Loaf ) );
```

Of course, it takes time to type all this information and to carefully indent all the aggregate items. In the long run, however, this extra effort will be rewarded. Your code will be easier to understand, maintain, and modify.

The preceding examples of aggregates do not violate the restriction that array aggregates cannot mix positional and named notation. This restriction applies only to portions of an aggregate that are in the same parenthetical grouping in a multi-dimensional aggregate. For instance, look at the aggregate shown in Combination 2. The outer aggregate covering the rows (Days_Open) and each subaggregate covering the columns (Meal_Type) are considered different parenthetical groupings. Therefore, if the Wed row is referenced using named notation, the Thurs, Fri, and Sat rows must also be referenced using named notation. However, the three meals for Wed might use named notation, while the three meals for Thurs use positional notation, and so on.

Using named notation effectively documents which value is being assigned to which array component. However, named notation is only effective if descriptive names have been assigned to the index values. Arrays that use integer indexes, which are not typically descriptive, should usually employ positional notation for their aggregates. Consider the following two-dimensional array:

```
type Matrix_Type is array (1..2, 1..3) of Integer;
Matrix: Matrix_Type;
```

We can initialize `Matrix` just using positional notation (Combination 1), as follows:

```
Matrix := (  ( 1, 2, 3 ),
             ( 4, 5, 6 ) );
```

This aggregate is easy to read. The following aggregates (Combination 2, followed by Combination 3) use positional and named notation:

```
Matrix := (  1 =>  ( 1, 2, 3 ),              -- rows are named
             2 =>  ( 4, 5, 6 ) );

Matrix := (  (1 => 1,  2 => 2,   3 => 3 ), -- columns are named
             (1 => 4,  2 => 5,   3 => 6 )  );
```

The worst-looking aggregate (Combination 4) uses named notation for the rows and the columns:

```
Matrix := (  1 => ( 1 => 1,   2 => 2, 3 => 3),
             2 => ( 1 => 4,   2 => 5, 3 => 6) );
```

In the `Matrix` examples, Combination 1 is the easiest to read; Combination 4 is the hardest to read. In the previous two-dimensional `Special` array, the reverse is true. The difference, again, has to do with whether or not the index values of the array have descriptive names. In the `Special` array, `Wed` and `Lunch` are descriptive names. In the `Matrix` array, the index values 1, 2, and 3 have no meaning except as indicators of position, and position is best conveyed using positional notation.

## ANONYMOUS ARRAYS

Anonymous arrays are arrays that do not belong to any named type. Each anonymous array is considered to be a one-of-a-kind array whose type is anonymous (nameless). To better understand anonymous arrays, let us first look once more at an array that belongs to a named type. For contrast, we will then make this array an anonymous type.

```
type Items_In_Stock is new Integer range 0..1_000;
type Item is (Computers, CRTs, Printers, Disk_Drives);
type Inventory is array (Item) of Items_In_Stock;
March_Inventory, April_Inventory: Inventory;
```

Note that `April_Inventory` and `March_Inventory` are two arrays that belong to the array type named `Inventory`. Since these arrays belong to the same type, they are assignment compatible and may be tested for equality, inequality, and other relationships that will be discussed later:

```
March_Inventory :=  (Computers => 27, CRTs => 9, Printers => 5,
                     Disk_Drives => 10);
April_Inventory := March_Inventory;
      -- OK, since both arrays are of the same type
```

The effect of this array assignment is to assign each component value of `March_Inventory` to the corresponding component of `April_Inventory`. This one assignment statement, in other words, does the work of the following four assignment statements:

```
April_Inventory (Computers)    := March_Inventory (Computers);
April_Inventory (CRTs)         := March_Inventory (CRTs);
April_Inventory (Printers)     := March_Inventory (Printers);
April_Inventory (Disk_Drives) := March_Inventory (Disk_Drives);
```

Whereas more than one array may belong to the same named type, every anonymous array belongs to its own unique anonymous type. This is true even when the anonymous arrays are defined in the same declaration:

```
March_Inventory, April_Inventory: array (Item) of
    Items_In_Stock; -- anonymous arrays
```

`March_Inventory` and `April_Inventory` are declared as arrays, but not as arrays of any specific array type (such as type `Inventory` above). Thus, they belong to different anonymous types. Due to type incompatibility, these arrays cannot be assigned or compared to one another. Thus, the following assignment is illegal:

```
April_Inventory := March_Inventory; -- Illegal; type mismatch
```

Type conversion cannot be used to circumvent this type incompatibility, since these arrays do not have a type name that can be used as a type conversion operator. (Type conversion will be discussed in this chapter in "Operations on Arrays.") Note, however, that since the components of these anonymous arrays belong to type `Items_In_Stock`, no type incompatibility results in assigning components of one array to the other:

```
April_Inventory (Computers) := March_Inventory (CRTs); -- OK
```

Anonymous arrays, therefore, should be used only when one does not need more than one array of the same type and when one's sense of data abstraction does not require a common abstract array type. Discussions of other restrictions that apply to anonymous arrays will be deferred to the relevant chapters in this book.

## DYNAMIC ARRAYS

Dynamic arrays are arrays whose size are not determined until runtime. Suppose that the upper bound of an index of an array named Dynamic is interactively set at runtime by the user of the program. If the user, for example, enters 1000, then Dynamic will have an index range from 1 to 1000. A first attempt at writing this code might result in the following:

```ada
procedure Dynamic_Array is
    Limit: Positive;
    Get (Limit);  -- compilation error; executable code cannot be
                  -- placed in declarative part
    Dynamic: array (1..Limit) of Float;
begin
    ...
end Dynamic_Array;
```

The problem with this code, as indicated, is that it is illegal to place an executable statement, Get (Limit), in the declarative part of a procedure. Yet this statement must be executed before the value of Limit is used to set the array bounds of Dynamic. (The declarative part includes all the code between the keywords **is** and **begin**.)

A second attempt at writing this code might result in the following:

```ada
procedure Dynamic_Array is
    Limit: Positive;
begin
    Get (Limit);
    Dynamic: array (1..Limit) of Float;  -- compilation error;
        -- declarations cannot be placed in statement part
        ...
end Dynamic_Array;
```

This code is also illegal, because a declaration cannot be placed in the statement part of a procedure. (The statement part includes all the code between the keywords **begin** and **end**.) A third and successful attempt at writing this code follows:

```ada
procedure Dynamic_Array is
    Limit: Positive;
begin
    Get (Limit);
    declare
        Dynamic: array (1..Limit) of Float;
    begin
        -- executable statements go here
        ...
    end;
end Dynamic_Array;
```

The problem of placing a declaration within the statement part of the code is solved by using a block statement. A block statement is an executable statement that begins with the keyword **declare**, followed by declarations; then the keyword **begin**, followed by executable statements; then the keyword **end.** The block statement is useful in situations like the previous example because the block statement contains a declarative part and yet can be placed wherever executable statements are allowed. Thus, declarations can be placed in the statement part of a procedure if the declarations are embedded in the declarative part of a block statement. More information on block statements will be given in Chapter 6.

## UNCONSTRAINED ARRAY TYPES

Ada excels at data abstraction, and the unconstrained array type is a paragon of data abstraction. Unconstrained array types allow Ada programmers to declare arrays that differ in size (the number of index values in a given dimension) to be the same type. An unconstrained array type, then, does not include information about the size of the array; that is, the array indexes are not constrained to a particular range of values. Determination of the array size is deferred until an array is declared to belong to this unconstrained array type. As we will see in Chapter 6, unconstrained array types allow general-purpose subprograms to be created for manipulating similar arrays that have differing sizes.

The following is an example of an unconstrained array type:

```
type Row is array (Integer range <>) of Integer;
```

Instead of supplying a discrete range after the keyword **range**, we use the symbol, <>, called a box, to indicate that no constraint is imposed on the range of integer index values. When arrays are declared to belong to type Row, array index bounds must be supplied. These index bounds, or index constraints, take the form of a discrete range, which is appended to Row:

```
Row_Of_3: Row(1..3);
Row_Of_4: Row(1..4);
Row_Of_5: Row(0..4);
Row_Of_6: Row(-3..2);
```

Row_Of_3 has a length (size) of 3, Row_Of_4 has a length of 4, Row_Of_5 has a length of 5, and Row_Of_6 has a length of 6. Even though these arrays have different lengths (and in some cases, different lower index bounds), they all belong to the same type, Row. In essence, each of these arrays belong to different subtypes of Row, each constrained to a different index range. For example, Row_Of_3 belongs to the implicit subtype of Row, whose index is constrained from 1 to 3. In fact, instead of constraining each array as it is declared, an explicit subtype can be used to set a constraint. As the following example illustrates, the subtype Row_Of_4 constrains the index to values from 1 to 4. Arrays A, B, and C are then declared to be of this subtype:

```
type Row is array (Integer range <>) of Integer;
subtype Row_Of_4 is Row (1..4);
A, B, C: Row_Of_4;  -- each array has index values 1 to 4
```

**Ada 95 ▶**    Another way that an array object can be constrained is by initializing the object when it is declared. The size of the object is then inferred from the size of the aggregate being assigned to it:

```
type Row_Type is array (Positive range <> ) of Integer;
Row: Row_Type := (1, 7, 5); -- Index constraint for Row is 1..3
```

In this declaration, Row's index is implicitly constrained from 1 to 3. This constraint is derived from the length of the aggregate being assigned to Row. (In Ada 83, providing index constraints through initialization is only allowed for array constants, never for array variables.)

Implicit index constraints are handy, but caution must be exercised, as shown in the following code:

```
declare
    type Row_Type is array (Integer range <> ) of Integer;
    Row: Row_Type := (1, 7, 5);
begin
    Row (1) := 2; -- Constraint error; index value out of range
    Row (Integer'First) := 2;  -- OK
end;
```

The important difference between this code and the preceding example is that in this code, the unconstrained array type Row_Type has an integer index instead of a positive index. This difference seems innocuous, but the consequence of using an integer index may surprise you. If you try to access the first component of the array Row by writing Row (1), the compiler will raise a constraint error. The problem is that since no explicit constraint is imposed on the index of Row, the compiler makes Integer'First the first index value. On a standard 16-bit computer, Integer'First is not 1 but -32,768! This is not a problem in our original example, where we declare the index to be Positive, because Positive'First is 1.

We can overcome this problem by declaring the index type to be Positive or by initializing Row using named notation:

```
Row: Row_Type := (1 => 1,  2 => 7, 3 => 5);  -- Index range is
                                              -- 1..3
```

This use of named notation forces the index range of Row to be 1..3 instead of Integer'First..(Integer'First + 2). Alternatively, we can supply an index constraint:

```
Row: Row_Type (1..3) := (1, 7, 5);   -- Index range is 1..3
```

Unconstrained arrays may be one-dimensional, as in the preceding examples, or multidimensional, as in the following example:

```
type Matrix_Type is array (Positive range <>,
                           Positive range <> ) of Integer;
Four_By_Four: Matrix_Type (1..4, 1..4);
Three_By_Three: Matrix_Type (1..3, 1..3);
subtype Two_By_Three_Group is Matrix_Type (1..2, 1..3);
A, B, C: Two_By_Three_Group;
```

This example is like the preceding examples, except that two array indexes must be constrained. By the way, if one index is unconstrained, all indexes must be unconstrained. Constrained and unconstrained notation may not appear in the same type definition. For example, Matrix_Type cannot be declared as follows:

```
type Matrix_Type is array (Positive range 1..5, -- Illegal
                           Positive range <>) of Integer;
```

**Ada 95 ▶**   As we have seen, each array belonging to an unconstrained array type belongs to a subtype of that unconstrained array type. The subtype is determined by its index constraint. When an array is assigned an aggregate value, the aggregate is sometimes implicitly converted to a new subtype. This implicit subtype conversion is called "sliding." Sliding, however, does not occur in all cases. In particular, sliding never occurs on an array aggregate with an **others** choice. In the following code, for example, sliding only occurs when A is assigned an aggregate value, but not B or C:

```
declare
    type Vector_Type is array (Positive range <>) of Float;
    A, B, C: Vector_Type (1..7);
begin
    A: Vector_Type := (5..7 => 0.0, 8..11 => 1.0);
        -- Aggregate "slides" so that
        -- A(1) to A(3) have value 0.0
        -- A(4) to A(7) have value 1.0

    B := (5..7 => 0.0, others => 1.0);
        -- No sliding so that
        -- B(1) to B(4) have value 1.0
        -- B(5) to B(7) have value 0.0

    C := (0.0, 0.0, 0.0, others => 1.0);
        -- No sliding so that
        -- C(1) to C(3) have value 0.0
        -- C(4) to C(7) have value 1.0
        ...
end;
```

For A, its index range determines how the aggregate slides. The index range of A is 1..7. The index range of the aggregate being assigned to A is 5..11. The assignment causes the aggregate to slide, so that A(1) gets the aggregate component with the index of 5, A(2) gets the aggregate component with the index of 6, and so on. As a result, A(1) to A(3) receive the value 0.0, and A(4) to A(7) receive the value 1.0. For B, however, no sliding occurs because the **others** clause is used. Since B has an index range 1..7 and since B(5) to B(7) are explicitly given the value 0.0, the **others** clause just covers B's remaining index values, 1 to 4. Thus, after the assignment to B, B(1) to B(4) have the value 1.0 and B(5) to B(7) have the value 0.0. Since the aggregate assigned to C has an **others** clause, once again no sliding occurs. By position, C(1) to C(3) are assigned 0.0. The **others** clause covers the remaining components, C(4) to C(7), so these components are assigned 1.0.

**Ada 95 ▶**     Although unconstrained arrays typically belong to a named array type, it is possible to declare an unconstrained anonymous array, as long as it is initialized to an aggregate:

```
A: array (Integer range <>) of Boolean := ( 2..4   => True,
                                             5       => False );
```

In this example, the index of A is constrained to 2..5. This range is deduced from the initial aggregate being assigned.

---

## STRINGS

**Ada 95 ▶**     Strings are discussed in this chapter on arrays because a string is an unconstrained one-dimensional array of characters. In the Ada package Standard, strings are defined as follows:

```
-- defined in the package Standard
type String is array (Positive range <>) of Character;
type Wide_String is array (Positive range <>) of Wide_Character;
```

Type String is provided for type Character, and type Wide_String is provided for type Wide_Character. (In this book, examples use types String and Character, but they could just as easily use Wide_String and Wide_Character.)

Because a string is an unconstrained array type, constraints must be supplied when an object is declared to be a string. (Or, as mentioned previously, subtypes or initial values can be used to set a constraint.) For example, in the declaration that follows, My_Cat is defined as a string variable constrained to a length of 13:

```
My_Cat: String (1..13);
```

An array aggregate containing 13 characters can then be assigned to My_Cat:

```
My_Cat := (   'M', 'e', 'o', 'w', ' ','T', 's', 'e', '-', 't',
            'u', 'n', 'g' );
```

This notation is unnatural and awkward. In most computer languages, the entire string is placed in quotes. Ada allows the same convention:

```
My_Cat := "Meow Tse-tung";
```

A double quote that is part of the string is indicated with two double quotes:

```
Put ("Physicists say that ""strings are super!""");
```

This statement outputs: Physicists say that "strings are super!"
Let us now declare a few more strings:

```
My_Boa: String (1.. 15)          := "Julius Squeezer";
My_Cobra: String (1.. 11)        := "Herman Hiss";
My_Canary: String (1..4)         := "Pete";
My_Second_Canary: String(1..6)   := "Repete";
```

Note that the string variables are given a size constraint that exactly matches the size of the string aggregates (also called string literals) that are being assigned to them. For instance, My_Boa, which is a string variable of length 15, is assigned the value "Julius Squeezer", which is 15 characters long. Strings, as well as other kinds of arrays, can only be assigned to one another if they have the same size. Consider this declaration:

```
Pet_Name: String (1..5);
```

Because Pet_Name is a string variable of length 5, the following assignments are illegal:

```
Pet_Name := "Pete";    -- illegal;
                       -- "Pete" contains less than 5 characters


Pet_Name := "Repete"; -- illegal;
                       -- "Repete" contains more that 5 characters
```

(Programmers needing variable length strings can use the services of Ada's pre-defined package Ada.Strings, which is briefly discussed at the end of this section.)
When working with strings, it is sometimes useful to select a substring, or in Ada's terminology, a string slice. String slices are taken by specifying the desired index range. For example, consider the declaration

```
My_Cobra: String (1..11) := "Herman Hiss";
```

The following slice can be made:

```
My_Husband: String (1..6) := My_Cobra (1..6);
   -- assigns the value "Herman"
```

In this declaration, `My_Cobra (1..6)` is a string slice, consisting of the first 6 characters ("Herman") of the 11-character string `My_Cobra`. This slice is then assigned to the string variable `My_Husband`.

In the next declaration, the string slice `My_Cobra (8..11)` yields the 4-character string "Hiss", which is assigned to the string variable `My_Favorite_Sound`:

```
My_Favorite_Sound: String (1..4) := My_Cobra (8..11);
    -- assigns the value "Hiss"
```

A slice can be dynamically set; that is, the upper or lower bound of a slice can be set at runtime. If the upper bound is less than the lower bound, then the slice is null. The result is a null string, indicated by two double quotes with nothing between them: "". Null strings are legal; no compiler error is generated.

Strings are the most common types of arrays to slice. However, in Ada, any type of one-dimensional array can be sliced. Other examples of array slicing are given in this chapter in "Operations on Arrays."

In addition to array slicing, catenation is another common string operation. Catenating strings means to join them. In Ada, the catenation operator is the ampersand symbol, &. Consider these declarations:

```
My_Canary: String (1..4) := "Pete";
My_Second_Canary: String (1..6) := "Repete";
```

The following catenation yields the value `"Pete and Repete"`, which is then assigned to the string `My_Birds`:

```
My_Birds: String (1..15) := My_Canary & " and " &
                            My_Second_Canary;
    -- assigns "Pete and Repete"
```

Any type of one-dimensional array may be catenated, not just strings. An example of an integer array catenation appears in "Operations on Arrays."

When a string slice is assigned a value, the rest of the string is not automatically padded with blanks. This is shown in the following code:

```
declare
    My_Boa: String (1.. 15) := "Julius Squeezer";
    My_Cobra: String (1.. 11) := "Herman Hiss";
begin
    My_Boa (1..6) := My_Cobra (1..6);
        -- My_Boa = "Herman Squeezer", not "Herman        "
end;
```

Although `My_Boa (1..6)` is assigned the value `"Herman"`, the remaining slice, `My_Boa (7..15)`, still contains `" Squeezer"`. The entire string, `My_Boa (1..15)`, therefore has the value "Herman Squeezer". If only the value "Herman" is desired, then the remainder of the string must be padded with blanks:

```
My_Boa := My_Cobra (1..6) & "                      ";
```

Failing to pad a string with blanks is one common programming pitfall. Another common pitfall is confusing strings of length 1 with a character. Strings and characters are distinct types. Consider the following declaration:

```
My_Newt: String (1..16) := "Sir Isaac Newton";
```

Given this declaration, the string slice My_Newt (1..1) is not the same as My_Newt (1). The string slice My_Newt (1..1) yields the string "S", whereas My_Newt (1) yields the value of the first component of My_Newt, which is the character 'S'. Thus, My_Newt (1..1) and My_Newt (1) may not be assigned or compared to one another:

```
if My_Newt (1..1) /= My_Newt (1) then    -- will not compile;
                                          -- mixed types
    My_Newt (1..1) := My_Newt (1);        -- same problem
end if;
```

Even though strings and characters are different types, the catenation operator can operate on either of them. Thus, "Ad" & 'a' yield "Ada". (Technically, there exists four "overloaded" versions of "&": one catenates a string with a string; another, a character with a string; another, a string with a character; and another, a character with a character. All four versions return a string as a result.)

Another common pitfall is to break a single string across multiple lines. In Ada, this is illegal:

```
Put ("EGOIST, n. A person of low taste, more interested in
        himself than in me. (Ambrose Bierce)" );
        -- will not compile; cannot break up a string
```

Therefore, string catenations are particularly handy when a string cannot fit on one line:

```
Put ( "EGOIST, n. A person of low taste, more interested in " &
        "himself than in me. (Ambrose Bierce)" ); -- legal
```

Now that we have discussed string slicing and catenation, let us consider a program that uses both operations:

```
with Ada.Text_IO; use Ada.Text_IO;
procedure String_Search is
    Search_String: String (1..45) :=
        "Self-actualization through programming in Ada";
    Target: String (1..2) := "ro"; -- forbid null strings
    subtype Loop_Bounds is Natural
        range 1 .. (Search_String'Length - Target'Length + 1);
```

```
        Upper: constant Natural := Target'Length - 1;
        Times_Found: Natural := 0;
begin

    for Lower in Loop_Bounds loop
        if Search_String (Lower..(Lower + Upper)) = Target then
            Times_Found := Times_Found + 1;
        end if;
    end loop;

    Put_Line ("The target word, """ & Target & """, was found"
                    & Natural'Image (Times_Found) & " times.");
end String_Search;
```

This procedure searches a string, "Self-actualization through programming in Ada", for a target string, "ro", and counts the number of times that the target string is found. When this program is run, the following is output:

The target word, "ro", was found 2 times.

During each iteration through the **for** loop, a successive dynamic substring—`Search_String(1..2)`, `Search_String(2..3)`, `Search_String(3..4)`, `..., Search_String(44..45)`—is compared with the target string "ro". Whenever a match is found, `Times_Found` is incremented. Note how the expression `Natural'Image (Times_Found)` is catenated with the strings. By using this `Image` attribute to convert a natural number to its string representation, we are able to output our answer using only one `Put_Line` statement instead of multiple `Put` statements. By using the `Image` attribute, we also avoid having to generically instantiate the `Integer_IO` package in order to output the integer value `Times_Found`.

Before introducing additional array operators, let us consider how string slices and catenations can be used to handle dynamically sized strings. Since a string variable can only be assigned a string of a particular length, how can such a variable be

**Ada 95 ▶** assigned a value whose length is unknown until runtime? One solution is to allow the string variable to implicitly assume the size of the value being assigned:

```
    Str: String := Integer'Image (N);
```

This solution works fine if the size of `Str` can be set to the length of the assigned value. But what if `Str` must be of a specific length? For example, what if `Integer'Image (N)` must be assigned to `Str` that has a length of 9? How can the amount of padding be determined? As the following code illustrates, since the value of `N` is unknown until runtime, the amount of padding required must be dynamically calculated:

```
declare
    N: Integer := 45;
```

```
        Integer_Image: constant String := Integer'Image(N);
        -- Integer'Image returns " 45" (note the leading blank)
        Str: String (1..9);
    begin
        Str := Integer_Image &
                 (1..(Str'Length - Integer_Image'Length) => ' ');
            -- In this case, pads with 6 trailing blanks
        Put_Line (Str);  -- outputs □45□□□□□□
                            -- where □ represents a blank space
    end;
```

(Since the length of the string returned by Integer'Image(N) is unknown until runtime, compilers do not know how much memory to reserve at compile time. In such situations, compilers typically allocate the required memory dynamically as the program is running.)

In addition to the catenation operator, there are other useful operators, called relational operators: =, /=, <, <=, >, >=. These relational operators can be used to compare strings of the same length or of different lengths. The following Boolean

**Ada 95 ▶** expressions are all True. Note that qualification is required in Ada 95 to distinguish between types String and Wide_String.

```
String'("PETE") < String'("REPETE")
Wide_String'("ADA") <= Wide_String'("AGUSTA")
String'("?") > String'("+")
```

The last expression is True because Ada lists the character '+' before '?'. As we show in "Operations on Arrays," these relational operators can apply to any one-dimensional discrete array, not just to strings.

In addition to the predefined string types contained in the package Standard, there may be user-defined string types that only include certain characters. For instance, one can define the set of Morse code characters as an array of characters consisting only of dots, dashes, and spaces:

```
    procedure User_Defined_String is
        type Dots_Dashes_And_Spaces is ('.', '-', ' ');
        type Morse_Code is array (Positive range <>) of
            Dots_Dashes_And_Spaces;
        ADA: Morse_Code (1..10);
        A: constant Morse_Code := ".- ";
        B: constant Morse_Code := "-... ";
        C: constant Morse_Code := "-.-. ";
        D: constant Morse_Code := "-.. ";
    begin
        ADA := A & D & A;       -- assigns ".- -.. .- "
    end User_Defined_String;
```

Note that string literals of the user-defined type Morse_Code may be placed within a pair of double quotes, just like literals of the predefined types String and Wide_String.

**Ada 95 ▶**    For most applications, the string operations discussed in this section should suffice. For applications that require extensive string manipulation, Ada provides a predefined package, `Ada.Strings`. This package, together with its many child packages, offers a multitude of string-handling subprograms for both fixed length strings and variable length strings. For example, subprograms are provided to search a string for various kinds of patterns. Other subprograms are provided for overwriting, deleting, inserting, or replacing substrings. These packages are quite large and would take many pages to describe. Programmers needing these specialized services are, therefore, encouraged to read about these packages in their *Ada 95 Reference Manual*.

## BOOLEAN VECTORS

A vector is just a fancy name for a one-dimensional array. `Boolean` vectors are one-dimensional arrays with `Boolean` components, such as the following:

```
type Boolean_Vector is array (Positive range <>) of Boolean;
```

`Boolean` vectors are not of a predefined type; they are user defined.

`Boolean` vectors are mentioned in a separate section because they are the only type of array that can be operated on by the logical operators **and, or, xor**, and **not**. With the exception of **not**, these logical operators operate on two one-dimensional `Boolean` vectors of the same type and length:

```
declare
    type Boolean_Vector is array (Positive range <> ) of Boolean;
    T: constant Boolean := True;
    F: constant Boolean := False;
    A: Boolean_Vector (1..4) := (T, F, T, F);
    B: Boolean_Vector (1..4) := (T, F, F, T);
    C: Boolean_Vector (1..4);
begin
    C := not A;      -- yields (F, T, F, T)
    C := A and B;    -- yields (T, F, F, F)
    C := A or B;     -- yields (T, F, T, T)
    C := A xor B;    -- yields (F, F, T, T)
end;
```

After the unconstrained array `Boolean_Vector` is declared, the constants `T` and `F` are initialized to the `Boolean` literals `True` and `False`, respectively. Throughout the rest of the code, `T` and `F` can then be used for `True` and `False`. As can be inferred from this code, the logical operators apply to each of the corresponding `Boolean` components of the two arrays, and the result is an aggregate, not a single `Boolean` value. For instance, the result of `A` **and** `B` is the aggregate `(T, F, F, F)`, as shown below:

```
    (T, F, T, F)        -- Value of A
and (T, F, F, T)        -- Value of B
    (T, F, F, F)        -- Value of A and B
```

---

## ARRAY OF ARRAYS

In Ada, it is possible to have an array of arrays. It is even possible to have an array of arrays of arrays, and so on, although these data structures soon get too complex to easily comprehend. The following is an example of an array of arrays:

```
declare
    Int_Value: Integer;
    type Two_By_Three is array (1..2, 1..3) of Integer;
    type Array_Of_2_By_3 is array (1..3) of Two_By_Three;
    Array_Of_Array: Array_Of_2_By_3 :=
            (  (   (1, 2, 3),
                   (4, 5, 6) ),

               (  (7,  8,  9),
                  (10, 11, 12) ),

               (  (13, 14, 15),
                  (16, 17, 18) ) );
begin
    Int_Value := Array_Of_Array (3) (1, 2); -- assigns 14
        -- first row, second column of third 2 by 3 array

    ...

end;
```

`Array_Of_Array`, as we can see from the aggregate being assigned to it, consists of 3 components. Each component is a 2 by 3 array of type `Two_By_Three`.

The last statement of the preceding code contains some unusual syntax. The expression `Array_Of_Array(3)(1, 2)` selects a component of a component. That is, the expression selects the integer value in the first row, second column, of the third 2 by 3 array. This is more easily shown by introducing an intermediate variable. The following two statements are logically equivalent to the last line of code in the preceding example:

```
Intermediate_Variable := Array_Of_Array (3);
Int_Value := Intermediate_Variable (1, 2);
```

`Intermediate_Variable`, which is assumed to belong to type `Two_By_Three`, is first set to the third 2 by 3 array:

```
(   (13, 14, 15),
    (16, 17, 18)  )
```

Then, the variable `Int_Value` is set to the first row, second column, of this array aggregate. The value in this position is 14.

In Ada, an array of arrays is not the same thing as a multidimensional array. Thus, the following statement is not allowed:

```
Int_Value := Array_Of_Array (1, 2, 3); -- not allowed
```

Furthermore, by declaring an array of an array, more structures can be referenced than by declaring a single multidimensional array. For example, the following structures of `Array_Of_Array` can be referenced:

```
Array_Of_Array            -- refers to entire structure
Array_Of_Array(N)         -- refers to the Nth 2 by 3 array
Array_Of_Array(N)(A, B)   -- refers to row A, column B of the
                          -- Nth 2 by 3 array
```

For contrast, consider the following three-dimensional array:

```
type Three_Dim_Array is array (1..2, 1..3, 1..3) of Integer;
Three_Dim: Three_Dim_Array;
```

Unlike `Array_Of_Array`, for `Three_Dim`, only two different structures can be referenced:

```
Three_Dim          -- refers to entire structure
Three_Dim(A, B, N) -- refers to row A, column B, of the Nth 2 by
                   -- 3 array
```

## ARRAY ATTRIBUTES

Array attributes are characteristics of arrays. Arrays have four frequently used attributes: `First`, `Last`, `Range`, and `Length`. These attributes apply to arrays and to constrained array types. Furthermore, these attributes give characteristics of the array index, not characteristics of the array components.

Consider the following one-dimensional array, `Conductor`, which stores information on how well various materials carry electric current:

```
type Material is (  Wood, Glass, Water, Saltwater, Plastic,
                    Superconductor, Rubber, Metal );
type Rating is ( Perfect, Excellent, Good, Middling, Fair,
                 Poor, Worthless );
Conductor: array (Material) of Rating :=
```

```
(    Wood                => Poor,
     Glass               => Worthless,
     Water               => Fair,
     Saltwater           => Middling,
     Plastic             => Worthless,
     Superconductor      => Perfect,
     Rubber              => Worthless,
     Metal               => Excellent );
```

In Chapter 2, we saw how the attributes `First` and `Last` apply to scalar types. These attributes can also apply to arrays. The attributes `First` and `Last` give the first and last index values of an array. `Conductor'First`, therefore, gives `Wood`, and `Conductor'Last` gives `Metal`. Note that `Wood` and `Metal` are the first and last index values of the array, not the first and last component values of the array, which in this case are `Poor` and `Excellent`.

The attribute `Length` gives the length (number of components) of the array. Because the `Conductor` array has an index that can assume any of 8 possible values, `Conductor'Length` is 8.

In Chapter 3, we applied the `Range` attribute to scalar types. This attribute can also apply to arrays, and once again, `P'Range` is always equivalent to `P'First..P'Last`. Thus, when P is an array, `P'Range` gives P's index range. In our previous example, `Conductor'Range` gives the range `Wood..Metal`. This means that `Conductor'Range` can be used wherever the range `Wood..Metal` can be used—for instance, in **for** loops, or as constraints in declarations. The following two **for** loops are therefore logically equivalent:

```
for Substance in Wood..Metal loop
    Conductor (Substance) := Poor;
end loop;

for Substance in Conductor'Range loop  -- Wood..Metal
    Conductor (Substance) := Poor;
end loop;
```

The array attributes `First`, `Last`, `Length`, and `Range` apply to arrays of any dimension. In multidimensional arrays, the attributes are followed by a number in parentheses, sometimes called a parameter. This parameter specifies the array dimension to which the attribute refers. The parameter does not refer to a particular index value but to an index range defining a dimension.

Consider an anonymous 2 by 6 (2 rows, 6 columns) integer array named `Matrix`:

```
Matrix: array (1..2, 0..5) of Integer :=
    (  (12, 24, 15, 33, 11, 43),
       (72, 91, 54, 26, 56, 81) );
```

The `Matrix` array contains two index ranges, `1..2` and `0..5`. The range `1..2` refers to the first dimension (the rows) of `Matrix`, and the range `0..5` refers to the second dimension (the columns) of `Matrix`. When we apply an array attribute to `Matrix`, we can specify the array dimension to which the attribute applies. We select the first or second dimension by placing 1 or 2 in parentheses, following the array attribute. `Matrix'First(1)` yields the value of 1, because it refers to the lower bound of the first dimension of `Matrix`, that is, the first index value in the range `1..2`. `Matrix'Last(2)` yields the value of 5, because it refers to the upper bound of the second dimension of `Matrix`, that is, the last index value in the range `0..5`. `Matrix'Range(1)` yields the discrete range `1..2` of the first dimension of `Matrix`. `Matrix'Length(2)` yields the value of 6, because it refers to the length of the second dimension, that is, the number of values in the second index range, `0..5`.

The following is a list of array attributes as they apply to `Matrix`:

```
Matrix'First (1)         -- yields 1
Matrix'First (2)         -- yields 0
Matrix'Last (1)          -- yields 2
Matrix'Last (2)          -- yields 5
Matrix'Length (1)        -- yields 2
Matrix'Length (2)        -- yields 6
Matrix'Range (1)         -- yields 1..2
Matrix'Range (2)         -- yields 0..5
Matrix'First      -- yields 1, same as Matrix'First (1)
Matrix'Range      -- yields 1..2, same as Matrix'Range (1)
```

As illustrated in the last two cases, when the attribute parameter is omitted, the first dimension is assumed. In other words, `Matrix'First` is the same as `Matrix'First (1)`, `Matrix'Range` is the same as `Matrix'Range (1)`, and so on. It is considered good programming practice, however, not to omit the attribute parameter when using multidimensional arrays, except, perhaps, when the omission makes no difference. For example, the length of the diagonal of a 5 by 5 array can just as meaningfully be determined with `Length (1)` as with `Length (2)`. Hence, the parameter for `Length` may be omitted. One-dimensional arrays, of course, do not need an attribute parameter because there is only one dimension that can be selected.

The `Range` attribute is frequently used when looping through the indexes of a multidimensional array. In the two-dimensional array `Matrix`, we can explicitly use the discrete ranges `1..2` and `0..5`:

```
for Row in 1..2 loop           -- row index
   for Column in 0..5 loop     -- column index
      Matrix (Row, Column) := 0;
   end loop;
end loop;
```

However, it is better to use `Matrix'Range(1)` instead of `1..2` and `Matrix'Range(2)` instead of `0..5`:

```
for Row in Matrix'Range(1) loop         -- row index
   for Column in Matrix'Range(2) loop   -- column index
      Matrix (Row, Column) := 0;
```

```
        end loop;
    end loop;
```

Array attributes generalize code and help localize changes that may be needed in the future. For instance, suppose that `Matrix` is redefined so that the row index has a range `1..3` and the column index has a range `1..5`. If the attributes `Matrix'Range(1)` and `Matrix'Range(2)` are consistently used throughout the code, then the modified ranges are automatically handled. `Matrix'Range(1)` will now be `1..3`, and `Matrix'Range (2)` will now be `1..5`.

In the preceding example, array attributes improve the code but are not absolutely required. However, there are certain cases where array attributes are required. In the following example, the nested procedure `Print_Sum_Of_Components` must use array attributes:

```
with Ada.Text_IO; use Ada.Text_IO;
procedure Main is
    package Int_IO is new Integer_IO (Integer);
    use Int_IO;
    type Vector is array (Integer range <>) of Integer;
    Vector_Of_3: Vector (1..3) := (3, 1, 6);
    Vector_Of_4: Vector (2..5) := (9, 2, 5, 7);

    procedure Print_Sum_Of_Components (V: Vector) is
        Sum : Integer := 0;
    begin
        -- An array attribute is needed since the actual size of
        -- array V can vary from call to call
        for J in V'Range loop
            Sum := Sum + V (J);
        end loop;
        Put (Sum);
    end Print_Sum_Of_Components;

begin -- Main
    Print_Sum_Of_Components (Vector_Of_3); -- prints 10
    Print_Sum_Of_Components (Vector_Of_4); -- prints 23
end Main;
```

In this program, the procedure `Print_Sum_Of_Components` is placed within the declarative part of the procedure `Main`. The procedure `Main` uses `Print_Sum_Of_Components` to add all the components of a vector.

The first line of the declaration of `Print_Sum_Of_Components` merits closer scrutiny:

```
procedure Print_Sum_Of_Components (V: Vector) is...
```

This line introduces some subtle concepts that will be further explained in the next chapter. The parameter, `V`, is a "dummy" parameter that is passed an actual value when `Print_Sum_Of_Components` is invoked (activated). Since `V` belongs to an unconstrained array type, Vector, V can be passed arrays of different sizes. The procedure Print_Sum_Of_Components takes these different-sized arrays and adds their components. To accomplish this, the attribute V'Range (which is the same as V'First .. V'Last) is used. The attribute V'Range takes the index range of the array being passed in as an actual parameter value. For instance, when Print_Sum_Of_Components is called with the parameter Vector_Of_3, V'Range has the value 1..3. When Print_Sum_Of_Components is called with the parameter of Vector_Of_4, V'Range has the value 2..5.

## OPERATIONS ON ARRAYS

As we have shown in preceding sections of this chapter, many different operations on arrays are possible. Some operations can apply only to a specific kind of array; other operations can apply to any array. The term "operations" is used in a liberal sense to include all the following: array attributes, logical operations, catenation, array slicing, assignments, type conversions, relational operations, and membership tests.

We have already discussed four frequently used array attributes in the section on array attributes. These array attributes can apply to any array or constrained array type. We have also discussed logical operators in the section on Boolean vectors. The logical operators apply only to one-dimensional Boolean arrays of the same length.

In addition, we have seen how catenation and array slicing are used in the section on strings. Although these operations are most frequently used on strings, they can be similarly applied to any one-dimensional array:

```
declare
    type Vector is array (Integer range <>) of Integer;
    V1: Vector (1..4)    := (1, -2, 3, -5);
    V2: Vector (-2..1)   := (-3, -4, -1, 0);
    V3: Vector (0..3);
begin
    V3 := V1 (1..2) & V2 (0..1);   -- yields (1, -2, -1, 0)
        ...
    V1 := V1 (3..4) & V1 (1..2);   -- yields (3, -5, 1, -2)
end;
```

In this code, V3 is assigned the catenated values of the array slice V1 (1..2) and the array slice V2 (0..1). The slice V1 (1..2) yields the aggregate (1, -2). The slice V2 (0..1) yields the aggregate (-1, 0). [Be careful with the slice V2 (0..1). Because the index range of V2 is -2..1, the index range 0..1 covers the last two index values of V2, not the first two index values.] Therefore, V1(1..2) & V2(0..1) yields (1, -2) & (-1, 0), which yields the final result, (1, -2, -1, 0). In the last statement, V1 is assigned the catenated values of the array slice V1 (3..4) and the array slice V1 (1..2). The result is (3, -5) & (1, -2), which yields the final result, (3, -5, 1, -2). The index bounds of the result of

**Ada 95 ▶**

the catenation is $1..4$, which covers the full index range of V1. The range $1..4$ is the combination of the ranges of V1's slices $1..2$ and $3..4$. (In Ada 83, the bounds of the result of the catenation yielded $3..6$, which caused a Constraint_Error since 6 is greater than V1'Last. This behavior seemed counterintuitive and was, therefore, corrected.)

The next array operation to be considered is the assignment. We have already seen examples where one array is assigned to another array. In general, two arrays of the same type may be assigned to each other if they have the same shape and size (the same number of index values in each dimension). Consider the following example:

```
declare
    type Matrix_Type is array (    Integer range <>,
                                   Integer range <> ) of Integer;
    P : Matrix_Type (0..1, 2..5)  := (   (1, 3, 8, 9),
                                         (2, 5, 7, 6) );
    Q : Matrix_Type (3..4, 1..4);
    R : Matrix_Type (1..5, 1..3);
begin
    Q := P;      -- OK
    R := Q;      -- illegal; the arrays have different shapes
end;
```

In this code, array P can be legally assigned to array Q, even though the range of their corresponding indexes differs: the range of the first index of P is $0..1$, and the range of the first index of Q is $3..4$. The second indexes also have different corresponding ranges. Even though the ranges are different, P can be assigned to Q because P'Length (1) = Q'Length (1) and P'Length (2) = Q'Length (2). However, Q cannot be assigned to R since Q is a 2 by 4 array and R is a 5 by 3 array.

Another array operation is type conversion. Arrays that belong to different types cannot be assigned or compared to one another. This restriction can sometimes be circumvented by performing type conversion. An array can be converted to another type of array, however, only when each array has the same shape and size, the same component type, and the same or convertible corresponding index types. In the next example, arrays A, B, and C belong to different types but have the characteristics just mentioned. Therefore, array B may be assigned to array A if array B is first converted to the same type as array A, and vice versa. Array A belongs to type Row_A. Array B can be converted to type Row_A by using the type name Row_A as a type conversion operator:

```
declare
    type Row_A is array (Integer range <>) of Float;
    type Row_B is array (Integer range <>) of Float;
    A: Row_A (1..4)  := (1.0, 2.0, 3.0, 4.0);
    B: Row_B (1..4)  := (5.0, 6.0, 7.0, 8.0);
    C: array (1..50) of Float := (others => 0.0);
begin
```

```
    A := B;                    -- illegal; mixed types
    A := Row_A (B);            -- OK; B converted to type Row_A
    B := Row_B (A);            -- OK; A converted to type Row_B
    A := Row_A (C (41..44)); -- OK
        -- slice of anonymous array C converted to type Row_A
end;
```

Note that the slice of the anonymous array, C, can be type converted to Row_A. However, there is no way to assign A or B to C, because C has no type name associated with it that can be used for type conversion. (Components of A or B, however, can be assigned to C since the components of each array belong to type Float.)

We have already seen how the relational operators, =, /=, <, >, <=, and >=, are used on strings. These operators can also be used on other types of arrays. Any two arrays, not just strings, can be tested for equality (=) and inequality (/=), as long as they belong to the same type. The other relational operators, however, impose a further restriction. These other operators (<, >, <=, >=) can be used only on one-dimensional discrete arrays. Thus, we cannot test whether multidimensional arrays are greater than or less than one another. Neither can we test whether one-dimensional real arrays are greater than or less than one another.

There is a specific method for testing whether one array is greater than or less than another array. This method is a generalization of the way that words are alphabetized. This is as expected, since words are strings, which are arrays of characters. Two arrays are compared by comparing, in turn, each of their corresponding components, from left to right, until a difference is found, or until all the components of one or both arrays have been exhausted. If a difference in a corresponding component is detected, then the array possessing the component with the smaller value is considered to be "less than" the other array, regardless of what components may follow. Thus, "DO" < "IF", and (2,5) < (9,3). Also, "ADA" < "ALL", and (2, 3, 1) < (2, 4, 8). Now assume that all of the components of one array have been exhausted and no difference in a corresponding component has been detected. If additional components remain for the second array, then the first array is considered to be "less than" the second array. Thus, "DO" < "DONE", and (2,5) < (2,5,2,3). Finally, two arrays are considered to be equal if they have the same number of components and all corresponding components are equal. Thus, "DONE" = "DONE", and (3,1,2) = (3,1,2).

Another array operation that is available is the membership test that we introduced in Chapter 2. Consider, for example, the following declarations:

```
type Matrix is array ( Positive range <>,
                       Positive range <>) of Boolean;
M: Matrix (1..2, 1..3);
subtype Two_By_Three is Matrix (1..2, 1..3);
```

Suppose that we want to know whether the variable M has the same index range in each dimension as the subtype Two_By_Three. This is equivalent to asking whether M is "in" (belongs to) subtype Two_By_Three. Thus, the following membership test can be used:

```
M in Two_By_Three -- yields True
```

Since M is in the subtype Two_By_Three, this membership test yields True. This membership test is far more concise than this equivalent Boolean expression:

```
M'First(1)    =    Two_By_Three'First(1)    and
M'Last(1)     =    Two_By_Three'Last(1)     and
M'First(2)    =    Two_By_Three'First(2)    and
M'Last(2)     =    Two_By_Three'Last(2)
```

Table 4.1 summarizes our discussion of the various array operations and the restrictions that apply. Note that Ada's strong typing mandates that binary operators operate only on arrays of the same type. Keep in mind, though, that this restriction can sometimes be circumvented by using type conversion. Also keep in mind that if two arrays are of the same type, then it follows that their component types are the same and their corresponding index types are the same. However, it does not follow that the arrays are the same size or that their corresponding index ranges are the same.

This concludes our discussion of arrays. Both arrays and records are composite types, that is, types that consist of multiple components. Whereas every component of an array must belong to the same type, components of a record may belong to different types. The next chapter discusses records.

**Table 4.1**   Operations on Arrays

| Operation | Restrictions |
|---|---|
| Array Attributes (First, Last, Length, Range) | None |
| Logical Operators (not, and, or, xor) | Must be one-dimensional Boolean arrays of same length and type |
| Catenation (&) | Must be one-dimensional arrays of same type |
| Array Slicing | Must be one-dimensional array |
| Assignments (:=) | Must be same size and type |
| Type Conversions | Must be same size with the same component types and the same or convertible index types |
| Relational Operators (<, >, <=, >=) | Must be one-dimensional discrete arrays of same type |
| Equality Testing (=, /=) | Must be same type |
| Membership tests | Must be same type |

## EXERCISES

1. Use array attributes to minimize the use of integer literals in the following code:

```
declare
    type Matrix_Type is array (0..2, 1..4) of Integer;
    Matrix: Matrix_Type;
begin
    for Row in 0..2 loop
        for Column in 1..4 loop
            ...
        end loop;
    end loop;
    -- assign the first matrix component the value of
    -- the number of array components
    Matrix (0, 1) := 12;
end;
```

2. Use array aggregate assignments to make the following code potentially more efficient and simpler.

   a.
```
declare
    Vector: array (1..6) of Boolean;
begin
    Vector(1) := False;    Vector(2) := True;
    Vector(3) := True;     Vector(4) := True;
    Vector(5) := False;    Vector(6) := False;
end;
```

   b.
```
declare
    type Matrix_Type is array (0..2, 1..4) of Float;
    Matrix: Matrix_Type;
begin
    for Row in Matrix'Range(1) loop
        for Column in Matrix'Range(2) loop
            Matrix (Row, Column) := 0.0;
        end loop;
    end loop;
end;
```

   c.
```
declare
    N: Natural;
begin
    Get (N);
    declare
        Powers: array (0..5) of Integer;
    begin
        for K in Powers'Range loop
            Powers (K) := N ** K;
```

```
            end loop;
            ...
        end;
    end;
d.  for Row in 1..3 loop
        for Column in 1..3 loop
            if Row = Column then
                Matrix (Row, Column) := 1.0;
            else
                Matrix (Row, Column) := 0.0;
            end if;
        end loop;
    end loop;
```

3. Given these declarations

```
type Vector is array (1..100) of Float;
Row: Vector;
```

initialize Row with the following values:

| Index | Component Values |
|---|---|
| 1 | 3.0 |
| 2 | 1.0 |
| 3 | 2.0 |
| 4 to 6 | 3.0 |
| 7 | 2.0 |
| 8 | 3.0 |
| 9 | 1.0 |
| 10 to 16 | 3.0 |
| 17 to 24 | 0.0 |
| 25 to 33 | 3.0 |
| 34 to 67 | 2.0 |
| 68 to 100 | 3.0 |

4. Which one of the following is *not* allowed when initializing a one-dimensional integer array with integer indexes from 1 to 4?

```
a.  A : Array_Type := (1, 2, 0, 0 );
b.  A : Array_Type := (1, 2, others => 0);
c.  A : Array_Type := (1, 2, 3..4 => 0);
d.  A : Array_Type := ( 2 => 2, 1 => 1, 4 => 0, 3 => 0);
e.  A : Array_Type := ( 1 => 1, 2 => 2, 3..4 => 0);
```

5. Replace the following **case** statement with code that selects the proper number-word by indexing into an array. (Blanks may be added to number-words to make them the same size.)

```
case N is
   when 1    => Put ("One");
   when 2    => Put ("Two");
   when 3    => Put ("Three");
   when 4    => Put ("Four");
end case;
```

Which implementation do you prefer, and why do you prefer it?

6. Use array slices to eliminate component-by-component assignments in the following code:

```
declare
   type Vector is array (1..9) of Boolean;
   A, B: Vector;
begin
   . . .
   B(5) := A(1);  B(6) := A(2);  B(7) := A(3);
   B(8) := A(4);  B(9) := A(5);
end;
```

7. Replace the executable statement part of the following code with an array slice:

```
declare
   type Index_Type is range 1..9;
   A: array (Index_Type) of Character;
begin
   . . .
   for Index in A'First..A'Last-1 loop
      -- A is an array of characters
      A (Index) := A (Index + 1);
   end loop;
   A (A'Last) := '_';
   . . .
end;
```

8. Which of the following is *not* allowed when initializing the two-dimensional array Snow?

Declarations:

```
type Location is (Los_Angeles, Seattle, Fargo);
subtype Year is Integer range 1987 .. 1989;
type Snow_Array is array (Location, Year) of Boolean;
Snow: Snow_Array;
```

```
a.  Snow := (  ( False,   False,   False ),
               ( False,   True,    True  ),
               ( True,    True,    True  ) );
```

**b.** Snow := (     Los_Angeles   => (   1987 => False,
                                       1988 => False,
                                       1989 => False ),
               Seattle      => (   1987 => False,
                                         1988 => True,
                                       1989 => True ),
               Fargo        => (   1987 => True,
                                       1988 => True,
                                       1989 => True ) );

```
b. Snow := (     Los_Angeles  => (   1987 => False,
                                     1988 => False,
                                     1989 => False ),
                 Seattle      => (   1987 => False,
                                     1988 => True,
                                     1989 => True ),
                 Fargo        => (   1987 => True,
                                     1988 => True,
                                     1989 => True ) );
c. Snow :=    ( Los_Angeles  => (  others     => False ),
                Seattle      => (  1987       => False,
                                   1988       => True,
                                   1989       => True    ),
                Fargo        => (  others => True ) );
d. Snow :=    ( others       => (  others => True ) );
e. Snow :=    ( Los_Angeles  => ( 1987 | 1989  => False,
                                  1988          => True ),
                others       => ( 1987 .. 1989 => True ) );
f. Snow :=    ( Los_Angeles  => (   1987 => False,
                                    1988 => False,
                                    1989 => False ),
                             (   1987 => False,
                                 1988 => True,
                                 1989 => True ),
                             (   1987 => True,
                                 1988 => True,
                                 1989 => True )   );
g. Snow := ( (  others       => False ),
             (  1987         => False,
                1988 | 1989  => True    ),
                others       => ( others => True )   );
```

9. Consider the following declarations:

```
type Boolean_Vector is array (Positive range <> ) of Boolean;
A: Boolean_Vector (1..4) := (True, True, False, False);
B: Boolean_Vector (1..4) := (True, False, False, True);
```

Evaluate each of the following expressions:

**a.** A **xor** B
**b.** A **and** B
**c.** A **or** B
**d.** **not** (A **and** B)
**e.** A **or** (**not** B **xor** A)

10. Consider the following declarations:

```
type Days_Of_Week is (Mon, Tues, Wed, Thurs, Fri, Sat, Sun);
type Days_Open is array (Days_Of_Week) of Boolean;
Open : Days_Open;
```

Which, if any, attempts to represent the discrete range Mon to Sun are illegal?

   **a.**  `Mon .. Sun`
   **b.**  `Days_Of_Week` **range** `Mon .. Sun`
   **c.**  `Open'Range`
   **d.**  `Open'First..Open'Last`
   **e.**  `Days_Of_Week'First .. Days_Of_Week'Last`
   **f.**  `Days_Of_Week`
   **g.**  `Days_Of_Week'Range`
   **h.**  `Days_Open'Range`

11. Evaluate each of the following expressions. If the expression results in an error, then give the reason for the error.

    Assumed Declarations:

    ```
    type Solar_System is (  Mercury, Venus, Earth, Mars,
                            Jupiter, Saturn, Uranus,
                            Neptune, Pluto );
    type Planets is array (Solar_System) of Boolean;
    Ringed_Planets: constant Planets := (False, False,
        False, False, True, True, True, True, False);
    type Matrix_Type is array (0..1, 2..5) of Integer;
    Matrix: Matrix_Type :=  ( (1, 2, 3, 4),
                              (5, 6, 7, 8) );
    ```

       **a.**  `Solar_System'Pos (Mercury)`
       **b.**  `Solar_System'Succ (Pluto)`
       **c.**  `Solar_System'Val(1)`
       **d.**  `Solar_System'First`
       **e.**  `Ringed_Planets'Range`
       **f.**  `Ringed_Planets'First`
       **g.**  `Ringed_Planets'Succ (Jupiter)`
       **h.**  `Ringed_Planets'Length`
       **i.**  `Planets'First`
       **j.**  `Planets'Range`
       **k.**  `Matrix'Last (2)`
       **l.**  `Matrix'Length (1)`
       **m.**  `Matrix'Range (2)`
       **n.**  `Matrix'First`
       **o.**  `Matrix_Type'Range (1)`
       **p.**  `(Pluto < Uranus)` **xor** `(Matrix (1, 2) < Matrix (0, 2))`

12. State whether each of the following code segments is correct. If it is incorrect, explain what is wrong.

       **a.**
    ```
    declare
        C, D : array (1..3) of Float;
    begin
        C := (1.1, 2.2, 3.3);
        D := C;
    end;
    ```

**b.** SUPER : String (1..20) := "Symmetry";

**c.** **declare**
```
    type Matrix is array (Integer range <>,
                          Integer range <>) of Float;
    A : Matrix (1..2, 0..1);
    B : Matrix (5..6, 1..2) := (  ( 1.0, 2.0),
                                  ( 4.0, 5.0) );
```
**begin**
```
    A := B;
```
**end**;

**d.** **declare**
```
    type List is array (Integer range <>) of Integer;
    type Row is array (Integer range <>) of Integer;
    L: List (1..5) := (7, 2, 0, 1, -2);
    R: Row (-2..2);
```
**begin**
```
    R := Row (L);
```
**end**;

13. What will the following code fragment output?

**declare**
```
    Language: String(1..3) := "ADA";
    Sensor: String(1..5) := "ROVER";
```
**begin**
```
    Sensor (2..4) := Language;
    Put_Line (Sensor);
```
**end**;

14. What is the value of V3?

**declare**
```
    type Vector is array (Integer range <>) of Integer;
    V1: Vector (0..4) := (1, 2, 3, 4, 5);
    V2: Vector (1..5) := (6, 7, 8, 9, 10);
    V3: Vector (2..6);
```
**begin**
```
    V3 := V1 (0..1) & V2 (2..3) & V2 (1..1);
       . . .
```
**end**;

15. Consider the following declarations:

```
type Int is array (Integer range <>) of Integer;
A: Int (1..2) := (3, 2);
B: Int (0..1) := (5, 0);
C: Int (1..4) := (3, 2, 1, 1);
D: Int (1..2) := (5, 0);
E: Int (1..2) := (5, 3);
F: Int (0..3) := (3, 2, 1, 0);
```

Which one of the following Boolean expressions is False?

**a.** A < B
**b.** C < B
**c.** B <= D
**d.** C < A
**e.** F < C
**f.** E >= D
**g.** F > A

16. Which eight of the following lines contains errors?

```
declare
    type Math_OP is ('+', '-', '*', '/');
    type P is array (1..3) of Math_OP;
    P1, P2: P := ('*', '+', '-');
    type Q is array (0..2) of Math_OP;
    Q1, Q2: Q;
    type R is array (Positive range <>) of Math_OP;
    R1: R;
    R2: R := ('-', '-', '-');
    R3: constant R := "++--**//";
begin
    Q1:= '-';
    Q2 := "***";
    Q1 (3) := '/';
    Q1 (1) := '&';
    Q1 := R3;
    Q1 := R3 (1..3);
    Q1 := Q (R3 (1..3));
    R3 (1) := '+';
    if R2 < R3 then
        Put ("R2 is less than R3");
    end if;
    if R2(1..1) = R2(1) then
        Put ("This is amazing!");
    end if;
end;
```

17. Write a program that reads 10 real numbers, finds the smallest of these numbers, subtracts this smallest number from each of the other 9 numbers, and prints the results.

18. Consider the following types:

```
type Strange_Claims is (UFOs, Unicorns, Ghosts, ESP,
    Astrology, Santa_Claus, Channeling,
    Psychic_Surgery, Bigfoot, Loch_Ness_Monster);

type Likelihood is (Certain, Very_Likely, Likely,
    Fifty_Fifty, Unlikely, Very_Unlikely,
    Impossible, No_Opinion);
```

Declare an array called `Believe_In` and store what you believe is the likelihood of each of these strange claims. For a unicorn hunter, for instance, `Believe_In (Unicorns)` might have the value of `Certain`.

19. Rewrite each of these anonymous arrays as named arrays:

    a. `Minimal_Energy:` **array** `(Animal)` **of** `Kilo_Calories;`
    b. `Pixel_On:` **array** `(X_Coord, Y_Coord)` **of** `Boolean;`
    c. `Present:` **array** `(Character` **range** `<>)` **of** `Boolean`
       `:= (  'A'..'V' => True, 'W'..'Z' => False);`

20. Show six different ways that each component of the following anonymous array can be initialized to `True`:

    `A:` **array** `(1..4)` **of** `Boolean;`

21. What is wrong with the following code?

```
Get (N); -- Assume N is an integer
declare
    type Text is array (Integer range <>) of Character;
    Answer: Text := Integer'Image (N);
begin
    if Answer (1) = '2' then ...
    ...
end;
```

22. Write a program that outputs a list of available seats in a theater that are unreserved balcony seats. Suppose that the seats in a theater are numbered 1 to 50. Reserved seats are 1, 8, 16, 24, 32, and 50. Balcony seats are 30 to 50.

# 5

# Records

Ada has two kinds of composite objects that consist of multiple components: arrays and records. The previous chapter discussed arrays; this chapter will discuss records.

Arrays and records have certain basic features in common. An entire array or record is referenced by a single identifier. An individual component may also be specified. In addition, both arrays and records can be assigned an aggregate, which is a complete set of values for the composite object. An aggregate can be written using positional or named notation.

The essential difference between arrays and records is that every component of an array must be of the same type, whereas the components of a record may be of different types. An array, for example, cannot have both integer and character components. A record, however, may have an integer component, a character component, a Boolean component, and so on.

This chapter is divided into two main sections: record types and discriminated record types. Records belonging to the same type must have identical components, unless that type is a discriminated record type. Discriminated record types enable records of the same type to have components that differ from one another with respect to kind, number, or size.

## RECORD TYPES

Record types are declared as follows:

```
type record name is
   record
      record components
   end record;
```

The keyword **type** is followed by the record name and the keywords **is record**. The declaration ends with the keywords **end record**. The record components are declared between **record** and **end record**. These record component declarations appear exactly like variable declarations. Each component has a unique identifier and can assume values of the specified type. Consider, for example, the following record type declaration, which defines Position in terms of an X coordinate and a Y coordinate:

```
type Position is
   record
      X_Coord: Integer;
      Y_Coord: Integer;
   end record;
```

The identifiers X_Coord and Y_Coord, which appear to the left of a colon, name the record components. Both record components are declared to be of type Integer.

Once type Position is defined, records of this type can be declared. In the following declaration, an entire record is represented by the identifier, Point:

```
Point: Position;
```

The individual components of Point, X_Coord and Y_Coord, may be selected using dot notation. The first component of Point is selected by writing Point.X_Coord. The second component of Point is selected by writing Point.Y_Coord. Once selected, operations can be performed on these components as if they were regular integer variables. For instance, the components may be assigned values:

```
Point.X_Coord := 1;
Point.Y_Coord := 2;
```

As an alternative to separately assigning values to each component of a record, an entire record can be assigned an aggregate:

```
Point := (1, 2); -- positional notation
```

Record aggregates closely resemble array aggregates. The previous aggregate is written using positional notation. Since the value 1 appears first, this value is assigned to the first record component, X_Coord. The second value is assigned to the second record component, Y_Coord.

Just as with array aggregates, named notation may also be used:

```
Point := (X_Coord => 1, Y_Coord => 2);  -- named notation
```

The name of the record component appears to the left of the arrow, =>. The value being assigned to this component is placed to the right of the arrow. When using named notation, the order in which items are listed is irrelevant. The preceding aggregate may therefore be written as follows:

```
Point := (Y_Coord => 2, X_Coord => 1);  -- named notation
```

Since coordinate values are frequently written as ordered pairs of numbers, positional notation works well in this case. Usually, however, named notation is preferred over positional notation because it helps document what is represented by each component value of the record. In addition, aggregates written with named notation do not need to be changed if the order of the record components changes.

In previous chapters, we have seen that variables can be initialized at the point they are declared, or they can be assigned a value later on in the executable statement part of the code. Record variables are no exception. Like an array variable, a record variable such as Point can be initialized to an aggregate when it is declared:

```
Point: Position := (1, 2);
```

Also like array aggregates, record aggregates, under certain conditions, may use the vertical bar, |, or the keyword **others**. In our example, since both components of Position belong to the same type, the vertical bar may be used to assign the same value to both components:

```
Point := (X_Coord | Y_Coord => 2);
   -- if component is X_Coord or Y_Coord, assign it 2
```

The same result may also be accomplished with the keyword **others**:

```
Point := (others => 2); -- assigns 2 to both components
```

As with array aggregates, **others** must always appear as the last item in a record aggregate. Unlike array aggregates, however, the **others** clause must always refer to at least one component.

So far, we have mentioned the similarities between array aggregates and record aggregates. Let us now consider two differences. One difference is that, unlike array aggregates, record aggregates may mix named and positional notation. The only restriction is that all the items listed in positional notation precede the items listed in named notation. The following mixed notation is legal:

```
Point := (1, Y_Coord => 2);    -- mixed notation
```

The next assignment, however, is illegal because named notation is used before positional notation:

```
Point := (X_Coord => 1, 2);    -- illegal;
   -- positional notation must be used before named notation
```

Another difference is that, unlike array aggregates, record aggregates may not use a discrete range:

```
Point := (X_Coord..Y_Coord => 2); -- illegal; cannot use ranges
```

Now that we have discussed similarities and differences between array and record aggregates, let us discuss a feature of record types that no other data type in Ada possesses: record types can be assigned an initial default value. Consider the following code:

```
type Position is
   record
       X_Coord: Integer range 0..1023 := 0; -- initialized to 0
       Y_Coord: Integer range 0..1023 := 0; -- initialized to 0
   end record;
```

When a record of type `Position` is declared, both its components assume the default value of 0 unless this default is overridden:

```
Point_1: Position;
   -- both record components have default values of 0

Point_2: Position := (1, 1);
   -- default component values overridden
```

Note that we also included a range constraint in the component declarations: **range** `0..1023`. If values of `X_Coord` or `Y_Coord` wander outside this range, a constraint error is raised.

Whenever two or more record components have the same type definitions, the definitions may be combined in the same declaration. The previous version of `Position` may thus be written as follows:

```
type Position is
   record
       X_Coord, Y_Coord: Integer range 0..1023 := 0;
   end record;
```

Let us now consider the predefined operations for records. Fewer such operations exist for records than for arrays. For instance, whereas one may test whether one array is greater than or less than another array, such relational operations are not defined for records. The only predefined operations that may be performed on records are assignments, and tests for equality and inequality. Illegal and legal record operations are shown in the following code:

```
-- assumes Position is visible
declare
    Point_1: Position := (3, 1);
    Point_2: Position := Point_1;
begin
    if Point_1 /= Point_2 then
        Put_Line ("Not equal, but will make equal");
        Point_2 := Point_1;
    elsif Point_1 > Point_2 then -- illegal;
        -- ">" is undefined for records
```

```
            Put_Line ("Point_1 is greater then Point_2");
        end if;
    end;
```

In this code, the following assignment statement replaces the value of `Point_2` with a new record value:

```
    Point_2 := Point_1;
```

Such an assignment is logically equivalent to the following two component assignments:

```
    Point_2.X_Coord := Point_1.X_Coord;
    Point_2.Y_Coord := Point_1.Y_Coord;
```

In addition to declaring record variables, such as `Point_1` and `Point_2`, a programmer may also declare record constants:

```
    Home: constant Position := (0, 0);
```

As with all constants, `Home` can be read from but not written to (given a value):

```
    Home.X_Coord := 1;   -- error; Home is a constant
```

By making `Home` a constant, each of its components becomes a constant. Ada does not allow individual components of a record to be declared as constants:

```
    type Position is
        record -- record components cannot be declared as constants
            X_Coord: constant Integer := 0; -- illegal
            Y_Coord: constant Integer := 0; -- illegal
        end record;
```

However, as we shall illustrate later in this chapter, individual record components can act as constants when they are declared as "discriminants."

Whereas both components of `Position` belong to the same type, components of a given record can belong to different types. This is illustrated by the following record, which stores information about galaxies:

```
    type Galaxy_Classification is (Spiral, Elliptical, Barred,
        Irregular);

    type Galaxy is
        record
            Galaxy_Name: String (1..10) := (others => ' ');
            Distance: Float range 0.0..1_000.0;
                -- millions of light years
            Classification: Galaxy_Classification;
        end record;
```

```
Neighbor: Galaxy := (  Galaxy_Name     => "Andromeda ",
                       Distance        => 2.2,
                       Classification  => Spiral );
```

The three components—Galaxy_Name, Distance, and Classification—belong to three different types: String, Float, and Galaxy_Classification. Consider the first type, String. Recall that a string is a one-dimensional unconstrained array of characters. To select the first character of the string assigned to the Galaxy_Name component of Neighbor, we can write

```
Neighbor.Galaxy_Name(1) -- selects 'A' from "Andromeda "
```

Not only can an array, such as Galaxy_Name, be a component of a record; a record can also be a component of a record. Such a nested record is shown in the following declarations:

```
type Language_Type is (Pascal, Ada, FORTRAN, COBOL, C);

type Software_Engineering_Principles is
   record
      Strong_Typing: Boolean;
      Information_Hiding: Boolean;
      Concurrent_Processing: Boolean;
      Exception_Handling: Boolean;
   end record;

type Computer_Language is
   record
      Language: Language_Type;
      Features: Software_Engineering_Principles; -- nested
                                                 -- record
      ISO_Standard: Integer range 1955 .. 2010;  -- adoption
                                                 -- date
   end record;

Official_DOD_Language: Computer_Language;
```

Note that Features is a record that is a component of another record, Computer_Language. To reference a component of the nested record, Features, one must use dot notation twice:

```
if Official_DOD_Language.Features.Information_Hiding then
   -- references a component of a component
   Put (Official_DOD_Language.Language);
   Put (" is a strongly typed language");
end if;
```

Nested records may be assigned aggregates in a similar manner as records that are not nested. The aggregate for the inner nested record is placed within the aggregate for the outer record:

```
-- positional notation
Official_DOD_Language: Computer_Language :=
   ( Ada, (True, True, True, True), 1994 );
```

As shown, the nested aggregate is placed in parentheses. Positional notation is used throughout this nested aggregate. Named notation can also be used, as follows:

```
-- named notation
Official_DOD_Language:  Computer_Language :=
   (  Language   =>    Ada,
      Features   => (  Strong_Typing           => True,
                       Information_Hiding       => True,
                       Concurrent_Processing    => True,
                       Exception_Handling       => True ),
      ISO_Standard => 1994 );
```

The notation used in an aggregate is independent of the notation used in any of its nested aggregates. In the following example, a record aggregate uses named notation, and its nested aggregate uses positional notation:

```
Official_DOD_Language: Computer_Language :=
   (  Language    => Ada,
      Features    => (True, True, True, True),
      ISO_Standard => 1994 );
```

In the previous chapter on arrays, we mentioned arrays of records. Now that we understand records, we can show how such a data structure is declared:

```
type Array_Of_Languages is array (1 .. 10) of
   Computer_Language;
   -- assumes Computer_Language is visible

Language_List: Array_Of_Languages;
```

To reference, for instance, the Language component of the first record in the array Language_List, we write:

```
Language_List(1).Language
```

To reference the Information_Hiding component of the Features component of the third record in the array, we write:

```
Language_List(3).Features.Information_Hiding
```

As can be seen, referencing a deeply nested data structure can require lengthy expressions. In order to make code less verbose and easier to read, such lengthy expressions can be renamed to a simple Boolean variable:

```
Info_Hiding: Boolean renames
   Language_List(3).Features.Information_Hiding;
```

Note that **renames** is a keyword. Also note that `Info_Hiding` is declared as a `Boolean` variable. The type `Boolean` must be used since `Info_Hiding` is renaming a `Boolean` expression. If `Info_Hiding` were renaming, for instance, an `Integer` expression, then it would have to be declared as an `Integer` variable.

The term renaming is a bit misleading because the original expression is still available after it has been renamed. The variable just becomes an alternative name for the expression.

(For the advanced reader: it may appear that renaming a complex expression to a simple variable and then using that variable throughout the code could make the code execute faster. Instead of evaluating the same complex expression each time it appears, the compiler could just evaluate the expression once and then read the value of the variable renaming the expression. However, mature Ada compilers frequently perform this optimization—known as common subexpression elimination—even when renaming is not used.)

In the examples presented so far, records of a given type have exactly the same kind of components and number of components. The next section will show how record types with discriminants can be used to declare records that differ from one another in the kind of components, number of components, or size of components.

## DISCRIMINATED RECORDS

Record types with discriminants can be used to define records to be of the same type even though the kind, number, and size of the components may differ between records. The notion of "sameness" is thus raised to a higher level of abstraction. Objects can conceptually be of the same type even if their internal structure differs. The criterion for deciding which objects belong to the same type can therefore be based on conceptual considerations without concern for the object's physical structure.

Record types with discriminants are used frequently to declare variant records. Variant records of the same type can have a different set of components from one another. In addition, record types with discriminants can be used to declare records whose component size varies. These two uses of discriminated record types will be discussed in the following subsections. Less common uses for discriminated record types will be covered in a third subsection.

### Variant Records

The following problem illustrates the need for variant records. Suppose that a record type is needed to store information about a collection of music recordings. These recordings are on three different media: phonograph records, cassettes, and compact disks. We could tackle this problem by using three different record types without discriminants: a first to store information about phonograph recordings, a second to store information about cassette recordings, and a third to store information about compact disk recordings:

```
type Music_Type is (Classical, Jazz, New_Age, Bluegrass, Folk, Pop);
subtype Year is Integer range 1920 .. 2020;
type Speed_Type is (LP, Forty_Five);
type Phonograph_Recording is -- phonograph record information
    record
        Music: Music_Type;
        Year_Recorded: Year;
        Speed: Speed_Type;
        Scratched: Boolean;
    end record;
type Length_Type is (Sixty_Minute, Ninety_Minute);
type Tape_Type is (Metal, Chromium_Oxide, Normal);
type Cassette_Recordings is -- cassette information
    record
        Music: Music_Type;
        Year_Recorded: Year;
        Length: Length_Type;
        Tape: Tape_Type;
        Noise_Reduction: Boolean;
    end record;


type Compact_Disk_Recording is -- compact disk information
    record
        Music: Music_Type;
        Year_Recorded: Year;
    end record;
```

The three record type declarations have two components in common: `Music` and `Year_Recorded`. The other components are different for each record type, because different information needs to be stored depending on the recording medium. Information about being scratched, for instance, applies only to phonograph records, and information about being made with chromium oxide applies only to cassette tapes. Because different information is needed for each record type, the internal structure of each record type differs.

Even though the internal structure of the three record types differs, it still makes conceptual sense to categorize the three types as a single type. This single type can be used to store any information about music recordings. To create a single record type to hold information about recordings made on phonograph records, cassette tapes, and compact disks, a discriminant should be used. (Without a discriminant, "merging" all three record types into one type would be contrived and confusing, because for each recording medium, some of the components would not apply.) A discriminant is a record "parameter" whose value determines which set of alternative components a record acquires. The following record type, `Recording`, has a discriminant, `Device`, of type `Recording_Medium`. The values of `Device`—`Phonograph_Record`, `Cassette`, and `Compact_Disk`—select the set of record components appropriate for each of these recording media:

```ada
type Music_Type is (Classical, Jazz, New_Age, Bluegrass, Folk, Pop);
subtype Year is Integer range 1920 .. 2020;
type Recording_Medium is ( Phonograph_Record, Cassette, Compact_Disk);
type Speed_Type is (LP, Forty_Five);
type Length_Type is (Sixty_Minute, Ninety_Minute);
type Tape_Type is (Metal, Chromium_Oxide, Normal);

type Recording ( Device: Recording_Medium ) is -- variant record
    record
        Music: Music_Type; -- invariant part
        Year_Recorded: Year;

        case Device is -- variant part
            when Phonograph_Record => -- variant with two components
                Speed: Speed_Type;
                Scratched: Boolean;
            when Cassette => -- variant with three components
                Length: Length_Type;
                Tape: Tape_Type;
                Noise_Reduction: Boolean;
            when Compact_Disk => -- variant with no components
                null;
        end case;

    end record;
```

The record type `Recording` consists of two parts: the invariant part and the variant part. The invariant part consists of components that do not vary. These components are common to every record belonging to type `Recording`. In this example, the invariant part consists of the components `Music` and `Year_Recorded`.

The variant part consists of alternative sets of components, which are selected according to the value of the discriminant, `Device`. This variant part closely resembles the structure of a **case** statement. The four rules that govern the **case** statement, presented in Chapter 3, also apply here. However, unlike a **case** statement, which controls the execution of code, this structure controls the declaration of record components.

Note that the variant part follows the invariant part. This ordering is required. Thus, the components `Music` or `Year_Recorded` cannot be declared after the keywords **end case**.

Let us now examine the variant record type, `Recording`, in detail. `Recording` has a discriminant, `Device`, of type `Recording_Medium`:

```ada
type Recording ( Device: Recording_Medium ) is ...
```

This discriminant, which is a record component that acts like a record parameter, can assume the values `Phonograph_Record`, `Cassette`, and `Compact_Disk`. These discriminant values determine which group of components is selected from the variant part of the record type. In essence, each value of the discriminant defines a subtype of type `Recording`, where each subtype has a specific set of components. (This is analogous to subtypes of an anonymous array, where each subtype has a specified index range.) Discriminant values are supplied when a record of type `Recording` is declared:

```
Songs_For_101_Ukuleles: Recording ( Cassette );
New_Wave_Accordian: Recording ( Phonograph_Record );
The_Shmatta_Rag: Recording ( Compact_Disk );
```

These discriminants may optionally be written using named notation, as follows:

```
-- named notation
Songs_For_101_Ukuleles: Recording (Device => Cassette);
New_Wave_Accordian: Recording (Device => Phonograph_Record);
The_Shmatta_Rag: Recording (Device => Compact_Disk);
```

In named notation, the name of the discriminant is placed to the left of the arrow, and the discriminant value, to the right of the arrow.

Once a record is declared with a discriminant, it is constrained. This means that the value of the discriminant may never be changed. For example, since the record, `Songs_For_101_Ukuleles`, is declared with the discriminant `Cassette`, this record may only be used to store information about cassette recordings.

The record, `Songs_For_101_Ukuleles`, has six components. The first component, `Device`, is the discriminant. The next two components, `Music` and `Year_Recorded`, are taken from the invariant part of the record type and do not depend on the value of the discriminant `Device`. The remaining components, however, are selected from the variant part of the record type, according to the value of `Device`. Since the value of `Device` is `Cassette`, the **when** clause for `Cassette` is chosen, and the three components listed in that **when** clause are selected: `Length`, `Tape`, and `Noise_Reduction`.

The record `New_Wave_Accordian` is declared with a discriminant value of `Phonograph_Record` and therefore has five components: the discriminant, `Device`; the two invariant components, `Music` and `Year_Recorded`; plus two components in the variant part, `Speed` and `Scratched`. The record `The_Shmatta_Rag` is declared with a discriminant value of `Compact_Disk`. The **when** clause for `Compact_Disk` does not have any components. Therefore, `The_Shmatta_Rag` only consists of the discriminant `Device`, plus the invariant components `Music` and `Year_Recorded`.

A **when** clause with no components requires the "do nothing" keyword **null**, because it is illegal to have an "empty" **when** clause. Furthermore, the **when** clause for `Compact_Disk` is required even though `Compact_Disk` has no components in the variant part. The **when** clause is needed since, as with the regular **case** statement, every possible discriminant value—`Phonograph_Record`, `Cassette`, and `Compact_Disk`—must be explicitly covered. If one or more **when** clauses use the keyword **null**, they may be combined by using the keyword **others**:

```
when others => null;
```

This **when others** clause thus handles all the discriminant values that do not select any components in the variant part.

Once `Songs_For_101_Ukuleles` and the other records are declared with a discriminant, their components may be selected. Once selected, operations can be performed on these components as if they were regular variables. For instance, the components may be assigned values:

```
Songs_For_101_Ukuleles.Tape := Metal;
New_Wave_Accordian.Speed := LP;
The_Shmatta_Rag.Music := Pop;
```

If an attempt is made to access a record component that does not exist for the record's particular discriminant value, then a constraint error is raised:

```
Songs_For_101_Ukuleles.Scratched := True;
    -- constraint error; record does not have this component
New_Wave_Accordian.Tape := Chromium_Oxide;
    -- constraint error; record does not have this component
```

Since the discriminant, `Device`, is a record component, it may be selected just like any other record component:

```
if Songs_For_101_Ukuleles.Device = Phonograph_Record then ...
```

An error, however, will be raised if one attempts to assign a value to only the discriminant component:

```
Songs_For_101_Ukuleles.Device := Phonograph_Record;
    -- constraint error; cannot change the discriminant,
New_Wave_Accordian.Device := Phonograph_Record;
    -- cannot even reassign the same value to a discriminant
```

Discriminant values cannot be changed because, as previously mentioned, these records are constrained.

Instead of separately assigning values to each record component, an aggregate may be assigned to the entire record. As shown in the following three examples, the aggregate must be complete and must therefore contain every record component, including the value of the discriminant:

```
Songs_For_101_Ukuleles :=
    (  Device           => Cassette,
       -- discriminant with value Cassette required
       Music            => Pop,
       Year_Recorded    => 1955,
       Length           => Ninety_Minutes,
       Tape             => Normal,
       Noise_Reduction  => False );
```

```
New_Wave_Accordian :=
   (  Device            => Phonograph_Record,
      -- discriminant with value Phonograph_Record required
      Music             => New_Age,
      Year_Recorded     => 1989,
      Speed             => Forty_Five,
      Scratched         => True );

The_Shmatta_Rag :=
   (  Device            => Compact_Disk,
      -- discriminant with value Compact_Disk required
      Music             => Jazz,
      Year_Recorded     => 1957 );
```

As indicated in the comments, the value of the discriminant used in the aggregate must match the discriminant that was used to constrain the record. For instance, recall that when `The_Shmatta_Rag` was declared, it was constrained to `Compact_Disk`. An attempt to alter this discriminant value, such as changing it to `Cassette`, results in a constraint error:

```
The_Shmatta_Rag :=
   (  Device            => Cassette, -- constraint error
         -- cannot change discriminant
      Music             => Jazz,
      Year_Recorded     => 1957 );
```

In addition to being used in assignment statements, aggregates may be used in declarations:

```
The_Shmatta_Rag: Recording (Compact_Disk) :=
   (Compact_Disk, Jazz, 1957);
```

In this declaration, positional notation is used. Note that the discriminant, `Compact_Disk`, must appear on both sides of the assignment operator. On the left side, the discriminant constrains the record. On the right side, the discriminant appears as one of the record components required to make the aggregate complete. The discriminant, of course, must appear the same on both sides of the operator.

In all of the examples seen so far, the discriminant of the record cannot change. Records can be declared, however, whose discriminants can change. The discriminant of a record can be changed only if the record is unconstrained. A record is unconstrained only if it is declared without a discriminant constraint. A record can be declared without a discriminant constraint only if its record type is declared with a default discriminant value. Consider, for example, the following record type declaration, in which the discriminant `Poisonous` is given the default value of `True`:

```
type Venom_Type is (Hemotoxic, Neurotoxic);
type Snake (Poisonous: Boolean := True) is -- given default
```

```
record
    case Poisonous is
        when True =>
            Venom: Venom_Type;
        when False =>
            Constrictor: Boolean;
    end case;
end record;
```

As a result of the default value given to `Poisonous`, a record of type `Snake` can be declared with or without a discriminant constraint. The following declaration does not have a discriminant constraint:

```
Green_Mamba: Snake; -- unconstrained record
    -- initially takes default discriminant value
```

Since a discriminant constraint is not provided, `Green_Mamba` is an unconstrained record that takes the default discriminant value of `True`. This discriminant value may later be overridden and changed as many times as desired. When overriding this discriminant value, however, one cannot just change the discriminant since this could render the other component values invalid:

```
Green_Mamba.Poisonous := False; -- error;
    -- to change discriminant, assign value of entire record
```

To override this discriminant value, one must change the value of the entire record. The compiler can thus guarantee that a record's discriminant value is always in agreement with the record's components. The value of the entire record may be changed by assigning it a record object or a record aggregate:

```
declare
    My_Snake: Snake := ( Poisonous   => False, -- unconstrained
                         Constrictor => True );
    Your_Snake: Snake; -- unconstrained
begin -- in both statements, an entire record value is assigned
    Your_Snake := My_Snake;
    My_Snake := ( Poisonous => True,
                  Venom     => Hemotoxic );
end;
```

In the first declaration, `My_Snake` is declared and initialized to an aggregate with the discriminant value `False`. This value overrides the default discriminant value of `True`. Note that even though a discriminant value is provided to the right of the assignment operator, no discriminant constraint is provided to the left of the operator. The record is thus unconstrained.

The second declaration defines the record `Your_Snake`. Since no discriminant is provided, the default value of `True` is assumed. The next line assigns the record, `My_Snake`, to `Your_Snake`. This assignment is legal since an entire record value is being assigned. As a result of this assignment, the discriminant value of Your_Snake, which had the default value True, is assigned the value False. The last statement assigns a record aggregate to My_Snake, which changes the discriminant value of My_Snake to True.

Records belonging to the type Snake may thus be declared as unconstrained records. Records belonging to this type, however, may optionally be declared as constrained records. To declare a constrained record, provide a discriminant constraint, just as if the record belongs to a record type without a default discriminant value. When the discriminant constraint is provided, the default value of True is overridden. The following record, Boomslang, is declared with a discriminant value of True:

```
Boomslang: Snake (Poisonous => True); -- constrained record
```

Even though the discriminant constraint, True, is the same as the default value, the effect is to constrain the record. Thus, Boomslang must spend the rest of its life with this discriminant value of True. (Of course, Boomslang could have been initially constrained with the discriminant value of False.)

Discriminated records can also be constrained by using subtypes:

```
declare
    subtype Poisonous_Snake is Snake ( Poisonous => True );
    -- all records of this subtype are constrained
    Green_Mamba: Poisonous_Snake := (True, Neurotoxic);
begin
    Green_Mamba := ( False, False ); -- constraint error;
        -- cannot change discriminant
end;
```

As shown, Green_Mamba is constrained since it is declared to be a record of a constrained record subtype. Note that the use of subtypes does not allow us to omit the discriminant value from the record aggregate.

Discriminated records can be constrained using types as well as subtypes:

```
type Poisonous_Snake is new Snake ( Poisonous => True );
```

Of course, since this declaration introduces a new type, objects of type Poisonous_Snake are type incompatible with objects of type Snake.

In Chapter 4, we showed how a membership test can be used to determine whether a array is within a specified array subtype. Similarly, a membership test can be used to determine whether a record is within a specified record subtype:

```
declare
    ...
    subtype Poisonous_Snake is Snake ( Poisonous => True );
    Green_Mamba: Snake (Poisonous => True);
begin
    if Green_Mamba in Poisonous_Snake then ...-- membership test
```

```
                    -- yields True
        end;
```

Since the subtype Poisonous_Snake sets Poisonous to True, the membership test yields True if Green_Mamba.Poisonous is also True.

As mentioned, whenever an attempt is made to change the discriminant of a constrained record, a constraint error is raised. To avoid raising such an error, if you want to change the discriminant of a record but are uncertain whether the record is constrained, use the Constrained attribute:

```
if not Green_Mamba'Constrained then
    Green_Mamba := ( False, False );
            -- only changes discriminant if Green_Mamba is
            -- unconstrained
end if;
```

The expression Green_Mamba'Constrained is True when Green_Mamba is constrained; otherwise, this expression is False.

The following code illustrates the rules governing constrained and unconstrained records:

```
-- assume type Snake is visible
declare
    A: Snake;                               -- unconstrained
    B: Snake := (True, Hemotoxic);          -- unconstrained
    C: Snake (True);                        -- constrained
    D: Snake (False) := (False, False);     -- constrained
begin
    A := B;     -- OK
    C := B;     -- OK; discriminant not changed
    C := D;     -- constraint error; can't change discriminant
    A := D;     -- OK
    D := B;     -- constraint error; can't change discriminant
    B := D;     -- OK
    B := (False, True);     -- OK
    D := (False, True);     -- OK
    C := (False, False);    -- constraint error
            -- can't change discriminant
end;
```

Records are constrained or unconstrained according to the conditions shown in Figure 5.1.

**Ada 95 ▶**    Recall that an object belonging to an unconstrained array type can be constrained by assigning it an aggregate. The index constraint is determined by the size of the aggregate. Similarly, an object belonging to a discriminated record type without default discriminant values can be constrained by assigning it an aggregate. The discriminant constraint is determined by the discriminant value within the aggregate:

Record Type

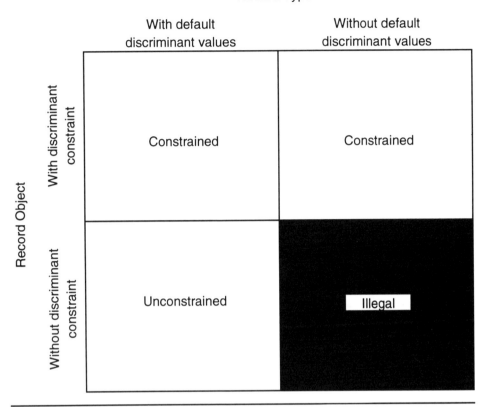

**Figure 5.1** Conditions under which record objects are constrained or unconstrained.

```
type T (A: Boolean) is
    record
        case A is
            when True    => B: Character;
            when False   => C: Integer;
        end case;
    end record;
Rec: T := (A => True, B => 'A'); -- OK;
    -- Rec is constrained by aggregate
```

Again, constraining a record through initialization only works when the discriminated record type T has no default discriminant; otherwise, the aggregate assignment would not constrain Rec. (In Ada 83, a discriminant constraint cannot be provided by the initial value.)

Whether a variant record is constrained or unconstrained, certain restrictions apply. One restriction was already mentioned: the variant part of a record must follow the invariant part. Another restriction is that variant records may only include a single variant part. In other words, the record type declaration may contain only a single **case** construct. The following code, which contains two **case** constructs, is therefore illegal:

```ada
type Programmer_Type is (System, Application);
type Project_Language is (Ada, Pascal);

type Project (   Programmer: Programmer_Type;
                 Language: Project_Language ) is
   record
      case Programmer is
         when System      => Compiler_Experience: Boolean;
         when Application => Graphics_Experience: Boolean;
      end case;

      case Language is -- illegal; cannot have another case
                       -- construct
         when Ada      => Years_Of_Ada_Experience: Boolean;
         when Pascal   => Months_Of_Pascal_Experience: Boolean;
      end case;

   end record;
```

One **case** construct, however, can be nested in another case construct:

```ada
type Furniture_Type is (Coffee_Table, Dining_Table);
type Material_Type is (Wood, Glass);
type Wood_Type is (Mahogany, Maple, Cedar, Walnut, Teak, Paduka);
type Hardness_Scale is (Soft, Medium, Hard);
type Color_Type is (Green, Gray, Colorless);

type Sale_Items   ( Furniture: Furniture_Type   := Coffee_Table;
                    Material: Material_Type      := Wood ) is
   record
      case Furniture is
         when Coffee_Table =>
            case Material is -- nested case construct
               when Wood =>
                  Kind: Wood_Type;
                  Hardness: Hardness_Scale;
               when Glass =>
                  Clear: Boolean;
                  Beveled: Boolean;
                  Color: Color_Type;
            end case;
         when Dining_Table =>
            Thickness: Float range 0.1 .. 3.0;
      end case;
   end record;
```

The record type `Sale_Items` has two discriminants, `Furniture` and `Material`, each with two possible values. Thus, four combinations of these values exist. These combinations are illustrated by the following declarations:

```
Table_1: Sale_Items :=
   (  Furniture    => Coffee_Table,
      Material     => Wood,
      Kind         => Teak,
      Hardness     => Medium );

Table_2: Sale_Items :=
      (  Furniture => Coffee_Table,
         Material  => Glass,
         Clear     => False,
         Beveled   => True,
         Color     => Gray     );

Table_3: Sale_Items :=
   (  Furniture    => Dining_Table,
      Material      => Wood,
      Thickness    => 2.0    );

Table_4: Sale_Items :=
      (  Furniture => Dining_Table,
         Material  => Glass,
         Thickness => 0.5 );
```

There are some restrictions that apply to all discriminated records types, including variant records. One restriction is that if any discriminant is assigned a default value, then all the discriminants, assuming there is more than one, must be assigned default values. Thus, in our previous example, `Sale_Items` cannot provide a default to the discriminant `Furniture` without also providing a default value to `Material`:

```
-- illegal; defaults must be provided for all discriminants or
-- none of the discriminants
type Sale_Items ( Furniture: Furniture_Type   := Coffee_Table;
                  Material: Material_Type ) is
```

There is another restriction that applies to all records but is most likely to cause problems with variant records: every component of a record type must have a unique identifier. This restriction applies even if the record components are within different **when** clauses:

```
type Country is (USA, France);
type American_Money is (Dollar, Cents);
type French_Money is (Franc, Centimes);
type Money_Type (Nation: Country) is
   record
```

```
       case Nation is
          when USA =>
             Money: American_Money;
          when France =>
             Money: French_Money; -- illegal
                   -- record component Money appears twice
       end case;
    end record;
```

The problem with this record type is that the record component Money appears twice. Although multiple components with the same name cannot appear in the same record type, each component may appear in a different record type. In addition, an object can be declared with the same name as a record component. The following code illustrates how different objects called X can appear without any name clash:

```
procedure P is -- each X is a different object
   X: integer;
   type R1 is
      record
          X: Float:
      end record;
   Y: R1;
   type R2 is
      record
          X: Character
      end record;
   Z: R2;
begin
   -- no name clash
   X := 3;        -- procedure P's variable X
   Y.X := 2.9;   -- Y's component X
   Z.X := 'A';   -- Z's component X
end P;
```

No ambiguity arises since the name of the record must always be included when accessing one of its components.

## Records with Different-Sized Components

We have seen how discriminants can be used to declare variant records; that is, records with different kinds and numbers of components. There is another common use for discriminants: to set the size of a record component. This can be done if the component belongs to an unconstrained array type. In such cases, a discriminant may be used to set the size of the array. Consider, for instance, the following record type:

```
type Instructor (Name_Length: Positive := 10) is
   record
```

```
        Name: String (1 .. Name_Length);
    end record;
```

This record type has a discriminant, `Name_Length`, which is used to set the size of the array of characters (string), `Name`. (Recall that a string is defined as a one-dimensional unconstrained array of characters.) The following code declares two records to belong to record type `Instructor`:

```
    declare
        -- assume type Instructor is visible
        My_Ada_Instructor, My_Pascal_Instructor: Instructor;
    begin
        My_Ada_Instructor.Name := "Augusta ";
            -- takes default length of 10
        My_Pascal_Instructor := ( Name_Length  => 6,
                                  Name         => "Blaise");

        . . .
    end;
```

Since the record `My_Ada_Instructor` is declared without a discriminant value, the default value of 10 applies and `Name` is assigned the string `"Augusta    "`. (This string must be padded with 3 blanks so that its total length is 10.) The record `My_Pascal_Instructor` overrides the default value by assigning 6 to `Name_Length`, thereby setting the length of `Name` to fit the length of "Blaise." (Thus, no padding is required.)

Recall that every object (variable or constant) belonging to an unconstrained array type must be constrained. In other words, there are unconstrained array types, but not unconstrained array objects. (In Chapter 6, however, we will see that a formal subprogram parameter or function return value may be unconstrained.) Thus, the index range of an array object is fixed throughout its lifetime. However, when an array such as `Name` is a component of an unconstrained record such as `My_Pascal_Instructor`, then the size of the array is not fixed, but can dynamically change throughout its lifetime by resetting the value of the record discriminant, `Name_Length`. Thus, `My_Pascal_Instructor` can be assigned

```
    My_Pascal_Instructor := ( Name_Length  => 6,
                              Name         => "Blaise");
```

and then later assigned

```
    My_Pascal_Instructor := ( Name_Length  => 13,
                              Name         => "Blaise Pascal");
```

Note that `Name_Length` is changed to from 6 to 13 and Pascal's full, 13-character name is assigned to `My_Pascal_Instructor.Name`.

Beware of a common pitfall that programmers encounter when an unconstrained record uses a discriminant to set an array size. In this situation, some compilers will consume a great deal of computer memory. The reason is that, for ease of implementation, these compilers will reserve enough memory to hold the largest possible record value. (Other implementations, instead of reserving memory at compile time, may dynamically allocate memory as needed when the size of the record component changes.) Consider, for instance, the preceding declaration of `My_Ada_Instructor`. As just discussed, since this record is unconstrained, its discriminant, `Name_Length`, may assume various values throughout its life. The largest possible value is

```
My_Ada_Instructor := ( Name_Length  => Positive'Last,
                       Name         => ( others => '!' ) );
```

On a standard 16-bit computer, `Positive'Last` might be 32,767. An Ada compiler might thus reserve storage space needed to hold a record with an array of this length. To avoid such a possible waste of memory, use types or subtypes to limit the range of values that a discriminant may assume:

```
subtype Name_Range is Integer range 1 .. 20;
type Instructor (Name_Length: Name_Range := 10) is
    record
        Name: String (1 .. Name_Length);
    end record;
```

Since the discriminant has a maximum value of 20, the Ada compiler should reserve no more storage space than is needed to hold a record with an array of length 20.

In the previous record type, a single discriminant sets the index bounds of a one-dimensional array component. In the next record type, two discriminants are used to set the index bounds of a two-dimensional array:

```
subtype Size is Integer range 1 .. 20;
type Matrix_Type is array (Size range <>, Size range <>)
    of Integer;

type Table_Type (Rows, Columns: Size) is
    record
        Matrix: Matrix_Type (1 .. Rows, 1.. Columns);
    end record;
M1: Table_Type (Rows => 2, Columns => 4); -- named notation
M2: Table_Type (3, 7); -- positional notation
```

`Table_Type` has two discriminants. The first discriminant, `Rows`, is used to set the number of rows for `Matrix`. The second discriminant, `Columns`, is used to set the number of columns for `Matrix`. `M1`. Variable `Matrix` is declared with 2 rows and 4 columns, and `M2.Matrix` is declared with 3 rows and 7 columns.

In the preceding example, the record component `Matrix` is declared to belong to the type `Matrix_Type`. Usually, one has the option of declaring an array object, such as `Matrix`, as an anonymous array type. This cannot be done for arrays in component declarations of a record:

```
subtype Size is Integer range 1 .. 20;
type Table (Rows, Columns: Size) is
   record
      Matrix: array (1 .. Rows, 1 .. Columns) of Integer;
         -- illegal; record component cannot be declared
         -- as an anonymous array
   end record;
```

Let us consider yet another restriction that applies to discriminated records: discriminants may only appear by themselves; they may not be part of a larger expression:

```
subtype Size is Integer range 0 .. 20;
type Matrix_Type is array (Size range <>, Size range <>) of
   Integer;

type Table_Type (Rows, Columns: Size) is
   record
      Matrix: Matrix_Type (0 .. Rows - 1, 0 .. Columns - 1);
         -- illegal; discriminant cannot be part of expression
   end record;
```

The problem with this example is that the discriminants `Rows` and `Columns` do not appear by themselves. They are used as part of the larger expressions, `Rows - 1` and `Columns - 1`.

## Three Other Uses of Discriminated Records

As we have seen, discriminants can be used to create variant records and records with different-sized components. There are three other uses of discriminants. First, a discriminant may be used to initialize a record component:

```
type Test_Score ( Score: Natural ) is
   record
      Top_Score: Natural := Score;
   end record;

Ada_Class: Test_Score (97);
```

`Ada_Class` is declared with a discriminant value of 97. This discriminant value is used to initialize the record component, `Top_Score`. To reference this top score, select the `Top_Score` component of the `Ada_Class` record:

```
Ada_Class.Top_Score -- has the value 97
```

Second, a discriminant can be used to constrain a record component that is itself a discriminated record:

```
type Size is new Integer range 1..9;
type Matrix_Type is array (Size range <>, Size range <>) of
   Float;

type Square_Matrix (Length: Size := 2) is
   record
      Matrix: Matrix_Type (1..Length, 1..Length);
   end record;

type Pair_Of_Square_Matrixes (Side: Size) is
   record
      Matrix_One: Square_Matrix (Length => Side);
      Matrix_Two: Square_Matrix (Length => Side);
   end record;

Matrix_Pair: Pair_Of_Square_Matrixes (Side => 4);
```

Note that the components, Matrix_One and Matrix_Two, of the record type Pair_Of_Square_Matrixes, are themselves discriminated records. Also note that Side, which is the discriminant of Pair_Of_Square_Matrixes, is used to constrain the components Matrix_One and Matrix_Two.

Nested discriminated records, such as those of type Pair_Of_Square_Matrixes, are initialized like nested records without discriminants. Just remember to include the values for the discriminants in addition to the values for the other components:

```
Matrix_Pair :=
   (  Side        => 4,
      Matrix_One => ( Length => 4,
                      Matrix => (others => (others => 0.0))),
      Matrix_Two => ( Length => 4,
                      Matrix => (others => (others => 0.0))) );
```

Since the discriminant value of Side is also used as the discriminant value of Length, the values of Size and Length must be the same.

Third, a discriminant can be used to create records with components that act like constants. In the following example, a value must be provided for the discriminant Sex when objects of type Person are declared. This component value acts like a constant since it cannot change during the life of the object:

```
type Gender is (Male, Female);
type Person (Sex: Gender) is
   record
      Age: Years;       -- Assume component types
      Weight: Pounds;   -- were previously declared
   end record;
```

```
-- the age and weight of Bob and Mary can change, but not their
-- sex
Bob: Person (Sex => Male);
Mary: Person (Sex => Female);
```

Note the Sex is used as a discriminant but is not referenced anywhere in the record type.

In summary, discriminants may be used five ways: to form variant records, records with different-sized components, records with a component initialized to the discriminant, and records with a component constrained by its discriminant, and records with components that act as constants. These are the only ways that discriminants can be used. Avoid the common pitfall of attempting to use a discriminant as, for instance, a range constraint in a variable declaration:

```
type Grade ( Perfect_Score: Positive ) is
    record
        Score: Integer range 0 .. Perfect_Score;
        -- illegal; cannot use a discriminant
        -- as a range constraint for a variable declaration
    end record;
```

This concludes our discussion of records. The next chapter will discuss blocks, procedures, and functions.

---

## EXERCISES

1. Explain the differences between records and arrays.

2. Define a record type that may be used to represent fractions.

3. Initialize the components of the record type defined in Exercise 2 so that the default value of the numerator is 0 and the default value of the denominator is 1.

4. Define a record type whose components represent the year, month, and day.

5. Which three of the following assignments are illegal?
```
declare
    type Complex is
        record
            Real, Imaginary: Float;
        end record;
    C: Complex;
begin
    C.Real := 1.0; C.Imaginary := 3.2;
    C := (2.4, 9.9);
    C := (others => 0.0);
```

```
        C := (Real .. Imaginary => 0.0);
        C := (Real | Imaginary => 0.0);
        C := (5.2, Imaginary => 1.8);
        C := (3.2, Real => 3.1);
        C := (Imaginary => 2.2, Real => 1.1);
        C := (Real => 3.2, 5.1);
    end;
```

6. Use record aggregate assignments to make the following code simpler and probably more efficient:

```
declare
    type Four_Values is
        record
            One: Integer;
            Two: Boolean;
            Three: Character;
            Four: Float;
        end record;
    T: Four_Values;
begin
    T.One    := 7;        T.Two  := False;
    T.Three  := 'A';    T.Four := 7.8;
end;
```

7. Consider the following declarations:

```
type Record_Type is
    record
        A1: Positive;    A2: Positive;
        A3: Positive;    A4: Positive;
        B1: Float;       B2: Float;
        B3: Float;       B4: Float;
        C: Character;
    end record;
R: Record_Type;
```

Suppose that record components A1 to A4 are related and must often be assigned values as a group. Suppose that the same is true with components B1 to B4. Since "record slices" such as

```
    R (A1..A4) := (4, 7, 8, 5); -- illegal
```

are not supported by Ada, component-by-component assignments are necessary. Replace Record_Type with a different record structure so that all the A components and B components can be assigned aggregate values.

8. What will each of the following Put statements output?

```
with Ada.Text_IO; use Ada.Text_IO;
procedure Output is
    type Philosopher is
        record
            Name: String (1..12) := "HERACLITUS ";
        end record;
```

```
      Pre_Socratic: Philosopher;
      Modern: Philosopher := (Name => "WITTGENSTEIN" );
begin
   Put (  Pre_Socratic.Name (2)      &
          Modern.Name (9..10)        &
          Pre_Socratic.Name (3)      &
          Modern.Name (12)           &
          Pre_Socratic.Name (4)      &
          Pre_Socratic.Name (6)      &
          Pre_Socratic.Name (12)     &
          Modern.Name (3)            &
          Pre_Socratic.Name (3)      &
          Pre_Socratic.Name (9)      &
          Modern.Name (4)            &
          Pre_Socratic.Name (1)   );
   New_Line;
end Output;
```

9. Consider the following declarations:

```
type R1 is
   record
        D: Integer range 1 .. 10;
        E: Character range 'A' .. 'Z';
   end record;

type R2 is
   record
        A: Boolean;
        B: Float;
        C: R1;
   end record;
R: R2;
```

Given these declarations, which one of the following record aggregates is illegal? Why?

**a.** `R := ( True, 2.4, (5, 'C') );`
**b.** `R := ( A => True,`
`        B => 2.4,`
`        C => ( D => 5, E => 'C' ) );`
**c.** `R := ( True, 2.4, C => (5, 'C') );`
**d.** `R := ( A => True,`
`        B => 2.4,`
`        C => (5, 'C') );`
**e.** `R := ( True, 2.4, ( D => 5, E => 'C' ) );`
**f.** `R := ( True, 2.4, C => (5, E => 'C' ) );`
**g.** `R := ( A => True, B => 2.4, (D => 5, E => 'C' ) );`

10. Modify the following records so that there are fewer redundant components.

```
type  Phonograph_Recording is
   record
        Music: Music_Type;
```

```
        Year_Recorded: Year;
        Instrumental: Boolean;
        Quality: Evauation_Type;
        Scratched: Boolean;
    end record;

type   Cassette_Recording is
   record
        Music: Music_Type;
        Year_Recorded: Year;
        Instrumental: Boolean;
        Quality: Evauation_Type;
        Noise_Reduction: Boolean;
    end record;

type   Compact_Disk_Recording is
   record
        Music: Music_Type;
        Year_Recorded: Year;
        Instrumental: Boolean;
        Quality: Evauation_Type;
        Digitally_Recorded: Boolean;
    end record;
```

11. Consider the following declarations:

```
type Gender is (Male, Female, Neither);
type Adult (Sex: Gender) is
   record
        Age: Integer range 0..120;
        case Sex is
           when Male =>
              Male_Chauvinist: Boolean;
              Bearded: Boolean
           when Female =>
              Use_Perfume: Boolean;
           when Neither =>
              null;
        end case;
    end record;

Cosmologist: Adult (Female);
Cosmetologist Adult (Male);
Cosmogonist: Adult (Neither);
```

Assign each of the three records—Cosmologist, Cosmetologist, and Cosmogonist—a legal set of aggregate values.

12. Modify the variant record type, Adult, of Exercise 11, so that unconstrained records may be declared. Declare several different unconstrained records and assign them aggregate values that change their default discriminant values.

13. Find the errors in this code:

```
declare
    type Rec (Val: Boolean) is
        record
            case Val is
                when True =>
                    X: Integer;
                when False =>
                    Y: Character;
            end case;
        end record;

    A: Rec;
    B: Rec (True);
    C: Rec (False);
    D: Rec := (True, 7);
    E: Rec (True) := (True, 9);
    F: Rec (True) := (False, 'X');
begin
    B := (True, 12);
    C := (True, 25);
    E := (False, 'S');
    B := (True, 'B');
    C := (False, 6);
end;
```

14. Consider the following record type:

```
type Rec (Val: Boolean := True) is
    record
        case Val is
            when True =>
                X: Integer;
            when False =>
                Y: Character;
        end case;
    end record;
```

Given the preceding declaration, which of the following records, A to G, are constrained?

```
A: Rec;
B: Rec (True);
C: Rec (False);
D: Rec := (True, 7);
E: Rec := (False, 'A');
F: Rec (True) := (True, 9);
G: Rec (False) := (False, 'C');
```

15. Which of the following assignment statements raise a constraint error?

```
declare
    type Alternative is (Rent, Buy);
```

```
    type Option (Choice: Alternative := Rent ) is
        record
            case Choice is
                when Rent =>
                    Monthly_Rate: Positive;
                when Buy =>
                    Fixed_Rate: Boolean;
            end case;
        end record;

    Risky: Option;
    Popular: Option := (Buy, True);
    Worst: Option (Rent);
    Best: Option (Buy) := (Buy, False);
begin
    Risky := Popular;
    Risky := Best;
    Worst := (Buy, False);
    Worst := (Rent, 1200);
    Worst := Popular;
    Worst := Best;
    Best := Popular;
    Popular := Best;
    Popular := (Buy, True);
    Popular := (Rent, 750);
    Best := (Buy, True);
    Best := (Rent, 375);
end;
```

16. Explain what is wrong with each of the following record types (every example contains an error):

a.
```
    type Rec ( Val1, Val2: Boolean ) is
        record
            case Val1 is
                when True =>
                    W: Integer;
                when False =>
                    X: Character;
            end case;

            case Val2 is
                when True =>
                    Y: Integer;
                when False =>
                    Z: Character;
            end case;
        end record;
```

b.
```
    subtype Size is Integer range 1..100;
    type Rec ( Limit: Size ) is
```

```
      record
          Row: array (1 .. Limit) of Boolean;
      end record;
```

c.
```
   subtype Size is Integer range 1..100;
   type Row_Type is array (Size range <>) of Boolean;
   type Rec ( Limit: Size ) is
      record
          Row: Row_Type (1 .. Limit + 1);
      end record;
```

d.
```
   type Rec ( Limit: Positive ) is
      record
          Int: Integer range 1 .. Limit;
      end record;
```

e.
```
   type Rec ( Val: Boolean ) is
      record
         case Val is
            when True =>
                X: Integer;
            when False =>
                X: Character;
         end case;
      end record;
```

f.
```
   type Selection is (Alpha, Beta, Gamma);
   type Rec ( Val: Selection ) is
      record
         case Val is
            when Alpha =>
                X: Integer;
            when Gamma =>
                Y: Character;
         end case;
      end record;
```

**17.** Use renaming to simplify the following complex expression:

```
RCA(J, K)(X) := RCA(J, K)(X) ** 2 - RCA(J, K)(X) + 1;
```

Assume that RCA(J, K)(X) is an integer expression.

**18.** Correct all the errors in the following code:

```
type Employee is
   record
       ID: String (1..5) := (others => 'X');
       Name: String (1..20) := (others => ' ');
   end record;
type Sizes is (Small, Medium, Large);

type Software_House (Size: Sizes := Small) is
   record
```

```
          Lead_Programmer: Employee;
          case Size is
             when Small =>
                 null;
             when Medium =>
                 President: Employee;
                 Project_Engineer: Employee;
                 Marketing_Analyst: Employee;
             when Large =>
                 President: Employee;
                 Vice_President: Employee;
                 Project_Engineer: Employee;
                 System_Engineer: Employee;
                 Marketing_Analyst: Employee;
          end case;
      end record;
```

**19.** Correct all the errors in the following code:

```
type Pizza_Type is (Basic, Vegetable, Meat);
type Pizza (Kind: Pizza_Type) is
   record
       Cheese: Cheese_Type;
       Sauce: Sauce_Type;
       case Kind is
          when Basic =>
              null;
          when Vegetable =>
              Veggie: Veggie_Type;
          when Meat =>
              Veggie: Veggie_Type;
              Meat: Meat_Type;
              Hold_The_Anchovy: Boolean;
       end case;
   end record;
```

CHAPTER

# 6

# Blocks, Procedures, and Functions

**B**locks, procedures, and functions are units of code that contain a declarative part, an executable statement part, and an optional exception handler part. (Exception handlers will be discussed in Chapter 10.) Packages and tasks also contain these three parts, but will be discussed in later chapters. The declarative part contains declarations of such items as types, subtypes, variables, constants, procedures, functions, and packages. When the compiler elaborates these declarations, objects (variables and constants) are brought into existence, computer memory is allocated to store them, and, when requested, objects are initialized. These objects are local: they exist only as long as the block, procedure, or function in which they reside is active. When the unit of code in which they reside is finished executing, these local objects cease to exist. The executable statement part, which we will refer to as simply the statement part, contains executable statements such as assignments and control statements. At least one statement must appear in the statement part of a block, procedure, or function. The "do-nothing" statement, **null**, satisfies this requirement.

Blocks are primarily used to group declarations that are only needed locally. By localizing these declarations, programmers are prevented from mistakenly accessing them from other regions of code. Also, there is less code that needs to be examined in order to understand its inner workings.

Procedures and functions, collectively known as subprograms, are used to carry out an action. Subprograms are the basic executable units of Ada programs. To execute a subprogram, it must be called (invoked) by name. The name of the subprogram represents a group of statements that implements some high-level operation. Users view the operation through the subprogram name as if it were a single action. For example, the subprogram name `Prompt_The_User_For_Input` could be viewed as a single action even though a sequence of statements is required to implement this action.

To understand code that invokes a subprogram, one needs to know what the subprogram does, not how it does it. By assigning a meaningful name to a subprogram, it should be quite obvious what it does. Since at the point a subprogram is called, its implementation can be ignored, its implementation is hidden inside the subprogram body. Well-named subprograms, therefore, help manage the complexity of a program by reducing the amount of code that must be understood at any one time.

Although blocks and subprograms are covered in this chapter, there are three basic differences between them. First, subprograms can be separately compiled. Blocks cannot be separately compiled but must be embedded in some larger unit that is compilable. Second, subprograms can be called. Blocks cannot be called. To call a subprogram is to activate it. Subprograms can be called as many times as needed from wherever in the code they are needed. A subprogram is called by a single command. Whenever the subprogram is finished executing, control passes to the statement following the command that called it. Thus, the need for redundant code is reduced. On the other hand, since a block statement cannot be called, it must be duplicated wherever it is needed in the code. The third basic difference between blocks and subprograms is that the code that implements a subprogram must be placed in the declarative part of a unit, while the code that invokes a subprogram must be placed in the statement part. In contrast, the code that implements a block must be placed in the statement part of a unit.

This chapter continues the discussion of blocks, procedures, and functions. Specific features of procedures and functions will then be covered.

## BLOCKS

Blocks, or block statements, were introduced in Chapter 2. Recall that a block has the following structure:

```
declare
    declarations
begin
    statements
end;
```

A block begins with the keyword **declare**, followed by a declarative part containing declarations of local objects. After the declarative part is the keyword **begin**, followed by one or more executable statements. After the executable statements, the block statement terminates with the keyword **end**. If there are no declarations, then the keyword **declare** is optional. Blocks without declarations, however, do not serve any purpose unless they contain exception handlers.

An entire block is considered to be an executable statement, even though it contains a declarative part. Thus, a block can appear wherever an executable statement is allowed. A block can even be placed in the executable part of another block:

```
--Assume Put is visible
declare
```

```
    A: Integer := 1;
    B: Integer := 2;
begin
    Put (A);  -- outputs 1
    Put (B);  -- outputs 2

    declare    -- beginning of inner block
        C: Integer := 3;
        D: Integer := 4;
    begin
        Put (A);  -- outputs 1
        Put (B);  -- outputs 2
        Put (C);  -- outputs 3
        Put (D);  -- outputs 4
    end;          -- end of inner block

    Put (A);  -- outputs 1
    Put (B);  -- outputs 2
    Put (C);  -- error, C is not available
    Put (D);  -- error, D is not available
end;
```

Note that the inner block can access objects A and B, which are declared in the outer block. However, the outer block cannot access objects C and D, which are declared in the inner block and only exist within this inner block. As soon as the inner block is finished executing, C and D cease to exist and are, therefore, inaccessible to the outer block.

An inner block, then, can access objects that are declared in an outer block. But what happens when an inner block declares an object with the same name as one of the objects declared in an outer block? This situation is illustrated in the following code:

```
declare
    A: Integer := 1;
    B: Integer := 2;
begin
    Put (A);  -- outputs 1
    Put (B);  -- outputs 2

    declare        -- beginning of inner block
        A: Integer := 3;
    begin
        Put (A);  -- outputs 3
        Put (B);  -- outputs 2
    end;            -- end of inner block

    Put (A);  -- outputs 1
    Put (B);  -- outputs 2
end;
```

Note that both the inner block and the outer block have declared a variable A. In such situations, within the inner block, the inner A "hides" the outer A. In other words, if the variable A is accessed within the inner block, it is the inner A that is accessed. This allows a programmer to freely choose a suitable name for items declared within a block without worrying about unintended clashes with names introduced elsewhere in the program (although, in general, duplicate names should be avoided to minimize confusion).

But what if, within the inner block, we want to access the A declared in the outer block? To do this, a name (identifier) is assigned to the outer block, just as a name was assigned to a loop statement in Chapter 3. The name, which can be any valid Ada identifier, can then be used to reference hidden variables like the outer A. For instance, we can identify the outer block as Outer, by placing

```
Outer:
```

before the keyword **declare**. The identifier Outer must also be placed at the end of the block, after the keyword **end**. (Although a block identifier or a loop identifier *must* be placed after the keyword **end**, placement of a subprogram identifier after the keyword **end** is optional.) When an identifier, such as Outer, is given to the outer block, then the outer variable A can be accessed by the inner block through the use of dot notation: Outer.A:

```
Outer:
declare
    A: Integer := 1;
    B: Integer := 2;
begin
    Put (A);        -- outputs 1
    Put (B);        -- outputs 2

    Inner:                      -- beginning of inner block
    declare
       C: Integer := A; -- A here is Outer A
       A: Integer := 3;
    begin
        Put (A);            -- outputs 3
        Put (B);            -- outputs 2
        Put (C);            -- outputs 1
        Put (Inner.A);     -- outputs 3
        Put (Outer.A);     -- outputs 1
    end Inner;              -- end of inner block

    Put (A);        -- outputs 1
    Put (B);        -- outputs 2
    Put (C);        -- error; C not available
    Put (Inner.A);  -- error; Inner.A not available
    Put (Outer.A);  -- outputs 1
end Outer;
```

Note that we gave the name, Inner, to the inner block. This name, which is not required, makes code more readable by allowing the programmer to explicitly state which variable A is being accessed. Even with the notation Inner.A, however, the outer block still cannot access the inner A. Also note that, within the inner block, C is declared before A. Since the outer A is not hidden until after C is declared, when C is initialized to A, it is initialized to the outer A. Thus, the order of declarations is significant. If these two declarations were written in reverse order, C would be initialized to the value of the inner A. This is because the outer A would be hidden by the inner A before C was declared.

The preceding discussion reflects Ada's scope and visibility rules. According to Ada's scope rules, the scope of an object extends from the end of its declaration to the end of the block in which it is declared. In the previous example, the scope of the outer A extends from the point in the code after it is declared to the end of the outer block. The scope of the inner A extends from the point after it is declared to the end of the inner block. The scope of B and C is similarly defined.

According to the visibility rule, an object is visible from the end of its declaration to the end of the block in which it is declared, except when hidden by objects with the same name. In the previous example, the variable A declared in the outer block is thus directly visible in the outer block but not within areas of the inner block where the inner A is visible. An object is "directly visible" if it can be directly accessed simply by using its name without dot notation. The variable B declared in the outer block, however, is directly visible to the end of the code because it is not hidden by any declarations in the inner block. These scope and visibility rules apply to nested subprograms as well as to nested block statements (see Exercise 4 of this chapter).

Because a block is an executable statement that may contain a declarative part, a block enables us to place declarations within the statement part of the code. An example of this use of a block was shown in Chapter 4, in the discussion of dynamic arrays. Another such example follows, in which the subtype Percent_Range is given an upper limit at runtime:

```
declare
    subtype Percent is Integer range 0 .. 100;
    Highest_Percent: Percent;
begin
    Put ("Enter the greatest possible percent.");
    Get (Highest_Percent);
    declare
        subtype Percent_Range is Percent range
                Percent'First.. Highest_Percent;
            . . .
    begin
        . . .
    end;
end;
```

At runtime, a user enters the highest possible percentage value that needs to be considered. This value is then used to place an upper bound on the subtype

`Percent_Range`. The inner block is needed here because the declaration of `Percent_Range` must follow the executable statement `Get (Highest_Percent)`. Without this inner block, in other words, the subtype declaration for `Percent_Range` would be illegal, because it would be located in the executable part of the code instead of the declarative part.

## PROCEDURES

A procedure is an executable program unit that is invoked as a statement. In general, procedures should be named with active verb phrases, such as `Turn_On_Lights`, `Read_Tracking_Data`, and `Start_Countdown`.

Procedures were first introduced in Chapter 1 and then used in succeeding chapters. The structure of a procedure should, therefore, be familiar:

```
procedure procedure name (parameter definitions ) is
    declarations
begin
    statements
end procedure name;
```

A procedure is composed of two parts: the procedure specification and the procedure body. The procedure specification begins with the keyword **procedure**, followed by the procedure name and parameter definitions, if any, which are enclosed in parentheses. The procedure body begins with the keyword **is** and terminates with the keyword **end**, followed by an optional procedure name. As discussed in the beginning of this chapter, the procedure body is also divided into two parts: the declarative part and the statement part. The declarative part contains local declarations, which are placed between the keywords **is** and **begin**. The statement part contains executable statements that are placed between the keywords **begin** and **end**.

Procedures are frequently written with the specification and body combined into one unit. It is possible, however, to separate the procedure specification from its body and to compile each unit separately:

```
procedure procedure name (parameter definitions);
    --specification
```

```
procedure procedure name (parameter definitions) is -- body
    declarations
begin
    statements
end procedure name;
```

The line indicates two separate compilation units. Each compilation unit is normally placed in its own file and compiled by itself. Note that the procedure body is written exactly as if the procedure specification had not been separated from it. The body, in other words, must duplicate the information contained in its specification.

The main advantage of separating a procedure specification from its body and placing each in a separate file is to reduce the amount of compilation needed when the procedure body changes. By keeping the specification and body separate, the body can be modified and recompiled without requiring those library units that invoke the procedure to be recompiled.

The main disadvantage of separating a procedure specification from its body is the creation of an excessive number of compilation units, half of which only contain a single line of code (the procedure specification). As we will see in Chapter 7, the solution to this problem is to place related procedures into a common package. The package specification contains all the externally callable procedure specifications, while the package body contains all the procedure bodies. Only two compilation units are created—the package specification and the package body. Thus, a package allows procedure specifications and bodies to be separated to minimize recompilation while minimizing the number of compilation units.

Before showing an example of a procedure, let us see how a procedure is invoked, which will be contrasted with how a function is invoked. A procedure is invoked as a statement. For instance, consider the procedure `Square_Root`, which calculates the square root of a real number. This procedure, whose implementation is not shown, can be invoked as follows:

```
Square_Root (9.0, Result);
```

The first parameter, `9.0`, is passed to the procedure `Square_Root`, which then calculates the square root of `9.0`. The procedure returns the answer, `3.0`, through the second parameter, `Result`. Thus, the first parameter passes in a value to the procedure, and the second parameter returns a value from the procedure back to the caller. As we will see later in this chapter, the procedure defines how the parameters are to be used.

Whereas a procedure is invoked as a statement, a function is invoked as an expression. Thus, if procedure `Square_Root` is instead written as a function, it can be invoked as follows:

```
Result := Square_Root (9.0);
```

Unlike the procedure, this function has only a single parameter. This is because the result is not returned through a parameter; rather, it is returned through the function identifier `Square_Root`. The function identifier appears on the right side of the assignment operator because it is an expression that yields a result. The square root of `9.0` is calculated, and the result, `3.0`, is returned through the identifier, `Square_Root`. The result is then assigned to the real variable, `Result`. In general, when a subprogram returns a single value to the caller and does not modify the external environment (for example, does not modify global variables or perform input or output), then it should be implemented as a function, not as a procedure. Thus, `Square_Root` is better written as a function. However, note that regardless of whether `Square_Root` is a procedure or function, to invoke it, no knowledge is required of how it works.

Let us now examine a procedure that swaps the values of two integer variables. This procedure is implemented as follows:

```
procedure Swap (Pre, Post: in out Integer) is
   Temp: Integer := Pre;
begin
   Pre := Post;
   Post := Temp;
end Swap;
```

The parameter definitions of this procedure—Pre, Post: **in out** Integer—define two formal parameters, Pre and Post, to be **in out** parameters of type Integer. A formal parameter is a name that is only manipulated within the body of a subprogram. An actual parameter is the particular object associated with the corresponding formal parameter when the subprogram is invoked. The keywords **in out** define the parameter mode. (Parameter modes will be discussed in detail in a subsequent section.) An **in out** formal parameter is passed an actual value when the subprogram is invoked; it then returns a result when the subprogram is finished executing. (This differs from the Square_Root procedure, whose first parameter is used for passing in a value, and whose second parameter is used for returning a result.) Thus, at runtime, the two formal parameters, Pre and Post, are passed actual parameters, A and B, when the procedure Swap is invoked:

```
declare
   A: Integer := 5;
   B: Integer := 3;
begin
   Swap (A, B);      -- invocation of Swap
   . . .
end;
```

When Swap is invoked, A has a value of 5 that is passed to the formal parameter Pre, and B has a value of 3 that is passed to the formal parameter Post. The swap procedure then swaps these two values and returns the results to A and B. After Swap is invoked, therefore, A has the value of 3, and B has the value of 5. Note that the actual parameter names, A and B, do not have to be the same as the formal parameter names, Pre and Post. An actual parameter, however, must belong to the same type as its associated formal parameter. Thus, if one attempted to pass Swap noninteger values, one would get a compile time error.

## FUNCTIONS

A function is an executable program unit that is invoked as an expression and returns a single value to the caller. Functions should generally be named with nouns, such as Square_Root, End_Of_File, and Count. Functions that return a Boolean value should be named with a phrase implying a condition that can be either true or false, such as Is_Empty and End_Of_File_Reached.

The structure of a function is the same as the structure of a procedure, except that the function includes the keyword **return,** followed by the type of result that the function returns:

```
function function name (parameter definitions) return type is
    declarations
begin
    statements
end function name;
```

As with procedures, parameter definitions are optional. Functions without parameters, in other words, are acceptable and are written without parentheses.

Like a procedure, a function is composed of two parts: the function specification and the function body. The function specification begins with the keyword **function,** followed by the function name and parameter definitions, if any, which are enclosed in parentheses. Next is the keyword **return,** followed by the type of the result that the function returns. The function body begins with the keyword **is** and terminates with the keyword **end,** followed by an optional function name. The function body is also composed of two parts: the declarative part and the statement part. The declarative part contains declarations of local objects, which are placed between the keywords **is** and **begin**. The statement part contains executable statements, which are placed between the keywords **begin** and **end**.

As with procedures, the function specification and function body can be written as two separate program units that are compiled separately. This is done in the same manner as that described for procedures. Therefore, the information will not be repeated in this section.

Let us consider a simple function that uses the membership test to check whether a character is an uppercase letter:

```
function Is_Upper (Char: in Character) return Boolean is
begin
    return Char in 'A' .. 'Z';
end Is_Upper;
```

This function has a formal **in** parameter called Char that is of type Character. An **in** parameter is passed an actual value when a function is invoked; it cannot be used to return a result. In fact, unlike procedure parameters, a function parameter must be an **in** parameter and therefore can never be used to return a result back to the caller. Rather, a result can only be returned through the function identifier. Since a function can only return a result through its identifier, only a single value can be returned. (This single value, however, may be an array or record aggregate with multiple component values.)

In the preceding function, the identifier, Is_Upper, gets set to a Boolean value by the **return** statement:

```
return Char in 'A' .. 'Z';
```

If `Char` is in the range from `'A'` to `'Z'`, then `Is_Upper` is set to `True`; else `Is_Upper` is set to `False`. The **return** statement then returns control to the program unit that called this function, and execution resumes with the statement following the function call.

Functions must contain at least one **return** statement. Procedures, however, do not require **return** statements, because no value is being returned through the procedure identifier and because the procedure automatically returns control to the calling unit when the procedure is finished executing. Even though procedures do not require **return** statements, they sometimes use **return** statements when a return to the calling unit is desired before the end of the procedure is reached. Unlike function returns, when a procedure employs a **return** statement, no value or expression follows the keyword **return**.

Let us now embed the preceding function, `Is_Upper`, in a complete Ada program. In the following program, the function `Is_Upper` is used to test whether a `Character` input by a user is an uppercase letter:

```
with Ada.Text_IO; use Ada.Text_IO;
procedure Input_Character is

   Letter: Character;
   function Is_Upper (Char: Character) return Boolean is
   begin
      return Char in 'A' .. 'Z';
   end Is_Upper;

begin

   Put ("Enter a character.");
   Get (Letter);

   if Is_Upper (Letter) then
      Put_Line ("You entered an uppercase letter.");
   else
      Put_Line ("You didn't enter an uppercase letter.");
   end if;

end Input_Character;
```

This procedure begins by prompting the user for a character. If the character is an uppercase letter, the procedure outputs "You entered an uppercase letter." Otherwise, the procedure outputs "You didn't enter an uppercase letter."

The procedure `Input_Character` uses the function `Is_Upper` as a `Boolean` expression in its **if** statement. When `Is_Upper` is invoked, the actual parameter `Letter` is passed to the formal parameter `Char`. A membership test is then performed to check whether `Letter` is an uppercase letter. If the letter is uppercase, then the function returns the value `True`; otherwise, it returns the value `False`.

Note that `Is_Upper` is embedded in the declarative part of the procedure

`Input_Character` and is then invoked from the statement part of this procedure. Languages such as Pascal also use this structure. Any number of subprograms, whether functions or procedures, can be placed in the declarative part of another subprogram and then can be invoked from the statement part of that subprogram.

**Ada 95 ▶**    Since no general-purpose language such as Ada can anticipate all the possible functions needed by programmers, programmers must frequently define their own functions. However, certain functions are needed often enough for Ada to provide them. The function `Is_Upper`, for example, is provided in the predefined child package `Ada.Characters.Handling`, along with functions that determine whether a character is a lowercase character, a control character, a graphic character, a letter, a digit, and so on. Functions are also provided for converting characters and characters within strings to uppercase or lowercase. Programmers needing such functions should read about package `Ada.Characters.Handling` in the *Ada 95 Reference Manual*.

## FEATURES OF PROCEDURES AND FUNCTIONS

This section covers the features common to procedures and functions: parameter modes, positional and named notation, default parameter values, subunits, subprogram library units, overloading, returning composite values, recursive subprograms, inlined subprograms, and renamed subprograms.

### Parameter Modes

Subprogram parameters are used to pass data to or from subprograms. Passing data through parameters is generally preferable to sharing global data between subprograms. The use of global data tends to make code less maintainable and less reliable because it makes the interfaces between the program units more complex.

Ada provides three different parameter modes for controlling the direction in which data can flow between the calling subprogram (the caller) and the subprogram being called: **in**, **out**, and **in out**. All three parameter modes apply to procedures, but only the **in** parameter mode applies to functions. If no mode is specified, the **in** mode is taken as the default. The **in** mode, as well as the **in out** mode, has already been introduced. Briefly, an **in** parameter allows data to flow in only one direction: from the caller to the subprogram being called. The caller passes a parameter value to the called subprogram, but this parameter cannot return any value back to the caller. An **out** parameter allows data to flow in the opposite direction: from the called subprogram back to its caller. The called subprogram assigns the **out** parameter some value, which is passed back to the caller after the subprogram finishes executing. An **in out** parameter allows data to flow in both directions. A value is passed to a subprogram. The subprogram can read this value and modify it. When the subprogram is finished executing, the updated value is then passed back to the caller.

Parameter modes will be examined from two perspectives: first, from the perspective of the code that does the calling; second, from the perspective of the subprogram that is called.

For the first perspective, consider a procedure that takes two values and then calculates the square of their difference:

```
procedure Square_Of_Difference ( X, Y :     in Integer;
                                  Answer :   out Natural ) is
begin
   Answer := (X - Y) ** 2;
end Square_Of_Difference;
```

The following block statement shows how this procedure can and cannot be called:

```
-- assume Square_Of_Difference is visible
declare
   A: Integer := 2;
   B: Integer;
   C: constant Integer := 3;
begin
   Square_Of_Difference (C, 6, A);                   -- OK
   Square_Of_Difference (2, B, A);                   -- Error
      -- B must be initialized
   Square_Of_Difference (C+1, A, B);                 -- OK
   Square_Of_Difference (3, 1, 4);                   -- illegal
      -- cannot return a value to the literal 4
   Square_Of_Difference (A, A, C);                   -- illegal
      -- cannot change the value of constant C
   Square_Of_Difference (A, C, 1+2);                 -- illegal
      -- cannot return a value to expression 1 + 2
end;
```

The first invocation, or call, to `Square_Of_Difference`, is legal:

```
Square_Of_Difference (C, 6, A);
```

The value of the constant C is passed in to the formal parameter X, 6 is passed in to Y, and the value of Answer is returned through the variable A. It does not matter that A is initialized to 2. The result of the procedure call, in this case, 9, is passed to variable A and replaces the value 2.

The second call contains an error:

```
Square_Of_Difference (2, B, A);
```

Since parameters of mode **in** (and **in out**) provide values to the called subprogram, the caller must initialize the variable B before making the call. If B is uninitialized, when the procedure `Square_Of_Difference` reads the associated formal parameter, Y, it will be reading an undefined value. In practice, most Ada compilers will not detect the error of reading an uninitialized parameter unless the "garbage" value happens to fail a range check.

The third call is legal:

```
Square_Of_Difference (C + 1, A, B);
```

The expression C + 1 is passed in to X, the value of A is passed in to Y, and the result, 4, is returned through the variable B. Note that in this case, B does not need to be initialized. For a parameter of mode **out**, the caller is not required to initialize the parameter since **out** parameters do not provide values to the called subprogram.

The fourth call is illegal:

```
Square_Of_Difference (3, 1, 4);
```

The problem is with the third parameter, 4. The literal 4 cannot be used as an actual **out** (or **in out**) parameter since the procedure result cannot be returned to a literal. In other words, the value of a literal, such as 4, cannot be changed.

The fifth call is also illegal:

```
Square_Of_Difference (A, A, C);
```

Again the problem is with the third parameter. C cannot be used to store the result of the procedure call, because C is a constant whose value cannot be changed.

The sixth call also has a problem with the third parameter:

```
Square_Of_Difference (A, C, 1 + 2);
```

The expression 1 + 2 cannot be assigned a value returned from the procedure call.

In summary, for parameters of mode **in**, the caller can supply an actual parameter that is a literal, constant, initialized variable, or expression. For parameters of mode **out** (or **in out**), however, the caller must supply an actual parameter that is a variable. The reason for this is that a value will be returned via the parameter, and only variables can accept the returned value.

So far we have been considering the first perspective: parameter modes from the viewpoint of the calling code. Now let us consider the second perspective: the viewpoint of the subprogram being called. Consider, for instance, the following procedure:

```
procedure Callee ( In_Param      : in      Integer;
                   Out_Param     :     out Integer;
                   In_Out_Param  : in out Integer ) is
begin

   Out_Param := 0;  -- OK

   Out_Param := Out_Param + 1;    -- OK to read Out_Param since
                                  -- it was just initialized
```

```
        In_Param := 1;                      -- illegal; can't write to an
                                            -- in parameter

        In_Out_Param := In_Out_Param + In_Param; -- OK
           . . .
    end Callee;
```

The first statement in procedure `Callee` is legal and initializes an **out** parameter to 0.

```
    Out_Param := 0;
```

Initializing **out** parameters is not only legal, it is required. An **out** parameter has no initial value and must be assigned a value before the procedure is finished executing. If a value is not assigned, then when the calling program reads the returned value, it will be reading a value that is undefined. As previously mentioned, most Ada compilers will not detect the error of reading an uninitialized parameter unless the "garbage" value happens to fail a range check.

**Ada 95 ▶**   The second statement is also legal:

```
    Out_Param := Out_Param + 1;
```

Be very careful, however, when reading an **out** parameter. Unlike parameters of mode **in** and **in out,** which are set by the caller, the value of an **out** parameter is not set by the caller. In order to avoid reading an uninitialized parameter, an **out** parameter needs to be initialized by the called subprogram before the called subprogram reads it. In our example, since `Out_Param` was previously initialized to 0, it can be safely read. (In Ada 83, an **out** parameter cannot be read by the called subprogram, even after the called subprogram initializes it. This restriction is dropped in Ada 95.)

The third statement is illegal:

```
    In_Param := 1;
```

Since **in** parameters cannot be used to return values to the caller, the called subprogram can read **in** parameters but cannot modify their value. Such parameters, in other words, act like constants because they are in a read-only mode. An **in** parameter, then, can never appear on the left side of the assignment operator.

The fourth statement is legal:

```
    In_Out_Param := In_Out_Param + In_Param;   -- OK
```

Parameters of mode **in** and **in out** can be read (can appear on the right side of the assignment operator) since they have a value supplied by the caller. An **in out** parameter may appear on the left side of the assignment operator as well as on the right side, since it can be written to, as well as read from. A called subprogram typically needs to modify the value of an **in out** parameter, unless the caller is to be returned the same parameter value that it passed in.

Whereas procedures can use **in**, **out**, and **in out** parameter modes, functions can only use **in** parameters, in order to limit their "side effects." A function is said to have a side effect if it impacts any nonlocal entities. Since functions cannot have **out** or **in out** parameters, they cannot modify a nonlocal variable via parameter passing. Of course, functions could produce side effects by directly modifying the value of some global variable, or by outputting a message to the terminal. Although these side effects usually make programs harder to understand, they are not prohibited by the Ada language.

The rest of the information in this section is for the advanced reader, and may be skipped if desired. There are two ways that parameters can be passed: by value or by reference. When parameters are passed by value, values are copied between the actual and formal parameters, depending on the parameter mode. For example, if the parameter mode is **in**, then the actual parameter is copied to the formal parameter of the called subprogram. When parameters are passed by reference, the actual and formal parameters reference the same object. In Ada, scalar types must be passed by value. Composite types can either be passed by value or by reference. (Most implementations will pass large composite types by reference since passing by value would be inefficient.) Some types covered in later chapters—such as tagged types, task types and protected types—are always passed by reference.

Avoid code, such as the following, whose results differ, depending on whether composite types are passed by value or by reference:

```
with Ada.Text_IO; use Ada.Text_IO;
procedure Parameter_Passing is
   S: String (10 .. 19);
   procedure Side_Effect (T: out String) is
   begin
      T := (T'Range => 'X');
      S := (others => 'Y');
   end Side_Effect;
begin
   Side_Effect (S);
   Put_Line (S);
   -- If pass by copy, outputs Xs
   -- If pass by reference, outputs Ys
end Parameter_Passing;
```

The problem arises because the same string, S, is being referenced in two different ways: through Side_Effect's parameter T, and directly within Side_Effect's body. In other words, when the procedure Side_Effect is called, the identifiers T and S name the same string. Such "aliasing" is undesirable because the results differ, depending on the parameter-passing mechanism. This makes code nonportable. If parameters are passed by value, then T and S are separate copies of the same string. In this case, modifying S does not change the value of T. The output is what one undoubtedly expects: "XXXXXXXXXX". On the other hand, if parameters are passed by reference, then T and S are two different names for the same exact string. In this case, modifying $S$ immediately changes the value of $T$. This results in the unexpected output: `"YYYYYYYYYY"`. (Aliasing may also occur when the same variable is used as an actual parameter twice in the same procedure call and the parameters are not both specified as **in** mode.)

## Positional and Named Notation

Recall from Chapters 4 and 5 that array aggregates and record aggregates can be written using positional notation or named notation. Similarly, subprogram calls can be written using either positional or named notation. More precisely, when a procedure or function is invoked, the association between its formal parameters and actual parameters may be indicated by position or name. Consider, for example, the following declarations:

```
type Bean_Type is (Colombian, Kenyan, Jamaican, Costa_Rican);
type Roast_Type is (Light, Medium, Dark);
procedure Coffee (Bean: Bean_Type; Roast: Roast_Type);
```

Note that since the parameter modes of `Bean` and `Roast` are not explicitly given, Ada assumes that they both are **in** parameters. Given these declarations, the procedure `Coffee` can be called as follows:

```
Coffee (Kenyan, Medium);    -- positional notation
Coffee (Bean => Kenyan, Roast => Medium);    -- named notation
Coffee (Roast => Medium, Bean => Kenyan);    -- named notation
Coffee (Kenyan, Roast => Medium);            -- mixed notation
```

These four procedure calls are logically equivalent. The first procedure call uses positional notation. The compiler associates the actual parameter that is listed first, `Kenyan`, with the formal parameter that is listed first, `Bean`. The compiler also associates the second actual parameter, `Medium`, with the second formal parameter, `Roast`. The second procedure call uses named notation. The arrow, `=>`, associates the formal procedure parameter to the left of the arrow with the actual parameter to the right of the arrow. Thus, `Bean => Kenyan` associates the formal parameter `Bean` with the actual parameter `Kenyan`. The third procedure call also uses named notation. This call shows that, with named notation, the order in which the parameters are listed does not matter. The fourth procedure call shows that named and positional notation may be mixed. In this case, the first parameter uses positional notation, and the second parameter uses named notation. This order of notation, positional notation followed by named notation, must be observed whenever mixed notation is used. The following procedure call is illegal because this order is reversed:

```
Coffee (Bean => Jamaican, Medium); -- illegal
```

There are two advantages of calling procedures and functions using named notation. First, the order in which the formal parameters are listed does not need to be considered; just their names need to be known. Second, if the formal parameters are assigned meaningful names, named notation helps document what the actual parameters represent. This means that, when possible, programmers should carefully select meaningful names for formal subprogram parameters so that programmers calling the subprogram can benefit from using named notation.

## Default Parameter Values

A useful feature that is available only for **in** parameters is the assignment of default parameter values. If a procedure or function initializes its **in** parameters to a default value, then whenever the procedure or function is called, the default value can either be accepted or overridden with a new value. Consider the following example of a function that takes from two to five parameters and returns the sum of their cubes:

```
function Sum_Of_Cubes (A, B      : in Integer;
                       C, D, E  : in Integer := 0) return
                       Integer is
begin
    return (A**3 + B**3 + C**3 + D**3 + E**3);
end Sum_Of_Cubes;
```

Note that the first two parameters, A and B, do not have default values. Therefore, these parameters must always be passed values when the function is called. However, the remaining parameters, C, D, and E, are initialized to a default value of 0, so do not need to be passed values. Therefore, this function can be called with two to five parameters:

```
Sum_Of_Cubes (2)                        -- illegal;
    -- at least 2 parameters are required
Sum_Of_Cubes (2, 3)                      -- returns 35
Sum_Of_Cubes (-2, 3, 4)                  -- returns 83
Sum_Of_Cubes (1, 1, 1, 1)                -- returns 4
Sum_Of_Cubes (2, 4, 3, 1, 2)             -- returns 108
```

In all these function calls, if a value is not provided for parameters C, D, or E, then the default value of 0 is used. The first call is illegal since at least two parameters must be provided. The second call passes the value 2 for A and 3 for B. All the other parameters are defaulted to 0. Thus, the returned value is $2^3 + 3^3 + 0^3 + 0^3 + 0^3$, which is 35. The third call passes the value of -2 to A, 3 to B, and 4 to C. All the other parameters are assigned the default value of 0. Thus, the returned value is $(-2)^3 + 3^3 + 4^3 + 0^3 + 0^3$, which is 83. Skipping to the last call, values are passed to all the parameters: A, B, C, D, and E. Therefore, all of the default values are overridden. Thus, the returned value is $2^3 + 4^3 + 3^3 + 1^3 + 2^3$, which is 108.

Let us consider another example that uses default parameter values:

```
type Body_Type is (Station_Wagon, Van, Sedan, Hatchback,
     Coupe, Convertible);
type Color_List is (Aqua, Mauve, Fuchsia, Passion_Pink,
     Chartreuse, Lavender, Magenta);
```

```
procedure Purchase_Car
   (   Body             :  in Body_Type    := Convertible;
       Color            :  in Color_List   := Chartreuse;
       Is_Fully_Loaded  :  in Boolean      := True );
```

Note that the **in** parameter Body is initialized to the default value Convertible; Color, to the default value Chartreuse; and Is_Fully_Loaded, to the default value True. It is useful to provide such default values when one particular value is used much more often than any other value.

Given the previous declarations, the following procedure calls can be made:

```
Purchase_Car; -- convertible, chartreuse, true

Purchase_Car (Van); -- van, chartreuse, true

Purchase_Car (Color => Fuchsia); -- convertible, fuchsia, true

Purchase_Car (   Is_Fully_Loaded  => False,
                 Body             => Station_Wagon );
   -- station wagon, chartreuse, false

Purchase_Car (Sedan, Passion_Pink, True);
   -- sedan, passion pink, true

Purchase_Car (Coupe, Color => Aqua, Is_Fully_Loaded => True);
   -- coupe, aqua, true

Purchase_Car (   Body             => Van,
                 Color            => Aqua,
                 Is_Fully_Loaded  => True );
   -- van, aqua, true
```

These procedure calls work in the same way as those of the previous function, Sum_Of_Cubes. For example, the first procedure call does not pass in any parameters, so all the default values are used: Body is Convertible, Color is Chartreuse, and Is_Fully_Loaded is True. The second call passes in the parameter Van, so only the default values Chartreuse and True are used. All of the other calls work similarly.

If we wish to override the default values of parameters that are listed sequentially from the beginning of the list, then positional notation can be used. Thus, positional notation can be used in the following cases: when the default for Body is overridden but not the defaults for Color or Is_Fully_Loaded; when the defaults for both Body and Color are overridden but not the default for Is_Fully_Loaded; and when the defaults for all three parameters are overridden. In all other cases where one or more defaults are overridden, named notation must be used. If, for example, we want to accept the default for Color but want to override the defaults for Body and Is_Fully_Loaded, then the following procedure call can be used:

```
Purchase_Car (Body => Hatchback, Is_Fully_Loaded => False);
```

There is no way to accomplish this by using positional notation. That is, we cannot use positional notation and skip the second parameter by leaving it blank:

```
Purchase_Car (Hatchback, ,False); -- illegal
```

Now let us consider two other incorrect uses of positional and named notation:

```
Purchase_Car (Passion_Pink);           -- illegal
Purchase_Car (Body => Sedan, True);   -- illegal
```

In the first procedure call, because positional notation is used, `Passion_Pink` is incorrectly associated with the formal parameter `Body`. In the second call, named notation is used before positional notation, which is illegal.

## Subunits

The Ada programs we have seen thus far have been structured similarly to this example:

```
procedure Main is

   -- Constants, types, and variables for P1, F1, and Main
   Flag: Boolean := True;

   procedure P1 (Item: in Boolean) is   -- can reference Flag
      -- Constants, types, and variables for P1
   begin
      -- Executable statements for P1
   end P1;

   function F1 return Boolean is -- can reference Flag and P1
      -- Constants, types, and variables for F1
   begin
      -- Executable statements for F1
   end F1;

begin -- beginning of Main
   ...
   Flag := F1;
   P1 (Flag);
end Main;
```

The structure of procedure `Main` is adequate if procedure `P1` and function `F1` are relatively short subprograms, and if enough information is known to write the bodies of `P1` and `F1` at the time `Main` is written. But what if `P1` and `F1` are large subprograms? If we embed both of these subprograms in the declarative part of procedure `Main`, the result is a huge program unit that requires substantial time to compile and is difficult to maintain and read. Or what if the implementation details of `P1` and `F1` are not sufficiently established to write the bodies of `P1` and `F1` at the time `Main` is written? We would not be able to finish writing `Main`.

To avoid these problems, we should defer writing the bodies of `P1` and `F1`. However, we should still be able to write all of `Main` and compile it, so that the compiler can check for completeness and consistency. Fortunately, Ada has a mechanism by which the bodies of `P1` and `F1` can be removed from `Main` and implemented later, while still allowing `Main` to be written and compiled. This mechanism is called the subunit. Subunits are subprogram (or package or task) bodies that are separated from the declarative part of the program unit in which they are embedded and made into a separate compilation unit. A placeholder, called a "stub," is placed in the declarative part of the program unit to indicate where the subunit belongs. Thus, instead of placing subprogram bodies in `Main`, we can use stubs, which each consist of the subprogram specification, followed by the keywords **is separate**. The bodies of `P1` and `F1` can then each eventually be written as separately compiled units. This is shown in the following code (where the lines indicate separate compilation units):

```
procedure Main is

    -- constants, types, and variables for Main
    Flag: Boolean := True;

    procedure P1 (Item: in Boolean) is separate;  -- stub for P1
    -- can still reference Flag

    function F1 return Boolean is separate;        -- stub for F1
    -- can still reference Flag and P1

begin -- beginning of Main
    ...
    Flag := F1;
    P1 (Flag);
end Main;
```

---

```
separate (Main)
procedure P1 (Item: in Boolean) is
    -- constants, types, and variables for P1
begin
    -- executable statements for P1
end P1;
```

---

```
separate (Main)
function F1 return Boolean is
    -- constants, types, and variables for F1
begin
    -- executable statements for F1
end F1;
```

To help the compiler associate P1 and F1 with the parent unit, Main, a separate clause appears at the beginning of P1 and F1. This clause consists of the keyword **separate**, followed by the name of the parent unit, Main, enclosed in parentheses. No semicolon follows the parentheses.

Making P1 and F1 subunits does not change the behavior of the program. Subprograms P1 and F1 operate just as before and still have access to data defined in Main, such as the variable Flag. The only difference is that P1 and F1 can have their own **with** clause, since they are now separate compilation units:

```
with Whatever;    -- This clause only applies to P1
separate (Main)
procedure P1 (Item: in Boolean) is
    -- constants, types, and variables for P1
begin
    -- executable statements for P1
end P1;
```

The preceding **with** clause only applies to P1, not to Main or F1. Note that limiting the scope of the **with** clause to just P1 is only possible by making P1 a subunit.

As previously mentioned, subunits can reference items appearing above their body stub. For example, P1 and F1 can reference their parent's variable Flag. Subunits are thus dependent on their parent. This means that subunits must be compiled after their parent is compiled. If the parent is modified and recompiled, then all of the parent's subunits become candidates for recompilation. Fortunately, however, if a subunit's body is modified and recompiled, its parent does not need to be recompiled. Thus, the creation of subunits can significantly reduce the amount of recompilation needed when code is modified. (Compilation order and compilation dependencies will be discussed in detail in Chapter 9.)

**Ada 95 ▶**     Note that if neither subprograms P1 nor F1 need to reference variable Flag, then Flag should be placed at the end of the declarative part of Main to ensure that this does not mistakenly happen:

```
procedure P1 (Item: in Boolean) is separate;
function F1 return Boolean is separate;
-- Flag can no longer be referenced by P1 or F1
Flag: Boolean := True;
```

[In Ada 83, it is illegal to place a variable (or constant, type, or subtype) after the declaration of a subprogram.] By making Flag inaccessible to P1 and F1, the compiler can also generate more efficient code by storing Flag in a register instead of placing it in memory. (A register is used for storing temporary values that need to be referenced quickly.)

Also note that since F1 is declared after P1, F1 can call P1, but P1 cannot call F1. This is because a subprogram can only be called after its declaration has been elaborated. But what if P1 and F1 need to call each other? It seems that we are caught in a "chicken and egg" problem since each must be placed before the other. The solution is to place the specifications for P1 and F1 before their bodies (or body stubs):

```
procedure Main is

   Flag: Boolean := True;

   -- specifications for P1 and F1
   procedure P1 (Item: in Boolean); -- spec for P1
   function F1 return Boolean;       -- spec for F1

   -- bodies for P1 and F1 (in this case body stubs)
   procedure P1 (Item: in Boolean) is separate;
   function F1 return Boolean is separate;

begin -- beginning of Main
   ...
   Flag := F1;
   P1 (Flag);
end Main;
```

```
separate (Main)
procedure P1 (Item: in Boolean) is
   A: Boolean;
begin
   A := F1;          -- P1 invokes F1
   ...
end P1;
```

```
separate (Main)
function F1 return Boolean is
begin
   P1 (False);       -- F1 invokes P1
   ...
end F1;
```

Function F1 can call P1 as long as P1's specification appears before F1's body. Similarly, procedure P1 can call F1 as long as F1's specification appears before P1's body.

In the previous code, procedure Main is the parent of the subunits P1 and F1. A subunit can itself be a parent of other subunits. To place a subunit within another subunit, place the stub for the inner subunit in the declarative part of the outer subunit. For instance, the preceding subunit, P1, can contain a stub for another subunit, as follows:

```
separate (Main)
procedure P1 (Item: in Boolean) is
   Y: Integer;
   function F2 return Integer is separate; -- stub for F2
begin
   Y := F2;
```

```
      . . .
   end P1;
```

---

```
separate (Main.P1)
function F2 return Integer is
      -- constants, types, and variables for F2
begin
      -- executable statements for F2
end F2;
```

Note the **separate** clause that appears at the beginning of function F2: **separate** (Main.P1). This clause tells the compiler that F2 has the parent, P1, which in turn has the parent Main. The compiler must be given this complete family relationship.

## Subprogram Library Units

So far, we have only considered structures where subprograms, or their stubs, are placed in the declarative part of another program unit. There is another kind of structure, where the entire subprogram is compiled separately, becoming a library unit that can be accessed by other library units. The preceding nested subprogram F1, for instance, can be made into a library unit by being separately compiled without the **separate** clause. F1 can then be accessed by any other library unit that lists F1 in its **with** clause. The subprogram P1 can also be made into a library unit. This process is shown in the following example. Procedure Main, which is the last compilation unit listed, accesses P1 and F1 by simply listing P1 and F1 in its **with** clause:

```
procedure P1 (Item: in Boolean) is
      -- constants, types, and variables for P1
begin
      -- executable statements for P1
end P1;
```

---

```
function F1 return Boolean is
      -- constants, types, and variables for F1
begin
      -- executable statements for F1
end F1;
```

---

```
with P1, F1; -- makes P1 and F1 available to Main
                -- use clause cannot be employed
procedure Main is
      -- constants, types, and variables for Main
      Flag: Boolean := True;
begin
      . . .
      Flag := F1;
      P1 (Flag);
end Main;
```

Note that by making P1 and F1 library units, they can be accessed not only by procedure Main, but by any other library unit that mentions them in a **with** clause. (Of course, by making P1 and F1 library units instead of embedding them in Main, they can no longer reference items such as Flag that are defined in Main.) In general, subunits are preferred when the code should only be available to its parent because it is too specialized to be used by other program units. However, library units rather than subunits are preferred for general-purpose code that can be used by different library units or even reused by other programs.

Since procedure Main mentions P1 and F1 in its **with** clause and then calls P1 and F1, P1 and F1 must be compiled before Main is compiled. This compilation order is enforced by the Ada compilation system. Furthermore, if P1 or F1 is modified and recompiled, then Main needs to be recompiled. However, procedure Main can be modified and recompiled without requiring P1 or F1 to be recompiled. Thus, by making P1 and F1 library units instead of subunits, compilation dependencies between Main and the subprograms P1 and F1 are reversed. (In Chapter 9, we shall see that compilation dependencies can be further reduced by separately compiling the specifications and bodies of P1 and F1.)

Note that Main has a **with** clause but no **use** clause. It is illegal to mention a subprogram in a **use** clause. The **use** clause applies only to packages in order to make the internal resources of the package directly visible to the users. Subprograms, unlike packages, do not offer internal resources to users. So the **use** clause, even if allowed, would accomplish nothing.

## Overloading

As mentioned in previous chapters, the term overloading means that the same name denotes more than one entity. In Ada, entities that are subprograms, operators, and enumeration literals can be overloaded, as long as the compiler can determine from the context which particular overloaded entity is being referenced. In this chapter, we will further explore overloading.

Subprograms can be overloaded as long as they are not library units (units that can be listed in a **with** clause), and as long as the compiler can determine which particular overloaded subprogram is being invoked. Typically, overloaded subprograms are distinguished by having different parameter types or number of parameters. If the overloaded subprograms are functions, then the distinguishing characteristic could be the type of value being returned. Even differing formal parameter names can be used to distinguish one overloaded subprogram from another. Distinguishing one overloaded entity from another is called overload resolution. (Features such as parameter modes, which are not apparent in a subprogram call, are not considered to be distinguishing characteristics.) Consider, for instance, the following function, Minimum, which returns the smaller of two integer values:

```
function Minimum (X, Y: Integer) return Integer is
begin
   if X < Y then
      return X;
```

```
    else
        return Y;
    end if;
end Minimum;
```

Consider also a function that is needed to return the smaller of two real numbers. Because the processing in these two functions is the same, it makes sense to give this function the same name, Minimum, as the previous function:

```
function Minimum (X, Y: Float) return Float is
begin
    if X < Y then
        return X;
    else
        return Y;
    end if;
end Minimum;
```

The two preceding versions of Minimum cannot both be made into library units by being separately compiled, because library units cannot be overloaded. Every library unit must have a unique identifier. These two functions, however, may be embedded in the same program unit:

```
with Ada.Text_IO; use Ada.Text_IO;
procedure Overload is

    package Int_IO is new Integer_IO (Integer);
    package Real_IO is new Float_IO (Float);
    use Int_IO, Real_IO;

    function Minimum (X, Y: Integer) return Integer is
    begin
        if X < Y then
            return X;
        else
            return Y;
        end if;
    end Minimum;

    function Minimum (X, Y: Float) return Float is
    begin
        if X < Y then
            return X;
        else
            return Y;
        end if;
    end Minimum;

begin -- Overload
```

```
Put (Minimum (5, 2) );      -- outputs 2
Put (Minimum (3.6, 8.5) ); -- outputs 3.6

end Overload;
```

Ada determines which of the two overloaded `Minimum` functions is being invoked by examining their parameters. If `Minimum` is invoked with integer parameters, then the version of `Minimum` that compares integers is used. If `Minimum` is invoked with real parameters, then the version of `Minimum` that compares real numbers is used.

On rare occasions, overloaded subprograms cannot be distinguished, and the compiler cannot resolve the ambiguity. Consider, for example, the following declarations:

```
type Triangle is (Obtuse, Right, Acute);
type Person is (Obtuse, Normal, Acute);

function Sharper_Than_Most (T: Triangle) return Boolean;
function Sharper_Than_Most (P: Person) return Boolean;

Preferable: Boolean;
```

Given these declarations, consider the following function calls:

```
Preferable := Sharper_Than_Most (Right);    -- OK
Preferable := Sharper_Than_Most (Normal);   -- OK
Preferable := Sharper_Than_Most (Acute);    -- ambiguous
Preferable := Sharper_Than_Most (Obtuse);   -- ambiguous
```

There is no problem with the first and second function calls. In both calls, the `Sharper_Than_Most` function that is needed can be determined by examining the type of parameter. The third and fourth calls, however, are ambiguous, and the compiler has no way of resolving the ambiguity. In the third call, the compiler has no way of determining whether `Acute` refers to an `Acute` person or an `Acute` triangle. In the fourth call, the compiler has no way of determining whether `Obtuse` refers to an `Obtuse` person or an `Obtuse` triangle. Fortunately, such ambiguity can be resolved by qualifying `Acute` and `Obtuse`, that is, by explicitly stating their type:

```
Preferable := Sharper_Than_Most ( Triangle'(Acute) ); -- OK
Preferable := Sharper_Than_Most ( Person'(Obtuse) );  -- OK
```

Recall from Chapter 3 that a qualifier consists of the type or subtype name followed by a tick mark, `'`, followed by the literal enclosed in parentheses. `Triangle'(Acute)`, for instance, selects the enumeration literal `Acute` that is of type `Triangle`. Since two different formal parameters, `T` and `P`, are used by the functions `Sharper_Than_Most` in their declarations, the preceding ambiguities can also be resolved by specifying the formal parameter name with named notation:

```
Preferable := Sharper_Than_Most (T => Acute); -- OK
-- selects Acute triangle
```

In addition to overloading subprograms, we can overload special kinds of functions, called operators. Overloading operators, such as +, −, >, =, is not a new idea. Even the primordial language FORTRAN has, for instance, an overloaded addition operator. In FORTRAN, the addition operator that is used when one writes 2 + 3 is not the same as the addition operation that is used when one writes 2.4 + 3.1. FORTRAN, in other words, uses different addition operators, represented by the same plus symbol, for adding integers and for adding real numbers. Even though overloading operators is not a new idea, what is new is that in Ada, programmers can define overloaded operators.

Let us consider an example of a user-defined overloaded operator. In the following procedure, the user defines an addition operator—which can already be used to add integers and real numbers—to add two matrices:

```
procedure Overload_Operator is

    type Matrix_Type is array (1..2, 1..3) of Integer;
    X, Y, Z : Matrix_Type;

    --user-defined addition operator for adding two matrices
    function "+" (A, B: Matrix_Type) return Matrix_Type is
        C: Matrix_Type;
    begin
        for J in Matrix_Type'Range (1) loop
            for K in Matrix_Type'Range (2) loop
                C (J, K) := A (J, K) + B (J, K);
            end loop;
        end loop;
        return C;
    end "+";

begin -- Overload_Operator

    X := ( (1, 2, 3),
           (4, 5, 6) );

    Y := ( (7, 5, 4),
           (1, 0, 2) );

    Z := X + Y;   -- yields    (  ( 8, 7, 7),
                  --              ( 5, 5, 8) );

end Overload_Operator;
```

The overloaded addition operator is a special kind of function. In the function specification, the function identifier is in quotes: "+". The identifier is then followed by the parameter definitions, just as if this were a regular function.

Overloading the addition operator makes sense when matrix addition is needed, because two matrices can then be added using the same familiar notation that is used in mathematics:

```
Z := X + Y;
```

We could also add two matrices by defining a function called `Add_Matrices` instead of overloading the addition operator. However, we would have to use the less natural notation:

```
Z := Add_Matrices (X, Y);
```

The difference between the two preceding notations is not simply a difference between the function identifiers `"+"` and `Add_Matrices`. There is also a difference between the two kinds of notation: infix notation and prefix notation. Infix notation, like `X + Y`, has one operand (object that is being operated on), `X`, to the left of the addition operator and another operand, `Y`, to the right of it.

Using infix notation to invoke the addition operator is optional. We can invoke the addition operator using the regular prefix notation for invoking functions:

```
Z := "+" (X, Y);
```

In prefix notation, the identifier, "+", appears first, followed by a list of parameters in parentheses. Note that the addition operator appears in quotes. As we can see, this prefix notation is not as readable as the familiar infix notation.

**Ada 95 ▶**     In the preceding example, the addition operator was overloaded. In Ada, any of the arithmetic, logical, or relational operators can be overloaded: **\*\*, \*, /, +, –, mod, rem, abs, not, and, or, xor, =, <, <=, >, >=,** and **&.** Note that this list excludes the assignment operator (:=), the short-circuit logical operators (**or else** and **and then**), and the inequality operator (/=). The assignment operator can never be overloaded, although a form of user-defined assignment is provided through "controlled types," which are covered in Chapter 13. The short-circuit logical operators can never be overloaded. The inequality operator, /=, cannot be overloaded when the corresponding "=" operator returns a `Boolean` type. In this case, the inequality operator is implicitly provided. However, if an overloaded equality operator is defined that returns a non-`Boolean` type, then a corresponding inequality operator is not automatically provided and may be defined explicitly. [In Ada 83, the equality operator had to return a `Boolean` type, and could only be overloaded for limited private types (to be discussed in Chapter 7). The inequality operator could never be explicitly overloaded.]

**Ada 95 ▶**     The following code defines the overloaded operators "=" and "/=" for the type `Three_Valued_Logic`:

```
type Three_Valued_Logic is (False, True, Unknown);

function "=" (Left, Right: in Three_Valued_Logic)
    return Three_Valued_Logic is
begin
```

```
   if Three_Valued_Logic'Pos (Left) =
      Three_Valued_Logic'Pos (Unknown) or else
      Three_Valued_Logic'Pos (Right) =
      Three_Valued_Logic'Pos (Unknown) then
      return Unknown;
   elsif
      Three_Valued_Logic'Pos (Left) =
      Three_Valued_Logic'Pos (Right) then
      return True;
   else
      return False;
   end if;
end "=";

function "/=" (Left, Right: in Three_Valued_Logic)
   return Three_Valued_Logic is
begin
   if Three_Valued_Logic'Pos (Left) =
      Three_Valued_Logic'Pos (Unknown) or else
      Three_Valued_Logic'Pos (Right) =
      Three_Valued_Logic'Pos (Unknown) then
      return Unknown;
   elsif
      Three_Valued_Logic'Pos (Left) =
      Three_Valued_Logic'Pos (Right) then
      return False;
   else
      return True;
   end if;
end "/=";
```

At first sight, this code seems unnecessarily complex. For example, instead of the expression

```
Three_Valued_Logic'Pos (Left) = Three_Valued_Logic'Pos (Unknown)
```

why not use this simpler expression?

```
Left = Unknown
```

The reason is that the "=" operator in the simper expression would result in a recursive call. That is, "=" would be calling itself over and over since Left, Right, and Unknown belong to the same type, Three_Valued_Logic, as the parameter type of "=". (If this is confusing, do not despair; recursion will be covered later in this chapter.)

Another point to notice is that if the "/=" operator is not explicitly defined, it would not be implicitly provided. The "/=" is only implicitly provided when its associated "=" returns a value of type Boolean. Finally, note that since these overloaded "=" and "/=" operators do not return Standard.Boolean, statements such as the following are illegal:

```
declare
   type Three_Valued_Logic is (False, True, Unknown);
   Value_Converges: Three_Valued_Logic := True;
begin
   if Value_Converges then ...    -- illegal;
        -- not of type Standard.Boolean
end;
```

The values `True` and `False` that are contained in type `Three_Valued_Logic` are distinct from the `True` and `False` contained in the predefined type `Boolean`.

For another example of overloaded equality and inequality operators, Exercise 24 uses an overloaded `"="` operator for componentwise vector comparisons that return a `Boolean` vector.

There are four restrictions that apply to overloaded operators. First, the number of parameters for a user-defined overloaded operator must be the same as for the standard operator, which is defined in the package `Standard`. For example, the relational operator, `>`, is defined in the package `Standard` as a binary operator—one that operates on two objects. Thus, `>` can only be overloaded with a user-defined operator that has two parameters.

Two operators exist, `+` and `−`, that programmers can overload with operators that have either one or two parameters. A glance at the package `Standard` shows why this is the case. In the package `Standard`, the operator `+` is overloaded four times, as follows:

```
function "+" (Left, Right: Integer'Base) return Integer'Base;
function "+" (Left, Right: Float) return Float;

function "+" (Right: Integer'Base) return Integer'Base;
function "+" (Right: Float) return Float;
```

As we can see, the first two overloaded `"+"` operators are binary operators that operate on `Integer` and `Float` numbers, respectively. The second two overloaded `"+"` operators are unary operators that operate on `Integer` and `Float` numbers, respectively. As a binary operator, `"+"` is an addition operator that adds two numbers, such as 7 + 2. As a unary operator, `"+"` is a positive operator that is used to indicate a positive number, such as +4. The operator `"−"` can similarly be used as either a binary subtraction operator or a unary negative operator.

Consider the following overloaded function specifications:

```
function "+" (A: Matrix_Type) return Matrix_Type;      -- OK
function "+" (A, B: Matrix_Type) return Matrix_Type;  -- OK
function "+" (A, B, C: Matrix_Type) return Matrix_Type;
     -- illegal
```

The first overloaded `"+"` is a unary operator because it has only one parameter, A. This specification is legal because the package `Standard` contains a unary `"+"` operator. The second overloaded `"+"` is a binary operator, because it has two parameters: A and B. This specification is also legal. The third overloaded `"+"`, however, has three parameters. This specification is illegal because there is no corresponding "+" operator in the package `Standard` that has three parameters.

The second restriction that applies to overloaded operators is that they cannot be library units. Overloaded operators must always be embedded in another unit such as a procedure, function, or package.

The third restriction is that a procedure identifier cannot be an operator; only a function identifier can be an operator.

The fourth restriction is that overloaded operators cannot have default parameter values. This makes sense, since infix notation requires that both operands be provided.

As we have seen in this chapter and previous chapters, subprograms, operators, and enumeration literals can be overloaded. Other entities, such as objects and types, cannot be overloaded. In the following code, for example, `Diamonds` is the name of an enumeration literal of type `Suit` as well as a `Boolean` variable. An enumeration literal cannot be overloaded with a variable, and the error is caught at compile time.

```
type Suit is (Clubs, Diamonds, Hearts, Spades);
Diamonds: Boolean; -- illegal; overloading not allowed
```

**Ada 95 ▶**   As mentioned in the second restriction on overloaded operators, subprograms can be overloaded, but not as library units. Thus, one cannot compile two subprograms with the same name. But what about subunits? Can multiple subunits have the same name? The answer is that subunits can have the same name as long as their expanded names are unique. However, this is not considered overloading. For example, the following two subunits are considered to have unique expanded names, `Parent_1.P` and `Parent_2.P`:

```
separate (Parent_1)
procedure P is ...

separate (Parent_2)      -- OK, expanded names Parent_1.P and
procedure P is ...       -- Parent_2.P are unique
```

(In Ada 83, subunits must have unique names; it is not enough that their expanded names are unique.)

## Returning Composite Values

The addition operator shown in the previous section returns an array aggregate. In addition to operators, regular functions and procedures can also return composite values that are array or record aggregates. The following procedure declares a function, `Array_Of_Abs`, that returns an array aggregate:

```
procedure Return_Composite is

    type Vector is array (Positive range <>) of Integer;
    Row_Of_4, V4: Vector (1..4);
    Row_Of_6, V6: Vector (1..6);
    Int: Integer;
```

```
                  --overloaded unary operator that returns a composite result
                  function Array_Of_Abs (V: Vector) return Vector is
                     Result: Vector (V'Range);
                  begin
                     for J in V'Range loop
                        Result (J) := abs V(J);
                     end loop;
                     return Result;
                  end Array_Of_Abs;

               begin -- Return_Composite

                  V4 := (-31, -12, 39, -9);
                  V6 := (26, -83, -1, 0, 73, -122);

                  Row_Of_4 := Array_Of_Abs (V4);    -- (31, 12, 39, 9)
                  Row_Of_6 := Array_Of_Abs (V6);    -- (26, 83, 1, 0, 73, 122)
                  Int := Array_Of_Abs (V4) (1);     -- 31
                       . . .
               end Return_Composite;
```

In this example, `Array_Of_Abs(V4)` returns the array aggregate `(31, 12, 39, 9)`, and `Array_Of_Abs(V6)` returns the array aggregate `(26, 83, 1, 0, 73, 122)`.

Note that the formal parameter of the function `Array_Of_Abs` is an unconstrained array. By using a formal parameter that is an unconstrained array, the function can accept arrays of the type `Vector` that are of any length. Of course, when the function is invoked, the array object being passed in as an actual parameter must be constrained (its length must be set). This is because every array object must be declared with an index constraint. However, a formal parameter may be specified as an unconstrained array type. The formal parameter, `V`, then acquires the index range of the actual array parameter. For example, when `Array_Of_Abs` is invoked with the parameter `V6`, because `V6'Range` is `1..6`, `V'Range` is also `1..6`.

Also note the expression `Array_Of_Abs(V4)(1)`. This expression immediately selects the first component of the array aggregate returned by the function `Array_Of_Abs`. In other words, the expression returns the first component of the aggregate `(31, 12, 39, 9)`, which is `31`.

## Recursive Subprograms

A recursive subprogram is a subprogram that calls itself. Ada supports both recursive procedures and recursive functions. In order to better understand this concept, let us consider a recursive definition, that is, a definition that defines a word in terms of itself. A recursive definition does not have to be "viciously" circular any more than a recursive subprogram has to keep calling itself forever. A condition may be reached that ends the cycle.

Recursive definitions are sometimes used in mathematics. For instance, a factorial function is often recursively defined as follows:

N! is equal to 1 if N = 1
N! is equal to N * (N–1)! if N > 1

For those who have forgotten about factorial numbers, consider this example: 9! is equal to 9 * 8 * 7 * 6 * 5 * 4 * 3 * 2 * 1, which equals 362,880. In general, for any positive integer N, N! is equal to N * (N-1) * (N-2) * (N-3), and so on, until the last term becomes 1.

The behavior of the preceding recursive definition can be illustrated, as follows:

```
9!  =  9 * 8!
    =  9 * 8 * 7!
    =  9 * 8 * 7 * 6!
    =  9 * 8 * 7 * 6 * 5!
    =  9 * 8 * 7 * 6 * 5 * 4!
    =  9 * 8 * 7 * 6 * 5 * 4 * 3!
    =  9 * 8 * 7 * 6 * 5 * 4 * 3 * 2!
    =  9 * 8 * 7 * 6 * 5 * 4 * 3 * 2 * 1!
    =  9 * 8 * 7 * 6 * 5 * 4 * 3 * 2 * 1
```

Each line represents a "cycle" through the recursive definition. We begin with N being set to 9. While N > 1, we keep following the second condition of our recursive definition, replacing N! with N * (N-1)!. Thus, 9! gets replaced with 9 * (9-1)!, which is 9 * 8!. In the second line, 8! gets replaced with 8 * (8-1)!, which is 8 * 7!, and so on, until we finally reach 1!. When N becomes 1, we follow the first condition of our recursive definition, and replace 1! with 1. Our processing now ends, since a factorial number is no longer defined in terms of other factorial numbers.

To illustrate recursive subprograms, we will first write a factorial function that is iterative (uses a loop):

```ada
with Ada.Text_IO; use Ada.Text_IO;
procedure Iterative is
   package Int_IO is new Integer_IO (Positive);
   use Int_IO;

   function Factorial (N: Positive) return Positive is
      Fact: Positive := 1;
   begin
      for J in reverse 1 .. N loop
         Fact := Fact * J;
      end loop;
      return Fact;
   end Factorial;

begin -- Iterative
   Put (Factorial (3));      -- outputs 6
end Iterative;
```

Now let us see how this same function looks when it is written recursively:

```
with Ada.Text_IO; use Ada.Text_IO;
procedure Recursive is
    package Positive_IO is new Integer_IO (Positive);
    use Positive_IO;

    function Factorial (N: Positive) return Positive is
    begin
        if N = 1 then
            return 1;
        else
            return N * Factorial (N-1);
        end if;
    end Factorial;

begin -- Recursive
    Put (Factorial (3)); -- outputs 6
end Recursive;
```

The main difference between the iterative and recursive versions of the function Factorial is that the iterative function uses a loop, and the recursive function "cycles" by repeatedly calling itself. Note that the recursive version closely follows the recursive mathematical definition of factorial.

Here is how the recursive Factorial function works. The procedure Recursive invokes Factorial with a parameter value of 3. Factorial(3) needs to return the result 3 * Factorial(2). However, this result cannot be returned until Factorial(2) is evaluated. Factorial(2) needs to return the result 2 * Factorial(1). Again, this result cannot be returned until Factorial(1) is evaluated. Factorial(1) finally resolves to 1. So far, this function has been "winding itself up," calling itself again and again. Now that Factorial(1) is ready to return the result 1, we can start to "unwind." The result 1 is returned to Factorial (1); then the result 2 * Factorial(1), or 2, is returned to Factorial(2); then the final result 3 * Factorial(2), or 6, is returned to our original invocation, Factorial(3). This winding and unwinding is shown in Figure 6.1. The winding is represented by the arrows pointing downward. The unwinding is represented by the arrows pointing up and to the left.

## Inlined Subprograms

As we have seen, subprograms are a very important language feature that should be used frequently to improve the readability of programs and to reduce the amount of redundant code. Numerous subprogram calls, however, may slow down a program's execution speed. In fact, for very small subprograms, more time may be taken setting up the subprogram call than executing the subprogram body. For time-critical applications, this slowdown might be unacceptable. **Pragma** Inline is a possible solution. **Pragma** Inline is just one of the many pragmas

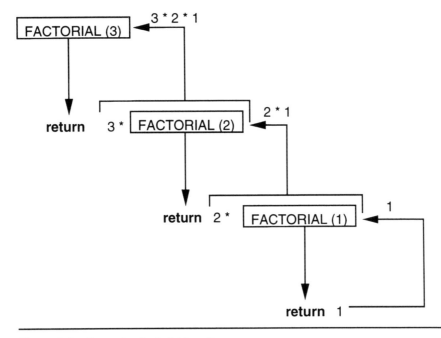

**Figure 6.1**   Recursive factorial function.

available in Ada. Pragmas allow programmers to convey requests to the compiler. **Pragma** `Inline` instructs the compiler to expand the subprogram's body inline at each point the subprogram is called. This has the advantage of reducing the overhead associated with calling a subprogram.

**Pragma** `Inline` takes one or more parameters that specify the names of the subprograms to be inlined:

```
pragma Inline (A, B, C, D); -- inline subprograms A, B, C, and D
```

Note that only the subprogram names are listed, not their parameter definitions.

Although inlining subprograms often results in faster code, there are two disadvantages: expanded code size and additional compilation dependencies. The size of executable code is increased since the executable code for a subprogram's body is duplicated each place the subprogram is called. Additional compilation dependencies are created since a subprogram cannot be inlined unless its body has already been compiled. The following procedure, for example, cannot be compiled unless the subunit for `P1` has been compiled:

```
procedure Main is
   procedure P1;
   pragma Inline (P1);
   procedure P1 is separate;
begin
```

```
      P1; -- Calls to P1 cannot be inlined when the
          -- body of P1 is not yet available.
   end Main;
```

Normally, Main can be compiled without the subunit P1. Main's compilation dependency on P1 is created since the inlined subprogram call to P1 cannot be compiled unless the compiled code for P1's body is available for inlining. This compilation dependency means that if P1's body is modified, then Main has to be recompiled.

## Renamed Subprograms

Recall from Chapter 5 that expressions can be renamed. In Ada, subprograms can also be renamed. Renaming a subprogram does not bring a new subprogram into existence or replace one name with another. Renaming merely provides an alternative name. A subprogram can be renamed to any valid Ada identifier. For example, Text_IO.Put can be renamed to Print:

```
   procedure Print (Value: in Character) renames Text_IO.Put;
```

Notice that the formal parameter name of the renamed subprogram can differ from the formal parameter name of the original subprogram. In particular, the formal parameter name Value is used instead of Put's formal parameter name, Item. A renamed subprogram can also provide a new default value for an **in** parameter.

Some attributes, such as Succ and Pred, are defined as functions and can therefore be renamed as functions:

```
   function Next_Character (Item: in Character) return Character
      renames Character'Succ;
```

Even enumeration literals can be renamed as functions:

```
   type Rainbow is (Red, Orange, Yellow, Green, Blue, Indigo, Violet);
   function Rot return Rainbow renames Red;
   function Rouge return Rainbow renames Red;
```

The value Red can now also be referenced with the name Rot or Rouge. (The reason that an enumeration literal can be renamed as a function is because Ada specifies that enumeration literals be implemented as functions.)

As we will see throughout this book, many other entities besides subprograms can be renamed, and renaming has many different uses.

As mentioned in the beginning of this chapter, blocks, procedures, and functions are units of code that contain a declarative part, a statement part, and optional exception handlers. There are other such units of code, like packages. Packages are discussed in the next chapter.

## EXERCISES

1. Write a function that returns the square root of a real number, X. As a first approximation, use X/2. Keep applying the following formula until the difference between two consecutive approximations is less than 0.001.

```
Next_Approximation =
    0.5 (Last_Approximation + X / Last_Approximation)
```

2. Write an Ada program that illustrates the "twin paradox" that is a consequence of Einstein's Theory of Special Relativity. Consider two twins, where one gets into a spaceship and travels near the speed of light, while the other stays on earth. Upon returning to earth, the traveler will be younger than the twin who stayed behind.

   This "time dilation" is calculated with the following formula:

$$A = T \times \sqrt{1 - \left[\frac{P}{100}\right]^2}$$

where   A is the number of years that the traveler will age
        P is the percent of the speed of light that the traveler will be traveling
        T is the number of earth-years that the trip takes

Have your Ada program prompt the user to enter the percent of the speed of light, P, that the traveler will travel, and the number of Earth years, T, that the traveler will be traveling. Have the program then calculate and output the number of years, A, that the traveler will age during the trip. You may use the square root function you developed for Exercise 1.

   If the traveler goes 99.999% the speed of light, how much older will the traveler be upon returning to earth 100 earth-years later? Try other values to see how little the traveler ages compared to the time that has elapsed on earth. Make sure, however, that the traveler does not exceed the "cosmic speed limit" of light.

3. Consider the following code:

```
Outer:
declare
    X : Integer := 9;
    Y : Integer := 2;
begin -- Outer
    Inner:
    declare
        X : Integer := Y;
        Y : Integer := 5;
    begin -- Inner
        Put (X);
        Put (Y);
        Put (Outer.X);
```

```
                    Put (Outer.Y);
                end Inner;
                Put (X);
                Put (Y);
            end Outer;
```

Write the six values that the code will output, in the order in which the values will be output: ____ ____ ____ ____ ____ ____

4. Consider the following program:

```
with Ada.Text_IO; use Ada.Text_IO;
procedure Outer is
    package Int_IO is new Integer_IO (Integer);
    use Int_IO;
    A, B, C, D: Integer := 1;

    procedure Middle is
        B, C: Integer := 2;

        procedure Inner is
            C, D: Integer := 3;
        begin
            Put (A);
            Put (B);
            Put (C);
            Put (D);
            Put (Outer.C);
            Put (Middle.C);
            Put (Middle.B);
        end Inner;

    begin -- Middle
        Inner;
        Put (A);
        Put (B);
        Put (C);
        Put (D);
        Put (Outer.B);
    end Middle;

begin -- Outer
    Middle;
    Put (A);
    Put (B);
    Put (C);
    Put (D);
end Outer;
```

What will this program output? Test your answer by running the program.

5. Assume that you are given the following declarations:

```
type Bean_Type is (Colombian, Kenyan, Jamaican, Costa_Rican);
type Roast_Type is (Light, Medium, Dark);
procedure Coffee (   Bean:  in Bean_Type  := Colombian;
                     Roast: in Roast_Type := Dark       );
```

What values do each of the following procedure invocations assign to the parameters Bean and Roast?

a. `Coffee ( Roast => Light);`
   **Bean** is set to _____
   **Roast** is set to _____

b. `Coffee;`
   **Bean** is set to _____
   **Roast** is set to _____

c. `Coffee (Costa_Rican, Roast => Medium);`
   **Bean** is set to _____
   **Roast** is set to _____

d. `Coffee (Roast => Medium, Bean => Jamaican);`
   **Bean** is set to _____
   **Roast** is set to _____

6. Consider this procedure specification:

```
procedure Check (   First: in Integer;
                    Second: in out Integer;
                    Result: out Boolean );
```

Consider these declarations:

```
X : Integer := 1;
Y : constant Integer := 3;
B : Boolean;
```

Which six of the following calls to Check are illegal, and why?

a. `Check;`
b. `Check (9, X, B);`
c. `Check (Y, X, B);`
d. `Check (X, Y, B);`
e. `Check (X, 2, B);`
f. `Check (2, X, True);`
g. `Check (9, X, Result => True);`
h. `Check (First := 7, Second := X,  Result := B);`
i. `Check (First => 7, Result => B,  Second => X);`

7. Which of the following statements are illegal, and why?

```
procedure Demo ( In_Param     : in Integer;
                 Out_Param    : out Integer;
                 In_Out_Param : in out Integer ) is
begin
   Out_Param := 4;
   In_Param := 4;
   if Out_Param /= In_Param then
```

```
        Out_Param := Out_Param - In_Param;
    elsif In_Param = In_Out_Param then
        In_Param := In_Param + 1;
    else
        In_Out_Param := In_Out_Param - In_Param;
    end if;
end Demo;
```

8. Simplify the following code by introducing calls to function `Max` that return the larger of two values:

   a.
   ```
   if X1 > Y1 then
       R1 := X1;
   else
       R1 := Y1;
   end if;
   ...
   if X2 > Y2 then
       R2 := X2;
   else
       R2 := Y2;
   end if;
   ...
   if X3 > Y3 then
       R3 := X3;
   else
       R3 := Y3;
   end if;
   ```

   b.
   ```
   if X > Y then
       if Z > X then
           Result := Z;
       else
           Result := X;
       end if;
   else -- Y >= X
       if Z > Y then
           Result := Z;
       else
           Result := Y;
       end if;
   end if;
   ```

9. Write a procedure that outputs a specified number of blanks to the terminal.

10. Write a function that converts lowercase letters to uppercase letters. Write a main program that uses this function to convert lowercase letters entered from the keyboard into uppercase letters. You may wish to use the `Is_Upper` function presented in this chapter.

**11.** Use the function written for Exercise 10 to write a procedure that converts a string of characters to all uppercase values.

**12.** When the following recursive Ada procedure is invoked with `Recursion (4)`, what values will be output? _____

```
procedure Recursion (P: in Positive) is
begin
    if P = 1 then
        return;
    else
        Put (P);
        Recursion (P - 1);
    end if;
    Put (P);
end Recursion;
```

**13.** Write overloaded functions, "*", that allow a value of type `Integer` to be multiplied by type `Float` and vice versa. The value returned by such mixed multiplication is type `Float`.

**14. a.** Write an overloaded function "+" that adds two complex numbers. Define your complex number as a record:

```
type Complex_Number is
    record
        Real      : Float;
        Imaginary : Float;
    end record;
```

**b.** Embed the overloaded addition operator in the declarative part of a procedure. Have this procedure use the overloaded addition operator to calculate and output the sum of complex numbers A and B, where A `:= (7.9, 6.5)` and B `:= (-5.2, 1.9)`.

**15.** Write a function that, given a number from 1 to 12, returns the name of the month corresponding to that position.

**16.** Which three of the following four specifications are illegal, and why are they illegal?

**a.** `function Square_Root ( Value: in Float;`
`                            Imaginary: out Boolean)`
`                            return Float;`

**b.** `-- assume types Months_Of_Year and Days_In_Month`
`-- are visible`
`procedure Days_In_Month`
`    ( Month: in Months_Of_Year   := January;`
`        Days:   out   Days_In_Month := 31 );`

**c.** `function Get_Response return Boolean;`

**d.** -- assume type Complex is visible

```
procedure ">" (Left, Right: in Complex;
                Result: out Boolean);
```

17. Explain the problem with the following code. Will the compiler necessarily detect this problem?

```
procedure Discriminant (   A, B, C:         in Float;
                           Discrim:         out Float;
                           Real_Solution:   out Boolean ) is
   Answer: Float;
begin
   Answer := B ** 2 - 4 * A * C;
   if Answer >= 0 then
      Discrim := Answer;
      Real_Solution := True;
   else
      Real_Solution := False;
   end if;
end Discriminant;
```

18. Write a procedure, Sum_Of_Abs, that takes from 2 to 6 integer values and outputs the sum of their absolute values. For example, Sum_Of_Abs (-2, 3) returns 5, and Sum_Of_Abs (2, -3, 4, -5, 6, -1) returns 21. (Hint: Use default parameter values for the last four parameters.)

19. When a rocket is launched upward, how high it goes depends on its height and speed at "burnout," the moment at which its propellant is used up. A formula for this is

$$h = a + r^2 / 20.$$

where h is how high the rocket goes, a is its height at burnout, and r is its speed at burnout.

Write a program to determine how high a rocket goes if it is 3421.12 meters high at burnout and traveling at a speed of 132.11 meters per second.

20. Write a recursive function, F(N), that calculates the Nth element in the sequence of numbers: 1, 5, 9, 13, 17, ... Note that this sequence begins with 1 and each successive number is 4 more than its predecessor. Here is the recursive definition for this sequence:

F(N) is equal to 1         if N = 1
F(N) is equal to 4 + F(N-1)    if N > 1

Thus, F(1) evaluates to 1; F(2) evaluates to 4 + F(1), which equals 5; F(3) evaluates to 4 + F(2), which equals 9; and so on.

21. Write a recursive function, F(N), that calculates the Nth element in the sequence of numbers: 3, 5, 9, 17, 33, ... Note that this sequence begins with 3 and each successive number is 1 less than twice its predecessor. Here is the recursive definition for this sequence:

F(N) is equal to 3                     if N = 1
F(N) is equal to 2 * F(N-1) - 1        if N > 1

Thus, F(1) evaluates to 3; F(2) evaluates to 2 * F(1) - 1, which equals 5; F(3) evaluates to 2 * F(2) - 1, which equals 9; and so on.

22. In the `Return_Composite` procedure presented in the "Returning Composite Values" section of this chapter, replace the `Array_Of_Abs` function with an overloaded "+" defined as an unary operator. Be careful rewriting `Array_Of_Abs (V4) (1)`. This expression becomes "+" `(V4) (1)`, not + `V4 (1)`. Since the component selection has precedence over the "+" operator, +V4 `(1)` is the same as `Standard. "+" (V4 (1) )`, which is + (-31) or -31.

23. How does the output of the following procedure differ when parameters are passed by copy or by reference?

```
with Ada.Text_IO; use Ada.Text_IO;
procedure Main is
    type Record_Type is
        record
            Field: Integer := 0;
        end record;
    Main_Record: Record_Type;
    package Int_IO is new Integer_IO (Integer);
    use Int_IO;
    procedure Inner (Inner_Record: in out Record_Type) is
    begin
        Inner_Record.Field := 1;
        Put (Main_Record.Field);
    end Inner;
begin
    Put (Main_Record.Field);
    Inner (Main_Record);
    Put (Main_Record.Field);
end Main;
```

24. Define a componentwise overloaded "=" and "/=" operator for some integer array type that returns an array of `Boolean`s. Separately overload the inequality operator. For example, if the integer array A has the value (1, 3, 8, 2) and B has the value (3, 3, 9, 2), then A = B yields (False, True, False, True) and A /= B yields (True, False, True, False).

# 7

# Packages

$P$ackages are an essential part of Ada because they determine the structure of Ada programs. The modules that make up an Ada program typically consist of a parameterless main procedure plus many packages (or generic packages). The interfaces between these packages embody the design and structure of the Ada program. The bodies of these packages contain the implementation of the program. Packages are also an essential part of Ada because they provide the primary mechanism for "hiding" implementation details from the users of the package.

In their simplest form, packages are used to bundle together related resources that provide users with a well-defined service. These resources can consist of functions; procedures; other packages; and declarations of constants, variables, types, subtypes, and so on. For example, the predefined `Ada.Text_IO` package provides input and output services through procedures such as `Put` and `Get` and through nested generic packages such as `Integer_IO`.

**Ada 95 ▶** The math package `Elementary_Functions` provides trigonometric functions such as `Sin` and `Cos`. Package `Elementary_Functions` is a child package of `Numerics`, which, in turn, is a child package of `Ada`. Besides predefined packages such as `Ada.Text_IO` and `Elementary_Functions`, programmers may also write their own packages. For instance, a graphics package might be written that allows users to draw different shapes. Once such general-purpose packages are written, their services are easily made available to any program unit.

This chapter begins with a discussion of package specifications and package bodies. The division of packages into a specification and body has certain implications for software design. These implications are explored. Next is a detailed examination of the **with** clause and the **use** clause, followed by a discussion of when to employ the **use** clause. Embedded packages are then presented. The chapter concludes with an exploration of two kinds of types that may only appear in package specifications: private types and limited private types.

## PACKAGE SPECIFICATIONS AND BODIES

Packages have two parts—a specification and a body. The specification contains the visible interface to the package. The package body contains the hidden implementation. This division between interface and implementation is analogous to hardware. Consider, for example, that ubiquitous piece of hardware, the television. To use a television, only its user interface needs to be understood. This interface includes the power button, volume control, and channel selector. Users of the television do not need to understand its inner workings. The inner workings only need to be understood by those building or fixing televisions. Therefore, the inner workings are placed inside the television where they are hidden from viewers. Similarly, to use a package, only its user interface (defined in its specification) needs to be understood. Users of the package do not need to understand its inner workings any more than users of a television need to understand how signals are converted into images on the screen. The package's inner workings only need to be understood by those developing or maintaining the package. Therefore, the inner workings are placed inside the package body, where they are hidden from the package users.

Continuing with this television analogy, the inner workings of a television can be fixed, enhanced, or replaced without affecting how viewers watch television. Similarly, a package body can be fixed, enhanced, or replaced without affecting how clients use the package. In fact, when a package body is modified and recompiled, not only do existing clients not have to modify their code to accommodate the changes, they do not even have to recompile their code. All they eventually need to do is relink the program. Relinking is required to generate an executable image reflecting the updated package body.

Users of a package, therefore, only form a dependency on the package specification, not the body. Only when the specification changes may users be required to modify and recompile their code. The body of the package can be modified with full assurance that users are not impacted. This is typically not the case with other languages, where an innocuous change to the implementation can unexpectedly have a massive impact on users.

Package specifications and bodies have the following form:

```
-- package specification
package package name is
   visible declarations
end package name;

-- package body
package body package name is
   hidden declarations
begin -- initialization
   statements
end package name;
```

The package specification begins with the keyword **package**, followed by the package name and the keyword **is**. Next comes the declarations, which may include definitions of constants, variables, types, subtypes, and subprogram specifications. The package specification ends with the keyword **end**, followed optionally by the package name.

The package body begins with the keywords **package body**, followed by the package name and the keyword **is**. Next comes the declarative part of the body. As with package specifications, the declarative part of a package body may include definitions of constants, variables, types, subtypes, and subprogram specifications. Unlike package specifications, the declarative part of a package body may also contain subprogram bodies. Following the declarative part of the package body is the keyword **begin**, the executable statement part (in a package, usually referred to as the initialization part), and the keyword **end**, optionally followed by the package name.

As alluded to with the television analogy, there are two critical distinctions between a package specification and a package body. One critical distinction is that the specification is the visible part of a package and the body is the hidden part. By "visible" we mean accessible. Items in the specification can be accessed by the package users as well as by the package body. By "hidden" we mean inaccessible, not out of sight. Users of the package might be able to view a package body, but since items in the body are inaccessible, cannot base their code on what is viewed. The other critical distinction is that the package specification contains the interface to the package resources, whereas the package body contains the underlying implementation of these resources. The specification contains everything that the user needs to know: the resources the package has to offer and how to use these resources. The body contains the underlying implementation that does not concern the user. To use the resources of a package, one does not have to know how the package works.

Although a package usually consists of a specification and a body, the following user-defined package consists of only a specification:

```
package Houses is -- package consisting of a specification
   type Styles is ( Queen_Anne, Gothic, Craftman,
       Prairie_Style, English_Tudor, Mediterranean,
       French_Norman, Spanish_Colonial, Art_Deco, High_Tech,
       Streamline_Moderne);
end Houses;
```

**Ada 95 ▶** Package Houses is as simple as a package can get; it just contains a declaration of an enumeration type. Since the enumeration type is complete and does not require any underlying implementation to be specified, no package body is allowed. (If a package body is, nevertheless, desired, then **pragma** Elaborate_Body must be placed in the package specification and a body must then be provided.)

Once package Houses is written, it may either be compiled independently or as part of a larger program unit, in which it is embedded. Packages that are separately compiled become library units, which can be referenced by other program units. Embedded packages, however, have more limited use, because they are only available to the unit in which they are embedded. (This is not true, however, for packages embedded within a package specification.) Until the discussion of embedded packages later in this chapter, we will assume that all packages presented are library units. This is the usual case, since the benefits of packages may be fully exploited when they are library units.

After package Houses is compiled as a library unit, its resources become available to other program units. Other program units can reference these resources by using a **with** clause and optionally a **use** clause:

```
with Ada.Text_IO, Houses; use Ada.Text_IO, Houses;
procedure Taste is
   -- Styles and High_Tech imported from package Houses
   package House_IO is new Enumeration_IO (Styles);
   use House_IO;
   House: Styles;
begin
   Get (House);
   if House = High_Tech then
      Put_Line ("Remember that God is in the details");
   end if;
end Taste;
```

The **with** clause, optionally followed by the **use** clause, is known as the context specification. The context specification defines the environment of a program unit. The environment consists of all the library units available to the program unit.

The **with** clause consists of the keyword **with**, followed by a list of program units. When the **with** clause is encountered, the Ada library is searched for the listed program units. In our example, the program units consist of the packages Ada.Text_IO and Houses. When these packages are found in the Ada library, their resources are made available to procedure Taste. Thus, unlike items appearing in subprograms that can only be used locally, items appearing in a package specification can be exported to clients of the package.

Whereas the **with** clause makes these resources available, the **use** clause makes these resources directly visible. By directly visible, we mean that a resource, such as the enumeration type Styles, can be referenced simply by using its name, Styles. If we omit the **use** clause, resources such as Styles can only be referenced using dot notation: Houses.Styles. This dot notation tells the compiler that Styles is found in the package Houses. (As we will see later in this chapter, if the **use** clause is omitted, even items such as the equality operator must be referenced using dot notation.)

Now that we have seen an example of a package specification, let us examine a package that has a body as well as a specification. The following package contains resources to calculate the areas of circles, rectangles, and triangles. Since the package specification contains the specifications for various functions, a package body is required to hold the bodies of these functions:

```
package Area_Calculations is -- package specification
   type Distance is new Float range 0.0 .. 100.0;
```

```
    function Circle_Area (Radius: Distance) return Float;
    function Rectangle_Area (Length, Width: Distance) return Float;
    function Triangle_Area (Base, Height: Distance) return Float;
end Area_Calculations;

package body Area_Calculations is -- package body

    function Circle_Area (Radius: Distance) return Float is
        PI: constant Float := 3.1415927;
    begin
        return PI * Radius * Radius;
    end Circle_Area;

    function Rectangle_Area (Length, Width: Distance) return
        Float is
    begin
        return Length * Width;
    end Rectangle_Area;

    function Triangle_Area (Base, Height: Distance) return Float is
    begin
        return 0.5 * Base * Height;
    end Triangle_Area;

end Area_Calculations;
```

The package specification of `Area_Calculations` contains the declaration of the type `Distance` and the specifications of the functions used to calculate the areas of circles, rectangles, and triangles. Since these functions are provided to external users, they must be placed in the public part of the package, the package specification. Only the function specifications—not the function bodies—can be placed in the package specification. This is because function specifications contain interface information (information required to call the function), which belongs in the package specification. This interface information includes the name of the function, followed by parameter definitions (in parentheses) and the type of value returned by the function. This is the only information needed by the user of this package, except for comments describing the services that the package offers. The user does not need to know how the functions are implemented. The implementations of these functions are therefore contained in the function bodies, which are hidden in the package body. Keep in mind that these function bodies may be invoked from outside the package only because their corresponding function specifications are contained in the package specification.

Once the preceding package, `Area_Calculations`, is independently compiled, it may be referenced by another program unit that mentions this package in its **with** clause:

```
with Ada.Text_IO, Area_Calculations;
use Ada.Text_IO, Area_Calculations;
procedure Output_Areas is
```

```
type Shape is (Circle, Rectangle, Triangle);
Object: Shape;
package Real_IO is new Float_IO (Float);
package Shape_IO is new Enumeration_IO (Shape);
use Real_IO, Shape_IO;
Radius, Length, Width, Base, Height: Distance;

begin -- Output_Areas

   Put_Line ("Do you want to find the area of a circle, " &
         "rectangle, or triangle?");
   Get (Object);

   case Object is

      when Circle =>
         Put_Line ("Enter the radius as a real number: ");
         Get (Radius);
         Put ("The area of the circle is ");
         Put ( Circle_Area (Radius), 0, 3, 0 );
         New_Line;


      when Rectangle =>
         Put_Line ("Enter the length as a real number: ");
         Get (Length);
         Put_Line ("Enter the width as a real number: ");
         Get (Width);
         Put ("The area of the rectangle is ");
         Put ( Rectangle_Area (Length, Width), 0, 3, 0 );
         New_Line;

      when Triangle =>
         Put_Line ("Enter the base as a real number: ");
         Get (Base);
         Put_Line ("Enter the height as a real number: ");
         Get (Height);
         Put ("The area of the triangle is ");
         Put ( Triangle_Area (Base, Height), 0, 3, 0 );
         New_Line;

   end case;

end Output_Areas;
```

When procedure Output_Areas executes, the user is prompted for the type of object—Circle, Rectangle, or Triangle—whose area is to be calculated. The user response is assigned to the variable `Object`, which is declared to be of type `Shape`. A **case** statement then selects a group of statements to execute, based on the value of `Object`. If, for instance, `Object` has the value of `Circle`, then the user is prompted for the radius of the circle. The area is calculated by making a call to the `Circle_Area` function, and the result is output with an appropriate message.

A sample run of this program may appear, as follows:

```
Do you want to find the area of a circle, rectangle, or
triangle?
> circle

Enter the radius of the circle as a real number:
> 2.0

The area of the circle is 12.566
```

The user responses follow the prompt, >. Note that the answer is rounded off to the nearest thousandth. This output format is specified by the `Put` statements that output the areas of the various objects. For example, the area of a circle is output by the following statement:

```
Put ( Circle_Area (Radius), 0, 3, 0 );
```

The second parameter, 0, provides space for 0 digits to the left of the decimal point. Since Ada syntax requires that at least one digit appear to the left of the decimal point, a field width of 0 is never enough. Whenever a specified field is too small, the compiler chooses the minimum width required for the value being output. No blanks are added. The third parameter, 3, specifies that 3 digits are to follow the decimal point. The fourth parameter, 0, specifies that no digits are to be used for an exponent; that is, an exponent is not to be used. Without such a format specification, the output would appear in awkward scientific notation, such as 1.256637E+01. Formatted output will be discussed in detail in Chapter 14.

Each time one of the functions in package `Area_Calculations` is called, the calculated area is returned to the caller. No information is retained in the package between each of the calls. Quite often, however, a package body hides data structures that retain their values between subprogram calls. These data structures are protected. They can only be manipulated through the subprograms provided in the package specification.

The following example illustrates such a package, where the hidden data structure is an array used to stack integer values. Before showing the code, let us briefly describe a stack.

A stack is a "last in, first out" (LIFO) data structure. Items are "pushed" on (placed in) the stack and "popped" off (taken from) the stack just as individual plates in a cafeteria are placed in a stack or removed from a stack. The plate that is removed from the top of the stack is the one that was most recently added to the stack.

The following stack package maintains an integer stack whose values can be pushed and popped using subprograms provided by the package:

```
package Stack is     -- specification
   -- this package can be used to stack up to 1,000 values of
   -- type Stack_Item
   type Stack_Item is new Integer range -10_000 .. 10_000;
   procedure Push (Item: in Stack_Item);
   function Pop return Stack_Item;
end Stack;

package body Stack is    -- body
   -- declaration part
   Stack_Size: constant Integer := 1_000;
   Stack_Array: array (1 .. Stack_Size) of Stack_Item;
   Top: Integer range 0 .. Stack_Size;

   procedure Push (Item: in Stack_Item) is
   begin
      Top := Top + 1;
      Stack_Array (Top) := Item;
   end Push;

   function Pop return Stack_Item is
   begin
      Top := Top - 1;
      return Stack_Array (Top + 1);
   end Pop;

begin -- initialization part
   Top := 0;
end Stack;
```

The package specification contains the declaration of the type Stack_Item, and the specifications of the procedure Push and the function Pop. Procedure Push pushes an object belonging to Stack_Item onto the stack, and function Pop pops an object belonging to Stack_Item from the stack and returns the value of the object.

Now let us consider the package body, which contains the hidden implementation details. The declarative part of the package body contains the declarations of the constant Stack_Size, the anonymous array Stack_Array, and the integer variable Top.

Stack_Size is set to 1000, which places an upper limit on the number of integers that can be stacked. Stack_Array is used to hold all the integer values in the stack. These integer values belong to the type Stack_Item. The type Stack_Item, declared in the package specification, is thus directly visible to the corresponding package body. Note that although the stack is implemented as an array, this fact is hidden from the users of the package. Whether the stack is implemented as an array or as some other data structure should be of no concern to the user, because this does not affect how the package is used.

Next, the integer variable `Top` is declared. `Top` is the index value of the last item placed in `Stack_Array`. `Top` must therefore be updated whenever integers are added to or removed from the array. Following the declaration of `Top` are the bodies of the subprograms `Push` and `Pop`. Since subprogram bodies contain implementation details rather than interface information, they must be placed in the package body rather than in the package specification. The procedure `Push` increments `Top` and assigns the item to be pushed on the stack to the array component `Stack_Array(Top)`. The function `Pop` decrements the value of `Top` and returns the last value in the stack before `Top` was decremented.

After the function `Pop` comes the executable statement part of the `Stack` package body, which initializes `Top` to 0. The statement part of a package body is unlike the statement part of subprograms. The statement part of subprograms, which must contain at least one statement, is critical because it implements the actions that the subprogram is designed to accomplish. The statement part of a package body, however, plays a minor role and is often omitted (along with the keyword **begin**). When such a part does exist, it typically just contains a few statements that initialize some of the variables, such as `Top`, previously declared in the package. For this reason, the statement part of a package body is often known as the initialization part. The statement part of packages plays such a minor role because, unlike subprograms, a package is not invoked or passed parameters. (However, as in our `Stack` package, a package may contain subprograms that can be invoked and passed parameters.) Therefore, unlike the statement part of a subprogram, which is executed whenever the subprogram is invoked, the statement part of a package is executed only when the package is elaborated (brought into existence). If the package is a library unit, this elaboration occurs only once, before the main program begins to execute. `Top` is thus initialized only once. Thereafter, every time a call is made to `Push` or `Pop`, `Top` is updated but never again initialized to 0.

Instead of initializing `Top` in the statement part of the package body, we could have initialized `Top` in the declarative part of the body:

```
Top: Integer range 0 .. Stack_Size := 0;
```

The effect is the same as before: `Top` is only initialized once, when the package is first brought into existence.

Now that we have examined the `Stack` package, let us consider the following program that uses its services:

```
with Stack, Ada.Text_IO; use Stack, Ada.Text_IO;
procedure Use_Stack is
    package Stack_Item_IO is new Integer_IO (Stack_Item);
    use Stack_Item_IO;
    X, Y: Stack_Item;
begin -- Use_Stack
    Push (5);
```

```
      X := 3;
      Push (X);
      Put ( Pop );  -- outputs 3
      Y := Pop;
      Put ( Y );    -- outputs 5
   end Use_Stack;
```

`Use_Stack` references all three items listed in the specification of `Stack`: `Stack_Item`, `Push`, and `Pop`. `Stack_Item` is used to instantiate `Integer_IO` and to declare variables `X` and `Y`. `Push` is used to push the integer values 5 and 3 onto the stack, and then `Pop` is used to pop these two values from the stack. Since a stack is a last in, first out data structure, the values are popped from the stack in the opposite order from which they were pushed onto the stack.

When a program unit such as `Use_Stack` references a package, this does not preclude other program units from referencing the package. An Ada program may have several different program units that mention `Stack` in their **with** clauses. Regardless of how many program units reference the `Stack` package, only one stack is created. Thus, each call to `Push` or `Pop` manipulates the same integer stack, regardless of which program unit makes the call. Furthermore, this integer stack exists throughout the lifetime of the main program. The values in the array `Stack_Array` and the value of `Top` are retained between calls to the subprograms `Push` and `Pop`. Therefore, whenever variables, such as `Stack_Array` and `Top`, need to be maintained throughout a program's life, place them in the declarative part of the package body. If the variables need to be made public, place them in the package specification.

As mentioned, unlike the items declared in the specification of `Stack`, items declared in the body of `Stack` are "hidden" from the users of this package. "Hidden" does not mean that the users are necessarily forbidden to examine the Ada code for the body of the `Stack` package. Rather, hidden means that, even if the code is examined, the items contained in the body cannot be accessed. Therefore, a program unit that mentions `Stack` in its **with** clause cannot access the items `Stack_Size`, `Stack_Array`, or `Top`:

```
with Stack; use Stack;
procedure Inaccessible_Items is
begin
   Stack_Array(1) := 7;    -- error; Stack_Array not available
   Top := 20;              -- error; Top not available
   Top := Stack_Size;      -- error; Stack_Size not available
end Inaccessible_Items;
```

By hiding implementation details from the user, the integrity of the package is protected. Users may only manipulate the stack using the subprograms mentioned in the specification: `Push` and `Pop`. Users cannot circumvent these subprograms and directly manipulate the underlying structure of the stack. For example, as shown in the preceding code, the users of a `Stack` cannot directly insert values into `Stack_Array` or reset the value of `Top`. This is fortunate; otherwise, the users could corrupt the stack or incorrectly extract items from the stack. Packages such as

Stack that encapsulate an object such as Stack_Array in its body are called "object managers." Package Stack manages access to the Stack_Array object via subprograms Push and Pop defined in its specification.

Another advantage of hiding items such as Stack_Array in a package body is that the package developer may change the implementation of the stack without impacting existing clients of the Stack package. As long as changes are restricted to the body of Stack, programmers that "**with**" Stack do not need to modify their code to accommodate the changes, or even to recompile their code. Nothing is required of the users of Stack until they wish to execute the Ada program that incorporates the latest changes to the package body. At that point, users need to relink the program in order to create a new executable image.

Information in the preceding discussion impacts how packages should be developed. When developing a package, carefully consider what items should be placed in the package specification and what items should be placed in the package body. The goal is to place as many items as possible in a package body. Only the items that must be visible to users of the package should appear in a package specification.

There are several reasons to place as few items as possible in a package specification. First, if extraneous implementation details are placed in the package specification, users of the package can base their code on these irrelevant details. If these details ever change, then users may have to modify their code to accommodate the change.

Second, if there are unnecessary items in the specification, users may unintentionally corrupt these items. For example, in the Stack package, if the declarations of Stack_Size, Stack_Array, and Top were relocated to the specification of Stack, the result would be a poorly structured package. The package would still work, because every item declared in a package specification is available to the corresponding package body. However, all of the illegal operations illustrated in the previous procedure, Inaccessible_Items, would unfortunately be legal. Such operations could easily lead to a stack of the wrong size or with incorrect values.

Third, placing as few items as possible in a package specification minimizes the amount of recompilation required when code is changed. As we will discuss in Chapter 9, changes made to a package body usually do not require other program units to be recompiled, just relinked. Changes made to a package specification, however, require that every program unit that mentions this package in its **with** clause be recompiled.

To realize the saving in recompilation time that occurs when only the package body changes, package specifications should be compiled separately from their bodies. If both are compiled together in the same file, then any changes that are made could require that every program unit referencing this package also be recompiled.

## PACKAGES AND SOFTWARE DESIGN

A package specification and package body may each be separately compiled as long as the specification is submitted to the compiler before its associated body. Separate compilation of a package specification and a package body is particularly useful when designing a program from the top down.

Top-down design is the traditional design methodology that embraces the "divide and conquer" strategy. In top-down design, one starts at the highest levels of abstraction and then decomposes the system into lower and lower levels. Through successive refinement, a program is eventually broken down into manageable, well-defined pieces, sometimes called modules. Each module should be self-contained and easy to understand, and the interfaces between modules should be simple and well-defined. Modules with these properties tend to be small and easy to implement, test, and maintain. In Ada, modules are naturally represented as packages.

In top-down design, all that is initially needed are the library level subprograms, including the main program, and interface information provided by package specifications. The specifications can be written and compiled without the associated bodies. In other words, program units that reference a package can be compiled, provided that the package specification has been compiled. The compiler checks the program design by testing the specifications for completeness and consistency. Completeness is checked by verifying that all the units mentioned in **with** clauses actually exist and contain the required resources. Consistency is checked by verifying that procedures and functions are called with the correct number and type of parameters, both within and across compilation units. The implementation details contained in the package bodies are deferred until the design has been tested by the compiler and is ready to be implemented. The package bodies do not need to be fully implemented until the program is ready to be linked and executed.

Thus, when developing Ada code using top-down design, carefully define the package specifications before worrying about the package bodies. Since the package specifications reflect the design of the program, much effort should be taken when developing the specifications. Regardless of how well the package bodies are implemented, without well-thought-out package specifications, a poorly designed program might result.

Ada also supports bottom-up design and object-oriented design. In bottom-up design, low-level modules are pieced together by **with** clauses to form larger chunks of code, which are in turn pieced together to form yet larger chunks of code, and so on, until an entire program eventually emerges. Bottom-up design is particularly useful when many of the modules already exist from other applications. Instead of rewriting these modules, they may be easily reused, thanks to the package construct and the **with** clause. When writing library packages, therefore, keep them as general as possible so that they can be reused in future applications.

Large systems are rarely developed using only top-down or bottom-up approaches. Typically both approaches are used.

In object-oriented design, objects are defined, together with the operations that can be performed on the objects. In Ada, objects are typically data structures. Packages encapsulate the objects and their operations. For example, our `Stack` package creates an object that is a stack, together with push and pop operations that can be performed on the stack. The implementation of the stack and the push and pop operations are hidden in the package body. In well-designed object-oriented code, the objects often mirror physical objects in the real world that they are meant to represent, and the operations often mirror physical operations that are performed on these physical objects.

Ada 95 fully supports object-oriented design and programming. Further discussion of this topic is deferred to Chapter 13, which is entirely devoted to object-oriented programming.

## THE WITH CLAUSE AND USE CLAUSE

Throughout this book, we have been employing the **with** clause and the **use** clause. This section explores these two clauses in detail. Recall that the **with** clause makes the resources of a package available, whereas the **use** clause makes these resources directly visible so that dot notation may be avoided. The **use** clause, therefore, does not determine which items are available to a program unit; it merely allows those items that are available to be referenced more concisely.

The **with** clause may mention any library unit, not just packages. A **with** clause, for example, can mention functions and procedures, as long as these functions and procedures are separately compiled to form library units. The **use** clause, however, may only mention a package. This is because the **use** clause makes the internal resources of a library unit directly visible to external clients, and the only kind of library unit that provides internal resources to clients is a package. A subprogram does not offer internal resources to an external client. Items declared within a subprogram can only be used locally and are never available to outside units. What is available to outside units is the subprogram name and formal parameters. The **with** clause alone renders all these items directly visible, so the **use** clause would have no purpose even if it were allowed.

Unlike the **use** clause, which may optionally be placed in the declarative part of a program unit, the **with** clause must be placed before the specification of the program unit. It cannot be embedded in a program unit:

```
procedure Outer is
   . . .
   with P; -- illegal; with clause cannot be embedded
   procedure Inner is
      . . .
```

When a **with** clause precedes a package specification, the clause automatically applies to the corresponding package body. The same **with** clause can also appear with the package body, but this has no additional effect. However, when a **with** clause appears with a package body but not the associated package specification, it only applies to the body:

```
with A; -- may use more than 1 with clause
with B;
package P is
   -- can access resources of A and B
end P;

with B;
with C;
```

```
package body P is
   -- can access resources of A, B, and C
end P;
```

A **use** clause may be placed after its associated **with** clause before the program unit specification, or in the declarative part of a program unit. When the **use** clause appears after the **with** clause, it applies throughout the program unit, rendering the resources of the package mentioned in the **use** clause directly visible. Dot notation, however, may still be employed to make the code more understandable or to eliminate ambiguity. When a **use** clause appears in the declarative part of a program unit, it takes effect from the point in the code after it is declared, throughout the scope of the unit. Consider the following code (where the line indicates separate compilation units):

```
package Houses is -- package consisting of a specification
   type Styles is (Queen_Anne, Gothic, Craftsman,
      Prairie_Style, English_Tudor, Mediterranean,
      French_Norman, Spanish_Colonial, Art_Deco, High_Tech,
      Streamline_Moderne);
end Houses;
```
_____
```
with Houses;
procedure Demo_Use_Clause is

   Your_House: Houses.Styles := Houses.French_Norman;
   -- needs dot notation for type Styles and enumeration
   -- literal French_Norman

   use Houses;
   -- takes effect from here to the rest of procedure

   My_House: Styles := Art_Deco;
   -- does not need dot notation

begin

   My_House := Streamline_Moderne;
   -- does not need dot notation

end Demo_Use_Clause;
```

Before the **use** clause is employed in the procedure Demo_Use_Clause, dot notation is needed, not only for the enumeration type Styles but also for the values of Styles, such as French_Norman. Once the **use** clause is employed, dot notation is no longer required from that point on to the end of the procedure.

The **use** clause does not always guarantee that dot notation can be avoided.

Sometimes dot notation is required to resolve ambiguity. Consider, for example, the following two packages that each have an identifier named C:

```
package P1 is
    A, B, C: Integer;
end P1;
```
---
```
package P2 is
    C, D: Integer;
end P2;
```

Suppose that a procedure mentions these two packages in a **with** clause and a **use** clause:

```
with P1, P2; use P1, P2;
procedure Q is
begin
    A := 1;              -- OK
    B := 2;              -- OK
    C := 3;              -- error; C is ambiguous
    P1.C := 3;           -- OK
    P2.C := 3;           -- OK
    D := 4;              -- OK
end Q;
```

As shown, the identifier C, written without dot notation, is ambiguous; it may refer to the C in package P1 or P2. The identifier C must therefore be written using dot notation, even though the **use** clause is employed.

In the previous example, identifiers having the same name appear in two different packages. Let us now consider what happens when identifiers with the same name appear in a package and in the program unit referencing the package:

```
package P is
    A: Integer;
end P;
```
---
```
with P; use P;
procedure Q is
    A: Integer;
begin
    A := 2;    -- refers to the local A
    Q.A := 2; -- explicitly selects the local A
    P.A := 3; -- selects the A imported from package P
end Q;
```

Even though the **use** clause is employed, the integer variable A defined in package P is not directly visible. It is not directly visible because it is hidden by the local declaration of the variable A in program Q. Local identifiers thus hide identifiers with the same name that are imported from packages. To reference the A in package P, one must write P.A.

Before ending this section, let us consider one more property of the **with** clause. In typical Ada programs, the **with** clause is often used to tie together many program units. A question that naturally emerges is whether **with** clauses allow program units to indirectly reference resources. In other words, if unit P3 **withs** P2, which **withs** P1, does P3 have access to the resources of P1? The answer is no. This is illustrated in the following code:

```
package P1 is
    subtype T1_Type is Integer range 1 .. 100;
end P1;
```

```
with P1; use P1;
package P2 is
    subtype T2_Type is T1_Type range 1 .. 10;
end P2;
```

```
with P2; use P2;
package P3 is
    A: T1_Type;    -- resources of P1 not available
    B: T2_Type;    -- OK
end P3;
```

Since P3 mentions P2 in its **with** clause, P3 can reference subtype T2_Type of P2. P2 can in turn reference subtype T1_Type of P1. This "chain" of references, however, does not enable P3 to reference the subtype T1_Type.

## WHEN TO EMPLOY THE USE CLAUSE

The issue of when to employ the **use** clause is controversial. Some Ada experts and software engineers believe that the **use** clause should never be employed. Without the **use** clause, code is better documented and therefore easier to understand. Code is better documented because every imported item must be referenced with dot notation. For example, at a glance, one can tell from Coordinate.X1 that X1 is a coordinate value defined in package Coordinate. Without dot notation, a reader of the code encountering X1 might have trouble figuring out what X1 represents or in what package it is defined. The following code illustrates this difficulty:

```
with A, B, C;    -- assume these are packages
use A;
package body P is
   use B;
   . . .
   procedure P1 is
      use C;
      . . .
```

```
begin
    Find_Me;   -- may be defined in P spec, P body, P1,
               -- A spec, B spec, or C spec
end P1;
end P;
```

Because of the **use** clauses in this code, the procedure Find_Me can be quite challenging to locate. Find_Me could be defined in the specification or body of P, in P1, or in the specifications of packages A, B, or C.

Another reason not to employ the **use** clause is that it can hide potential errors:

```
package P is
    A: Integer;
    B: Float;
end P;
```

```
with P; use P;
procedure Q is
    A: Integer;
begin
    A := 5;    -- intent may have been to use P.A instead of Q.A
    B := 7.9;  -- intent may have been to use Q.B that the
               -- programmer forgot to declare
end Q;
```

The programmer may have intended to assign 5 to the A that is imported from package P, forgetting that A is hidden by a locally declared A. The programmer may also have intended to assign 7.9 to a local B that he or she forgot to declare. Since the B from package P is directly visible, no error message is generated. Had the **use** clause been omitted, such programming errors would be detected or avoided. Without the **use** clause, the programmer's intent must be explicitly stated. If the A from package P is desired, A must be referenced as P.A. If a locally declared B is desired but does not exist, the Ada compiler generates an error message instead of referencing P.B.

Let us now consider the advantages of employing the **use** clause. By employing the **use** clause, items can be referenced without dot notation. Such "unexpanded" names are concise and therefore easy to read. For instance, the function call Square_Root(X) is easier to read than Math_Library.Square_Root(X).

Perhaps the biggest advantage of employing the **use** clause occurs when overloaded operators are imported. Consider, for instance, the following package, which contains overloaded operators for adding, subtracting, multiplying, and dividing complex numbers:

```
package Complex_Number is

    type Complex is
        record
            Real: Float;
```

```
                Imaginary: Float;
            end record;

            -- overloaded functions

            function "+" (Left, Right: Complex) return Complex;
            function "-" (Left, Right: Complex) return Complex;
            function "*" (Left, Right: Complex) return Complex;
            function "/" (Left, Right: Complex) return Complex;
            procedure Put (Item: in Complex);

end Complex_Number;

with Ada.Text_IO; use Ada;
package body Complex_Number is

    function "+" (Left, Right: Complex) return Complex is
    begin
        return ( Left.Real + Right.Real,
                 Left.Imaginary + Right.Imaginary);
    end "+";

    function "-" (Left, Right: Complex) return Complex is
    begin
        return ( Left.Real - Right.Real,
                 Left.Imaginary - Right.Imaginary);
    end "-";

    function "*" (Left, Right: Complex) return Complex is
    begin
        return ( Left.Real * Right.Real -
                 Left.Imaginary * Right.Imaginary,
                 Left.Real * Right.Imaginary +
                 Left.Imaginary * Right.Real );
    end "*";

    function "/" (Left, Right: Complex) return Complex is
        Denom: Float;
    begin
        Denom := Right.Real ** 2 + Right.Imaginary ** 2;
        return (( Left.Real * Right.Real +
                  Left.Imaginary * Right.Imaginary) / Denom,
                ( Left.Imaginary * Right.Real -
                  Left.Real * Right.Imaginary) / Denom );
    end "/";

    procedure Put (Item: in Complex) is
        package Flt_IO is new Text_IO.Float_IO (Float);
    begin
```

```
            Flt_IO.Put (Item.Real, 0, 0, 0);
            Text_IO.Put (" + ");
            Flt_IO.Put (Item.Imaginary, 0, 0, 0);
            Text_IO.Put ("i");
         end Put;
   end Complex_Number;
```

If you are not mathematically inclined, just think of a complex number as a record consisting of two components of type `Float`. You do not have to understand the package body to follow the discussion in this section.

Without the **use** clause, an external program unit must reference the overloaded operators `"+"`, `"-"`, `"*"`, and `"/"`, by employing their extended names, `Complex_Number."+"`, `Complex_Number."-"`, `Complex_Number."*"`, and `Complex_Number."/"`. This notation is unnatural and very difficult to read. To make matters worse, when dot notation is employed, the infix notation, where operands are placed on opposite sides of the operator, cannot be employed:

```
   Z := X Complex_Number."+" Y; -- illegal syntax
```

Instead, the standard prefix function notation must be used:

```
   Z := Complex_Number."+" (X, Y);
```

This defeats the reason for using overloaded operators, which is to provide natural mathematical notation, such as

```
   Z := X + Y;
```

The following procedure demonstrates the advantages of employing the **use** clause when overloaded operators are imported:

```
   with Complex_Number;
   procedure Demonstrate_Use_Clause is
      X, Y, Z: Complex_Number.Complex := (2.0, 3.0);
   begin
      -- without the use clause, one must employ dot notation
      -- and standard function notation
      Z := Complex_Number."+" (X, Y);

      declare
         use Complex_Number; -- only applies to following items
                             -- within this block statement
      begin
         -- with the use clause, one can omit dot notation
         -- and employ infix notation
         Z := X + Y;
      end;

   end Demonstrate_Use_Clause;
```

When the **use** clause is placed in the declarative part of a block statement, it applies only from the point in the code where it is declared to the end of the block. Thus, the overloaded operator, "+", imported from the package Complex_Number, may be referenced without dot notation only within the block statement. Throughout the rest of the code, dot notation is required.

The problem of referencing operators with dot notation not only arises when importing overloaded operators. The problem arises whenever predefined operators are used to manipulate items imported from external packages. For example, let us reconsider procedure Taste, presented in the beginning of this chapter, which references the package Houses. The following version of Taste omits the **use** clause:

```
with Ada.Text_IO, Houses; -- no use clause
procedure Taste is
   House : Houses.Styles := Houses.High_Tech;
   -- must use dot notation for enumeration type and literals
begin
   if Houses."=" (House, Houses.High_Tech) then
      -- must use dot notation for equality operator
      Ada.Text_IO.Put ("This person likes supermodern");
   end if;
end Taste;
```

This example shows that when the **use** clause is omitted, extended names are required not only for Styles and High_Tech, but also for the equality operator, "=", which compares values of type Styles. In other words, the equality operator, "=", must be written as Houses."=". Requiring dot notation may seem peculiar because all that can be seen in package Houses is the enumeration type Styles. The operator Houses."=" does not appear anywhere. To understand where Houses."=" is coming from, recall that a type not only defines a set of values, but also a set of predefined operations that apply to those values. In our example, the type Styles acquires all the operations—">", "<", and so on—that are predefined for enumeration types. Therefore, even though the operations on type Styles are not shown in package Houses, these operations are implicitly declared along with the type, as indicated in the code comments that follow:

```
package Houses is    -- package consisting of a specification
   type Styles is ( Queen_Anne, Gothic, Craftsman,
      Prairie_Style, English_Tudor, Mediterranean,
      French_Norman, Spanish_Colonial, Art_Deco, High_Tech,
      Streamline_Moderne);
   -- These operators are implicitly declared here
   -- function "=" (Left, Right: Styles) return Boolean;
   -- function ">" (Left, Right: Styles) return Boolean;
   -- function "<" (Left, Right: Styles) return Boolean;
   -- function ">=" (Left, Right: Styles) return Boolean;
   --      ... etc.
end Houses;
```

Such implicit operations must be referenced just as if they were explicitly defined. Without the **use** clause, therefore, procedure `Taste` must employ dot notation when referencing operations on `Styles`. (Unlike other operations, the assignment operation, `":="`, is directly visible without the **use** clause and is not implicitly defined in this package.)

In procedure `Taste`, the price to pay for not employing the **use** clause is high. Writing each enumeration literal with dot notation is cumbersome. More disturbing, however, is the loss of the natural notation for equality. As previously mentioned, once an operator such as `"="` is written with dot notation, `Houses."="`, infix notation can no longer be used. The required prefix function notation is very awkward and difficult to read.

Before giving up and employing the **use** clause, let us consider another alternative that allows natural notation for operations such as equality without employing the **use** clause:

```
with Ada.Text_IO, Houses;
procedure Taste is
    function "=" (Left, Right: Houses.Styles) return Boolean
        renames Houses."=";
    House : Houses.Styles := Houses.High_Tech;
begin
    if House = Houses.High_Tech then -- OK; uses the renamed "="
        Ada.Text_IO.Put ("This person likes supermodern");
    end if;
end Taste;
```

In order to use the natural notation for equality, this version of `Taste` renames `Houses."="` to `"="`. As mentioned in previous chapters, renaming does not bring new entities into existence or replace one name with another. Renaming merely provides an alternative name. In our example, as a result of renaming, the equality operator can be referenced either with the name `"="` or with dot notation as `Houses."="`. Renaming the equality operator is perhaps better than using dot notation, but renaming operators is still awkward and confusing. Moreover, if the code also employs operators such as `"<"` and `">"`, each of these would also need to be renamed. Finally, care must be taken that an operator is not mistakenly renamed to a different kind of operator. For instance, a programmer could mistakenly rename a greater-than operator as a less-than operator:

```
function ">" (Left, Right: Houses.Styles) return Boolean
    renames Houses."<"; -- a tough error for a programmer to detect
```

Since this code is fully acceptable by the rules of Ada, a programmer might have to spend considerable time tracking the problem down.

**Ada 95 ▶** Fortunately, there is yet another possible solution to our **use** clause dilemma: the type-based **use** clause. The type-based **use** clause avoids the harmful effects of the **use** clause without giving up infix notation of imported operators and without requiring the renaming of operators. The type-based **use** clause has the form:

```
use type type names;
```

The keywords **use type** are followed by a list of types. If a type is specified in a type-based **use** clause, dot notation is not required for any of its operators, although dot notation is still required for all other items imported from the **with**'d package. Applying the type-based **use** clause to our previous example results in the following code:

```
with Ada.Text_IO, Houses;
use type Houses.Styles; -- type based use clause
procedure Taste is
    House : Houses.Styles := Houses.High_Tech;
begin
    if House = Houses.High_Tech then -- OK;
        --"=" is directly visible
        Ada.Text_IO.Put ("This person likes supermodern");
    end if;
end Taste;
```

Note that infix notation is allowed for the "=" operator (and all other operators on Houses.Styles), but dot notation is required everywhere else. The type-based **use** clause is, therefore, the best solution to our problem.

The type-based **use** clause could also have been employed on the previous Complex_Number package in order to allow infix operations on type Complex:

```
with Complex_Number;
use type Complex_Number.Complex; -- type based use clause
procedure Demonstrate_Type_Based_Use_Clause is
    X, Y, Z: Complex_Number.Complex := (2.0, 3.0);
        -- dot notation is required for type Complex
begin
    Z := X + Y; -- OK
    Z := X - Y; -- OK
    Z := X * Y; -- OK
    Z := X / Y; -- OK

end Demonstrate_Type_Based_Use_Clause;
```

The type-based **use** clause allows operators to be written without expanded names, but what about variables, constants, subprograms, and packages? Typically, such items should be referenced with their expanded names. However, when desired, dot notation can be avoided through renaming. For example, the procedure Ada.Text_IO.Put can be renamed to Put:

```
procedure Put (Item: in Character) renames Ada.Text_IO.Put;
```

As a result of this rename, the identifier Put can be used instead of Ada.Text_IO.Put. Such renaming has some of the effect of a **use** clause. However, unlike the **use** clause, which applies to all the resources of a package, the renaming feature only applies to the individually renamed items. Furthermore, the newly introduced name is documented right in the code.

**Ada 95** ▶ While we are on the topic of renaming, let us consider a few other ways that renaming can be used. Subprogram bodies, for instance, can be provided in package bodies by renaming another subprogram:

```
package P is
    procedure Print (Item: in Character);
end P;

with Ada.Text_IO;
package body P is
    -- supply procedure body by renaming another procedure
    procedure Print (Item: in Character) renames
        Ada.Text_IO.Put;
    -- This is better than having procedure Print call
    -- Ada.Text_IO.Put
end P;
```

Of course, the renamed procedure `Print` must have the same number and type of parameters as `Ada.Text_IO.Put`. Since the renaming is performed in the package body, it is of no concern to those invoking `P.Print`. For the package developer, however, renaming provides an efficient and natural way of implementing one subprogram in terms of another subprogram. Without this rename, the body of `P.Print` would have to invoke `Ada.Text_IO.Put`, as the following illustrates:

```
with Ada.Text_IO;
package body P is
    -- without the rename
    procedure Print (Item: in Character) is
        Ada.Text_IO.Put(Item);
    end Print;
end P;
```

Care must be taken when items are renamed in a package specification, because renaming can change the item's scope. Recall that **with** clauses do not enable program units to indirectly reference resources. For example, if procedure `Main` **withs** P2, which **withs** P1, `Main` does not have access to the resources of P1. However, if the specification of P2 renames P1, then `Main` can access the resources of P1.

```
package P1 is
    type Signal is (Red, Yellow, Green);
    procedure Change_Signal (Current: in Signal);
end P1;
```

```
with P1;
package P2 is
```

```
        package Renamed_P1 renames P1;
            -- Renaming makes package P1 available to those who
            -- "with" P2
     end P2;
```

```
with P2;
procedure Main is
    -- Main can access package P1's resources just by
    -- "withing" P2
    Light: P2.Renamed_P1.Signal := P2.Renamed_P1.Red;
begin
    P2.Renamed_P1.Change_Signal (Current => Light);
    ...
end Main;
```

Instead of renaming package P1, P2 could have renamed procedure Change_Signal, or could have "renamed" type Signal by introducing a sub-type of Signal:

```
with P1;
package P2 is
    -- P1.Signal and P1.Change_Signal are available to those
    -- who "with" P2
    subtype Renamed_Signal is P1.Signal;
        -- Has the effect of a rename
    procedure Renamed_Change_Signal (Current: in Renamed_Signal)
        renames P1.Change_Signal;
end P2;
```

The "renamed" items, Renamed_Signal and Renamed_Change_Signal, are each made available to programmers that list P2 in a **with** clause. While renaming can result in items becoming available that should not be available, it can be put to good use. Renaming allows a package to "re-export" items from selected packages needed by its clients, without requiring its clients to "**with**" these other packages. In the previous example, package P2 re-exports to its clients Signal and Change_Signal from package P1.

This concludes our discussion of renaming. Let us now return to our main topic, the employment of the **use** clause. Considering the pros and cons of the **use** clause, it is suggested that type-based **use** clauses be considered to allow infix notation of operators, but that the "regular" **use** clause be employed judiciously. The regular **use** clause should be considered when items imported from a package are self-explanatory. For example, there is little danger of misunderstanding if the identifier Square_Root is used rather than Math_Package.Square_Root. The identifier Square_Root adequately explains what the function does. Furthermore, if one wishes to know where this function comes from, it should be obvious that it comes from the package named Math_Package, listed in the **with** clause. (Even in this case, however, a rename should be considered as a less dangerous alternative.) The **use** clause may also be considered when the imported items are well-known resources from one of the predefined packages, such as `Text_IO`. For example, there is little danger of confusion using the procedure call `Put("Hello")` instead of `Ada.Text_IO.Put("Hello")`. Anyone seeing this procedure call would automatically assume the `Put` statement from the `Ada.Text_IO` package was being used. Once again, however, a rename should be considered instead.

## EMBEDDED PACKAGES

So far we have only considered packages that are library units (independent program units). As previously mentioned, such packages are elaborated before the main program executes. The package then exists throughout the lifetime of the program, and its resources are available to any compilation unit that mentions the package in a **with** clause.

In contrast to packages that are library units, packages may be embedded (contained) within other units, such as block statements and subprograms. A package that is embedded in the declarative part of a block statement or subprogram comes into existence when it is elaborated with the rest of the declarations. It ceases to exist when the enclosing program unit ceases to exist. Embedded packages are thus re-created each time the enclosing unit is elaborated. In the beginning of each new re-creation, declarations in the package are elaborated, and the statements in the initialization part of the package are executed. No information in the package is retained from one re-creation to the next.

The following example shows a package that is embedded in the declarative part of a procedure:

```
procedure P is
   package Q is
      A: Integer := 1;
   end Q;
   B: Integer := Q.A;  -- dot notation required
   use Q;
   C: Integer := A; -- dot notation not required
begin
   A := B + C;
end P;
```

Package `Q` is brought into existence each time procedure `P` is invoked and `P`'s declarations are elaborated. The package ceases to exist, along with the other items declared in `P`, as soon as `P` is finished executing. If `P` is called again, the package is re-created. Any variables declared in the package have no "memory" of the values they held during their previous life. Furthermore, the resources of package `Q` are not available outside procedure `P`. Inside `P`, the resources are available from the point in the code where the package is declared to the end of `P`. In other words, the scope of the items declared within the package specification extends beyond the package, to the end of the procedure in which the package is declared. As shown in the example, however, unless the **use** clause is employed, items declared within the package specification are not directly visible outside the package.

In addition to being embedded in block statements and subprograms, packages can be nested within other packages. The lifetime of the inner package extends throughout the lifetime of the outer package. Packages can be nested within other packages in two ways. The inner package, including its specification and body, may be placed in the body of the outer package. Alternatively, the specification of the inner package may be placed in the specification of the outer package, and the body of the inner package may be placed inside the body of the outer package. Consider, for example, the following nested package specifications (which do not have bodies):

```
package Outer is
    subtype Outer_Spec is Integer;
    A: Outer_Spec;

    package Inner is
        B: Outer_Spec;
        ...
    end Inner;

end Outer;
```

Note that the inner package specification can reference the subtype declared in the outer package specification. A program unit that mentions Outer in its **with** clause can reference all the resources in the specification of Outer, including the resources of the specification of Inner. Suppose that procedure P mentions Outer in a **with** clause but not a **use** clause:

```
with Outer;
procedure P is
begin
    Outer.A := 1;
    Outer.Inner.B := 2;
end P;
```

To reference a variable such as B, the dot notation must include the full expanded name Outer.Inner.B. If the clause **use** Outer is employed, this variable can be referenced as Inner.B. If the clause **use** Outer.Inner is employed, then this variable can be simply referenced as B. The clause **use** Outer.Inner, however, does not provide a **use** Outer. In other words, the clause **use** Outer.Inner does not give direct access to A. The clause **use** Outer is needed:

```
with Outer;    -- cannot write with Outer.Inner;
use Outer;
use Outer.Inner; -- or, due to the previous use clause,
                 -- use Inner;
procedure P is
```

```
begin
    A := 1;     -- made possible by use Outer;
    B := 2;     -- made possible by use Inner.Outer;
end P;
```

As previously mentioned, to avoid dot notation, renaming can be used. The previous procedure P, for instance, can be written as follows:

```
with Outer;
procedure P is
    A: Integer renames Outer.A;
    B: Integer renames Outer.Inner.B;
begin
    A := 1;
    B := 2;
end P;
```

The integer variable A becomes an alternative name for Outer.A, and the integer variable B becomes an alternative for Outer.Inner.B. Such renaming is particularly handy when the expanded names become unmanageably long.

## PRIVATE TYPES

As we have seen, by placing a subprogram specification in a package specification and the associated subprogram body in the package body, the subprogram is visible, but its underlying implementation is hidden. In Ada, one can define private types, which are handled similarly. A private type is visible, but its underlying implementation—structure and values—is hidden. Hiding a type's implementation is called "encapsulating" the type. Users of a private type know how to use the type but not how the type is implemented.

Before showing how private types are declared, let us begin by demonstrating the need for private types. Consider, for example, the following package specification that defines operations on fractions:

```
package Frac_Pack is

    type Fraction is      -- Implementation of Fraction should
        record            -- be hidden
            Top: Integer;
            Bottom: Positive;
        end record;

    function "*" (Left, Right: Fraction) return Fraction;
    function "/" (Left, Right: Fraction) return Fraction;
    function "+" (Left, Right: Fraction) return Fraction;
    function "-" (Right: Fraction) return Fraction;
    function "-" (Left, Right: Fraction) return Fraction;
```

```
      function "=" (Left, Right: Fraction) return Boolean;
         -- "/=" is implicitly provided

      procedure Put (Item: in Fraction);
   end Frac_Pack;
```

This package represents fractions such as one-half or three-quarters as record values (1, 2) and (3, 4), respectively. The fraction operators return the result as a fraction. Thus, (1, 2) * (3, 4) should yield the fraction (3, 8). Note that we avoided the problem of fractions with 0 as a denominator by declaring the denominator, Bottom, to be of subtype Positive. Also note that an overloaded "=" function is provided. Without overloading "=", the package Frac_Pack would be exporting an implicitly defined "=" operator that would return the wrong result when the fractions were not reduced. For example, (1, 2) should equal (2, 4), but by the standard quality test for record values, these aggregates are not equal. To test whether two fractions, (a, b) and (c, d), are equal, cross-multiplication may be used: If a * d equals b * c, then the fractions are equal, else they are not equal. Recall from Chapter 6 that an inequality operator "/=" is implicitly provided when "=" is declared that returns a Boolean type. The operator "/=" cannot be explicitly overloaded, except when the associated "=" operator returns a value other than Boolean. An overloaded "=" that uses cross-multiplication is shown in the following implementation of the body of package Frac_Pack:

**Ada 95** ▶

```
   with Ada.Text_IO; use Ada;
   package body Frac_Pack is

      -- Reduce is only available for use within this package body
      function Reduce (F: Fraction) return Fraction is
         Divisor: Integer;

         function GCD (Left, Right: Integer) return Integer is
         begin
            if Right = 0 then
               return A;
            else
               return GCD (Right, Left mod Right);
            end if;
         end GCD;
      begin

         Divisor := GCD (F.Top, F.Bottom);
         return (F.Top / Divisor, F.Bottom / Divisor);
      end Reduce;

      function "*" (Left, Right: Fraction) return Fraction is
         Product: Fraction :=
            (  Left.Top * Right.Top, Left.Bottom * Right.Bottom );
```

```ada
begin
    return (Reduce (Product) );
end "*";

function "/" (Left, Right: Fraction) return Fraction is
    Quotient: Fraction :=
        (  Left.Top * Right.Bottom, Left.Bottom * Right.Top );
begin
    return (Reduce (Quotient) );
end "/";

function "+" (Left, Right: Fraction) return Fraction is
    Sum: Fraction :=
        (  Left.Top * Right.Bottom + Right.Top * Left.Bottom,
           Left.Bottom * Right.Bottom );
begin
    return (Reduce (Sum) );
end "+";

function "-" (Right: Fraction) return Fraction is
begin
    return (-Right.Top, Right.Bottom);
end "-";

function "-" (Left, Right: Fraction) return Fraction is
begin
    -- uses the previously defined "+" and "-"
    return Left + (-Right); -- Left - Right would be
                            -- infinitely recursive
end "-";

-- Since fractions may not be reduced, equality is tested by
-- "cross multiplication"
function "=" (Left, Right: Fraction) return Boolean is
begin
    return Left.Top * Right.Bottom = Left.Bottom * Right.Top;
end "=";

procedure Put (Item: in Fraction) is
    package Int_IO is new Text_IO.Integer_IO (Integer);
begin
    Int_IO.Put (Item.Top, Width => 0);
    Text_IO.Put ("/");
    Int_IO.Put (Item.Bottom, Width => 0);
end Put;
end Frac_Pack;
```

Function Reduce uses the recursive GCD function to reduce fractions. Reduce is then used by the fraction operators in order to return a fraction in reduced form.

For example, instead of returning the fraction (6, 15), the fraction is first reduced to (2, 5). Since the specification of Reduce is not in the specification of Frac_Pack, Reduce can only be used within the body of Frac_Pack, not by the users of Frac_Pack.

In Frac_Pack, the subtraction operator for fractions returns the expression Left + (-Right). The "+" and "-" operators used in this expression are those previously defined for fractions. This expression could not be replaced with the simpler expression Left - Right, because this would result in infinite recursion. In other words, the "-" would call itself without end.

Now that Frac_Pack has been explained, let us use this package to demonstrate the need for private types. Since the implementation of type Fraction is placed in the visible part of the package Frac_Pack, users may access components Top and Bottom. As the following code illustrates, this enables users to violate the intended use of type Fraction or to substitute the provided fraction operators with their own unsanctioned versions:

```
with Frac_Pack; use Frac_Pack;
procedure Abuse_Fractions is
    A, B, C: Fraction;
begin
    A := (3, 4);
    B := (1, 2);

    A.Top := B.Top + B.Bottom;
        -- this operation doesn't make sense

    C := (A.Top + B.Top, A.Bottom + B.Bottom);
        -- provided "+" substituted with this
        -- unsanctioned version
end Abuse_Fractions;
```

After initializing A and B to record aggregates, this code violates our concept of a fraction. Conceptually it makes no sense to assign the sum of the numerator and denominator of B to the numerator of A. Furthermore, the last statement bypasses the provided "+" operator for fractions defined in package Frac_Pack and employs the user's own unsanctioned version of fraction addition. In most computer languages, programmers can only trust that users of their code do not abuse their abstractions in this way. As we shall see, in Ada, programmers can prohibit such abuse by defining a Fraction to be a private type.

There is yet another problem with our Frac_Pack package. Clients of Frac_Pack are able to write code that depends on the specific implementation of type Fraction. If the implementor of this package changes the representation of type Fraction, not only will the clients of this package need to recompile, they may also have to recode to accommodate the change. For example, in the following version of Frac_Pack, a fraction is represented as an array instead of as a record:

```
package Frac_Pack is
    -- This new representation of type Fraction impacts
```

```
          -- users of the previous implementation
          type Fraction_Parts is (Top, Bottom);
          type Fraction is array (Fraction_Parts) of Integer;

          function "*" (Left, Right: Fraction) return Fraction;
          function "/" (Left, Right: Fraction) return Fraction;
          -- same as before except that division by 0 checks are needed
             ...
      end Frac_Pack;
```

Clients of this package must now reference the parts of a fraction as array components instead of record components. Ideally, clients of `Frac_Pack` should not depend on the underlying implementation of type `Fraction`. Fractions should be
thought of in an abstract mathematical manner that is divorced from their representation in Ada. Whether fractions happen to be implemented as records or arrays
is irrelevant to the concept of a fraction.

All of the cited problems with the `Frac_Pack` package can be solved in Ada
by making `Fraction` a private type. Private types require a special private region
of the package specification.

So far, we have only encountered packages that are neatly divided into a public
part, which is the package specification, and the private part, which is the package
body. The package specification, however, may itself contain a private part. This
private part is where the implementations of private types are placed:

```
     -- package specification with a private part
     package package name is
        public declarations
     private
        private declarations
     end package name;
```

The private part of a package specification begins with the keyword **private** and
extends to the end of the specification.

The following version of the `Frac_Pack` package specification makes type
`Fraction` a private type:

```
     package Frac_Pack is

         type Fraction is private; -- private type
            -- the only operations on private types are the ones
            -- defined in this package specification plus the
            -- operations =, /=, and :=
         function "*" (Left, Right: Fraction) return Fraction;
         function "/" (Left, Right: Fraction) return Fraction;
         function "+" (Left, Right: Fraction) return Fraction;
         function "-" (Right: Fraction) return Fraction;
         function "-" (Left, Right: Fraction) return Fraction;
         function "/" (Top: Natural; Bottom: Positive) return Fraction;
            -- This "/" is used to construct a fraction
```

```
function "=" (Left, Right: Fraction) return Boolean;
-- "/=" is implicitly provided

procedure Put (Item: in Fraction);

private                -- private part
   -- this information is not available to users of the package
   type Fraction is
      record
         Top: Integer;
         Bottom: Positive;
      end record;

end Frac_Pack;
```

Type Fraction is declared to be private with the keywords **is private**:

```
type Fraction is private;
```

Private types can only be declared in package specifications. The name of the private type appears in the public part of the package specification and is available to package users. The implementations of these private types are defined in the private part of the package specification. Within this private part, private types must be fully specified, just as an ordinary type. In our example, Fraction is specified to be a record with two components.

From a user's perspective, even though items placed in the private part of a package specification can be visually examined, these items are hidden (inaccessible), just as if they were placed in the package body. Of course, the question that arises is, so why are these items not placed in the package body? Who benefits from the information contained in the private part of a package specification? The answer is that the compiler benefits. The implementation of a private type such as Fraction is placed in the private part of the package specification, rather than in the package body, because the compiler needs to know how Fraction is implemented. The compiler must know what kind of object is being declared as private and how much memory needs to be allocated for such an object. This information cannot be obtained from the package body because code that lists package Frac_Pack in its **with** clause just needs the specification of Frac_Pack in order to compile.

When the implementation of Fraction is placed in the private part of the package specification, users of the package are encouraged to think of fractions in the abstract mathematical sense and to ignore the fact that the fractions are implemented using a record. From the user's perspective, it makes no difference whether the fractions are implemented as records, arrays, or some other data structure. Let us now revisit the procedure Abuse_Fractions and see how it is affected by the new version of Frac_Pack, where Fraction is now a private type:

```
with Frac_Pack; use Frac_Pack;
procedure Abuse_Fractions is
   A, B, C: Fraction;
```

```
begin

    -- use the "/" to construct fractions
    A := 3 / 4;       -- A := (3, 4); is illegal
    B := 1 / 2;       -- B := (1, 2); is illegal


    A.Top := B.Top + B.Bottom;
        -- illegal; cannot access Top or Bottom


    C := (A.Top + B.Top, A.Bottom + B.Bottom);
        -- illegal; cannot access Top or Bottom


end Abuse_Fractions;
```

Users of this new version of `Frac_Pack` can now reference fraction variables and constants as a whole but cannot reference their numerator (`Top`) and denominator (`Bottom`) components. This means that a fraction cannot be initialized to a record aggregate:

```
A := (3, 4); -- illegal;
```

This assignment is illegal because it is based on the knowledge that `Fraction` is implemented as a record with two integer components. This information cannot be used. To initialize a fraction, the following version of the function " / " was added to the `Frac_Pack` package:

```
function "/" (Top: Natural; Bottom: Positive) return Fraction;
```

The body of " / ", which must be placed in the body of `Frac_Pack`, appears as follows:

```
-- This overloaded "/" allows fractions to be constructed
function "/" (Top: Natural; Bottom: Positive) return Fraction is
begin
    return (Top, Bottom);
end "/";
```

This function simply returns, as a fraction, the numerator and denominator components that were passed in as parameters. This function makes use of information in the private part of `Frac_Pack`'s specification. No problem arises since this information is available to the body of Frac_Pack.

The next two statements in `Abuse_Fractions`, the objectionable assignments, are now illegal, as desired:

```
A.Top := B.Top + B.Bottom;                        -- now illegal
C := (A.Top + B.Top, A.Bottom + B.Bottom); -- now illegal
```

These assignments are illegal because, once again, the components of `Fraction` cannot be accessed.

By declaring a type to be private, we not only make the underlying components of the type inaccessible; we also restrict the predefined operations that can be performed on objects of this type. The only predefined operations that can be performed on objects of a private type are assignments and tests for equality and inequality. A few attributes can also apply to private types, along with membership tests. The " = " operator was overloaded, so the only predefined fraction operation available to users of the package is the assignment operator. Any additional operations must be explicitly provided in the package specification where the private type is declared. In our example, the additional operations—" / ", " + ", " - ", and so on—are explicitly provided in the package specification of `Frac_Pack`.

As just mentioned, only assignments and equality tests can be performed on objects of a private type. In our example, however, this is not a restriction since the private type `Fraction` is implemented as a record, and records are already restricted to these predefined operations. If a private type, though, is implemented as an integer type, then users of the package are still restricted to these operations. They cannot employ the operations usually allowed for integers, such as addition, subtraction, multiplication, and division, unless these operations are explicitly provided in the package.

As we have seen, the private part of the package specification of `Frac_Pack` only contains the full declaration of the private type `Fraction`. Other items, however, may be placed in this private part. For example, we may declare each component of the record `Fraction` to belong to a user-defined subtype:

```
   . . .
private

    subtype Top_Type is Integer range -1_000 .. 1_000;

    subtype Bottom_Type is Positive range 1 .. 1_000;

    type Fraction is
        record
            Top: Top_Type;
            Bottom: Bottom_Type;
        end record;

end Frac_Pack;
```

Subtypes `Top_Type` and `Bottom_Type` are declared in the private part of the package specification. This is appropriate since these subtypes are merely provided to implement type `Fraction` and do not concern users of the package. (Although subtypes may appear in the private part of a package specification, private types such as `Fraction` cannot be declared as subtypes.)

Another point to consider is that, except for subprogram bodies, every item in the declarative part of a package body can be relocated to the private part of its corresponding package specification. This is not advised, however, because changes to a package are best made in the package body rather than in the package specification. As previously mentioned, changes to the package body usually do not require any other unit of code to be recompiled, whereas changes to a package specification typically require that every program unit that mentions the specification in its **with** clause also be recompiled.

Once a type is declared to be private, constants of this private type can be declared in the public part of the package specification, so they will be available to users. Declaring such constants, however, creates a dilemma. Thus far in this book, we have seen that all constants must be initialized when they are declared. Constants that belong to a private type, however, cannot be assigned an initial value because the full implementation of the private type has not yet been provided. For example, suppose that we wish to declare the constant One_Half and initialize it to the record aggregate (1, 2). We cannot initialize One_Half when it is declared, because the implementation of type Fraction has not yet been provided:

```
package Frac_Pack is

   type Fraction is private;
   One_Half: constant Fraction := (1, 2);   -- illegal;
      -- the implementation of Fraction has not yet
      -- been defined
      ...
```

The solution to our dilemma is to use deferred constants. When a deferred constant is declared, the specification of its value is deferred until after the private type to which it belongs is fully declared:

```
package Frac_Pack is

   type Fraction is private;
   One_Half: constant Fraction; -- deferred constant

   function "*" (Left, Right: Fraction) return Fraction;
   function "/" (Left, Right: Fraction) return Fraction;
   -- plus other functions declared as before
      ...
private

   type Fraction is
      record
         Top: Integer;
         Bottom: Positive;
      end record;

   One_Half: constant Fraction :=
         (Top => 1, Bottom => 2); -- full declaration of constant

end Frac_Pack;
```

The full declaration of the constant One_Half, including its value, is placed in the private part of the package specification, following the full declaration of Fraction. In our example, the deferred constant, One_Half, belongs to a private type, but Ada allows deferred constants to be of any type. (In Ada 83, deferred constants are only allowed for private types.)

**Ada 95** ▶

In summary, private types permit designers of a package to impose their data abstractions upon users of the package. This is accomplished in two ways. First, a private type is visible, while its underlying implementation is hidden. Users of the package can then reference a private type but cannot fiddle around with irrelevant implementation details. Second, a private type restricts the kind of operations that can be performed on its objects. Thus, only operations that make sense for a particular abstract type are allowed. (Within the package itself, however, such restrictions do not apply. The underlying representation of the private type is visible, and any operations normally available can be used.)

## LIMITED PRIVATE TYPES

As previously mentioned, from outside a package, the only predefined operations that automatically apply to private types are assignments and tests for equality and inequality. The designer of the package may even forbid these operations by declaring a limited private type. With a limited private type, the only operations allowed are those provided in the package along with the type. (A few attributes can apply to private types or to limited private types, such as P'Address, which yields the address where a P is stored.) The programmer thus takes complete control over how objects of a limited private type are used. This control allows a programmer to define a type whose operations include those and only those that are needed.

Limited private types are declared just like private types, except that the keywords **is limited private** are used. The private part of the package specification is still denoted by the keyword **private**. The next example is a version of the Stack package that defines a stack as a limited private type:

```
package Stack is

    type Stack_Type (Stack_Size: Natural) is limited private;
        -- limited private means that the only operations on
        -- stacks are the ones defined in this package specification

    function Is_Empty (S: in Stack_Type) return Boolean;
    function Is_Full (S: in Stack_Type) return Boolean;

    procedure Push (S: in out Stack_Type; Item: in Integer);
    procedure Pop (S: in out Stack_Type; Item: out Integer);

    function "=" (Left, Right: in Stack_Type) return Boolean;
    procedure Copy (From: in Stack_Type; To: out Stack_Type);
    procedure Clear (S: in out Stack_Type);
```

```ada
private
    -- this information cannot be accessed by the
    -- users of the package

    type Integer_Array is array (Natural range <>) of Integer;

    type Stack_Type (Stack_Size: Natural) is
        record
            Stk: Integer_Array (1 .. Stack_Size) := (others => 0);
            Top: Natural := 0;
        end record;
end Stack;

with Ada.Text_IO; use Ada.Text_IO;
package body Stack is

    function Is_Empty (S: in Stack_Type) return Boolean is
    begin
        return S.Top = 0;
    end Is_Empty;

    function Is_Full (S: in Stack_Type) return Boolean is
    begin
        return S.Top = S.Stack_Size;
    end Is_Full;

    procedure Push (S: in out Stack_Type; Item: in Integer) is
    begin
        if Is_Full (S) then
            Put_Line ("ERROR: Stack Overflow");
        else
            S.Top := S.Top + 1;
            S.Stk (S.Top) := Item;
        end if;
    end Push;

    procedure Pop (S: in out Stack_Type; Item: out Integer) is
    begin
        if Is_Empty (S) then
            Put_Line ("ERROR: Stack Underflow");
        else
            Item := S.Stk (S.Top);
            S.Top := S.Top - 1;
        end if;
    end Pop;

    function "=" (Left, Right: in Stack_Type) return Boolean is
    begin
        -- only compares valid part of stacks
```

```
        return Left.Top = Right.Top and then
          (Left.Stk (1 .. Left.Top) = Right.Stk (1 .. Right.Top));
    end "=";

    procedure Copy (From: in Stack_Type; To: out Stack_Type) is
    begin
        -- checks whether there is room in the destination stack
        -- for a copy
        if From.Top > To.Stack_Size then
            Put_Line ("ERROR: Stack Overflow");
        else
            -- copies stack items
            To.Top := From.Top;
            To.Stk (1 .. From.Top) := From.Stk (1 .. From.Top);
        end if;
    end Copy;

    procedure Clear (S: in out Stack_Type) is
    begin
        -- only resets Top; does not fill array with zeros
        S.Top := 0;
    end Clear;

end Stack;
```

Outside of the package, objects belonging to a limited private type may not even be assigned to one another or tested for equality or inequality. (These restrictions, however, do not apply within the package in which the limited private type is declared.) To compensate for these missing operations, the equality operator "=" and the procedure Copy have been added to the package. With the operator "=", users of the package can test whether objects of the limited private type Stack_Type are equal. (The inequality operator "/=" is implicitly provided when "=" is declared.) Unlike the equality operator, the assignment operator, ":=", can never be overloaded. (As we will see in Chapter 13, however, user-defined assignments can be implemented with "controlled types.") The procedure Copy, which has the effect of an assignment operator, is thus provided. For example, assuming that A and B are variables of Stack_Type, the following procedure assigns the value of A to the variable B:

```
Copy (From => A, To => B);
```

The restriction against employing the assignment operator for objects of a limited private type extends to other operators where values are copied. For instance, users of a package may not declare an object of a limited private type with an assigned initial value. This means that outside of the package, constants belonging to a limited private type cannot be declared. (Once again, these restrictions only apply to external users of the package, not within the package containing the limited private type.) However, objects of a limited private type can be passed as parameters (without default parameter values), and a function can return a value of a limited private type.

This previous version of package `Stack` is an example of a type manager, as opposed to the original version presented in this chapter, which was an object manager. Whereas the object manager version creates and manages a single stack object that exists throughout the lifetime of the program, this package provides and manages a type, `Stack_Type`, that allows users to declare their own stacks within their own code. These user-declared stacks can then be manipulated using the services such as `Push` and `Pop` provided in this package. Since users of this package may declare different stacks, `Push` and `Pop` must have a parameter indicating which stack to manipulate. The particular stack to be manipulated is passed to `Push` or `Pop` via the formal parameter S. Since S is updated, and then returned to the caller, this parameter must have an **in out** mode.

This version of a stack package is more complete than the original stack package. We have added resources such as `Is_Empty`, which informs us whether a stack is empty; `Is_Full`, which informs us whether a stack is full; the equality operator "="; the procedure `Copy`, which replaces the assignment operator; and the procedure `Clear`, which empties the stack. Furthermore, `Push` and `Pop` (`Pop` is now a procedure) contain two parameters instead of one. The added parameter specifies the particular integer stack to manipulate.

The functions `Is_Full` and `Is_Empty` can be invoked not only by clients of package `Stack`; they are also invoked by procedures `Push` and `Pop`. `Push` and `Pop` invoke the functions `Is_Full` and `Is_Empty`, respectively, before attempting to push or pop an item. For example, if the stack is empty and `Pop` is called, then `Pop` determines that the stack is empty and outputs an error message. (In Chapter 10, we will see that a better way to handle such overflow or underflow conditions is by raising user-defined exceptions.)

Note that the limited private type, `Stack_Type`, is implemented as a variant record type. The record discriminant, `Stack_Size`, sets the size of the stack and is visible to the package users. Therefore, users of this package may declare different-sized integer stacks, as follows:

```
My_Stack: Stack_Type (Stack_Size => 50);
    -- creates an integer stack of size 50


Your_Stack: Stack_Type (Stack_Size => 33);
    -- creates an integer stack of size 33
```

To push or pop an item, include the name of the desired stack:

```
Push (My_Stack, 10);    -- pushes the value 10 on My_Stack
Push (Your_Stack, 5);   -- pushes the value 5 on Your_Stack
Pop (My_Stack, Item);   -- pops the value 10 from My_Stack and
                        -- returns this value in the integer
                        -- variable Item
```

Note that, as with package `Frac_Pack`, package `Stack` needs to provide an overloaded "=" operator because the predefined "=" that operates on records does not yield the desired result. (And since `Stack_Item` is a limited private type, the predefined "=" is not available anyway.) The overloaded "=" operator provided for stacks first checks that the stacks are the same size at the time the comparison is made. If they are not the same size, then they are not equal—no further examination is needed. If the stacks are equal in size, then only the portion of the stacks that contains valid stack items is compared. The portion of the stacks beyond `Top` that contains undefined data is not used in the comparison.

In our `Frac_Pack` package, where `Fraction` is declared to be a private type instead of a limited private type, the only predefined operation available to the package users is the assignment operator. [The predefined "=" (and "/=") would have been available had they not been overridden.] Allowing users of `Frac_Pack` to employ the assignment operator presents no problems. In the case of package `Stack`, however, the predefined assignment operator for records yields incorrect results. By declaring `Stack_Type` to be a limited private type, this assignment operator becomes unavailable and is replaced by the `Copy` procedure. `Copy` first checks that the destination stack is large enough to accommodate the copied stack. If there is enough room, it then copies over the value of `Top` and the portion of the stack that contains valid stack items.

The `Clear` procedure simply sets the top of the stack to zero. It does not need to zero out the stack; doing so would just waste processing time.

**Ada 95 ▶** In the preceding `Stack` package, a limited private type, `Stack_Type`, is implemented as a discriminated record whose discriminant is visible. A limited private type (or private type) can also be implemented as a discriminated record whose discriminant is hidden. The hidden discriminant, however, must be given a default value. As shown below, the discriminant value takes the default provided in the private implementation:

```ada
package Reptiles is
   type Snake is limited private; -- discriminant is not visible
   ...
private
   type Venom_Type is (Hemotoxic, Neurotoxic);
   type Snake (Poisonous: Boolean := True) is
      record
         case Poisonous is
            when True =>
               Venom: Venom_Type;
            when False =>
               Constrictor: Boolean;
         end case;
      end record;
end Reptiles;
```

```ada
with Reptiles;
procedure Ophideophobia is
```

```
My_Snake: Reptiles.Snake;
        -- takes the default discriminant value of True from the
        -- private implementation
begin
    ...
end Ophideophobia;
```

As a final brief note, any type can be declared as a private or limited private type. However, record types (and only record types) can be declared as limited without being private. As limited types, one cannot use the predefined record operations of assignment and tests for equality. In Chapter 15, we shall see that task types and protected types are automatically limited but not necessarily private.

Although the packages presented in this chapter may be very useful, they are not general purpose or flexible enough to be offered as reusable software components. For example, the previous stack package, although allowing stacks of different sizes to be created, only allows integer values to be stacked. To stack floating point values, or enumeration values, or records values, the package must be modified.

Generics is a powerful tool for making packages, and other program units, general purpose and very flexible. A generic stack package, for example, can be written that not only allows stacks of different sizes to be created, but allows practically any type of object to be stacked. Generics is the subject of the next chapter.

---

## EXERCISES

1. When, if ever, would you employ the **use** clause? Defend your position.

2. How do packages differ from subprograms? How do package specifications differ from package bodies?

3. Write a package that contains an enumeration type `Personal_Computers` that consists of brands of various personal computers. Include a constant of type `Personal_Computers` called `Best_Computer`.

4. Find all the errors in the following packages, ignoring the fact that the package bodies would rarely serve any purpose. (Lines indicate separate compilation units.)

```
package P1 is
    pragma Elaborate_Body;
    subtype P1_Spec is Integer range 1 .. 10;
    A: P1_Spec;
end P1;
```

---

```
package body P1 is
    B: P1_Spec;
    subtype P1_Body is Character range 'A' .. 'Z';
    C: P1_Body;
end P1;
```

```
with P1; use P1;
package P2 is
   pragma Elaborate_Body;
   D: P1_Spec;
   E: P1_Body;
   subtype P2_Spec is Integer range 1 .. 10;
   F: P2_Spec;
end P2;
```

```
package body P2 is
   G: P1_Spec;
   H: P1_Body;
   I: P2_Spec;
   subtype P2_Body is Character range 'A' .. 'Z';
   J: P2_Body;
end P2;
```

5. Find all the errors in declarative part of procedure Q, ignoring the fact that the package bodies would rarely serve any purpose:

```
procedure Q is

   package P1 is
      pragma Elaborate_Body;
      subtype P1_Spec is Integer range 1 .. 10;
      A: P1_Spec;
   end P1;

   B: P1.P1_Spec;
   use P1;
   C: P1_Spec;
   subtype Outside is Float range 0.0 .. 5.0;

   package P2 is
      pragma Elaborate_Body;
      D: P1_Spec;
      E: Outside;
      subtype P2_Spec is Integer range 1 .. 10;
      F: P2_Spec;
   end P2;

   package body P1 is
      G: P1_Spec;
      H: P2_Spec;
      I: Outside;
      subtype P1_Body is Character range 'A' .. 'Z';
      J: P1_Body;
   end P1;

   package body P2 is
      K: P1_Spec;
```

```
        L: P1_Body;
        M: P2_Spec;
    end P2;
begin  -- Q
    null;
end Q;
```

6. Which variables, A to M, are available to the executable statement part of procedure Q in exercise 5?

7. Find all the errors in the following code:

```
package P1 is
    subtype P1_Spec is Integer range 1 .. 10;
end P1;
```

---

```
with P1; use P1;
package P2 is
    A: P1_Spec;
    subtype P2_Spec is Character range 'A' .. 'Z';
end P2;
```

---

```
with P2; use P2;
package P3 is
    pragma Elaborate_Body;
    B: P1_Spec;
    C: P2_Spec;
    subtype P3_Spec is Integer range 0 .. 10;
end P3;
```

---

```
with P1; use P1;
package body P3 is
    D: P1_Spec;
    E: P2_Spec;
    F: P3_Spec;
end P3;
```

8. What will each of the following Put statements in procedure Q output? (Note: one of these Put statements contains an error.)

```
package P1 is
    A, B, C, D: Character := 'X';
end P1;
```

---

```
package P2 is
    C, D, E: Character := 'Y';
end P2;
```

---

```
with Ada.Text_IO, P1, P2; use Ada.Text_IO, P1, P2;
procedure Q is
    B, C: Character := 'Z';
begin
    -- one of these is illegal
```

```
      Put (A); New_Line;
      Put (B); New_Line;
      Put (C); New_Line;
      Put (D); New_Line;
      Put (E); New_Line;
   end Q;
```

9. Fix the errors in the following code *without* employing the **use** clause:

```
package D_Scale is
   type D_Major is (D, E, F_Sharp, G, A, B, C_Sharp);
end D_Scale;
```

```
with Ada.Text_IO;
with D_Scale;
procedure Noteworthy is
   package Scale_IO is new Enumeration_IO (D_Major);
   Note: D_Major := D;
begin
   Get (Note);
   if Note = D_Major'First then
      Put_Line ("First note of scale");
   end if;
end Noteworthy;
```

Show what `Noteworthy` looks like when it employs the type-based **use** clause:

```
use type D_Scale.D_Major;
```

10. Rewrite the `Complex_Number` package presented in this chapter, making type `Complex` a private type. Add a subprogram to the package to allow users to assign a value (literal) to objects of type `Complex`. If the private implementation of type `Complex` changed from a record type

```
type Complex is
   record
      Real: Float;
      Imaginary: Float;
   end record;
```

to the following array type

```
type Complex_Components is (Real, Imaginary);
type Complex is array (Complex_Components) of Float;
```

then what impact would this change have on existing clients of package `Complex_Number`?

11. Modify the package you wrote for Exercise 10 so that the type `Complex` is a limited private type. Add new subprograms to the package to allow users to perform assignment operations and to test complex numbers to determine whether they are equal. Does it make sense to make type `Complex` a limited private type instead of just a private type?

12. Consider the following package that contains a private type:

```ada
package Counter is
   type Element is private;
   function Set_Element return Element;
   function Increment (Item: Element) return Element;
private
   type Element is new Integer;
end Counter;

package body Counter is
   function Set_Element return Element is
   begin
      return 1;
   end;

   function Increment (Item: Element) return Element is
   begin
      return Item + 1;
   end Increment;
end Counter;
```

Which of the following statements illegally attempt to reference items from the package Counter that are hidden?

```ada
with Ada.Text_IO, Counter; use Ada.Text_IO, Counter;
procedure Demo is
   X, Y, Z: Element;
begin
   Z := Set_Element;
   Y := Increment (Z);
   X := Z;
   if X = Y then
      Put_Line ("Equal");
   end if;
   if X = 2 then
      Put_Line ("Equals 2");
   end if;
   X := 4;
   Y := Set_Element + 1;
end Demo;
```

13. Which statements in Exercise 12 would be illegal if Element were a limited private type?

14. Can clients of package Frac_Pack shown in this chapter declare their own constants of type Fraction? If so, show how this can be done.

15. **Pragma** Elaborate_All specifies that the listed compilation unit needs to be elaborated before continuing. Explain why it is desirable to place **pragma** Elaborate_All in the following code:

```
package A is
    function Initialize return Integer;
end A;
...
with A;
pragma Elaborate_All (A);
package body B is
    J: Integer := A.Initialize;
end B;
```

16. In the following code, should different variables, Temp, be defined in procedures P1, P2, and P3, as shown, or should each procedure reference a single variable, Temp, placed above P1? What are the advantages and disadvantages?

```
package body Demo is
    --  Temp: Integer;
    --  Should a single Temp be placed here instead of
    --  the separate variables, Temp, in each procedure below?
    procedure P1 is
        Temp: Integer;
    begin
        Temp := 1;
        ...
    end P1;

    procedure P2 is
        Temp: Integer;
    begin
        Temp := 2;
        ...
    end P2;

    procedure P3 is
        Temp: Integer;
    begin
        Temp := 3;
        ...
    end P3;
end Demo;
```

17. Replace the body of Q by renaming procedure External.P:

```
package External is
    procedure P;
end External;

package Use_P_Body is
    procedure Q;
end Use_P_Body;

with External;
```

```
package body Use_P_Body is
   procedure Q is          -- Replace with a rename
   begin
      External.P;
   end Q;
end Use_P_Body;
```

18. Implement the private part of the specification and the body of the following queue package:

```
package Queue_Pack is

   type Queue_Type (Queue_Size: Positive) is limited private;

   function Is_Empty (Queue: in Queue_Type) return Boolean;
   function Is_Full (Queue: in Queue_Type) return Boolean;

   procedure Add ( Queue: in out Queue_Type;
                   Item:  in      Integer);
   procedure Remove ( Queue: in out Queue_Type;
                      Item:      out Integer);

   function "=" (Left, Right: in Queue_Type) return Boolean;
   procedure Copy (From: in Queue_Type; To: out Queue_Type);
   procedure Clear (Queue: in out Queue_Type);

private
   -- your own implementation
end Queue_Pack;
```

19. Implement the body of the following string package:

```
package String_Manipulation is
   Max_Length: constant Positive := 40;
   subtype Index is Natural range 0 .. Max_Length;
   type Variant_String (Max_Size: Index := Max_Length) is
      private;
   function To_Variant_String (Str: String)
      return Variant_String;
   procedure Append ( Str: in out Variant_String;
                      Item_To_Append: in Variant_String );
   function Size (Str: Variant_String) return Index;
   function Extract_String (Str: Variant_string)
      return String;
   -- additional operations can be added here
private
   type Variant_String (Max_Size: Index := Max_Length) is
      record
         Length: Index := Index'First;
         Text: String (1 .. Max_Size) := (1..Max_Size => '');
      end record;
end String_Manipulation;
```

**20.** Implement the body of the following package that converts a Roman numeral to an integer.

```ada
package Convert is
   type Roman is ('I', 'V', 'X', 'L', 'C', 'D', 'M');
   type Roman_Numeral is array (Positive range <>) of Roman;
   -- converts a roman numeral to an integer value
   function To_Integer (Numeral: Roman_Numeral) return
      Positive;
end Convert;
```

Write the function To_Integer so that it properly converts roman numerals such as "IV" and "VI". (If you want to get fancy, reject illegally constructed Roman numerals such as "VX".)

# 8

# Generics

**G**enerics, or generic units, act as a template from which actual nongeneric units can be created. What makes generic units useful is that they can greatly reduce the amount of redundant code. Furthermore, they allow the creation of flexible, general-purpose code that can be easily reused on different software projects.

Generics eliminate redundant code in a manner similar to the way a form letter program eliminates the need to write redundant letters. A form letter is written like a regular letter except that data that can vary, such as a person's name and address, are marked by special symbols. When letters are printed, these symbols are replaced with actual names and addresses. The letter is thus written only once, and many copies, differing only in certain information, are created.

Similarly, a generic is written like a regular program unit, except that data can vary. For example, a parameter type is marked by a special symbol. When actual program units are generated, the special symbol is replaced with an actual type. The generic is thus written only once, and many copies, differing only in the parameter type, are created. This process of making an instance of a generic is known as instantiating a generic. The special symbol is called a generic formal parameter. Different users of a generic can create code that is customized to their particular needs simply by instantiating the generic with the appropriate data.

Note that a generic cannot be used like an actual program unit any more than a form letter template can be used like an actual letter. Generics, as well as form letter templates, can only be used to create copies that can vary in specific ways. In particular, generic functions and procedures cannot be invoked; only the actual functions and procedures created by instantiating these generics can be invoked. Similarly, the resources of a generic package cannot be accessed; only the resources of its instantiated copies may be accessed.

The simplest example of a form letter is the "degenerate case," where there are no symbols to replace. Each instance of the form letter is thus identical. Similarly, generics can be written that have no symbols (generic parameters) to replace. Each instantiation of the generic results in an identical program unit.

Procedures, functions, and packages can be made generic. To make a procedure, function, or package a generic, simply begin with the keyword **generic**:

```
generic          -- a generic procedure
procedure Proc (X: in Float);

generic          -- a generic function
function Func (N: Integer) return Boolean;

generic          -- a generic package
package Pack is
    type T is (Alpha, Beta, Gamma);
end Pack;
```

The preceding generics can be instantiated as follows:

```
procedure My_Proc is new Proc;
procedure Your_Proc is new Proc;
function My_Func is new Func;
function Your_Func is new Func;
package My_Pack is new Pack;
package Your_Pack is new Pack;
```

As a result of these instantiations, two copies of `Proc`, `Func`, and `Pack` are created. Since no generic parameters are provided (no symbols to be substituted), each instantiation of a particular generic produces an identical program unit. In our example, `My_Proc` and `Your_Proc` are identical procedures, `My_Func` and `Your_Func` are identical functions, and `My_Pack` and `Your_Pack` are identical packages. Thus, both `My_Pack` and `Your_Pack` contain an enumeration type `T` with the three values: `Alpha`, `Beta`, and `Gamma`.

Although generics can be written without any generic parameters, this is unusual. The real power of generics comes from providing generic parameters so that instances of a generic differ from one another in certain respects. There are five kinds of generic parameters: type parameters, derived type parameters, object parameters, subprogram parameters, and package parameters. Each of these will be discussed in the following sections.

## GENERIC TYPE PARAMETERS

To illustrate how generics can be used to eliminate redundant code, we will consider three different nongeneric functions. Each of these functions does the same processing but on objects of different types. We will then see how a generic function enables us to eliminate the redundant code by writing the implementation of these functions only once instead of three times.

The first function compares two integers and returns the value of the larger integer:

```
function Larger_Integer (X, Y: Integer) return Integer is
begin
    if X > Y then
        return X;
    else
        return Y;
    end if;
end Larger_Integer;
```

Note that this function only returns the larger of two *integer* values. If we need a function that returns the "larger" of two character values, then a new function must be written. This is our second function, Max_Character:

```
function Max_Character (X, Y: Character) return Character is
begin
    if X > Y then
        return X;
    else
        return Y;
    end if;
end Max_Character;
```

For a third example, consider a function that, given two planets, returns the planet that is farthest from the sun. (Ignore the fact that during unusual times, Pluto is closer to the sun than Neptune.)

```
type Solar_System is (Mercury, Venus, Earth, Mars, Jupiter,
    Saturn, Uranus, Neptune, Pluto);
function Outer_Planet (X, Y: Solar_System) return
    Solar_System is
begin
    if X > Y then
        return X;
    else
        return Y;
    end if;
end Outer_Planet;
```

The three functions–Larger_Integer, Max_Character, and Outer_Planet–basically do the same thing: they return the larger of two values. The only difference between the functions is that they operate on different types of data: integers, characters, and planets. Writing different functions to handle each data type, as we have done, results in redundant code. Redundant code is not a major problem if the functions are as short as these three examples. However, if the functions require many lines of code, then redundant code is a problem. First, redundant code is error prone because errors can be easily introduced when duplicating many lines of source code. Second, redundant code is difficult to maintain, because if one function containing this code needs to be modified, every other function containing the same code will probably have to be modified. Code is also difficult to maintain because it is difficult to understand. A lot of code might be examined before one spots the redundancy. Third, and least important, redundant code wastes computer storage space because more space is needed to store all the duplicate source code (Ada code). (As we will discuss later, generics may or may not reduce the amount of executable object code.)

Some computer languages partially avoid redundant code by allowing data types to be passed in at runtime as parameters to regular subprograms. In strongly typed languages like Ada, however, types cannot be passed in at runtime because the type of every data object must be determined at compilation time. (A special exception to this, dynamic dispatching, will be discussed in Chapter 13.)

Although data types cannot be passed to subprograms during runtime, they can be "passed" to generic units during compilation time when these units are instantiated. The result of this generic instantiation is the creation of an actual program unit, such as a function, that can reference the type that was passed in. There is, therefore, no uncertainty at compilation time about the type to which any object belongs.

Let us now return to the problem of redundant code illustrated by the three preceding functions: `Larger_Integer`, `Max_Character`, and `Outer_Planet`. Instead of having three copies of essentially the same function, a single generic function can be written. From this single generic function, the three functions can be instantiated.

A generic function has two parts, a generic specification and a body:

```
-- generic specification
generic
    generic formal parameters
function function name (parameter definitions) return type;

-- body
function function name (parameter definitions) return type is
    declarations
begin
    statements
end function name;
```

The first part of the generic unit is the generic specification. The generic specification is the visible part that acts as an interface to those who instantiate the generic function. The generic specification begins with the keyword generic, followed by a list of formal generic parameters. Formal generic parameters act like place holders, or replaceable dummy names. When a generic unit is instantiated, these formal generic parameters are replaced by actual parameters. Following the formal generic parameters is the standard function specification.

The second part of the generic unit is the body, which is indistinguishable from the body of a regular nongeneric function. The generic body, like the generic specification, contains the function specification.

The generic function from which `Larger_Integer`, `Max_Character`, and `Outer_Planet` can be instantiated appears as follows:

```
generic          -- generic specification
   type Item is (<>);
function Maximum (X, Y: Item) return Item;

function Maximum (X, Y: Item) return Item is    -- body
begin
   if X > Y then
      return X;
   else
      return Y;
   end if;
end Maximum;
```

The first part of this generic function, Maximum, is its specification. The specification has a single formal generic parameter called Item:

```
type Item is (<>);
```

The keyword **type** tells us that Item is a formal generic type parameter. The actual type that will replace Item is determined when this generic function is instantiated. The notation (<>) indicates that the actual type that will replace Item must be a discrete type. Thus, the compiler will reject any attempt to instantiate this generic with a nondiscrete type, such as Float. (As we will see, other notation is used for restricting the actual parameter types to integer types, etc.) Following the formal generic parameter is a standard function specification for Maximum.

The second part of the function Maximum is its body. The body of Maximum contains the implementation of the function and is the same as the bodies of functions Larger_Integer, Max_Character, and Outer_Planet. Note, however, that X and Y are of type Item. Since item is the name of the formal generic type parameter, it will be replaced with an actual type when the generic is instantiated. The body, then, can operate on objects whose types are determined at the time the generic unit is instantiated.

Given this generic function Maximum, the functions Larger_Integer, Max_Character, and Outer_Planet can all be created by instantiating Maximum as follows:

```
function Larger_Integer is new Maximum (Item => Integer);
function Max_Character is new Maximum (Item => Character);
function Outer_Planet is new Maximum (Item => Solar_System);
```

As we can see, a generic instantiation of a function begins with the keyword **function**, followed by the user-supplied function name, followed by the keywords **is new**. Next comes the name of the generic function that is to be instantiated. Note that generic functions can only be instantiated to create functions, never to create procedures or packages. Following the name of the generic function, Maximum, and placed within parentheses, are the actual generic parameters: Integer, Character, and Solar_System. At the time of instantiation, these actual generic parameters are matched, either through positional or named notation, with the formal generic parameter Item. The three preceding instantiations use named notation, denoted by the arrow, =>. In the first instantiation, for example, the actual generic parameter, Integer, is matched, using named notation, with the formal generic parameter Item. The actual type, Integer, therefore, replaces every occurrence of the "dummy" type Item. Within the generic function Maximum, variables X and Y, which were declared to belong to type Item, are now variables of type Integer. Therefore, in the body of Maximum, when a test is made whether X > Y, the values of two integer variables, X and Y, are being compared.

Be careful not to confuse the formal parameters of Maximum, which are X and Y, with its generic formal parameter, Item. As we have seen, the generic formal parameter Item is passed a value when Maximum is generically instantiated. The formal parameters X and Y, however, are passed actual values at runtime when the three functions created by instantiating Maximum are invoked.

As shown in the following code, once the functions Larger_Integer, Max_Character, and Outer_Planet are created through generic instantiations, they can be used as if they were created "normally":

```
declare
    Int_1: Integer := 8;
    Int_2: Integer := 2;
    Char_1: Character := 'A';
    Char_2: Character := 'Z';
    My_Planet: Solar_System := Earth;
begin  -- assume Int, Char, and Planet
       -- were previously declared
    Int := Larger_Integer (X => Int_1, Y => Int_2);
       -- returns 8
    Char := Max_Character (X => Char_1, Y => Char_2);
       -- returns 'Z'
    Planet := Outer_Planet (X => My_Planet, Y => Venus);
       -- returns Earth
       . . .
end;
```

Our problem of code redundancy is now solved. The source code that implements three functions is now contained in only one place: in the body of the generic function Maximum. The object code, however, is handled differently by different compilers. Some compilers create the object code for the generic only once, no matter how many times this generic is instantiated. Each function created by instantiating the same generic thus shares the same object code. This typically results in less object code but slower execution speed. Other compilers create (expand) the object code each time the generic is instantiated. Each program unit created by instantiating the same generic thus has its own copy of the object code. This typically results in more object code but faster execution speed. The preferable approach depends on which is more important, computer memory or execution speed. An ideal compiler allows either option. (There are other factors that also affect memory and execution speed, such as the size of the generic, the number of times it is instantiated, and the kind of generic formal parameters it has.)

With some Ada compilation systems, the user "tells" the Ada compiler whether space or time is more important by placing a pragma called Optimize in the declarative part of a program unit. (A pragma is a compiler directive.) Optimize has two possible parameter values, Space and Time. The following statement tells the compiler that whenever there is a trade-off between space and time, space should be the overriding concern:

```ada
pragma Optimize (Space);
```

Alternatively, the following statement tells the compiler that time should be the overriding concern:

```ada
pragma Optimize (Time);
```

Generic procedures are handled like generic functions. To demonstrate the need for generic procedures, let us again begin by considering several nongeneric procedures that perform the same tasks but on different data types. The following nongeneric procedure, Print_Solar_System, prints all the planets of the solar system:

```ada
with Ada.Text_IO; use Ada.Text_IO;
procedure Print_Solar_System is
    type Solar_System is (Mercury, Venus, Earth, Mars, Jupiter,
        Saturn, Uranus, Neptune, Pluto);
    package Solar_System_IO is new
        Enumeration_IO (Solar_System);
    use Solar_System_IO;
begin
    for Planet in Solar_System loop
        Put (Planet);
        New_Line;
    end loop;
end Print_Solar_System;
```

Similarly, the next procedure, Print_Music_Types, prints all the different kinds of music listed in the enumeration type Music_Types:

```ada
with Ada.Text_IO; use Ada.Text_IO;
procedure Print_Music_Types is
    type Music_Types is (Jazz, Folk, Blues, Bluegrass, Klezmer,
        Pop);
    package Music_Type_IO is new Enumeration_IO (Music_Types);
    use Music_Type_IO;
begin
    for Music in Music_Types loop
        Put (Music);
        New_Line;
    end loop;
end Print_Music_Types;
```

These two procedures, `Print_Solar_System` and `Print_Music_Types`, do the same thing: they output the items of an enumeration type. The only difference between the procedures is that they output different enumeration types: planets and types of music. Writing different procedures to handle each data type results in redundant code. This redundant code can be eliminated by writing a single generic procedure. Instead of showing this generic procedure out of context, we will show how it fits into a complete Ada program. In this program, the generic procedure `Print_Enumeration_Type` is embedded in the procedure `Main`:

```ada
with Ada.Text_IO; use Ada;
procedure Main is

   type Solar_System is (Mercury, Venus, Earth, Mars, Jupiter,
      Saturn, Uranus, Neptune, Pluto);

   type Music_Types is (Jazz, Folk, Blues, Bluegrass, Klezmer,
      Pop);

   generic -- generic specification
      type Enum_Type is (<>);
   procedure Print_Enumeration_Type;

   procedure Print_Enumeration_Type is  -- body
      package Enum_Type_IO is new Text_IO.Enumeration_IO
         (Enum_Type);
   begin
      for Item in Enum_Type loop
         Enum_Type_IO.Put (Item);
         Text_IO.New_Line;
      end loop;
   end Print_Enumeration_Type;

   procedure Print_Solar_System is new  -- generic instantiation
      Print_Enumeration_Type (Enum_Type => Solar_System);

   procedure Print_Music_Types is new   -- generic instantiation
      Print_Enumeration_Type (Enum_Type => Music_Types);

begin -- Main
   Print_Solar_System;-- prints the planets of the solar system
   Print_Music_Types; -- prints the kinds of music in
                      -- Music_Types
end Main;
```

The first two declarations in procedure `Main` define the enumeration types `Solar_System` and `Music_Types`. These two declarations are followed by the generic specification and body of `Print_Enumeration_Type`. Once these items have been defined, `Print_Enumeration_Type` is instantiated, using the actual parameter values `Solar_System` and `Music_Types`. The procedures `Print_Solar_System` and `Print_Music_Types` are thus created and are available to the body of procedure `Main`. When `Main` invokes `Print_Solar_System`, all the planets of the solar system from `Mercury` to `Pluto` are output. When `Main` invokes `Print_Music_Types`, all the types of music from `Jazz` to `Pop` are output.

Note once again that we have created two procedures—`Print_Solar_System` and `Print_Music_Types`—but have coded the implementation of these procedures just once, in the body of `Print_Enumeration_Type`. We could create an indefinite number of these same procedures, each one outputting a different enumeration type, by simply instantiating `Print_Enumeration_Type` with different actual generic parameters.

Let us consider one more example of a generic procedure. This time, instead of first reviewing various versions of nongeneric procedures, we will immediately show the generic version. This generic procedure swaps the values of two objects:

```
generic    -- generic specification
    type Item is private;
procedure Swap_Them (Left, Right : in out Item);

procedure Swap_Them (Left, Right : in out Item) is    --body
    Temp: Item;
begin
    Temp    := Left;
    Left    := Right;
    Right   := Temp;
end Swap_Them;
```

In the preceding generic specification, note the new kind of formal generic parameter:

```
type Item is private;
```

Our previous examples used the symbol (`<>`) instead of the keyword **private**. The difference between (`<>`) and **private** has to do with the types with which the generic can be instantiated.

As previously mentioned, the symbol (`<>`) means that the generic unit can be instantiated only with discrete types (integer types and enumeration types). Because of this restriction (enforced by the Ada compiler), the body of the generic unit may perform operations on objects of type `Item` that are available for discrete types. These are the relational operators =, /=, >, >=, <, and <=; the assignment operator := ; and attributes such as `Pred`, `Succ`, `First`, and `Last`.

The keyword **private** means that the generic procedure `Swap_Them` can be instantiated with any type except a **limited** type or an unconstrained type. Thus, `Swap_Them` can be instantiated with scalar types (`Integer`, `Float`, `Boolean`, etc.) and even with records types and constrained array types. But there is a price that the developer of the generic must pay. Because the generic can be instantiated with practically any type, the body of the generic may only perform operations on objects of type `Item` that apply to all these types. Only equality testing (=, /=) and assignments (:=) meet this stringent requirement. For the body of the generic procedure Swap_Them, however, this limited choice of operators is no problem because only the assignment operator is needed.

The following code shows how the generic procedure Swap_Them can be instantiated with integer types, character types, enumeration types, record types, and array types:

```ada
declare
    procedure Swap is new Swap_Them (Item => Integer);
    procedure Swap is new Swap_Them (Item => Character);
    type AI is (Neural_Networks, Expert_Systems);
    procedure Swap is new Swap_Them (Item => AI);
    type Complex is
        record
            Re, Im : Float;
        end record;
    procedure Swap is new Swap_Them (Item => Complex);
    type Vector is array (1..5) of Float;
    procedure Swap is new Swap_Them (Item => Vector);
    Int_1: Integer := 5;
    Int_2: Integer := 7;
    Char_1: Character := 'A';
    Char_2: Character := 'D';
    AI_1: AI := Neural_Networks;
    AI_2: AI := Expert_Systems;
    Comp_1: Complex := (3.5, 2.1);
    Comp_2: Complex := (4.4, 1.0);
    Vect_1: Vector := (1.0, 2.0, 3.0, 4.0, 5.0);
    Vect_2: Vector := (6.0, 7.0, 8.0, 9.0, 10.0);
begin
    Swap (Left => Int_1, Right => Int_2);
    Swap (Left => Char_1, Right => Char_2);
    Swap (Left => AI_1, Right => AI_2);
    Swap (Left => Comp_1, Right => Comp_2);
    Swap (Left => Vect_1, Right => Vect_2);
        . . .
end;
```

In this code, five overloaded "copies" of Swap are created by instantiating the generic procedure Swap_Them. To determine which Swap procedure is being used, the compiler checks the parameters of Swap. For instance, if the actual parameters are integer variables, then the version of the Swap procedure that swaps integer values is used.

**Ada 95 ▶**    Note that Swap_Them cannot be instantiated with an unconstrained type such as an unconstrained array type. (As we will see in Chapter 13, tagged classwide types are also unconstrained.) For example, since String is an unconstrained array type, the following instantiation will not compile:

```ada
procedure Swap is new Swap_Them (Item => String); -- illegal
```

**Ada 95 ▶** To allow Swap_Them to also be instantiated with unconstrained types (as well as all the other types), its formal generic parameter must have a box in parentheses immediately following the type name:

```
generic
    type Item (<>) is private; -- allows unconstrained types
procedure Swap_Them (Left, Right : in out Item);

-- this body, however, will no longer compile
procedure Swap_Them (Left, Right : in out Item) is    --body
    Temp: Item;   -- illegal
                  -- Item cannot be an unconstrained type
begin
    Temp   := Left;
    Left   := Right;
    Right  := Temp;
end Swap_Them;
```

In this case, however, the body of Swap_Them will not compile. Since a generic with an unconstrained formal type parameter can be instantiated with a constrained as well as an unconstrained type, any operation must be avoided whose legality depends on whether or not the type is constrained. The problem with the body of Swap_Them is that Temp is declared without a constraint. This declaration is allowed only if type Item is constrained. On the other hand, if a type constraint were explicitly provided, the code would still be illegal because of the incorrect assumption that type Item is an unconstrained type:

```
    Temp: Item (Left'Range);   -- assumes Item is unconstrained
```

A mechanism is required for constraining Temp when needed, without making any assumptions about Temp's particular type. Such a mechanism is available by implicitly providing a constraint through initialization:

```
-- this body will work
procedure Swap_Them (Left, Right : in out Item) is
    Temp: Item := Left;
        -- No assumption is made about Item's type
        -- If Item is unconstrained, Temp'Range = Left'Range
begin
    Left   := Right;
    Right  := Temp;
end Swap_Them;
```

This body of Swap_Them will work, regardless of Item's particular type. If, for instance, Swap_Them is instantiated with type String, then the index range of Temp will be implicitly given Left'Range.

In addition to the keyword **private** and the symbol (<>), there are other type specifications that can be used in formal generic parameters. Table 8.1 lists these formal generic type parameters, together with the operations allowed in the generic body and the types allowed as actual generic parameters. Examples of some of these kinds of formal generic type parameters have already been provided or will be shown later in this chapter. Types, such as fixed, decimal, modular, and access, will be discussed in later chapters.

Once again, note that as we allow a greater variety of types to be used as actual generic parameters, fewer operations can be used in the body of the generic. This is because the more types that are allowed, the fewer operations remain that can be performed on all these types. For instance, if a generic unit allows itself to be instantiated with any discrete type, it can use the operators greater than (>) and less than (<). If the generic unit, however, also allows itself to be instantiated with records, then these operators can no longer be used, since Ada does not define such operations on records. As we will see later, however, such comparisons may be defined by the programmer.

**Ada 95 ▶**     As an aside, recall from Chapter 7 that Ada allows a subprogram body to be provided by renaming another subprogram. Ada also allows a subprogram body to be provided by a generic instantiation:

```
generic
    type Item is private;
procedure Swap (Left, Right: in out Item);


package P is
    procedure Swap_Integer (Left, Right: in out Integer);
end P;


with Swap;
package body P is
    procedure Swap_Integer is new Swap (Item => Integer);
    -- body supplied by generic instantiation
end P;
```

**Ada 95 ▶**     As another aside, recall from previous chapters that subprograms, variables, and packages can be renamed. As illustrated below, generic units can also be renamed:

```
with Ada.Text_IO;
Procedure P is
    generic package Enum_IO renames Ada.Text_IO.Enumeration_IO;
    package Bool_IO is new Enum_IO (Boolean);
        -- instead of
        --     package Bool_IO is new
        --         Ada.Text_IO.Enumeration_IO (Boolean);
    ...
end P;
```

As a result of the rename, Enum_IO becomes an alternative name for Ada.Text_IO.Enumeration_IO. In addition to generic packages being renamed, generic procedures and generic functions can be renamed.

**Table 8.1**  Generic Type Parameters

| Formal Parameter Types | Operations Allowed in Generic Body | Actual Parameter Types |
|---|---|---|
| **type** Any_Type **is limited private**; | None | Any type |
| **type** Nonlimited_Type **is private**; | =, /=, := | Discrete, Float, constrained array, record, private |
| **type** General_Type (<>) **is private**; | =, /=, := | Discrete, Float, any array, record, private |
| **type** Discrete_Type **is** (<>); | =, /=, :=, >, >=, <, <=, Pred, Succ, First, Last | Discrete |
| **type** Integer_Type **is range** <>; | Integer operations | Integer |
| **type** Float_Type **is digits** <>; | Real operations | Floating point |
| **type** Fixed_Type **is delta** <>; | Fixed operations | Fixed |
| **type** Decimal_Type **is delta** <> **digits** <>; | Decimal operations | Decimal type |
| **type** Modular_Type **is mod** <>; | Modular integer operations | Modular integer |
| **type** Derived_Type **is new** Parent_Type; | Parent_Type operations | Any type derived from Parent_Type |
| **type** Tagged_Type **is new** Parent_Type **with private**; | =, /=, := | Any tagged type derived from Parent_Type |
| **type** Access_Type **is access** Any_Type; | =, /=, := | Any access type to same object type |
| **type** Array_Type **is array** (Index) **of** Any_Type; | Array operations | Constrained array of same index and component types |
| **type** Array_Type **is array** (Index **range** <>) **of** Any_Type; | Array operations | Unconstrained array of same index and component types |
| **type** Tagged_Type **is tagged private**; | =, /=, := | Tagged type |
| **type** Limited_Type **is tagged limited private**; | None | Any tagged type |
| **type** Abstract_Type **is abstract** . . .; | None | Any abstract type |

Throughout this book, we have been instantiating the generic input/output packages contained in package `Text_IO`. Now that we understand generics, let us examine these packages more closely.

The `Text_IO` package is used for inputting or outputting strings and characters. The generic packages within `Text_IO` are used for inputting and outputting

**Ada 95 ▶** other kinds of data. Package `Text_IO` contains a total of six generic packages: `Integer_IO`, `Modular_IO`, `Float_IO`, `Fixed_IO`, `Decimal_IO`, and `Enumeration_IO`. These packages are used for inputting or outputting integer values, modular (unsigned) integer values, floating point values, fixed point values, decimal fixed point values, and enumeration values. (Packages `Modular_IO` and `Decimal_IO` are new to Ada 95.) Each of these six generic packages has a single formal generic type parameter. This parameter is used to specify the particular type to be input or output.

First, let us examine the `Enumeration_IO` package. If we examine the `Text_IO` package that contains all the generic packages, we can see that the generic package specification for the `Enumeration_IO` package begins as follows:

```
generic
    type Enum is (<>);
package Enumeration_IO is...
```

Recall that the notation `(<>)` indicates that any discrete type can be used as an actual generic type parameter. Technically, this includes integer and character types, although in practice, this is rarely done. Input and output of character values is directly supported by package `Text_IO` (and `Wide_Text_IO`); input and output of integer values is supported by the generic package `Integer_IO`. The Ada language does not define what happens when `Enumeration_IO` is instantiated with an integer type. When `Enumeration_IO` is instantiated with a character type, then the `Put` statement outputs the character value and includes the single quotes.

Second, let us examine the `Integer_IO` package. The specification of the `Integer_IO` package appears in `Text_IO`, as follows:

```
generic
    type Num is range <>;
package Integer_IO is...
```

The notation **range** `<>` indicates that any `Integer` type or subtype can be used as an actual generic type parameter. Consider the following code:

```
declare
    -- assume Text_IO is visible
    type Housing_Starts is new Natural range 0..10_000_000;
    type Programmer_IQ is new Integer range 100..200;
    Absolutely_Shure: Positive := Positive'First;
    Short_Fall: Short_Integer := 5; -- assumes Short_Integer is
                                    -- available
```

```
        July_Housing: Housing_Starts := 100;
        Ada_Programmer_IQ: Programmer_IQ := Programmer_IQ'Last;


        package Positive_IO is new Text_IO.Integer_IO (Positive);
        package Short_Int_IO is new Text_IO.Integer_IO
            (Short_Integer);
        package Houses_IO is new Text_IO.Integer_IO
            (Housing_Starts);
        package Programmer_IQ_IO is new Text_IO.Integer_IO
            (Programmer_IQ);
    begin
        -- Each Put statement outputs a different integer type
        Positive_IO.Put (Absolutely_Sure);
        Short_Int_IO.Put (Short_Fall);
        Houses_IO.Put (July_Housing);
        Programmer_IQ_IO.Put (Ada_Programmer_IQ);
        Positive_IO.Put (July_Housing); -- illegal; wrong type
    end;
```

If values of each of these distinct integer types need to be input or output, then
`Integer_IO` must be separately instantiated with every one of the types. Thus,
`Integer_IO` is instantiated with the predefined subtype `Positive`, the predefined type `Short_Integer`, and the user-defined integer types
`Housing_Starts` and `Programmer_IQ`. Each of the four packages created by
instantiating `Integer_IO` (`Positive_IO`, `Short_Int_IO`, `Houses_IO`, and
`Programmer_IQ_IO`) has its own version of `Put`, which only accepts values of the
specified type. As illustrated in the last statement of the previous code, if a parameter of the wrong integer type is passed to `Put`, then the code will not compile.

**Ada 95 ▶**      When a generic is instantiated with a subtype such as `Positive`, the formal
parameter acquires the range constraint imposed by the subtype. If the body of
the generic needs temporary variables to perform intermediate calculations, they
may need to be unconstrained. At times, it may be desirable for even the results to
be unconstrained. Consider, for example, the predefined `Ada.Numerics.`
`Generic_Elementary_Functions` package. This package is a generic version
of the nongeneric `Ada.Numerics.Elementary_Functions` package discussed
in Chapter 2:

```
generic
    type Float_Type is digits <>;
package Ada.Numerics.Generic_Elementary_Functions is
    function Sqrt (X: Float_Type'Base) return Float_Type'Base;
        -- many other functions follow
        ...
end Ada.Numerics.Generic_Elementary_Functions;
```

Note that the parameter and result of the function `Sqrt` belong to type
`Float_Type'Base`. As a consequence, if the package is instantiated with a constrained subtype, the calculations and the returned value are not so constrained.

## GENERIC DERIVED TYPE PARAMETERS

**Ada 95 ▶** Even though generic derived type parameters are a kind of generic type parameter, they merit their own section because they are quite different from the other type parameters. Generic derived type parameters allow a generic to be instantiated with a type or any of its derivatives.

Consider the following derived types:

```
type Inventory is new Integer range -2**31 .. 2**31 - 1;
type Negative_Inventory is new Inventory
   range Inventory'First..-1;
type Positive_Inventory is new Inventory
   range 1..Inventory'Last;
```

Keeping these declarations in mind, consider the following generic specification:

```
generic
    type Inventory_Range is new Inventory;
package Stock is

   ...

end Stock;
```

As illustrated below, this generic can be instantiated with the parent type Inventory, or with any type derived from Inventory, such as Negative_Inventory or Positive_Inventory:

```
package Deficit is new
   Stock (Inventory_Range => Negative_Inventory );
package Surplus is new
   Stock (Inventory_Range => Positive_Inventory );
package Quantity is new
   Stock (Inventory_Range => Inventory );
```

As we have seen, the format of a generic formal type parameter indicates what class of types it can be matched with. For example, the generic formal parameter

```
type T is (<>);
```

indicates that T can only be matched with types in the class of discrete types. The class of discrete types is defined by the Ada language. Generic derived type parameters allow programmers to define their own class of types. Thus, the format of the generic formal parameter

```
type Inventory_Range is new Inventory;
```

indicates that Inventory_Range can only be matched by types in the class of types directly or indirectly derived from type Inventory. The developer of the generic can, thus, use operations and values that are common to all types in this class.

Ada provides another version of generic derived type parameters that ends with the keywords **with private**:

```
type Inventory_Range is new Inventory with private;
    -- for tagged types (to be covered in Chapter 13)
```

In this version, `Inventory_Range` must be a tagged type. Tagged types are used for object-oriented programming and will be covered in Chapter 13.

## GENERIC OBJECT PARAMETERS

So far, we have only considered generic type parameters. Another kind of generic parameter is the generic object parameter. Object parameters allow a generic to be passed an object instead of a type. Consider the following generic, `Membership_Test`, that tests whether every character within a string is within a specified range of character values:

```
procedure Process_Text (Text: in String) is
    generic
        Beginning, Ending: Character;-- generic object parameters
    function Membership_Test (Str: String) return Boolean;

    function Membership_Test (Str: String) return Boolean is
    begin
        for K in Str'Range loop
            if Str(K) not in Beginning..Ending then
                return False;
            end if;
        end loop;
        return True;
    end Membership_Test;

    function Entirely_Upper_Case is new
        Membership_Test ( Beginning  => 'A',
                          Ending     => 'Z' );
    function Entirely_Lower_Case is new
        Membership_Test ( Beginning  => 'a',
                          Ending     => 'z' );
    function Entirely_Decimal_Digits is new
        Membership_Test ( Beginning  => '0',
                          Ending     => '9' );
begin

    if Entirely_Upper_Case (Text) then
        -- do appropriate processing
```

```
        elsif Entirely_Lower_Case (Text) then
           -- do appropriate processing
        elsif Entirely_Decimal_Digits (Text) then
           -- do appropriate processing
        else
           -- do appropriate processing
        end if;
     end Process_Text;
```

Note that when `Membership_Test` is instantiated, its object parameters `Begin-ning` and `Ending` are passed character values. Also note that by implementing `Membership_Test` as a generic, functions such as `Entirely_Upper_Case` can be created whose purpose is clearly indicated by its name. Had `Membership_Test` alternatively been implemented as a regular, nongeneric function, its purpose would not be so easily identified:

```
     -- A nongeneric version
     function Membership_Test ( Beginning, Ending: Character;
                                Str: String) return Boolean is
     begin
        for K in Str'Range loop
           if Str(K) not in Beginning..Ending then
              return False;
           end if;
        end loop;
        return True;
     end Membership_Test;
```

As shown in the following code, using the nongeneric version of `Membership_Test` to test for uppercase characters is not as readable as using the previously created function `Entirely_Upper_Case`. This is because the intended use of the nongeneric version is not specified by name but implied by the parameter values `'A'` and `'Z'` for `Beginning` and `Ending`:

```
     if Membership_Test ( Beginning  => 'A', -- check for all
                           Ending     => 'Z', -- uppercase
                           Str        => Text ) then ...
```

Let us now consider another example that uses an object parameter. Recall from Chapter 7 that a stack is a "last in, first out" (LIFO) data structure. With just a few more lines of code, the first example of a stack that was presented in that chapter can be rewritten as a generic package:

```
     generic
        type Item is private;
        Stack_Size: Positive;
     package Stack is
```

```
      procedure Push (A: in Item);
      function Pop return Item;
end Stack;

package body Stack is
    Stack_Array: array (1..Stack_Size) of Item;
    Top: Integer range 0 .. Stack_Size;

    procedure Push (A: in Item) is
    begin
        Top := Top + 1;
        Stack_Array (Top) := A;
    end Push;

    function Pop return Item is
    begin
        Top := Top - 1;
        return Stack_Array ( Top + 1);
    end Pop;

begin -- Stack
    Top := 0;
end Stack;
```

For details on how this package works, read the discussion on stacks in Chapter 7. (As seen in Chapter 7, we could also add checks for overflow and underflow and add a subprogram to clear the stack.)

Unlike the nongeneric version of the stack in Chapter 7, which can only be used to stack up to 1000 integer values, this generic version can be used to stack up to any specified number of values of any specified type. Depending on how the generic is instantiated, a package can be created to stack up to 100 integers, or 500 characters, or 2000 real numbers, or 20 Boolean values, and so on. Packages can even be created to stack arrays and records.

Note that the preceding generic stack package has two formal generic parameters:

```
type Item is private;
Stack_Size: Positive;
```

When the Stack is instantiated, a type is passed to Item, and a positive value is passed to Stack_Size. The type passed to Item determines the type of items that can be stacked. The value passed to Stack_Size sets an upper limit to the size of the stack. The value passed to Stack_Size is fixed at the time of instantiation and can be read by the generic but not modified by the generic. A formal object parameter, unlike other kinds of generic formal parameters, can have the parameter modes **in** and **in out**, but not **out**. Like subprograms, the **in** mode is assumed unless otherwise specified.

The following code illustrates different ways that Stack can be instantiated and how objects can be pushed and popped from the various stacks created by instantiating `Stack`:

```
declare

    type Smoke_Types is (Cigarette, Pipe, Cigar);
    type Smoke is array (Smoke_Types) of Boolean;

    package Stack_Real is new Stack (Float, 20);
    package Stack_100 is new Stack (Integer, 100);
    package Stack_10 is new Stack (Integer, 10);
    package Smoke_Stack is new Stack (Smoke, 20);
    use Stack_Real, Stack_100, Stack_10, Smoke_Stack;

    X, Y: Float := 1.2;
    A, B: Integer := 5;
    P: Smoke :=  ( Cigarette => True, Pipe => False,
                   Cigar => False );
begin
    . . .
    Push (X);            -- Stack_Real.Push
    Y := Pop;            -- Stack_Real.Pop
    Stack_10.Push (A);   -- must qualify to avoid ambiguity
    B := Stack_100.Pop;  -- must qualify to avoid ambiguity
    Push (P);            -- Smoke_Stack.Push
    . . .
end;
```

In this code, the generic package `Stack` is instantiated four times. Each instantiation creates a stack package with its own version of `Push` and `Pop`. The first instantiation creates a stack capable of stacking up to 20 numbers of type `Float`:

```
package Stack_Real is new Stack (Float, 20);
```

The second instantiation creates a stack capable of stacking up to 100 integers:

```
package Stack_100 is new Stack (Integer, 100);
```

The third instantiation creates a stack capable of stacking up to 10 integers:

```
package Stack_10 is new Stack (Integer, 10);
```

Finally, the fourth instantiation creates a stack capable of stacking up to 20 arrays of type `Smoke`:

```
package Smoke_Stack is new Stack (Smoke, 20);
```

After the four preceding stack packages are created, their `Push` and `Pop` subprograms are used. Because each of these four stack packages contain their own

`Push` and `Pop` subprograms, `Push` and `Pop` are each overloaded four times. Since the **use** clause is employed, when dot notation is not used for `Push` and `Pop`, the compiler must determine which versions to call. For example, since `X` belongs to type `Float`, the compiler realizes that `Push(X)` calls the `Push` procedure in package `Stack_Real`. No ambiguity arises because `Stack_Real` is the only package containing a `Push` procedure for values of type `Float`. However, the call, `Push (A)`, is ambiguous. There are two packages that have a `Push` procedure for pushing values of type `Integer`: `Stack_10` and `Stack_100`. The compiler has no way of determining which version of `Push` to call. As shown in the preceding code, this ambiguity is resolved by using dot notation, `Stack_10.Push(A)` or `Stack_100.Push(A)`, to inform the compiler which version to call. Similarly, dot notation must be used when `Pop` is assigned to the integer variables `A` or `B`.

In the generic package `Stack`, the formal object parameter `Stack_Size` could have been assigned a default value:

```
Stack_Size : Positive := 100;
```

In this case, if the `Stack` package is instantiated without an actual object parameter, then the default of `100` is used:

```
package Default_Size is new Stack (Integer);
```

As with subprogram parameters, a default value can only be assigned to a formal object parameter that is an **in** parameter.

We have seen that generic **in** parameters enable a generic to be passed a value determined during instantiation. The generic can then use this value as a constant. In contrast, generic **in out** parameters enable a generic to be passed a variable that is external to the generic. The generic can then read and modify this external variable. In the following example, the generic procedure `Increment` can access the actual parameter `N` through the formal parameter `In_Out`:

```
generic
    In_Out: in out Positive;
procedure Increment;

procedure Increment is
begin
    if In_Out = Positive'Last then
        In_Out := Positive'First;
    else
        In_Out := In_Out + 1;
    end if;
end Increment;
```

```
with Increment;
with Ada.Text_IO; use Ada.Text_IO;
procedure P is
    N: Positive := Positive'Last;
```

```
      procedure My_Inc is new Increment (In_Out => N);
      procedure Your_Inc is new Increment (In_Out => N);
   begin
      My_Inc;   Put_Line (Positive'Image (N)); -- outputs 1
      My_Inc;   Put_Line (Positive'Image (N)); -- outputs 2
      Your_Inc; Put_Line (Positive'Image (N)); -- outputs 3
   end P;
```

Note that the procedures `My_Inc` and `Your_Inc` can read or modify the external variable `N`, simply by reading or modifying the parameter `In_Out`. Such upward references to `N` are usually undesirable, however, since they create obscure dependencies between the subprograms `My_Inc` and `Your_Inc`.

## GENERIC SUBPROGRAM PARAMETERS

Thus far in this chapter, we have discussed two kinds of generic parameters: type parameters and object parameters. We will now discuss a third kind of generic parameter: a subprogram parameter. Subprogram parameters are functions or procedures that are passed in when the generic unit is instantiated. To better understand the need for generic subprogram parameters, let us compare the private types discussed in this chapter (those used in generic specifications) with the private types encountered in Chapter 7 (those used in package specifications).

Recall from Chapter 7 that private types can be used in packages to hide the underlying structure or implementation of a type contained in the package specification. In both package specifications and generic specifications, operations on private types are restricted to assignments and to tests for equality and inequality. There is, however, this difference in perspective: users of a package containing a private type cannot assume anything about the private type. Therefore, the users can only perform assignments and tests for equality and inequality on objects of this private type. Developers of the package, however, know the actual makeup of the private type and can exploit this knowledge to perform additional operations on objects of this type. This situation is reversed when private types are used in generic specifications. Users who instantiate a generic unit know everything about the type they are passing in to match the private type. Developers of the generic unit, however, cannot know what actual type the user will be passing in to match the private type.

Thus, the following dilemma is created. If the users of a generic unit do not have any restrictions imposed and can instantiate the generic unit with any data type, then the developers are very restricted. They are limited to only using operations that apply to all data types. Conversely, if the developers wish to use operations that cannot apply to every data type, then the users of the generic unit are restricted. They can only instantiate this generic unit with certain data types. Ada solves this dilemma by using generic subprogram parameters.

First, to illustrate the dilemma, let us return to the generic function `Maximum` that we discussed at the beginning of this chapter. The specification of this function is as follows:

```
generic
    type Item is (<>);
function Maximum (X, Y: Item) return Item;
```

This generic specification uses the symbol (<>) to indicate that this generic unit can be instantiated only with discrete types. But what if we want to have this function work on real numbers, and even on arrays and records? We could try replacing the symbol (<>) with the keyword **private**, which results in the following version of the generic function Maximum:

```
generic
    type Item is private;
function Maximum (X, Y: Item) return Item;

function Maximum (X, Y: Item) return Item is
begin
    if X > Y then     -- illegal operation on private types
        return X;
    else
        return Y;
    end if;
end Maximum;
```

Because our generic formal parameter, Item, is a **private** type, we can instantiate this function with real numbers, arrays, records, or any other type except **limited** types. However, there is a problem. The only operations allowed on **private** types are assignments and tests for equality and inequality, yet the body of this generic function uses the greater than operator, >. This is illegal, and the compiler will issue an error.

Fortunately, there is a solution to our dilemma. We can let our generic formal parameter, Item, remain a **private** type and can also allow the operator, >, to appear in the generic body. To do this, however, we must place a special burden on those who instantiate this generic function. Whoever instantiates this package must define what is meant by the operator, >. Thus, users of this generic function Maximum may instantiate Maximum with a record type, but they must also define what is meant when one record is "greater than" another record. As the following code illustrates, such a definition is supplied to the generic unit through the formal generic subprogram parameter:

```
generic
    type Item is private;
    with function ">" (Left, Right: Item) return Boolean;
function Maximum (X, Y: Item) return Item;

function Maximum (X, Y: Item) return Item is -- generic body
begin
    if X > Y then
        return X;
```

```
    else
        return Y;
    end if;
end Maximum;
```

The generic function, Maximum, has two parameters, a generic type parameter, Item, and a generic subprogram parameter, ">". These parameters are processed sequentially and must be placed in the order shown because the subprogram parameter, ">", references the type parameter, Item.

The formal generic subprogram parameter, ">", is preceded by the keyword **with**. (This keyword is unrelated to the **with** used in context specifications.) This keyword is used to remove ambiguity, so that the compiler knows that the function ">" is a generic subprogram parameter and not the name of the generic function itself. If the keyword **with** is not included, the code appears as follows:

```
generic
    type Item is private;
function ">" (Left, Right: Item) return Boolean;
```

The compiler then interprets the name of this generic function to be ">", not Maximum.

When our generic function Maximum is instantiated, the formal subprogram parameter, ">", which serves as a placeholder, is replaced with an actual function. This is illustrated in the following example, in which the generic function Maximum is instantiated to create actual functions that compare whether one record is "greater than" another record:

```
with Maximum;
procedure Compare_People is

    type Personality_Type is (Loathsome, Tolerable, Lovable);
    type Adult is
        record
            Age: Integer range 0..130;     -- years
            Height: Integer range 36..86; -- inches
            Personality: Personality_Type;
        end record;

    Melba: Adult := ( Height      => 67,
                      Personality => Tolerable,
                      Age         => 28 );

    Zelda: Adult := ( Height      => 60,
                      Personality => Loathsome,
                      Age         => 55 );

    Gilda: Adult := ( Height      => 77,
                      Personality => Lovable,
                      Age         => 87 );

    Older_Person, Taller_Person, Nicer_Person: Adult;
```

```
    function Older_Than (X, Y: Adult) return Boolean is
    begin
        return X.Age > Y.Age;
    end Older_Than;

    function Taller_Than (X, Y: Adult) return Boolean is
    begin
        return X.Height > Y.Height;
    end Taller_Than;

    function Nicer_Than (X, Y: Adult) return Boolean is
    begin
        return X.Personality > Y.Personality;
    end Nicer_Than;

    function Older is new Maximum
        (Item => Adult, ">" => Older_Than);

    function Taller is new Maximum
        (Item => Adult, ">" => Taller_Than);

    function Nicer is new Maximum
        (Item => Adult, ">" => Nicer_Than);

begin -- Compare_People

    Taller_Person := Taller (Melba, Gilda);
            -- returns Gilda
    Older_Person := Older (Melba, Zelda);
            -- returns Zelda
    Nicer_Person := Nicer (Melba, Zelda);
            -- returns Melba
    Nicer_Person := Nicer (Nicer_Person, Gilda);
            -- returns Gilda
    ...
end Compare_People;
```

The procedure Compare_People compares people on the basis of their age, height, and personality. This procedure determines whether one person is older, taller, or nicer than another person.

The first line of this code makes the generic unit Maximum available through the context specification **with** Maximum. This is possible because generic units such as Maximum can be made into a library unit by being separately compiled as a "top-level" program unit. The generic function Maximum is used by the procedure Compare_People to create, through generic instantiation, three new functions: Older, Taller, and Nicer.

Procedure Compare_People works as follows. Several people—Melba, Zelda, and Gilda—are defined as records, of type Adult, that have three components: Age, Height, and Personality. These three components are then used by three functions: `Older_Than`, `Taller_Than`, and `Nicer_Than`. These functions define what it means to say that one adult is older, taller, or nicer than another adult. For instance, function `Older_Than` can determine whether `Melba` is older than `Zelda` by checking whether `Melba.Age > Zelda.Age`. Similarly, the function `Taller_Than` can determine whether `Melba` is taller than `Zelda` by checking whether the record components `Melba.Height > Zelda.Height`. The function `Nicer_Than` can determine whether `Melba` is nicer than `Zelda` by checking whether `Melba.Personality > Zelda.Personality`. This last comparison yields the desired result because values of the enumeration type `Personality_Type` are specifically listed in order of increasing niceness: `Loathsome`, `Tolerable`, and `Lovable`.

The functions `Older_Than` , `Taller_Than`, and `Nicer_Than` are used as actual subprogram parameters when the generic function `Maximum` is instantiated. The function `Taller`, for example, is created by generically instantiating `Maximum` with the type `Adult` and the function `Taller_Than`. The function `Taller` resembles the template, `Maximum`, from which it was created, except for these differences: `X` and `Y` that were declared in `Maximum` to be of type `Item` are now of type `Adult`. In addition, the function `">"` that appears in the body of `Maximum` is replaced by the function `Taller_Than`. The function `Taller`, therefore, behaves as if its body were written as follows, where `Taller_Than(X, Y)` is `True` or `False` depending on whether or not `X.Height > Y.Height`:

```
function Taller (X, Y: Adult) return Adult is
begin
   if Taller_Than(X, Y) then
      return X;
   else
      return Y;
   end if;
end Taller;
```

Within `Compare_People`, the actual generic subprogram parameters used to instantiate `Maximum` are `Older_Than`, `Taller_Than`, and `Nicer_Than`. But what if we just want to use the predefined function `">"`, contained in the package `Standard`, as the actual subprogram parameter for comparing integers? This can be accomplished by instantiating the generic function `Maximum`, as follows:

```
function Larger_Int is new Maximum   (Item => Integer,
                                       ">"  => ">" );
```

This instantiation creates a function called `Larger_Int` that can be used to return the larger of two integers. In the peculiar notation `">" => ">"`, the `">"` to the left of the arrow represents the formal generic subprogram parameter. The `">"` to the right of the arrow represents the actual generic subprogram parameter. We can use dot notaton on the actual subprogram parameter, `">"`, as follows: `Standard. ">"`. This dot notation clarifies the code by explicitly stating that the `">"`  function, which is being passed to the generic procedure `Maximum`, is the standard `">"` function contained in the `Standard` package and not a user-defined overloaded function.

Let us consider another example that uses subprogram parameters. Such parameters are sometimes used in mathematical programs. The following program creates the functions `Average_Square`, `Average_Cube`, and `Average_Poly` by instantiating the generic function `Average` with the function parameters `Square`, `Cube`, and `Polynomial`:

```ada
with Ada.Text_IO; use Ada.Text_IO;
procedure Average_Term is
   package Real_IO is new Float_IO (Float);
   use Real_IO;

   function Square (X: Integer) return Integer is
   begin
      return X ** 2;
   end Square;

   function Cube (X: Integer) return Integer is
   begin
      return X ** 3;
   end Cube;

   function Polynomial (X: Integer) return Integer is
   begin
      return 2*(X**2) + 5*X - 7;
   end Polynomial;

   generic
      with function Values (Param: Integer) return Integer;
   function Average (Beginning, Ending: Integer) return Float;

   function Average (Beginning, Ending: Integer) return Float is
      Sum_Of_Terms: Natural := 0;
   begin
      for Index in Beginning .. Ending loop
         Sum_Of_Terms := Sum_Of_Terms + Values (Index);
      end loop;
      return Float (Sum_Of_Terms)
               / Float (Ending - Beginning + 1);
   end Average;

   function Average_Square is new Average (Values => Square);
   function Average_Cube is new Average (Values => Cube);
   function Average_Poly is new Average (Values => Polynomial);

begin
   Put ( Average_Square (Beginning => 1, Ending => 4));
   New_Line;
   Put ( Average_Cube (Beginning => 10, Ending => 15));
   New_Line;
   Put ( Average_Poly (Beginning => 1, Ending => 3));
   New_Line;
end Average_Term;
```

In this program, the function call

```
Average_Square (Beginning => 1, Ending => 4)
```

returns the average value of $N^2$ for values of N from 1 to 4:

```
(12 + 22 + 32 + 42) / 4
```

The function call

```
Average_Cube (Beginning => 10, Ending => 15)
```

returns the average value of $N^3$ for values of N from 10 to 15:

```
(103 + 113 + 123 + 133 + 143 + 153) / 6
```

The function call

```
Average_Poly (Beginning => 1, Ending => 3)
```

returns the average value of $2N^2 + 5N - 7$ for values of N from 1 to 3:

```
((2*12 + 5*1 - 7) + (2*22 + 5*2 - 7) + (2*32 + 5*3 - 7)) / 3
```

Note that each of these function calls returns the average value of its terms by adding all its terms and then dividing by the number of terms.

The generic function `Average` was designed with a single generic subprogram parameter, `Values`. Alternatively, the parameters `Beginning` and `Ending` could also have been generic parameters instead of regular function parameters:

```
generic
    Beginning, Ending: Integer;
    with function Values (Param: Integer) return Integer;
function Average return Float;
```

This new implementation, however, is less flexible than the previous implementation because the range of terms is fixed for each instantiation. For example, the following instantiation of the new implementation of `Average` creates a function `Average_Square` that can only take the average square of terms from 1 to 4:

```
function Average_Square is new
    Average ( Beginning => 1,
              Ending    => 4,
              Values    => Square);
```

The original implementation of `Average_Square` is more flexible because the range of terms is specified each time the function `Average_Square` is called.

Before ending our discussion of subprogram parameters, let us see how these parameters can be given a default name. In the preceding generic function Average, for instance, the clause

```
with function Values (Param: Integer) return Integer;
```

could be replaced with

```
with function Values (Param: Integer) return Integer is Square;
```

This second version uses the function name Square as a default name for the actual subprogram parameter. To use Square as a default name, Square must be visible at the point where the generic unit, Average, is declared. This requirement is satisfied in the procedure Average_Term. Given this second version, Average can be instantiated without a generic parameter:

```
function Average_Square is new Average;
```

In this case, since the formal subprogram parameter is omitted, the default Square is used.

There is another method for giving a subprogram parameter a default name. This method uses, as a default, a subprogram that is visible at the point where the generic is instantiated, rather than where the generic unit is declared:

```
with function ">" (Left, Right: Item) return Boolean is <>;
```

This strange-looking notation with the box, <>, at the end makes the name of the default subprogram parameter the same as the name of the formal subprogram parameter. In this example, therefore, the default subprogram name is ">". This default, ">", could be the one defined in package Standard, one that is implicitly created when a type is declared, or one that is explicitly overloaded. Whichever one it is, it must be visible at the point of instantiation.

The default, ">", can effectively be used for instantiating the generic Maximum to return the larger of two integer values. Recall that we originally performed the instantiation, as follows:

```
function Larger_Int is new Maximum   (Item => Integer,
                                      ">"  => Standard.">" );
```

Since we are just using Standard.">", which is visible at the point of instantiation, we can leave off this subprogram parameter, ">", and accept the default:

```
function Larger_Int is new Maximum (Item => Integer);
   -- uses default Standard.">"
```

For another example of generic subprogram parameters, consider this second version of a generic stack package:

```ada
generic
   type Stack_Element is private;
package Stack is

   type Stack_Type (Stack_Size: Natural) is limited private;

   function Is_Empty (S: in Stack_Type) return Boolean;
   function Is_Full (S: in Stack_Type) return Boolean;

   procedure Push (S: in out Stack_Type; Item: in Stack_Element);
   procedure Pop (S: in out Stack_Type; Item: out Stack_Element);

   function "=" (Left, Right: in Stack_Type) return Boolean;
   procedure Copy (From: in Stack_Type; To: out Stack_Type);
   procedure Clear (S: in out Stack_Type);

   generic-- nested generic
      with procedure Apply_To_Stack_Elements
          (Element: in out Stack_Element);
   procedure Traverse_Stack (S: in out Stack_Type);

private

   type Stack_Array is array (Natural range <>) of Stack_Element;

   type Stack_Type (Stack_Size: Natural) is
      record
         Stk: Stack_Array (1..Stack_Size);
         Top: Natural := 0;
      end record;
end Stack;
```

Whereas the generic stack shown earlier in this chapter was an object manager, this generic stack package is a type manager. As explained in Chapter 7, a type manager package allows clients to use the type (in this case, Stack_Type) to declare and manipulate any number of stacks. Furthermore, since this package is generic, a client can create stacks whose elements are of any nonlimited type:

```ada
package Float_Stack is new Stack (Stack_Element => Float);
My_Flt_Stack: Float_Stack.Stack_Type(Stack_Size => 20);
Your_Flt_Stack: Float_Stack.Stack_Type(Stack_Size => 80);
   ...
Float_Stack.Push (My_Flt_Stack, 3.2);
Float_Stack.Push (Your_Flt_Stack, 8.2);
```

```ada
package Integer_Stack is new Stack (Stack_Element => Integer);
My_Int_Stack: Integer_Stack.Stack_Type(Stack_Size => 10);
Your_Int_Stack: Integer_Stack.Stack_Type(Stack_Size => 70);
   ...
```

```
Integer_Stack.Push (My_Int_Stack, 2);
Integer_Stack.Push (Your_Int_Stack, 8);
```

The most interesting aspect of the preceding generic stack package is that it contains the nested generic, `Traverse_Stack`. Once the outer generic, `Stack`, is instantiated, the inner generic, `Traverse_Stack`, can be instantiated. This inner generic allows any user-specified operation to be applied to each element of the stack. For example, a procedure to print the entire floating point stack declared above can be created by instantiating `Float_Stack.Traverse_Stack` with the procedure `Print`. The resulting procedure, `Print_Stack`, can then be used to output every floating point component of any stack created with package `Float_Stack`:

```
-- assume Float_IO was properly instantiated
procedure Print (Item: in out Float) is
    -- mode in out needed to match parameter mode of
    -- Apply_To_Stack_Elements
begin
    Put (Item, 0, 0, 0); Put (" ");
end Print;

procedure Print_Stack is new
    Float_Stack.Traverse_Stack (Apply_To_Stack_Elements =>
        Print);
    ...
Print_Stack (My_Flt_Stack);    -- outputs My_Flt_Stack
                               -- using procedure Print
Print_Stack (Your_Flt_Stack); -- outputs Your_Flt_Stack
                               -- using procedure Print
```

Of course, to work properly, the body of `Traverse_Stack` (contained in the body of `Stack`) must invoke `Apply_To_Stack_Elements` with every valid item in the stack array `S.Stk`:

```
procedure Traverse_Stack (S: in out Stack_Type) is
begin
    for K in S.Stk'First..S.Top loop
        Apply_To_Stack_Elements (K);
    end K;
end Traverse_Stack;
```

When `Traverse_Stack` is instantiated with procedure `Print`, the procedure `Apply_To_Stack_Elements` is replaced with procedure `Print`.

In our final example of how generic subprogram parameters can be used, consider a method for sorting items, sometimes called an insertion sort. An insertion sort, probably the simplest of all the sorting algorithms, works in the same way that you sort the cards you are dealt during a game of cards. You start with one item (which is considered already sorted). Then you get a second item and insert it where it belongs. Then you get a third item and insert it where it belongs. You keep getting and inserting items until every item is inserted. While the insertion sort is not the most efficient sort, it performs well for lists of less than 100 items, and it is easy to implement.

Before showing the generic insertion sort procedure, let us consider a nongeneric version that sorts integer arrays of type `Vector`:

```ada
type Vector is array (1 .. 10) of Integer;
```

Arrays of type `Vector` have a length of 10 and index values that range from 1 to 10. The nongeneric sort procedure appears as follows:

```ada
-- nongeneric version of an insertion sort for integer arrays
-- of length 10
procedure Insertion_Sort (V: in out Vector) is
   J: Integer;
   Temp: Integer;
begin
   -- loop invariant: V(1 .. K - 1) is already sorted
   for K in 2..10 loop
      J := K;
      Temp := V(J);

      while J > 1 and then V(J - 1) > Temp loop
         V(J) := V(J - 1);
         J := J - 1;
      end loop;

      V(J) := Temp;

   end loop;
end Insertion_Sort;
```

Now let us consider the generic version of the insertion sort:

```ada
-- generic version of an insertion sort
generic
   type Item is private;
   type Index is (<>);
   type Vector is array (Index range <>) of Item;
   with function ">" (Left, Right: Item) return Boolean is <>;
procedure Insertion_Sort (V: in out Vector);

procedure Insertion_Sort (V: in out Vector) is
   J: Index;
   Temp: Item;
begin
   -- loop invariant: V( First..Pred(K)) is already sorted
   for K in Index'Succ(V'First)..V'Last loop
      J := K;
      Temp := V(J);

      while J > V'First and then V (Index'Pred( J )) > Temp loop
         V (J) := V ( Index'Pred( J ));
```

```
        J := Index'Pred(J);
      end loop;

      V(J) := Temp;
   end loop;
end Insertion_Sort;
```

To make the insertion sort generic, attributes are extensively used. For example, `Index'Succ(V'First)` is used instead of the second index value 2 (in the nongeneric version) for the lower bounds of the **for** loop. In addition, `V'Last` is used instead of the last index value, 10. These attributes enable this generic sort procedure to be used for arrays with index ranges other than from 1 to 10. For instance, if an array has index values from 5 to 15, then `Index'Succ(V'First)` yields the second index value, 6, and `V'Last` yields the last index value, 15. But this generic version will even work for noninteger index values. For example, if the values of `Index` belong to the enumeration type `Day` that contains the values `Monday` to `Sunday`, then this generic procedure still works! `Index'Succ(V'First)` yields the second index value, `Tuesday`, and `V'Last` yields the last index value, `Sunday`.

The only limitation of this generic procedure is that it does not work for indexes that are enumeration types with only one value, such as the following:

```
type One is (Lonely);
```

In other words, this generic program assumes that `Index'Succ(V'First)`, which yields the second index value, is always legal. Since it is rather ridiculous to sort arrays that can never have more than one item, this is not an unreasonable limitation.

The previous example of a generic `Insertion_Sort` procedure has a long list of generic formal parameters. The first parameter, `Item`, is used to specify the kind of items that are to be sorted. The second parameter, `Index`, is used to specify an index range. The third parameter, `Vector`, is an unconstrained array of type `Item` with an index of type `Index`. As can be seen, unlike subprogram parameters, Ada allows generic parameters to "build" upon previously declared parameters. Thus, type `Vector` references the previously listed type parameters `Index` and `Item`, and the fourth parameter, function `">"`, references the previously listed type `Item`.

The fourth parameter, `">"`, allows the programmer to define what it means for a value of type `Item` to be greater than another value. This generic procedure can therefore be used to sort items such as records for which the relational operators are not predefined. Furthermore, although the formal parameter name `">"` implies that the array items are sorted in ascending order, one may instantiate `Insertion_Sort` so that the sort is performed in descending order. To accomplish this, match the formal generic parameter, `">"`, with the actual parameter, `"<"`:

```
">" => "<"
```

Now that we have discussed `Insertion_Sort`'s generic formal parameters, let us consider how they are matched with actual parameters. Since `Vector` is an unconstrained array type, the actual array parameter must also be unconstrained. Furthermore, the relationships between the formal parameters must correspond to the relationships between the actual parameters. Thus, the component type of the actual array must be the type that was matched with Item, and its index type must be the type that was matched with Index.

The following procedure instantiates the generic Insertion_Sort and uses its instance, Sort, to sort an array of planets:

```ada
with Ada.Text_IO, Insertion_Sort; use Ada.Text_IO;
procedure Sort_List is
    type Solar_System is (Mercury, Venus, Earth, Mars, Jupiter,
               Saturn, Uranus, Neptune, Pluto);
    subtype Index_Type is Integer range 0..100;
    type Planets is array (Index_Type range <>) of Solar_System;
    procedure Sort is new
        Insertion_Sort ( Item   => Solar_System,
                         Index  => Index_Type,
                         Vector => Planets );
                         -- takes Sort_List.">" implicitly
                         -- defined for Solar_System
    Sort_Me: Planets (5..13) :=
        ( Jupiter, Mars, Pluto, Earth, Mercury, Venus, Saturn,
          Neptune, Uranus );

    package Solar_System_IO is new Enumeration_IO (Solar_System);
    use Solar_System_IO;

begin

    for Heavenly_Body in Sort_Me'Range loop
        Put (Sort_Me (Heavenly_Body));    -- outputs planets in
        New_Line;                         -- unsorted order
    end loop;
    New_Line;

    Sort (Sort_Me);   -- returns array sorted by planet's
                      -- position from sun

    for Heavenly_Body in Sort_Me'Range loop
        Put (Sort_Me (Heavenly_Body));    -- outputs planets in
        New_Line;                         -- sorted order
    end loop;

end Sort_List;
```

The planets are first output in their unsorted order. The Sort procedure is then used to sort the planets, and they are output in their correct order.

When Insertion_Sort is instantiated, the compiler checks that Solar_System is a nonlimited type, that Index_Type is a discrete type, and that Planets is a one-dimensional unconstrained array whose index type is Index_Type and whose component type is Solar_System.

Note that procedure Sort_List provides no parameter for the ">" function, so the default is taken. The default is the `">"` for type `Item` that is visible at the point of instantiation. Since type `Item` is passed the enumeration type `Solar_System`, the `">"` that is visible is the one that Ada implicitly defines for type `Solar_System`.

Procedure `Insertion_Sort` defines its generic type parameter, `Vector`, as an unconstrained array type. `Vector` is thus matched with some unconstrained array type. However, `Vector` could have been declared as a constrained array type:

```
-- This version only sorts Constrained array types
generic
    type Item is private;
    type Index is (<>);
    type Vector is array (Index) of Item;    -- Constrained
    with function ">" (Left, Right: Item) return Boolean is <>;
procedure Insertion_Sort (V: in out Vector);
```

Since `Vector` is constrained, it can only be matched with some constrained array type. Thus, the following attempt to match `Vector` with the unconstrained array type, `String`, is illegal:

```
type String_Sort is new Insertion_Sort
    (  Item   => Character,
       Index  => Positive,
       Vector => String,    -- illegal
       ">"    => ">" );
```

So far, all the formal generic subprogram parameters have been passed subprograms or operators. In special cases like the one illustrated below, formal generic subprogram parameters may be passed attributes that are treated as functions :

```
generic
    type Item is private;
    with function Image (A: Item) return String;
package P is ...

package Q is new P ( Item  => Integer,
                     Image => Integer'Image );
```

Note that Table 8.1 indicates that no operations are allowed on limited private generic type parameters. This may seem strange. Without any available operations, how can the developer of the generic do anything with the type? Actually, operations may be allowed, but these must be provided as generic subprogram parameters. For example, the body of the following generic, `Demo`, can only operate on objects of type `Any_Type` using the subprograms `F` and `P`:

```
generic
    type Any_Type is limited private;
    with function F return Any_Type;
    with procedure P (X: in Any_Type);
procedure Demo;
```

## GENERIC PACKAGE PARAMETERS

**Ada 95 ▶**  Generic package parameters facilitate the creation of a hierarchy of generic packages whereby types and operations from one generic can be exported to another generic. This other generic can then define additional types and operations in terms of those it imported.

Items from one generic package are passed to another via generic package parameters. Suppose, for example, that we have an existing generic package, `Frac_Ops`, that defines basic operations on fractions whose numerator (top value) and denominator (bottom value) are of some user-specified integer type:

```
generic
   type Some_Integer is range <>;
package Frac_Ops is
   type Fraction is private;
   function "*" (L, R: Fraction) return Fraction;
   function "/" (L, R: Fraction) return Fraction;
   function "+" (L, R: Fraction) return Fraction;
   function "-" (R: Fraction) return Fraction;
   function "-" (L, R: Fraction) return Fraction;
   function "/" (L, R: Some_Integer) return Fraction;
   function "=" (L, R: Fraction) return Boolean;
   procedure Put (Item: in Fraction);
private
   type Fraction is
      record
         Top: Some_Integer;
         Bottom: Some_Integer;
      end record;
end Frac_Ops;
```

Suppose that another generic package is needed, `Extend_Frac_Ops`, that is an extension of `Frac_Ops`. Specifically, `Extend_Frac_Ops` needs to use the types `Some_Integer` and `Fraction`, and the fraction operations defined in the generic `Frac_Ops`, to implement additional fraction operations. This is accomplished in the following code with a formal generic package parameter `Frac_Pack`:

```
with Frac_Ops;
generic
   with package Frac_Pack is new Frac_Ops (<>);
package Extend_Frac_Ops is
   -- Other types and operations go here
                 . . .
end Extend_Frac_Ops;
```

Everything that is declared in the specification of `Frac_Ops` is now available to `Extend_Frac_Ops`, including the generic parameter `Some_Integer`.

The parameter `Frac_Pack` can be matched with any package created by instantiating `Frac_Ops`. The following is an example of such a match:

```
package Long_Frac is new
    Frac_Ops (Some_Integer => Long_Integer);
```

Since Long_Frac was created by instantiating Frac_Ops, it can now be used to instantiate package Extend_Frac_Ops:

```
package Long_Extend_Frac is new Extend_Frac_Ops
    ( Frac_Pack => Long_Frac );
```

Generics, as well as subprograms and packages, can be separately compiled as "top-level" program units. The next chapter discusses how such program units fit into the structure of Ada programs.

## EXERCISES

1. When should generic units be used?

2. Replace the following function specification with a generic function specification that allows square root operations on any floating point type, not just type Float.

    ```
    function Square_Root (X: in Float) return Float;
    ```

    Show how your generic can be instantiated to create two overloaded square root functions, one that calculates the square root of Float and the other that calculates the square root of a type derived from Float.

3. Rewrite your solution to Exercise 2 so that the parameter and return value of function Square_Root is unconstrained. (Hint: use the Base attribute.)

4. Consider the following specification:

    ```
    generic
        type Item_List is (<>);
        type Items_In_Stock is range <>;
        type Item_ID is private;
    procedure Stock;
    ```

    Which of the following instantiations are illegal, and why?

    a.  type Bluegrass_Instruments is (Guitar, Bass, Fiddle,
            Banjo, Mandolin);
        subtype Category_Type is Integer range 0 .. 20;
        procedure Number_Of_Bluegrass_Instruments is new
            Stock
            (   Item_List          => Bluegrass_Instruments,
                Items_In_Stock     => Natural,
                Item_ID            => Category_Type );
    b.  type Harmonicas is (Diatonic, Chromatic, Chord,
                Bass);
        type ID is
            record
```
```

```
                    Make: String (1..15);
                    Model: Integer range 1..999;
                 end record;
            procedure Harmonicas_In_Stock is new Stock
                         (   Item_List         => Harmonicas,
                             Items_In_Stock    => Integer,
                             Item_ID           => ID );
        c.  type Mandolin_Types is (Mandolin, Mandola,
               Mandocello, Mandobass);
            procedure Mandolins_Available is new Stock
                 (   Item_List         => Mandolin_Types,
                     Items_In_Stock    => Float,
                     Item_ID           => Positive );
```

5. Write a generic procedure called `First_And_Last` that returns the first and last values of an enumeration type. Instantiate this procedure using several user-defined enumeration types of your choice. For example, you can create the procedure `End_Months` by instantiating this generic unit with the enumeration type consisting of the months of the year. The procedure call

   `End_Months (First, Last);`

   would then return `January` for the parameter `First` and `December` for `Last`.

6. Consider the following generic package specification:

```
generic
    Upper_Bounds: Positive := 80; -- default of 80
package Characters_Per_Line is
    Line: array (1 .. Upper_Bounds) of Character;
end Characters_Per_Line;
```

   Write a program that instantiates this generic package with a generic parameter value of 40. Have the program then use the array, `Line`, to output a 40-character message.

7. Consider the following generic procedure:

```
generic
    with function Func (A: Integer) return Integer;
procedure Output_Term (Term: in Integer);

with Ada.Text_IO; use Ada.Text_IO;
procedure Output_Term (Term: in Integer) is
begin
    Put_Line ("Parameter: " & Integer'Image (Term) );
    Put_Line ("Function value: " & Integer'Image(Func(Term)));
end Output_Term;
```

   Write a program that instantiates this generic procedure with a function

   $$F(N) = N^3 - 2N^2 + 5N - 6$$

   Using this instantiated procedure, have the program output the parameter 3 and F(3), which evaluates to 18.

8. Implement a generic function that, for any discrete type, returns its second successor. If the value is the last or next to last value, have the function wrap around to the first value. Use the following generic specification:

```
generic
    type Enum is (<>);
function After_Next (Item: Enum) return Enum;
```

9. Generalize the generic function written for Exercise 8 by having it return the N[th] successor, where the value for N is passed as a generic object parameter. Use the following generic specification:

```
generic
    type Enum is (<>);
    N: Positive := 1;    -- used to specify the Nth item
function After_N (Item: Enum) return Enum;
```

10. Rewrite the generic stack package presented in this chapter as a generic queue package.

11. Implement the following generic Queue package:

```
generic
    type Item is private;
package Queue_Pack is
    type Queue_Type (Queue_Size: Positive) is limited private;
    procedure Add ( Queue: in out Queue_Type,
                    Value: in      Item );
    procedure Remove ( Queue: in out Queue_Type;
                       Value:     out Item );
private
    -- implementation goes here
end Queue_Pack;
```

12. Replace the following package specification with a generic version:

```
package Trig_Functions is
    function Sin (Angle: Float) return Float;
    function Cos (Angle: Float) return Float;
    function Tan (Angle: Float) return Float;
end Trig_Functions;
```

13. Given the generic specification

```
generic
    type Might_Be_Unconstrained (<>) is private;
    type Cannot_Be_Unconstrained is private;
procedure P;
```

explain the problem, if any, with the following generic instantiations:

```
procedure Q is new P
    ( Might_Be_Unconstrained => String,
      Cannot_Be_Unconstrained=> String );

subtype Constrained is string (1..20);
procedure R is new P
```

```
(  Might_Be_Unconstrained  => Constrained,
   Cannot_Be_Unconstrained => Constrained );
```

**14.** What is wrong with the following code?

```
generic
    type Might_Be_Unconstrained (<>) is private;
    type Cannot_Be_Unconstrained is private;
procedure P;

Procedure P is
    A: Might_Be_Unconstrained;
    B: Cannot_Be_Unconstrained;
begin
    ...
end P;
```

**15.** What are the trade-offs between these three different generic stack packages?

```
generic
    Size : Positive;
    type Item is private;
package Stack is
    procedure Push (A : in Item);
    function Pop return Item;
end Stack;

generic
    Size : Positive;
    type Item is private;
package Stack is
    type Stack_Type is limited private;
    procedure Push    (  To:    in out Stack_Type;
                         Value: in Item );
    procedure Pop     (  From:  in out Stack_Type;
                         Value: out Item );
private
    type Item_Array is array (1..Size) of Item;
    type Stack_Type is
        record
            Stk: Item_Array;
            Top: Natural := 0;
        end record;
end Stack;

generic
    type Item is private;
package Stack is
    type Stack_Type (Stack_Size: Natural) is
        limited private;
    procedure Push    (  To:    in out Stack_Type;
                         Value: in Item );
```

```
      procedure Pop    (   From:  in out Stack_Type;
                           Value: out Item );
private
   type Item_Array is array (Natural range <>) of Item;
   type Stack_Type (Stack_Size: Natural) is
      record
         Stk: Item_Array (1..Stack_Size);
         Top: Natural := 0;
      end record;
end Stack;
```

# 9

# Compilation Units

**C**ompilation units are units of code that are separately compiled. Separately compiled does not mean independently compiled, because type checking is performed both within and *across* compilation units. Thus, a compilation unit will fail to compile if an item imported from another compilation unit belongs to an incompatible type. In addition, a compilation unit will fail to compile if the units upon which it depends need to be compiled first.

There are several advantages to breaking code up into separate compilation units. First, when a change is made to a compilation unit, possibly only that unit will need to be recompiled. If the code is not broken up into compilation units but is written as one monolithic structure, then any change, no matter how minor, requires recompilation of the entire program. Second, code can be more easily farmed out to programmers working on the same project. Programmers can work on their own compilation units without fear of undoing the work of others. Third, code is easier to read and maintain because the modular structure of the program is easier to discern. Fourth, code written as a compilation unit is more likely to be reused, than had the code been hiding within larger chunks of code. Fifth, the use of separate compilation units encourages a modular approach to design and development. This is because modules are physically represented as separate compilation units. And since Ada clearly distinguishes a compilation unit's interface from its implementation, programmers are encouraged to keep the interconnections between modules simple and well-defined.

Not every unit of code is a compilation unit. Block statements, for instance, cannot be separately compiled; they must always be embedded in a larger unit of code. However, subprograms (procedures and functions), packages, and generics can be separately compiled.

In this chapter, we will first discuss the differences between two kinds of compilation units: primary units, also known as library units, and secondary units. (Throughout the book, we have used the term library unit instead of primary unit.

In this chapter, however, since we are continually contrasting primary units with secondary units, the alternative name seems more appropriate.) Next, we will discuss compilation dependencies and how these dependencies affect the order in which units must be compiled or recompiled. The impact of these compilation dependencies on compiling and developing entire Ada programs will also be discussed. The remainder of this chapter is then devoted to hierarchical libraries, which allow child units to be declared. Ada's hierarchical library system enables software to be incrementally developed without impacting existing code or the clients of existing code. Hierarchical libraries also allow different interfaces to be provided to different clients, allow private types to be shared among multiple packages, and allow large systems to be divided into subsystems whose members can be private to the subsystem. We conclude our discussion of the hierarchical library system by explaining how child units can be renamed, and how child units can have parents that are generic packages.

## PRIMARY UNITS AND SECONDARY UNITS

Recall that compilation units—subprograms, packages, and generics—are each divided into two parts: a specification and a body. (The body is further broken down into a declarative part and a statement part; however, this level of division is irrelevant to this chapter.) A specification defines how the user interfaces with the program unit. A body contains the implementation of the program unit.

Typically, the specification is a primary unit, and the body is a secondary unit. The differences between primary units and secondary units are most easily conveyed by example. The following examples show primary and secondary compilation units in procedures, functions, packages, generics, generic instantiations, and subunits.

*Procedures*

Primary Unit:
```
-- specification
procedure Greetings;
```

Secondary Unit:
```
-- body (with specification)
procedure Greetings is
begin
    Put ("Hello");
end Greetings;
```

or

Primary Unit:
```
-- body (with specification)
procedure Greetings is
begin
    Put ("Hello");
end Greetings;
```

Secondary Unit:     Same as primary unit

### Functions

Primary Unit:

```
--specification
function Cube (A: Integer) return Integer;
```

Secondary Unit:

```
--body (with specification)
function Cube (A: Integer) return Integer is
begin
    return A ** 3;
end Cube;
```

or

Primary Unit:

```
-- body (with specification)
function Cube (A: Integer) return Integer is
begin
    return A ** 3;
end Cube;
```

Secondary Unit: Same as primary unit

### Packages

Primary Unit:

```
-- specification
package Computer_Languages is
    type Language is (FORTRAN, Pascal, Ada);
    function Better_Language (A, B: Language)
        return Language;
end Computer_Languages;
```

Secondary Unit:

```
-- body
package body Computer_Languages is
    function Better_Language (A, B: Language)
        return Language is
    begin
        if A > B then
            return A;
        else
            return B;
        end if;
    end Better_Language;
end Computer_Languages;
```

### Generics

Primary Unit:

```
-- specification
generic
    type Item is (<>);
function Maximum (X, Y: Item) return Item;
```

Secondary Unit:

```
-- body
function Maximum (X, Y: Item) return Item is
begin
```

```
                    if X > Y then
                        return X;
                    else
                        return Y;
                    end if;
                end Maximum;
```

*Generic Instantiations*

Primary Unit:
```
with Ada.Text_IO; use Ada;
package Int_IO is new
    Text_IO.Integer_IO(Integer);
```

Secondary Unit:   None

*Subunits*

Primary Unit:     None

Secondary Unit:
```
-- body (with specification)
separate (Main)
procedure Subunit is
begin
    Put ("I am a subunit");
end Subunit;
```

Note that procedures and functions may be submitted for compilation in two different ways. Consider, for instance, the previous example of procedure Greetings:

```
procedure Greetings is
begin
    Put ("Hello");
end Greetings;
```

The body of this procedure actually begins with the keyword **is**. However, this procedure body cannot be compiled without its specification **procedure** Greetings. Thus, a procedure body always contains its own specification. Procedure specifications, however, can be written without their bodies. This means that a procedure body may form either a primary unit or a combined primary/secondary unit. The compiler determines which option to take, as follows. If the specification is submitted to the compiler before the body, the body becomes a secondary unit when it is submitted to the compiler. This is rarely done. More commonly, the procedure body is interpreted as a combined primary/secondary unit. This is done by submitting only the body to the compiler.

Functions may also be submitted for compilation in the two ways just described for procedures. In general, then, subprogram bodies may either form primary units or primary/secondary units, depending on whether the subprogram specification is compiled first.

As shown, packages are broken down into primary and secondary units in a straightforward manner. When a package specification is compiled, it becomes a primary unit. When the corresponding package body is later compiled, it becomes a secondary unit. Recall that there may not be an associated package body. A package that has no body just consists of a primary unit.

As with packages, generics are also broken down into primary and secondary units in a straightforward manner. When a generic specification is compiled, it becomes a primary unit. When the corresponding generic body (which is indistinguishable from a regular body) is later compiled, it becomes a secondary unit. (Some implementations require that the primary and secondary units of a generic unit be submitted in the same file.)

Generic instantiations can serve as primary units. As previously illustrated, one can compile the generic instantiation of `Text_IO.Integer_IO`. The package created from the instantiation, `Int_IO`, is a primary unit that has no associated secondary unit. (As a result, programmers needing `Int_IO` for integer input or output can just mention `Int_IO` in a **with** clause.)

Subunits are bodies that are separated from the declarative part of the program unit in which they are embedded and made into separate compilation units. Subunits are unique because they are the only secondary units that do not have a corresponding primary unit. Subunits do not have corresponding primary units because the only possible candidate for being a primary unit—the specification of the subunit—is not even a compilation unit. The specification of the subunit (and body stub of the subunit) must be contained in the subunit's parent unit.

Subunits that are subprogram bodies were shown in Chapter 6. Subunits, however, may also be package bodies:

```
procedure Main is
   package P is

      . . .

   end P;
   package body P is separate;     -- body stub
begin
   . . .

end Main;
```

```
-- subunit P
separate (Main)
package body P is

   . . .

end P;
```

In this case, the body of P is removed from the declarative part of Main and replaced by a body stub, consisting of the package name followed by the keywords **is separate**. Subunit P is separately compiled and forms a secondary unit without a corresponding primary unit. Note that, as with subunits that are subprogram bodies, subunits that are package bodies must begin with the **separate** clause. The **separate** clause gives the name of the subunit's parent unit, which contains the subunit's body stub and corresponding specification.

In summary, primary units usually consist of compilation units that are package specifications, generic specifications, generic instantiations, and subprogram bodies (which include their specifications). Secondary units are compilation units that usually consist of package bodies, generic bodies, or subunits.

## COMPILATION DEPENDENCIES

Now that we have shown the differences between primary and secondary units, let us see how compilation dependencies between these units are created. Compilation dependencies—whereby the compilation of one unit depends on the prior compilation of another unit—are created in three different ways.

First, compilation dependencies are created through the use of subunits. A subunit is dependent on its parent. This makes sense since a subunit may reference items declared in its parent (that precede the subunit stub).

Since a subunit can reference items declared in its parent, the parent must be compiled first. Furthermore, if the parent is modified and recompiled, then the subunit may also have to be recompiled. However, since a parent is not dependent on its subunit, a subunit can be modified and recompiled without requiring its parent to recompile.

Second, compilation dependencies are created whenever a unit is written that consists of both a primary and secondary unit. In such cases, the secondary unit (the body) depends on its associated primary unit (its specification). This makes sense since the secondary unit may reference items declared in the primary unit.

Since a secondary unit can reference items in its corresponding primary unit, the primary unit must be compiled first. Furthermore, if the primary unit is modified and recompiled, then the secondary unit may also have to be recompiled. However, since a primary unit is not dependent on its secondary unit, a secondary unit can be modified and recompiled without requiring its primary unit to recompile.

Third, compilation dependencies are created through the use of the **with** clause. A unit is dependent on other units that are mentioned in its **with** clause. This dependency created by using the **with** clause, however, is formed on a primary unit, not on a secondary unit. Thus, if a **with** clause of a procedure mentions a package, then the procedure only depends on the package's primary unit (its specification), not on the package's secondary unit (its body).

Since a unit can reference the primary units listed in its **with** clause, the listed units must be compiled first. Furthermore, if the primary unit being **with**'d is modified and recompiled, then the unit doing the **with**ing may also have to be recompiled. However, since the **with**'d unit is not dependent on the unit **with**ing it, the unit **with**ing it can be modified and recompiled without requiring the **with**'d unit to recompile.

As we have seen, a unit must be compiled before all other compilation units that depend on it. This makes sense, since units must be compiled before they are available to other units. We have also seen that when a unit is modified and recompiled, units that depend on it may also have to recompile. Note that we said "may." Whether or not recompilation is required depends on the kind of change made and on the "intelligence" of the particular Ada library system. Almost all systems are smart enough to recognize that adding comments to a unit never requires other units to recompile. However, a system must be far more intelligent to determine which dependent units do not need to recompile when, for example, a type is removed from a package specification.

Compilation order can be summarized as follows. A subunit must be compiled after its parent, a secondary unit must be compiled after its associated primary unit, and a unit that has a **with** clause must be compiled after the primary unit mentioned in this clause. To illustrate these compilation orderings, consider the following Ada program, which consists of six separate compilation units. (A line is used to indicate separate compilation units.)

```
with P1;            -- P1 specification (spec) must be compiled
procedure Main is   -- before Main
begin

   . . .

end Main;
```

```
-- package P1 spec
with P2;            -- P2 must be compiled before P1 spec
package P1 is       -- P1 spec must be compiled before P1 body

   . . .

end P1;
```

```
-- package P1 body
package body P1 is

   . . .

end P1;
```

```
procedure P2 is     -- P2 must be compiled before P3
   procedure P3 is separate;
begin

   . . .

end P2;
```

```
-- subunit P3
separate (P2)
procedure P3 is     -- P3 must be compiled before P4
   procedure P4 is separate;
begin

   . . .

end P3;
```

```
-- subunit P4
separate (P2.P3)
procedure P4 is
begin

   . . .

end P4;
```

In this program, because package P1 appears in the **with** clause of procedure Main, Main is dependent on the primary unit of P1 (P1's specification) and must be compiled after the specification for P1 is compiled. The package P1 specification, in turn, mentions procedure P2 in a **with** clause and is thus dependent on P2. P2, therefore, must be compiled before the specification of P1. Note that the package P1 specification also has an associated body. Specifications must always be submitted for compilation before their associated bodies. Now let us examine procedure P2. Note that P2 contains a procedure body stub for P3. This means that the subunit, P3, depends on its parent unit, P2. P2, therefore, must be compiled before P3. Finally, note that P3, in turn, contains a procedure body stub, in this case, for P4. Procedure P3 must therefore be compiled before P4. The pairs of compilation orderings that we have discussed are listed below:

$$
\begin{array}{lll}
P1_{spec} & \textbf{before} & Main \\
P2 & \textbf{before} & P1_{spec} \\
P1_{spec} & \textbf{before} & P1_{body} \\
P2 & \textbf{before} & P3 \\
P3 & \textbf{before} & P4
\end{array}
$$

The compilation orderings listed above show direct (immediate) dependencies. Many indirect dependencies are inferred from these direct dependencies. For example, since P2 must be compiled before P3 and P3 must be compiled before P4, P2 must be compiled before P4.

Now that we understand compilation orderings, let us consider the consequences of modifying and recompiling various compilation units. As a first example, let us assume that, in the preceding program, Main, the specification for package P1 is modified and recompiled. Since Main and the body of P1 depend on the specification of P1, both of these compilation units may need to be recompiled.

As a second example, let us suppose that procedure P3 is modified and then recompiled. Because the subunit P4 depends on P3, P4 may also need to be recompiled. No other units depend on P3, so no other units need to be recompiled.

As a third example, suppose that procedure P2 is modified and recompiled. Potentially, this could require that the entire program be recompiled. The specification of P1, and the subunit P3, may need to be recompiled since these directly depend on P2. If so, then Main and P1's body may need to recompile since they directly depend on the specification of P1, and P4 may need to recompile since it directly depends on the subunit P3.

As a fourth example, let us suppose that the package P1 body is modified and recompiled. In this case, because no other unit depends on the package P1 body, no other unit needs to be recompiled. Of course, this is assuming that the changes made to the body do not require changes to the specification.

The four examples just discussed are realistic since units of code are usually compiled as they are written or modified. At times, however, the compilation of an entire Ada program consisting of many compilation units is required. For instance, complete recompilation is required when an Ada program is ported to a different Ada compiler or when a new version of the Ada compiler is received that is incompatible with the previous version. When compiling an entire program such as Main, all of the immediate compilation orderings previously listed must be satisfied. However, these orderings can be satisfied in different ways, such as the following:

P2 **before** P3 **before** P4 **before** P1$_{\text{spec}}$ **before** P1$_{\text{body}}$ **before** Main
  or
P2 **before** P1$_{\text{spec}}$ **before** Main **before** P1$_{\text{body}}$ **before**P3 **before** P4
  or
P2 **before** P3 **before** P1$_{\text{spec}}$ **before** Main **before** P4 **before** P1$_{\text{body}}$

Any of these complete orderings works, since each satisfies all the immediate compilation orderings. (Some Ada compilation systems provide what is often called a "make facility," which automatically compiles all units in a workable order.)

As we have seen, when a unit is modified and recompiled, all the units that depend on it may also have to recompile. To reduce the amount of potential recompilation, it is important to isolate compilation dependencies as much as possible. For example, if the specification of a package mentions a procedure in its **with** clause, then this specification directly depends on the procedure. The corresponding body of the package indirectly depends on this procedure. That is, the package body depends on the package specification, which in turn depends on the procedure. In contrast, if only the body of a package mentions a procedure in its **with** clause, then this body directly depends on the procedure. The corresponding specification of the package does not depend on the procedure. Therefore, to minimize potential recompilation, whenever possible, apply the **with** clause to a package's body instead of to its specification:

```
with A;          -- If the spec of B withs A, then if A changes,
                 -- P and the spec and body of B might need
                 -- recompiling

package B is
   . . .
end B;

with A;          -- If only the body of B withs A, then if A
                 -- changes, only the body of B might need
                 -- recompiling

package body B is
   . . .
end B;

with B;
procedure P is ...
```

Note that if the specification of B **with**'s A, then if A changes, P and the specification and body of B must be recompiled. However, if only the body of B **with**'s A, then if A changes, only the body of B must be recompiled.

As previously stated, a unit is dependent on the primary unit that is mentioned in its **with** clause. However, when **pragma** Inline is used (see Chapter 6), a dependency may also be formed on the secondary unit:

```
package A is
   procedure P;
   pragma Inline(P);
end A;

package body A is    -- Since P is inlined, changes to this body
   procedure P is    -- could require that the spec of A and
   begin             -- Main recompile
      ...
   end P;
end A;

with A;
procedure Main is    -- depends on the body of A.P
begin
   A.P;
   ...
end Main;
```

As a result of **pragma** Inline, clients of A that invoke procedure P form a compilation dependency not only on A's specification, but also on A's body. The reason that **pragma** Inline adds this new dependency is that for Main to compile, the body of procedure P that resides in the body of A must be available for inlining. In other words, the body of procedure P is needed so that its call can be inlined.

**Ada 95 ▶**        To make this situation somewhat better, Ada allows subunit stubs to be placed in the private part of a package:

```
package A is
   procedure P;
   pragma Inline(P);
   ...
private
   procedure P is separate;
end A;
```

In this case, instead of forming a dependency on the specification and body of package A, Main forms a dependency on the specification of A and the subunit P. The trade-off is therefore between forming a dependency on a package body or a subunit. The subunit is preferable because whereas the subunit only implements P, the package body typically contains the implementation of P, together with many other items.

In most computer languages, if a compilation unit is modified and recompiled, it is up to the programmers to make sure that all the units that depend on the modification are also recompiled. If one forgets to recompile all the dependent units, then the linker may generate a corrupted executable image (object code that can execute on the hardware). It may take considerable debugging time before this error is uncovered. In Ada, however, this cannot happen. The Ada compilation system will not allow an executable image to be built from out-of-date units.

It is fortunate that the Ada compilation system keeps track of all the compilation dependencies, because this task would be difficult without computer assistance. But how does the Ada compiler system enforce a compilation order that is consistent with all the dependencies that exist between a program's compilation units? The *Ada 95 Reference Manual* does not specifically answer this question. A user-friendly compiler system might automatically recompile, in proper order, all the units that need to be recompiled. A less friendly compiler system might instruct a user to manually recompile each unit that needs to be recompiled, perhaps one unit at a time.

## DEVELOPING ADA PROGRAMS

Let us now consider how the development of Ada programs is affected by the fact that primary units do not depend on secondary units. When a program is developed, the compiler can test the design before the implementation details are written. To have the compiler test the design, only the primary units need to be compiled. (This is possible since, barring **pragma** Inline, primary units never depend on secondary units.) The primary units contain all of the information on how units interface with one another. This interface information embodies the program design. The secondary units, which contain the underlying program implementation, do not need to be written and compiled until the program is ready to run.

During compilation, the compiler system tests the program design by making consistency, completeness, and circularity checks. Consistency checks guarantee that subprograms are being called with the correct number and type of parameters, both within and across compilation units. Completeness checks guarantee that the primary units mentioned in a **with** clause actually exist, and that if the units are packages, they contain all of the resources one is counting on. Circularity checks guarantee that circular dependencies do not exist. Circular dependencies occur when two primary units mention each other in **with** clauses. This is illegal since each unit requires that the other be compiled first. In the following example, the specifications of P1 and P2 depend on each other:

```
--illegal circularity
with P2;
package P1 is -- depends on P2
    -- public part
end P1;
```

```
with P1
package P2 is -- depends on P1
    -- public part
end P2;
```

One way to avoid this circularity is to relocate one or both **with** clauses to the package bodies:

```
-- legal
package P1 is
```

```
         -- public part
      end P1;
```

```
      package P2 is
         -- public part
      end P2;
```

```
      with P2;
      package body P1 is
         -- private part
      end P1;
```

```
      with P1;
      package body P2 is
         -- private part
      end P2;
```

The body of P1 now depends on the specification of P2, and the body of P2 depends on the specification of P1. This does not result in a circularity problem. A consequence of the solution, however, is that the resources of P1 are only available to the *body* of P2, and the resources of P2 are only available to the *body* of P1. If the package specifications require each other's resources, then this solution will not work. In such cases, the packages must be restructured or combined so that circularity between their specifications is avoided.

Circular dependencies are not always as obvious as A **with**ing B and B **with**ing A. A circular dependency can be created through a long chain of **with**ing. For example, a circular dependency is created if A **with**'s B, which **with**'s C, which **with**'s D, which **with**'s E, which in turn **with**'s A.

## HIERARCHICAL LIBRARIES

**Ada 95** ▶ Large programs are rarely developed in one fell swoop. Typically, they evolve over many years from smaller systems. Such evolutionary development of large software systems is called "programming-in-the-large."

Ada's hierarchical library system supports "programming-in-the-large" by allowing incremental development of software without impacting existing code or the clients of existing code. Specifically, hierarchical library units enable extensions to be added to the existing software without requiring the existing software to be modified or even to be recompiled, and without requiring clients of the existing software to modify or recompile their code.

Hierarchical library units form a tree of units: parent units have children, that have children, and so on. As shown in Figure 9.1, each tree is rooted at the ultimate ancestor of all its children.

Not all library units can have child units. Only library units that are packages can have child units. These child units can be any kind of compilation unit, not just packages. Child units are named similarly to the way subunits are named: the name of the child is prefixed with the parent's name:

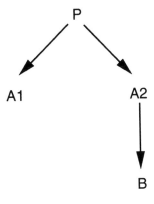

**Figure 9.1**   Hierarchical library.

```
package P is ... -- parent unit

-- The following children can be added without
-- modifying or recompiling P or P's clients
procedure P.A1;      -- child procedure of P
package P.A2 is ...  -- child package of P
procedure P.A2.B;    -- child procedure of P.A2
```

A child can be added to a parent without impacting the parent or the parent's existing clients. Specifically, the system consisting of package P can be extended with the child units P.A1 and P.A2 without requiring P to be modified or recompiled and without impacting the existing clients of P. Similarly, the system consisting of P.A2 can be extended with the child unit P.A2.B without requiring P.A2 to be modified or recompiled and without impacting existing clients of P.A2. Since adding a child unit has no impact on its parent or its parent's clients, the parent should not even need to be retested, except in conjunction with the newly developed child units. Finally, recompilation is minimized since extensions composed of child units can be compiled without their parents being recompiled.

Although a child unit is compiled separately, it is logically nested in its parent. In this respect, child units resemble subunits. Furthermore, both child units and subunits depend on their parent and must therefore be compiled after their parent is compiled. But despite these similarities, significant difference exist. A significant difference between child units and subunits is that the parent of a child unit is a package specification, whereas the parent of a subunit is a unit body. More specifically, the declaration of a child unit is logically located in its parent package, right at the end of the its parent's private part. In contrast, a subunit is logically located at its body stub within the declarative part of a unit's body. Another significant difference is that child units can be attached to a parent unit without any modification to the parent unit and without impacting existing clients of the parent unit. Child units can be added without even recompiling the parent unit. In contrast, a subunit can be attached to a parent only if the parent contains a subunit stub (an **is separate** clause).

This means that when new subunits are attached to an existing parent, the parent must be modified and recompiled. Finally, a child unit is made available to any unit that **with**'s it. However, a subunit cannot be listed in a **with** clause.

A client can select library units by listing those desired in its **with** clause. For example, if a client only needs P but none of its children, only P should be **with**'d. If a client needs P and P.A1, then only P.A1 needs to be **with**'d. This is because when P.A1 is **with**'d, P is implicitly **with**'d:

```
with P.A1;    -- implicitly provides a with P
```

If P, P.A2, and P.A2.B are needed, then only P.A2.B needs to be **with**'d:

```
with P.A2.B; -- implicitly provides a with P and a with P.A2
```

In general, by **with**ing a child, all of its ancestors also become available.

Without employing the **with** clause, a child unit can only access its ancestor's resources. (Details about the availability of resources will be covered later in this chapter.) Thus, in Figure 9.1, A1 and A2 can reference P, and B can reference A2 and P. However, A1 cannot access A2 or B because A2 and B are on a different "branch of the tree." In other words, A2 and B are relatives of A1 but not ancestors. If A1 needs to access A2 or B, then A1 must **with** them. A library unit can list a relative in a **with** clause as long as the relative's specification has been compiled.

The **use** clause behaves differently from the **with** clause. When the **use** clause is applied to a child package, only that package's resources becomes directly visible, not the resources of its ancestors. For example, see the tree of units in Figure 9.1. The following **use** clause only makes the resources of P.A2.B directly visible, not the resources of P or P.A2:

```
use P.A2.B;   -- does not provide a use P or a use P.A2
```

The rules governing the **with** and **use** clauses are illustrated by the following code:

```
package A is
   procedure A1;
end A;

package A.B is
   procedure B1;
end A.B;

with A.B;     -- Implicitly provides with A
use A.B;      -- Doesn't provide use A
procedure P1 is
begin
   A.A1;  -- Extended name required
   B1;    -- OK
end P1;
```

```
with A.B;
use A;
procedure P2 is
begin
    A1;    -- OK
    B.B1;  -- Extended name required
end P2;

with A.B;
use A; use B;
procedure P3 is
begin
    A1;    -- OK
    B1;    -- OK
end P3;
```

Now that we understand the concept of child units, let us consider how the Ada environment is organized. In Ada 95, package `Standard` is the ultimate ancestor of all other packages. Package `Standard` has three predefined child packages—`Ada`, `Interfaces`, and `System`. All other predefined Ada compilation units are children of one of these three packages. Package `Ada` has by far the most children.

Package `Standard` is not only the ultimate ancestor of Ada's predefined packages. Even user-defined top-level library packages are considered implicit children of package `Standard`. This explains why the resources in `Standard` such as types `Integer`, `Float`, `Character`, `Wide_Character`, `String`, `Wide_String`, `Duration`, `Boolean`, and the predefined exceptions `Constraint_Error`, `Program_Error`, `Storage_Error`, and `Tasking_Error`, are always accessible.

As we have seen, child units support programming-in-the-large by allowing programs to be incrementally developed without impacting the existing code or its clients. Child units are also important because they allow different interfaces to be provided for different clients and allow a private type to be shared among multiple packages. In addition, a special kind of child unit—a private child—enables large systems to be divided into subsystems. We shall discuss each of these uses of child units, in turn.

## Multiple Interfaces

Child units enable different interfaces to be provided to different clients. For example, the following stack package provides one interface (the specification of `Stack`) for those needing to push or pop items on a stack, and another interface (the specification of `Stack.Debug_Support`) for those debugging code that uses the stack:

```
package Stack is -- parent package
    -- Children can be added without modifying or recompiling
    -- this package or its existing clients
    subtype Stack_Item is Integer range -10_000 .. 10_000;
```

```ada
      Stack_Size: constant Integer := 1_000;
      procedure Push (Item: in Stack_Item);
      function Pop return Stack_Item;
   private
      Stack_Array: array (1 .. Stack_Size) of Stack_Item;
      Top: Integer range 0 .. Stack_Size := 0;
   end Stack;


package body Stack is

      procedure Push (Item: in Stack_Item) is separate;
      function Pop return Stack_Item is separate;
   end Stack;


package Stack.Debug_Support is -- child package of Stack
      procedure Output_Stack;
      procedure Output_Entire_Stack_Array;
   end Stack.Debug_Support;


with Ada.Text_IO; use Ada;
package body Stack.Debug_Support is -- body of child package
      package Int_IO is new Text_IO.Integer_IO (Stack_Item);

      procedure Output_Stack is
      begin
         for Index in Stack_Array'First..Top loop
            Int_IO.Put (Stack_Array (Index)); Text_IO.New_Line;
         end loop;
      end Output_Stack;

      procedure Output_Entire_Stack_Array is
      begin
         for Index in Stack_Array'Range loop
            Int_IO.Put (Stack_Array (Index)); Text_IO.New_Line;
         end loop;
      end Output_Entire_Stack_Array;
   end Stack.Debug_Support;


separate (Stack) -- subunit
procedure Push (Item: in Stack_Item) is
begin
   Top := Top + 1;
   Stack_Array (Top) := Item;
end Push;


separate (Stack) -- subunit
function Pop return Stack_Item is
begin
   Top := Top - 1;
   return Stack_Array (Top + 1);
end Pop;
```

The package `Stack` is like the simple one shown in Chapter 7. It allows clients to push integers on a stack or pop integers from a stack. The child package `Stack.Debug_Support` allows the values of a stack to be dumped. `Stack.Debug_Support` contains two procedures, `Output_Stack` and `Output_Entire_Stack_Array`. The procedure `Output_Stack` dumps the values stored on the stack. Procedure `Output_Entire_Stack_Array` dumps the entire stack array, including garbage values, beyond the index of `Top`.

Whereas the package `Stack` is provided to programmers needing stack services, the child package `Stack.Debug_Support` provides debug support to programmers debugging code. This child package is not meant for general users of the `Stack` package. Child units such as `Stack.Debug_Support` thus allow interfaces to be created for specialized clients.

Before leaving this `Stack` package, note how Ada's visibility rules apply. The visible part of the parent, `Stack`, is visible throughout the specifications and bodies of its child, `Stack.Debug_Support`. The body of `Stack`, however, is not visible to any of its children. The private part of `Stack`'s specification is visible to the private part and body of its children, but not to the visible specifications of its children. Since `Stack_Array` and `Top` needs to be accessed by the body of the child package `Stack.Debug_Support`, `Stack_Array` and `Top` are placed in the private part of `Stack` instead of in `Stack`'s body.

## Sharing Private Types

Besides supporting programming-in-the-large and allowing different interfaces to be provided for different clients, child units allow private types to be shared among multiple child packages.

Recall from Chapter 7 that the implementation of a private type is only available to the package body, not to external clients. Since all operations on private types require access to the type's implementation, these operations must reside in the package body. All operations on a private type must, therefore, reside in the same package, possibly making the package excessively large. In addition, extending the operations of the private type impacts the existing system. The modified package must be recompiled and retested, and all units that list the package in their **with** clause must recompile. Furthermore, the extended operations must be made available to all users of the package, even to those who do not need them.

All these problems are solved by child packages. Instead of all of a private type's operations being defined in one package, the operations can be distributed among one or more child packages. Clients can choose which set of operations are needed by **with**ing the appropriate child packages. Finally, as requirements are added, new child packages can be developed to extend the private type's operations without impacting any of the existing code.

The following code illustrates how a child package, `Fraction_Ops.Extension`, can access its parent's private type `Fraction`, in order to provide additional fraction operations:

```
package Fraction_Ops is
   type Fraction is limited private;
```

```ada
      function "+" (Left, Right: in Fraction) return Fraction;
      function "-" (Left, Right: in Fraction) return Fraction;
      function "*" (Left, Right: in Fraction) return Fraction;
      function "/" (Left, Right: in Fraction) return Fraction;
      function "=" (Left, Right: in Fraction) return Boolean;
      procedure Copy (From: in Fraction; To: out Fraction);
   private
      type Fraction is
         record
            Numerator: Natural;
            Denominator: Positive;
         end record;
end Fraction_Ops;


-- Child package
package Fraction_Ops.Extension is
   function "/" (   Top: in Natural;
                    Bottom: in Positive) return Fraction;
   function Get_Numerator (Left: in Fraction) return Natural;
   function Get_Denominator (Left: in Fraction) return Positive;
   procedure Put (Item: in Fraction);
end Fraction_Ops.Extension;

-- This body has access to the private part of Fraction
with Ada.Text_IO; use Ada;
package body Fraction_Ops.Extension is

   function "/" (   Top: in Natural;
                    Bottom: in Positive) return Fraction is
   begin
      return (Numerator => Top, Denominator => Bottom);
   end "/";

   function Get_Numerator (Left: in Fraction) return Natural is
   begin
      return Left.Numerator;
   end Get_Numerator;

   function Get_Denominator (Left: in Fraction) return Positive
      is
   begin
      return Left.Denominator;
   end Get_Denominator;

   procedure Put (Item: in Fraction) is
   begin
      Text_IO.Put_Line (  Natural'Image(Item.Numerator) &
         " / " & Positive'Image(Item.Denominator) );
   end Put;

end Fraction_Ops.Extension;
```

Note that the body of the child package accesses the implementation of `Fraction`, which is hidden in the private part of its parent. In general, the hidden part of a child (its body or private part of its specification) can access either the visible or hidden parts of its parent specification. However, the visible part of the child package can only access the visible part of its parent. This restriction prevents a child from indirectly exporting items in its parent's hidden part to external clients. Finally, neither the visible nor the hidden part of a child package can access the body of its parent. These scope restrictions are depicted in Figure 9.2.

By allowing the operations on private types to be distributed across multiple packages, the needs of application programmers who are end users of a package and the developers who are the reusers of a package are satisfied. The end user **with**'s a package and invokes the operations that are supplied for its private types. Since the end user uses the package "as is," the underlying implementations of the private types are hidden. In contrast to end users, reusers typically need to extend the operations that apply to private types in order to satisfy the requirements of a particular application. Such an extension is only possible if the reuser has access to the underlying implementation of the private types. The least disruptive way for the reuser to gain such access is through child packages. This solution enables the implementation of private types to remain hidden from end users, but at the same time, to be fully accessible to reusers.

Interestingly, child units render private types less private than implied in Chapter 7. Any program unit can declare itself a child of some package and thereby gain

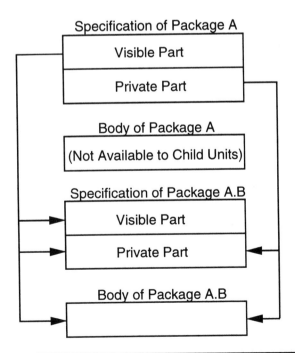

**Figure 9.2** Accessibility of parent units.

access to the implementation of the package's private types. And there is no way that a package can prohibit child units from attaching to it. When this is undesirable, however, there is one trick that the developer of a package can employ. When a private type is implemented as an access type, then the definition of the type being accessed can span the package's specification and body. The specification can contain the incomplete type, while the body contains the full type definition:

```
package Parent is
   type Some_Type is private;
   -- visible operations on Some_Type go here
   ...
private
   type Deferred;   -- incomplete type that is hidden from
                    -- all of Parent's children
   type Some_Type is access Deferred;
end Parent;

package body Parent is
   type Deferred is ('+', '-', '*'); -- full type
   ...
end Parent;

package body Parent.Child is
   A: Deferred; -- Illegal; child units cannot access this type
   ...
end Parent.Child;
```

Since type `Deferred` is implemented in the package body, the child units of `Parent` cannot access `Deferred`, thus enforcing the absolute privacy of this type.

## Private Child Units and Subsystems

As we have seen, child units support programming-in-the-large, allow different interfaces to be provided for different clients, and allow private types to be shared among multiple child packages. There is a special kind of child unit—the private child unit—that allows the creation of packages that are visible within a subsystem, but not to clients outside the subsystem.

Large software systems are often divided into different subsystems. A subsystem is a group of library units that are ancestors of the same root parent. Figure 9.1, for example, shows a subsystem rooted at parent P. Usually, the units making up a subsystem are not only available within the subsystem, but also to external clients of the subsystem. Recall that a client that **with**'s a member of a subsystem also has access to all the ancestors of that member.

Although it is often desirable for members of a subsystem to be available to external clients, some members are designed to be only used within the subsystem. Such members should be declared as private child units. A child unit is declared to be private by placing the keyword **private** at the beginning of its declaration. In Figure 9.3, package A.B is a private child.

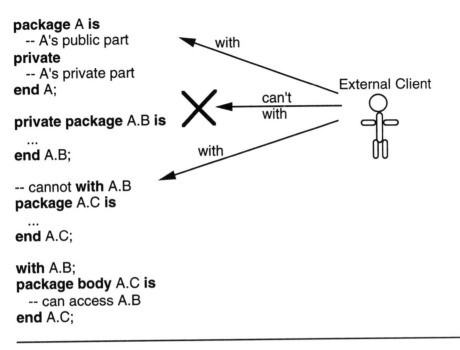

**package** A **is**
    -- A's public part
**private**
    -- A's private part
**end** A;

**private package** A.B **is**

    ...

**end** A.B;

-- cannot **with** A.B
**package** A.C **is**

    ...

**end** A.C;

**with** A.B;
**package body** A.C **is**
    -- can access A.B
**end** A.C;

with

can't
with

External Client

with

**Figure 9.3**  Private child.

As shown by the arrows in Figure 9.3, external clients cannot **with** the private child A.B. The resources defined in A.B can only be used within the subsystem. To guarantee this, restrictions apply so that members of the subsystem cannot indirectly export items in A.B to their external clients. Thus, as indicated in Figures 9.3 and 9.4, the specification of package A.C cannot list the private package A.B in its **with** clause. However, since the body of package A.C cannot be accessed by external clients, this body can list A.B in its **with** clause.

As illustrated in Figure 9.4, the specification (and body) of a private child can access its parent's private parts as well as its public part. It is safe for the specification of a private child to access its parent's private parts since the private child cannot be accessed by external clients and can therefore never indirectly export items declared in its parent's private parts.

In addition to the rules illustrated in Figure 9.4, a private child can be **with**'d from the specification or body of any other private child units within the same subsystem.

## Renaming Child Units

In Ada 95, packages such as Text_IO are children of package Ada. In Ada 83, however, child units are not supported. For upward compatibility, Ada 95 renames Ada.Text_IO to Standard.Text_IO. As a result, in Ada 95, the context clause

```
with Text_IO;
```

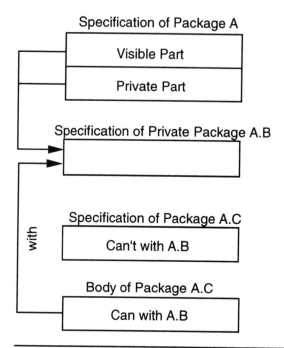

**Figure 9.4**   Accessing private child from within subsystem.

is equivalent to

```
with Ada.Text_IO;
```

although the latter context clause reminds us that `Text_IO` is a child package. Besides the predefined renaming of child packages such as `Text_IO`, programmers do their own renaming.

Since the tree of child units can contain many branches, the names of child units can get excessively long. To shorten these names, programmers can rename a child unit. For example, child package `A.B.C.D` can be renamed to `D`, as follows:

```
with A.B.C.D;
package D renames A.B.C.D;
```

Since package `D` is a library unit, other library units can list `D` in their **with** clause:

```
with D; -- this is equivalent to "withing" A.B.C.D
package body P is ...
```

Besides providing shortened names, renamed library units can also be used to select different package bodies with the same interface. For example, suppose that there are two different implementations of a sorting package: `My_Sort_Package` and `Your_Sort_Package`. Both packages have identical specifications but different bodies. In order to easily change implementations, a package called `Sort` can be introduced that is a rename of either `My_Sort_Package` or `Your_Sort_Package`. Program units needing the sort package can list package `Sort` in their **with** clauses. To change an implementation of `Sort`, only the **renames** statement needs to be modified:

```
-- assume these packages have the same interface
package My_Sort is ...
package Your_Sort is ...

-- To change the implementations, just change these
-- two statements
with My_Sort;                    -- with Your_Sort;
package Sort renames My_Sort; -- package Sort renames
                                 -- Your_Sort;

-- all users "with" Sort to get the current implementation
with Sort;
procedure User_1 is ...

with Sort;
procedure User_2 is ...

with Sort;
procedure User_3 is ...
   ...
```

## Child Units and Generics

So far, we have only shown child units of regular packages. Ada also supports child units of generic packages. All children of a generic package must themselves be a generic unit–either a generic package or a generic subprogram. A generic child unit can then either be instantiated inside the body of its parent, or instantiated as a child of an instance of its parent. The following code illustrates the latter case:

```
generic                           -- generic parent
   type Int is range <>;
package Generic_Parent is ...

generic
package Generic_Parent.Child is ... -- generic child unit

with Generic_Parent;
pragma Elaborate_All (Generic_Parent);
package Parent_Instance is new Generic_Parent (Int => Integer);

with Generic_Parent.Child;
pragma Elaborate_All (Generic_Parent.Child);
-- Generic_Parent.Child is instantiated as a child
-- of an instance of its parent
package Parent_Instance.Extensions is new Generic_Parent.Child;
```

As a precaution, **pragma** `Elaborate_All` should be used to ensure that the
**Ada 95 ▶** specified units (plus everything they need) have previously been elaborated. (This
**pragma** replaces Ada 83's **pragma** `Elaborate`.)

As we have seen, a generic package can have children. In addition, a child can
be an instantiation of a generic:

```
package Relationships is
  type Marital_Status is (Ideal, Complacent, Needs_Work,
    Free_To_Be_You_And_Me);
end Relationships;
```

```
with Ada.Text_IO;
-- child package created through a generic instantiation
package Relationships.IO is new
    Ada.Text_IO.Enumeration_IO(Marital_Status);
```

The bodies of compilation units–procedures, functions, and packages–as well
as blocks and tasks, contain a declarative part and a statement part. There is an
optional third part that we have not yet discussed: exception handlers. The next
chapter will explore these exception handlers.

## EXERCISES

1. Answer true or false.
   a. Block statements can be separately compiled.                        T   F
   b. Primary units are also known as library units.                      T   F
   c. The body of a subprogram may form either a primary or a             T   F
      primary/secondary unit.
   d. Every secondary unit must have a corresponding primary unit.        T   F
   e. The compiler can test the design of a program before the            T   F
      implementation details are written.
   f. A subunit is dependent on its parent.                               T   F
   g. A primary unit usually consists of a body.                          T   F
   h. Ada protects the integrity of its library.                          T   F
   i. A unit is dependent on other units that are mentioned in            T   F
      its **with** clause.
   j. A subunit must be compiled before its parent unit is compiled.      T   F
   k. For a compiler to test the design of a program, only the            T   F
      primary units need to be compiled.
   l. The Ada standards require that the specification of a generic       T   F
      unit be separately compilable.
   m. A package body may be compiled before its corresponding            T   F
      specification.
   n. Compilation units have two parts: a specification and a body.       T   F
      The body contains a declarative part and a statement part.
   o. Every primary unit must have a corresponding secondary unit.        T   F

p.  In general, changes made to secondary units do not require    T    F
that other units be recompiled.

q.  Typically, only one compilation ordering is possible for a    T    F
program consisting of many compilation units.

r.  In general, primary units often depend on other primary    T    F
units but rarely on secondary units.

s.  Secondary units often depend on primary units, but may    T    F
depend on other secondary units.

2.  Explain three ways that compilation dependencies are created.

3.  Given the following compilation units, write all pairs of immediate compilation dependencies:

```
with P1, P2;
procedure Main is
begin
   . . .
end Main;
```

```
with P3;
procedure P1 is
begin
   . . .
end P1;
```

```
package P3 is
   . . .
end P3;
```

```
package P2 is
   procedure P4;
end P2;
```

```
package body P2 is
   procedure P4 is separate;
end P2;
```

```
separate (P2)
procedure P4 is
begin
   . . .
end P4;
```

4.  List two different complete compilation orderings that satisfy all of the immediate compilation orderings in Exercise 3.

5.  Correct the errors in the following code by employing dot notation when necessary:

```
package Relationships is
   type Marital_Status is (Ideal, Complacent, Needs_Work,
```

```
                    Free_To_Be_You_And_Me);
        end Relationships;

    package Relationships.People is
        type Married_Person is
            record
                Status: Marital_Status;
                Years_Married: Integer range 0..60;
            end record;
    end Relationships.People;

    with Relationships.People;
    procedure Statistics is
        Average_Marriage: constant Relationships.Marital_Status :=
            Relationships.Free_To_Be_You_And_Me;
    begin
        declare
            use Relationships.People;
        begin
            Unusual_Marriage: constant Maritial_Status := Ideal;
            Unusual_Person: Married_Person :=
                ( Status           => Unusual_Marriage,
                  Years_Married  => 50);
            declare
                use Relationships;
            begin
                Typical_Marriage: Marital_Status :=
                    Average_Marriage;
            end;
        end;
    end Statistics;
```

6. Write several new interfaces to the `Stack` package appearing in the Multiple Interfaces section of this chapter.

7. Which of the following statements are illegal?

```
    package Parent is
        type T is private;
        function F return T;
    private
        type T is new Integer;
    end Parent;

    package body Parent is
        X: T := 9;
        function F return T is separate;
    end Parent;

    procedure Parent.Child_1 is
        A: T := F;
        B: T;
```

```
begin
   X := 2;
   B := 7;
end Parent.Child_1;

package Parent.Child_2 is
   A: T := F;
   B: T := 2;
   procedure P (V: in T);
end Parent.Child_2;

package body Parent.Child_2 is
   procedure P (V: in T) is separate;
begin
   A := F;
   B := 5;
   X := 3;
end Parent.Child_2;

private package Parent.Child_3 is
   A: T := F;
   B: T := 8;
end Parent.Child_3;
```

# 10

# Exceptions

In most computer languages, when a problem is encountered during program execution, such as dividing by zero or running out of memory, the program abruptly terminates and control is passed to the runtime environment. Such behavior, however, is unacceptable in systems that must operate reliably. For example, a computer program that controls the radar on a plane or the cooling system of a nuclear power plant must be very reliable since people's lives depend on the system working properly. Ada places particular emphasis on software reliability and, therefore, provides a mechanism for intercepting problems encountered during program execution. When such problems are intercepted, code is run that attempts to recover from the problems and continue normal processing, or at least to minimize the damage before terminating the program.

In Ada, exceptions are errors, faults, or other unanticipated conditions that occur at runtime. They are called exceptions because they are exceptions to the normal, expected processing. During runtime, for example, an array index may go out of bounds, or the value of a variable may go out of range. Errors that are encountered as code is being compiled are not called exceptions.

An exception causes normal processing to be abandoned and a special action to be taken in response. Ada constructs that respond to an exception are called exception handlers. Exception handlers determine the kind of exception that was raised (announced) and then take appropriate action. By using exception handlers, an otherwise fatal error that causes a program to abort can be intercepted. Remedial action can then be taken to allow the program to continue running, if possible. The remedial action could be to repair the cause of the error, to make another attempt to accomplish whatever it was that caused the exception to be raised, to try another approach, or to give up and gracefully terminate the program.

This chapter will discuss predefined exceptions and user-defined exceptions. Information will be included on how to handle both kinds of exceptions with exception handlers. The propagation of exceptions will then be explored. Exception occurrences, which identify and provide information about exceptions, will next be covered. The chapter will conclude with a discussion of suppressing exceptions.

## PREDEFINED EXCEPTIONS

There are four predefined exceptions in the package `Standard` that is supplied with every Ada compiler. Each of these exceptions is identified with a name:

```
Constraint_Error
Storage_Error
Tasking_Error
Program_Error
```

These predefined exceptions are automatically raised when certain runtime errors are encountered. The `Constraint_Error` is raised whenever a value goes out of bounds. For instance, an attempt may be made to assign an out-of-range value to an array index or a variable. Or an attempt may be made to assign one array to another array of a different size. You have undoubtedly received messages mentioning constraint errors whenever such errors caused your programs to abort. The `Storage_Error` is raised when the computer runs out of available memory. For example, an attempt may be made to allocate space for a huge dynamic array. The `Tasking_Error` is raised, for instance, when a call is made to a task that is no longer active. (Tasks will be covered in Chapter 15.) The `Program_Error` is raised for exceptions that don't fall into the categories of constraint, storage, or tasking errors. For instance, the `Program_Error` is raised when the end of a function is reached without a **return** statement having been encountered. `Program_Error` may also be raised when an attempt is made to read an uninitialized variable. For a more complete description of these predefined exceptions, consult the *Ada 95 Ref-*

**Ada 95 ▶** *erence Manual.* (Ada 83 also defined `Numeric_Error`, but it proved very difficult to distinguish between the conditions that raise the `Constraint_Error` and those that raise the `Numeric_Error`. For upward compatibility, in Ada 95, `Numeric_Error` is just another name for `Constraint_Error`.)

Without the use of exception handlers, whenever one of these exceptions is raised, the program aborts, usually with a message from the Ada runtime environment, stating which of these four exceptions is raised. (The Ada runtime environment is the runtime system provided with the Ada compiler.) Consider the following block:

```
-- assume the Get for integers is visible
declare
   Input: Integer range 1..10;
begin
   Put_Line ("Enter an integer from 1 to 10");
   Get (Input);
   New_Line;
   Put_Line ("Good for you!");
end;
```

This block instructs the user to enter an integer within the range from 1 to 10. The value entered is given to the variable Input, which is constrained to values in the range from 1 to 10. If the user enters a value such as 11, then a Constraint_Error is raised, because the variable Input is assigned a value that is out of range. If the Ada program that includes this block does not contain exception handlers, then the program aborts, and control returns to the Ada environment. Instead of allowing the program to automatically abort, the programmer can take control by placing in this block an exception handler that deals with constraint errors. After the exception is handled, the program can then continue to execute.

Exception handlers are placed at the end of a block, or at the end of the body of a subprogram, package, generic unit, or task. In each of these cases, the keyword **exception** is used to indicate that an exception handler follows. The exception handler, then, resides between the keywords **exception** and **end**. Exception handlers are placed in a block, as follows:

```
declare
    declarations
begin
    statements
exception
    exception handler
end;
```

Consider the following block, which contains an exception handler:

```
declare
    Input: Integer range 1..10;
begin
    Put_Line ("Enter an integer from 1 to 10");
    Get (Input);
    New_Line;
    Put_Line ("Good for you!");
exception
    when Constraint_Error =>
        New_Line;
        Put_Line ("I said from 1 to 10!");
end;
```

When this segment of code executes, if a user enters a value from 1 to 10, then the code outputs the message "Good for you!" The exception handler is then bypassed, and control passes to the line of code (not shown) following this block. Here is a sample run of this block (with the user response indicated by the prompt, >):

```
Enter an integer from 1 to 10
>7
Good for you!
```

Now let us examine what happens when the user enters a value outside the range of 1 to 10:

```
Enter an integer from 1 to 10
>11
I said from 1 to 10!
```

When the user enters the value `11`, a `Constraint_Error` is raised. As soon as the error is raised, the remaining statements in the statement part of the block are by-passed, and the exception handler is executed. Within the exception handler, the **when** clause for `Constraint_Error` is chosen, and the message `"I said from 1 to 10!"` is output.

As shown, a `Constraint_Error` is raised when the entered value is a legal integer value but is out of range. But what if a user enters a letter or some garbled data that cannot be interpreted as an integer value? In this case, the exception `Data_Error` is raised. `Data_Error` is not one of the predefined exceptions in package `Standard`. Rather, `Data_Error` is provided, along with many other input/output exceptions, in package `Text_IO`. Exceptions defined for input or output operations will be covered in Chapter 14.

Note that an exception handler enhances readability because it is separated from the code that handles normal execution. To understand what happens during normal execution, therefore, a code reviewer can ignore the exception handler, which is conveniently placed at the end of the code.

Within the exception handler, which is similar to a **case** statement, the keyword **when** is followed by the name of an exception, an arrow, and the statements to be executed whenever the exception is raised. (Also, the exception handler, like the **case** statement, may use the vertical bar and the **when others** clause.)

The exception handler, wherever it appears, has the following structure:

```
exception
    when exception choice => statements
    when exception choice => statements
        . . .
    when exception choice => statements
end;
```

After an exception handler is done executing, control passes beyond the unit that contains the exception handler. For blocks, "beyond the unit" means to the statement following the block.

In the previous example, the user is only given one opportunity to enter a valid integer, because after the exception is raised and handled, control passes to the statement following the block. This is user unfriendly. Let us attempt to modify the code so that the user is given unlimited chances to enter a valid integer:

```
declare
    Input: Integer range 1..10;
begin
    << Try_Again >>
    Put_Line ("Enter an integer from 1 to 10");
```

```
      Get (Input);
      New_Line;
      Put_Line ("Good for you!");
   exception
      when Constraint_Error =>Put_Line ("I said from 1 to 10!");
      goto Try_Again; -- will not compile
   end;
```

This code seems to be just what is needed. When a constraint error is raised, an error message is output and a **goto** statement passes control back to the statement that prompts the user for input. However, this code will not work. When the exception handler is done executing, control always passes beyond the unit that raised the exception. The Ada standards explicitly forbid the **goto** statement to jump from one part of a control structure to another. In the previous block, the **goto** illegally attempts to jump from the exception handling part of a block to the executable statement part.

The solution to the problem is to place the entire block statement that contains the exception handler in a loop. If an exception is raised, the exception handler executes, the block statement is exited, and we loop back to the beginning of the block statement, where the user is once again prompted for input. This is demonstrated in the following Ada program:

```
with Ada.Text_IO; use Ada.Text_IO;
procedure Try_Again is
    package Int_IO is new Integer_IO (Integer);
    use Int_IO;


begin

    loop    -- keep looping until valid input is entered

        declare
            Input: Integer range 1..10;
        begin
            Put_Line ("Enter an integer from 1 to 10");
            Get (Input);
            New_Line;
            Put_Line ("Good for you!");
            exit;  -- valid input received, so exit loop
        exception
            when Constraint_Error =>
                New_Line;
                Put_Line ("I said from 1 to 10!");
        end;

    end loop;

end Try_Again;
```

## USER-DEFINED EXCEPTIONS

As we have seen, predefined exceptions are automatically raised whenever there are constraint, storage, tasking, or program errors. In addition to these predefined exceptions, programmers can define their own customized exceptions. The following program contains two such user-defined exceptions:

```ada
with Ada.Text_IO; use Ada.Text_IO;
procedure User_Defined_Exception is

    Age: Float range 0.0..120.0;
    Too_Young, Too_Old: exception; -- user-defined exceptions
    package Real_IO is new Float_IO (Float);
    use Real_IO;

begin  -- User_Defined_Exception

    Put_Line ("Enter your age in years");
    Get (Age);
    if Age < 18.0 then
        raise Too_Young;
    elsif Age > 80.0 then
        raise Too_Old;
    end if;
    Put_Line ("You qualify for skydiving");

exception -- exception handler

    when Constraint_Error =>
        Put_Line ("You are not being serious");
    when Too_Young =>
        Put_Line ("Sorry, you must be at least 18 to do"
            & " skydiving");
    when Too_Old =>
        Put_Line ("Sorry, you cannot do skydiving if you are"
            & " over 80");

end User_Defined_Exception;
```

Before discussing how this program works, note that the exception handler belongs to a procedure, not to a block. As with block statements, exception handlers in procedures (and functions) are placed between the keywords **exception** and **end**:

```ada
procedure procedure name (parameter definitions) is
    declarations
begin
    statements
exception
    exception handler
end procedure name;
```

In the preceding procedure, `User_Defined_Exception`, two user-defined exceptions are declared: `Too_Young` and `Too_Old`. These user-defined exceptions appear in the declarative part of the program unit as identifiers that are declared as exceptions:

```
Too_Young, Too_Old: exception;
```

The syntax, then, resembles the syntax used to declare variables. Do not, however, be mislead into thinking that exceptions can be treated like variables. Unlike variables, exception identifiers are not objects; they cannot be used in assignment statements, in expressions, or as subprogram parameters. Also note that instead of a type name appearing to the right of the colon, as with a variable, the keyword **exception** appears.

Unlike the four predefined exceptions, which are automatically raised, user-defined exceptions are not automatically raised because the compiler has no idea when to raise them. The programmer must decide when to raise these exceptions. In the program `User_Defined_Exception`, the exception `Too_Young` is raised when someone enters a valid age (between `0.0` and `120.0`) that is less than `18.0` years old, and the exception `Too_Old` is raised when someone enters a valid age that is over `80.0` years old. These user-defined exceptions are explicitly raised by employing the keyword **raise**, followed by the name of the exception. (A predefined exception can also be explicitly raised, for example, **raise** `Constraint_Error`. However, this is not recommended, since it may be hard to determine whether the exception was raised automatically by the compiler or explicitly by the programmer.)

The exception handler in `User_Defined_Exception` handles the exceptions `Too_Young` and `Too_Old` by outputting appropriate messages. When the user-defined exception `Too_Young` is raised, the program outputs "`Sorry, you must be at least 18 to do skydiving.`" When `Too_Old` is raised, the program outputs "`Sorry, you cannot do skydiving if you are over 80.`" In addition to the two user-defined exceptions, the exception handler handles a predefined exception, the `Constraint_Error`. This exception is automatically raised whenever a user enters an age that lies outside of the range `0.0` to `120.0`. In this case, the program outputs the message, "`You are not being serious.`" (Exceptions should only be raised in abnormal or emergency situations; it is debatable whether such situations exist in this program.)

## PROPAGATION OF EXCEPTIONS

In the last few examples, the program unit that raises an exception contains an exception handler that handles that exception. Once the exception is handled and the unit is exited, processing proceeds normally. But what if the unit that raises an exception does not contain an exception handler? In such situations, the exception is not forgotten. Rather, the exception propagates (passes) one level beyond the unit. The meaning of "one level beyond the unit" varies, depending on whether the exception propagates from a main program, a block, or a subprogram. (Packages will be discussed later in this section.) As we have seen, when an exception propagates from a main program, it propagates to the Ada runtime environment, and the program aborts. When an exception propagates from a block, it propagates to the unit enclosing the block. When an exception propagates from a subprogram, it propagates to the unit that invoked the subprogram. In each of these cases, the exception propagates to one level beyond the unit. If the unit at this new level contains the appropriate exception handler, the exception is handled. If not, the exception is automatically propagated to yet a higher level. If an exception is raised in a program that has no exception handler at any level, then the exception continues being propagated until it reaches the main program, which propagates it to the runtime environment.

The following example unconditionally raises an exception to show how exceptions raised in a procedure are propagated to the unit that called the procedure:

```
with Ada.Text_IO; use Ada.Text_IO;
procedure Handle_Exception is
    We_Are_In_Deep_Kimchee: exception;

    procedure Raise_An_Exception is
    begin
        raise We_Are_In_Deep_Kimchee;
    end Raise_An_Exception;

begin
    Raise_An_Exception;
    Put ("This sentence will never be outputted");
exception
    when We_Are_In_Deep_Kimchee =>
        Put_Line ("We are in deep kimchee!");
end Handle_Exception;
```

In this example, the procedure `Handle_Exception` calls the procedure `Raise_An_Exception`, which raises the user-defined exception `We_Are_In_Deep_Kimchee`. Since `Raise_An_Exception` does not have an exception handler, control passes back to `Handle_Exception`, and its exception handler is immediately executed. Thus, when this program runs, the message "`We are in deep kimchee!`" is output.

As we have seen, exceptions are propagated when the unit that raises the exception does not have an exception handler. There are two other situations where exceptions are propagated. An exception is propagated when the unit that raises an exception has an exception handler, but this exception handler does not handle the particular exception that is raised. This is possible because, although exception handlers resemble **case** statements, they differ in this respect: in **case** statements, every possible value of the **case** expression must be covered in a **when** clause; in exception handlers, it is not necessary for every possible exception that can be raised to be covered in a **when** clause. (Similarly to the **case** statement, however, the same exception cannot be covered by more than one **when** clause.) Finally, an exception is propagated when the exception handler itself raises an exception. We will consider these last two situations, in turn.

In the preceding example, the exception handler contains a handler for the exception `We_Are_In_Deep_Kimchee`. Consider what happens, however, if the exception handler of this example appears as follows:

```
exception
    when Constraint_Error => Put ("Constraint error raised");
end Handle_Exception;
```

In this case, even though an exception handler exists, it does not handle the particular exception that is raised. Therefore, the exception is automatically propagated just as if there were no exception handler.

Now let us consider the final way that an exception is propagated: when an exception handler raises an exception. Thus far, we have only seen exceptions being explicitly raised outside the exception handler. However, programmers may raise an exception *within* an exception handler. This is typically done when the exception handler cannot fully handle the exception. Let us explain this process in greater detail.

In general, an exception handler should attempt to recover from each possible exception so that damage to the data structures, disk files, and so on, is minimized and program execution can continue. However, such a full recovery is not always possible for a single exception handler. In such cases, an exception handler may require the assistance of other exception handlers in higher level units. To get this assistance, an exception handler may reraise the exception (raise the same exception again) or raise a new exception. The raised exception then propagates to a higher unit that may have its own exception handler. This other exception handler has the same option of raising the exception. Thus, multiple levels of exception handlers may be required to fully handle an exception. (As a general rule, though, exceptions should not be raised any higher than required to be fully handled.)

To raise an exception within an exception handler, the keyword **raise** is used, optionally followed by an exception identifier:

```
exception
    when Storage_Error =>
        Put_Line ("Out of memory");
        raise Overflow;
            -- propagates this exception
    end;
```

After the message "Out of memory" is output, the user-defined `Overflow` exception is raised. This raised exception propagates to a higher unit that may be better equipped to deal with this emergency.

If the keyword **raise** used within an exception handler is not followed by an exception identifier, then the same exception is raised that caused the exception handler to be executed:

```
exception
    when Storage_Error =>
        Put_Line ("Out of memory");
```

```
          raise; -- propagates Storage_Error
     end;
```

In this case, Storage_Error is reraised.

As previously mentioned, when an exception handler exists that does not handle the particular exception that is raised, the exception is automatically propagated just as if there were no exception handler. To avoid such automatic propagation, exception handlers must be written to handle every possible exception, including exceptions that are anonymous. An exception is anonymous if its identifier is not visible to the exception handler. An identifier is not visible to the exception handler when the exception handler lies beyond the scope of the unit in which the exception is declared. However, even though an identifier is not visible beyond the scope of the unit in which it is declared, the exception itself can be propagated beyond the unit.

The only way to write an exception handler to handle such anonymous exceptions is to use the **when others** clause. Before showing how this clause is used, we will give an example of an anonymous exception. The following modified version of the Handle_Exception program is an example in which, because of Ada's scoping rules, an exception handler contained in an outer unit cannot access an exception identifier that is declared in an inner unit:

```
with Ada.Text_IO; use Ada.Text_IO;
procedure Handle_Exception is

   procedure Raise_An_Exception is
      We_Are_In_Deep_Kimchee: exception;
   begin
      raise We_Are_In_Deep_Kimchee;
   end Raise_An_Exception;

begin
   Raise_An_Exception;
   Put ("This sentence will never be outputted");
exception
   when We_Are_In_Deep_Kimchee =>
      Put ("We are in deep kimchee!");
         -- will not compile because this exception
         -- is not visible here
end Handle_Exception;
```

In this program, the exception identifier, We_Are_In_Deep_Kimchee, is declared in the inner procedure, Raise_An_Exception, but is unavailable to the outer procedure, Handle_Exception. The exception We_Are_In_Deep_Kimchee still propagates to the outer procedure, but its identifier is not visible to the outer procedure. Thus, the exception becomes anonymous. (Anonymous exceptions lose their anonymity if they are eventually propagated to a unit where their identifier is once again visible.) Because this exception is anonymous, it cannot be explicitly mentioned in an exception handler. As previously stated, the only way for an exception handler to capture such anonymous exceptions is through a **when others** clause. This clause works similarly to the **when others** clause in the **case** statement. The clause is executed whenever an exception is raised that is not explicitly covered by the other **when** clauses. The following exception handler contains a **when others** clause that is executed whenever an exception is raised that is not a Storage_Error or a Constraint_Error:

```
exception
   when Storage_Error =>
      Put_Line ("Out of memory");
   when Constraint_Error =>
      Put_Line ("Illegal entry");
   when others =>
      Put_Line ("Some other exception was raised");
      raise; -- propagate the exception
end Handle_Exception;
```

The **when others** clause must appear on its own; in other words, it cannot be combined with other exception identifiers through use of a vertical bar. In addition, when the **when others** clause is used, it must appear as the last **when** clause in the exception handler.

As shown in the previous exception handler, using **raise** without an identifier is the only way that anonymous exceptions can be reraised. If the **when others** clause is entered, the message "Some other exception was raised" is output, and the exception, whatever it is, is raised again. (Note that **raise** without an exception identifier can only appear inside an exception handler.)

We have seen how exceptions raised in blocks and subprograms are propagated. Now let us consider how exceptions that are raised in packages are propagated. In a package, an exception handler is placed in the package body, as follows:

```
package body package name is
   hidden declarations
begin -- initialization
   statements
exception
   exception handler
end package name;
```

The exception handler in a package can only handle errors in the statement part (initialization part) of the package body. For an example, consider the following stack package:

```
package Stack is
   procedure Push (A : in Integer);
   function Pop return Integer;
   Stack_Overflow: exception;
   Stack_Underflow: exception;
end Stack;
```

```
package body Stack is
   Stack_Size: constant := 1_000;
   Stack_Array : array (1 .. Stack_Size) of Integer;
   Top: Integer range 0 .. Stack_Size;

   procedure Push (A: in Integer) is
   begin
      if Top = Stack_Size then
         raise Stack_Overflow;
      end if;
      Top := Top + 1;
      Stack_Array (Top) := A;
   end Push;

   function Pop return Integer is
   begin
      if Top = 0 then
         raise Stack_Underflow;
      end if;
      Top := Top -1;
      return Stack_Array ( Top + 1);
   end Pop;

begin  -- Stack initialization
   Top := 0;
end Stack;
```

This package is identical to the first example of a package presented in Chapter 7, except that exception handling features have been added. This package contains two user-defined exceptions, Stack_Overflow and Stack_Underflow, which are exported to users of the package. These two exceptions are raised within the bodies of subprograms Push and Pop, which reside in the package body. Stack_Overflow is raised by Push whenever an attempt is made to push an item onto a stack that is full. Stack_Underflow is raised by Pop whenever an attempt is made to pop an item from a stack that is empty.

Suppose that the following exception handler is placed in the body of this Stack package:

```
   . . .
begin  -- Stack initialization
   Top := 0;
exception  -- only executed when Top is assigned an illegal
           -- value
   when Constraint_Error =>
      Put_Line ("Stack package initialization error");
end Stack;
```

Although an exception handler is contained in the package body, the user-defined exceptions raised by the subprograms Push and Pop are not handled by this exception handler. Whenever these user-defined exceptions are raised, they propagate to the unit that last invoked these subprograms. The exception handler of the package is only executed when an exception is raised in the statement part of the package body. In the preceding example, there is only one statement in this part of the package:

```
Top := 0;
```

Thus, unless `Top` is assigned a value that is out of range, the exception handler is never executed.

Let us now illustrate how the `Stack` package can be used:

```
with Ada.Text_IO, Stack; use Ada.Text_IO, Stack;
procedure Stack_Demo is

    package Int_IO is new Integer_IO (Integer);
    use Int_IO;
    Int: Integer;

begin  -- Stack_Demo

    -- place 2 integers in the stack
    Push (8);
    Push (4);

    Int := Pop;
    Put ( Int );  -- outputs 4

    Int := Pop;
    Put ( Int );  -- outputs 8

    Int := Pop;  -- raises Stack_Underflow exception
    Put ( Int );

exception

    when Stack_Overflow => Put_Line ("Stack is full");
    when Stack_Underflow => Put_Line ("Stack is empty");
    when others => Put_Line ("An unknown error occurred.");

end Stack_Demo;
```

In this program, two integers are pushed onto the stack and then popped from the stack. When an attempt is made to pop a third integer from the stack, the `Stack_Underflow` exception is raised by the procedure `Pop`. The exception handler contained in `Stack_Demo` is then executed, and the message "Stack is empty" is output to the screen.

Since the exception identifiers `Stack_Overflow` and `Stack_Underflow` are exported (along with the subprograms `Push` and `Pop`) to clients of the `Stack` package, these clients have full control over what code to execute, if one of these exceptions should be raised. This flexibility is important since the appropriate response to stack overflows or underflows can vary, depending on how the stack is being used.

So far, we have only considered exceptions that are raised as statements are being executed. Exceptions may also be raised as declarations are being elaborated. The following example raises an exception when the variable N is elaborated:

```
with Ada.Text_IO; use Ada.Text_IO;
procedure Outer is
   -- declarations
   procedure Inner is
      N: Positive := 0;   -- constraint error during
                          -- elaboration
   begin
      null;
   exception
      when Constraint_Error =>
         Put_Line ("Constraint error handled in procedure"
            & " Inner");
   end Inner;

begin  -- Outer
   Inner; -- raise a constraint error produced during
          -- elaboration
exception
   when Constraint_Error =>
      Put_Line ("Constraint error handled in procedure Outer");
end Outer;
```

When this program executes, only this single message is output: "Constraint error handled in procedure Outer". Even though the constraint error is raised in procedure Inner, and even though Inner has an exception handler that handles constraint errors, the exception handler is never executed. This is because the constraint error is raised as the declarations in Inner are elaborated. Whenever an exception is raised during the elaboration of declarations, instead of being handled by the exception handler of that unit, the exception propagates to one level beyond the unit. This propagation policy is reasonable since when an elaboration fails, the body of that unit would behave unpredictably. Therefore, in our example, the exception raised in the procedure Inner is immediately propagated to the procedure that last invoked Inner, namely, Outer. Similarly, a block that raises an exception during elaboration propagates this exception to the unit enclosing the block. However, a library package that raises an exception when the declarative part of its body is elaborated, propagates the exception to the runtime environment, and the program is aborted. In this case, there is no way that the exception can be captured by an exception handler:

```
-- example of an exception that cannot be handled
package body P is
```

```
      N: Positive := 0;    -- exception propagated to runtime
                           -- environment and program aborts
      ...
   begin
      ...
   exception
      when Constraint_Error => ...   -- this handler will NOT
                                     -- capture the above exception
      ...
   end P;
```

Since the exception cannot be handled, it is propagated to the runtime environment, and the program aborts before the main program begins to execute. Such exceptions are, therefore, dangerous. To avoid the possibility of raising exceptions that cannot be handled, N can be initialized in the executable statement part of the package so that if any exceptions are raised, they can be handled in the package's exception handler:

```
   -- example of an exception that can be handled
   package body P is
      N: Positive;
      ...
   begin -- executable statement (initialization) part
      N := 0; -- raises Constraint_Error
      ...
   exception
      when Constraint_Error =>       -- this handler will capture
         Put_Line ("Holy halitosis!"); -- the above exception
      ...
   end P;
```

It is important to understand that the Constraint_Error is raised and the exception handler outputs the message "Holy halitosis!" when the package is elaborated (created). Library packages (primary units) such as P are elaborated once, before the execution of the main program. This means that P will output its error message before the first statement in the main program executes.

## EXCEPTION OCCURRENCES

**Ada 95 ▶** An exception occurrence is the specific instance of a raised exception. The predefined package Ada.Exceptions enables programmers to identify an exception occurrence and obtain information about it, such as where in the code the exception was originally raised and why it was raised. Such information can be logged in a file to help with debugging or can be used to determine the appropriate response to the exception.

Package Ada.Exceptions defines a limited private type, Exception_Occurrence, plus functions Exception_Name, Exception_Message, and Exception_Information that provide information about the exception occurrence. All these functions take a parameter of type `Exception_Occurrence` and return a printable `String`. Function `Exception_Name` returns the full expanded name of the exception that was raised. The expanded name (using dot notation) indicates where the exception is declared. The function `Exception_Message` returns, as a "one-liner," the name of the exception and a brief description of the exception. The function `Exception_Information` returns a string describing the exception and why it was raised. The specific information returned by `Exception_Message` and `Exception_Information` can vary, depending on the Ada compilation system. Typical information includes the location where the exception was first raised and the kind of failure that caused the exception to be raised. Other information may be provided, such as a traceback showing the propagation path of the exception, or the values of the machine registers when the exception occurred.

As illustrated in the following code, a value of type `Exception_Occurrence` is not explicitly declared as a variable, but is provided by a "choice parameter":

```
with Ada.Exceptions, Ada.Text_IO; use Ada;
procedure Demo_Exceptions is
begin
   . . .
exception
   . . .
   when Nasty_Occurrence: others =>
   -- Nasty_Occurrence is a choice parameter of
   -- type Exception_Occurrence

      Text_IO.Put_Line ("Unknown error in Demo_Exceptions: " &
         Ada.Exceptions.Exception_Information
            (Nasty_Occurrence));
            -- Outputs a description of the exception
   end Demo_Exceptions;
```

The identifier `Nasty_Occurrence`, which appears in the exception handler between **when** and **others**, is a choice parameter. Like **for** loop counters, choice parameters are not explicitly declared. However, unlike for loop counters, choice parameters are constants that automatically belong to the limited private type `Ada.Exceptions.Exception_Occurrence`. Choice parameters can, therefore, be passed as parameters to the subprograms `Exception_Name`, `Exception_Message`, and `Exception_Information`. In the exception handler of procedure `Demo_Exceptions`, `Nasty_Occurrence` is passed as a parameter to the function `Exception_Information`, and the returned information about the exception occurrence is output.

Since `Exception_Occurrence` is a limited private type, assignments cannot be used to save an exception occurrence for later analysis. However, this missing functionality is provided in package `Ada.Exceptions` by two versions of the subprogram `Save_Occurrence`.

Package `Ada.Exceptions` also contains procedure `Raise_Exception` that allows a programmer to attach a message to the raising of an exception. The following code uses `Raise_Exception` to raise the exception `System_Error` with a string attached as a message:

```
with Ada.Exceptions, Ada.Text_IO;
procedure Exception_With_Message is
    System_Error: exception;
    Help_Is_Available: Boolean := True;
begin
    ...
    if Help_Is_Available then
        Ada.Exceptions.Raise_Exception
            ( E       => System_Error'Identity,
              Message => "For immediate and friendly help,"
                & " please call project manager anytime"
                & " at home: 222-1131.");
    else
        Ada.Exceptions.Raise_Exception
            ( E       => System_Error'Identity,
              Message => "Sorry, you are on your own.");
    end if;
    ...

exception
    ...
    when Help: System_Error =>
        Ada.Text_IO.Put_Line (Ada.Exceptions.Exception_Message
            (Help));
            -- will output either of the above messages
end Exception_With_Message;
```

The exception handler will output either "For immediate and friendly help, please call project manager anytime at home: 222-1131." or "Sorry, you are on your own.", depending on which occurrence of `System_Error` was raised in the **if** statement.

Note that `Raise_Exception` has two parameters. The first parameter belongs to type `Exception_Id` that is used to identify an exception. As illustrated in the previous code, the `Identity` attribute applies to an exception identifier and yields its `Exception_Id` value. The second parameter of `Raise_Exception` belongs to type `String` and is passed the string message to be associated with the raised exception.

## SUPPRESSING EXCEPTIONS

One advantage of Ada is that many checks are performed at runtime to ensure that array indexes do not go out of bounds, that variables do not get assigned a value that is out of range, and so on. However, there is a price to pay: larger object code and slower execution speed. In real-time applications where there are stringent space and time constraints, runtime error checking may be too costly. A solution, although a controversial one, is to use exception suppression.

Exception suppression turns off various runtime error checking. This should only be considered when execution speed or object code size is critical, because once exceptions are turned off, previously detectable errors go undetected. This is why exception suppression is controversial. As all seasoned programmers know, any large chunk of code might have nasty errors lurking around, even if the code has been successfully executing for years. (Exception suppression, of course, should never be used to deliberately hide errors.)

Some Ada compilers allow exception suppression to be specified when code is compiled. Exceptions may then be turned on or off each time the code is compiled, without the need to alter Ada source code. This feature, however, is outside of the language requirements of Ada. The Ada language requirements do specify a pragma (a compiler directive) called `Suppress`, which turns off runtime error checks. This pragma, however, is an optional Ada feature and, therefore, may not be fully implemented on your compiler. If it is not implemented, the compiler will ignore the pragma and issue a warning.

In Ada, many different kinds of runtime error checking can be suppressed. For a full list of all pragmas that turn off runtime error checking, consult the *Ada 95 Reference Manual*. The following is a list of pragmas that turn off all checks, range checks, and index range checks:

**Ada 95 ▶**

```
pragma Suppress (All_Checks);
   -- suppresses all checks

pragma Suppress (Range_Check);
   -- suppresses range checking

pragma Suppress (Range_Check, Integer);
   -- suppresses range checking only for objects of type integer

pragma Suppress (Range_Check, X);
   -- suppresses range checking only for object X

pragma Suppress (Index_Check);
   -- suppresses index range checking for arrays
```

**Ada 95 ▶** If these pragma specifications are placed in the declarative part of a program unit, then they only affect that program unit. If these pragma specifications are placed before the first compilation unit listed in a file, then they apply to all the program units in the file. (Pragmas that can be located this way are called configuration pragmas.)

An example of exception suppression follows:

```
declare
    pragma Suppress (Range_Check);
    subtype One_Or_Two is Integer range 1..2;
    M, N: One_Or_Two;
```

```
        Out_Of_Bounds: Integer := 3;
    begin
        M := Out_Of_Bounds; -- no exception raised
        N := Out_Of_Bounds; -- no exception raised
            ...
    end;
```

In this block, all range checking is suppressed. Therefore, when M and N are assigned values that are out of range, no exception is raised.

The next example of exception suppression is similar to the previous example, except that range checking is only suppressed for the variable M. Therefore, when M and N are assigned values that are out of range, an exception is raised only when N is assigned the out-of-range value:

```
    declare
        subtype One_Or_Two is Integer range 1..2;
        M, N: One_Or_Two;
        pragma Suppress (Range_Check, M);
        Out_Of_Bounds: Integer := 3;
    begin
        M := Out_Of_Bounds; -- no exception raised
        N := Out_Of_Bounds; -- constraint error raised
            ...
    end;
```

The ability to suppress exceptions for a particular object, such as a variable, may seem peculiar, but it does have uses. Programs often spend a significant amount of time running the same few statements over and over again. Suppressing exception checks on particular objects within this code can make a significant difference in the overall execution speed of the program. Besides localizing exception suppression to particular objects or types, exception suppression may be localized to objects within a block. The advantage of localizing exception suppression is that careful analysis and thorough testing may first be performed to ensure that the code in question can never raise an exception.

Although runtime checking takes time, a good optimizing compiler can often avoid many runtime checks, especially if the Ada programmer writes proper Ada code. Proper Ada code uses appropriate types and subtypes, uses attributes, and avoids literals. Consider, for instance the following code that violates these recommendations:

```
    declare
        subtype Years is Integer range 1935 .. 1985;
        Recession: array (Years) of Boolean;
        Special_Year: Integer := 1950;
    begin
        ...
        for Year in 1935 .. 1985 loop
            Put (Recession (Year));        -- index check performed
        end loop;
```

```
      Put (Recession (Special_Year));  -- index check performed
   end;
```

Each time through the loop, an index range check is performed on the `Recession` array. An index range check on `Recession` is also performed on the statement following the loop. All of these index range checks can be eliminated when a good optimizing compiler is given the following version of the code:

```
declare
    subtype Years is Integer range 1935 .. 1985;
    Recession: array (Years) of Boolean;
    Special_Year: Years := 1950;
begin
    ...
    for Year in Recession'Range loop
        Put (Recession (Year)); -- No index range check needed
    end loop;

    Put (Recession (Special_Year)); -- No index range check
                                    -- needed
end;
```

Range checking can be eliminated since the array index variables, `Year` and `Special_Year`, belong to the same subtype, `Years`, as the array index. For example, if `Special_Year` is out of `Recession`'s index range, the problem is caught when `Special_Year` is initialized and does not have to be rechecked when `Special_Year` is used to index `Recession`. Furthermore, since the range of the **for** loop counter, `Year`, is specified with the `Range` attribute, the compiler selects `Recession`'s index values and, therefore, does not need to check its own selection of index values within the loop.

In this chapter, we discussed exceptions and exception handlers. The next chapter will cover access types.

## EXERCISES

1. Consider the following function:

```
function Flawed (A: Integer; OK: Boolean) return Integer is
    Answer: Integer range 0..100;
    Oops: exception;
    Yikes: exception;
begin
    if OK then
        Answer := 100 / A;
        return Answer;
    elsif A >= 0 then
        raise Oops;
```

```
        else
            raise Yikes;
        end if;
    exception
        when Constraint_Error => return -1;
        when Oops => return -2;
        when others => return -99;
    end Flawed;
```

Given this function, what is the result of the following expressions?

**a.**  `Flawed (1, True)`
**b.**  `Flawed (-10, True)`
**c.**  `Flawed (-10, False)`
**d.**  `Flawed (0, True)`
**e.**  `Flawed (0, False)`

2. Consider the following procedure:

```
with Ada.Text_IO; use Ada.Text_IO;
procedure Monitor_Temperature is
    Temperature: Integer range -30..1_000;
    Too_Hot, Too_Cold: exception;
begin
    loop
        Read_Temperature (Temperature);
        -- assume this procedure is visible
        if Temperature > 800 then
            raise Too_Hot;
        elsif Temperature < (-10) then
            raise Too_Cold;
        end if;
    end loop;
exception
    when Too_Hot =>
        Put_Line ("Sound alarm");
    when Too_Cold =>
        Put_Line ("Turn on heater");
    when others =>
        Put_Line ("Evacuate building");
end Monitor_Temperature;
```

What, if anything, does `Monitor_Temperature` output when the procedure `Read_Temperature` returns the following `Temperature` values?

**a.**  500
**b.**  950
**c.**  0
**d.**  1020
**e.**  −14
**f.**  −32

3. What will the following code output?

**a.**
```
-- assume package Text_IO is visible
declare
    Neg: Integer := -10;
    Pos: Positive := 10;
begin
    Pos := Neg;
    Put_Line ("Will this be output?");
exception
    when Constraint_Error => Put_Line
        ("Out of bounds");
end;
```

**b.**
```
with Ada.Text_IO; use Ada.Text_IO;
procedure Main is
    package Real_IO is new Float_IO (Float);
    use Real_IO;
    Pi: constant Float := 3.14159;

    function To_Degrees (Angle: in Float) return
        Float is
        Degrees: Float range 0.0 .. 360.0;
    begin
        Degrees := 180.0 * Angle / Pi;
        return Degrees;
    exception
        when Constraint_Error =>
            Put_Line
                ("Angle not in the range 0 to 2 Pi");
            return -99;
    end To_Degrees;

begin
    Put_Line ( To_Degrees ( Pi / 4.0 ) );
    New_Line;
    Put_Line ( To_Degrees ( 3.0 * Pi ) );
    New_Line;
    Put_Line ( To_Degrees ( Pi ) );
    New_Line;
exception
    when others =>
        Put_Line ("Error occurred");
end Main;
```

**c.**
```
with Ada.Text_IO; use Ada.Text_IO;
procedure Main is
    package Real_IO is new Float_IO (Float);
    use Real_IO;
    Pi: constant Float := 3.14159;
```

```
        function To_Degrees (Angle: in Float) return
            Float is
            Degrees: Float range 0.0 .. 360.0;
        begin
            Degrees := 180.0 * Angle / Pi;
            return Degrees;
        end To_Degrees;

    begin
        Put_Line ( To_Degrees ( Pi / 4.0 ) );
        New_Line;
        Put_Line ( To_Degrees ( 3.0 * Pi ) );
        New_Line;
        Put_Line ( To_Degrees ( Pi ) );
        New_Line;
    exception
        when Constraint_Error =>
            Put_Line ("Angle not in the range 0 to 2 pi");
        when others =>
            Put_Line ("Error occurred");
    end Main;
```

4. What is wrong with the following code?

```
with Ada.Text_IO; use Ada.Text_IO;
procedure Main is
    procedure Error is
        Oops: exception;
    begin
        raise Oops;
    end Error;
begin
    Error;
exception
    when Oops =>
        Put_Line ("Oops");
end Main;
```

5. What will the following procedures output?

   a.
```
    with Ada.Text_IO; use Ada.Text_IO;
    procedure Main is
    begin
        declare
            Zikes: exception;
        begin
            raise Zikes;
        end;
```

```
      exception
         when others => Put_Line
            ("A problem has occurred");
      end Main;
b.
   with Ada.Text_IO; use Ada.Text_IO;
   procedure Outer is
      procedure Middle is
         procedure Inner is
            Oops: exception;
         begin  -- Inner
            raise Oops;
         end Inner;
      begin  -- Middle
         Put_Line ("Calling Inner");
         Inner;
         Put_Line ("Finished calling Inner");
      end Middle;
   begin  -- Outer
      Put_Line ("Calling Middle");
      Middle;
      Put_Line ("Finished calling Middle");
   exception
      when Constraint_Error => Put_Line
         ("Constraint error");
      when others => Put_Line
         ("A problem has occurred");
   end Outer;
c.
   with Ada.Text_IO, P; use Ada.Text_IO, P;
   -- Package P follows
   procedure Main is
   begin
      Q; -- defined in package P
   exception
      when Constraint_Error =>
         Put_Line ("A problem has occurred");
   end Main;
```

---

```
   package P is
      procedure Q;
   end P;
```

---

```
   with Ada.Text_IO;    use Ada.Text_IO;
   package body P is
      Pos: Positive;
      procedure Q is
```

```
      begin
          Pos := -5;
      end Q;
   begin -- P initialization
      Pos := -10;
   exception
      when Constraint_Error =>
          Put_Line ("Bad initialization");
   end P;
```

6. Write a procedure that checks the amount of change received after an item is purchased. If the amount received is too little, then have the procedure raise the user-defined exception `Short_Changed`. If the amount received is too much, then have the procedure raise the user-defined exception `Over_Paid`. Incorporate an exception handler that takes appropriate action whenever one of these exceptions is raised.

7. Place an exception handler in the following procedure that handles possible numeric overflow:

```
function Cube_Of_Sum (Left, Right: Float) return Float is
begin
    return (Left + Right) ** 3;
end Cube_Of_Sum;
```

8. Write code that prompts the user to enter a positive integer value and employs an exception handler to handle incorrect input. Allow the user four tries at correctly entering a positive integer value. On the first three failures, output the message "Invalid response: Try again." After the fourth failure, output: "I give up!" and assume a value of 1.

9. Which of the following implementations of procedure Push do you prefer? Why?

```
procedure Push (A: in Integer) is
begin
    if Top = Stack_Size then
        raise Stack_Overflow;
    end if;
    Top := Top + 1;
    Stack_Array (Top) := A;
end Push;


procedure Push (A: in Integer) is
begin
    Top := Top + 1;
    Stack_Array (Top) := A;
exception
    when Constraint_Error =>
        raise Stack_Overflow;
end Push;
```

**10.** Explain the behavior of the following code:

```ada
package Bar is
    P: Positive := 0;
end Bar;

with Bar; Ada.Text_IO; use Ada;
procedure Foo is
begin
    Text_IO.Put_Line ("I'm running!");
    ...
end Foo;
```

# 11

# Access Types

Access types are used to declare pointers. Pointers can point to objects, subprograms, and tasks. Pointers to objects are very useful in the creation of linked data structures such as linked lists, binary trees, and directed graphs. An example of a linked list will be provided later in this chapter. Pointers to subprograms allow subprogram references to be passed as runtime parameters or to be stored in data structures such as arrays or records. Through these data structures, subprograms can be dynamically selected for execution. Pointers to tasks will be covered in Chapter 15.

In many languages, the value of a pointer is simply the address of the entity that it is pointing to. A pointer can point to any entity by being assigned the address of that entity. Furthermore, a pointer is typically allowed to point willy-nilly to any memory address. Therefore, it is the programmer's responsibility to make sure that a pointer is pointing to an valid entity, instead of pointing to a memory location containing a "garbage value."

In Ada, pointers are very different from these other languages. So different, that instead of talking of pointers pointing to objects, Ada talks of access values designating objects. With this different lingo, Ada attempts to dissociate itself from any preconceived notions about what pointers are and how they operate. Having noted this, however, this book will use the familiar terminology and talk of pointers pointing to objects or accessing objects.

So how do Ada pointers differ from the pointers of other languages? Programmers using computer languages that equate a pointer value with an address need to know how addresses are implemented. Ada, however, does not specify how the address type, `System.Address`, is implemented. Do not assume that addresses are implemented as unsigned integer values. Typically they are, but exceptions exist. (For example, hardware that contains different segments or domains of memory may represent an address as a record consisting of a segment identifier and a memory offset within that segment.) If you are curious how your compiler implements addresses, search for type `Address` in your `System` package. Be aware, however, that your compiler may implement type `Address` as a private type. Fortunately, for most applications, Ada programmers do not need to be concerned with how addresses are implemented. In fact, unlike many other languages, the value of a pointer is not guaranteed to be the address of the object it is pointing to. Typically it is, but not always. Pointers to dynamically sized objects, for example, often contain the address of a type descriptor that contains a description of the type, not the address of the object itself. In any case, pointers cannot be assigned addresses because pointers belong to access types that are type incompatible with type `System.Address`. Again, this differs from many other languages where pointers are routinely assigned address values. Thus, instead of thinking of pointers as representing addresses, Ada encourages programmers to think of pointers as entities that can point to specific types of objects.

Another important difference between pointers in Ada and pointers in many other languages has to do with program reliability. Ada avoids a common pitfall that programmers often encounter when working with pointers: the dangling pointer. Dangling pointers (or dangling references) are those that attempt to point to objects that no longer exist. The result is a pointer that points to meaningless garbage values. In Ada, this cannot happen because Ada's scoping rules guarantee that a pointer never outlives the object it points to.

There are two kinds of objects that pointers can point to: dynamically allocated objects and declared objects. The following section discusses pointers to dynamically allocated objects. We will then discuss pointers to declared objects. Next we will cover pointers to subprograms. Finally, the chapter concludes with access parameters.

## POINTERS TO DYNAMICALLY ALLOCATED OBJECTS

Pointers typically point to dynamically allocated variables. Dynamically allocated variables differ from the declared variables presented so far in this book. A declared variable is brought into existence when its declaration is elaborated:

```
Whole_Number: Integer;
```

In this case, `Whole_Number` is declared to be a variable of type `Integer`. Once the variable is declared, it may be referenced by its name, `Whole_Number`.

In contrast to a declared variable, a dynamically allocated variable is brought into existence at runtime by the execution of what is known as an allocator. Allocators will be discussed later in this section. Furthermore, unlike declared variables, dynamically allocated variables are referenced, not by a name, but by a pointer to the variable.

As we have seen throughout this book, Ada is a strongly typed language, and pointers are no exception to this rule. A pointer can only point to objects of a particular type. The particular type is determined by the pointer's access type. Pointers of an `Integer` access type can only point to objects of type `Integer`, pointers of a `Character` access type can only point to objects of type `Character`, pointers of a `String` access type can only point to objects of type `String`, and so on. An

Integer_Pointer

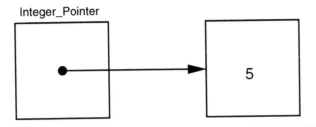

**Figure 11.1**   An integer pointer.

`Integer` pointer can no more point to a character value than an `Integer` variable can be assigned a character value.

In Figure 11.1, `Integer_Pointer` belongs to an integer access type and points to an integer variable whose value is 5. The variable containing the integer 5 is a dynamically allocated variable and therefore is not associated with a name; it can only be referenced through a pointer. If `Integer_Pointer` is reset to point to a different integer variable, then this variable containing 5 can no longer be referenced. The compiler is free to reuse the memory that was allocated to store this variable.

We have shown a single pointer pointing to a single object. More than one pointer can point to the same object, as shown in Figure 11.2. In such cases, the two pointers are said to be equal.

Two pointers can also point to different objects with the same value, as shown in Figure 11.3. In such cases, the two pointers are *not* equal.

The access type to which a pointer belongs is determined when the pointer is declared. The following code declares `Pointer_1` and `Pointer_2` to belong to the access type `Integer_Access_Type`:

Pointer_1

Pointer_2

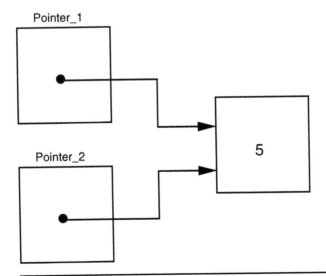

**Figure 11.2**   Two integer pointers that are equal.

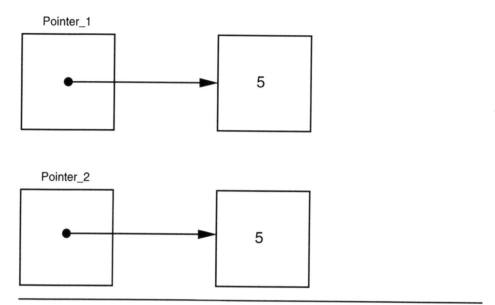

**Figure 11.3**   Two integer pointers that are not equal.

```
type Integer_Access_Type is access Integer;
Pointer_1, Pointer_2: Integer_Access_Type;
```

The first declaration defines type `Integer_Access_Type`. The keyword **type** is followed by the type identifier and the keywords **is access**. After the keyword **access** is the type name, `Integer`, which specifies the type of objects that may be pointed to. The second declaration defines the variables, `Pointer_1` and `Pointer_2`, to be of type `Integer_Access_Type`. This means that `Pointer_1` and `Pointer_2` may point only to objects of type `Integer`.

Optional constraints may be specified in access type declarations:

```
type Integer_Access_Type is access Integer range 1..10;
Pointer_1, Pointer_2: Integer_Access_Type;
```

In the preceding declarations, `Pointer_1` and `Pointer_2` can only point to variables of type `Integer` containing values in the range from 1 to 10. If an attempt is made to point to an integer value outside of this range, then a constraint error is raised.

Note that `Pointer_1` and `Pointer_2` are declared to be integer pointers, but they do not yet actually point to any integer variables. When a pointer is not pointing to anything, we say that it is a **null** pointer. Every pointer has an initial default value of **null**. (Access types are the only types where Ada defines an implicit default value.) Pointers can also be explicitly made into **null** pointers by being initialized to the keyword **null**:

```
Pointer_1, Pointer_2: Integer_Access_Type := null;
```

**Null** is a legal value for all pointers.

In addition to being initialized to **null**, pointers may also be initialized to point to a variable:

```
type Character_Access_Type is access Character;
Character_Pointer: Character_Access_Type := new Character;
```

The first declaration defines the character access type `Character_Access_Type`. The second declaration defines the variable, `Character_Pointer`, to be of type `Character_Access_Type`. Note the use of the keyword **new**, which is called an allocator. An allocator dynamically allocates memory for the variable and returns the access pointer value. In our example, the allocator creates a character variable that is pointed to by `Character_Pointer`. Note that no character value has been assigned to this character variable. The result of these two declarations is shown in Figure 11.4. The box pointed to is left blank to indicate a character variable whose value is undefined.

When pointers are declared, the variable to which they point can be assigned an initial value:

```
Pointer_1, Pointer_2: Integer_Access_Type := new Integer'(5);
```

The allocator, **new**, is followed by a qualified expression that provides initial values of 5 to each of the dynamically allocated variables that are being pointed to. The type name, `Integer`, is followed by a tick mark, `'`, then the value 5 in parentheses. As a result of this declaration, `Pointer_1` and `Pointer_2` each point to a different integer variable containing the value of 5 (as shown in Figure 11.3).

So far, we have seen the allocator **new** used when pointers are declared. The allocator **new** can also be used in assignment statements:

```
declare
    type Large_Star is (Betelgeuse, Antares, Herculis, Ceti,
        Pegasi, Alderbaran, Arcturus);
    type Star_Access_Type is access Large_Star;
    Star_Pointer: Star_Access_Type;
begin
    Star_Pointer := new Large_Star'(Betelgeuse);
        -- assignment statement using allocator new
end;
```

Character_Pointer

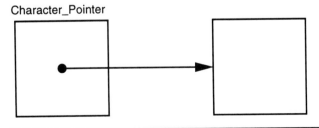

**Figure 11.4**   Pointer that points to variable whose value is undefined.

As a result of the assignment statement, `Star_Pointer` points to a variable containing the value `Betelgeuse`.

With assignment statements, the same pointer can be made to point to different objects throughout execution of the code:

```
Integer_Pointer := new Integer'(7);
Integer_Pointer := new Integer'(9);
Integer_Pointer := new Integer'(6);
```

In each of these assignment statements, memory is dynamically allocated for different integer variables containing different values. First, the integer variable containing the value 7 is created, then the integer variable containing the value 9, then the variable containing 6. Each time a new variable is created, the previous variable becomes inaccessible because `Integer_Pointer` is no longer pointing to it. (We are assuming that the variable is not being pointed to by another pointer.) But what happens to the memory that was allocated to store an object once the object is no longer accessible? Some Ada compilers do nothing, and the memory remains allocated as long as the program is running. Other Ada compilers will automatically reclaim the memory for other uses. Such "garbage collecting," however, is not required by the Ada standards, and in some applications is undesirable. Automatic garbage collecting may be undesirable because it occurs at unpredictable moments and can be quite time consuming. In real-time applications, events must be carefully scheduled, so such unpredictable slowdowns in execution are unacceptable. Ada provides pragma `Controlled` to prevent any automatic garbage collection.

Besides pragma `Controlled`, Ada provides a generic procedure, `Unchecked_Deallocation`, that allows the programmer to explicitly deallocate objects. This generic has the following specification:

```
generic
   type Object is limited private;
   type Name is access Object;
procedure Unchecked_Deallocation (X: in out Name);
```

When `Unchecked_Deallocation` is instantiated, a procedure is created that deallocates the storage occupied by the object being pointed to:

```
with Unchecked_Deallocation;
procedure P is
   type Integer_Access_Type is access Integer;
   Pointer: Integer_Access_Type := new Integer'(7);
   procedure Free is new Unchecked_Deallocation
      (  Object => Integer,
         Name   => Integer_Access_Type );
begin
   ...
   Free (Pointer);   -- deallocates storage occupied by object
                     -- pointed to by Pointer
   ...
end P;
```

Unchecked_Deallocation is useful if garbage collecting is desired but one's Ada compiler does not provide this service, or if, due to real-time constraints, a programmer wants to do his or her own garbage collecting. Unchecked_Deallocation allows a programmer to explicitly deallocate objects when they are no longer needed, allowing the memory for these objects to be reclaimed. However, as the term "unchecked" insinuates, using Unchecked_Deallocation is dangerous: no check is made, before deallocating the object, that a dangling pointer is not thereby created. A dangling pointer can easily be created when a programmer deallocates the object being pointed to, forgetting that other pointers are also pointing to that object. After the object is deallocated, these other pointers are pointing to the "lands where the Jumblies live."

**Ada 95 ▶**   Programmers needing full control over how objects are dynamically allocated and deallocated should refer to Chapter 13 of the *Ada 95 Reference Manual*. In essence, programmers can override the default implementation of allocators and Unchecked_Deallocation with their own storage management procedures. Allocators and Unchecked_Deallocation still appear in the code, but when encountered, the user-defined procedures for allocation and deallocation are automatically invoked.

So far, we have seen how to assign a value to the object that the pointer points to. Now let us see how to access that value. This is done by using a dot followed by the keyword **all**, as shown in the following program:

```
with Ada.Text_IO; use Ada.Text_IO;
procedure Demo is
    type Character_Access_Type is access Character;
    Character_Pointer: Character_Access_Type;
begin
    Character_Pointer := new Character'('Z');
    Put (Character_Pointer.all);
        -- outputs Z (the value of the object being pointed to)
    New_Line;
end Demo;
```

As shown in Figure 11.5, Character_Pointer.**all** represents the value of the variable pointed to by Character_Pointer. Referencing the value being pointed to is known as "dereferencing" the pointer.

Be careful not to confuse the value of a pointer with the value of the variable that it points to. Consider the following code:

```
declare
    type Boolean_Access_Type is access Boolean;
    Pointer_1: Boolean_Access_Type := new Boolean'(True);
    Pointer_2: Boolean_Access_Type := new Boolean'(False);
begin
    Pointer_1.all := Pointer_2.all;
        -- the variable pointed to by Pointer_1 is assigned the
        -- value of the variable pointed to by Pointer_2
    Pointer_1 := Pointer_2;
```

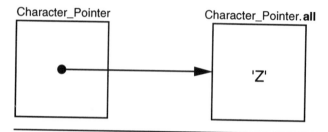

Character_Pointer                    Character_Pointer.**all**

'Z'

**Figure 11.5**   Using **.all** to reference the value of a variable pointed to.

```
                        -- Pointer_1 now points to the same variable as Pointer_2
        end;
```

Note how the assignment statement `Pointer_1`.**all** := `Pointer_2`.**all** differs from the assignment statement `Pointer_1 := Pointer_2`. The first statement assigns the value of the variable pointed to by `Pointer_2` to the variable pointed to by `Pointer_1`. The value being assigned is the `Boolean` value `False`. The second statement assigns the value of the pointer `Pointer_2` to `Pointer_1`. The result is that `Pointer_1` now points to the same object as pointer `Pointer_2`. The difference between these two assignment statements is shown in Figure 11.6.

Throughout this book, we have seen that objects of different types may not mix. This restriction applies to pointers as well. As illustrated below, even though pointers `Char_Ptr_1` and `Char_Ptr_2` both point to objects of type `Character`, they are incompatible since one belongs to access type `Char_Access_1` and the other belongs to type `Char_Access_2`:

```
        declare
            type Char_Access_1 is access Character;
            type Char_Access_2 is access Character;
            Char_Ptr_1: Char_Access_1 := new Character'('A');
            Char_Ptr_2: Char_Access_2 := new Character'('B');
        begin
            Char_Ptr_1 := Char_Ptr_2;           -- illegal; mixed types
            Char_Ptr_1.all := Char_Ptr_2.all; -- OK
        end;
```

Note that the second assignment is legal because the types are not mixed: a `Character` variable, `Char_Ptr_2`.**all**, is assigned to a `Character` variable, `Char_Ptr_1`.**all**.

So far, all the pointers that we have declared have been variables. Pointers may also be declared as constants:

```
        declare
            type Integer_Access_Type is access Integer;
            Constant_Pointer: constant Integer_Access_Type := new
                Integer'(6);
```

Initial Condition

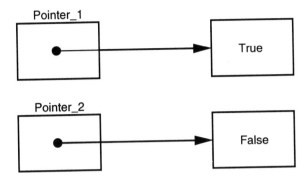

Pointer_1.**all** := Pointer_2.**all**;

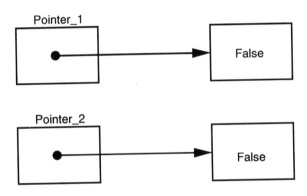

Pointer_1 := Pointer_2;

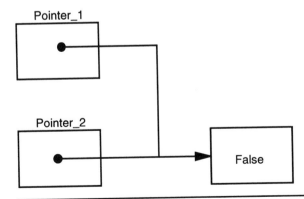

**Figure 11.6**   Value of pointer versus value of accessed variable.

```
        Integer_Pointer: Integer_Access_Type := new Integer'(1);
    begin
        Constant_Pointer := Integer_Pointer;
            -- illegal; cannot change where it points
        Constant_Pointer.all := Integer_Pointer.all; -- OK
            -- only changes value of the variable being pointed to
        Constant_Pointer.all := 7; -- also OK
    end;
```

The first executable statement, `Constant_Pointer := Integer_Pointer`, is illegal because a constant pointer must forever point to the same object. The second and third executable statements, however, are legal, because only the value of the variable being pointed to is being changed. Thus, a constant pointer must only be constant with respect to what variable it points to, not with respect to the value of the variable being pointed to.

When using pointers, be careful to allocate a variable before attempting to reference it:

```
declare
    type Access_Int is access Integer;
    A, B: Access_Int;
begin
    A := new Integer'(7);
    B.all := A.all;  -- null access violation
                     -- no variable has been allocated for B
end;
```

The problem with this code is that `B.all` attempts to access the variable "pointed to" by B before this variable exists! A `Constraint_Error` is raised in such situations where an attempt is made to dereference a **null** pointer. To correct this code, first allocate a variable for B to point to:

```
declare
    type Access_Int is access Integer;
    A, B: Access_Int;
begin
    A := new Integer'(7);
    B := new Integer; -- allocates a variable for B to point to
    B.all := A.all;
end;
```

As seen from the previous examples, pointers of the same type can be assigned to one another. The only other predefined operation for pointers is tests for equality (=) and inequality (/=). (Pointers, though, can be passed as subprogram parameters or returned as function results.) As the following code illustrates, pointers cannot be added to one another or checked to see whether one pointer is greater than another:

```
declare
    type Access_Int is access Integer;
```

```
   A, B: Access_Int := new Integer'(7);
begin
   -- Only assignments and tests for equality/inequality are
   -- allowed for pointers
   A := B;          -- OK
   B := A + B;      -- Illegal; "+" not defined for pointers
   if A = B then    -- OK
       Put_Line ("Pointers are equal");
   end if;
   if A > B then    -- Illegal; ">" not defined for pointers
       Put_Line ("Pointer A greater than B);
   end if;
end;
```

Pointers may not only point to scalar variables, such as integer, floating point, character, and Boolean variables. Pointers may also point to composite variables: arrays and records. The following example declares a pointer, Name, that points to an array of characters (a string):

```
with Ada.Text_IO; use Ada.Text_IO;
procedure String_Pointer is
   type Name_Access_Type is access String;
   Name_Pointer: Name_Access_Type;
begin
   Name_Pointer := new String'("Ada");
   Put_Line (Name_Pointer.all);   -- outputs "Ada"
   Put (Name_Pointer (2)); -- outputs 'd'
   New_Line;
end String_Pointer;
```

Name_Pointer points to a string variable with an initial value of "Ada". The value "Ada" can be referenced by using the keyword **all**:

```
Name_Pointer.all -- selects the value "Ada"
```

Rather than selecting the value of the entire array, we can select a component of the array. To do this, we specify an index, with or without the keyword **all**:

```
Name_Pointer.all (2)    -- selects character d
Name_Pointer (2)        -- also selects d
```

The keyword **all** is optional because, since the pointer is not a composite object, there is no doubt that we are referring to the object being pointed to rather than the pointer itself.

Recall that type String is defined in package Standard as an unconstrained array of characters. Since Name_Pointer points to objects of type String, it can point to strings of any size, as long as the required memory is allocated:

```
Name_Pointer := new String'("Ada");
Name_Pointer.all := "Pascal";            -- Constraint error
```

```
                  -- Only space for a 3 character string has been allocated
      Name_Pointer := new String'("Pascal");   -- OK
```

Note that the allocator **new** is needed each time Name_Pointer points to a string of a different size. Without re-evaluating the allocator, Name_Pointer can only point to strings of the size allocated.

A final point about the String_Pointer procedure is that when an allocator is applied to an unconstrained array type, either an initial value or an index constraint must be provided:

```
      Name_Pointer := new String'("Babbage"); -- OK
         -- allocates space for 7 character string
      Name_Pointer := new String (1..3);       -- OK
         -- allocates space for a 3 character string
      Name_Pointer := new String; -- illegal, no size provided
```

The last assignment is illegal because the amount of space to be dynamically allocated cannot be determined.

Pointers are most frequently used to point to records. (The reason for this will become apparent in the next section.) In the following code, pointers Star_Ptr_A and Star_Ptr_B point to records of type Star_Record:

```
with Ada.Text_IO; use Ada.Text_IO;
procedure Star_Size is

    type Large_Star is (Betelgeuse, Antares, Herculis, Ceti,
        Pegasi, Alderbaran, Arcturus);
    subtype Larger_Than_Our_Sun is Integer range 10 .. 1_000;
        -- diameter of star as compared with our sun
    subtype Distance_In_Parsecs is Integer range 4 .. 500;
        -- 1 parsec = 3.26 light years distance

    type Star_Record is
        record
            Name: Large_Star;
            Size: Larger_Than_Our_Sun;
            Distance: Distance_In_Parsecs;
        end record;

    type Star_Access_Type is access Star_Record;

    package Star_IO is new Enumeration_IO (Large_Star);
    package Int_IO is new Integer_IO (Integer);
    use Star_IO, Int_IO;
    Star_Ptr_A, Star_Ptr_B: Star_Access_Type;

begin
```

```
    Star_Ptr_A := new Star_Record'(  Name      => Betelgeuse,
                                      Size      => 700,
                                      Distance  => 150 );

    Star_Ptr_B := new Star_Record;
    Star_Ptr_B.all := Star_Ptr_A.all;
    Put ( Star_Ptr_B.Name );         -- outputs Betelgeuse
    New_Line;                        -- same as Star_Ptr_B.all.Name
    Put ( Star_Ptr_B.Size );         -- outputs 700
    New_Line;                        -- same as Star_Ptr_B.all.Size
    Put ( Star_Ptr_B.Distance );    -- outputs 150
    New_Line;                -- same as Star_Ptr_B.all.Distance
end Star_Size;
```

As shown in this code, an entire record aggregate may be accessed using the notation .all. Individual components of the record are selected by using a dot followed by the name of the component. As with arrays, when selecting a record component, the keyword all is optional but is generally not used.

Besides pointing to regular records such as Star_Record, pointers can also point to discriminated records:

```
-- assume all types and objects are previously defined
declare
    type Device_Type is (Printer, Disk, CRT);
    type Peripheral (Device: Device_Type := CRT) is
        record
            Status: Device_State;
            case Device is
                when Printer | CRT =>
                    Line_Count: Natural range 0..Page_Length;
                when Disk =>
                    Cylinder: Cylinder_Index;
                    Track: Track_Number;
            end case;
        end record;

    type Unconstrained_Pointer is access Peripheral;
    type Constrained_Pointer is access Peripheral (Device => CRT);
    Peripheral_Ptr: Unconstrained_Pointer;
    CRT_Ptr: Constrained_Pointer;
begin
    -- this pointer can point to any device, as long as the
    -- allocator is reevaluated
    Peripheral_Ptr := new Peripheral'(  Device    => Disk,
                                        Status    => Ready,
                                        Cylinder  => 1,
                                        Track     => 3 ); -- OK
    ...
    Peripheral_Ptr := new Peripheral'(  Device     => Printer,
                                        Status     => Ready,
                                        Line_Count => 0 ); -- OK
```

```
                -- this pointer can only point to CRTs
                CRT_Ptr := new Peripheral'(    Device        => CRT,
                                              Status        => Ready,
                                              Line_Count    => 0 );  -- OK

                CRT_Ptr := new Peripheral' ( Device    => Disk,   -- constraint
                                             Status    => Ready, -- error
                                             Cylinder => 1,
                                             Track     => 3 );
          end;
```

Since the discriminated record type, Peripheral, provides a default value for its discriminant, access types that point to peripheral can either be constrained or unconstrained. The access type Unconstrained_Pointer is unconstrained because it does not provide a value for the discriminant Device. The access type Constrained_Pointer is constrained because it sets Device to CRT. (If this is confusing, review discriminated records in Chapter 5.) Since Peripheral_Ptr belongs to type Unconstrained_Pointer, it can point to any kind of peripheral device (Printer, Disk, or CRT), as long as the required memory is allocated each time the device changes. On the other hand, since CRT_Ptr belongs to type Constrained_Pointer, it can only point to peripherals that are CRTs.

The examples shown so far in this chapter have limited use. Pointers, however, can be very useful because they can connect objects to form linked data structures such as linked lists, binary trees, and directed graphs. In this section, we will show how pointers are used to create the simplest and most common of these data structures, the linked list. A linked list is a data structure where one item points to another item, which in turn points to another item, and so on. The result is a list of items that are linked together with pointers, as shown in Figure 11.7. Each item of a linked list is typically a record. One of the components of the record is a pointer that points to the next record in the list.

Linked lists have several advantages over alternative data structures, such as arrays of records. A primary advantage of a linked list over an array of records is that computer memory is conserved because memory is dynamically allocated only as needed. In other words, for each record added to the linked list, the memory needed to store the new record is dynamically allocated. Furthermore, as records are removed from the linked list, memory can be dynamically deallocated,

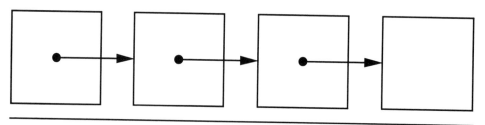

**Figure 11.7**   Linked list.

that is, given back to the computer to be used as needed. In contrast, the size of an array of records must be established before it is used. Once the array size is established, it cannot change as the program executes. Thus, when using an array of records, a fixed amount of storage is allocated, which is often much greater than the amount of storage needed. Or conversely, the array may overflow if too many records are added and the size of the array is exceeded. When this happens, code must be modified and recompiled to accommodate the extra array components that are needed.

Another advantage of a linked list is that items may be added to or removed from any location within the list simply by resetting a few pointer values. Thus, the order of items in the list can be maintained with minimal processing. For an array of records, however, if an item needs to be added at a particular location in the array, then all of the array components from that point on need to be shifted to the right to make room for the new item. Similarly, when an item is removed from an array of records, shifting to the left may be required to close the "hole."

Despite these advantages of linked lists over arrays of records, linked lists do have a few disadvantages. For instance, more memory is needed to store a record in a linked list than to store a record component of an array, because extra memory is required to store the pointers. More important, however, is that an item in a linked list cannot be directly referenced. It can only be referenced by traversing the list from the beginning, until the item is found. In an array of records, a component can be directly referenced with an index value.

Let us now consider a linked list where each item is a record that contains information about a restaurant. Once such a list is constructed, we will write procedures that can manipulate the list. One procedure will be able to search the list for a particular restaurant record. Another procedure will be able to add a restaurant record to the list; another procedure, to delete a restaurant record from the list; and another, to output the entire list.

As shown in Figure 11.8, each record of the linked list contains four components: a restaurant name; the type of food served; the average price per meal; and a pointer, Next, which points to the next record in this list.

Since the fourth component in the list is a pointer, it must belong to an access type that specifies the type of object it can point to. The type of object it can point to are records that belong to this linked list. The pointer is therefore a component of

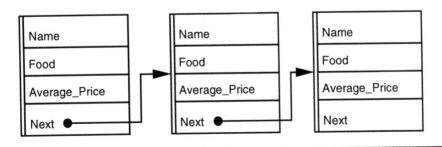

**Figure 11.8**   Linked list of records.

the very type of object that it can point to. This creates a dilemma, as shown in the following declarations:

```
type Ethnicity is (Chinese, Japanese, French, Korean,
    Mexican, Italian, Jewish, American, German);
subtype Name_Type is String ( 1 .. 20 );
subtype Price_Type is Float range 0.0 .. 150.0;

type Restaurant_Record is
    record
        Name: Name_Type;
        Food: Ethnicity;
        Average_Price: Price_Type;
        Next: access Restaurant_Record;
            -- illegal; cannot refer to Restaurant_Record
            -- until after it is fully declared
    end record;
```

The fourth component is the problem. The fourth component is a pointer, Next, of the Restaurant_Record access type. This pointer is a component of the same record type to which it points. Therefore, the declaration for this pointer must reference the very record type of which it is a component. This, unfortunately, is illegal. Restaurant_Record cannot be referenced by one of its own components. Restaurant_Record can only be referenced after it has been fully declared, that is, after the keywords **end record**.

Let us try a different approach to defining Restaurant_Record. Instead of defining the access type in the component declaration for Next, let us define the access type before the record type:

```
type Ethnicity is (Chinese, Japanese, French, Korean,
    Mexican, Italian, Jewish, American, German);
subtype Name_Type is String ( 1 .. 20 );
subtype Price_Type is Float range 0.0 .. 150.0;

type Restaurant_Access_Type is access Restaurant_Record;
    -- illegal; Restaurant_Record has not yet been defined
type Restaurant_Record is
    record
        Name: Name_Type;
        Food: Ethnicity;
        Average_Price: Price_Type;
        Next: Restaurant_Access_Type;
    end record;
```

Unfortunately, this approach also fails. Restaurant_Record needs to be defined before it is used in the declaration of Restaurant_Access_Type.

We are thus caught in a "chicken and egg" problem. The access type and the record type reference each other. A type must be declared before it can be referenced. Therefore, the access type must be defined before the record type can reference it, and vice versa. Fortunately, there is a solution to this dilemma, which involves the use of an incomplete type declaration:

```
type Ethnicity is (Chinese, Japanese, French, Korean,
    Mexican, Italian, Jewish, American, German);
subtype Name_Type is String ( 1 .. 20 );
subtype Price_Type is Float range 0.0 .. 150.0;

type Restaurant_Record; -- incomplete type declaration
type Restaurant_Access_Type is access Restaurant_Record;
type Restaurant_Record is -- complete type declaration
    record
        Name: Name_Type;
        Food: Ethnicity;
        Average_Price: Price_Type;
        Next: Restaurant_Access_Type; -- pointer
    end record;
```

In this example, the incomplete type declaration consists of the single statement:

```
type Restaurant_Record; -- incomplete type declaration
```

This incomplete declaration makes the identifier, Restaurant_Record, available to subsequent declarations without defining the nature of the type. The complete declaration of Restaurant_Record must follow the incomplete declaration. Note that the access type, Restaurant_Access_Type, is placed between the incomplete declaration and the complete declaration. Between these two declarations, only access types can reference the incomplete type declaration.

Now that we have defined the record type for our linked list, let us define a few records and link them together. The first record contains information about the Chinese restaurant "Wok N Roll" and is placed at the head of the list with the following declaration:

```
Head: Restaurant_Access_Type := new
    Restaurant_Record'( Name => "Wok N Roll            ",
                        Food => Chinese,
                        Average_Price => 9.45,
                        Next => null);
```

Since this record does not point to any other record, we initialize the pointer, Next, to **null**. This is shown pictorially in Figure 11.9.

Let us now add the German restaurant "Frank N Stein" as the second record in our list:

```
Head.Next := new
    Restaurant_Record'( Name => "Frank N Stein          ",
                        Food => German,
                        Average_Price => 12.75,
                        Next =>    null );
```

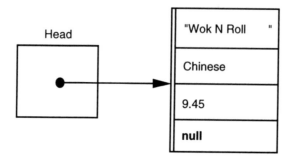

**Figure 11.9**    Linked list with one record.

After this statement is executed, the pointer of "Wok N Roll" (Head.Next) now points to the newly allocated record, "Frank N Stein". This is shown in Figure 11.10.

Now that we understand the structure of linked lists, let us create a package that contains procedures for adding items to a linked list, deleting items from this list, searching this linked list, and outputting this linked list:

```
package Restaurant_Linked_List is

    subtype Name_Type is String (1..20);
    type Restaurant_Record is private;

    procedure Add_To_List (New_Entry: in Restaurant_Record);
    procedure Get (New_Restaurant: out Restaurant_Record);
    procedure Delete_From_List (Target: in Name_Type);
    procedure Search_List (Target: in Name_Type);
    procedure Output_List;
private
    type Ethnicity is (Chinese, Japanese, French, Korean,
        Mexican, Italian, Jewish, American, German);
    subtype Price_Type is Float range 0.0 .. 150.0;
        -- this should be a decimal fixed type (see Chapter 12)
```

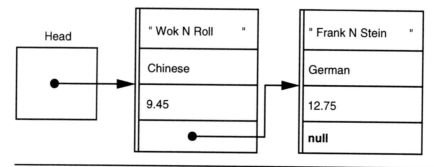

**Figure 11.10**    Linked list with two records.

```ada
   type Restaurant_Record; -- incomplete type declaration
   type Restaurant_Pointer is access Restaurant_Record;
   type Restaurant_Record is -- complete type declaration
      record
         Name: Name_Type;
         Food: Ethnicity;
         Average_Price: Price_Type;
         Next: Restaurant_Pointer;
      end record;
end Restaurant_Linked_List;

with Ada.Text_IO; use Ada.Text_IO;
package body Restaurant_Linked_List is

   Head, Tail: Restaurant_Pointer := null;

   package Food_IO is new Enumeration_IO (Ethnicity);
   package Price_IO is new Float_IO (Price_Type);
   use Food_IO, Price_IO;

   -- procedure to add a record to the linked list
   procedure Add_To_List (New_Entry: in Restaurant_Record) is
      Item_To_Add: Restaurant_Pointer;
   begin
      Item_To_Add := new Restaurant_Record'(New_Entry);
      Tail.Next := Item_To_Add;
      Tail := Item_To_Add;
      Put_Line (". . . Added");
   end Add_To_List;

   -- procedure to get information for a record
   procedure Get (New_Restaurant: out Restaurant_Record) is
   begin
      Put_Line ("Enter restaurant name:");
      Get (New_Restaurant.Name);
      Put_Line ("What kind of food is served?");
      Get (New_Restaurant.Food);
      Put_Line ("What is the average price per meal?");
      Get (New_Restaurant.Average_Price);
   end Get;

   -- procedure to delete a record from the linked list
   procedure Delete_From_List (Target: in Name_Type) is
      Previous: Restaurant_Pointer := Head;
      Current: Restaurant_Pointer := Head.Next;
   begin
      if Current = null then
         -- if null list, then nothing to delete
         Put_Line ("Cannot delete; list is empty");
         return;
      end if;
```

```
    loop
        if Current.Name = Target then -- found it
            if Current.Next = null then
                -- Target is last item in list
                Previous.Next := null;
                Tail := Previous;
            else
                -- Target is within list
                Current := Current.Next;
                Previous.Next := Current;
            end if;
            Put_Line (". . . Deleted");
            return;
        end if;
        if Current.Next = null then
            -- end of list and item not found
            Put_Line ("Item not found);
            return;
        end if;
        Previous := Current;          -- advance pointers
        Current := Current.Next;
    end loop;
end Delete_From_List;


-- procedure to search the linked list for record with
-- specified restaurant name
procedure Search_List ( Target: in Name_Type ) is
    -- search from the head
    Restaurant: Restaurant_Pointer := Head;
begin
    Put ("RESTAURANT");
    Set_Col (25); -- advance to column 25 (see Chapter 14)
    Put ("FOOD SERVED");
    Set_Col (43);
    Put ("AVERAGE PRICE");
    New_Line;
    loop
        if Restaurant.Name = Target then  -- found it
            Put (Restaurant.Name);
            Set_Col (25);
            Put (Restaurant.Food, 18);
            Put (Restaurant.Average_Price, 3, 2, 0);
            New_Line;
            exit;
        elsif Restaurant.Next = null then-- not found
            Put_Line ("Restaurant " & Target & " not found.");
            exit;
        else
            Restaurant := Restaurant.Next; -- still need to
                                           -- search
```

```
            end if;
         end loop;
      end Search_List;

      -- procedure to output all the information in the linked list
      procedure Output_List is
         -- start with record after dummy header
         Restaurant: Restaurant_Pointer := Head.Next;
      begin
         Put ("RESTAURANT");
         Set_Col (25);
         Put ("FOOD SERVED");
         Set_Col (43);
         Put ("AVERAGE PRICE");
         New_Line;
         while Restaurant /= null loop
            Put (Restaurant.Name);
            Set_Col (25);
            Put (Restaurant.Food, 18);
            Put (Restaurant.Average_Price, 3, 2, 0);
            New_Line;
            Restaurant := Restaurant.Next; -- point to next item
         end loop;
      end Output_List;

   begin -- initialization part
      -- create linked list, initialize pointers,
      -- create "dummy" header entry
      Head := new Restaurant_Record;
      Head.Name := "GOURMAND'S DATABASE ";
      Tail := Head;
   end Restaurant_Linked_List;
```

This package defines a linked list of records, plus operations that may be performed on this list. The operations are provided by five procedures: Add_To_List, which adds an item to the linked list; Get, which gets information for a record; Delete_From_List, which deletes a specified record from the list; Search_List, which searches for a specified record; and finally, Output_List, which outputs the information contained in each record of the linked list.

Note that the package body contains an executable statement (initialization) part. In this part, two pointers, Head and Tail, are initialized to point to a "dummy" header record:

```
Head := new Restaurant_Record;
Head.Name := "GOURMAND'S DATABASE ";
Tail := Head;
```

The effect of this code is shown pictorially in Figure 11.11. To make Figures 11.11 through 11.18 less cluttered, the record components dealing with the kind of food

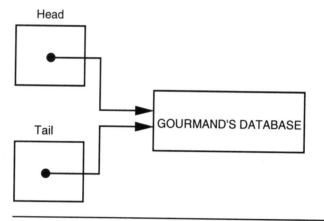

**Figure 11.11**  Initial condition of linked list.

and the average price per meal are not shown. Furthermore, the names of restaurants are not placed in quotes, and trailing blanks are ignored.

The header record does not contain actual information about a restaurant but contains a title for the linked list: GOURMAND'S DATABASE. By having a header record, the linked list can be created and initialized without requiring meaningful record information. Both pointers, Head and Tail, are kept updated so that Head always points to the dummy header record and Tail always points to the last record in the list. Let us now discuss each procedure contained in the package.

The Add_To_List procedure adds a record to the end of the linked list. When Add_To_List is invoked with, for example, the restaurant record for "Wok N Roll", this record value is passed to the formal parameter New_Entry. The following statement then creates a pointer Item_To_Add, which points to the new entry, "Wok N Roll":

```
Item_To_Add := new Restaurant_Record'(New_Entry);
```

The result of this assignment is shown in Figure 11.12.

Next, the pointer of the header record (Tail.Next) is changed to point to the new record:

```
Tail.Next := Item_To_Add;
```

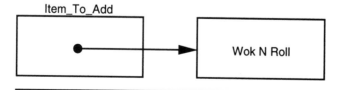

**Figure 11.12**  Pointer to a record to be added to linked list.

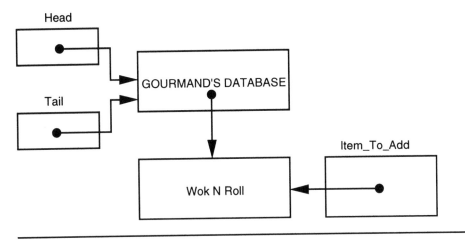

**Figure 11.13**    Header record updated to point to new record.

The result of this assignment is shown in Figure 11.13.
Finally, Tail is updated to point to the new record:

```
Tail := Item_To_Add;
```

The result of this assignment is shown in Figure 11.14. Item_To_Add is left pointing to the last item, with no ill effects.

Suppose that Add_To_List is invoked once again, this time with the record for "Frank N Stein." A pointer to "Frank N Stein", Item_To_Add, is created, and the last record in the list, "Wok N Roll", is directed to point to this new record (Figure 11.15).

Finally, Tail is updated to point to the new record (Figure 11.16). Item_To_Add is left pointing to the last item, with no ill effects.

The next procedure defined in Restaurant_Linked_List is Get. This pro-

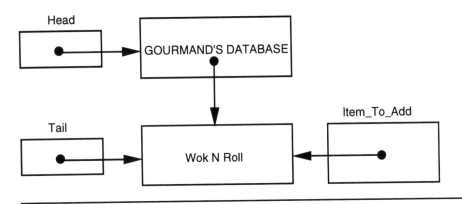

**Figure 11.14**    Tail updated to point to end of list.

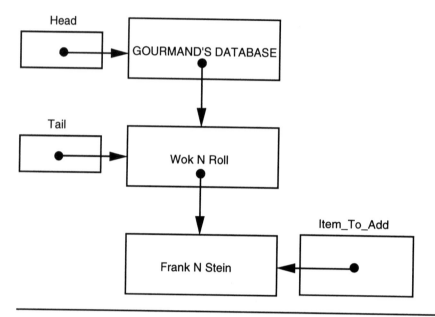

**Figure 11.15** Last record in list updated to point to new record.

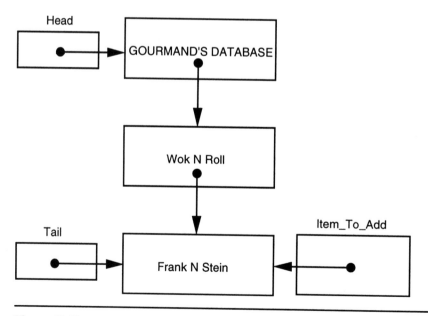

**Figure 11.16** `Tail` updated to point to last record.

cedure simply prompts the user for information needed to initialize a new record. This new record may then be added to the list by the `Add_To_List` procedure.

The next procedure, `Delete_From_List`, removes a record with the specified restaurant name from the list. Removing a record from the list is a bit more complex than adding a record to the list. Two pointers, `Previous` and `Current`, traverse the list together. `Previous` points to the record listed immediately before the record pointed to by `Current`. Initially, `Previous` points to the dummy header record, and `Current` points to the next record (or to **null** if there is no such record):

```
Previous: Restaurant_Pointer := Head;
Current: Restaurant_Pointer := Head.Next;
```

Now assume the initial situation shown in Figure 11.17. Suppose that we wish to delete the record "Wok N Roll". To do this, `Delete_From_List` is invoked with the restaurant name "Wok N Roll". This name is passed to the formal parameter `Target`. `Delete_From_List` then checks whether the list is empty (except, of course, for the header record):

```
if Current = null then...
```

If the list is empty, then no records can be deleted. A message is output, and the procedure terminates. If the list is not empty, then a loop is entered and a check is made to see whether `Current` is pointing to the target record, "Wok N Roll":

```
if Current.Name = Target then...
```

In the situation shown in Figure 11.17, the target record has been found.

At this point, different actions are taken depending on whether or not the record to be deleted is at the end of the list. If the record is not at the end of the list, then `Current` is advanced to the next record. The record pointed to by `Previous` is updated to point to the same object pointed to by `Current`:

```
Current := Current.Next;
Previous.Next := Current;
```

This is shown in Figure 11.18. Since no record components point to "Wok N Roll", this record is inaccessible. A compiler can thus use the memory taken up by "Wok N Roll" for other purposes.

If the record to be deleted is at the end of the list, then the pointer of the preceding record is set to **null**:

```
Previous.Next := null;
```

`Tail` is then set to point to this preceding record:

```
Tail := Previous;
```

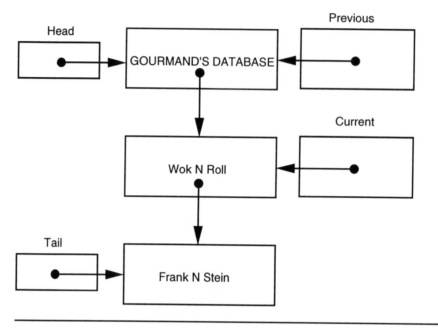

**Figure 11.17**    Initial condition for `Delete_From_List`.

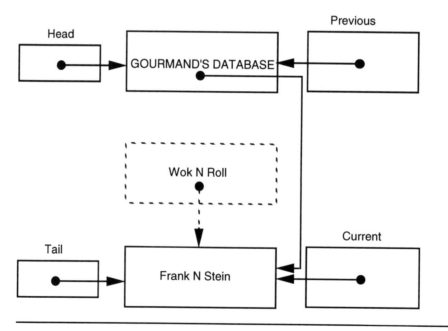

**Figure 11.18**    Pointers of `Current` and header records updated.

If the end of the list is reached and the record still is not found, then a message is output that the record does not exist.

The next procedure, Search_List, searches for a record with the specified restaurant name. Search_List keeps traversing the linked list until either it reaches the end without finding the record or until it finds the record. If the record is found, the information for this record is output. Search_List traverses the list using the statement:

```
Restaurant := Restaurant.Next;
```

Each time this statement is executed, Restaurant.Next points to the next record in the list.

The procedure Search_List uses several different features to format the output into columns. The procedure Set_Col places output at a specified column. The Put procedure used for outputting the kind of food contains a second parameter, which specifies the minimum field width for the output. The Put procedure used for outputting the average price contains a second, third, and fourth parameter used for formatting. The second parameter specifies the minimum field width to the left of the number's decimal point. The third parameter specifies the number of digits to the right of the decimal point. The fourth parameter, when set to 0, specifies that scientific notation (exponentiation) is not to be used. These formatting features, plus many others, will be discussed in Chapter 14.

The last procedure, Output_List, uses the same method of traversing the list as Search_List and outputs the information contained in all the records of the list, except the dummy header record.

Now that we have examined the contents of the Restaurant_Linked_List package, let us consider how a program can use this package:

```
with Ada.Text_IO, Restaurant_Linked_List;
use Ada.Text_IO, Restaurant_Linked_List;
procedure Restaurants is

    Choice: Integer range 1.. 5;
    New_Restaurant: Restaurant_Record;
    Restaurant_Name: Name_Type;
    package Int_IO is new Integer_IO (Integer);
    use Int_IO;

begin

    Put_Line ("T H E    G O U R M A N D ' S    D A T A B A S E");

    loop
        New_Line;
        Put_Line ("Enter your choice (1 to 5):");
        Put_Line ("  1. Enter a new restaurant.");
```

```
          Put_Line ("  2.  Delete a restaurant entry.");
          Put_Line ("  3.  Search for a restaurant entry.");
          Put_Line ("  4.  List all of the entries.");
          Put_Line ("  5.  Exit the program.");
          Get (Choice);

          case Choice is
             when 1 => -- enter new restaurant
                Get ( New_Restaurant ); -- overloaded Get
                Add_To_List ( New_Restaurant );
             when 2 => -- delete a restaurant
                Put_Line ("Enter name of restaurant to delete:");
                Get (Restaurant_Name);
                Delete_From_List ( Restaurant_Name );
             when 3 => -- search for restaurant
                Put_Line ("Enter name of restaurant to search:");
                Get (Restaurant_Name);
                Search_List ( Restaurant_Name );
             when 4 => -- list all restaurants
                Output_List;
             when 5 => -- exit program
                exit;
          end case;

       end loop;

       Put_Line ("Have a gastronomically rewarding day!");
    end Restaurants;
```

This program mentions the `Restaurant_Linked_List` package in its **with** clause and uses all of the procedures in this package. The procedures are invoked depending on the selections made by the user. The program keeps prompting the user with a list of choices until the user decides to exit the program. The following is a sample run of this program:

```
THE   GOURMAND'S   DATABASE

Enter your choice (1 to 5):
    1.  Enter a new restaurant.
    2.  Delete a restaurant entry.
    3.  Search for a restaurant entry.
    4.  List all of the entries.
    5.  Exit the program.
 > 1
Enter restaurant name:
 > "Tortured Taco          "
What kind of food is served?
 > Mexican
What is the average price per meal?
 > 7.75
```

```
Enter your choice (1 to 5):
    1.  Enter a new restaurant.
    2.  Delete a restaurant entry.
    3.  Search for a restaurant entry.
    4.  List all of the entries.
    5.  Exit the program.
>  1
Enter restaurant name:
>  "Quark Soup              "
What kind of food is served?
>  American
What is the average price per meal?
>  15.85

Enter your choice (1 to 5):
    1.  Enter a new restaurant.
    2.  Delete a restaurant entry.
    3.  Search for a restaurant entry.
    4.  List all of the entries.
    5.  Exit the program.
>  1
Enter restaurant name:
>  "Casa de Corned Beef     "
What kind of food is served?
>  Jewish
What is the average price per meal?
>  8.95

Enter your choice (1 to 5):
    1.  Enter a new restaurant.
    2.  Delete a restaurant entry.
    3.  Search for a restaurant entry.
    4.  List all of the entries.
    5.  Exit the program.
>  4

RESTAURANT                FOOD SERVED       AVERAGE PRICE
Tortured Taco             MEXICAN           7.75
Quark Soup                AMERICAN          15.85
Casa de Corned Beef       JEWISH            8.95

Enter your choice (1 to 5):
    1.  Enter a new restaurant.
    2.  Delete a restaurant entry.
    3.  Search for a restaurant entry.
    4.  List all of the entries.
    5.  Exit the program.
>  2

Enter name of restaurant to delete:
>  "Quark Soup              "
. . . Deleted
```

```
Enter your choice (1 to 5):"
    1. Enter a new restaurant.");
    2. Delete a restaurant entry.");
    3. Search for a restaurant entry.");
    4. List all of the entries.");
    5. Exit the program.");
> 3


Enter name of restaurant to search:
> "Casa de Corned Beef    "


RESTAURANT               FOOD SERVED      AVERAGE PRICE
Casa de Corned Beef      JEWISH           8.95


Enter your choice (1 to 5):
    1. Enter a new restaurant.
    2. Delete a restaurant entry.
    3. Search for a restaurant entry.
    4. List all of the entries.
    5. Exit the program.
> 5
Have a gastronomically rewarding day!
```

## POINTERS TO DECLARED OBJECTS

**Ada 95 ▶** In addition to pointing to dynamically allocated objects, pointers can point to declared objects. These pointers are useful when interfacing with non-Ada languages that use pointers. In addition, pointers to declared objects allow linked data structures such as linked lists and trees to be created without dynamically allocating memory. Dynamic memory allocation has several potential disadvantages. First, runtime code is required to dynamically allocate and initialize dynamically allocated variables. This runtime code slows down the execution speed of a program and increases object code size. Second, objects allocated by **new** are dynamically created in a special region of memory known as the "heap." In applications such as real-time embedded systems, heap space is often in short supply, and execution speed is of critical importance. Thus, dynamic memory allocation may be unacceptable.

To get a pointer to point to a declared object, the object must be declared as an "aliased" object:

```
Whole_Number: aliased Integer; -- only declared objects that are
                               -- aliased can be pointed to
```

The keyword **aliased** means that Whole_Number can be referenced in either of two ways: through its name, Whole_Number, or through a pointer. Objects that are not declared to be aliased cannot be referenced by a pointer. Since only aliased objects can be pointed to, no overhead is incurred for objects that are not declared as aliased.

Aliased objects can be referenced by pointers, but not by just any kind of pointer. The pointer must belong to a "general" access type. A general access type is declared like a regular access type, except with the additional keyword **all** (or, as discussed later, **constant**):

```
type Integer_Pointer is access all Integer;
   -- general access type
Int_Ptr: Integer_Pointer; -- general pointer
```

The keyword **all** indicates that pointers of this type can point to declared objects as well as to dynamically declared objects. The keyword **all** also indicates that the object being pointed to is a variable rather than a constant. Such types are called "general" access types to distinguish them from the "pool-specific" access types previously discussed in this chapter.

In order to get `Int_Ptr` , of type `Integer_Pointer`, to point to `Whole_Number`, the `Access` attribute is required:

```
Int_Ptr: Integer_Pointer := Whole_Number'Access;
```

Using the `Access` attribute guarantees that `Int_Ptr` is properly pointing to `Whole_Number`. Dangling references cannot arise because Ada checks at compile time that `Int_Ptr` cannot outlive the object being pointed to, namely, `Whole_Number`.

As the following code illustrates, general pointers, like `Bool_Pointer`, can point to dynamically allocated objects as well as to declared objects:

```
declare
   type Boolean_Access_Type is access all Boolean;
      -- a general access type
   Bool_Pointer: Boolean_Access_Type; -- a general pointer
   Flag: aliased Boolean := True;
begin
   Bool_Pointer := Flag'Access;
      -- points to declared object
   Bool_Pointer := new Boolean'(False);
      -- points to dynamically allocated object
end;
```

So far, all our examples have shown general pointers to declared scalar objects. General pointers can also point to declared composite objects and their components, as long as the item in question is declared as aliased. Consider, for instance, the following declarations:

```
type States is (AL, AK, AZ, AR, CA, CO, CT, DE, DC, FL, GA, HI,
   ID, IL, IND, IA, KS, KY, LA, ME, MD, MA, MI, MN, MS, MO, MT,
   NE, NV, NH, NJ, NM, NY, NC, ND, OH, OK, ORE, PA, RI, SC, SD,
   TN, TX, UT, VT, VA, WA, WV, WI, WY);
```

```
type State_Statistics is        -- Record type isn't aliased
   record
      State: aliased States;
      Population: aliased Natural;
      Square_Miles: Natural; -- This component isn't aliased
   end record;

Largest_State: State_Statistics; -- not aliased
```

Note that `Largest_State` is not aliased, but two of its three components are aliased: `State` and `Population`. The `Access` attribute can, therefore, apply to these components:

```
Largest_State.State'Access        -- OK; State is aliased
Largest_State.Population'Access   -- OK; Population is aliased
```

However, the `Access` attribute cannot apply to `Largest_State` or its component, `Square_Miles`, since neither is aliased:

```
Largest_State'Access              -- Error; not aliased
Largest_State.Square_Miles'Access -- Error; not aliased
```

The previous example shows how general pointers can point to a declared record and its components. The next example shows how general pointers can point to a declared array and its components. The following declarations reference the previously defined enumeration type `States`:

```
type State_Number is new Integer range 1..51;
type Growing_States is array (State_Number range <>) of
   aliased States; -- States defined previously
Notable_States: Growing_States (1..3);
Important_States: aliased Growing_States (1..5);

type Stable_States is array (State_Number range <>) of States;
Insignificant_States: Stable_States (1..5);
```

Since `Notable_States` is an array of aliased `States`, each component of the array is aliased. The `Access` attribute can, therefore, apply to every component. `Notable_states` itself, however, is not aliased. In contrast, `Important_States` is a aliased array with aliased components. Thus, the `Access` attribute can apply to either the array or its components. Finally, `Insignificant_States` is not aliased and neither are its components; therefore, the `Access` attribute cannot apply to either:

```
Notable_States'Access             -- Error; not aliased
Notable_States(1)'Access          -- OK

Important_States'Access           -- OK
Important_States(1)'Access        -- OK
```

```
Insignificant_States'Access          -- Error; not aliased
Insignificant_States(1)'Access       -- Error; not aliased
```

General access types can be declared as read-write or as read-only. The examples shown so far have been read-write general access types. They contain the keyword **all**:

```
type Read_Write_Pointer_Type is access all Float;
    -- read-write general access type
```

Pointers of such types can be used to both read and write to objects that they point to. Since read-write access is allowed, such pointers can point to variables, but not to constants:

```
Const: aliased constant Float := 0.0;
type Read_Write_Pointer_Type is access all Float;
    -- read-write general access type
Read_Write_Pointer: Read_Write_Pointer_Type := Const'Access;
    -- illegal; cannot write to a constant
```

Read-only general access types contain the keyword **constant**, instead of the keyword **all**:

```
type Read_Only_Pointer_Type is access constant Float;
    -- read-only general access type
```

Pointers of such types can point to either a variable or a constant, but the variable or constant cannot be modified. In other words, the object being pointed to is viewed as a constant, regardless of whether it is a constant or a variable. The following code illustrates these issues:

```
declare
    type Read_Only_Access is access constant Integer;
    -- Access restricted to read-only
    -- Can point to a constant, or a variable viewed as a constant
    Read_Only_Pointer: Read_Only_Access;

    Var: aliased Integer := 5;
    Const: aliased constant Integer := 12;
begin
    Read_Only_Pointer := Var'Access;      -- OK
    Read_Only_Pointer := Const'Access;    -- OK

    -- cannot write to object pointed to
    Read_Only_Pointer.all := 7;           -- Illegal
end;
```

General pointers that are read-only are useful for pointing to constants or to objects that are statically allocated to read-only memory. For example, the following code uses read-only general pointers to create a static "ragged array":

```
declare
   type Quote_Ptr is access constant String;
   Mies_Van_Der_Rohe: aliased constant String :=
      "Less is more.";
   Robert_Venturi: aliased constant String :=
      "Less is a bore.";
   David_Naiditch: aliased constant String :=
      "Less is more than a bore.";

   -- Array elements point to statically declared
   -- varying length strings
   Architectual_Wisdom: constant array (1..3) of Quote_Ptr
         := (   Mies_Van_Der_Rohe'Access,
                Robert_Venturi'Access,
                David_Naiditch'Access   );
begin
   for Quote in Architectual_Wisdom'Range loop
      -- Output architectural words of wisdom
      Put_Line (Architectual_Wisdom(Quote).all );
   end loop;
end;
```

Architectual_Wisdom is called a ragged array because each of its components differ in size. Architectual_Wisdom(1), Architectual_Wisdom(2), and Architectual_Wisdom(3) are constant strings of lengths 13, 15, and 25, respectively.

Let us now consider how type conversion can be used for pointers. A pointer belonging to a pool-specific access type can be converted to a general access type, as long as the type of object being pointed to is compatible:

```
declare
   type General_Access_Type is access all Character;
   type Pool_Specific_Access_Type is access Character;
   General: General_Access_Type;
   Pool: Pool_Specific_Access_Type;
begin
   Pool := new Character'('A');
   General := General_Access_Type (Pool);   -- OK
      -- type conversion from a pool-specific access type to a
      -- general access type
end;
```

In addition to the Access attribute, the Unchecked_Access attribute provides pointer access to declared objects. The difference is that when Access is used, the compiler guards against the possibility of dangling pointers. To accomplish this, the compiler checks that the object pointed to remains in existence at least as long as the access type. On the other hand, when Unchecked_Access is used, it is the programmer's responsibility to avoid dangling pointers because Ada imposes no accessibility restrictions. The difference between attributes Access and Unchecked_Access is illustrated below:

```
declare
    type Char_Access_Type is access all Character;
    Safe_Ptr: Char_Access_Type;
    Unsafe_Ptr: Char_Access_Type;
    Char: Character;
begin
    declare
        Local: aliased Character;
    begin
        Unsafe_Ptr := Local'Unchecked_Access; -- OK
        Unsafe_Ptr.all := 'A';                    -- Legal and safe

        Safe_Ptr := Local'Access;                 -- Illegal
        ...
    end;


    -- Unsafe_Ptr becomes a dangling pointer since the
    -- object pointed to (Local) no longer exists
    Char := Unsafe_Ptr.all; -- Legal but erroneous
    ...
end;
```

In the preceding code, the inner block references the pointers (`Unsafe_Ptr` and `Safe_Ptr`), whose access type, `Char_Access_Type`, is declared in the outer block. `Unsafe_Ptr` is then assigned `Local'Unchecked_Access`. This code is potentially dangerous because once the inner block is exited, the object pointed to, `Local`, ceases to exist and `Unsafe_Ptr` becomes a dangling pointer. Dereferencing this dangling pointer, `Unsafe_Ptr.all`, yields an undefined value. Since the `Access` attribute guards against the possibility of such dangling pointers, `Safe_Ptr` cannot be assigned `Local'Access`.

## POINTERS TO SUBPROGRAMS

**Ada 95** ▶ In addition to pointing to objects, Ada pointers may point to subprograms. Pointers to subprograms make it possible to indirectly pass subprograms as parameters to other subprograms. Pointers to subprograms also make it easy to dynamically select and invoke a subprogram and to store references to subprograms in data structures such as arrays or records. (For those dealing with X Window systems, pointers to subprograms allow installing "call-backs.")

Access types that point to subprograms are created as follows:

```
type P is access procedure;
    -- Pointers of type P can point to ANY parameterless procedure


type Q is access procedure (A: out Integer);
    -- Pointers of type Q can point to any procedure
    -- with a single out parameter of type Integer
```

```
type R is access function (B: in Character) return Boolean;
   -- Pointers of type R can point to any function with
   -- a single character parameter that returns a Boolean type
```

As the comments indicate, pointers of type P can point to any parameterless procedure. Pointers of type Q can point to any procedure with a single **out** parameter of type Integer. Pointers of type R can point to any function with a single character parameter that returns a Boolean type. Note that no subprogram name follows the keywords **procedure** or **function** since these are access types to any subprogram with the specified parameters, not to a specific subprogram.

The ability to point to a subprogram is provided through the Access attribute that was previously discussed:

```
declare
    function Tan (X: in Float) return Float is...
    type Trigonometrics is access function (F: in Float) return
        Float;
    Trig_Function: Trigonometrics;
       -- Can access conforming subprograms
    Flt: Float := 45.0;
begin
    Trig_Function := Tan'Access;
       -- Trig_Function points to function Tan
       ...
    Flt := Trig_Function (Flt); -- Same as Trig_Function.all(Flt);
       -- Tan is indirectly called when dereferenced
end;
```

As illustrated in the preceding code, Tan is indirectly called by dereferencing the pointer, Trig_Function. The pointer Trig_Function is dereferenced by either Trig_Function(Flt) or Trig_Function.**all**(Flt).

Let us now return to the access types P, Q, and R that were previously introduced. The following illustrates how pointers of these types can be used to indirectly invoke subprograms A, B, and C:

```
declare
    type P is access procedure;
    type Q is access procedure (A: out Integer);
    type R is access function (B: in Character) return Boolean;

    procedure A is ...
    procedure B (N: out Integer) is ...
    function C (X: in Character) return Boolean is ...

    Ptr_1: P := A'Access;
    Ptr_2: Q := B'Access;
    Ptr_3: R := C'Access;

    Bool: Boolean := Ptr_3 ('A'); -- indirectly invokes C
                                  -- Same as Ptr_3.all ('A');
```

```
      Result: Integer;

   begin
      Ptr_1.all;        -- indirectly invokes A
                        -- .all required since parameterless
      Ptr_2 (Result);  -- indirectly invokes B
                        -- same as Ptr_2.all (Result);
   end;
```

Note again that a subprogram is indirectly invoked via a pointer by dereferencing the pointer. Pointers to subprograms are dereferenced similarly to pointers to composite objects. If the subprogram being pointed to has parameters, then it can be invoked by following the pointer name with a parameter value. Thus, procedure B has a parameter and can be invoked via the pointer Ptr_2 as follows:

```
   Ptr_2 (Result);   -- same as Ptr_2.all (Result);
```

The compiler realizes that the procedure Ptr_2 points to is being invoked, and that an attempt is not being made to invoke the pointer itself. Note that the keyword **all** could be used, but is not required and is typically omitted. The keyword **all** is only required when the subprogram is parameterless. Thus, the parameterless procedure A must be invoked via the pointer Ptr_1 using the keyword **all**:

```
   Ptr_1.all;    -- all required since A is parameterless
```

Pointers to subprograms can be used for indirectly passing subprograms as runtime parameters. In the following code, function P is passed as a runtime parameter to the function Sum_Of_Terms:

```
   declare
      Total: Integer;

      function P (N: in Integer) return Integer is
      begin
         return (N ** 2) + (5 * (N - 7));
      end;

      type Polynomial is access function (N: in Integer) return
         Integer;

      function Sum_Of_Terms (Poly: in Polynomial;
                       From, To: in Integer ) return Integer is
         Sum: Integer := 0;
      begin
         for Term in From..To loop
            Sum := Sum + Poly (Term);
         end loop;
         return Sum;
      end Sum_Of_Terms;
```

```
begin
    Total := Sum_Of_Terms ( Poly => P'Access,
                             From => 3,
                             To   => 8 );
        -- Returns P(3) + P(4) + ... + P(8)
end;
```

Note that using pointers to pass subprograms as runtime parameters is an alternative to using generics to pass subprograms as compile time parameters.

As a final example, suppose a programmer wishes to sequentially call the procedures Eat, Drink, and Be_Merry. Instead of invoking each subprogram in turn, it is possible loop through an array of pointers to these procedures:

```
Procedure Life is
    procedure Eat is separate;
    procedure Drink is separate;
    procedure Be_Merry is separate;
    type Activities is access procedure;
    Live_Life: array (1..3) of Activities :=
        (Eat'Access, Drink'Access, Be_Merry'Access);
begin
    for Index in Live_Life'Range loop
        -- successively calls Eat, Drink, and Be_Merry
        Live_Life(Index).all;
    end loop;
end Life;
```

The first time through the loop, Live_Life(1) points to procedure Eat. When this pointer is dereferenced, Live_Life(1).all, procedure Eat is indirectly called. This process continues until each of the three subprograms Eat, Drink, and Be_Merry, are invoked, in turn.

Note that the same compile time scoping rules that guard against dangling pointers also ensure that a subprogram that no longer exists cannot be indirectly called by dereferencing a pointer.

## ACCESS PARAMETERS

**Ada 95 ▶** An access parameter is a special kind of formal parameter. This parameter can be matched with a pointer of any access type that points to objects of the specified type. In other words, parameter matching is based on the type of object being pointed to, not on the access type itself.

Do not confuse parameters of a specific access type with access parameters. The following code illustrates the difference:

```
procedure Demo_Access_Parameter is
    type Access_Bool is access Boolean;
    type Another_Access_Bool is access Boolean;
```

```
type Yet_Another_Access_Bool is access all Boolean;

Bool: aliased Boolean := True;

Bool_Ptr: Access_Bool := new Boolean'(False);
Another_Bool_Ptr: Another_Access_Bool := new Boolean'(True);
Yet_Another_Bool_Ptr: Yet_Another_Access_Bool := Bool'Access;

Procedure P (X: in Access_Bool) is separate;
    -- X is a parameter of an access type Access_Bool
procedure Q (Y: access Boolean) is separate;
    -- Y is an access parameter

begin
    ...
    -- P's parameter can only be matched with pointers of
    -- type Access_Bool
    P (Bool_Ptr);                   -- OK
    P (Another_Bool_Ptr);           -- illegal; type mismatch
    P (Yet_Another_Bool_Ptr);       -- illegal; type mismatch

    -- Q's parameter can be matched with any pointer
    -- that points to a Boolean object
    Q (Bool_Ptr);                   -- OK
    Q (Another_Bool_Ptr);           -- OK
    Q (Yet_Another_Bool_Ptr);       -- OK
end Demo_Access_Parameter;
```

Procedure P has a parameter X of the specific access type `Access_Bool`. Therefore, P's parameter can only be matched with pointers of type `Access_Bool`. In contrast, procedure Q has an access parameter. Q's parameter can be matched with any pointer that points to a `Boolean` object. Since pointers `Bool_Ptr`, `Another_Bool_Ptr`, and `Yet_Another_Bool_Ptr` each point to `Boolean` objects, Q can be passed any of these pointers. By the way, note that `Yet_Another_Bool_Ptr` is a general pointer, while the other pointers are pool specific.

Access parameters have a few unusual characteristics. An access parameter must be a formal **in** parameter. Modes of **out** or **in out** are not allowed. Also, since access parameters do not specify a particular access type, they belong to an anonymous access type. Variables, however, cannot be declared as anonymous access types:

```
Procedure Q (X: access Boolean) is    -- X belongs to an
                                      -- anonymous access type
begin
    A: access Boolean := X; -- illegal
        -- can't declare variables of an anonymous access type

end Q;
```

Finally, access parameters can never have a **null** value. For example, if procedure Q is passed a **null** value, then the exception, `Constraint_Error`, is raised. Thus, the body of procedure Q never needs to check whether its parameter X is **null**.

Once again, accessibility restrictions apply, to ensure that no dangling pointers can arise. However, in the case of access parameters, the check is made at runtime, not at compile time. (Specifically, the object pointed to by the actual parameter must live at least as long as type of the anonymous formal parameter that is implicitly declared at the point of the call.)

Access parameters provide a convenient way to generate a call by reference (see Chapter 6). However, as we will see in Chapter 13, the main use for access parameters is to allow runtime dispatching on access values.

Besides access parameters, Ada also supports access discriminants. Access discriminants, like access parameters, are primarily used in object-oriented programming and will therefore be covered in Chapter 13.

Access types are one of Ada's more advanced types. The next chapter considers other advanced types, such as modular integer types, fixed point types, and decimal fixed point types.

---

## EXERCISES

1. Which of the following statements contain errors? Explain the errors.

   ```
   declare
       type Character_Pointer is access Character;
       type Integer_Pointer is access Integer range 1 .. 9;
       Char_Ptr: Character_Pointer;
       Int_Ptr: Integer_Pointer;
   begin
       Char_Ptr := new Character'('A');
       Int_Ptr := new Integer'(11);
   end;
   ```

2. Pictorially show the difference between the two assignment statements in the statement part of this block:

   ```
   declare
       type Integer_Access_Type is access Integer;
       Int_Pointer_1: Integer_Access_Type := new Integer'(1);
       Int_Pointer_2: Integer_Access_Type := new Integer'(2);
   begin
       Int_Pointer_1.all := Int_Pointer_2.all;
       Int_Pointer_1 := Int_Pointer_2;
   end;
   ```

3. What values do each of the following Put statements output?

   ```
   with Ada.Text_IO; use Ada.Text_IO;
   procedure Output_Items is
       type String_Access_Type is access String;
   ```

```
        String_Pointer: String_Access_Type;
    begin
        String_Pointer := new String'("Sesquipedalian");
        Put (String_Pointer.all);
        New_Line;
        Put (  String_Pointer (10) &
               String_Pointer (9)  &
               String_Pointer (13)     );
        New_Line;
    end Output_Items;
```

4. Which of the following statements contain errors? Explain the errors.

```
    declare
        type Natural_Pointer is access Natural;
        type Positive_Pointer is access Positive;
        Nat: Natural_Pointer := new Natural'(0);
        Pos: Positive_Pointer := new Positive'(1);
    begin
        Nat := Pos;
        Pos := Nat;
        Pos.all := Nat.all;
        Nat.all := Pos.all;
    end;
```

5. What will the following program output?

```
    with Ada.Text_IO; use Ada.Text_IO;
    procedure Demo is
        package Int_IO is new Integer_IO (Integer);
        use Int_IO;
        type R is
            record
                A: Integer;
                B: Character;
            end record;
        type R_Pointer is access R;
        Pointer: R_Pointer := new R'(2, 'C');
    begin
        Put (Pointer.A);
        New_Line;
        Put (Pointer.B);
        New_Line;
    end Demo;
```

6. Find the error in the following code:

```
    declare
        type R is
            record
                A: Integer;
                B: Character;
            end record;
```

```
      type R_Pointer is access R;
      P1, P2: R_Pointer;
   begin
      P1 := new R'(A   => 5,
                   B   => 'a' );
      P2.all := P1.all;
   end;
```

7. Consider the following code:

```
type Inner is
   record
         A: Boolean;
         B: Character;
   end record;

type Outer is
   record
         P: Integer;
         Q: Inner;
   end record;

type Outer_Ptr is access Outer;
Ptr: Outer_Ptr := new Outer'
   (P => 3, Q => (A => True, B => 'g') );
```
Show how assignments can be made to change the values of P, A, B, or Q.

8. Modify the program `Restaurants` and the package `Restaurant_Linked_List` presented in this chapter so that the program asks the user to enter the type of food desired and then prints all the restaurants that feature that kind of food.

9. Modify the program `Restaurants` and the package `Restaurant_Linked_List` presented in this chapter so that the program prompts the user for both the type of food desired and the maximum average price per meal. Have the program then output all the restaurants, if any, that satisfy these requirements.

10. Modify the package `Restaurant_Linked_List` to add items to the front of the list (after the header record) instead of to the back of the list.

11. Consider the following declarations:

```
type Proc_Ptr is access function (A: in Character) return
   Boolean;
function Is_Upper (Char: in Character) return Boolean is
begin
   return Char in 'A'..'Z';
end Is_Upper;

Ptr: Proc_Ptr := Is_Upper'Access;
```

```
function Q (V: in Proc_Ptr) return Boolean is
begin
    return V('B');
end Q;
```

Is the following expression `True` or `False`?

```
Q(Ptr) = Is_Upper('B')
```

12. Replace the following loop with a single assignment:

```
declare
    type Vector is array (1..100) of Float;
    type Vector_Pointer is access Vector;
    To_Pointer, From_Pointer: Vector_Pointer;
begin
    ...
    for K in Vector'Range loop
        To_Pointer(K) := From_Pointer(K);
    end loop;
end;
```

13. Replace the following assignment statements with aggregate assignments:

```
declare
    type Int_Ptr is access Integer;
    A: array (1..8) of Int_Ptr;
    B: array (1..4) of Int_Ptr;
begin
    A(1) := new Int_Ptr'(3);    A(2) := new Int_Ptr'(7);
    A(3) := new Int_Ptr'(9);    A(4) := new Int_Ptr'(3);
    A(5) := new Int_Ptr'(3);    A(6) := new Int_Ptr'(3);
    A(7) := new Int_Ptr'(1);    A(8) := new Int_Ptr'(3);
    B(1) := new Int_Ptr;        B(2) := new Int_Ptr;
    B(3) := new Int_Ptr;        B(4) := new Int_Ptr;
end;
```

14. Rewrite the following generic (presented in Chapter 7) as a nongeneric function. Hint: Instead of passing the function, `Values`, via a generic parameter, pass a pointer to the function as a runtime parameter. What are the advantages and disadvantages of using generics?

```
generic
    with function Values (Param: Integer) return Integer;
function Average (Beginning, Ending: Integer) return Float;

function Average (Beginning, Ending: Integer) return Float is
    Sum_Of_Terms: Integer := 0;
begin
    for Index in Beginning .. Ending loop
        Sum_Of_Terms := Sum_Of_Terms + Values (Index);
    end loop;
    return Float (Sum_Of_Terms) /
        Float (Ending - Beginning + 1);
end Average;
```

15. Using the static array `Architectual_Wisdom` declared in this chapter, write a package body that implements the following package specification.

```
package Architectual_Quotes is
    type Quote_Code is new Integer range 1..3;
    function Get_Quote (Code: in Quote_Code) return String;
end Architectual_Quotes;
```

16. Explain why the second assignment to X is illegal:

```
package A is
    type T is access all Integer;
    VV: aliased Integer;
end A;

with A;
procedure P is
    X: A.T;
    V: aliased Integer;
begin
    X := VV'Access;
    X := V'Access;
end P;
```

17. Explain the problems, if any, with the following procedure:

```
procedure Demo_Access_Parameter is
    type Some_Float_Access_Type is access all Float;
    type Another_Float_Access_Type is access all Float;
    procedure Proc (Access_Param: access Float) is separate;

    Some_Ptr: Some_Float_Access_Type;
    Another_Ptr: Another_Float_Access_Type;
    Flt: aliased Float := 0.0;
begin
    Proc (Access_Param => Flt'Access);
    Some_Ptr := Flt'Access;
    Proc (Access_Param => Some_Ptr);

    Another_Ptr := new Float'(2.0);
    Proc (Access_Param => Another_Ptr);
end Demo_Access_Parameter;
```

18. Which assignment statements have errors?

```
declare
    type Char_Access is access all Character;
    type Const_Access is access constant Character;
    Ptr_1: Char_Access;
    Ptr_2: Const_Access;
    Char: aliased Character := 'A';
    Const: aliased constant Character := 'B';
begin
    Ptr_1 := Char'Access;
```

```
      Ptr_2 := Char'Access;
      Ptr_1 := Const'Access;
      Ptr_2 := Const'Access;
      Ptr_1.all := 'C';
      Ptr_2.all := 'C';
   end;
```

19. Consider the following declarations:

```
type Rec is
   record
      A: aliased Character;
      B: aliased Natural;
      C: Float;
   end record;

X: aliased Rec;
Y: Rec;
```

Which of the following expressions have errors?

```
X.A'Access
X.B'Access
X.C'Access
X'Access
Y.A'Access
Y.B'Access
Y.C'Access
Y'Access
```

# More About Types

In this chapter, we discuss some of the more advanced aspects of types. The first section covers portable numeric types, which have the same range of values on every Ada compiler. Next, we discuss derived types that introduce new discriminants. We then examine Ada's support of inheritance, whereby a derived type inherits its parent's operations. Inheritance plays a major role in object-oriented programming and will, therefore, be covered in far greater detail in Chapter 13. The next topic is modular integer types. These types are always positive and their values, instead of going out of range, wrap around to their starting value. We next explore fixed point types, followed by decimal fixed point types. These types are real numbers whose decimal point is at a fixed location. This chapter concludes with universal types. Universal types consist of numeric literals and special kinds of constants called named numbers.

## PORTABLE NUMERIC TYPES

This section discusses how to create numeric types that are portable from one Ada compiler to another.

The sizes of all the numeric types in package `Standard` are implementation defined and, therefore, are not fully portable from one Ada compiler to another. Ada, for example, does not require that type `Integer` be a 32-bit type or that `Integer'First` equal $-2^{31}$ and `Integer'Last` equal $2^{31} - 1$. On the positive side, implementations can support integer types that naturally map to the hardware. Forcing all Ada compilers to support, for instance, a 32-bit integer type is undesirable because on some hardware, 32-bit integer types may be very inefficient. On the negative side, however, portability of Ada code is compromised because numeric objects have different sizes and ranges of values on different Ada compilers. For example, consider tests that measure how fast different Ada compilers multiply objects of type `Float`. It is unfair to compare the test result of one Ada compiler that defines `Float` as a 16-bit number with another that defines `Float` as a 32-bit number. For code running on the same computer, a compiler using a 32-bit `Float` type may be unfairly penalized.

The solution to this problem is to avoid referencing the numeric types in package `Standard`. At first, this may seem impossible, because derived types must eventually be derived from a predefined numeric type such as `Float` or `Integer`. However, there is an alternative. Code can be made more portable by using special forms of the derived type declarations, called integer type definitions and floating point type definitions.

To illustrate the need to make code more portable, consider the following regular derived type declaration:

```
type Inventory is new Integer range 0 .. 50_000;
```

This derived type declaration works on an Ada compiler where `Integer'Last` is at least `50,000`, but it raises a constraint error on an Ada compiler where `Integer'Last` is less than `50,000`.

We could attempt to make the preceding declaration more portable by using the predefined integer type `Long_Integer`:

```
type Inventory is new Long_Integer range 0 .. 50_000;
```

The range of values for type `Long_Integer` is implementation dependent; however, when available, type `Long_Integer` provides a greater range of values than type `Integer`. Thus, `Long_Integer` is more likely to include `50,000` than `Integer`.

However, there are two problems with this solution. First, type `Long_Integer` is not supported by every Ada compiler. Unlike type `Integer`, which must be supported, type `Long_Integer` is an optional type. Second, if this code is ported to an Ada compiler where `Integer'Last` exceeds `50,000`, then deriving type `Inventory` from `Long_Integer` wastes computer memory. Instead of storing objects of type `Inventory` as, for instance 32-bit integers, we may be storing them as 64-bit integers.

In summary, defining the parent type of `Inventory` as `Integer` has the disadvantage of not being very portable. On the other hand, defining the parent type of `Inventory` as `Long_Integer` is also not very portable and has the disadvantage of potentially wasting computer memory. The solution to this dilemma is to use an integer type definition:

```
-- integer type definition
type Inventory is range 0 .. 50_000;
    -- enhances portability by letting the compiler decide
    -- whether the parent type is Short_Integer, Integer,
    -- Long_Integer, etc.
```

Integer type definitions differ from other derived type declarations as follows: the specification of a parent type, such as **new** `Integer`, is omitted. Because of this omission, the compiler selects the most appropriate parent type to handle the range of values on the particular computer. In other words, the programmer does not select the parent type; instead, the selection is made by the compiler. On some computers, the Ada compiler may select type `Integer` as the parent type; on other computers, the compiler may select `Short_Integer` as the parent type; on other computers, `Long_Integer`; on others, yet a different integer type. By letting the compiler select the parent type, we not only increase code portability; we also trust the compiler to select the most efficient representation of the type on the particular computer.

In addition to integer type definitions, there are floating point type definitions, which are also special forms of the derived type. The following floating point type definition has an accuracy constraint:

```
-- floating point type definition with accuracy constraint
type Tiny_Real is digits 3;
   -- enhances portability by letting compiler decide whether
   -- the parent type is Short_Float, Float, Long_Float, etc.
```

In floating point type definitions, words such as **new** `Float`, which appear in other derived type declarations, are omitted. As with integer type definitions, the result of this omission is that the programmer does not select the parent type; the selection is made by the compiler. Note the accuracy constraint: **digits** 3. This accuracy constraint indicates that the values of the type `Tiny_Real` need not be accurate to more than 3 significant digits. An object of `Tiny_Real`, therefore, might not distinguish between the values 3.111 and 3.112 since the 3 significant digits only consist of 3.11, not the last digit.

To further illustrate what significant digits are, consider the following real literals:

```
3.11,  2.22E7,   0.00452,  12.3E-3,  745000.0
```

Each of these literals contain 3 significant digits. Note that leading and trailing zeros, as well as exponents, do not count as significant digits.

Floating point definitions may contain range constraints in addition to accuracy constraints:

```
-- floating point type definition with accuracy
-- and range constraint
type Portable_Float is digits 6 range -1.0E+38 .. 1.0E+38;
```

In this example, objects of type `Portable_Float` are represented by at least 6 significant digits and are constrained to the range from -1.0E+38 to 1.0E+38. Although floating point type definitions often have range constraints, the parent type is determined by the requested precision, not the range of values. This is different from integer type definitions, where the parent type is determined by the range of values.

**Ada 95 ▶**   In Chapters 2 and 8, we briefly discussed the `Base` attribute. When this attribute is applied to a type definition, it provides the range of the compiler-chosen parent type. Consider, for instance, the following code:

```
declare
   type Elevation is range -30_000 .. +30_000;
```

```
      A: Elevation;        -- constrained to values -30_000..+30_000
      B: Elevation'Base;   -- can take all values of Elevation's
                           -- parent type
  begin
      A := 31_000;  -- Constraint_Error raised
      B := 31_000;  -- OK if implementation chooses a 16 bit integer
                    -- type (or larger) as the parent of Elevation
  end;
```

As illustrated, assigning the value 31_000 to A raises a Constraint_Error since this value is beyond Elevation'Last. On the other hand, since B is declared to be of type Elevation'Base, it can assume any value in the range of its parent type. If the compiler chooses a 16-bit integer type as the parent of Elevation, then B can be assigned 31_000 since this value is less than Elevation'Base'Last, which is 32_767. In general, constraint checks apply to values assigned to A, but not to B. Values assigned to B only raise a constraint error if an overflow occurs.

This concludes our discussion of portability issues. The next section discusses derived types that introduce new discriminants.

## DERIVED TYPES THAT INTRODUCE NEW DISCRIMINANTS

Ada 95 ▶ An interesting feature of derived types is that they may introduce discriminants that do not belong to their parent. As illustrated, these new discriminants have the effect of renaming or constraining their parents' discriminants:

```
      type R1 (C: Character) is ...;
      type R2 (N1: Integer; N2: Integer) is ...;

      type New_R1 (V: Character) is new R1 (V);
      type New_R2 (I: Integer) is new R2 (I, 7);
      type Another_New_R2 (I: Integer) is new R2 (I, I);
```

Type New_R1 uses its discriminant V to specify the value of its parent R1's discriminant. Note that the derived types New_R2 and Another_New_R2 have only one discriminant, I, whereas their parent R2 has two discriminants, N1 and N2. Type New_R2 uses its discriminant I to specify the value of its parent R2's first discriminant and the literal 7 to set R2's second discriminant. Finally, Another_New_R2 uses its discriminant I to specify both its parent R2's discriminants.

By introducing new discriminants, the implementation of a private type with discriminants can be based on a preexisting discriminated type. For example, in the following code, type Hidden is implemented in the private part of the package as a derivative of R with the discriminant A replacing C:

```
      package P is
         type R (C: Character) is ...;
         type Hidden (A: Character) is private;
            ...
```

```
private
    -- Hidden is implemented using the existing type R
    type Hidden (A: Character) is new R (A);
        ...
end P;
```

## INHERITANCE

Derived types inherit basic predefined operations from their parent type. For example, a type derived from an enumeration type inherits the predefined relational operators (<, >, =, etc.), and a type derived from an integer type inherits the predefined arithmetic operators (+, -, *, etc.). Consider a derived type whose parent is type Integer:

```
declare
    type Stoves_In_Stock is new Integer range 0 .. 200;
    Number_Of_Stoves: Stoves_In_Stock := 25;
begin
    Number_Of_Stoves := 2 * Number_Of_Stoves + 1;
    -- OK; inherits arithmetic operations from the parent
    -- type, Integer
end;
```

In this example, the derived type Stoves_In_Stock inherits the arithmetic operations from its parent type, Integer.

Even though the parent type is not explicitly provided, inheritance is also supported for integer type definitions such as the previous type Inventory and floating point type definitions such as the previous Tiny_Real.

Besides inheriting basic predefined operations, a derived type may inherit operations defined in the visible part of a package where its parent type is declared. Consider, for example, the following package specification:

```
package Coordinates is
    type Point is
        record
            X_Coordinate : Float range 0.0 .. 10_000.0;
            Y_Coordinate : Float range 0.0 .. 10_000.0;
        end record;
    function Distance (Point_A, Point_B: in Point)
        return Float;
end Coordinates;
```

This package declares a type, Point, and a function, Distance, which operates on objects of type Point. Suppose that another program unit defines a derived type whose parent is Point. Since Distance is defined in the same package specification as type Point, the derived type inherits the function Distance. Distance may thus operate on objects belonging to this derived type, as shown in the following code:

```
with Ada.Text_IO, Coordinates ; use Ada.Text_IO, Coordinates;
procedure As_The_Crow_Flies is
    type Intersection is new Point;
    Hollywood_And_Vine: Intersection := (2_301.3, 198.1);
    Pico_And_Sepulveda: Intersection := (2_294.6, 203.0);
    package Real_IO is new Float_IO (Float);
    use Real_IO;
begin
    Put ("The distance between the corner of Hollywood and Vine "
        & "and the corner of Pico and Sepulveda is ");
    Put ( Distance ( Hollywood_And_Vine, Pico_And_Sepulveda ) );
        -- the function Distance is inherited from type Point
    New_Line ;
end As_The_Crow_Flies;
```

Now let us consider a situation where a derived type does not inherit all the operations of its parent type. The following package specification defines the function Square_Root but does not define the type Float, on which this function operates:

```
package Math_Library is
    function Square_Root (X: Float) return Float;
end Math_Library;
```

As illustrated below, types derived from Float do not inherit Square_Root:

```
with Math_Library; use Math_Library;
procedure Not_Inherited is
    type New_Float is new Float;
    X: New_Float;
    subtype Positive_Float is Float range 0.0 .. 1.0E6;
    Y: Positive_Float := 3.0;
begin
    Y := Square_Root (X);   -- illegal;
        -- New_Float does not inherit Square_Root
    Y := Square_Root (Y);   -- OK
end Not_Inherited;
```

The derived type, New_Float, does not inherit the function Square_Root because its parent type, Float, is not defined in the same package specification as Square_Root. (Float is defined in the package Standard.) Note that there is no problem invoking Square_Root with a parameter belonging to the subtype Positive_Float. The subtype Positive_Float has the same operations as its base type Float because, unlike a derived type, a subtype does not introduce a new type. A subtype just places an optional constraint on the range of values of its base type.

As we have seen, inheritable operations are tightly bound to a type because they are implicitly or explicitly declared together with the type. The function Distance is explicitly declared with type Point. Predefined operations such as = and

/= are implicitly declared with type Point. Such inheritable operations are called "primitive operations."

Although a derived type inherits all of its parent type's primitive operations, a programmer can override the ones not desired or define new ones. For example, a programmer can override the Distance function inherited by the derived type Intersection by providing a new version:

```
with Ada.Text_IO, Coordinates ; use Ada.Text_IO, Coordinates ;
procedure As_The_Crow_Flies is
    type Intersection is new Point;
    -- The following version of Distance overrides the version
    -- inherited from type Point
    function Distance (Point_A, Point_B: in Intersection)
        return Float is separate;
    -- The following procedure is only defined for type
    -- Intersection, not its parent type, Point
    procedure Print (Item: in Intersection) is separate;

        . . .
```

Also note that the function Print has been added, which applies to type Intersection but not to its parent type, Point.

## MODULAR INTEGER TYPES

**Ada 95 ▶** Modular integer types, also known as ordinal types or unsigned integer types, are special integer types that are always positive and have values that never go out of range. Instead of going out of range, the value wraps around to the beginning, starting at 0. To illustrate this behavior, consider the strange-looking dial in Figure 12.1.

Note that values are provided in the range from 0 to 7. When the dial goes beyond 7, it wraps around to 0 and starts over. Thus, setting the dial in the positive direction 8 notches from 0 returns it to 0, setting the dial 9 notches from 0 brings it to 1, setting the dial 10 notches brings it to 2, and so on. In mathematical terms, this dial operates in modulo (mod) 8 since there are 8 notches on the dial. Values that correspond to the same notch are said to be congruent. Thus, 0 is congruent to 8, 1 is congruent to 9, and 2 is congruent to 10.

In Ada, modular integer types are declared using the keywords **is mod**. For example, the following modular integer type, Dial_Type, exhibits the same wraparound behavior as our dial:

```
type Dial_Type is mod 8;   -- Modular integer type with
                           -- a range 0 to 7

Dial: Dial_Type;
```

In this example, all values of type Dial_Type are taken **mod** 8, which results in values in the range 0 to 7. Since Dial is a variable of type Dial_Type, if a value is

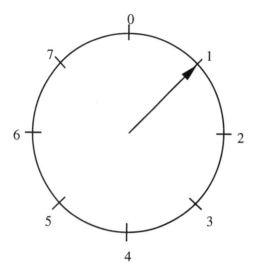

**Figure 12.1** Dial operating in modulo 8.

assigned to `Dial` that exceeds 7, then instead of raising a `Constraint_Error`, the value wraps around to 0 and continues:

```
Dial := 7;        -- assigned 7 (no wraparound)
Dial := 8;        -- assigned 0 because 8 mod 8 = 0
Dial := 9;        -- assigned 1 because 9 mod 8 = 1
Dial := 10;       -- assigned 2 because 10 mod 8 = 2
Dial := 17;       -- assigned 1 because 17 mod 8 = 1
```

As shown, 8 wraps around to 0 just like our dial. In mathematical terms, 8 **mod** 8 = 0. Similarly, 9 wraps around to 1, and 10 wraps around to 2. Note that assigning `Dial` the value 17 causes a double wraparound that ends at 1.

Modular integer types have all the operations that signed integer types have, but with automatic wraparound:

```
Dial := 9 + 9;    -- Assigned 2
```

Note that overflow does not occur since addition is performed **mod** 8.

Attributes such as `First`, `Last`, and `Succ` may also be applied to modular types. When `Succ` is applied to a modular number, wraparound occurs when the result exceeds the largest positive value.

```
Dial := Dial_Type'First;      -- assigned 0
Dial := Dial_Type'Last;       -- assigned 7
Dial := Dial_Type'Succ(10);   -- assigned 3
```

In addition to arithmetic operators and attributes, modular integer types have bitwise logical operators: **and, or, xor,** and **not**. These logical operators are bitwise because they operate on each bit, in turn, where bit 0 is interpreted as `False`, and bit 1 as `True`.

```
V1: Dial_Type := 2#101#;
V2: Dial_Type := 2#110#;
V3: Dial_Type := V1 and V2;   -- Assigned 2#100#
V4: Dial_Type := V1 or V2;    -- Assigned 2#111#
V5: Dial_Type := not V1;      -- Assigned 2#010#
```

Package `Interfaces` provides predefined modular integer types that are directly supported by the "target machine" or that are useful when interfacing between code written in Ada and code written in another language. (The target machine is the computer that executes the code generated by the compiler.) Left and right shifting and rotating subprograms are provided for these modular types.

When using `Text_IO` to input or output modular integers, the generic package `Modular_IO` must be instantiated. Package `Integer_IO` cannot be instantiated with a modular integer type:

```
package Mod_IO is new Ada.Text_IO.Modular_IO (Dial_Type);
```

Package `Modular_IO` begins in `Text_IO`, as follows:

```
generic
    type Num is mod <>;
package Modular_IO is ...
```

As shown, the generic formal type parameter for modular integer types uses the keyword **mod**, followed by the box, <>.

## FIXED POINT TYPES

Real types consist of floating point types and fixed point types. Numbers belonging to the floating point type were discussed in Chapter 2. We will now discuss numbers belonging to the fixed point type.

Unlike floating point numbers, where the decimal point can shift to different locations, in fixed point numbers, the decimal point is "fixed" to a particular location. In more technical terms, only the most significant digits of a floating point number are stored (its "mantissa"), together with a scale factor (exponent value), which represents the position of the decimal point within the stored digits. In contrast, fixed point numbers do not have a scale factor (exponent) because the position of the decimal point cannot move around. Also, whereas floating point numbers have a margin of error that is relative to the magnitude (absolute value) of the number, fixed point numbers have a margin of error that is a fixed quantity.

A fixed point type is not a predefined type; there is no predefined type identifier such as `Fix` that can be used in object declarations. Rather, the programmer must define a fixed point type by specifying a fixed point constraint and a range constraint (using real literals or static real expressions):

```
type Modification is delta 0.125 range 0.0..255.0;
   -- fixed point type declaration
```

Fixed point type declarations begin with the keyword **type**, followed by the name of the fixed point type, the keywords **is delta**, and the delta value (fixed point constraint). The delta value establishes the absolute margin of error (the largest amount by which the fixed point number may stray from its mathematically exact value). In this example, the absolute margin of error is specified as 0.125. This means that an object of type Modification may be inaccurate by no more than ±0.125. This is a maximum value. The actual margin of error chosen by the compiler may be smaller. The delta value is followed by the keyword **range** and a range constraint. In this example, the range constraint is 0.0..255.0.

When using Text_IO to input or output fixed point numbers, Fixed_IO must be instantiated. Neither Integer_IO nor Float_IO can be instantiated with a fixed point type:

```
package Modification_IO is new
   Ada.Text_IO.Fixed_IO (Modification);
```

Package Fixed_IO begins in Text_IO as follows:

```
generic
   type Num is delta <>;
package Fixed_IO is...
```

As shown, the generic formal type parameter for fixed point types uses the keyword **delta**, followed by the box ,<>.

## DECIMAL FIXED POINT TYPES

**Ada 95** ▶ As we have seen, the delta value of a fixed point type specifies a minimum amount of accuracy. A compiler may provide an actual delta value that is more accurate than requested. But what if we want an exact delta value? For example, programs involving monetary calculations require values to the exact cent in order to avoid round-off errors. In Ada, exact decimal computations are provided by decimal fixed point types. These types, however, can be rejected by an Ada compiler unless it conforms to the optional Information Systems Annex.

Decimal fixed point types are declared as follows:

```
-- Must be supported only if the optional Information Systems
-- Annex is supported
type Dollar_Amount is delta 0.01 digits 6 range 0.00..1_000.00;
   -- for exact monetary calculations
```

Unlike regular fixed point types, decimal fixed point types require a **digits** clause following the **delta** clause. Type Dollar_Amount can be used in monetary calculations since it provides values to the exact cent. Values of this type, in other words, are exact multiples of the **delta** value 0.01.

When converting a numeric type to a decimal fixed point type, the value is truncated towards zero. If rounding to the nearest value is desired instead, the attribute Round is available.

Unlike regular fixed point types, for decimal fixed point types, the **delta** value must be a power of 10: 0.1, 0.01, 0.001, and so on. The range constraint is optional:

```
-- without a range constraint
type Dollar_Amount is delta 0.01 digits 6;
```

In this case, Dollar_Amount provides 6 digits total: 2 digits for the cents and the remaining 4 digits for the dollar amount. Thus, Dollar_Amount has the range -9_999.99..9_999.99.

The optional Information Systems Annex defines a package, Ada.Text_IO.Pictures, for formatting decimal fixed point values. Formatting features include "floating" currency symbols, commas separating groups of digits, and suppressed decimal points when fractional parts are zero. Those interested in this package should consult the *Ada 95 Reference Manual*.

When using Text_IO to input or output decimal fixed point numbers, the generic package Decimal_IO must be instantiated. Neither package Float_IO nor Fixed_IO can be instantiated with a decimal fixed point type:

```
package Dollar_IO is new
    Ada.Text_IO.Decimal_IO (Dollar_Amount);
```

Package Decimal_IO begins in Text_IO as follows:

```
generic
    type Num is delta <> digits <>;
package Decimal_IO is ...
```

As shown, the generic formal type parameter for decimal fixed point types uses the keyword **delta**, followed by the box <>, followed by the keyword **digits**, followed by another box, <>. This syntax mirrors the syntax used in decimal fixed point type declarations.

## UNIVERSAL TYPES

Universal types include the universal integer type and the universal real type. The universal integer type consists of integer literals and integer named numbers. The universal real type consists of real literals and real named numbers. This classification of universal types is shown in Figure 12.2. Recall from Chapter 2 that integer literals are whole numbers that do not contain a decimal point, such as 7, 0, and 16#BAD#. Real literals are numbers that contain a radix point (fractional part), such

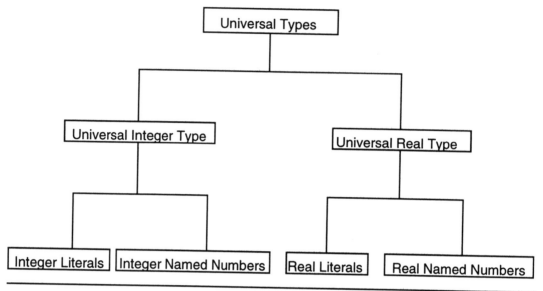

**Figure 12.2** Classification of universal types.

as $3.2, 0.0$, and $2\#1.01\#E2$. Integer literals automatically belong to type universal integer, and real literals automatically belong to type universal real.

Integer named numbers and real named numbers provide names for numeric values known at compile time. Named numbers are special kinds of constants. They are declared like regular constants, except that the name of a type is omitted. To contrast named number and constant declarations, consider the following regular constant declaration:

```
Dozen: constant Integer := 12; -- a regular constant
       -- belongs to type Integer
```

Now consider the following named number declaration:

```
Dozen: constant := 12; -- a named number
       -- belongs to type universal integer
```

Note that the keyword **constant** is not followed by the name of a type, such as Integer. Rather, the compiler determines whether the type belongs to universal integer or universal real by examining the value being assigned to Dozen. Because the integer literal 12 is assigned to Dozen, the compiler determines that Dozen belongs to the universal integer type. Constants of universal types are thus implicitly declared. Programmers cannot, for example, explicitly declare an object to belong to a universal integer or universal real type, because there are no predefined type identifiers, such as Universal_Integer or Universal_Real, which programmers can access. Therefore, variables cannot belong to a universal type.

Real named numbers are declared similarly to integer named numbers:

```
Pi: constant := 3.1415927; -- Pi is a named number that
-- belongs to type universal real
```

Since `Pi` is initialized to a real literal, it belongs to the type universal real.

The primary advantage of using named number declarations instead of regular constant declarations is that named number declarations are more portable between Ada compilers. Consider, for example, the following regular constant declaration:

```
Speed_Of_Light: constant Integer := 186_000;
```

This declaration is probably legal on a 32-bit computer but not on a 16-bit computer. On 32-bit computers, the Ada compiler typically makes `Integer'Last` 2_147_483_647, because this is the largest positive integer value that can be contained in a 32-bit word. The integer literal 186_000, used in the preceding declaration, is less than this maximum integer value, so no problems arise. On 16-bit computers, however, `Integer'Last` is typically 32_767, because this is the largest positive integer value that can be contained in a 16-bit word. On these 16-bit computers, the preceding regular constant declaration raises a constraint error, because we are attempting to initialize a constant to an integer value that is larger than `Integer'Last`.

To make the preceding regular constant declaration more portable, rewrite it as a named number declaration:

```
Speed_Of_Light: constant := 186_000;
```

By making `Speed_Of_Light` belong to a universal type, it is not limited to the range of values of the predefined type `Integer`. Rather, a named number can assume a range of values that must be at least as great as any of the predefined integer types, such as `Long_Integer`, that are supported by a particular compiler. To determine the smallest and largest integer values on a given system, access the package `System`, which contains system dependent constants, and output `System.Min_Int` and `System.Max_Int`. Similarly, objects belonging to the universal real type have a range that must be at least as great as any of the real types supported by a particular computer. The accuracy offered for universal reals is, therefore, the best an implementation of Ada can offer.

**Ada 95 ▶**     As illustrated in the following code, named numbers differ from regular constants because they provide names for numeric values known at compile time and therefore act as numeric literals. They cannot name values that must be determined at runtime:

```
Get (N); -- assume N is of type Integer
declare
    Dynamic_Integer_Constant: constant Integer := N;
    Static_Integer_Constant: constant Integer := 1;

    Named_Number: constant := Dynamic_Integer_Constant; -- illegal
        -- the value assigned to Named_Number must be static
        -- (determined at compile-time)
```

```
      Named_Number: constant := Static_Integer_Constant; -- OK
begin
   null;
end;
```

(Ada 83 is more restrictive than Ada 95; it is not enough for the value of a named number to be known at compile time, it also has to be of a universal type. Thus, assigning Named_Number the value Static_Integer_Constant is illegal in Ada 83 because Static_Integer_Constant does not belong to a universal type.)

It should be mentioned that certain attributes yield numeric values that belong to a universal type. For instance, the attribute Pos yields a universal integer that represents the position of an item in a discrete type, and the attribute Length yields a universal integer that represents the number of components of an array. Note that since Pos may have a dynamic parameter (one that is evaluated at runtime), when Pos appears in an expression, the expression might not be evaluated at compilation time. Hence, not every expression that yields a universal integer or a universal real result is evaluated at compilation time.

Before ending our discussion of universal types, let us consider universal types as they relate to strong typing. For reliability, Ada enforces strong typing with fanatic fervor. Objects of different types cannot be assigned or compared to one another and cannot appear in the same expression. However, universal types are an exception. Universal integers are compatible with objects of any integer type, and universal real numbers are compatible with objects of any real type. Thus, an expression such as N + 2 is legal regardless of whether N belongs to type Integer, Short_Integer, Long_Integer, or some user-defined integer derived type. We do not need to explicitly convert the literal 2 to N's type. Type compatibility of universal types is illustrated in the following code:

```
with Ada.Text_IO; use Ada.Text_IO;
procedure Type_Compatibility is

   Int: constant Integer := 1;
   Universal_Int: constant := 2;
   type New_Int_Type is new Integer;
   New_Int: constant New_Int_Type := 3;

   Floating: constant Float := 1.0;
   Universal_Real: constant := 2.0;
   type New_Float_Type is new Float;
   New_Float: constant New_Float_Type := 3.0;

   type Fixed_Type is delta 0.1 range 0.0..10.0;
   Fixed: constant Fixed_Type := 4.0;
   type Decimal_Fixed_Type is delta 0.1 digits 9;
   Decimal_Fixed: Decimal_Fixed_Type := 1.5;

   package Int_IO is new Integer_IO (Integer);
   package New_Int_IO is new Integer_IO (New_Int_Type);
```

```
    package Flt_IO is new Float_IO (Float);
    package New_Flt_IO is new Float_IO (New_Float_Type);
    package Fix_IO is new Fixed_IO (Fixed_Type);
    package Dec_Fix_IO is new Decimal_IO (Decimal_Fixed_Type);
begin
    -- all these expressions are OK
    New_Int_IO.Put (9 + New_Int); New_Line;
    Flt_IO.Put (6.3 + Floating); New_Line;
    Int_IO.Put (Universal_Int + Int); New_Line;
    New_Int_IO.Put (Universal_Int + New_Int); New_Line;
    Flt_IO.Put (Universal_Real + Floating); New_Line;
    New_Flt_IO.Put (Universal_Real + New_Float); New_Line;
    Fix_IO.Put (Universal_Real + Fixed); New_Line;
    Dec_Fix_IO.Put (Universal_Real + Decimal_Fixed); New_Line;
end Type_Compatibility;
```

In this code, the universal integers 9 and Universal_Int are type compatible with types Integer and New_Int_Type. In other words, universal integers are implicitly converted to the required integer types, in this case, Integer or New_Int_Type. Similarly, the universal real numbers are implicitly converted to the required real type–Float, New_Float_Type, Fixed_Type, or Decimal_Fixed_Type. Implicit conversion is handy since literals and named numbers may be used without the programmer having to worry about explicit type conversion. Furthermore, when a universal real type is implicitly converted, the compiler ensures conversion to the precision required.

Universal types provide a kind of static "polymorphism." An object belonging to a universal type is compatible with every type in its class. In this context, the word "class" either refers to the class of integer types or real types. We shall develop the notion of type class in the next chapter on object-oriented programming.

---

## EXERCISES

1. Describe the main differences between subtypes and derived types.

2. Which of the following declarations are illegal?

```
declare
    A: constant := 5.2;
    B: constant Float := A;
    C: constant := B;
    D: constant := A - 4.9;
    E: Integer := 5;
    F: constant := E;
begin
    null;
end;
```

3. What is the main advantage of the declaration

```
Ounces_In_Ton: constant := 35_274;
```

over the declaration

```
Ounces_In_Ton: constant Integer := 35_274;
```

4. Which of the following statements result in an error?

```
declare
    type Derived_Type is new Integer;
    Derived: Derived_Type := 6;
    Int: Integer := 9;
begin
    Int := 5;
    Derived := 5;
    Int := Derived + 5;
    Derived := Int + 5;
    Derived := Derived_Type (Int) + 5;
end;
```

5. Explain the main advantage of the declaration

```
type Infrared is range 7E3..1E6; -- Angstroms
```

over the declaration

```
type Infrared is new Integer range 7E3..1E6; - Angstroms
```

6. Consider the following package specification:

```
package Math_Resources is
    type Degree is range 0 .. 360;
    function Sine (Angle: Degree) return Float;
    function Factorial (N: Positive) return Positive;
end Math_Resources;
```

Explain what is wrong with the following procedure that references Math_Resources:

```
with Math_Resources; use Math_Resources;
procedure Math is
    type Quadrant_I is new Degree range 0 .. 90;
    type Small_Positive is new Positive range 1 .. 7;
    Angle: Quadrant_I := 45;
    P: Small_Positive := 1;
    N: Positive := 5;
    F: Float;
begin
    N := Factorial (N);
    F := Sine (Angle);
    P := Factorial (P);
end Math;
```

7. What values (from 0 to 15) are being assigned to Unsigned:

```
declare
    type Unsigned_4_Bits is mod 16;
    Unsigned: Unsigned_4_Bits;
begin
    Unsigned := 16;
    Unsigned := Unsigned_4_Bits'Last;
```

```
Unsigned := Unsigned_4_Bits'Last + 1;
Unsigned := Unsigned_4_Bits'First;
Unsigned := Unsigned_4_bits'First - 2;
Unsigned := 40;
Unsigned := 2 * 9 + 5;
Unsigned := Unsigned_4_bits'Succ (Unsigned_4_bits'Last);
Unsigned := Unsigned_4_bits'Pred (Unsigned_4_bits'First);
end;
```

8. Which of the following values is *not* congruent to 3 modulo 8?

    a.  11
    b.  19
    c.  −5
    d.  35
    e.  −13
    f.  26

9. What values are being assigned to `Unsigned`? (Give answer in base 2.)

```
declare
    type Unsigned_8 is mod 256;
    Unsigned: Unsigned_8;
    A: Unsigned_8 := 2#1010_0111#;
    B: Unsigned_8 := 2#1110_0010#;
begin
    Unsigned := A and B;
    Unsigned := A xor B;
    Unsigned := A or B;
    Unsigned := not A and B;
    Unsigned := not (A and B);
    Unsigned := (A and B) + 7;
end;
```

10. Define a type suitable for monetary calculations that has a range of values from 0.00 to 1_000.00.

11. What is the range of values of type `Deficit`?

```
type Deficit is delta 0.01 digits 11;
```

12. Find the errors, if any, in the following code:

```
Get (N);    -- assume N belongs to type Integer
declare
    Dozen: constant Integer := 12;
    Bakers_Dozen: constant := Dozen + 1;
    Dynamic: constant Integer := N;
    More_Dynamic: constant := Dynamic + 1;

    type My_Int_Type is new Integer;
    My_Int: My_Int_Type := 5;

    Int: Integer := 3;
begin
```

```
        Int := Int + Dozen;
        Int := Int + Bakers_Dozen;
        My_Int := My_Int + Dozen;
        My_Int := My_Int + Bakers_Dozen;
        My_Int := Bakers_Dozen - 6;
    end;
```

13. Correct the errors, if any, in the following code:

```
type Ordinal is mod 4;
type Decimal is delta 0.1 digits 4;
package Ordinal_IO is new Ada.Text_IO.Integer (Ordinal);
package Decimal_IO is new Ada.Text_IO.Fixed (Decimal);
```

# Object-Oriented Programming

**Ada 95 ▶** **A**da supports object-oriented programming in an efficient and reliable manner. In object-oriented programming, instead of thinking of a program as a sequence of operations, think of a program as a collection of objects, plus operations performed on these objects. In well-designed object-oriented code, the objects typically mirror physical objects in the real world that they are meant to simulate, and the operations typically mirror physical operations that are performed on these physical objects. For example, objects could be real-world entities such a person, an automobile, or a disk drive. Operations on these objects could include such activities as checking a person's identification, opening or closing an automobile's fuel injection valve, or accessing a specified file on disk.

Sometimes objects are not physical objects in the real world but abstract entities such as a stack [first in, first out (FIFO)] data structure. In this case, operations include pushing values on the stack and popping values from the stack. (This chapter assumes that the reader has a basic understanding of object-oriented programming. If not, the reader may wish to read a book on this subject before tackling this chapter.)

In Ada, each kind of object is typically implemented as a type (data structure). Specific objects are instances of these types. An object's operations are implemented as procedures or functions. Typically related types, plus their operations, are encapsulated in a package. In other words, the public part of the package specification provides an abstract interface to types and their operations, while the private part of the package specification hides the implementation of the types. In turn, the package body hides the implementation of the operations. For example, the following `Stack` package (taken from Chapter 7) encapsulates the kind of object called `Stack_Type`:

```
package Stack is -- from Chapter 7
   type Stack_Type (Stack_Size: Natural) is limited private;
```

```
      procedure Push (S: in out Stack_Type; Item: in Integer);
      procedure Pop (S: in out Stack_Type; Item: out Integer);
         ...
   private
      -- implementation of Stack_Type goes here
      ...
   end Stack;

   package body Stack is
      -- implementation of Push and Pop go here
      ...
   end Stack;
```

Ada 83 is somewhat suited to object-oriented programming because, as we have just illustrated, through information hiding, it allows objects and their operations to be encapsulated in packages. Since Ada was first defined in 1983, however, additional ingredients have become important to object-oriented programming, such as class-wide operations and runtime dispatching. These ingredients have been added to Ada 95 , making Ada 95 a fully object-oriented language.

This chapter begins by covering inheritance and type extension. Inheritance enables a new type to implicitly acquire the structure, values, and operations of an existing type. Type extension allows a new type to extend its inherited structure without impacting existing types. Private tagged types and private extensions are then introduced, which allow data to be hidden. This chapter continues with class-wide types and class-wide operations. A class-wide type represents a collection of types having similar properties. A class-wide operation is an operation that applies to all types within a specified class. Next, runtime dispatching is discussed. Runtime dispatching occurs when an operation is passed a parameter value whose specific type is not known until runtime. Based on the specific type, the appropriate version of the operation is automatically dispatched (invoked). Runtime dispatching is followed by a section on comparing tags. Values of a class-wide type have an implicit discriminant called a "tag," which identifies its specific type within the class. These tag values can be compared with one another. This chapter then continues with multiple inheritance. In its most common interpretation, multiple inheritance allows a type to directly inherit the properties of two or more types. Although Ada does not directly support multiple inheritance, the effect of multiple inheritance can be achieved through other means. After multiple inheritance, this chapter covers abstract types and abstract subprograms. Abstract types and subprograms serve as a "blueprint" from which actual types and subprograms can be built. This chapter concludes with a section on controlled types. Controlled types are a special kind of abstract type that provide programmers with user-defined assignments and user-defined cleanup operations when objects cease to exist.

## INHERITANCE AND TYPE EXTENSION

In Chapter 9, we saw how hierarchical libraries support incremental development of code with minimal impact to previously existing code. Object-oriented programming also supports incremental development, but through the mechanism of inheritance. Inheritance enables a new type to implicitly acquire (inherit) the properties of an existing type without affecting the existing type.

Recall from Chapter 12 that a derived type inherits its parent's values, operations, and structure. In the following example, type `Age` inherits from its parent type, `Integer`, a scalar structure, the values 0 to 120, and all the predefined integer operations:

```
type Age is new Integer range 0..120;
    -- Age inherits scalar structure, values 0..120, and integer
    -- operations from its parent type, Integer
```

Also recall from Chapter 12 that, besides inheriting predefined operations, a derived type inherits user-defined operations declared in the same package specification as its parent type. These user-defined operations are either subprograms with parameters of the parent type, or, if a function, a result belonging to the parent type.

Inheritance also occurs as follows: If a type appears in the same list of declarations as its parent type, then it inherits its parent's subprograms. For a parent's subprogram to be inherited, however, it must be specified before the derived type wishing to inherit it. Thus, in the following code, the derived types B and C inherit, from A, procedures P and Q but not procedure R:

```
type A is... -- some type
procedure P (X: in A);
procedure Q (X: in A);

type B is new A;        -- inherits P and Q
procedure P (X: in B);  -- overrides inherited P with its own
                        -- version
procedure S (X: in B);  -- S does not apply to type A

type C is new B;        -- inherits P, Q, and S
procedure P (X: in C);  -- overrides inherited P with its own
                        -- version

procedure R (X: in A);  -- not inherited by types B or C since
                        -- declared after B and C are declared
```

In general, a derived type inherits its parent's "primitive" operations. Recall that primitive operations are those that are "tightly bound" to the type, being either implicitly or explicitly declared at the point of the type declaration. If an inherited primitive operation is inappropriate, it can be overridden with a different version. Thus, in the previous example, types B and C define their own version of the operation (procedure) P that overrides the inherited version. If the inherited primitive operations are incomplete, new operations can be added. Thus, in the previous example, type B adds the operation (procedure) S not shared by its parent type A.

So far we have seen how a derived type inherits the primitive operations of its parent type. But how do subprograms with access parameters serve as primitive operations? (Recall from Chapter 11 that an access parameter can be matched by an actual parameter of any access type with the same designated type.) The answer is that a subprogram with an access parameter is a primitive operation of the designated type (type of object pointed to), not of some access type. This means that a type derived from the designated type inherits the subprogram with the access parameter. Therefore, in the following code, type New_T is derived from T and thus inherits procedure A:

```
type T is range 1..5;
procedure A (V: access T); -- a primitive operation of T
   ...
type New_T is new T; -- inherits procedure A
```

Thus, access parameters allow the creation of subprograms that are passed pointer values, yet are considered primitive operations of the designated type.

As we have seen, inherited primitive operations can be overridden or new operations can be added. But what about the inherited structure? Can the inherited structure be extended or must it be taken, "as is," from the parent type? The answer is that an inherited structure can be extended if the parent type is a "tagged" type.

Tagged types are record types (or private types implemented as record types) that are declared with the keyword **tagged**. Types derived from a tagged type are implicitly tagged and can extend their inherited structure with additional record components. (The names of these additional components, however, cannot have the same names as those of the parent type.) This is known as "type extension." In the following example, the tagged type Basic_Pizza is extended by type Veggie_Pizza, which is itself extended by type Meat_Pizza:

```
-- assume component types have been previously defined
type Basic_Pizza is tagged
   record
       Cheese: Cheese_Type;
       Sauce: Sauce_Type;
   end record;

procedure Make_Pizza (Pie: Basic_Pizza) is
begin
   Add_Topping (Pie.Cheese);
   Add_Topping (Pie.Sauce);
      ...
end Make_Pizza;

type Veggie_Pizza is new Basic_Pizza with
   record
       -- Inherits Cheese and Sauce components
       Veggie: Veggie_Type;
   end record;

procedure Make_Pizza (Pie: Veggie_Pizza) is
begin
```

```
        -- use type conversion to
        -- add cheese and sauce
        Make_Pizza (Basic_Pizza(Pie));
        Add_Topping (Pie.Veggie);
    end Make_Pizza;

    type Meat_Pizza is new Veggie_Pizza with
        record
            -- Inherits Cheese, Sauce, and Veggie components
            Meat: Meat_Type;
            Hold_The_Anchovy: Boolean;
        end record;

    procedure Make_Pizza (Pie: Meat_Pizza) is
    begin
        Make_Pizza (Veggie_Pizza(Pie)); -- add cheese, sauce, veggie
        Add_Topping (Pie.Meat);
        If not Pie.Hold_The_Anchovy then
            Add_Topping (Anchovy);
        end if;
            . . .
    end Make_Pizza;
```

As illustrated, types derived from a tagged type must include the keyword **with**, followed by the added record components placed between the keywords **record** and **end record**. This syntax is required even if no extra components are added:

```
    type My_Kind_Of_Pizza is new Meat_Pizza with null record;
```

As a result of this requirement, a tagged type can always be identified by either the keyword **tagged** (if it is a root type) or by the keyword **with** (if it is derived from a tagged type). Note that the phrase **with null record** is an allowed shorthand for

```
        ...with
    record
        null;
    end record;
```

In the previous example, Veggie_Pizza inherits the Cheese and Sauce components from its parent type, Basic_Pizza, and adds the component Veggie. Type Meat_Pizza inherits the Cheese, Sauce, and Veggie components from its parent, Veggie_Pizza, and adds the components Meat and Hold_The_Anchovy. Therefore, as illustrated by the following aggregates, Mid_West_Pizza has two components, California_Pizza has three components, and Chicago_Pizza has five components:

```
    Mid_West_Pizza: Basic_Pizza :=
        (   Cheese => Mozzarella,
            Sauce  => Tomato );
```

```
California_Pizza: Veggie_Pizza :=
    (  Cheese => Goat_Cheese,      -- Inherited
       Sauce  => Tahini,           -- Inherited
       Veggie => Tofu );
California_Pizza: Meat_Pizza :=
    (  Cheese => Mozzarella,       -- Inherited
       Sauce  => Tomato,           -- Inherited
       Veggie => Bell_Pepper,      -- Inherited
       Meat   => Pepperoni,
       Hold_The_Anchovy => False );
```

In the preceding example, Veggie_Pizza and Meat_Pizza each have their own version of Make_Pizza, which overrides the inherited versions. Note that Make_Pizza uses type conversion to delegate processing of its inherited components to its ancestor. That is, Make_Pizza converts its parameter, Pie, to its parent type, then passes this converted parameter value to its parent's version of Make_Pizza. For instance, Veggie_Pizza's version of Make_Pizza converts its parameter Pie to type Basic_Pizza, then passes this converted parameter value to Basic_Pizza's version of Make_Pizza:

```
Make_Pizza (Basic_Pizza(Pie));
                        -- type conversion is used to delegate
                        -- processing of inherited components
                        -- to ancestor
```

After this call, only the Veggie component that has been added by Veggie_Pizza  needs to be processed. Similarly, Meat_Pizza's version of Make_Pizza converts its parameter, Pie, to Veggie_Pizza, then passes this converted parameter value to Veggie_Pizza's version of Make_Pizza. After Meat_Pizza's version of Make_Pizza calls its parent's version of Make_Pizza, only components that have been added by Meat_Pizza  need to be processed: Meat and Hold_The_Anchovy.

In our example, a parameter of type Meat_Pizza is converted to Veggie_Pizza, and a parameter of type Veggie_Pizza is converted to type Basic_Pizza. In both cases, type conversion is performed toward the tagged root type Basic_Pizza. Conversions towards the root type automatically "drop off" the appropriate extended components (but do not change the value's "tag" identifying its specific type). For tagged types, type conversion is only allowed in this direction. Conversion away from the tagged root type is illegal since the new components introduced through type extension would be left with undefined values. Thus, using the pizza types previously declared, type conversion can only take place toward Basic_Pizza:

```
California_Pizza := Veggie_Pizza (Chicago_Pizza);
    -- components Meat and Hold_The_Anchovy are dropped

Chicago_Pizza := Meat_Pizza (California_Pizza); -- illegal
```

```
Chicago_Pizza := ( California_Pizza with
                   Meat => Pepperoni,
                   Hold_The_Anchovy => False);
 -- OK; an extension aggregate (named notation)
```

Note that although type conversion cannot be used to assign `California_Pizza` to `Chicago_Pizza`, an extension aggregate can be used. Extension aggregates thus overcome the limitation of not being able to convert a type away from the root type. The extension aggregate in our example adds the missing `Meat` and `Hold_The_Anchovy` components to the values of `California_Pizza`. Once extended, this aggregate contains all the components of type `Meat_Pizza` and can, therefore, be assigned to `Chicago_Pizza`.

As the following example illustrates, the ancestor type in an extension aggregate (the type placed before the **with**) need not be the immediate ancestor (parent) of the target type, but can be any ancestor:

```
Chicago_Pizza := ( Mid_West_Pizza with
                   Veggie => Bell_Pepper,
                   Meat => Pepperoni,
                   Hold_The_Anchovy => False );
  -- extension aggregate using indirect ancestor
```

An extension aggregate is required even when there are no missing components and hence no extension. In such cases, a null extension must be used:

```
type My_Kind_Of_Pizza is new Meat_Pizza with null record;
My_Pizza: My_Kind_Of_Pizza := (Chicago_Pizza with null record);
```

The astute reader may have noticed that nested records or variant records could serve as an alternative to type extension. However, as we shall see momentarily, there are two advantages to using type extension over these alternatives. First, type extension is simple to implement and, as illustrated by the previous aggregates, each extended type has a simple structure. In contrast, the alternatives to type extension result in a complex nesting of records or **case** constructs. Second, type extension can be performed without requiring the existing type to be modified. For example, `Veggie_Pizza` extends `Basic_Pizza` without requiring any changes to `Basic_Pizza`. In contrast, the variant record alternative to type extension requires changes to existing code.

To illustrate the advantages of type extension, consider the first alternative to type extension: the nested record. A record containing the components of a basic pizza can be nested in a record containing the additional components for a veggie pizza, which in turn can be nested in a record containing the additional components for a meat pizza:

```
type Basic_Pizza is
   record
      Cheese: Cheese_Type;
```

```
            Sauce: Sauce_Type;
         end record;

      type Veggie_Pizza is
         record
            Basic: Basic_Pizza;
            Veggie: Veggie_Type;
         end record;

      type Meat_Pizza is
         record
            Vegetable: Veggie_Pizza;
            Meat: Meat_Type;
            Hold_The_Anchovy: Boolean;
         end record;
```

A disadvantage of this triply nested record is its complexity. As the following example illustrates, aggregate values are difficult to read:

```
Chicago_Pizza: Meat_Pizza :=
   (   Vegetable => (   Basic  => (   Cheese => Mozzarella,
                                      Sauce  => Tomato ),
                        Veggie => Bell_Pepper   ),
       Meat        => Pepperoni,
       Hold_The_Anchovy => False );
```

Note how much simpler the aggregate for `Chicago_Pizza` appears when type extension is used:

```
Chicago_Pizza: Meat_Pizza :=
   (   Cheese => Mozzarella,
       Sauce  => Tomato,
       Veggie => Bell_Pepper,
       Meat   => Pepperoni,
       Hold_The_Anchovy => False );
```

Also note that with type extension, nesting is avoided, so that all record components are equally accessible. Thus, to access the `Sauce` component of `Chicago_Pizza`, one simply writes

```
Chicago_Pizza.Sauce
```

instead of the complex expression required when nested records are used:

```
Chicago_Pizza.Vegetable.Basic.Sauce
```

The second alternative to type extension is the variant record. Keeping with our pizza example, a variant record can be defined whose discriminant is used to distinguish between the three kinds of pizzas:

```
type Pizza_Type is (Basic, Vegetable, Meat);
type Pizza (Kind: Pizza_Type) is -- correct, but complex
   record
       Cheese: Cheese_Type;
       Sauce: Sauce_Type;
       case Kind is
           when Basic =>
               null;
           when Vegetable | Meat =>
               Veggie: Veggie_Type;
           case Kind is
               when Meat =>
                   Meat: Meat_Type;
                   Hold_The_Anchovy: Boolean;
               when others => null;
           end case;
       end case;
   end record;
```

A disadvantage of this variant record, as with the nested record, is its complexity. Although this variant record type eliminates the need for nested records, it requires nested **case** constructs. (This nesting arises from the requirement that every value of the discriminant, Kind, must be covered in one and only one **when** clause.) To make matters worse, these nested **case** constructs may need to be repeated whenever records of this variant record type are processed. For example, the following version of Make_Pizza processes the variant record type Pizza and contains a **case** statement that reflects the structure of this variant record type:

```
procedure Make_Pizza (Pie: Pizza) is
begin
   Add_Topping (Pie.Cheese);
   Add_Topping (Pie.Sauce);
   case Pie.Kind is     -- reflects structure of variant record
       when Basic =>
           null;
       when Vegetable | Meat =>
           Add_Topping (Pie.Veggie);
           case Pie.Kind is
               when Meat =>
                   Add_Topping (Pie.Meat);
                   If not Pie.Hold_The_Anchovy then
                       Add_Topping (Anchovy);
                   end if;
               when others => null;
           end case;
   end case;
   ...
end Make_Pizza;
```

Compare this complex version of `Make_Pizza` to the previous versions that process extended types.

Besides the added complexity, another disadvantage of using variant records is that variants can only be added by modifying existing code. For example, to add a new kind of pizza, a new value needs to be added to `Pizza_Type`. Also, the **case** construct for type `Pizza`, as well as the **case** statement in `Make_Pizza`, must be updated.

In summary, the main advantages of using type extension instead of nested records or variant records are that code is simpler and extensions can be provided without impacting existing code.

Before ending this discussion of type extension, we will show one more way that a tagged type may extend its parent type: by adding new components that are discriminants. Recall from Chapter 5 that a record discriminant is considered one of the record's components. (Derived types shown in the previous chapter that introduce discriminants not belonging to their parent are not considered cases of type extension.) As the following code illustrates, new discriminants are normally used to control new components defined in the extended type:

```
type Window is tagged record...end record;

type Labeled_Window (Length: Natural ) is new Window with
    record
        Label: String (1..Length);
    end record;
```

Type `Labeled_Window` extends its inherited structure by adding two new components: the discriminant component `Length` and the regular component `Label`. Note that `Length` is used to set the length of the component `Label`.

Note that the parent type, `Window`, has no discriminant, but its derived type, `Labeled_Window`, has a discriminant. It is also possible for a parent type to have a discriminant but for its derived type to have none:

```
type Another_Window is new Labeled_Window
    with null record;
```

Finally, both a parent type and the derived type may have discriminants:

```
type Double_Labeled_Window (Length_1: Natural;
                            Length_2: Natural)
    is new Labeled_Window   (Length => Length_1) with
    record
        Label_2: String (1..Length_2);
    end record;
```

Note that, unlike the previous versions, `Double_Labeled_Window` does not inherit its parent's discriminant `Length`, although it does inherit the component `Label`. Thus, `Double_Labeled_Window` has the components `Label`; two discriminant components, `Length_1`, `Length_2`; and component `Label_2`. Note that the discriminant of the parent type, `Length`, is provided the value `Length_1`. The discriminant of the parent type must be provided some value (although the value could even be a literal such as 9). Thus, the discriminant `Length` always has the same value as the discriminant `Length_1`. In essence, `Length_1` is a redefinition of `Length`.

## PRIVATE TAGGED TYPES AND PRIVATE EXTENSIONS

Information hiding is supported through private types, but also through private tagged types and private extensions. Private tagged types and private extensions allow record components to be hidden from external clients. Tagged types that are private must be implemented as tagged record types in the private part of the package. In addition to private tagged types, one can declare private type extensions. A private extension must also be implemented in the private part of the package. In the following code, for example, type `Linear_Point` is a private tagged type, and types `Planar_Point` and `Spatial_Point` have private extensions:

```
package One_Dim is
    type Linear_Point is tagged private; -- private tagged type
    function Current_Position return Linear_Point;
        . . .
private
    type Linear_Point is tagged
        record
            X: Float;
        end record;
end One_Dim;

package One_Dim.Two_Dim is
    type Planar_Point is new Linear_Point with private;
        -- private extension
    function Current_Position return Planar_Point;
        . . .
private
    type Planar_Point is new Linear_Point with
        record
            Y: Float;
        end record;
end One_Dim.Two_Dim;

package One_Dim.Two_Dim.Three_Dim is
    type Spatial_Point is new Planar_Point with private;
        -- private extension
    function Current_Position return Spatial_Point;
        . . .
private
    type Spatial_Point is new Planar_Point with
        record
            Z: Float;
        end record;
end One_Dim.Two_Dim.Three_Dim;
```

The preceding code defines coordinates for a one-dimensional, two-dimensional, and three-dimensional space. A function, `Current_Position`, is defined that returns the position of a point in any of these spaces. Since `Linear_Point` is declared as a private tagged type, its components are hidden from external clients. Since types `Planar_Point` and `Spatial_Point` have private extensions, their components `Y` and `Z` are also hidden from external clients. Indeed, the extensions of a private type must also be private.

In Chapter 9, we learned how to create a hierarchy of library units through child units. In this chapter, we have seen how to create a hierarchy of types through type derivation. Well-structured object-oriented code is typically designed so that these two hierarchies coincide. As illustrated in the previous code, the hierarchies coincide by placing the root tagged type in a parent package and by placing the extended types in child packages. Specifically, the package declaring the extension of type `Linear_Point` is a child of the package declaring `Linear_Point`, and the package declaring the extension of type `Planar_Point` is a child of the package declaring `Planar_Point`. As discussed in Chapter 9, objects and types declared in the visible part of the parent package are automatically available to child packages. Items such as private extensions that are declared in the private part of a parent package are only available to the hidden parts of child packages.

## CLASS-WIDE TYPES AND CLASS-WIDE OPERATIONS

Ada supports three kinds of types: specific types, universal types, and class-wide types. Specific types cover a single type, whereas universal types and class-wide types cover many types. Universal types were covered in Chapter 12. Specific types were introduced in Chapter 1 and illustrated in succeeding chapters.

Recall that an object belonging to a universal type is compatible with objects of every type in its class. Thus, a named number or numeric literal belonging to the universal integer type is compatible with every type in the class of integer types, including types `Integer`, `Short_Integer`, `Long_Integer`, and all user-defined integer types. Similarly, a named number or numeric literal belonging to the universal real type is compatible with every type in the class of real types. (In addition to universal integer types and universal real types, Ada also defines a universal fixed point type.) Note that the word "class" is being used to designate the set of all integer types or the set of all real types. In general, a type class defines a group of types with similar properties and operations. If a type is in a certain class, then any type derived from it is also in that class. Thus, a type derived from an integer type must itself be an integer type, and a type derived from a floating point type must itself be a floating point type.

The concept of class-wide types builds off this idea of type class. Like universal types, a class-wide type covers all types within its class. However, unlike universal types, class-wide types can be created by the programmer. The programmer can create a class-wide type by deriving types from a tagged type. The tagged type, `T`, together with all types directly or indirectly derived from `T`, forms a class-wide type rooted at `T`. This class-wide type is denoted using the `Class` attribute as

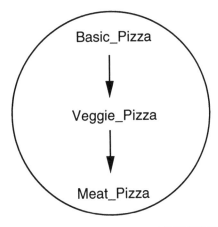

**Figure 13.1**   Basic_Pizza'Class.

`T'Class`. In our previous pizza example, `Basic_Pizza'Class` contains types `Basic_Pizza`, `Veggie_Pizza`, and `Meat_Pizza`, as shown in Figure 13.1.

As shown in Figure 13.2, class-wide types can contain many branches. Thus, `T'Class` contains types `T`, `A1`, `A2`, `A3`, `B1`, `B2`, `B3`, `C1`, and `D1`. Each of these tagged types forms its own class. Thus, `A1'Class` contains types `A1`, `B1`, `B2`, and `B3`. `A3'Class` contains types `A3`, `C1`, and `D1`. In fact, even types such as `D1` form the class `D1'Class`. Since no types are derived from `D1`, `D1'Class` only contains `D1`.

Since type `T` is a tagged type, all its derived types are tagged. Objects (variables or constants) of types within `T'Class` have an implicit discriminant, called a tag, which denotes the object's specific type within the class.

Objects of a class-wide type must be constrained to a specific type within their

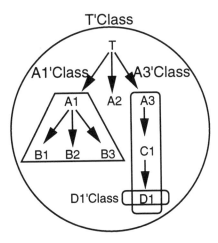

**Figure 13.2**   T'Class.

class. (Without this restriction, implementations would be inefficient, since an object's size could keep changing at runtime because the size of types in a class can vary without bounds.) In other words, an unconstrained object cannot be declared that is compatible with every type in a class. This is analogous to the way objects of an unconstrained array type must be constrained. Thus, the following declarations are illegal because they attempt to declare unconstrained objects:

```
-- cannot declare unconstrained objects
X: String;                        -- illegal
Y: T'Class;                       -- illegal

A: array (1..4) of String;    -- illegal
B: array (1..4) of T'Class;   -- illegal

type R is
   record
       A: String;                 -- illegal
   end record;
type S is
   record
       B: T'Class;             -- illegal
   end record;
```

Just as a string object may be constrained through initialization, an object of a tagged type may be constrained through initialization:

```
-- assume Str is a string variable and
-- V is a variable of a type in T'Class
X: String := Str;    -- OK; X'Range is set to Str'Range
Y: T'Class := V;     -- OK; Y's type is set to V's type
```

Whereas the string variable X is constrained to Str's index range, the class-wide object Y is constrained to V's tag, and thus, to the specific type that this tag denotes. (Unlike string variables that can alternatively be constrained with an index constraint, tagged objects cannot be similarly constrained since the tag is provided implicitly.) Once initialized, the variable Y must always belong to the same specific type to which the variable V belongs.

Although Ada does not allow unconstrained array objects or unconstrained class-wide objects, it does allow unconstrained formal subprogram parameters:

```
-- formal parameters can be unconstrained
procedure P (X: String);   -- OK
   -- X can be matched with a string of any index range
procedure Q (Y: T'Class);  -- OK
   -- Y can be matched with a variable of any type in T'Class
```

Whereas procedure P can be passed strings of any string index range, procedure Q can be passed values of any type within T'Class. Procedures such as Q that can operate on values of any type within a class are called class-wide operations.

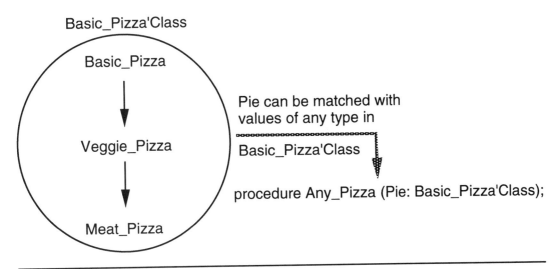

**Figure 13.3**   Class-wide operation.

In Figure 13.3, procedure `Any_Pizza` is a class-wide operation since its formal parameter `Pie` is declared to be of the class-wide type `Basic_Pizza'Class`. Because procedure `Any_Pizza` is a class-wide operation, it can be passed a value belonging to type `Basic_Pizza` or belonging to any of its derivative types:

```
Any_Pizza (Mid_West_Pizza);   -- OK
Any_Pizza (California_Pizza); -- OK
Any_Pizza (Chicago_Pizza);    -- OK
```

(Recall that `Mid_West_Pizza` belongs to type `Basic_Pizza`, `California_Pizza` belongs to type `Veggie_Pizza`, and `Chicago_Pizza` belongs to type `Meat_Pizza`.)

As previously mentioned, specific types have primitive operations that are inheritable. In contrast, class-wide types have no primitive operations, but enable users to declare their own class-wide operations using the `Class` attribute. In addition to declaring subprogram parameters as class-wide, programmers can declare functions that return a class-wide type:

```
procedure P (A: in T'Class);   -- can be passed values of any
                               -- type within T'Class
function F return T'Class;      -- can return values of any
                               -- type within T'Class
```

Whereas procedure `P` can be called with values of any type within `T'Class`, function `F` can return values of any type within `T'Class`. Since class-wide operations such as `P` and `F` apply to a class of related types, they eliminate the need to define separate, redundant operations for each specific type. In other words, class-wide operations factor out the differences between a collection of related types such that only their common properties are considered. As we shall see in the next section, class-wide operations are especially important because their formal parameters can be used to dynamically dispatch subprograms that have different implementations, depending on the specific type.

So far, we have seen how class-wide operations can be constructed using class-wide parameters or function results. Class-wide operations can also be constructed using access types to a class-wide type:

```
type Access_Pizzas is access Basic_Pizza'Class;
Pie_Pointer: Access_Pizzas;-- can point to values of any type
                           -- within Basic_Pizza'Class
```

As shown in Figure 13.4, Pie_Pointer can point to variables of type Basic_Pizza or to variables of any type derived from Basic_Pizza. If a linked data structure such as a linked list is created using Access_Pizzas, then items in the list can belong to different types within Basic_Pizza'Class. Furthermore, as the following code illustrates, an array of class-wide pointers can be declared whose components point to objects of different types within the class:

```
declare
    type Row_Of_Pies is array (Positive range <>) of
        Access_Pizzas;
    Row: Row_Of_Pies (1..3):=
        (   new Basic_Pizza'(Mid_West_Pizza),
            new Veggie_Pizza'(California_Pizza),
            new Meat_Pizza'(Chicago_Pizza));
begin

    . . .
    for Index in Row'Range loop
        Make_Pizza( Row(Index).all );
    end loop;
end;
```

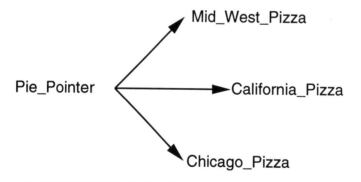

**Figure 13.4**  Class-wide pointer.

The array component `Row(1)` points to pizzas of type `Basic_Pizza`, `Row(2)` to pizzas of type `Veggie_Pizza`, and `Row(3)` to pizzas of type `Meat_Pizza`. Within the **for** loop, `Make_Pizza` is called with each one of these types of pizzas. The particular version of `Make_Pizza` that is dispatched (called) is determined at runtime by evaluating the type of pizza that `Row(Index)` is pointing to. Such runtime dispatching is the topic of the following section.

## RUNTIME DISPATCHING

Runtime dispatching (also called dynamic polymorphism) is one of the primary features of object-oriented programming. Runtime dispatching refers to the appropriate version of an operation being automatically invoked (dispatched) at runtime.

Ada supports runtime dispatching in an efficient and reliable manner. For efficiency, runtime dispatching does not severely slow down execution speed, and if not used, has no impact on execution speed. For reliability, compile time checks are made to guarantee that a call can never be made to a dispatching operation that does not exist. Furthermore, runtime dispatching does not render Ada less reliable by undermining strong typing. The class to which a tagged object belongs is known at compile time. The specific type within the class to which an object belongs is either determined at compile time or at runtime. The object's specific type is indicated by its associated tag. In fact, this tag provides the basis for runtime dispatching.

Runtime dispatching occurs when a subprogram with formal parameters of a specific tagged type is called with actual parameters of a class-wide type. For example, in the following code, the subprogram `Make_Pizza` is called with an actual parameter of the class-wide type `Basic_Pizza'Class`:

```
procedure Process_Pizza (Pie: Basic_Pizza'Class) is
begin
    . . .
    Make_Pizza (Pie);    -- dynamically dispatches to
    . . .                -- appropriate version of Make_Pizza
end Process_Pizza;
```

Recall that there are three versions of `Make_Pizza`, one for each of the types: `Basic_Pizza`, `Veggie_Pizza`, and `Meat_Pizza`. The particular version of `Make_Pizza` that `Process_Pizza` needs to invoke cannot be determined until `Process_Pizza` is invoked. For instance, if `Process_Pizza` is invoked with a value whose tag denotes type `Veggie_Pizza`, then `Process_Pizza` will invoke `Veggie_Pizza`'s version of `Make_Pizza`.

Thus, the value of `Pie`'s tag is used at runtime to determine which implementation of `Make_Pizza` to call. Parameters such as `Pie` that control which implementation of a subprogram is dispatched are called "controlling operands." Besides dispatching on an operand, it is also possible to dispatch on the result of a function call when the context determines the specific result type. Such a result is called a "controlling result." All controlling operands and results of a subprogram (if there are more than one) must have the same tag. If not, then a `Constraint_Error` is raised. (Without this restriction, it becomes unclear which type's primitive operation is being dispatched.) This rule, however, does not apply to the equality operator, "=", which returns `False` when the parameters have different tags. Thus, the two values can safely be compared without first checking that their tags are the same.

Not only must controlling operands and results of a call have the same tag; in order to avoid confusion, dynamically and statically determined tags cannot mix. All tags must either be statically or dynamically determined. For example, the following code is illegal since the tag of `Pie` is determined dynamically (at runtime), whereas the tag of `Veg` is determined statically (at compile time):

```
procedure Customize_Pizza (Pie: Basic_Pizza'Class) is
  procedure Add_Extra_Cheese (L: in Basic_Pizza'Class;
                              R: out Basic_Pizza'Class) is
    separate;
  Veg: Veggie_Pizza;
begin
    . . .
    Add_Extra_Cheese (Pie, Veg); -- illegal

end Customize_Pizza;
```

Of course, if `Pie` is converted to type `Veggie_Pizza`, then the tags of both parameters are statically determined and are the same. Thus, the following is legal:

```
Add_Extra_Cheese (Veggie_Pizza(Pie), Veg); -- OK
```

Type conversion could also have been used by `Process_Pizza` to avoid dynamic dispatching:

```
procedure Process_Pizza (Pie: Basic_Pizza'Class) is
begin
    . . .
    Make_Pizza (Veggie_Pizza(Pie));
        -- if Pie is of type Basic_Pizza, then a Constraint_Error
        -- is raised since types cannot be converted away
        -- from the root type Basic_Pizza
    . . .
end Process_Pizza;
```

Runtime dispatching does not occur since the class-wide parameter `Pie` is converted to the specific type `Veggie_Pizza` before `Make_Pizza` is invoked. In general, no runtime dispatching occurs when the type of parameter value being passed in is known at compile time. Thus, at compile time, it is determined that the implementation of `Make_Pizza` to be invoked is the one that handles parameters of type `Veggie_Pizza`.

When converting a parameter of a class-wide type to a specific type, care must be taken that conversion is not away from the root type. In our previous example, the formal class-wide parameter, `Pie`, can be matched with actual parameters of type `Veggie_Pizza` or `Meat_Pizza`. However, if `Pie` is matched with a value of type `Basic_Pizza`, then a `Constraint_Error` is raised when `Pie` is explicitly converted to type `Veggie_Pizza`. This is because conversion from `Basic_Pizza` to `Veggie_Pizza` is away from the root type.

## COMPARING TAGS

As we have seen, `Veggie_Pizza` and `Meat_Pizza` have their own versions of `Make_Pizza`, which overrides the version inherited from `Basic_Pizza`. The appropriate version of `Make_Pizza` can then be automatically dispatched, depending on the specific type that is passed to the formal parameter `Pie`. An alternative, although typically a less desirable approach, is to avoid dynamic dispatching by having only one version of `Basic_Pizza` that performs different processing, depending on `Pie`'s tag. This approach compares tag values using the `Tag` attribute or a membership test.

The `Tag` attribute returns the tag of a specific tagged type or an object of a tagged type. This attribute allows a tag of a class-wide object to be compared with a tag of another class-wide object or a tag of a specific type. For example, the following `Boolean` expression yields `False` since `Chicago_Pizza` and `California_Pizza` belong to different types and thus have different tag values:

```
Chicago_Pizza'Tag = California_Pizza'Tag -- yields False
```

Membership tests can be used to check whether a type is in a class-wide type. For example, the following membership test yields `True` since `Chicago_Pizza` is in the class-wide type `Basic_Pizza'Class`:

```
Chicago_Pizza in Basic_Pizza'Class -- True
```

The next membership test yields `False`, since `Mid_West_Pizza` is not in the class-wide type rooted at `Veggie_Pizza`:

```
Mid_West_Pizza in Veggie_Pizza'Class -- False
```

As previously mentioned, dynamic dispatching can be avoided by using a single version of `Make_Pizza` that performs different processing depending on the type of value passed to `Pie`:

```
procedure Make_Pizza (Pie: Basic_Pizza'Class) is
begin
    Add_Topping (Pie.Cheese);
    Add_Topping (Pie.Sauce);
    if Pie in Meat_Pizza'Class then
        Add_Topping (Pie.Meat);
        If not Pie.Hold_The_Anchovy then
            Add_Topping (Anchovy);
        end if;
```

```
        end if;
        if Pie in Veggie_Pizza'Class then
            Add_Topping (Pie.Veggie);
        end if;
    end Make_Pizza;
```

The main problem with this nonobject-oriented approach is that the introduction of new pizza types would require changes to `Make_Pizza`. By taking the object-oriented dispatching approach, new type extensions can be introduced without the need to update previous versions of `Make_Pizza`.

## MULTIPLE INHERITANCE

Unlike some object-oriented languages, Ada does not directly support multiple inheritance. In other words, Ada does not allow a type to have more than one parent type whose properties it inherits. Each type can only have a single parent. Multiple inheritance is not directly supported because it would make Ada's type model very complex and would significantly slow down program execution speed.

Although Ada does not directly support multiple inheritance, the effects of multiple inheritance can be achieved using generics or access discriminants. The following discussion is a brief introduction. Readers planning to implement this special feature should consult the *Ada 95 Rationale*.

There are different varieties of multiple inheritance. Here, we deal with the common notion of "mix-in" types, which inherit the properties or two or more types. (Other varieties of multiple inheritance can also be implemented in Ada.) For mix-in types, one can use generic formal tagged type parameters:

```
    type T is tagged private;
```

Generics with this kind of formal parameter can be only be instantiated with tagged types.

To illustrate how generics can provide the functionality of multiple inheritance, suppose that various tagged types need to be extended with a time stamp. A generic can be written that adds this extension to any tagged type that is passed to it:

```
with Ada.Calendar;
generic
    type Any_Tagged_Type is tagged private;
package Add_Time_Stamp is
    type Time_Stamp is new Any_Tagged_Type with private;
    procedure Stamp_It (Moment: in out Time_Stamp);
private
    type Time_Stamp is new Any_Tagged_Type with
        record
            Stamp: Ada.Calendar.Time;
        end record;
end Add_Time_Stamp;
```

```
package body Add_Time_Stamp is
   procedure Stamp_It (Moment: in out Time_Stamp) is
   begin
      Moment.Stamp := Ada.Calendar.Clock;
   end Stamp_It;
end Add_Time_Stamp;
```

The time stamp is made using the services of package Ada.Calendar. The values of type Time represent points of time, and the function Clock returns the time of day as a value of type Time. (We will return to package Calendar in Chapter 15.)

The following procedure instantiates the generic package Add_Time_Stamp:

```
with Add_Time_Stamp;
procedure Schedule is
   type Basic_Appointment is tagged
      record
         With_Whom: Person; -- assume Person previously declared
      end record;
   -- Basic_Appointment operations go here
      ...
   type Interview_Appointment is new Basic_Appointment with
      record
        Company: Companies;  -- assume companies previously
                             -- declared
      end record;
   -- Interview_Appointment operations go here
      ...

   package Appointment_Info is new Add_Time_Stamp
      (Any_Tagged_Type => Interview_Appointment);
      -- This adds a time stamp to type Interview_Appointment
   My_Interview: Appointment_Info.Time_Stamp;
      ...
begin
   Appointment_Info.Stamp_It (My_Interview);
   ...
end Schedule;
```

Objects of type Appointment_Info.Time_Stamp inherit the properties of two types: Interview_Appointment and Time_Stamp.

In addition to using generic formal tagged types for multiple inheritance, programmers can use record types with access discriminants:

```
type Mix_In; -- incomplete type definition
type First_Component (A: access Mix_In) is limited
   record...end record;
type Second_Component (B: access Mix_In) is limited
   record...end record;
type Mix_In is
```

```
record
    First: First_Component (A => Mix_In'Access);
    Second: Second_Component (B => Mix_In'Access);
end record;
```

Note that types `First_Component` and `Second_Component` are declared to be limited, which makes type `Mix_In` also limited. As illustrated, limited record types are allowed to contain access discriminants that are analogous to subprogram access parameters, discussed in Chapter 11. Access discriminants A and B are declared using the keyword **access**. The discriminants A and B are constrained to `Mix_In'Access`. Thus, components `First` and `Second` refer back to the enclosing record `Mix_In`. Objects of type `Mix_In`, therefore, inherit the properties of types `First_Component` and `Second_Component` that are accessed through the components of type `Mix_In`.

## ABSTRACT TYPES AND ABSTRACT SUBPROGRAMS

Abstract types and abstract subprograms serve as a "blueprint" from which actual types and subprograms are built. (Do not confuse abstract types with the very different notion of abstract data types, which Ada implements as private types.) This blueprint determines which operations go with which type, but does not specify how these operations or types are to be implemented. The implementation is up to those using the blueprint. Consider, for example, the following package that contains the abstract type `Point` and the abstract subprogram `Current_Position`:

```
-- This package serves as a blueprint for building derivations
package Base_Space is
    type Point is abstract tagged null record; -- Abstract type
        -- Nothing can be declared as type Point
    function Current_Position return Point is abstract;
        -- Abstract subprogram that has no body and cannot be
        -- called
end Base_Space;
```

Only abstract types such as `Point` can have abstract subprograms such as `Current_Position`. Type `Point` cannot have components, and objects of type `Point` cannot be declared or allocated. Function `Current_Position` cannot have a body and can never be invoked. (Also, since abstract subprograms cannot be invoked, they can never be mistakenly dispatched.)

Even though package `Base_Space` contains no implementations of its abstract types and abstract subprograms, `Current_Position` is nevertheless a primitive operation of type `Point` and therefore is inherited by types derived from type `Point`. Therefore, all types derived from an abstract type such as `Point` provide actual components and *must* override all of the inherited abstract operations with specific implementations:

```
package Base_Space.Space is
    type Linear_Point is new Point with
```

```
      record
          X: Float;
      end record;
   function Current_Position return Linear_Point; -- Required

   type Planar_Point is new Linear_Point with
      record
          Y: Float;
      end record;
   function Current_Position return Planar_Point;


   type Spatial_Point is new Planar_Point with
      record
          Z: Float;
      end record;
   function Current_Position return Spatial_Point;


end Base_Space.Space;
```

Abstract operations are useful because they have no implementations, yet define the primitive operations which must exist for all objects in a class of types. For the root type, implementations of the primitive operations often do not make sense. (Even if the implementation does make sense for the root type, it might not make sense for every type derived from this root type.) For example, in package Base_Space, no meaningful implementation can be given to the Current_Position function defined for the type Point in a "zero-dimensional" space. If a meaningless operation were provided, it would be inherited by all the derivative types that failed to override it. Abstract operations, however, do not provide any implementation and therefore must always be overridden.

## CONTROLLED TYPES

In practically every program, objects are declared or allocated, assigned values, and destroyed. Usually these operations work as desired and little thought is given to their inner workings. In special cases, however, programmers need to control these operations. Controlled types provide this needed control.

Two kinds of controlled types are defined in the package Ada.Finalization: Controlled and Limited_Controlled. The difference between these two abstract private types is that, as the name implies, Limited_Controlled is a limited type. This means that objects of such types cannot be assigned to one another or tested for equality.

Types Controlled and Limited_Controlled each have a version of procedures Initialize and Finalize. In addition, type Controlled has procedure Adjust.

Procedure Initialize has a single **in out** parameter. Immediately after an object of type Controlled or Limited_Controlled is declared or allocated, the Initialize procedure is automatically called with that object as a parameter. Procedure Initialize has a null, "do-nothing," body. Therefore, procedure Initialize should only be overridden when special processing needs to be performed as an object is created.

Procedure Finalize also has a single **in out** parameter. Just before an object ceases to exist, the procedure Finalize is automatically called with that object as a parameter. (An object ceases to exist when leaving its scope or upon deallocation.) Procedure Finalize has a null body and should only be overridden when special processing needs to be performed when an object ceases to exist.

Procedure Adjust applies to copy or assignment operations. Since such operations are not available to types derived from Limited_Controlled, procedure Adjust is only provided for type Controlled. Procedure Adjust has a single **in out** parameter. When assigning one object to another, Finalize is automatically called with the target object as a parameter (the object to the left of an assignment operator). The source object is copied, and then Adjust is automatically called with the updated target object as a parameter. Procedure Adjust has a null body and should only be overridden when special processing needs to be performed during copy or assignment operations.

As mentioned throughout the previous discussion, calls to Initialize, Finalize, and Adjust occur automatically, not explicitly, in the code. The following block illustrates how these three procedures are automatically called as the variable N is created, assigned a new value, and then destroyed:

```
-- assume T is derived from type Controlled
declare
   -- N is created
   N: T;                 -- Initialize (N)
begin
   N := New_Value;  -- Finalize(N), copy New_Value, Adjust (N)
end;                   -- Finalize(N);
-- N is destroyed
```

The object N is created when its declaration is elaborated. After N is created, procedure Initialize is automatically called with N as a parameter. (Procedure Initialize is not called if N is explicitly initialized in the code.) This procedure is defined by the programmer to provide automatic initialization of objects of type T. (Assume that type T is derived from the abstract type Controlled.) Before N is assigned a New_Value, procedure Finalize is automatically called with N as a parameter. Procedure Finalize is defined by the programmer to tidy up before the old value of N is overwritten and thus destroyed. After New_Value is assigned to N, procedure Adjust is automatically called with the updated value of N as a parameter. Procedure Adjust is defined by the programmer to do whatever is needed for the new value of N. When the end of the block statement is reached, procedure Finalize is called once again before N is destroyed. (The finalize procedure is called whenever leaving the scope of an object. In addition to leaving a block statement, as shown above, the scope of an object may be exited with a **return** statement or exception.)

There are other ways that objects are created, replicated, or destroyed, which are not shown in the previous example. For instance, the Adjust procedure is automatically called when returning from a function call. Specifically, Adjust is automatically called with the return value before Finalize is called as a result of leaving the function body. Procedure Finalize is invoked with the return value when the statement or declaration containing the function call completes.

As we have seen, the abstract types Controlled and Limited_Controlled have subprograms: Initialize and Finalize. In addition, type Controlled has procedure Adjust. Let us now explain how to override these subprograms and create code where these overridden subprograms are automatically invoked.

Controlled types are derived from the tagged abstract types Controlled and Limited_Controlled, which are defined in the package Ada.Finalization. Controlled types are controlled through subprograms that override the inherited procedures Initialize, Adjust, and Finalize. The following package uses a controlled type to maintain "reference counts":

```ada
with Ada.Finalization;
package Reference_Counts is
    type Audited is new Ada.Finalization.Controlled
        with null record;

    -- override inherited subprograms
    procedure Initialize (Object: in out Audited);
    procedure Adjust (Object: in out Audited);
    procedure Finalize (Object: in out Audited);

    -- returns the current reference count
    function Current_Count return Natural;
end Reference_Counts;

package body Reference_Counts is
    Instance: Natural := 0;

    procedure Initialize (Object: in out Audited) is
    begin
        Instance := 1;
    end Initialize;

    procedure Adjust (Object: in out Audited) is
    begin
        Instance := Instance + 1;
    end Duplicate;

    procedure Finalize (Object: in out Audited) is
    begin
        Instance := Instance - 1;
    end Finalize;
```

```
      function Current_Count return Natural is
      begin
         return Instance;
      end Current_Count;
   end Reference_Counts;
```

Type `Audited` extends the abstract type `Controlled` and therefore inherits the subprograms `Initialize`, `Adjust`, and `Finalize`. These three subprograms are then overridden with versions that modify the value of `Instance`. `Initialize` sets `Instance` to 1, `Adjust` increments it, and `Finalize` decrements it. The value of `Instance` thus reflects the number of times objects of type `Audited` are referenced. This value is made available through function `Current_Count`.

The next example illustrates how the `Ada.Finalization` package can be used to create strings of variable length:

```
with Ada.Finalization; use Ada;
package String_Support is
   type Variable_Length_Strings (Max_Length: Natural := 0)
      is new Finalization.Controlled with private;
   procedure Put (Str: in Variable_Length_Strings);
   -- other operations on Variable_Length_Strings go here
private
   -- these procedures are never explicitly called
   procedure Initialize (Str: in out
      Variable_Length_Strings);
   procedure Finalize (Str: in out
      Variable_Length_Strings);
   procedure Adjust (Str: in out
      Variable_Length_Strings);
   type String_Pointer is access String;
   type Variable_Length_Strings (Max_Length: Natural := 0)
      is new Finalization.Controlled with
   record
      Buffer: String_Pointer;
   end record;
end String_Support;


with Ada.Unchecked_Deallocation, Ada.Text_IO;
package body String_Support is

   procedure Free is new Unchecked_Deallocation (String,
      String_Pointer);

   procedure Initialize (Str: in out
      Variable_Length_Strings) is
   begin
      if Str.Max_Length > 0 then
         Str.Buffer := new String (1..Str.Max_Length);
      end if;
   end Initialize;
```

```
procedure Finalize (Str: in out
    Variable_Length_Strings) is
begin
    Free (Str.Buffer);
end Finalize;

procedure Adjust (Str: in out Variable_Length_Strings) is
begin
    Str.Buffer := new String'(Str.Buffer.all);
end Adjust;

procedure Put (Str: in Variable_Length_Strings) is
begin
    Put (Str.Buffer.all);
end Put;

end String_Support;
```

Note that the specifications of `Initialize`, `Finalize`, and `Adjust` are placed in the private part of the package specification. This guarantees that they will never be directly called, but still allows them to be implicitly called. Package `String_Support` implements variable length strings with a variant record consisting of a discriminant, `Max_Length`, and a pointer, `Buffer`, that points to a dynamically allocated string. The discriminant is used to set the maximum size of the string.

Procedure `Initialize` dynamically allocates a string of the maximum length. Procedure `Finalize` frees memory that was allocated for the string. To understand how procedure `Adjust` works, consider the following code:

```
A, B: String_Support.Variable_Length_Strings
    (Max_Length => 9);
    . . .
A := B;
```

Had procedure `Adjust` not been provided, then A and B would both be pointing to the same string. This is undersirable since if A changes the contents of the string, B would be impacted and vice versa. Procedure `Adjust` eliminates this problem by having A point to a copy of the string that B points to.

In the next chapter, we will examine the resources provided by the `Ada.Text_IO` package. In addition, we will examine other standardized input/output packages that are used for file manipulation.

## EXERCISES

1. Which assignments are illegal?

```
procedure Demo is
    type A is range 0..99;
    function F1 return A is separate;
    function F2 (U: A) return Boolean is separate;
```

```
    procedure P1 (W: in A) is separate;
    procedure Q1 (X: access A) is separate;

    type New_A is new A range 0..5;
    type New_A_Access is access New_A;
    procedure P2 (Y: in A) is separate;
    function F1 return New_A is separate;
    procedure P3 (Z: in New_A) is separate;
    OA: A := 5;
    NA: New_A := 0;
    Bool: Boolean;
    Ptr: New_A_Access := new New_A'(0);
begin
    OA := F1;
    NA := F1;
    Bool := F2 (OA);
    Bool := F2 (NA);
    P1 (NA);
    P1 (OA);
    P3 (NA);
    P3 (OA);
    P2 (NA);
    P2 (OA);
    Q1 (Ptr);
end Demo;
```

2. Which of the following type conversions will raise a `Constraint_Error`?

```
declare
    type Linear_Point is tagged
        record
            X: Float;
        end record;

    type Planar_Point is new Linear_Point with
        record
            Y: Float;
        end record;

    type Spatial_Point is new Planar_Point with
        record
            Z: Float;
        end record;

    On_Line: Linear_Point := (X => 1.2);
    On_Plane: Planar_Point := (X => 3.2, Y => 5.8);
    In_Space: Spatial_Point := (X => 2.6, Y => 8.9, Z => 2.1);
begin
    On_Line := Linear_Point (On_Plane);
    In_Space := Spatial_Point (On_Plane);
    On_Line := Linear_Point (In_Space);
    On_Plane := Planar_Point (On_Line);
end;
```

3. Replace the improper type conversions of the previous exercise using extension aggregates.

4. Consider the following records that contain redundant record components:

```
-- assume component types were previously declared
type Phonograph_Recording is
    record
        Music: Music_Type;
        Year_Recorded: Year;
        Instrumental: Boolean;
        Quality: Evaluation_Type;
        Scratched: Boolean;
    end record;

type Cassette_Recording is
    record
        Music: Music_type;
        Year_Recorded: Year;
        Instrumental: Boolean;
        Quality: Evaluation_Type;
        Noise_Reduction: Boolean;
    end record;

type Compact_Disk_Recording is
    record
        Music: Music_type;
        Year_Recorded: Year;
        Instrumental: Boolean;
        Quality: Evaluation_Type;
        Digitally_Recorded: Boolean;
    end record;
```

Eliminate the redundancy in the previous records by using nested records, then using variant records, and finally, by using type extensions.

5. Rewrite the following code using type extensions instead of a variant record:

```
package Business is
    type Employee is
        record
            ID: String (1..5) := (others => 'O');
            Name: String (1..20) := (others => ' ');
        end record;
    type Sizes is (Small, Medium, Large);

    type Software_House (Size: Sizes := Small) is
        record
            Lead_Programmer: Employee;
            case Size is
                when Small =>
```

```
                        null;
               when Medium | Large =>
                   President: Employee;
                   Project_Engineer: Employee;
                   Marketing_Analyst: Employee;
                   case Size is
                       when Large =>
                           Vice_President: Employee;
                           System_Engineer: Employee;
                       when others =>
                           null;
                   end case;
           end case;
       end record;

   procedure Output_Key_Personnel (Company: Software_House);

end Business;

with Ada.Text_IO; use Ada.Text_IO;
package body Business is
   procedure Output_Key_Personnel (Company: Software_House) is
   begin
       Put ("Lead programmer: ");
       Put (Company.Lead_Programmer.Name); New_Line;
       case Company.Size is
           when Small =>
               null;
           when Medium | Large =>
               Put ("President: ");
               Put (Company.President.Name); New_Line;
               Put ("Project engineer: ");
               Put (Company.Project_Engineer.Name); New_Line;
               Put ("Marketing Analyst: ");
               Put (Company.Marketing_Analyst.Name); New_Line;
               case Size is
                   when Large =>
                       Put ("Vice president: ");
                       Put (Company.Vice_President.Name);
                       New_Line;
                       Put ("System engineer: ");
                       Put (Company.System_Engineer.Name);
                       New_Line;
                   when others => null;
               end case;
       end case;
   end Output_Key_Personnel;
end Business;
```

6. Which version of the code in the previous exercise is easier to modify? Why?

7. In your solution to Exercise 5, illustrate how the proper version of procedure `Output_Key_Personnel` can be dispatched.

8. Replace the following code using type extensions instead of a variant record:

```
package Music is
    -- Supporting types go here
    type Recording (Device: Recording_Medium) is
        record
            Title: Title_Type;
            Music: Music_Type;
            Year_Recorded: Year;
            case Device is
                when Phonograph_Record =>
                    Speed: Speed_Type;
                    Scratched: Boolean;
                when Cassette =>
                    Length: Length_Type;
                    Tape: Tape_Type;
                    Noise_Reduction: Boolean;
                when Compact_Disk =>
                    null;
            end case;
        end record;
    procedure Play (Tune: in Recording);
end Music;


package body Music is
    procedure Play (Tune: in Recording) is
    begin
        Retrieve (Tune.Title); -- assume previously defined
        case Tune.Device is
            when Phonograph_Record =>
                Activate_Phono (Tune.Speed);
                if Tune.Scratched then
                    Set_Hi_Filter;
                end if;
            when Cassette =>
                Activate_Cassette (Tune.Tape);
                if Tune.Noise_Reduction then
                    Set_Dolby;
                end if;
            when Compact_Disk =>
                Activate_Compact_Disk;
        end case;
    end Play;
end Music;
```

9. In your solution to Exercise 8, illustrate how the proper version of procedure `Play` can be dispatched.

10. Explain the differences between the following declarations. Assuming that
    T is a tagged type, are all of these declarations legal?
    a. **procedure** P (X: **access** T);
    b. **procedure** P (X: **access** T'Class);
    c. **type** T_Class **is access** T'Class;
       **procedure** P (X: T_Class);

11. Write a linked list package that links together records of different tagged
    types.

12. Write the body of the following package:

```
package Math is
    type Rectangle is tagged
        record
            Length: Float;
            Width: Float;
        end record;
    function Interior_Space (R: in Rectangle) return Float;

    type Cuboid is new Rectangle with
        record
            Height: Float;
        end record;
    function Interior_Space (C: in Cuboid) return Float;
end Math;
```

Have the Interior_Space function for Cuboid call Interior_Space
(Rectangle(C)) instead of calculating C.Length * C.Width.

# Input/Output

**C**omputers process numbers and manipulate textual information at enormous speeds and with great accuracy. For computers to be useful, however, they must be able to communicate this information with the outside world. Data must be input to the computer and output from the computer. Such input/output (I/O) operations are the topic of this chapter.

I/O operations are not intrinsic to the Ada language. In other words, there are no built-in features of Ada that handle I/O. Instead, all I/O is handled through the resources contained in packages. Every Ada compiler, for instance, must supply a predefined `Ada.Text_IO` package that contains our familiar I/O procedures `Put`, `New_Line`, and `Get`.

**Ada 95 ▶** In this chapter, we will primarily discuss the contents of three standard predefined I/O packages: `Text_IO`, `Sequential_IO`, and `Direct_IO`. These I/O packages are children of package `Ada`. Package `Ada` is practically empty but is an "umbrella" (the parent package) for most of Ada's predefined packages. Since Ada 83 does not provide package `Ada` (or even support the parent package mechanism), for upward compatibility of Ada 83 with Ada 95, `Ada.Text_IO` has been renamed at the library level to `Text_IO`. Similarly, `Ada.Sequential_IO` has been renamed to `Sequential_IO`, and `Ada.Direct_IO` to `Direct_IO`. Therefore, when listing these packages in a **with** clause, the `Ada` prefix is optional:

```
with Text_IO, Sequential_IO, Direct_IO;
-- equivalent to:
-- with Ada.Text_IO, Ada.Sequential_IO, Ada.Direct_IO;
```

**Ada 95 ▶** Package `Text_IO` is a nongeneric package, although it contains six generic packages: `Integer_IO`, `Modular_IO`, `Float_IO`, `Fixed_IO`, `Decimal_IO`, and `Enumeration_IO`. (Packages `Modular_IO` and `Decimal_IO` are new to Ada 95.) Packages `Sequential_IO` and `Direct_IO` are generic packages, and must, therefore, be instantiated with a data type before I/O can be performed. After the discussion of these packages, we will explore the Ada.IO_Exceptions package, which contains the exceptions that may be raised during I/O operations. The chapter will conclude with a section on other I/O support.

## TEXT_IO PACKAGE

**Ada 95** ▶ The Text_IO package is used to input and output human readable text consisting of strings and characters. The Text_IO package also contains generic packages that are used to input and output integers, modular integers, floating point numbers, fixed point numbers, decimal fixed point numbers, and values belonging to enumeration types. The structure of the Text_IO package is shown in Figure 14.1. This package is the largest predefined I/O package. Many of its I/O services will be discussed for the first time in this chapter. Fortunately, some of the generic packages within Text_IO do not need to be separately discussed because they are practically identical to other generic packages. In particular, the generic package Modular_IO, which is used for modular integer I/O, is practically identical to package Integer_IO. In addition, Fixed_IO, which is used for fixed point I/O, and Decimal_IO, which is used for decimal fixed I/O, are practically identical to Float_IO. Therefore, these three packages are only briefly mentioned. However, the most commonly used packages, Integer_IO and Float_IO, are covered in detail.

Throughout this book, we have performed basic I/O operations using procedures such as Put and Get from the Text_IO package. By examining the Text_IO package and its nested generic packages, you will observe that Put and Get have many overloaded versions. There are 22 different overloaded Put procedures and 22 different overloaded Get procedures! In addition, these overloaded procedures have parameters that we have not yet discussed. Many of these parameters can be used for formatting I/O. Formatting I/O means specifying the physical layout of the data to be input or output. Formatted output is often used to produce visually pleasing reports. In such reports, numbers typically line up in vertical columns, floating point numbers have a set number of digits to the right of their decimal points, headers appear at specific lines and columns, and so on. Formatted input specifies the columns from which data is to be read by the computer. For example, for a particular input, columns 1 through 9 might contain social security numbers; columns 10 through 21, telephone numbers; and so on.

In addition to formatting I/O, many of the overloaded versions of Put and Get have a parameter that directs input and output to and from files rather than to and from the standard I/O device. (We have been assuming that the standard I/O device consists of a keyboard for inputting information and a video screen for outputting information.) A file consists of a collection of data, typically on a magnetic disk. Large amounts of data can be stored in files over long periods of time and can be read or updated, as needed.

We will begin by discussing the Text_IO services for formatting I/O. We will then discuss the Text_IO services for handling file I/O.

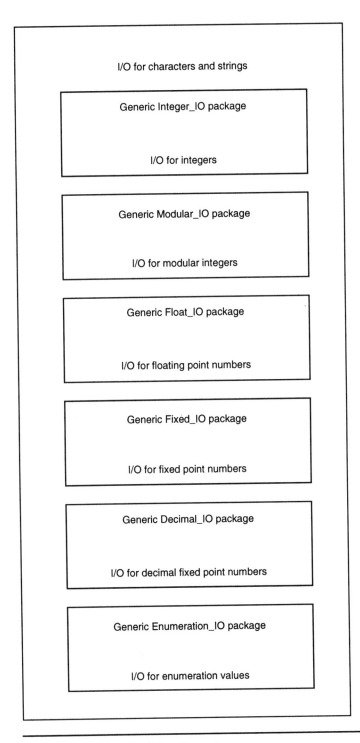

I/O for characters and strings

Generic Integer_IO package

I/O for integers

Generic Modular_IO package

I/O for modular integers

Generic Float_IO package

I/O for floating point numbers

Generic Fixed_IO package

I/O for fixed point numbers

Generic Decimal_IO package

I/O for decimal fixed point numbers

Generic Enumeration_IO package

I/O for enumeration values

**Figure 14.1** Structure of Text_IO package.

## Formatting I/O

The `Text_IO` package provides many services for formatting I/O. We will first discuss some of the overloaded `Put` and `Get` procedures. We will then cover `Put_Line` and `Get_Line`. Finally, we will explore controlling columns, lines, and pages.

**Ada 95** ▶  *PUT Procedures*  Out of the 22 overloaded `Put` procedures, 8 output to the standard output device. These 8 procedures output characters, strings, integers, modular integers, floating point numbers, fixed point numbers, decimal fixed point numbers, and enumeration values. Two of these 8 `Put` procedures are contained within the `Text_IO` package, outside of any nested generic packages. These 2 `Put` procedures output characters and strings:

```
-- assume Text_IO is visible
Put (Item => 'A');      -- outputs A (the character)
Put (Item => "Ada");    -- outputs Ada (the string)
```

Both these procedure calls employ named notation using the formal parameter `Item`.

Now let us consider the `Put` procedures contained in the generic packages. When outputting integers to the standard I/O device, the `Put` procedure contained in the generic `Integer_IO` package is used. Since this `Put` procedure is placed within a generic package, its instance (instantiated copy) is only available when the `Integer_IO` package is instantiated with some integer type parameter. Consider, for example, when the `Integer_IO` package is instantiated with a derived integer type, `Tiny_Positive`:

```
type Tiny_Positive is new Positive range 0 .. 100;
-- assumes that Text_IO is visible
package Pos_IO is new Ada.Text_IO.Integer_IO (Tiny_Positive);
```

This instantiation of `Integer_IO` creates an instance of the `Put` procedure for objects of type `Tiny_Positive`. Each instantiation of the `Integer_IO` package creates another overloaded instance of the `Put` procedure. For example, the following instantiation creates another instance of `Put`:

```
package Int_IO is new Ada.Text_IO.Integer_IO (Integer);
```

This new instance of `Put` is just like the preceding one but applies to objects of type `Integer` rather than to objects of type `Tiny_Positive`. As shown in the following code, each of these two newly created `Put` procedures can only output objects of the appropriate integer type:

```
with Ada.Text_IO; use Ada.Text_IO;
procedure Output is

   type Tiny_Positive is new Positive range 0 .. 100;
   package Pos_IO is new Integer_IO (Tiny_Positive);
   package Int_IO is new Integer_IO (Integer);
```

```
      -- there are two instances of Put: one for objects of type
      -- Tiny_Positive and one for objects of type Integer

      Pos: Tiny_Positive := 1;
      Int: Integer := -2;

begin

      Pos_IO.Put (Pos);    -- outputs 1
      Int_IO.Put (Int);    -- outputs -2
      Pos_IO.Put (Int);    -- error; parameter of wrong type

end Output;
```

In this example, each `Put` procedure is called with a single parameter. `Put` may also be called with two additional parameters , which have the formal parameter names `Width` and `Base`. These optional parameters specify the field width and number base. `Width` establishes the minimum number of spaces (columns) allotted to the outputted integer. If the integer fits in the allotted space with room to spare, then it is placed at the right end of the field, and the extra space is padded with blanks. Whenever columns of integers are required to line up on the right side, the width must be sufficient to accommodate all the integers being output. For negative integers, this includes an extra space for a minus signs. If the integer does not fit in the specified width, then the minimum number of spaces needed to output the integer is used. To guarantee that only as many spaces are used as needed, specify a field width of $0$. Setting the field width to $0$ is especially useful when an integer is embedded within text, because no extraneous spaces will precede the integer when it is output:

```
      -- assume Ada.Text_IO and needed instances of
      -- generic packages are visible
      Put ("Johnny is ");
      Put (Item => 8, Width => 0);
      Put (" years old.");
```

These three `Put` statements output

```
      Johnny is 8 years old.
```

If the width is not specified, the default width is used, resulting in an undesirable format such as the following:

```
      Johnny is           8 years old.
```

Within the `Integer_IO` package, the default for `Width` is `Num'Width`. `Num` is the name of `Integer_IO`'s formal generic parameter:

```
      type Num is range <>;
```

Num thus takes the integer type used to instantiate the Integer_IO package, and the attribute Width (not to be confused with the formal parameter name) yields the minimum width that is sufficient to accommodate any value of the particular integer type. Thus, when Integer_IO is instantiated with type Integer, Num'Width becomes Integer'Width, which represents the minimum width that is sufficient to accommodate all values of type Integer. Therefore, unless the integer value is close to Integer'First or Integer'Last, it is output with many leading blanks.

In addition to the parameter Width, Put may be called with the parameter Base, which specifies the number base. Any number base from 2 to 16 may be specified. Thus, based literals such as 16#BAD_BEEF#, 8#123#, and 2#101# may be output. When the base is not specified, the default base of 10 is used, and no base is indicated in the output. A base 10 number is never output as, for instance, 10#145#.

The following code demonstrates various ways that integer literals may be output:

```
-- assume needed instance of Integer_IO is visible
Put (Item => 32);                  -- outputs 32 using defaults
Put (Item => 25, Base => 10); -- outputs 25 (no base indicated)
Put (104, 5);                      -- outputs □□104, where □
                                   -- represents a blank space
Put (Item => -44, Base => 8); -- outputs -8#54#
Put (Item => 2#101_100#, Base => 8);        -- outputs 8#54#
Put (Item => 25, Width => 11, Base => 2);   -- outputs
                                            -- □□□2#11001#
Put (Item => 102, Width => 1);              -- outputs 102
```

In this code, an open box, □, indicates a blank space. Note that the formal parameters used in the named notation are Item, Width, and Base. Parameters must be specified in this same order when using positional notation. Also note that when integers are output, neither the plus sign nor scientific notation is used.

As previously mentioned, the default width is Num'Width, and the default base is 10. These defaults are set by the variables Default_Width and Default_Base in the Integer_IO package. These defaults may be overridden for a given instantiation by user-specified defaults:

```
-- assume instance of Integer_IO package, Int_IO, is visible
Int_IO.Default_Width := 10;   -- may need dot notation to avoid
Int_IO.Default_Base := 2;     -- ambiguity
Put (22);                     -- outputs □□2#10110#
Put (22, Width => 2, Base => 10); -- outputs 22
                                  -- (defaults overridden)
Default_Base := 8;
Put (22);                         -- outputs □□□□□8#26#
```

These user-specified defaults are employed each time a Put statement accepts the default width or base value; the defaults stay in effect until changed.

**Ada 95 ▶**    Modular integer types cannot be output using the `Put` defined in `Integer_IO`. A `Put` procedure for outputting modular integers is provided in the generic package `Modular_IO`. This `Put` procedure is identical to the one in `Integer_IO`.

Let us now consider the `Put` procedure used to output floating point numbers. This `Put` procedure is contained in the generic `Float_IO` package that is nested in the `Text_IO` package. Since this `Put` procedure is placed within a generic package, its instance (instantiated copy) is only available when the `Float_IO` package is instantiated with a floating point type parameter. Each instantiation of the `Float_IO` package creates another overloaded instance of this `Put` procedure.

When using a `Put` procedure to output floating point numbers, one may optionally use parameters to specify the number of columns to the left of the decimal point, to the right of the decimal point, and for the exponent. (Unlike the `Put` procedure for integers, there is no parameter that specifies the number base.) These optional parameters are frequently employed because without them, the default scientific notation is used. Scientific notation is normally avoided because, unless the numbers are very large or very small, it is difficult to read. The complete list of formal parameters for this `Put` procedure is `Item`, `Fore`, `Aft`, and `Exp`. This order must be observed when positional notation is used.

The parameter `Item` is passed the value to be output. The value of `Fore` determines the minimum number of columns allotted to the left of the decimal point. If the number of digits to the left of the decimal point is less than the allotted space, then leading blanks are used. If the number of digits to the left of the decimal point exceeds the allotted space, then the value of `Fore` is ignored and the required amount of space is taken. To ensure that the number of columns to the left of the decimal point is never more than required, set `Fore` to 0. Setting `Fore` to 0 is especially useful when a floating point number is embedded within text, because no extraneous spaces appear between the text and the number.

Note that when `Fore` is set to a value large enough to accommodate any numbers being output, columns of floating point numbers can be arranged with their decimal points aligned. Consider the following code:

```
with Ada.Text_IO; use Ada.Text_IO;
procedure Align_Decimal_Points is
    package Real_IO is new Float_IO (Float);
    use Real_IO;
    Flt: Float;
begin
    Flt := 1.23456;
    for Index in 1 .. 5 loop
        Put (Flt, Fore => 5, Aft => 5, Exp => 0);
        New_Line;
        Flt := Flt * 10.0;
    end loop;
end Align_Decimal_Points;
```

This program outputs the following column of numbers with aligned decimal points:

```
   1.23456
  12.34560
 123.45600
1234.56000
12345.60000
```

In the preceding program, the formal parameter `Aft` is set to 5. The value of `Aft` determines the exact number of digits to the right of the decimal point. Instead of padding the right side of the field with blanks, when necessary, it is padded with zeros. If `Aft` is set to 0, one digit still appears after the decimal point, as required by the syntax for floating point numbers. When `Aft` specifies fewer digits to the right of the decimal point than contained by the number to be output, then the number is rounded off, not truncated.

The value of `Exp` determines the minimum number of spaces allotted for the exponent that follows the `E` in scientific notation. When such an exponent is used, one significant digit is always placed to the left of the decimal point, and a plus or minus sign always precedes the exponent. When `Exp` is 0, no exponent is used. If the exponent does not fit in the allotted space, then the value of `Exp` is ignored, and the required space is taken.

The following code demonstrates the various ways that floating point literals may be output:

```
-- assume needed instance of Float_IO is visible
Put (32.0);                    -- outputs 3.2000000E+01 in
                               -- scientific notation
Put (  Item    => 44.212,      -- outputs □□44.21200
       Fore    => 4,           -- where □ is a blank
       Aft     => 5,
       Exp     => 0 );
Put (137.1, Fore => 2, Aft => 2, Exp => 0);      -- outputs 137.10
   -- Fore ignored and exponent not written
Put (-4.8, Fore => 0, Aft => 0, Exp => 0);       -- outputs -4.8
Put (15.628, Fore => 3, Aft => 2, Exp => 0);     -- outputs
                                                 -- □15.63
                                                 -- rounds off
Put (-67.028, Fore => 4, Aft => 2, Exp => 2);    -- outputs
                                                 -- □□-6.70E+1
Put (0.419, Fore => 3, Aft => 1, Exp => 2);      -- outputs
                                                 -- □□4.2E-1
Put (87.011, Fore => 3, Aft => 2, Exp => 5);     -- outputs
                                                 -- □□8.70E+0001
Put (931.871, Fore => 4, Aft => 1, Exp => 1);    -- outputs
                                                 -- □□□9.3E+2
```

Just as the variables `Default_Width` and `Default_Base` can be reset when outputting integers, the variables `Default_Fore`, `Default_Aft`, and `Default_Exp` may also be reset:

```
Default_Fore := 0;
Default_Aft  := 2;
```

```
Default_Exp  := 0;
Put (159.568);         -- outputs 159.57
```

**Ada 95 ▶**    Overloaded `Put` procedures for outputting fixed point numbers and decimal fixed point numbers are provided in the generic packages `Fixed_IO` and `Decimal_IO`, respectively. These `Put` procedures are practically identical to the one in `Float_IO`, except that the default parameter values differ. One result of this difference is that, by default, no exponents are used.

Now let us consider the `Put` procedure used to output objects belonging to an enumeration type. This `Put` procedure is contained in the generic `Enumeration_IO` package that is nested in the `Text_IO` package. Since this `Put` procedure is placed within a generic package, its instance (instantiated copy) is only available when the `Enumeration_IO` package is instantiated with some enumeration type parameter. Each instantiation of the `Enumeration_IO` package creates another overloaded instance of this `Put` procedure.

When using this `Put` procedure to output objects of an enumeration type, one may optionally specify the minimum field width and whether uppercase or lowercase letters are to be used. If the specified field width is greater than the length of the enumeration literal, then blank spaces are placed after the literal. If the specified width is less than the length of the enumeration literal, then the specified field width is ignored; as many spaces are taken as needed. The default width is 0, which means that only the exact space needed for each literal is used. The result is an enumeration literal without any trailing blanks. To specify uppercase or lowercase, use the values `Upper_Case` or `Lower_Case` for the third parameter, whose formal parameter name is `Set`. (The complete list of formal parameters is `Item`, `Width`, and `Set`. This order must be observed when positional notation is used.) Unless otherwise specified, enumeration literals are always output in uppercase letters. One cannot specify a mixture of uppercase and lowercase letters. The following example demonstrates the various ways that a `Put` procedure may output values of the predefined enumeration type `Boolean`:

```
-- assume needed instance of Enumeration_IO is visible
Put (False);                      -- outputs FALSE
Put (Item => True, Width => 6);   -- outputs TRUE□□
                                  -- (uses 6 columns)
Put (Item => False,               -- outputs false
     Width => 5,                  -- (in lowercase)
     Set  => Lower_Case);
Put (Item => True,                -- outputs TRUE
     Set  => Upper_Case);         -- (in uppercase)
Put (Item => True, Width => 1);   -- outputs TRUE
```

Within the `Enumeration_IO` package, the variables `Default_Width` and `Default_Setting` contain the default values for `Width` and `Set`. These default values may be overridden in the same way that the variables `Default_Width` and `Default_Base` can be overridden when outputting integers, or that the variables `Default_Fore`, `Default_Aft`, and `Default_Exp` can be overridden when outputting real numbers.

We have examined the overloaded Put procedures for outputting characters, strings, integers, modular integers, floating point numbers, fixed point numbers, decimal fixed point numbers, and enumeration values. The Get procedure is similarly overloaded for each of these data types.

*GET Procedures* Whereas Put procedures are used to output values, the Get procedures are used to input values. Unlike the Put procedures whose forms differ for each type of object being output, the Get procedure only has two forms. One form is represented by three procedures that, in turn, input characters, strings, or enumeration values. This form has only one parameter, Item, which receives the value of the object being input. Another form of Get is represented by five procedures that, in turn, input integers, modular integers, floating point numbers, fixed point numbers, and decimal fixed point numbers. This form has two parameters. The first parameter, Item, has already been described. The second parameter, Width, is optional and specifies the number of columns to examine for the object being inputted. The following example shows how these overloaded Get procedures are called:

```
with Ada.Text_IO; use Ada;
procedure Input is
   package Int_IO is new Text_IO.Integer_IO (Integer);
   package Flt_IO is new Text_IO.Float_IO (Float);
   package Bool_IO is new Text_IO.Enumeration_IO (Boolean);
   Int: Integer;
   Flt: Float;
   Bool: Boolean;
   Char: Character;
   Str: String (1 .. 5);
begin
   Text_IO.Get(Char);   -- input character value is assigned
                        -- to Char
   Int_IO.Get(Int);     -- inputs the next integer
   Text_IO.Get(Str);    -- inputs the next 5 characters
   Int_IO.Get(Item => Int, Width => 7);
      -- examines the next 7 columns for the value of Int
   Bool_IO.Get (Item => Bool);   -- input is case insensitive
      -- (i.e., False, false, FaLsE are equivalent)
   Flt_IO.Get (Item => Flt, Width => 4);
      -- examines the next 4 columns for the value of Flt
end Input;
```

A value of the second parameter, Width, is usually not specified. When this parameter is not specified, a default value of 0 is used. When Width is set to 0, unformatted input is accepted. In unformatted input, leading blanks are skipped, even across multiple lines, until the input is located. The located input is read, a character at a time, until the next character read would violate the syntax of the indicated type. For example, if N is an integer variable, then Get(N) reads the value 97 from the following input (□ represents a blank):

□□□□□97KILOBYTES

All the blanks are skipped, 97 is read, and the reading ends since the next charac-
**Ada 95 ▶** ter, 'K', is not a valid integer. (Those wishing to write their own versions of the
Get procedure need to be able to examine the next character, without removing it,
to determine whether this next character is valid. This specialized capability is provided by the procedure Look_Ahead.)

**Ada 95 ▶** When the Get procedure is used to input real values, a digit does not have to
appear on each side of the radix point. Furthermore, if no fractional part is specified, then the radix point may be omitted. Thus, one can enter the real value 5.0 as
5, and one can enter the real value 0.5 as .5.

The parameter Width of the Get procedures is only specified when input is
restricted to specific columns. (We will see an example of this later in the chapter in
the section on file I/O.)

**Ada 95 ▶** When the Get procedure is invoked, the program halts until the user enters data
and hits the return (enter) key. (We are assuming that the input device is the keyboard.) Until the return key is hit, each character that is keyed in is stored in a
"buffer." Ada also supplies a version of Get called Get_Immediate that does not
halt the program and does not buffer the input. Procedure Get_Immediate is
expecially useful for interactive applications where data needs to be entered a character at a time (without having to hit the return key) as the programming is running.

***Put_Line and Get_Line*** The procedures Put_Line and Get_Line perform line-
oriented I/O of strings. Put_Line (which has a single formal parameter, Item),
outputs a string and then advances to the next line. The procedure call

```
Put_Line ("omphaloskepsis");
```

is thus equivalent to

```
Put ("omphaloskepsis");
New_Line;
```

As mentioned, Put_Line is available only for outputting strings, not characters or
any other type.

The procedure Get_Line is used to input a line of text. Get_Line has two
parameters. The first parameter (Item) is a string variable that is assigned the inputted line of text. The second parameter (Last) returns the length of the inputted
line. Get_Line keeps reading characters and assigning them to the string variable,
until either the end of the line is reached or the string variable is full. If the end of
the line is reached, then one advances to the next line; otherwise, the next time Get
or Get_Line is invoked, reading will continue from the same line. Consider the
following program:

```
with Ada.Text_IO; use Ada.Text_IO;
procedure Using_Procedure_Get_Line is
   Name: String (1 .. 20);
   Name_Length: Natural;
begin
```

```
    Put_Line ("Enter your name");

    Get_Line (Name, Name_Length); -- inputs a line of text
    Put_Line ( Name (1 .. Name_Length) );
       -- outputs string slice containing the inputted line

  end Using_Procedure_Get_Line;
```

If the user of this program enters the name "Anaximander", the string variable
Name is assigned this string value, and the variable Name_Length returns the
length of the name, 11. This length is then used to output the string slice,
Name(1..Name_Length), containing "Anaximander". The remainder of the
string, Name(Name_Length+1..Name'Last), is not padded with blanks but is
left undefined.

***Controlling Columns, Lines, and Pages*** In addition to the procedures just discussed, the Text_IO package contains subprograms that specify formats using the
familiar concepts of columns, lines, and pages. With these subprograms, one may
advance to a column, line, or page; establish line and page lengths; and determine
the current position on the screen.

Six procedures provide the capability for advancing to lines and columns:
Set_Col, Set_Line, New_Line, New_Page, Skip_Line, and Skip_Page. If a
file is not specified as the first parameter (as will be shown later), Set_Col and
Set_Line can only be used to control output. If a file is specified, these procedures
may control input or output. The procedures New_Line and New_Page only control
output, and the procedures Skip_Line and Skip_Page only control input.

The procedure Set_Col advances from the current position to the specified
column. For example, the following call to Set_Col advances to the 24th column:

```
    Set_Col (24);
```

The parameter used by Set_Col belongs to the subtype Positive_Count of the
integer type Count, defined in the Text_IO package, as follows:

```
    type Count is range 0..implementation defined;
    subtype Positive_Count is Count range 1 .. Count'Last;
```

Procedure Set_Col must, therefore, be passed values of subtype
Positive_Count instead of type Integer:

```
    with Ada.Text_IO; use Ada;
    procedure Diagonal_Stars is -- creates a diagonal line of stars
       Number_Of_Stars: constant Text_IO.Positive_Count := 40;
    begin
       for Tab in Text_IO.Positive_Count range
          Text_IO.Positive_Count'First .. Number_Of_Stars loop
          Text_IO.Set_Col ( Tab );
          Text_IO.Put_Line ("*");
```

```
      end loop;
   end Diagonal_Stars;
```

Besides Set_Col, all the other subprograms in the Text_IO package that specify formatting in terms of columns and lines also require parameters belonging to Count or Positive_Count.

The procedure Set_Line operates like Set_Col, except that the current position advances to the specified line rather than to the specified column. For example, the following call to Set_Line advances the position to the 10th line of the current page:

```
Set_Line (10);
```

Both procedures Set_Col and Set_Line can only be used to advance the current position. If the current position is beyond the target position, then one advances to the target position on the next line or page. For instance, if the current position is column 7, Set_Col(5) will not backspace two positions. Rather, the position will be advanced to column 5 on the next line. If the current position is already at column 5, then Set_Col(5) does not change the position. Similarly, if the current position is line 15, Set_Line(14) does not go back one line. Rather, the position advances to line 14 of the next page.

Whereas the parameter of Set_Line specifies a particular line, the parameter of New_Line specifies the number of lines to advance from the current position. New_Line has a default parameter value of 1. Therefore, when New_Line is called without any parameter, one advances to the beginning of the next line. If a parameter value is supplied, then the default of 1 is overridden, and one advances the specified number of lines from the current position.

```
New_Line;        -- advances 1 line
New_Line(3);     -- advances 3 lines
```

The procedure New_Page is like New_Line, except that one advances to the beginning of a new page instead of to a new line:

```
New_Page; -- advances to beginning of next page
```

Unlike New_Line, however, New_Page has no parameters; one may advance only one page at a time.

The procedures Skip_Line and Skip_Page behave like New_Line and New_Page, respectively. The difference is that New_Line and New_Page control an output device, whereas Skip_Line and Skip_Page control an input device.

In addition to the procedures for advancing to a column, line, or page, two procedures are available that specify line and page lengths: Set_Line_Length and Set_Page_Length. The line and page lengths are usually set to correspond to the size of a particular terminal display. For example, the following two procedure calls set a page to a maximum of 40 columns (length of each line), 24 lines (length of the page):

```
Set_Line_Length(40);    -- 40 column maximum
Set_Page_Length(24);    -- 24 line maximum
```

Whenever output reaches the 40th column, the display automatically advances to the next line. Whenever output reaches the end of the 24th line, the display automatically advances to the next page.

If the line or page length is not explicitly set by the programmer, then the default is not to establish any maximum. In other words, the column and page lengths are unbounded. To explicitly specify an unbounded line or page length, call Set_Line_Length or Set_Page_Length with a parameter value of 0. Better yet, use the predefined constant, Unbounded (contained in the Text_IO package), which is set to 0:

```
Set_Line_Length (Unbounded);    -- no maximum line length
Set_Page_Length (Unbounded);    -- no maximum page length
```

Three functions are available for reporting the current position: Col, Line, and Page. The function Col returns the column number of the current position; Line returns the line number of the current position; and Page returns the page number of the current position. If a file is not specified as the first parameter, these functions report the current position of the output. If a file is specified, these functions may report the current position of the input or output.

Finally, two functions are available that return the current maximum line length and maximum page length: Line_Length and Page_Length. These functions only report information about the output. A value of 0 indicates that no maximum length was specified.

The following code shows how some of the preceding subprograms are used to arrange output by column, line, and page:

```
-- assume Ada.Text_IO is visible
-- sets screen size
Set_Line_Length (80);
Set_Page_Length (24);
New_Page;         -- line 1, column 1 of new page
Set_Col (31);     -- line 1, column 31
Put ("WISDOM OF THE AGES"); -- begins at line 1, column 31
New_Line (2); -- advances to line 3, column 1
Put ("Don't let your karma run over your dogma.");
    -- begins at line 3, column 1
Set_Line (5); -- line 5, column 1
Put ("You can lead a horse to water, but a pencil must be " &
     "lead.");
    -- begins at line 5, column 1
New_Line; -- advances to line 6, column 1
Put_Line ("Time flies like an arrow, but " & -- begins at line 6,
          "fruit flies like bananas.");    -- column 1
Put ("Every bird can build a nest, but " &   -- begins at line
     "not everyone can lay an egg");         -- 7, column 1
Set_Line (1); -- line 1, column 1 of next page
```

*File I/O*  Each of the preceding subprograms that handles I/O to and from a standard I/O device has an overloaded form that handles I/O to and from a file. These overloaded forms only differ from the preceding subprograms by having an extra parameter. This extra parameter, File, which appears as the first parameter, names the file to be manipulated. For example, the following procedures manipulate the file called Wisdom:

```
-- assume Text_IO is visible
Set_Line (Wisdom, 3);    -- advances to line 3, column 1 in
                         -- Wisdom file
Set_Col (Wisdom, 5);    -- advances to column 5, line 3
Put (Wisdom, "Where there's a will, there's a won't.");
    -- begin at line 3, column 5
New_Line (Wisdom, 2);   -- advances 2 lines
```

The procedures Set_Col, Set_Line, and the versions of Get with a width parameter are particularly useful when inputting data from specific fields. Suppose, for example, that integer values located at the following lines and columns need to be input from a file called Stats_File:

```
Line 2:    Columns   2  to 3   Height
           Columns   4  to 6   Weight
           Columns   8  to 10  IQ
Line 4:    Columns   8  to 13  Income
           Columns   14 to 16  Age
```

This file contains information about a person's height, weight, IQ, income, and age, expressed as integer values. Height is in line 2, columns 2 to 3; Weight is in line 2, columns 4 to 6; and so on. The following code reads each of these integer values from the file Stats_File:

```
-- assume Ada.Text_IO is visible
-- assumes the current position is line 1, column 1
Skip_Line (Stats_File);         -- skips to line 2
Set_Col ( Stats_File, 2);       -- advances to column 2, line 2
Get ( Stats_File, Height, 2);   -- inputs height in columns 2 to 3
Get ( Stats_File, Weight, 3);   -- inputs weight in columns 4 to 6
Get ( Stats_File, IQ);          -- inputs IQ in columns 8 to 10
   -- since spaces separate this value, the width is omitted
Set_Line ( Stats_File, 4);      -- advances to line 4
Set_Col ( Stats_File, 8);       -- advances to column 8, line 4
Get ( Stats_File, Income, 6);   -- inputs income in columns 8 to 13
Get ( Stats_File, Age, 3);      -- inputs age in columns 14 to 16
```

Since Stats_File is an input file, the procedure Skip_Line is used instead of its cousin New_Line. The procedures Set_Col and Set_Line, however, operate on both input and output files (when a file is provided as a parameter).

Now that we have seen how information can be input from a file, let us consider how files are created. Before file I/O can be performed, the file must be declared and created. Files are declared by using the predefined limited private type File_Type, contained in the Text_IO package. Files are created by using the procedure Create, also contained in the Text_IO package.

The following program declares and creates the file Wisdom, and then uses this file to store words of wisdom entered from the keyboard:

```ada
with Ada.Text_IO; use Ada.Text_IO;
procedure File_IO_With_Text_IO is
    Wisdom: File_Type;      -- declares the file
    Line: String (1..80);
    Line_Length: Natural;
begin

    Create (Wisdom, Out_File, "Wisdom.Text"); -- creates a file
       -- Wisdom is the internal Ada file name
       -- "Wisdom.Text" is the external system file name

    Put_Line ("Enter your words of wisdom");
    Put_Line ("(up to 80 characters).");
    Put_Line ("Enter ""DONE"" when you are finished.");
    Get_Line (Line, Line_Length);

    while Line (1 .. Line_Length) /= "DONE" loop
       Put_Line ( Wisdom, Line (1 .. Line_Length) );
          -- writes to file
       Get_Line (Line, Line_Length); -- reads from terminal
    end loop;

    Close (Wisdom); -- closes file
end File_IO_With_Text_IO;
```

The file Wisdom is first declared to belong to File_Type. Procedure Create is then used to physically create this file on a disk.

Procedure Create is declared in the Text_IO package, as follows:

```ada
procedure Create ( File: in out File_Type;
                   Mode: in     File_Mode := Out_File;
                   Name: in     String := "";
                   Form: in     String := "" );
```

Procedure Create has four formal parameters, three with default values. The first formal parameter, File, is passed the name of the file to be created.

**Ada 95 ▶**     The second formal parameter, Mode, belongs to the type File_Mode, which is defined in the Text_IO package, as follows:

```ada
type File_Mode is (In_File, Out_File, Append_File);
```

The value In_File declares the file to be in read-only mode. That is, a program may read from the file but not write to the file. The value Out_File declares a write-only mode. A program may write to the file but not read from it. A file may only be in one mode at a time. The parameter Mode has the default value of Out_File. When procedure Create is invoked, if this default value is overridden to In_File, then an exception will be raised at runtime. This is because, when a file is first created, no items exist in the file to be read. The third value of File_Mode, Append_File, is used to add items to the end of an existing file.

The third formal parameter of procedure Create, Name, is passed the external system name (physical name) of the file. This name differs from the internal file name (logical name) passed to the parameter File. The internal file name is a valid Ada name that is used within an Ada program to reference the file. In contrast, the external name is the name by which the file is known to the outside world. For instance, the external name is used by the operating system to perform the actual physical I/O operations. There are no standard naming conventions for external names. On some systems, the file name includes a file extension following a dot: "WISDOM.TEXT". On other systems, a file name may appear as "&WISDOM:DN:10", and so on. The value of Name, whatever form it takes on a particular system, is written as a string. This external file name is associated with the internal file name by the Create procedure.

In the procedure Create, the formal parameter Name is given a default value of a null (empty) string. The external system name is thus optional. When an external name is not supplied (or is supplied as a null string), the file is created as a temporary file that exists only as long as the program is executing. This is unlike named files, which remain in existence after the program terminates.

The fourth formal parameter of Create, Form, is used by some systems to supply special information about the file. This information might include a maximum file size, a read or write password, the number of days to save the file, and so on. Consult the reference manual for your compiler to determine what, if any, values must be supplied for this parameter. The parameter Form, like Name, is given a default value of a null string.

Now that we understand how files are declared and created, let us return to the previous program, File_IO_With_Text_IO. Once the file Wisdom is created, the user is repeatedly prompted for words of wisdom. These words are output to the Wisdom file until the user enters "DONE". On some systems, a special character, such as control-Z, indicates the end of the file. On such systems, the program may use the predefined function End_Of_File instead of the special word "DONE":

```
while not End_Of_File loop...
    -- uses the predefined Boolean function to test for the
    -- end of file
```

Usually, End_Of_File is used when reading files, because this function often does not work well with interactive I/O devices. When properly working, the function End_Of_File returns the value True when the end of file is reached; otherwise, it returns the value False. Since the user is inputting items from the keyboard (the

assumed standard input device), no file name is required after the function name
End_Of_File. Similar functions, End_Of_Line and End_Of_Page, are also provided by the Text_IO package.

Once the user of the program File_IO_With_Text_IO is done entering
words of wisdom and enters "DONE", the Wisdom file is closed with the procedure
Close. This procedure informs the operating system that the file is not currently
needed by the program, and the association between the internal and external file
names is broken. All open files should eventually be closed. Unlike some languages, Ada is not required to automatically close all files when the program ends.
On some systems, if a file is not closed with the procedure Close, data may be lost.

Once a file with an external name is created, the file is permanent. Unless it is
deleted, this file can be manipulated by different programs at different times. For
example, after the previous program creates the file Wisdom, another program
may later read the words of wisdom contained in this file, as follows:

```ada
with Ada.Text_IO; use Ada.Text_IO;
procedure Read_Existing_File_With_Text_IO is
   Insight: File_Type;
   Enlightenment: String (1 .. 80);
   Enlightenment_Length: Natural;

begin
   Open (Insight, In_File, "Wisdom.Text"); -- opens existing
                                           -- file
   Put_Line ("WISDOM OF THE AGES"); -- outputs to terminal,
   New_Line;                        -- not to file

   while not End_Of_File (Insight) loop
      Get_Line ( Insight, Enlightenment,
         Enlightenment_Length);       -- inputs from file
      Put_Line ( Enlightenment (1 .. Enlightenment_Length));
         -- outputs to terminal
   end loop;

   Close (Insight);
end Read_Existing_File_With_Text_IO;
```

Since the file containing words of wisdom already exists, this program opens the
file, using the procedure Open, instead of creating it. Whereas the program that
created the file "Wisdom.Text" gave it the internal name Wisdom, this program
gives it the internal name Insight. Like the procedure Create, Open associates a
file's internal name with its external name. In general, the internal name associated
with the external name of a file may be changed each time a program is run or even
during a single execution of a program by closing the file and then reopening it
with a different internal name.

The procedure Open is declared in the Text_IO package, as follows:

```ada
procedure Open ( File:  in out File_Type;
                 Mode:  in      File_Mode;
```

```
Name:   in      String;
Form:   in      String := "" );
```

The procedure `Open` uses the same parameters as `Create`, except that `Mode` and `Name` do not have default values. These values must therefore be supplied.

**Ada 95 ▶**      Whenever a file is opened, it must be in a read-only mode (`In_File`), in a write-only mode (`Out_File`), or in the append mode (`Append_File`). A file cannot be opened in multiple modes. In our example, since we are reading the words of wisdom from the file, the file is opened with the parameter value of `In_File`. A file opened in the `In_File` mode returns to the beginning of the file and only permits the file to be read. A file opened in the `Out_File` mode also returns to the beginning of the file, but only allows the file be written to. Each time a file is opened in the `Out_File` mode, it returns to the beginning and the contents of the file are overwritten. If one desires to append data to the end of a file instead of overriding existing data, then the `Append_File` mode must be selected. A file opened in the `Append_File` mode can only be written to:

```
Open (Insight, Append_File, "Wisdom.Text");
    -- goes to end of file and opens in write-only mode
```

Only existing files may be opened. If an attempt is made to open a file that does not exist, a `Text_IO.Name_Error` exception is raised. Most systems, however, allow a file that already exists to be created, as long as it is not open. In such cases, `Create` opens the file.

Let us return to the program `Read_Existing_File_With_Text_IO`. When the file `Insight` is opened, the current position is the beginning of the file. Each time the `Get_Line` procedure is invoked, the next line is read from the file. The file is thus traversed sequentially, from beginning to end. To reference a particular item, one must search each item in the file in order, until the desired item is found. Such files that may only be traversed sequentially are known as sequential files. The `Text_IO` package only supplies resources to handle sequential files. Another kind of file, known as a direct access (random access) file, is supported by the `Direct_IO` package. The direct access file will be discussed subsequently.

To change the file mode within a program, one may close the file and then reopen it in a different mode value:

```
Open (Insight, In_File, "Wisdom.Text");
    ...
Close (Insight);
    ...
-- changes mode from In_File to Out_File
Open (Insight, Out_File, "Wisdom.Text");
```

As an alternative to closing and then reopening a file, one may reset its mode by calling the `Reset` procedure:

```
Open (Insight, In_File, "Wisdom.Text");
    -- opens file in read-only mode
```

```
. . .
Reset (Insight, Out_File); -- returns to beginning of file
                           -- resets mode to write-only
```

**Ada 95 ▶**     In this example, `Reset` returns to the beginning of the file and resets the mode to write-only. If a file is reset to the `Append_File` mode, then instead of returning to the beginning, it advances to the end of the file.

There are two overloaded versions of `Reset`. The preceding version, which uses two parameters, resets the mode value. The alternative version only has one parameter, the name of the file. This alternative version just returns to the beginning of the file without changing the mode value:

```
Reset (Insight); -- returns to the beginning of file without
                 -- changing the mode
```

Before ending our discussion of the `Text_IO` package, let us briefly mention a few other subprograms that are used for file manipulation. More complete descriptions may be found in the *Ada 95 Reference Manual*.

The procedure `Delete` is used to delete a file:

```
Delete (Insight); -- deletes the Insight file
```

A file may only be deleted if it is open. Once a file is deleted, for all practical purposes, it ceases to exist.

**Ada 95 ▶**     Three functions—`Mode`, `Name`, and `Form`—are used to query the properties of a file. The function `Mode` returns the mode of the file. For files created with the `Text_IO` package, the value of `Mode` is `In_File`, `Out_File`, or `Append_File`. The functions `Name` and `Form` return strings that contain the external system name of the file and the form of the file.

The function `Is_Open` returns the value `True` or `False`, depending on whether the specified file is open:

```
-- if the file is not open, then opens it
if not Is_Open (Insight) then
   Open (Insight, Out_File, "Wisdom.Text");
end if;
```

This code avoids attempting to open a file that is already open since such an attempt raises the exception `Text_IO.Status_Error`.

Six subprograms are supplied that control the default destinations for input or output: `Set_Input`, `Set_Output`, `Standard_Input`, `Standard_Output`, `Current_Input`, and `Current_Output`. The procedure `Set_Input` establishes the default source of input, and the procedure `Set_Output` establishes the default destination of output. The functions `Standard_Input` and `Standard_Output` return the `File_Type` value of the standard I/O device. In interactive environments, `Standard_Input` is typically associated with the keyboard, and the `Standard_Output` with the terminal display. The functions `Current_Input` and `Current_Output` return the `File_Type` value of the current default source of input and the current default destination of output. The use of these subprograms is illustrated in the following code:

```
-- assume Text_IO is visible
Put ("Green");    -- outputs string to standard output device
Set_Output (Colors);
Put ("Red");      -- outputs to file Colors
Set_Output (Standard_Output);
    -- resets the default destination to the standard output device
Put ("Blue");     -- outputs to standard output device
```

Unlike the file `Colors`, `Standard_Input` and `Standard_Output` cannot be opened, closed, reset, or deleted.

**Ada 95 ▶**     In addition to reading from and writing to an external file, one may also read from and write to an internal character string. This service is provided by overloaded `Put` and `Get` procedures that are located in the generic packages `Integer_IO`, `Modular_IO`, `Float_IO`, `Fixed_IO`, `Decimal_IO`, and `Enumeration_IO`. In the following code, for example, `Put` procedures output an integer value, then a floating point value, then a `Boolean` value to an eight-character string, `Buffer`:

```
with Ada.Text_IO; use Ada.Text_IO;
procedure Internal_IO is
    package Int_IO is new Integer_IO (Integer);
    package Flt_IO is new Float_IO (Float);
    package Bool_IO is new Enumeration_IO (Boolean);
    use Int_IO, Flt_IO, Bool_IO;

    Buffer: String (1 .. 8);
begin

    Put (To => Buffer, Item => 7, Base => 2);
        -- outputs 2#111# to Buffer
    Put (Buffer); -- outputs the string □□2#111#
                    -- □ represents a blank

    Put (To => Buffer, Item => 3.412, Aft => 1, Exp => 0);
        -- outputs 3.4 to Buffer
    Put (Buffer); -- outputs the string □□□□□3.4

    Put (To => Buffer, Item => True, Set => Lower_Case);
        -- outputs a true to Buffer
    Put (Buffer); -- outputs the string true□□□□
end Internal_IO;
```

Note that instead of specifying the file that receives the output, the internal character string `Put` specifies the string that receives the output. These `Put` procedures do not include the `Fore` and `Width` parameters since these `Fore` and `Width` fields are determined by the length of the string.

**Ada 95 ▶**     Package `Text_IO` provides I/O services for types `Character` and `String`, but not `Wide_Character` and `Wide_String`. Input/output services for `Wide_Character` and `Wide_String` are provided by the package `Ada.Wide_Text_IO`. This package is analogous to `Text_IO` and therefore does not need to be separately discussed.

## SEQUENTIAL_IO PACKAGE

The `Text_IO` package enables one to read from, write to, and manipulate sequential files containing human readable text. Human readable text differs from its binary representation inside the computer. To output human readable text to a file, data such as numeric values or enumeration values must be converted (encoded) from their internal binary representations to character representations. Conversely, to input human readable numeric values or enumeration values from a file, they must be converted (coded) from their character representations to their internal binary representation. This coding and encoding are necessary if the files are to contain information that humans can read. Sometimes, however, the files do not need to be read by humans; they are only meant to be read by programs. In such cases, data can be efficiently input and output as a pattern of bits without any need for coding or encoding. The generic `Ada.Sequential_IO` package provides this service. When this package is used, data can be input or output with no (or minimal) conversion.

The `Ada.Sequential_IO` package allows a sequence of values belonging to the same type to be transferred to or from a file. This type may be an elementary type or a composite type, but not a limited private type, and in some implementations, not an access type. The following program, for instance, outputs records of type `Product_Type` to the file `Inventory_File`:

```ada
with Ada.Sequential_IO; -- must with this package
procedure Sequential_IO_Demo is

   type Product_Type is
      record
         ID: String (1..5);
         Quantity: Integer range 0 .. 1_000;
      end record;

   package Product_IO is new Ada.Sequential_IO (Product_Type);
      -- Ada.Sequential_IO is a generic package,

   Inventory_File: Product_IO.File_Type;

   Best_Selling_Computer: Product_Type :=
      (  ID          =>  "FV20D",
         Quantity  =>  789 );
   Best_Selling_Mouse: Product_Type :=
      (  ID          =>  "19BRR",
         Quantity  =>  223 );
```

```
        Product: Product_Type;

begin

        Product_IO.Create ( File => Inventory_File,
                            Name => "Inventory.List");
           -- takes default (and required) Mode value of Out_File

        Product_IO.Write (   File => Inventory_File, -- named notation
                             Item => Best_Selling_Computer);


        Product_IO.Write (   Inventory_File,         -- positional
                             Best_Selling_Mouse);    -- notation


        Product_IO.Reset (File => Inventory_File,    -- returns to
                          Mode => In_File);          -- beginning
                                                     -- of file and
                                                     -- resets
                                                     -- mode to
                                                     -- In_File

        Product_IO.Read (   File => Inventory_File, -- assigns value
                            Item => Product);       -- to Product

        Product_IO.Close (File => Inventory_File);

end Sequential_IO_Demo;
```

As shown in this example, the package Ada.Sequential_IO offers many of the same services as Text_IO. (Refer to the *Ada 95 Reference Manual* for a complete specification of these packages.) Both packages provide distinct versions of the predefined types File_Type and File_Mode. Both packages also contain distinct versions of the subprograms Create, Open, Close, Delete, Reset, Mode, Name, Form, Is_Open, and End_Of_File. However, there are differences between the two packages, primarily because Sequential_IO does not output human readable text. Unlike the Text_IO package, the Sequential_IO package does not contain subprograms that format I/O or manipulate a file by columns, lines, and pages. Also, unlike the Text_IO package, which performs I/O using the procedures Put and Get, the Ada.Sequential_IO package performs I/O using the procedures Read and Write. These different names are meant to remind us that, unlike Get and Put, no coding or encoding is being performed. Finally, unlike the Text_IO package, the Sequential_IO package is a generic package. Therefore, to perform sequential I/O on objects of a type, such as Product_Type, one must first instantiate the Ada.Sequential_IO package with this type. As a result of this instantiation, only objects of type Product_Type can be input or output to a file. Package Sequential_IO cannot be used to store objects of differ-

ent types to the same file. This is in sharp contrast to `Text_IO`, which can be used
to output objects of type `Integer`, `Float`, `Character`, etc., to the same file. Of
course all these types are translated and stored as human readable text.

   Let us examine that last point in more detail. As mentioned, each time the
`Ada.Sequential_IO` package is needed, it must be instantiated with a particular
type. The previous example instantiates the `Ada.Sequential_IO` package to
perform I/O on objects of the type `Product_Type`:

```
package Product_IO is new Ada.Sequential_IO (Product_Type);
```

As a result of this instantiation, every file, such as `Inventory_File`, belonging to
`Product_IO.File_Type` may only contain values of type `Product_Type`.

   Suppose that another instantiation of the `Ada.Sequential_IO` package is
performed using type `Boolean`:

```
package Boolean_IO is new Ada.Sequential_IO (Boolean);
```

`Boolean` objects may now be sent to any file of type `Boolean_IO.File_Type`.
As the following code illustrates, `Boolean_IO.File_Type` and `Product_IO.
File_Type` are distinct file types:

```
declare
    Boolean_File: Boolean_IO.File_Type;
    Inventory_File: Product_IO.File_Type;
begin
    Create (Boolean_File, "Boolean.File");
    Create (Inventory_File, "Inventory.File");

    Write (Boolean_File, True);
    Write (Inventory_File, Product);
       -- Product defined in Sequential_IO_Demo
    Write (Boolean_File, Product);    -- error
       -- may only output Boolean values
    Write (Inventory_File, False);    -- error
       -- may only output Product_Type values
end;
```

File `Boolean_File` may only contain values of type `Boolean`, and file
`Inventory_File` may only contain values of type `Product_Type`.

   Even though the `Ada.Sequential_IO` package may only be used to input
and output values belonging to a single type, this single type may be a variant
record type. In a sense, a variant record "combines" several record types into one.
For example, consider the following two record types that store two different sets
of information about men, depending on whether they are bachelors or married:

```
type Bachelor is
   record
      Misogynist: Boolean;
```

```
         Misogamist: Boolean;
      end record;


   type Married_Man is
      record
         Years_Married: Integer range 0 .. 100;
      end record;
```

Unfortunately, both these record types, `Bachelor` and `Married_Man`, cannot be output to the same file. However, this problem can be circumvented by combining both record types into a single variant record type:

```
   type Marital_Status_Type is (Married, Bachelor);


   type Male (Marital_Status: Marital_Status_Type := Bachelor) is
      record
         case Marital_Status is
            when Married =>
               Years_Married: Integer range 0 .. 100;
            when Bachelor =>
               Misogynist: Boolean;
               Misogamist: Boolean;
         end case;
      end record;
```

By instantiating the `Ada.Sequential_IO` package with the variant record type `Male`, information about both married men and bachelors may now be output to the same file:

```
   package Men_IO is new Ada.Sequential_IO (Male);
```

(Some implementations of Ada only permit this instantiation if the discriminant, `Marital_Status`, is given a default value.)

**Ada 95 ▶**    Those finding `Sequential_IO` to be too restrictive can gain total control over file I/O using the package `Ada.Streams.Stream_IO`. This specialized package will be briefly discussed at the end of this chapter.

---

## DIRECT_IO PACKAGE

The `Ada.Direct_IO` package is used to perform I/O on direct access (random access) files. A direct access file does not need to be traversed sequentially. One may jump around among the various items in the file. To reference a particular item in a direct access file, an index value may be specified. The first item in a direct access file has the index value of 1; the second item, the value 2; the third item, the value 3; and so on. It is also possible to perform file I/O sequentially without specifying the index value. When this option is taken, programs using the `Ada.Direct_IO` package appear very similar to programs using the `Ada.Sequential_IO` package. For example, rewriting the `Sequential_IO_Demo` program (which appeared at the beginning of the preceding section) using `Direct_IO` results in the following program:

```ada
with Ada.Direct_IO;
procedure Direct_IO_Demo is

    type Product_Type is
        record
            ID: String (1..5);
            Quantity: Integer range 0 .. 1_000;
        end record;
    package Product_IO is new Ada.Direct_IO (Product_Type);

    Inventory_File: Product_IO.File_Type;

    Best_Selling_Computer: Product_Type :=
        (  ID         =>  "FV2.0D",
           Quantity  =>  789 );
    Best_Selling_Mouse: Product_Type :=
        (  ID         =>  "19BRR",
           Quantity  =>  223 );

    Product: Product_Type;

begin

    Product_IO.Create
        (  File => Inventory_File, -- mode set for both reading
           Mode => Inout_File,     -- and writing
           Name => "Inventory.List" );

    Product_IO.Write (Inventory_File, Best_Selling_Computer);
    Product_IO.Write (Inventory_File, Best_Selling_Mouse);

    Product_IO.Reset (File => Inventory_File);
        -- returns to beginning of file; mode does not change

    Product_IO.Read (Inventory_File, Product);
    Product_IO.Close (Inventory_File);

end Direct_IO_Demo;
```

**Ada 95 ▶**  As shown in this example, the `Ada.Direct_IO` package is, in many ways, similar to the `Ada.Sequential_IO` package. Both packages are generic packages that provide the types `File_Type` and `File_Mode`. However, `Direct_IO` does not provide the `File_Mode` value `Append_File`, since this capability is provided by advancing to the end of the file using the index value. In addition, both packages provide the subprograms `Create, Open, Close, Delete, Reset, Mode, Name, Form, Is_Open, Read, Write,` and `End_Of_File`. Finally, both packages are used to input and output data that is not human readable text.

The `Direct_IO_Demo` procedure does not specify an index value when it reads from or writes to the file and, therefore, uses read and write procedures identical to the ones in the `Ada.Sequential_IO` package. (When indexes are used, different overloaded versions of `Read` and `Write` are invoked.) Note that the value of the file mode is `Inout_File`. This value, which is only provided in the `Direct_IO` package, means that the file is in a read and write mode. In other words, direct access files assigned the mode `Inout_File` can be written to and read from, without being closed or reset. This mode is the default file mode for the version of the `Create` procedure in the `Direct_IO` package.

As with sequential files, whenever a read or a write is performed on a direct access file, the file index is automatically incremented. As the following code illustrates, one may therefore alternate between reading from and writing to items of a file:

```
Read (Inventory_File, Product);    -- reads item n
Write (Inventory_File, Product);   -- writes to item n + 1, which
                                   -- now contains value of item
                                   -- n
Read (Inventory_File, Product);    -- reads item n + 2
Write (Inventory_File, Product);   -- writes to item n + 3, which
                                   -- now contains value of item
                                   -- n + 2
```

In addition to the `Read` and `Write` procedures just shown, which have two parameters, the `Direct_IO` package contains `Read` and `Write` procedures with three parameters. The third parameter specifies the index value of the item:

```
Read  (Inventory_File, Product, 25); -- reads the 25th item and
                                     -- writes
Write (Inventory_File, Product, 17); -- its value to the 17th
                                     -- item
Read  ( File => Inventory_File,      -- invokes Read using named
          Item => Product,           -- notation
          From => 6   );
Write ( File => Inventory_File,      -- invokes Write using named
          Item => Product,           -- notation
          To => 8   );
```

The formal parameters `From` in procedure `Read` and `To` in procedure `Write` are passed the index value of the item in the file that is to be read from or written to. This index value belongs to type `Count`. When a direct access file is empty, the index value is 0.

To better understand the use of index values in direct access files, consider a direct access file of records that contains information about books. The first record component stores the title of the book, and the second component stores the name of the book's author. The following package contains the procedure `Search`, which uses the index values of the records to locate a book with a particular title:

```ada
package Binary_Search is

   subtype Book_Title is String (1..20);
   subtype Book_Author is String (1 .. 12);

   type Book_Type is
      record
         Title: Book_Title;
         Author: Book_Author;
      end record;

   procedure Search ( File_Name:   in String;
                      Target_Book: in Book_Title );
end Binary_Search;
```

---

```ada
with Ada.Text_IO, Direct_IO; use Ada.Text_IO;
package body Binary_Search is
   package Book_IO is new Direct_IO (Book_Type);
   use Book_IO;

   procedure Search ( File_Name:   in String;
                      Target_Book: in Book_Title ) is

      Book_File: Book_IO.File_Type;
      Book: Book_Type;
      Lower_Bound: Book_IO.Count := 1;
      Upper_Bound: Book_IO.Count;
      Midpoint: Book_IO.Count;

   begin
      Open (Book_File, In_File, File_Name);
      Upper_Bound := Size (Book_File);

      loop
         if Upper_Bound < Lower_Bound then
            -- book not found
            Put_Line ("Not found");
            return;
         end if;

         Midpoint := (Lower_Bound + Upper_Bound) / 2;
            -- integer division

         Read (Book_File, Book, Midpoint);

         if Book.Title = Target_Book then
            -- book found
```

```
            Put_Line ("Author is " & Book.Author);
            return;
        end if;

        -- continues the search
        if Book.Title > Target_Book then
            -- selects first half of file
            Upper_Bound := Midpoint - 1;
        else
            -- selects second half of file
            Lower_Bound := Midpoint + 1;
        end if;

    end loop;
  end Search;
end Binary_Search;
```

A program unit that mentions the package `Binary_Search` in its **with** and **use** clauses may invoke the procedure `Search`, as follows:

```
Search ( File_Name    => "Psychology.books",
         Target_Book  => "The Primal Sigh      ");
```

When `Search` is invoked, it searches the file `"Psychology.books"` for the book with the title *The Primal Sigh*. The kind of search used, a binary search, is efficient but can only work if the books are listed in alphabetical order by title. Briefly, this binary search examines the middle item in the file. If this middle item is not the desired item, then a check is made whether the desired item comes before or after this middle item. If, for example, the desired item comes before the middle item, then only the first half of the file is considered and the process repeats. The item in the middle of the first half of the file is checked. If this item is not the desired item, then a check is made whether the desired item comes before or after it. The process keeps repeating until the desired item is found or until it is determined that the item is not contained in the file.

Note that the procedure `Search` invokes the function `Size`. This function, defined in `Direct_IO`, returns the current number of items in the file. The value returned belongs to type `Count`.

We will conclude this section with two other subprograms contained in package `Direct_IO`: `Set_Index` and `Index`. `Set_Index` is a procedure that sets the index to a specified value (which may lie beyond the end of the file):

```
Set_Index (Psychology_Books, 43); -- sets index to 43rd book
Set_Index (File => Psychology_Books, To => 21);   -- named
                                                  -- notation
```

`Index` is a function that returns the current index value of a direct access file:

```
Current_Book := Index ( File => Psychology_Books);
    -- current index
```

## IO_EXCEPTIONS PACKAGE

Package Ada.IO_Exceptions is a predefined library package that contains the exceptions that may be raised during I/O operations. Unfortunately, there is quite a variety of problems that can arise during I/O operations. For example, an attempt may be made to write to a read-only file, or to open a nonexistent file, or to read past the end of a file.

All three I/O package specifications—Text_IO, Sequential_IO, and Direct_IO—mention package Ada.IO_Exceptions in their **with** clauses. The specification of package Ada.IO_Exceptions contains the declarations of eight exceptions: Status_Error, Mode_Error, Name_Error, Use_Error, Device_Error, End_Error, Data_Error, and Layout_Error. We will briefly discuss these exceptions. Full descriptions may be found in the *Ada 95 Reference Manual*.

Before discussing the individual exceptions, note that a program unit that mentions Text_IO, Sequential_IO, or Direct_IO in its **with** clause automatically has available the exceptions listed in the Ada.IO_Exceptions package. This seems to violate the rule presented in Chapter 7 about packages not being able to indirectly reference the resources of other packages. In other words, if program P **with**s Text_IO, which in turn **with**s Ada.IO_Exceptions, program P cannot, on that basis alone, reference the resources of Ada.IO_Exceptions. The only reason program P can reference the exceptions defined in Ada.IO_Exceptions is because these exceptions are renamed in the package specification of Text_IO ( as well as in Sequential_IO and Direct_IO):

```
Status_Error  :   exception renames IO_Exceptions.Status_Error;
Mode_Error    :   exception renames IO_Exceptions.Mode_Error;
Name_Error    :   exception renames IO_Exceptions.Name_Error;
    . . .
```

Since this renaming occurs in the visible part of the I/O packages (their specifications), the alternative names—Status_Error, Mode_Error, Name_Error, and so on—are made visible to external program units that reference these I/O packages. As discussed in Chapter 7, renaming can thus alter the scope of the items being renamed, making them available to program units to which they would otherwise not be available.

Let us now briefly consider the conditions that raise the predefined I/O exceptions. Status_Error is raised whenever one attempts to manipulate an open file in a manner only appropriate to a closed file, or vice versa. For example, Status_Error is raised whenever one attempts to reset the mode of a file that is closed or attempts to open a file that is already open.

Mode_Error is raised whenever an attempted I/O operation is incompatible with the file's current mode. For example, this error is raised whenever one attempts to write to a file whose current mode is In_File.

Name_Error is raised when calling Create or Open with an invalid external file name. The external file name may be invalid because it is in the wrong form for a given computer system. Alternatively, the name may be invalid because an external file with this name does not exist.

Use_Error is raised whenever an I/O operation is attempted on a file where such an operation is not supported. For example, if the printer is declared as a file (as is often done), then one cannot open this file in a read mode.

Device_Error is raised whenever an I/O operation cannot be carried out because of some failure affecting the I/O device.

End_Error is raised whenever an attempt is made to read past the end of a file. This error is very common.

Data_Error is raised whenever input is in the wrong form. For example, this exception is raised when attempting to read an integer value but instead receiving a value of type Character.

Layout_Error is raised whenever the formatting operations supplied by the Text_IO package are illegally used. The Layout_Error is only available in the Text_IO package.

Recall that the function Is_Open allows a programmer to determine whether or not a particular file is open. No similar function is provided to determine whether a particular file exists; programmers must write their own function to accomplish this. Although exceptions should not usually be used to control the flow of a program, in this case, it is very convenient to allow Name_Error to be raised when a file cannot be opened because it does not exist:

```ada
with Ada.Text_IO; use Ada.Text_IO;
function File_Exists (File_In_Question: String) return Boolean is
    Internal_Name: Text_IO.File_Type;
begin
    Open (Internal_Name, In_File, File_In_Question);
    -- Since file successfully opened, it exists
    Close (Internal_Name);
    return True;
exception
    -- File cannot be opened so assume it does not exist
    when Name_Error => return False;
end File_Exists;
```

## OTHER I/O SUPPORT

This section briefly covers miscellaneous I/O support not previously discussed. Detailed information about any of this support can be found in the *Ada 95 Reference Manual*.

**Ada 95 ▶**    We begin by explaining how unprintable characters can be referenced from within one's code. Next, package Ada.Characters is discussed. This package provides support for character manipulation and processing. The next package covered is Text_IO.Pictures. This child package of Text_IO provides fine control over the output of real values. Such control is especially needed when generating financial reports requiring neat tabulation of monetary data. Finally, the

`Streams.Stream_IO` package is discussed. This is a specialized package that provides I/O on streams of storage units.

## Referencing Unprintable Characters

**Ada 95 ▶** Literals of type `Character` that are printable are written within a pair of single quotes: `'A'`, `'8'`, `'!'`, and so on (assuming that a particular computer can enter all the printable characters). The other characters values, called control characters, cannot be referenced as printable literals. Control characters function as line feeds, carriage returns, line terminators, page terminators, and so on. These control characters may be referenced by using the `Val` attribute. For instance, the control character for a line feed can be referenced as `Character'Val(10)` because the line feed is at position `10` in the enumeration type `Character`. This notation, however, is unclear and error prone because one cannot easily discern which character is being referenced. To allow programmers to reference these control characters in a more natural fashion, the child package `Ada.Characters.Latin_1` is provided. (This child package replaces Ada 83's `Standard.ASCII` package.) Package `Ada.Characters.Latin_1` assigns constant names to the characters belonging to the International Standards Organization (ISO) 8859-1 character set. The constant names for the control characters are two-letter or three-letter mnemonics. For example, to reference the carriage return, one merely writes `Ada.Characters.Latin_1.CR`. To reference the line feed, one writes `Ada.Characters.Latin_1.LF`. These character constants may be catenated with other characters or strings. Consider the following `Put` statement, where `BEL` is the constant name for bell:

```
Put ("Dinner is ready!" & Ada.Characters.Latin_1.BEL);
    -- outputs the message and rings the bell
```

Besides allowing the control characters to be easily referenced, the `Ada.Characters.Latin_1` package enables one to reference characters that might not be available on a particular keyboard. For instance, if a keyboard is missing the character tilde, `'~'`, one may reference this symbol with the constant `Ada.Characters.Latin_1.Tilde`. As we shall see in the next section, package `Ada.Characters` contains more than the child unit `Latin_1`.

## Characters Package

**Ada 95 ▶** The child package `Ada.Characters.Handling` provides support for character manipulation and processing. This package allows one to test whether or not a character is a control character, a graphic character, a letter, a lowercase letter, an uppercase letter, a decimal digit, a hexadecimal digit, and so on. For example, the `Is_Letter` function returns `True` or `False` depending on whether the value passed in is a letter (uppercase or lowercase) from A to Z.

In addition to functions that classify characters, package `Ada.Characters.Handling` also contains functions for converting characters to uppercase or lowercase. For example, function `To_Upper` returns the corresponding uppercase form of a character. If the character has no uppercase form, then this function simply returns the character value that was passed in.

Finally, package `Ada.Characters.Handling` also contains functions for converting between types `Wide_Character` and `Character`, and between types `Wide_String` and `String`.

## Editing Package

**Ada 95 ▶** Software written for business applications often generates financial reports where monetary data is carefully formatted. Therefore, business application programmers need control over such items as the placement of currency symbols, commas, signs, digits, decimal points, leading zeros, or other characters. Such control is provided by the child package `Ada.Text_IO.Editing`. (Package `Ada.Wide_Text_IO.Editing` is also provided.)

COBOL, a language especially designed for business applications, has very powerful features for formatting monetary data. These same features can be found in the generic package `Edited_Output` that is contained in `Ada.Text_IO.Editing`. These packages, however, are defined in the optional Information Systems Annex and, therefore, may not be supported by your compiler.

## Command_Line Package

**Ada 95 ▶** In every implementation of Ada, a parameterless procedure can always serve as a main program. In some implementations, a procedure with parameters or a function can serve as a main program. In such implementations, a mechanism must exist to pass parameters to the main program from the command line interpreter or to receive a return value upon program termination. Such a mechanism is supplied by the package `Ada.Command_Line`.

## Steams.Stream_IO Package

**Ada 95 ▶** None of the I/O packages presented in this chapter—`Text_IO`, `Sequential_IO`, or `Direct_IO`—allows objects of a class-wide type to be input or output. The problem is that objects in a class-wide type can belong to different specific types and often differ in size (number of components). Package `Text_IO` could be used to separately input or output each component of an object, but the object itself cannot be input or output. Packages `Sequential_IO` and `Direct_IO` are inadequate since, for a single file, they can only input or output objects of the same specific type. The solution to our problem is to use package `Ada.Streams.Stream_IO`.

Package `Ada.Streams.Stream_IO` views data files as "streams." A stream is a sequence of storage units (typically an 8-bit byte) comprising values from possibly different types. This package provides operations for reading streams from files and writing streams to files. Like `Text_IO`, package `Ada.Streams.Stream_IO` provides types `File_Type` for declaring files, and `File_Mode` for specifying whether the file's mode is `In_File`, `Out_File`, or `Append_File`. Like `Text_IO`, package `Ada.Streams.Stream_IO` also provides the subprograms `Create`, `Open`, `Close`, `Delete`, `Reset`, `Is_Open`, and `End_Of_File`.

The following program outputs an integer and a floating point value to the file Stream_File, resets the file, then reads these values back:

```ada
with Ada.Streams.Stream_IO;
use Ada.Streams.Stream_IO;
procedure Stream_IO_Demo is

   Stream_File: Stream_IO.File_Type;
   Stream_Ptr: Stream_Access;     -- pointer to
                                  -- streams
   Int: Integer := 2;
   Flt: Float := 2.5;
begin

   Create (  File => Stream_File,
             Mode => Out_File,
             Name => "Stream_File.List");

   Stream_Ptr := Stream (Stream_File);
      -- points to the stream associated
      -- with Stream_File

   -- output Int and Flt to the file via
   -- the stream pointer
   Integer'Output (Stream_Ptr, Int);
   Float'Output (Stream_Ptr, Flt);

   Reset (Stream_File, In_File);

   -- read values back via the
   -- stream pointer
   Int := Integer'Input (Stream_Ptr);
   Flt := Float'Input (Stream_Ptr);

   Close (Stream_File);

end Stream_IO_Demo;
```

With package Stream_IO, files are declared and created in the usual manner. However, when a file is created, a specific stream is implicitly associated with the file. The function call Stream (Stream_File) returns a pointer of type Stream_Access that points to the stream associated with Stream_File. This pointer is assigned to Stream_Ptr. The attributes Input and Output can then be used to read or write to the Stream_File. In the previous example, and integer value is written to the stream as follows:

```ada
Integer'Output (Stream_Ptr, Int);
```

Note that the first parameter is the pointer to the stream and the second parameter is the value to be output. A floating point value is similarly output:

```
Float'Output (Stream_Ptr, Flt);
```

After the file is reset, the integer and floating point values are read back using the `Input` attribute:

```
Int := Integer'Input (Stream_Ptr);
Flt := Float'Input (Stream_Ptr);
```

Note that `Integer'Input` and `Float'Input` are functions that take the pointer to the stream to be read from and returns the value read. When the attributes `Input` and `Output` are used to read and write values of a tagged type, the discriminants (if any) and tag are also read or written.

The I/O facilities described in this chapter are designed for code written as a single thread of control, where instructions are executed sequentially, one after the other. In Ada, however, code can be written with multiple threads of control. This allows units of code to be executed concurrently. Problems can arise when one unit of code, for instance, attempts to output a message at the same time as another unit of code is outputting a message. The messages can intermix, resulting in gibberish. Such issues arising from concurrent programming are discussed in the next chapter.

## EXERCISES

1. Perform the necessary instantiations of the generic I/O packages to output objects of the following types:

```
type Clouds is (Cirrus, Cirrostratus, Cirrocumulus,
    Altostratus, Altocumulus, Stratocumulus, Nimbostratus,
    Cumulus, Cumulonimbus, Stratus);
type More_Clouds is new Clouds;
type Hours is range 0 .. 23;
type My_Float is new Float;
```

2. Assuming that the needed instance of the `Integer_IO` package is visible, what will each `Put` statement output? (Show the correct format of this output.)

```
Put (Item => 15);
Put (Item => 15, Base => 2);
Put (Item => 7_250, Width => 2);
Put (Item => 2#1101#, Base => 16);
Put (Item => 30, Width => 5, Base => 16);
```

3. Assuming that the needed instance of the `Float_IO` package is visible, what will each `Put` statement output? (Show the correct format of this output.)

```
Put (Item => 15.0);
Put (Item => 25.6, Fore => 3, Aft => 2, Exp => 0);
Put (Item => 123.4, Fore => 2, Aft => 2, Exp => 0);
Put (Item => 175.8, Fore => 0, Aft => 0, Exp => 0);
```

```
Put (Item => 25.79, Fore => 4, Aft => 1, Exp => 0);
Put (Item => -50.16, Fore => 5, Aft => 1, Exp => 2);
Put (Item => 0.096, Fore => 0, Aft => 1, Exp => 3);
Put (Item => 2_974.12, Fore => 4, Aft => 2, Exp => 1);
```

4. Assuming that the needed instance of the `Enumeration_IO` package is visible, what will each `Put` statement output? (Show the correct format of this output.)

```
Put (Item => True);
Put (Item => True, Width => 1);
Put (Item => False, Width => 9);
Put (Item => True, Set => Lower_Case);
Put (Item => False, Width => 7, Set => Upper_Case);
```

5. Use the procedures `Set_Col`, `Set_Line`, `Skip_Line`, and the versions of `Get` with a width parameter, to input integer values from the following specified fields:

```
Line 3:    Columns    5 to 7      WEIGHT
           Columns    8 to 9      HEIGHT
           Columns    10 to 12    AGE
Line 5:    Columns    2 to 4      IQ
           Columns    7 to 11     INCOME
```

6. Write a program that uses the `Text_IO` package to store the values of the following enumeration type to a file.

```
type Airplane_Parts is (Radar, Cockpit, Engine, Engine_Pod,
   Pylon, Wing, Vertical_Stabilizer, Rudder, Tabs, Elevator,
   Horizontal_Stabilizer, Flaps, Spoilers, Aileron,
   Thrust_Reverser);
```

Write another program to read this file and output each of the enumeration literals in a column on the screen. (The data can be read as either enumeration values or strings.)

7. Rewrite the program in Exercise 6 using the `Ada.Sequential_IO` package instead of the `Text_IO` package. Directly examine the contents of the file and compare what you see with the contents of the file created with the program from Exercise 6.

8. Rewrite the program in Exercise 6 using the `Direct_IO` package instead of the `Text_IO` package. Directly examine the contents of the file and compare with the contents of the file created with the program from Exercises 6 and 7.

9. Explain the potential problem with the following code.

```
with Ada.Text_IO; use Ada;
package Int_IO is new Text_IO.Integer_IO (Integer);
```
---
```
with Int_IO;
procedure A is
```

```
begin
    Int_IO.Default_Base := 2;
    Int_IO.Put(7);
end A;
```

---

```
with Int_IO;
with A;
procedure Main is
begin
    A;
    Int_IO.Put(9);
end Main;
```

10. In the following code, explain what happens when a real value such as 39.5 is entered for N. (Be careful. The answer is tricky, so try it on a computer.)

```
declare
    N: Integer;
begin
    Get (N);   -- assume that 39.5 is entered

        ...
exception
    when Constraint_Error =>...
    when Int_IO.Data_Error =>...
        -- assume Int_IO is an instance of Integer_IO
end;
```

11. Write code that keeps prompting users for the abbreviation of their state until a valid response is made. Use the following type:

```
type States is
    (  AL, AK, AZ, AR, CA, CO, CT, DE, DC, FL, GA,
       HI, ID, IL, IND,IA, KS, KY, LA, ME, MD, MA,
       MI, MN, MS, MO, MT, NE, NV, NH, NJ, NM, NY,
       NC, ND, OH, OK, ORE,PA, RI, SC, SD, TN, TX,
       UT, VT, VA, WA, WV, WI, WY  );
```

# Concurrent Programming

**T**he computer programs presented in the preceding chapters sequentially perform one activity after another. In Ada, one can also write programs that perform more than one activity concurrently (during the same period of time). This concurrent processing is called tasking. The units of code that run concurrently are called tasks.

Ada is one of the few programming languages that directly supports concurrent programming with high-level language constructs such as tasks. Unlike the other languages, the concurrent programs in Ada do not need to directly invoke operating system services or develop supporting routines in assembly code. As a result, concurrent code written in Ada is portable and relatively easy to understand and maintain.

**Ada 95 ▶** Basic support for concurrent programming is provided in the core Ada language. Some real-time applications, however, require extremely efficient code that maximizes execution speed and minimizes code size. Such applications may also require fine control over the way the program executes. Special support for these kinds of applications is provided in the optional Real-Time Systems Annex. This annex itself depends on the optional Systems Programming Annex. (These annexes are primarily concerned with issues related to scheduling, priorities, task identification, concurrent access to shared variables, timing accuracy, and interrupt handling.) Any features contained in these annexes that are described in this chapter will be clearly indicated, since not all Ada compilation systems support these optional annexes.

There are two methods of concurrent processing: overlapped concurrency and interleaved concurrency. On computers with multiple processors, overlapped concurrency can be used. In overlapped concurrency, several tasks execute simultaneously, each on their own processor. On computers with a single processor, interleaved concurrency is used so that each task, in turn, is given a moment of processing time. This jumping around from task to task is typically performed so rapidly that an illusion is created that all tasks are running simultaneously. (Although this jumping around, or "time slicing," is a common way of handling interleaved concurrency, Ada allows alternative approaches. On a single processor system, for example, some implementations run a task to completion unless some higher priority task becomes eligible to run.) Whether overlapped or interleaved concurrency is used, from the programmer's perspective, the effect is the same. The programmer should think of each task as executing over the same period of time.

Tasks may thus be used when various activities need to be performed concurrently. For instance, in a program that controls a space station, one task might monitor the life support system, another might monitor solar activity, another might monitor the orientation of the space station, and so on. In addition, tasks may be used to simulate (model) events in the real world that occur at the same time. Tasks may also be used to increase execution speed, especially when the computer has multiple processors available.

The topic of tasking is very involved. Entire books have been devoted to this subject. It is beyond the scope of this book to give such an exhaustive discussion of tasking. Rather, this chapter stresses the features of Ada tasks; it does not discuss all of the complex issues surrounding the use of these features to solve real problems.

It is also beyond the scope of this book to illustrate all of the pitfalls of concurrent programming. Concurrent programs can fail to execute for reasons that cannot arise in sequential programs. For example, two tasks may suspend their activities, each waiting for the other to do something. Since each task is waiting for the other to act first, they end up waiting forever. Besides this deadlocking, "task starvation" is another problem that can arise. Starvation occurs when a task that is ready to run is never given the processor (or other resources required to run) because other tasks are hogging these resources.

Besides deadlock and starvation, there is yet another pitfall that concurrent programmers face: dependence on the speed of various tasks. The speed with which a task executes can vary, depending on fluctuations in the speed of the hardware and its peripheral devices. Therefore, attempt to write programs that are not dependent on the speed of any of their tasks. Also, attempt to write programs that are not dependent on a specific number of processors being available. In other words, the behavior of a program should not depend on whether it runs on a system with one processor, two processors, three, or more.

We begin this chapter by considering tasks that do not interface with each other. Next we consider tasks that do interface. Such tasks may or may not transfer data. We first explore tasks that do not transfer data, then tasks that do transfer data. The next two sections of this chapter cover the selective **accept** statements and selective entry call statements. These constructs permit greater control of task interaction. We then explore task attributes, entry families, and a useful pragma for prioritizing tasks. Next, we discuss task types, followed by a section on task interference, which is a common problem with concurrent processing. A solution to this problem is presented. Dynamically created tasks are then briefly covered, followed by timing considerations and protected objects. The chapter concludes with a discussion of the Real-Time Systems Annex and the Distributed Systems Annex.

---

## TASKS THAT DO NOT INTERFACE

Concurrent processing is commonly performed by the "computer" between our ears. Without too much mental strain, most of us can, for instance, chew gum, listen to the radio, and drive a car at the same time. Suppose that we attempt to have a computer simulate these activities by invoking the procedures Chew_Gum, Listen_To_Radio, and Drive_To_Mother:

```
procedure Noon_Activity is
begin
    Chew_Gum;
    Listen_To_Radio;
    Drive_To_Mother;
end Noon_Activity;
```

Noon_Activity is not as efficient as we are because the three procedures—Chew_Gum, Listen_To_Radio, and Drive_To_Mother—are performed sequentially, not concurrently. The execution of each procedure is completed before the next one starts. First the procedure Chew_Gum is executed, followed by Listen_To_Radio, followed by Drive_To_Mother. In order to execute all three procedures concurrently, we must use tasks:

```
procedure Noon_Activity is

    task Exercise_Jaw; -- task specification
    task body Exercise_Jaw is -- task body
    begin
        Chew_Gum;
    end Exercise_Jaw;

    task Experience_Music; -- task specification
    task body Experience_Music is -- task body
    begin
        Listen_To_Radio;
    end Experience_Music;

    task Visit_Mom; -- task specification
    task body Visit_Mom is -- task body
    begin
        Drive_To_Mother;
    end Visit_Mom;

begin -- Noon_Activity
    null; -- must always have at least one executable statement
end Noon_Activity;
```

Note that three tasks—Exercise_Jaw, Experience_Music, and Visit_Mom—are embedded within the declarative part of the procedure Noon_Activity. Tasks must always be embedded in the declarative part of other units; they cannot be separate compilation units. (A task body, however, may be separately compiled as a subunit.) The unit in which tasks are embedded is referred to as the "master unit." The tasks are said to "depend" on the master unit. Although a task cannot be a compilation unit, if a task needs to be shared among different compilation units, place the task specification in a package specification. Units that wish to access the task can then **with** this package.

Also note that the three procedures—Chew_Gum, Listen_To_Radio, and Drive_To_Mother—are each invoked from within a task. The procedure Chew_Gum is invoked from within the task Exercise_Jaw; the procedure Listen_To_Radio is invoked from within the task Experience_Music; and the procedure Drive_To_Mother is invoked from within the task Visit_Mom.

Each of the three tasks contained within Noon_Activity has a specification and a body. The specification consists of the keyword **task**, followed by the task name. (As we will discuss momentarily, tasks that interface with each other require a different form of specification.) The task body begins with the keywords **task body**, followed by the task name and the keyword **is**. Optional declarations are placed between the keywords **is** and **begin**. (There are no task declarations in the example.) Executable code is placed between the keywords **begin** and **end**. The keyword **end** is optionally followed by the task name. Tasks that don't interface thus have the following form:

```
task task name; -- specification

task body task name is -- body
   declarations
begin
   statements
end task name;
```

Let us now examine how procedure Noon_Activity works. First the three dependent tasks—Exercise_Jaw, Experience_Music, and Visit_Mom—are elaborated in the declarative part of procedure Noon_Activity. Then, as soon as Noon_Activity starts running (starting with the keyword **begin**), all three tasks start executing concurrently. (On a computer with a single processor, of course, one of these three tasks must receive the first "slice" of processing time. Which task receives this first slice is not defined by the Ada language.) Each task invokes one of the procedures: Chew_Gum, Listen_To_Radio, or Drive_To_Mother. As each of these procedures finishes executing, so does the task that invoked it. When the three tasks finish executing, so does the procedure Noon_Activity, in which they are embedded. Note that if Noon_Activity is not a main program but was called by another program unit, then Noon_Activity cannot return to the caller until after all of its dependent tasks have terminated.

Note that the three tasks in the example do not interface, that is, they do not exchange data or synchronize. ("Synchronize" means to meet at a predetermined point in the code.) Rather, each of these tasks operates independently of the other two tasks.

There is an alternative way of writing procedure Noon_Activity. Any of the procedures contained within the three tasks can instead be placed in the statement part of Noon_Activity, as follows:

```
procedure Noon_Activity is

    task Exercise_Jaw; -- task specification
    task body Exercise_Jaw is -- task body
    begin
        Chew_Gum;
    end Exercise_Jaw;

    task Experience_Music; -- task specification
    task body Experience_Music is -- task body
    begin
        Listen_To_Radio;
    end Experience_Music;

begin -- Noon_Activity
    Drive_To_Mother;
end Noon_Activity;
```

In this alternative, the task Visit_Mom is omitted, and the procedure, Drive_To_Mother, which was invoked by this task, is instead placed in the statement part of Noon_Activity. Either of the other two procedures could be alternatively placed in Noon_Activity. Any difference in performance between these alternative ways of writing Noon_Activity is unspecified by the Ada standards. Note that in this alternative, even though the master unit, Noon_Activity, is a procedure, it behaves like a task that concurrently executes Drive_To_Mother. Such master units are also called "master tasks," even though they may be subprograms. Noon_Activity does not terminate when Drive_To_Mother is finished executing, unless its dependent tasks, Exercise_Jaw and Experience_Music, are also done executing.

## TASKS THAT INTERFACE WITHOUT TRANSFERRING DATA

In the preceding section, we discussed tasks that do not interface. Now let us consider tasks that interface without transferring data. These tasks are used when only synchronization is required. Synchronization is sometimes required so that the execution of one task does not get too far behind or ahead of the execution of another task. Consider the following example:

```
procedure Visit_Mother is

    task Make_Mom_Happy is -- task specification
        entry Eat_Her_Food;
    end Make_Mom_Happy;
```

```
    task body Make_Mom_Happy is -- task body
    begin
        accept Eat_Her_Food do
            Chew_And_Swallow;
        end Eat_Her_Food;
    end Make_Mom_Happy;


    task Time_With_Mom; -- task specification

    task body Time_With_Mom is -- task body
    begin
        Make_Mom_Happy.Eat_Her_Food;
    end Time_With_Mom;

begin -- Visit_Mother
    null;
end Visit_Mother;
```

In this example, procedure `Visit_Mother` contains two tasks: `Make_Mom_Happy` and `Time_With_Mom`. Note that the task specification of `Make_Mom_Happy`, unlike that of `Time_With_Mom`, contains an **entry** clause. It is this clause that enables the task to be called, thereby synchronizing it with the task that does the calling. The general form of a task specification that contains an **entry** clause is as follows:

```
    task task name is
        entry entry name (parameter definitions);
    end task name;
```

This specification begins with the keyword **task**, followed by the task name and the keyword **is**. The specification ends with the keyword **end**, followed optionally by the task name. Two kinds of items may be placed in such a specification: certain pragmas (one of which will be discussed at the end of this chapter) and, as mentioned, **entry** clauses. An **entry** clause contains the keyword **entry**, the entry name, and optional parameter definitions.

The procedure `Visit_Mother` contains a single **entry** clause:

```
    entry Eat_Her_Food;
```

Since no parameters follow the entry identifier `Eat_Her_Food`, this **entry** clause is used only for synchronization, not for transferring data.

The **entry** clause associates an entry identifier in the task specification with one or more entry points inside the corresponding task body. These entry points, indicated by **accept** statements, are the actual points in the code where tasks synchronize and transfer data. Thus, for each **entry** clause in a task specification, one or more associated **accept** statements should appear in the corresponding task body. (The **accept** statement can only appear in a task body; it can never appear, for instance, in the statement part of a procedure.)

In the task `Make_Mom_Happy`, the **entry** clause `Eat_Her_Food` is associated with the **accept** statement having the same identifier:

```
accept Eat_Her_Food do
    Chew_And_Swallow;
end Eat_Her_Food;
```

An **accept** statement has the following form:

```
accept entry identifier (parameter definitions) do
    statements
end entry identifier;
```

The **accept** statement begins with the keyword **accept**, followed by the entry identifier (including any parameters), followed by the keyword **do**. It ends with the keyword **end**, followed by an optional entry identifier. Executable statements are placed between the keywords **do** and **end**. These executable statements can include a **return** statement that causes control to be passed back to the task that did the calling. An **accept** statement that has no executable statements can simply be written, with or without parameter definitions, as follows:

```
accept entry identifier (parameter definitions);
```

Now that we have discussed the structure of a task that interfaces with another task, we will describe how two tasks interface. In order for two tasks to interface, one task must call the other task. The task that does the calling is known as the calling task. The task that is called is known as the acceptor task. The **entry** clauses in the specification of the acceptor task provide interface information needed by other tasks to call the acceptor task. This interface information includes the entry identifiers and the optional parameter definitions, which specify how data is transferred.

Tasks are called in much the same way that procedures are called, except that the calling task must specify both the task identifier and the entry identifier. In the procedure `Visit_Mother`, the task `Time_With_Mom` is the calling task, and `Make_Mom_Happy` is the acceptor task. `Time_With_Mom` calls `Make_Mom_Happy`, as follows:

```
Make_Mom_Happy.Eat_Her_Food;
```

The call consists of the task identifier `Make_Mom_Happy`, followed by a dot, followed by the entry identifier `Eat_Her_Food`. Dot notation cannot be avoided by employing a **use** clause, because tasks may not be mentioned in a **use** clause. There is, however, a mechanism for avoiding dot notation. A task entry can be renamed as a procedure:

```
task body Time_With_Mom is -- body of calling task
    procedure Please_Mother renames Make_Mom_Happy.Eat_Her_Food;
        -- rename an entry as a procedure
begin
```

```
      Please_Mother; -- task entry called as a procedure
   end Time_With_Mom;
```

By renaming a task entry as a procedure, the task entry can optionally be called as a procedure. This allows a long, extended task entry name to be substituted with a short procedure name. In addition, it allows a task entry call that may be unfamiliar to beginning programmers to be substituted with a procedure call that is familiar to all Ada programmers. (However, as described in the *Ada 95 Reference Manual*, Ada syntax sometimes requires that a task entry name be used instead of the renamed procedure name). Although a task entry call appears to be similar to a procedure call and can even be renamed as a procedure call, the mechanism of the call is quite different. Procedures are executed upon demand. If several tasks simultaneously call the same procedure, then the procedure may be executed at the same time by different tasks. (This is allowed since Ada requires subprograms to be "reentrant.") In contrast, if several tasks simultaneously call the same task entry, only one of their calls is accepted. The other tasks must wait their turn for their call to be accepted.

Note the asymmetry between a calling task and an acceptor task. To call a task, one must know the name of the task and the name of its entry. On the other hand, the acceptor task does not know the identity of those who call it. It is just a passive server to any task that deigns to call it.

When an entry of a task is called, one of the task's associated **accept** statements is executed when that point in the code is reached. When the **accept** statement is executed, the group of statements contained within it is executed. This group of statements specifies the actions to be performed as the tasks are interfacing. In the acceptor task `Make_Mom_Happy`, the **accept** statement `Eat_Her_Food` only specifies one action to be performed: `Chew_And_Swallow`.

Now let us consider how the procedure `Visit_Mother` works. After the declarations of the procedure are elaborated and execution begins, the two tasks, `Make_Mom_Happy` and `Time_With_Mom`, are activated. The task `Time_With_Mom` calls the acceptor task `Make_Mom_Happy`. Depending on the execution speed of each task, there are three possible situations. First, the acceptor task might be prepared to accept a call before a call is made. Second, a call might be made before the acceptor task is prepared to accept it. Third, there is the unlikely event that the acceptor task becomes ready to accept a call the moment the call is made.

Consider the first situation, where the acceptor task is prepared to accept a call before a call is made. In this situation, the acceptor task waits until a call is eventually made. In terms of our example, the acceptor task, `Make_Mom_Happy`, reaches its **accept** statement before the calling task, `Time_With_Mom`, calls the associated task entry. `Make_Mom_Happy` then waits for a call to be made. When `Time_With_Mom` finally makes the entry call, `Make_Mom_Happy.Eat_Her_Food`, the wait of `Make_Mom_Happy` is over, and the two tasks "rendezvous."

The term "rendezvous" refers to the meeting of two tasks. During a rendezvous, the two tasks synchronize and optionally transfer data. (In this particular example, no data transfer takes place.) During the rendezvous, the acceptor task executes all the statements within its **accept** statement while the calling task is suspended. When all the statements within the **accept** statement are done executing, the rendezvous is finished. The tasks are once again free to go their separate merry ways.

Since the calling task is suspended until the **accept** statement finishes executing, the number of statements in the **accept** statement should be kept to a minimum. Statements that do not need to be executed during a rendezvous should be placed outside of the **accept** statement, so that the calling task is not suspended longer than necessary.

In terms of our example, when the calling task `Time_With_Mom` finally makes the entry call `Make_Mom_Happy.Eat_Her_Food`, `Make_Mom_Happy` executes the one statement within its **accept** statement: `Chew_And_Swallow`. `Time_With_Mom` waits until `Chew_And_Swallow` is done executing, at which time the rendezvous is finished. When the rendezvous is finished, the tasks `Make_Mom_Happy` and `Time_With_Mom` disassociate and continue executing independently. Figure 15.1 shows the rendezvous process when an acceptor task is prepared to accept a call before the call is made.

Let us now consider the second situation that may result when one task calls another task: a call might be made before the acceptor task is prepared to accept it. In this situation, the calling task waits until its call is eventually accepted.

Applying this situation to the example, the calling task, `Time_With_Mom`, makes the entry call `Make_Mom_Happy.Eat_Her_Food` before the acceptor task, `Make_Mom_Happy`, reaches the associated **accept** statement. `Time_With_Mom`

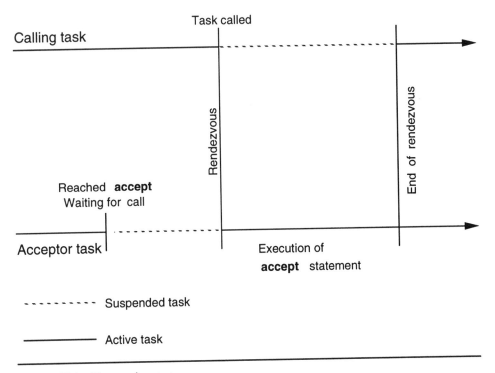

**Figure 15.1**   The rendezvous.

waits until Make_Mom_Happy reaches the **accept** statement and accepts its call. When Make_Mom_Happy accepts the call, a rendezvous is initiated.

In the third situation, a call is made at the same moment that the acceptor task is prepared to accept it. In this situation, a rendezvous is immediately initiated; neither task waits. This situation is rare. Since tasks progress at their own rate, it is unlikely for them to reach their rendezvous point at exactly the same time. (When is the last time you and another person arrived at your rendezvous point at exactly the same time?)

The meeting of two tasks is thus similar to the meeting of two people. The first task to arrive at a rendezvous point must wait for the other task to arrive.

Note that, in the preceding example, the task Make_Mom_Happy is called only once, and its **accept** statement is reached only once. Suppose, however, that the programmer needs to call Make_Mom_Happy twice:

```
procedure Visit_Mother is

    task Make_Mom_Happy is
       entry Eat_Her_Food;
    end Make_Mom_Happy;

    task body Make_Mom_Happy is
    begin
       accept Eat_Her_Food do -- error; entry called twice,
          Chew_And_Swallow;   -- but accept executed once
       end Eat_Her_Food;
    end Make_Mom_Happy;

    task Time_With_Mom;

    task body Time_With_Mom is
    begin
       Make_Mom_Happy.Eat_Her_Food;  -- calls Make_Mom_Happy
    end Time_With_Mom;

begin -- Visit_Mother
    Make_Mom_Happy.Eat_Her_Food;    -- calls Make_Mom_Happy
end Visit_Mother;
```

This example illustrates a tasking error that arises because Make_Mom_Happy reaches its **accept** statement only once yet is called twice: once from the task body Time_With_Mom and once from the statement part of the procedure Visit_Mother. Let us see how this problem arises. Suppose that the task Time_With_Mom first calls Make_Mom_Happy. In this case, if Visit_Mother makes its call while Time_With_Mom and Make_Mom_Happy are in a rendezvous, then it must wait. Only two tasks can participate in a rendezvous. After the rendezvous is finished, the task Make_Mom_Happy reaches its **end** statement and terminates. The predefined exception Tasking_Error is raised because Visit_Mother is now attempting to rendezvous with a task that has terminated.

It is perfectly legitimate for a task entry to be called twice. However, to avoid a `Tasking_Error` exception, the body of the acceptor task must be written so that the associated **accept** statement is also reached twice. This may be accomplished, for instance, by looping over the **accept** statement twice or by simply writing the **accept** statement twice:

```
task Make_Mom_Happy is
    entry Eat_Her_Food;
end Make_Mom_Happy;

task body Make_Mom_Happy is
begin

    accept Eat_Her_Food do
        Chew_And_Swallow;
    end Eat_Her_Food;


    . . .
    accept Eat_Her_Food do
        Chew_And_Swallow;
    end Eat_Her_Food;

end Make_Mom_Happy;
```

The single task entry, `Eat_Her_Food`, is now associated with the two **accept** statements within the task body. The first task entry call is accepted by the first **accept** statement; the second task entry call is accepted by the second **accept** statement.

Now that we have seen how a `Tasking_Error` exception can be raised, let us briefly see how exception handlers can be used to handle such an exception. In Chapter 10, we showed how exception handlers may be placed in block statements, subprograms, and packages. Exception handlers may also be placed in a task body:

```
task body Time_With_Mom is
begin
    Make_Mom_Happy.Eat_Her_Food; -- call Make_Mom_Happy
exception
    when Tasking_Error => Ask_For_Seconds;
end Time_With_Mom;
```

In this example, whenever a `Tasking_Error` is raised, the exception handler invokes the procedure `Ask_For_Seconds`. If the task is running and an exception is raised that is not handled by this exception handler, then the task automatically terminates; the exception does not propagate as it does for block statements, subprograms, and packages. This behavior, however, only applies to exceptions that are raised as tasks are executing and if no rendezvous is in progress.

A full description of how exceptions are propagated by tasks is beyond the scope of this book. The following brief description is for the advanced reader. Since a rendezvous involves two tasks, an unhandled exception that is raised during a rendezvous is propagated to both the calling task and the acceptor task. For the acceptor task, the exception is propagated at the end of the **accept** statement. For the calling task, the exception is propagated at the point of the call. Exceptions that are raised during a rendezvous, however, do not have to propagate. Such exceptions can be captured in an exception handler for the **accept** statement:

**Ada 95** ▶

```
accept Eat_Her_Food do
   Chew_And_Swallow;
exception
   when others => Heimlich_Maneuver;
end Eat_Her_Food;
```

If an exception is raised during the elaboration of a task body, then the exception Tasking_Error propagates to the point where the task was activated.

Now that we have briefly described exception propagation, let us return to our main discussion. As we have seen in a previous example, a task entry can be called multiple times. In such situations, the acceptor task may not be able to accept all the entry calls as they are made. Thus, a backlog of entry calls may form. This backlog of entry calls is stored in a queue for that task entry. Each task entry has its own queue. When the acceptor task is ready to accept a call to an entry, it accepts the calls on the entry queue on a first in first out (FIFO) basis. In other words, calls are accepted in the order in which they arrived. A task whose call is in an entry queue is suspended until its call is accepted and the rendezvous completes. (As we will show later in this chapter, an acceptor task may use the Count attribute to inquire about the number of entry calls that have been placed in an entry queue.)

## TASKS THAT INTERFACE AND TRANSFER DATA

Now that we have discussed tasks that rendezvous without transferring data, we will explore tasks that rendezvous and transfer data:

```
task Gas_Station_Attendant is -- task specification
   entry Service_Island (Car: Car_Type);
end Gas_Station_Attendant;

task body Gas_Station_Attendant is -- task body
begin
   loop
      accept Service_Island (Car: Car_Type ) do
         Fill_With_Gas (Car);
      end Service_Island;
   end loop;
end Gas_Station_Attendant;
```

Speaking loosely, the acceptor task Gas_Station_Attendant waits for a car to arrive at the service island. When a car arrives, it is filled with gas, and the "gas station attendant" waits for the next car to arrive. Since an infinite loop is used, this process continues nonstop, 24 hours a day, 7 days a week, with no time off.

More specifically, here is how this task works. When Gas_Station_Attendant runs, the infinite loop in the task body is entered and the **accept** statement Service_Island is reached. The task waits until the associated task entry Service_Island is called by an external unit. Note that the task entry has a parameter definition: Car is declared to be a formal **in** parameter of type Car_Type, which we assume has been previously defined. (Parameter modes for task entries are like those for procedures: when the parameter mode is omitted, an **in** parameter is assumed.) When a call is made to the Service_Island entry, an actual parameter must be passed to the formal parameter Car. It is through such parameter passing that data is transferred between tasks:

```
Gas_Station_Attendant.Service_Island (My_Car);
```

When the rendezvous is initiated, the calling task passes the value of the parameter My_Car to the **accept** statement, Service_Island, within the acceptor task. The **accept** statement then invokes the procedure Fill_With_Gas with this parameter value. After the procedure Fill_With_Gas is done executing, the rendezvous is finished.

The formal parameter, Car, only exists within the **accept** statement. Since the procedure Fill_With_Gas accesses this parameter, this procedure must be placed within the **accept** statement. Anyway, a car cannot be filled with gas while continuing down the road. The motorist must wait at the service island while the gas tank is being filled. In other words, the calling task must wait until Fill_With_Gas is finished executing.

Note that the data transfer that occurs in this example is from the calling task to the acceptor task. Data may also be transferred from the acceptor task to the calling task. This is accomplished just as it is for procedures—by using **out** or **in out** parameter modes.

Consider an **accept** statement that has an **in** parameter and an **out** parameter:

```
accept Parameter_Modes (   In_Param: in Positive;
                           Out_Param: out Character) do
   if In_Param in Character'Pos ('A')..Character'Pos ('Z')
   then
      Out_Param := Character'Val (In_Param);
   else
      Out_Param := ' ';
   end if;
end Parameter_Modes;
```

When the **accept** statement is executed, the actual parameter value in the entry call is passed to In_Param. This value is then used by the **if** statement within the **accept** statement. If the value of In_Param lies within the range of 65 to 90 (which are the positions of the uppercase letters in the character set), then Out_Param is set to the character at that position, else Out_Param is set to a blank character.

After the statements in the **accept** statement are done executing, the result stored in Out_Param is then passed back to the calling task, and the rendezvous ends.

Since the formal parameters, In_Param and Out_Param, are accessible only within the **accept** statement, and since the calling task must wait for the final value of Out_Param to be calculated, all of the previous code must be placed within the **accept** statement, not after it. In general, the only code that should appear in an **accept** statement (and hence, that will be executed during the rendezvous), are those statements that refer to entry parameters, or those statements that must be executed while the calling task is suspended. Any additional code placed in the **accept** statement results in the unnecessary suspension of the calling task.

Note that task entry calls are similar to procedure calls in that they both may use positional or named notation. Thus, assuming that the previous **accept** statement is in the body of task T (which is not shown), the following task entry calls are equivalent:

```
-- assume Char is a character variable)
T.Parameter_Modes (65, Char); -- positional notation

T.Parameter_Modes (In_Param => 65, Out_Param => Char);
   -- named notation
```

So far, every task presented has contained, at most, one **entry** clause. As the following example shows, tasks may contain multiple entries:

```
task Gas_Station_Attendant is -- task specification
   entry Service_Island (Car: Car_Type);
   entry Garage (Car: Car_Type);
end Gas_Station_Attendant;

task body Gas_Station_Attendant is -- task body
begin
   loop
      accept Service_Island (Car: Car_Type) do
         Fill_With_Gas (Car);
      end Service_Island;
      accept Garage (Car: Car_Type) do
         Fix (Car);
      end Garage;
   end loop;
end Gas_Station_Attendant;
```

Each of the two task entries, Service_Island and Garage, has a formal parameter of type Car_Type. Again, speaking loosely, the gas station attendant waits for a car to arrive at the service island. When a car arrives, it is filled with gas. The attendant then waits for a car to enter the garage. When a car enters the garage, it is fixed. The process then repeats: the attendant waits for a car to arrive at the service island, then for a car to enter the garage, and so on. Of course, this is no way to run a gas station. The attendant insists on going back and forth between the service island and the garage, regardless of the number of cars waiting for each kind of service. For example, after a car enters the service island and is filled with gas, the attendant then waits for a car to enter the garage. The attendant keeps waiting even if a long line of cars forms at the service island. (This task is modeled after my neighborhood gas station.)

More specifically, the code works as follows. Once the infinite loop in the task body is entered and the first **accept** statement, `Service_Island`, is reached, the task waits until the corresponding task entry is called. When a call is made, a rendezvous occurs, and the **accept** statement then invokes the procedure `Fill_With_Gas`. After the procedure is done executing, the rendezvous is finished, and the second **accept** statement, `Garage`, is reached. The task waits until the `Garage` task entry is called. When a call is made, a rendezvous occurs, and the **accept** statement then invokes the procedure `Fix`. When `Fix` is done executing, the rendezvous is finished, and the loop returns us to the **accept** statement for `Service_Island`, where the process repeats.

In order to write a more reasonable version of task `Gas_Station_Attendant`, a selective **accept** statement can be used.

## SELECTIVE ACCEPT STATEMENTS

Selective **accept** statements are used by acceptor tasks to control how they accept entry calls. The kind of selective **accept** statement that we need to improve task `Gas_Station_Attendant` has the following form:

```
select
    accept statement
        . . .
or
    accept statement
        . . .
or
    accept statement
        . . .
end select;
```

The **selective accept** statement begins with the keyword **select** and ends with the keywords **end select**. Within this variation of the **select** statement are multiple **accept** statements, each separated by an **or**. An **accept** statement must be placed immediately after the keyword **select** or the keyword **or**. Any statements can be placed after the **accept** statement.

The above selective **accept** statement selects any of the **accept** statements whose associated entry has been called. It does not wait for a particular entry call if other entries have been called. Applying this variation of the selective **accept** statement to the previous version of `Gas_Station_Attendant`, we obtain the following:

```
task Gas_Station_Attendant is -- task specification
   entry Service_Island (Car: Car_Type);
   entry Garage (Car: Car_Type);
end Gas_Station_Attendant;

task body Gas_Station_Attendant is -- task body
begin
   loop
      select
         accept Service_Island (Car: Car_Type) do
            Fill_With_Gas (Car);
         end Service_Island;
      or
         accept Garage (Car: Car_Type) do
            Fix (Car);
         end Garage;
      end select;
   end loop;
end Gas_Station_Attendant;
```

Again speaking loosely, if a car arrives at the service island and no car is at the garage, then the gas station attendant fills the car with gas. Conversely, if a car is at the garage and no car is at the service island, then the attendant fixes the car. If a car is waiting at both the service island and the garage, then the attendant arbitrarily (not necessarily randomly) selects one car or the other to service. If no car is either at the service island or the garage, then the attendant waits for the first car to arrive.

More specifically, once the **select** statement within the infinite loop is reached, the acceptor task accepts whichever task entry was called. If both task entries were called, Ada does not specify which entry will be selected. If neither entry was called, the acceptor task waits for whichever entry is called first.

As we have seen, either a calling task or an acceptor task may get suspended. If a calling task calls another task that is not ready to rendezvous, then the calling task is suspended. If an acceptor task reaches a **select** statement and no calls have been made to any of its entries, then the acceptor task is suspended. Although in both situations a task is suspended, there is an important difference. The difference is that a calling task waits for a single event—for its call to be accepted. In contrast, an acceptor task may wait for any one of many different events—for any task to call any of its entries in the **select** statement. Since the calling task waits for a single event while the acceptor task may wait for any one of many events, a calling task is typically at greater risk of being suspended for a long time. When designing concurrent systems, therefore, a task that must quickly respond to many events and cannot afford to wait for any single event should be an acceptor task. Only a task that can afford to wait for its call to be accepted should be a calling task.

One of the problems with the last version of Gas_Station_Attendant is that we are assuming that gas is always available. As everyone knows, this is not the case. The next version of the task, which uses another variation of the selective **accept** statement, deals with this problem by placing a **when** clause before the **accept** statement for Service_Island:

```
task Gas_Station_Attendant is -- task specification
    entry Service_Island (Car: Car_Type);
    entry Garage (Car: Car_Type);
end Gas_Station_Attendant;

task body Gas_Station_Attendant is -- task body
begin
    loop
        select
            when Gas_Available =>
                accept Service_Island (Car: Car_Type) do -- guarded
                    Fill_With_Gas (Car);
                end Service_Island;
        or
            accept Garage (Car: Car_Type) do -- unguarded
                Fix (Car);
            end Garage;
        end select;
    end loop;
end Gas_Station_Attendant;
```

An **accept** statement preceded by a **when** clause is said to be "guarded." In other words, the **when** clause acts as a "guard," permitting or not permitting the acceptor task to reach the guarded **accept** statement. The **when** clause consists of the keyword **when**, followed by a Boolean expression, and an arrow. The Boolean expression is evaluated only at the top of the **select** statement, which means once each time through the loop. If the Boolean expression has the value True, then the guard permits the **accept** statement to be reached. In such cases, the alternative containing the **accept** statement is "open" and is a possible candidate for a rendezvous. If the Boolean expression has the value False, then the alternative containing the **accept** statement is "closed" and cannot be considered for a rendezvous. In the example, the guard contains the Boolean function Gas_Available. If Gas_Available returns True, then the select alternative is open, and the **accept** statement for Service_Island can be considered for a rendezvous, just as if the **when** clause were not present. If Gas_Available returns False, then this alternative is closed, and the **accept** statement for Service_Island cannot be considered for a rendezvous (although the entry within a closed alternative may still be called by other tasks or already have calling tasks waiting).

When gas is available, this version of Gas_Station_Attendant behaves just like the previous version. The gas station attendant either accepts a car at the service station or at the garage, depending on which request is made first. If both requests are made, then one request is arbitrarily selected. If neither request is made, then the attendant waits.

Suppose, however, that gas is not available. In this case, only cars entering the garage are considered. If no car enters the garage, the gas station attendant just waits; no attempt is made to take a car at the service island.

Care must be taken when all of the alternatives in a **select** statement are guarded. Consider, for example, the following version of Gas_Station_Attendant:

```
task Gas_Station_Attendant is -- task specification
   entry Service_Island (Car: Car_Type);
   entry Garage (Car: Car_Type);
end Gas_Station_Attendant;

task body Gas_Station_Attendant is -- task body
begin
   loop
      select -- program error might be raised
         when Gas_Available =>
            accept Service_Island (Car: Car_Type) do -- guarded
               Fill_With_Gas (Car);
            end Service_Island;
      or
         when Garage_Available =>
            accept Garage (Car: Car_Type) do      -- guarded
               Fix (Car);
            end Garage;
      end select;
   end loop;
end Gas_Station_Attendant;
```

Each **accept** statement in this example is guarded. When the **select** statement is entered, each guard is evaluated and only open alternatives are considered. If there are no open alternatives (all the guards are `False`), then instead of letting `Gas_Station_Attendant` suspend itself forever, the predefined exception, `Program_Error`, is raised. In the example, therefore, one must be sure that the `Boolean` functions, `Gas_Available` and `Garage_Available`, can never both be `False`. If this cannot be guaranteed, then the possibility of an exception being raised can be avoided by using an **else** clause within the **select** statement. The following example is yet another variation of the selective **accept** statement:

```
task Gas_Station_Attendant is -- task specification
   entry Service_Island (Car: Car_Type);
   entry Garage (Car: Car_Type);
end Gas_Station_Attendant;

task body Gas_Station_Attendant is -- task body
begin
   loop
      select
         when Gas_Available =>
            accept Service_Island (Car: Car_Type) do -- guarded
               Fill_With_Gas (Car);
            end Service_Island;
      or
         when Garage_Available =>
            accept Garage (Car: Car_Type) do      -- guarded
               Fix (Car);
            end Garage;
```

```
        else
            Tidy_Up_Gas_Station;
        end select;
    end loop;
end Gas_Station_Attendant;
```

In this example, the **select** statement contains three alternatives, which are separated by the keywords **or** and **else**. The first two alternatives are guarded as before. The third alternative, however, is preceded by the keyword **else**. This alternative can contain a sequence of one or more statements, such as a call to the procedure Tidy_Up_Gas_Station. This third alternative is only selected when, for whatever reason, one of the other two alternatives cannot be selected. These other alternatives cannot be selected either when they are closed or when they are open but their associated task entries have not been called.

Speaking loosely again, the gas station attendant first checks to see if gas is available and if the garage is available. If neither is available, then the attendant tidies up the gas station. If, however, gas is available and/or the garage is available, then before considering tidying up the gas station, the attendant checks whether any cars are waiting for whatever service is available. If a car is waiting for an available service, then instead of tidying up the gas station, the attendant services the car. Finally, if one or both services are available but no cars are waiting to be serviced, then the attendant tidies up the gas station; he does not wait for an available service to be requested. Note that by using the **else** clause, the attendant never waits around doing nothing.

In the examples shown so far, when an acceptor task arrives at a rendezvous point before the calling task, it either waits indefinitely for a calling task to make a call, or it shows ultimate impatience by refusing to wait for even a moment. There is an alternative to these two extremes. A programmer may specify how long an acceptor task must wait. This variation of the selective **accept** statement uses the keyword **delay**:

```
task Gas_Station_Attendant is -- task specification
    entry Service_Island (Car: Car_Type);
    entry Garage (Car: Car_Type);
end Gas_Station_Attendant;

task body Gas_Station_Attendant is -- task body
begin
    loop
        select
            accept Service_Island (Car: Car_Type) do
                Fill_With_Gas (Car);
            end Service_Island;
        or
            accept Garage (Car: Car_Type) do
                Fix (Car);
            end Garage;
        or
```

```
            delay 3_600.0;  -- wait 1 hour before taking a break
            Take_A_Break;
        end select;
    end loop;
end Gas_Station_Attendant;
```

In this example, when the **select** statement is reached, the gas station attendant checks whether a car requests service at the service island or at the garage. If neither service is requested, the attendant waits up to 1 hour. If a car arrives before the hour is up, then the attendant provides it with the requested service. If the hour expires without a car arriving, the attendant stops waiting and takes a break.

Since the **delay** statement in this code immediately follows an **or** clause of a **select** statement, it does not behave like the **delay** statements shown in Chapter 3, or later in this chapter in the section on timing considerations. The previously encountered **delay** statements express the actual amount of time to wait, whereas this **delay** statement expresses the maximum amount of time that waiting is tolerable. Specifically, when the **select** statement is reached, if no calls have been made to the task entries Service_Island or Garage, then the task waits up to the amount of time specified in the **delay** statement. In the preceding code, for instance, instead of unconditionally waiting 1 hour (3600 seconds), the **delay** statement acts as a timer that is interrupted the moment a unit calls one of the task entries in the **select** statement. Suppose, for example, that after waiting 50 minutes, a task calls the Garage task entry. As soon as this call is made, the task Gas_Station_Attendant stops the timer, accepts the call, and the rendezvous is initiated. After the rendezvous is finished, the **select** statement is exited (without calling the procedure Take_A_Break). The call to Take_A_Break is only made if a full hour elapses without any task calling the task entries within the **select** statement.

The **delay** statement must immediately follow the keyword **or** in order for it to work as a timer. If an unconditional delay is desired, then a construct such as the following is required:

```
    . . .
else
    . . .                 -- statements may go here
    delay 3_600.0;    -- an unconditional delay
end select;
```

Instead of a **delay** statement, a **terminate** statement may also be placed after the **or** in a **select** statement:

```
task Gas_Station_Attendant is -- task specification
    entry Service_Island (Car: Car_Type);
    entry Garage (Car: Car_Type);
end Gas_Station_Attendant;

task body Gas_Station_Attendant is -- task body
begin
    loop
```

```
select
   accept Service_Island (Car: Car_Type) do
      Fill_With_Gas (Car);
   end Service_Island;
or
   accept Garage (Car: Car_Type) do
      Fix (Car);
   end Garage;
or                    -- when service is no longer required,
   terminate;    -- terminate this task
end select;
   end loop;
end Gas_Station_Attendant;
```

In this example, if no call has been made, or ever can be made, to the Service_Island or Garage task entries, then the task Gas_Station_Attendant terminates. This task is terminated with the **terminate** statement, which just consists of the keyword **terminate** immediately following the **or**. (The **terminate** statement may be guarded, although this is infrequently done.)

The terminate alternative is "safe" since it is only taken if there is no possibility of another task generating a Tasking_Error by calling Gas_Station_Attendant after Gas_Station_Attendant has terminated. This means that the **terminate** alternative can only be selected if Gas_Station_Attendant's master task (not shown) is ready to terminate, and if any other tasks directly or indirectly dependent on this master task have terminated or are ready to terminate. If every acceptor task (dependent on the same master) is waiting on a **terminate** alternative in its **select** statement, then they all terminate together. (Ada does not define when tasks terminate when their master is a library package.) This safely orchestrated termination using the **terminate** statement is in sharp contrast to the **abort** statement. The **abort** statement (not a form of the selective **accept** statement) terminates a task "midstream."

Unlike the **terminate** statement, the **abort** statement usually brings task execution to a screeching halt. The **abort** statement should only be used in emergencies when one must "slam on the brakes," because, despite language-imposed precautions, the aborted task may leave incomplete and perhaps corrupted results in its wake. Furthermore, unlike the **terminate** statement, there is no guarantee that an attempt will not be made to call a task after it has aborted.

The **abort** statement consists of the keyword **abort**, followed by a list of tasks to be aborted. If, for example, our gas station attendant works too hard and goes berserk, we can take emergency measures and abort the task, as follows:

```
abort Gas_Station_Attendant;
```

Unlike the **terminate** statement that terminates the task from within, the **abort** statement aborts external tasks.

Usually the tasks listed after the keyword **abort** are quickly aborted; however, they may not be the only program units that are aborted. All tasks that depend on the aborted tasks are aborted as well, in addition to all the active subprograms that the aborted tasks invoked.

The exact behavior of the **abort** statement depends on the activity taking place at the time. Tasks listed after the keyword **abort** are promptly aborted unless the task is engaged in certain critical operations such as executing a call on a task entry (or on a protected operation, to be discussed later), or a call on an `Initialize` or `Finalize` operation for a controlled type. Tasks are also not aborted when waiting in an entry queue. Task abortion is disallowed in such circumstances to prevent seized resources from not being released or to prevent data from being left in a corrupted state. As soon as such critical activities have completed, the task immediately aborts. Despite these safety checks, however, aborting a task is still risky business.

In addition to the **terminate** and **abort** statements, a task can be terminated by calling a task entry designed to terminate the task. For example, the following version of `Gas_Station_Attendant` can be terminated by calling the entry `Close_Station`:

```
task Gas_Station_Attendant is -- task specification
   entry Service_Island (Car: Car_Type);
   entry Garage (Car: Car_Type);
   entry Close_Station;
end Gas_Station_Attendant;


task body Gas_Station_Attendant is -- task body
begin
   loop
      select
         accept Service_Island (Car: Car_Type) do
            Fill_With_Gas (Car);
         end Service_Island;
      or
         accept Garage (Car: Car_Type) do
            Fix (Car);
         end Garage;
      or
         when Service_Island'Count = 0 and Garage'Count = 0 =>
            accept Close_Station;
            exit; -- exit loop and terminate task
      end select;
   end loop;
end Gas_Station_Attendant;
```

After a call to `Close_Station` is accepted, the **exit** statement jumps out of the loop and `Gas_Station_Attendant` terminates. Note that the `Count` attribute is used in the guard for `Close_Station`. The `Count` attribute appends to the name of a task entry and may only reside within the acceptor task body. This attribute yields the number of calls in the specified entry queue. The guard uses the `Count` attribute to make sure that calls to `Close_Station` can only be accepted if there are no pending calls to `Service_Island` or `Garage`. However, even if there are no pending calls, the danger is that future calls may be made after the `Close_Station` entry is accepted and the `Gas_Station_Attendant` is terminated. A **terminate** statement would guarantee that this could not happen. However, in this example, the programmer must guarantee that this cannot happen.

We have seen variations of the selective **accept** statement that have the following special **select** alternatives: an **else** clause, a **delay** statement, or a **terminate** statement. Three rules apply when using these special alternatives. First, no more than one of these special alternatives may be contained in a single **select** statement. The **terminate** alternative, for example, may not appear in the same **select** statement with a **delay** alternative or an **else** clause. Second, a **select** statement cannot solely consist of a special alternative; it must include at least one **accept** statement. Third, these special alternatives are selected only when none of the other alternatives can be selected.

Before leaving this section, let us consider how tasks can be combined with generics. Even though a task cannot be a generic, it can be declared within a generic package and reference the generic parameters. This is illustrated in the following generic queue package that allows concurrent updates to a queue. Note that the task entries `Insert` and `Remove` access the package's formal generic parameter `Queue_Type`:

```
generic
    type Item_Type is private;
package Queue_Service is
    task Queue is
        entry Insert (Item: in Item_Type);
        entry Remove (Item: out Item_Type);
    end Queue;
end Queue_Service;


package body Queue_Service is
    task body Queue is
        Max_Size: constant := 1_000;
        type Size_Range is range 0 .. Max_Size;
        Head, Tail: Size_Range := 1;
        Queue_Array: array (Size_Range) of Item_Type;
        Length: Natural range 0 .. Max_Size := 0;
    begin
        loop
            select
                when Length < Max_Size =>  -- prevents overflow
                    accept Insert (Item: in Item_Type) do
                        Queue_Array (Tail) := Item;
                    end Insert;
                    Tail := Tail mod Max_Size + 1; -- wrap around
                    Length := Length + 1;
            or
                when Length > 0 =>          -- prevents underflow
                    accept Remove (Item: out Item_Type) do
                        Item := Queue_Array (Head);
```

```
                        end Remove;
                        Head := Head mod Max_Size + 1; -- wrap around
                        Length := Length - 1;
                  end select;
              end loop;
          end Queue;
      end Queue_Service;
```

This package works as follows. The queue is implemented as an array, `Queue_Array`, of `1,000` elements. One index of the array, `Head`, "points" to the head of the queue, and another index, `Tail`, "points" to the tail. Items are removed from the head of the queue and added to the tail of the queue. The index values "wrap around" from the last component to the first component. Task entries are used to insert and remove items from the queue. If adding an item to the queue would cause the tail index to overtake the head index (queue overflow), then the calling task is suspended until additional items are removed from the queue. If removing an item would cause the head index to overtake the tail index (queue underflow), then the calling task is suspended until additional items are added to the queue. Guards are used to suspend the calling task.

Depending on how `Queue_Service` is instantiated, different types of objects can be queued. For example, the following instantiation creates a queue to store character values:

```
package Character_Queue is new Queue_Service
    (Item_Type => Character);
```

To add the character `'A'` to the queue, the `Insert` entry is called:

```
Character_Queue.Queue.Insert (Item => 'A');
```

To remove an entry from the queue, the `Remove` entry is called:

```
Character_Queue.Queue.Remove (Item => Char);
    -- assume Char is a character variable
```

Since only one task at a time can rendezvous with the generic instance of `Queue_Service`, concurrent updates to the queue can be made without conflicts. As we will see later in this chapter, unless software is designed for concurrent access, tasks may interfere with each other.

## SELECTIVE ENTRY CALL STATEMENTS

So far we have seen how a form of the **select** statement, called the selective **accept** statement, can be used within the acceptor task. Now we will discuss the selective entry call statement, which may only appear in the calling task. Selective entry call statements come in three forms: conditional entry calls, timed entry calls, and asynchronous **select** statements. Let us first examine the conditional entry call.

## Conditional Entry Calls

The following conditional entry call simulates the behavior of the impatient motorist who leaves one gas station in search of another if service is not immediately provided:

```
select -- conditional entry call
    Gas_Station_Attendant.Service_Island (My_Car);
else
    Try_Another_Gas_Station;
end select;
```

This code first attempts to call the task entry `Service_Island`, in task `Gas_Station_Attendant`. If the call is not immediately accepted by the task, then the **else** clause is executed, which invokes the procedure `Try_Another_Gas_Station`.

## Timed Entry Calls

Let us now consider the timed entry call. The motorist in the following example is not quite as impatient as the motorist in the preceding example. This motorist waits 5 minutes before leaving one gas station in search of another:

```
select -- timed entry call
    Gas_Station_Attendant.Service_Island (My_Car);
or
    delay 300.0; -- wait 5 minutes
    Try_Another_Gas_Station;
end select;
```

The code calls the task entry `Service_Island`. If the call is not immediately accepted by the task `Gas_Station_Attendant`, then a **delay** statement that acts as a 5-minute (300-second) timer is activated. If the entry call is accepted before the 5 minutes are over, then the timer is abruptly halted, and a rendezvous takes place. Note that the **delay** only measures the time spent waiting for the rendezvous to start, not the time spent executing the rendezvous. After the rendezvous is finished, the **select** statement is exited. On the other hand, if the entry call is not accepted within 5 minutes, then the entry call is removed from the `Service_Island` entry queue, and the procedure `Try_Another_Gas_Station` is executed. After the procedure is finished executing, the **select** statement is exited.

## Asynchronous Select Statements

**Ada 95 ▶** There is yet another form of the selective entry call statement—the asynchronous **select** statement—that uses the **then abort** clause. This clause causes an activity to be abandoned when some condition arises that requires an alternative action to be taken. For example, anyone cooking their first turkey on Thanksgiving may not realize how much time is required to cook the turkey. The following code illustrates this problem:

```
select -- asynchronous select statement
    delay 10_800.0; -- wait 3 hours for turkey to be cooked
    Dine_Out_For_Thanksgiving;
then abort
    Cook_The_Turkey;
end select;
```

This code begins executing by cooking the turkey. If the turkey is not cooked in 3 hours (10,800 seconds), then the cooking is abandoned and the alternative of dining out for Thanksgiving is taken instead. On the other hand, if the turkey is cooked within the 3 hour limit, then the **select** statement is finished executing and the delay is cancelled. This form of **select** statement is useful whenever a missed deadline requires that the current activity be abandoned for a new activity.

In the previous example, the **delay** statement determines when the cooking of the turkey should be abandoned. The expiration of the delay triggers the transfer of control from the Cook_The_Turkey procedure to the Dine_Out_For_Thanksgiving procedure. Besides the expiration of a **delay** statement, the acceptance of a task entry call can also act as a trigger for transferring control. The following code illustrates this form of the asynchronous **select** statement:

```
begin
    Read_Card (Card_Data);
    select -- asynchronous select statement
        Keyboard.Cancel_Pressed;
        raise Transaction_Cancelled;
    then abort
        Validate_Card (Card_Data);
    end select;
    Perform_Transaction (Card_Data);
exception
    when Transaction_Cancelled =>
        Display_Cancellation_Notice;
        Return_Card;
end;
```

This example consists of a block statement with no declarations and hence no **declare** clause. Such "degenerate" block statements are useful for localizing an exception handler. This block statement implements a simple "bank teller" program. First, the procedure Read_Card reads the data from a user's bank card. An attempt is then made to validate the data by calling Validate_Card. If the user presses the cancel button on the bank teller machine while the card is in the process of being validated, then validation is abandoned, and the exception Transaction_Cancelled is raised. Within the exception handler, procedure Display_Cancellation_Notice then displays a cancellation notice, and the procedure Return_Card returns the card to the customer. On the other hand, if the customer does not press the cancel button during card validation, then Perform_Transaction is called to perform the transaction.

Note that the triggering event that causes the card validation to be abandoned is the acceptance of the call to `Keyboard.Cancel_Pressed`. This task entry call is accepted when the customer presses the cancel button.

## TASK ATTRIBUTES

There are several attributes that relate to tasks. We have already mentioned the `Count` attribute, which tells us how many entry calls are waiting in an entry queue. Other useful attributes that relate to tasks are `Terminated` and `Callable`. Both these attributes append to task names.

To understand these attributes, let us consider the five states of a task: running, ready, blocked, completed, and terminated. (There is actually a short-lived sixth state, abnormal, that arises when the **abort** command is issued.) A running task has been assigned a processor and is actively performing its duties. A ready task is ready to run but is waiting for a processor to become available on which to run. A blocked task is a previously running task that is delayed or waiting for a rendezvous. A completed task has reached its final **end** statement, but must wait until other tasks that depend on it (i.e., are contained within it) have terminated before it can terminate. A terminated task has reached its final **end** statement, and no tasks that depend on it are running.

Keeping these definitions in mind, the attribute `P'Terminated`, where P is the task name, is `True` or `False`, depending on whether task P has terminated. The attribute `P'Callable` is `True` or `False`, depending on whether task P is callable. A task is callable only if it has not completed or terminated. If an attempt is made to call a task that has either completed or terminated, then the `Tasking_Error` exception is raised. Therefore, when in doubt about the state of a task, use the `Callable` attribute immediately before attempting to call the task:

```
if Gas_Station_Attendant'Callable then
   Gas_Station_Attendant.Garage (My_Car);
else -- cannot call task because it completed or terminated
   Fix_Car_Myself;
end if;
```

In this **if** statement, the `Callable` attribute is used to determine whether the task `Gas_Station_Attendant` is callable. If this task is callable, then a call is made to the `Garage` entry of this task. If this task is not callable, then the procedure `Fix_Car_Myself` is invoked. Note that we cannot safely replace `Gas_Station_Attendant'Callable` with **not** `Gas_Station_Attendant'Terminated`. The replacement cannot be safely made because, to be callable, a task must not only have not terminated, it must also have not completed.

The astute reader may have noticed that the preceding code is not foolproof. It is possible that the task is callable when the `Callable` attribute is executed, but then ceases to be callable by the time the task is actually called. Of course, to reduce the risk of this happening, call a task as soon as possible after the callable check is made.

## ENTRY FAMILIES

Entry families resemble one-dimensional arrays. Recall from Chapter 4 that with arrays, a single identifier can refer to many related objects. Similarly, by using entry families, a single entry identifier can refer to many related entries. The following task specification shows the need for entry families:

```
task Multiple_Entries is
    entry Point_1 (On: in Boolean);
    entry Point_2 (On: in Boolean);
    entry Point_3 (On: in Boolean);
    entry Point_4 (On: in Boolean);
    entry Point_5 (On: in Boolean);
    entry No_Emergency;
    entry Emergency;
end Multiple_Entries;
```

This task specification contains two kinds of related entries. There are entry points 1 to 5 that have Boolean **in** parameters, and entries that deal with emergencies. These two kinds of entries may be written more concisely by using two entry families, each family representing a group of related entries:

```
task Multiple_Entries is
    entry Point (1 .. 5) (On: in Boolean);
        -- entry family of 5 entries each with a Boolean parameter
    entry Emergency (Boolean);
        -- entry family of 2 entries each with no parameters
end Multiple_Entries;
```

The entry family Point has integer index values that range from 1 to 5 and a formal parameter of type Boolean. The entry family Emergency has Boolean index values that range from False to True, and no parameters. Given this task specification, the body of the task may provide **accept** statements such as the following:

```
accept Point (3) (On: in Boolean);    -- third member of entry
                                      -- family
accept Emergency (True);-- second member of entry family
```

External tasks can then call entries in these entry families, as follows:

```
Multiple_Entries.Point (3) (On => True);
    -- call the third member of entry family with a
    -- parameter of True
Multiple_Entries.Emergency (True);
    -- call the second member of entry family
    -- (without any parameter)
```

Do not confuse the entry family index with the entry parameter. In the first task entry call, the value True is an entry parameter that is needed whether or not entry families are used. The number 3 is the entry family index. In the second task entry call, the value True is not an entry parameter but an entry family index. The index values for this entry family range from False to True, so the index value of True selects the second member of the entry family.

## PRAGMA PRIORITY

There are only two kinds of items that may be placed in a task specification: **accept** statements and certain pragmas, such as the **pragma** Priority. Recall that a pragma is a compiler directive. **Pragma** Priority directs the compiler to prioritize tasks from the least important to the most important. This pragma must appear in the declarative part of a task to which it applies. This pragma can also appear in the declarative part of a main program and then applies to the main program.

Prioritizing tasks can be useful when the number of active tasks exceeds the processing resources, such as the number of available processors. In such situations, the processors must somehow be allocated to the tasks. By prioritizing tasks, the programmer controls the allocation of available processors so that a ready task with a higher priority is always selected over a ready task with a lower priority. Note, however, that **pragma** Priority does not affect the manner in which calling tasks are stored in a task entry queue. Tasks are queued on a first-come, first-served basis, regardless of their relative priorities. This is analogous to a queue to see a movie. To line up for a movie, one goes to the back of the line in the order arrived, regardless of one's position (priority) in life.

A task is assigned a priority by placing the **pragma** Priority in its specification. The keyword **pragma** is followed by the word Priority, then by an integer priority number enclosed in parentheses. In the following task specifications, Important and Not_So_Important are assigned the priority levels of 9 and 1, respectively:

```
task Important is
    pragma Priority (9);
    entry Monitor_Patient;
end Important;

task Not_So_Important is
    pragma Priority (1);
    entry Heat_Coffee;
end Not_So_Important;
```

Note that a larger integer value denotes a higher priority level. The priority value belongs to the subtype Priority defined in package System. The number of priority levels allowed is implementation dependent. (However, the optional Real-Time Systems Annex mandates at least 31 priority values.)

**Ada 95 ▶**     Task priorities are static; that is, they cannot be changed as a program is running. As we will see, however, the optional Real-Time Systems Annex supports dynamic priorities that can be modified in response to changing runtime conditions.

## TASK TYPES

It was pointed out in Chapter 2 that an exotic type exists called a task type. All tasks belong to a task type. However, the tasks presented so far in this chapter are not explicitly declared to belong to any task type. As a result, these tasks are one of a kind, each implicitly belonging to a different anonymous task type. (This is analogous to arrays that implicitly belong to an anonymous array type, as discussed in Chapter 4.) As we shall illustrate momentarily, task types enable identical instances of a task to be created, allow tasks to be stored in a data structure such as an array or record, allow tasks to be passed as subprogram parameters, and enable tasks to have discriminants. As we will show in a later section of this chapter, task types also allow the creation of pointers to dynamically created tasks.

Syntactically, task type declarations appear just like the task specifications we have encountered, except that the keyword **type** follows the keyword **task**:

```
task type Resource is   -- task type declaration
   entry Seize;
   entry Release;
end Resource;
```

The task body corresponding to a task type declaration is the same as the body of tasks that are not declared as task types.

Once a task type is specified, objects that are particular tasks can then be declared to belong to this task type:

```
Laser_Printer, Dot_Matrix: Resource; -- declares two tasks
```

Both tasks, `Laser_Printer` and `Dot_Matrix`, are declared to belong to the same task type, `Resource`. This means that both these tasks have identical characteristics. One such characteristic is that both tasks have the same task entries. Another shared characteristic is that both tasks perform the same processing, but do so independently. Also, both tasks declare the same variables and constants, although these variables and constants are not actually shared between the tasks. Each task, in other words, has its own copy of these variables and constants. Therefore, whenever two or more copies of the identical task are needed, instead of writing each task separately, simply define a single task type, and declare as many tasks as needed.

Task types are limited types (see Chapter 7). Thus, task objects cannot be assigned or compared to one another. However, tasks can be passed as subprogram parameters, and an array or record of task objects may be declared:

```
task type Message_Type;
type Message_Array is array (1..5) of Message_Type;
Message: Message_Array; -- an array of 5 tasks
procedure Output (Unit: in Message_Type);
```

**Ada 95 ▶**    Task types, like all composite types except array types, can have discriminants. Task discriminants allow a task to be passed an initial value that informs the task of its identity, sets the task's priority, or controls the task's execution. As with other discriminants, the discriminant value is provided when the task object is declared:

```
task type Check (Device: in Device_Type);
Check_Device: Check (Device => Printer);
    -- Check_Device is initialized to Printer
```

Without task discriminants, initial values such as `Printer` would have to be passed through an initial rendezvous. Thus, in the following code,

```
task type Check is
    entry Get_Device (Device: in Device_Type);
end Check;
Check_Device: Check;
```

a rendezvous is required so that `Check_Device` receives the value `Printer`:

```
Check_Device.Get_Device (Device => Printer);
```

Such an initial rendezvous is too time consuming and cumbersome to use for such simple purposes.

## TASK INTERFERENCE

Writing Ada programs that use tasks can be tricky. As mentioned in the beginning of this chapter, there are many pitfalls and unexpected side effects of using tasks. One of the more common pitfalls is task interference. Task interference may occur when two or more tasks concurrently use the same resource, such as a terminal screen, printer, or disk drive. In the following example, two tasks interfere with each other as they concurrently output the same message to the screen:

```
with Ada.Text_IO; use Ada.Text_IO;
procedure Print is
    task type Message_Type;
    Copy_1, Copy_2: Message_Type;
    task body Message_Type is
    begin
        Put ("...now that we have gigantic computers, "
            & "programming has become an equally gigantic problem. "
            & "-- E.W. Dijkstra");
        New_Line;
    end Message_Type;
begin -- both tasks, Copy_1 and Copy_2, are activated here
    null;
end Print;
```

`Copy_1` and `Copy_2` are declared to be tasks of type `Message_Type`. Both these tasks concurrently output the same message when they are activated. As with previous examples, the tasks are activated when the keyword **begin** is reached.

Try running this code and see what happens. On most computer systems, when the services of `Text_IO` are concurrently used to output messages to the same device, the tasks interfere with each other. Thus, instead of outputting two consecutive copies of the message, the copies are intertwined, resulting in gobbledygook. A few letters of one copy are output, then a few letters from the other copy, and so on.

This problem of task interference can be solved by the following task type:

```
task type Resource is
   entry Seize;
   entry Release;
end Resource;
```

The two entries, `Seize` and `Release`, are called by other tasks in order to seize or release a resource such as the screen, printer, or disk drive. This prevents other tasks from using the same resource at the same time. Thus, when a task needs to use a resource, it seizes control of it by calling the task entry `Seize`. When it is done with the resource, it releases control by calling the task entry `Release`. The resource is then once again available for other tasks to seize. Task interference is therefore avoided because a task cannot seize control of a resource unless the task that previously used the resource has relinquished control.

Assume that `Screen` is declared to be a task of type `Resource`. A task can then seize the screen by calling `Screen.Seize` and can release the screen by calling `Screen.Release`. After incorporating these calls, the task body of `Message_Type`, which was in procedure `Print`, appears as follows:

```
separate (Print)
task body Message_Type is
begin
   Screen.Seize; -- seizes control of the screen
   Put ("...now that we have gigantic computers, programming "
      & "has become an equally gigantic problem. "
      & "-- E.W. Dijkstra");
   New_Line;
   Screen.Release; -- releases control of the screen
end Message_Type;
```

Note that this task body has been made into a separate compilation unit called a subunit. (Subunits are discussed in Chapters 6 and 9.)

Now that we have explained how the task type `Resource` can be used to eliminate task interference, let us examine how it works. The following shows the specification and body of `Resource`:

```
task type Resource is
   entry Seize;
```

```
         entry Release;
      end Resource;

      task body Resource is
         In_Use: Boolean := False;
      begin
         loop
            select
               when not In_Use =>
                  accept Seize do
                     In_Use := True;
                  end Seize;
            or
               when In_Use =>
                  accept Release do
                     In_Use := False;
                  end Release;
            or
               terminate;
            end select;
         end loop;
      end Resource;
```

The task body of Resource (an instance of it) begins by initializing the Boolean variable In_Use to False. When the **select** statement is reached, the alternative containing the guarded **accept** statement, Seize, is therefore open, but the alternative containing the guarded Release alternative is closed. A rendezvous is thus made with whichever task first calls the task entry Seize. Suppose that tasks A and B (not shown) both try to seize the same resource and that task A calls the task entry Seize before task B. During the rendezvous with task A, In_Use is set to True. The rendezvous then ends, and the loop returns us to the beginning of the **select** statement. Since In_Use is now set to True, the select alternative containing the entry Seize is closed, but the alternative containing Release is open. Thus, Resource waits for a call to the entry Release, which is the only entry call that it can accept. By this time, let us assume that the Seize entry was called by the slower task B. Task B is placed on the Seize queue even though the guard for Seize is currently False. Once task A finishes outputting its message and calls the task entry Release, In_Use is set to False. The rendezvous ends, and task A terminates. Meanwhile, Resource loops to the beginning of the **select** statement, a rendezvous is made with task B, and In_Use is again set to True. The loop once again returns to the beginning of the **select** statement. Even though all the entry queues are now empty, the **terminate** alternative is not selected because task B is still active and can potentially call Resource. Indeed, after task B finishes outputting its message, it calls the entry Release and then terminates. The loop returns us once again to the beginning of the **select** statement. This time, since there are no calls waiting on either entry queue, and since the only two tasks that could have called Resource have already terminated, the **terminate** alternative is selected.

As we have just seen, task interference may occur when two or more tasks concurrently use the same output device. Task interference can also occur when two or more tasks attempt to concurrently update the same global data. Normally, data that needs to be shared between tasks is protected by being placed in the private parts of protected objects (to be discussed later in this chapter) or updated from within task **accept** statements. (Since the calling task is suspended when code in the **accept** statement is executed, no task interference can occur.) Alternatively, the previous `Resource` task can be used: every task seizes the global data before accessing it and, when finished, releases the global data for other tasks to use. However, situations occasionally arise where, because of efficiency or other concerns, the shared data is made directly accessible to each task without having to invoke any subprograms or task entries. As mentioned, the greatest danger with this approach is that concurrent updates of the global data may produce unpredictable results due to task interference. Suppose, for example, that one task increments a global integer variable, N, by 1:

```
N := N + 1;
```

And suppose that other task decrements N by 1:

```
N := N - 1;
```

If N is initialized to 0, and if both tasks attempt to modify N concurrently, the resulting value of N could be –1, 0, or 1, depending on the order of operations. If each task fully executes its assignment statement in turn, then N becomes 0:

```
Step 1:            N := N + 1;   -- Result is the same when steps
Step 2:            N := N - 1;   -- 1 and 2 are reversed
Value of N:   0
```

Note that N evaluates to 0 even if Steps 1 and 2 are reversed. So far, the results are probably as the programmer expects. Consider what happens, however, if each task evaluates the expression to the right of the assignment operator and then, before carrying out the assignment, control is passed to the other task. In this case, the expressions N + 1 and N – 1 are evaluated before either assignment operation is performed. The value of N then becomes either 1 or –1, depending on the order of assignment. If the assignment associated with N – 1 is performed last, then N will be set to –1:

```
Step 1:       Evaluate N + 1 and N - 1
Step 2:       N := 1;       -- 1 is the value of N + 1
Step 3:       N := -1;      -- -1 is the value of N - 1
Value of N:   -1
```

If the assignment associated with N + 1 is performed last, then N will be set to 1:

```
Step 1:       Evaluate N + 1 and N - 1
Step 2:       N := -1;      -- -1 is the value of N - 1
Step 3:       N := 1;       -- 1 is the value of N + 1
Value of N:   1
```

Again, the reason the value of N can vary is because the previous assignment statements are not performed "atomically," that is, they are not indivisible. They are performed in stages, which gives other tasks the opportunity to intervene. In Ada, no operation, regardless of how simple it appears, can be assumed to be atomic. An operation is only atomic if the generated machine code is atomic. (The previous discussion is therefore simplified since we should have discussed machine code and not Ada source code.)

**Ada 95 ▶**     To help minimize the risk of task interference, Ada provides the **pragma** Atomic. This pragma is defined in the optional Systems Programming Annex. **Pragma** Atomic requests that all reads and writes to the specified object be indivisible. This means that the machine code generated to read or write the data consists of a single (atomic) instruction. This guarantees that only one task is actually accessing the data at any particular moment.

**Ada 95 ▶**     There is another situation where concurrent access to global data leads to task interference. Assume that two tasks are concurrently updating the value of a global variable. If the variable is always directly accessed from memory, no problem arises. As an optimization, however, a task may keep a local copy of a global variable (or temporarily store its value in a register). If another task directly updates the global variable, then the local copy will be out of date. **Pragma** Volatile addresses this problem by requesting that all reads or writes to the specified global variable be made directly to or from memory. (**Pragma** Volatile replaces Ada 83's **pragma** Shared.) Pragmas Atomic_Components and Volatile_Components are like pragmas Atomic and Volatile except they apply to array types and make all of the array components atomic or volatile.

## DYNAMICALLY CREATED TASKS

In all the examples given so far, tasks have been created statically. However, tasks may also be created dynamically. In other words, while a program is executing, tasks can be created (and disposed of) as they are needed. Dynamically created tasks are thus especially useful when the number of tasks needed for a particular application depends on runtime conditions and therefore cannot be known in advance. The topic of dynamically created tasks is an advanced one that is only briefly introduced in this section.

Dynamically created tasks are brought into existence like other dynamically created objects—by using access types and allocators:

```
procedure Dynamic_Tasks is
   task type Plot is
      entry Position (X, Y: in Natural);
   end Plot;

   type Position_Ptr is access Plot;
   Ptr_1: Position_Ptr := new Plot;
      -- allocator new activates task pointed to by Ptr_1
   Ptr_2: Position_Ptr;
```

```
        type Plot_Array_Type is array (1..9) of Plot;
        Plot_Array: Plot_Array_Type;

    begin -- Plot_Array(1) to Plot_Array(9) are activated here
        ...
        Ptr_1.Position (2, 4);
        ...
        Plot_Array(3).Position (3, 5);
        ...
        Ptr_2 := new Plot;
            -- allocator new activates task pointed to by Ptr_2
        ...
        Ptr_2.Position (4, 9);
    end Dynamic_Tasks;
```

Once the task type Plot is defined, an access type, Position_Ptr, is declared that accesses type Plot. The pointers Ptr_1 and Ptr_2 are then declared. These are pointers to dynamically created tasks of type Plot. Note that when Ptr_1 is declared, it is initialized using an allocator **new**. The task pointed to by Ptr_1 is therefore dynamically created as the declaration for Ptr_1 is elaborated. This allocator not only dynamically creates a task for Ptr_1 to point to, it also activates the task. Only dynamically allocated tasks are activated by allocators. Tasks such as Plot_Array(1) to Plot_Array(9) that are not dynamically allocated are activated when the **begin** is reached. Note that unlike Ptr_1, which is initialized as it is declared, Ptr_2 is initialized with an assignment statement. The task pointed to by Ptr_2 is therefore created and activated in the executable statement part of procedure Dynamic_Tasks.

As illustrated in the previous code, a task entry is indirectly called through a pointer by following the pointer's name with a dot and the task entry name:

```
    Ptr_1.Position (2, 4); -- calls task pointed to by Ptr_1
        -- same as Ptr_1.all.Position (2, 4);
```

As the comments indicate, the keyword **all** is optional.

## TIMING CONSIDERATIONS

When running tasking programs, periodic delays in execution are often required. Reconsider the **for loop** used in procedure Launch, shown in Chapter 3:

```
    for Counter in Count_Down loop
        Count_Down_IO.Put (Counter);
        Text_IO.New_Line;
        delay 1.0; -- wait at least 1 second
    end loop;
```

Recall that type Count_Down is an enumeration type:

```
type Count_Down is (Ten, Nine, Eight, Seven, Six, Five, Four,
          Three, Two, One, Blast_Off);
```

As mentioned in Chapter 3, the **delay** statement indicates that the procedure is eligible to resume execution after 1 second has expired. However, the procedure is not guaranteed to run the moment it becomes eligible to run because the computer might be busy with other work. It can take a while for a busy computer to get back to procedure Launch, notice that the **delay** has expired, and then resume the execution of Launch.

The **delay** statement takes values of the fixed point type Duration that is defined in package Standard. The delay statement must take values up to at least 86,400 seconds (one day). If a negative value is supplied, it is treated as a zero value.

There are different ways that a program can be delayed. The **delay** statement puts the program "to sleep" rather than executes a "busy wait." Putting the program to sleep means that the process is suspended until an event occurs; in this case, the expiration of a **delay**. While the program is sleeping, the computer is free to do other work. On the other hand, a busy wait means that the program is using processing resources without doing any useful work. It ties up the computer. Here is an example of a busy wait:

```
-- This is poor code
Procedure Wait (Cycle_Count: in Positive) is
   type Counter is range 1..10_000;
   N: Counter := Counter'First;
   Cycle: Positive := 1;
begin
   -- a busy wait whose waiting time is machine dependent
   while Cycle <= Cycle_Count loop
      if N = Counter'Last then
         N := Counter'First;
         Cycle := Cycle + 1;
      else
         N := N + 1;
      end if;
   end loop;
end Wait;
```

This code uses a busy wait that not only wastes processor time, but whose waiting time is machine dependent. This code assumes that looping a specific number of times will delay the execution of the program the desired amount of time. This assumption is dangerous. If, for example, the processor is upgraded to a faster version, then this code will no longer wait as long as desired.

It may seem curious that the busy wait in the previous example keeps incrementing N until it reaches the value Counter'Last and then wraps around to the beginning value, Counter'First. Why not simply use the following loop with nothing in it?

```
-- this code could be "optimized away" so no delay occurs
for Pause in 1 .. 10_000 * Cycle_Count loop
```

```
        null;
    end loop;
```

As the code comments indicate, a compiler might optimize away this do-nothing **for** loop. Of course, what is eliminated is not the source code **for** this loop, but the executable object code. If no executable code is generated for this loop, then no delay will occur.

As previously discussed, the Launch procedure delays at least 1 second each time through the loop. After 11 cycles through the loop, the extra delay time can accumulate. For example, assume that the average extra delay is 0.001 seconds. After 11 times through the loop, the total time delayed is 0.011 seconds greater than the 11 seconds requested. This imprecision may be intolerable in hard real-time systems where timing must be extremely precise. The following procedure prevents time from drifting as the program cycles through the loop:

```
with Ada.Text_IO;
with Ada.Calendar;   -- If available, package Real_Time is
                     -- preferable
use Ada; use Calendar;
procedure Better_Launch is

    type Count_Down is (Ten, Nine, Eight, Seven, Six, Five,
        Four, Three, Two, One, Blast_Off);
    package Count_Down_IO is new
        Text_IO.Enumeration_IO (Count_Down);
    Pause: constant Calendar.Day_Duration := 1.0;
    Target_Time: Calendar.Time := Calendar.Clock;
        -- set to current time of day
begin -- Blast_Off

    for Counter in Count_Down loop
        Count_Down_IO.Put (Counter); Text_IO.New_Line;
        Target_Time := Target_Time + Pause;
        delay until Target_Time;-- delays until specified time
    end loop;

end Better_Launch;
```

**Ada 95 ▶**    Although Better_Launch does not avoid the possibility of the **delay** being extended beyond the specified 1 second, it does avoid the problem of time drifting as the program cycles through the loop. This is accomplished by using the **delay until** and package Calendar. Whereas the **delay** statement is used to delay a specified amount of time, the **delay until** statement is used to delay until a specified time is reached. The problem of time drift is avoided because if a particular delay is a fraction of a second longer than the 1 second requested, then the next loop cycle automatically lessens its delay by this amount. The delay is lessened because it is based on the time that the next loop cycle should start.

Package Ada.Calendar includes, among other features, a Time type whose values represent points of time, and a function `Clock` that returns the time of day as a value of type `Time`. (Package `Ada.Real_Time` provides better timing than package `Calendar` but may not be available unless the optional Real-Time Systems Annex is provided.) Note that the procedure, `Better_Launch`, references `Day_Duration`. `Day_Duration` is a subtype of the fixed point type `Duration` that is defined in package `Standard`. (Fixed point types were covered in Chapter 12.) `Duration` represents intervals of time expressed in seconds, and subtype `Day_Duration` constrains the range from 0.0 to 86_400.0 (the number of seconds in a day).

## PROTECTED OBJECTS

**Ada 95 ▶** Although tasks are powerful high-level abstractions that simplify concurrent programming, they do have their limitations. One limitation is that switching control from task to task may significantly slow down execution. Therefore, programs that contain many tasks that rendezvous with one another may be too slow for time-critical applications.

Another limitation of tasks is that rendezvous are synchronous and do not naturally map to asynchronous communication. Synchronous communication means the tasks must meet in order to communicate. This is analogous to two people exchanging information by meeting face to face at a rendezvous point. On the other hand, asynchronous communication means that tasks do not need to meet in order to communicate. This is analogous to two people exchanging information by placing notes in a mailbox. When one person places a note in the mailbox, he or she does not need to wait around for the other person to arrive. The other person retrieves notes from the mailbox whenever convenient.

Yet another limitation of tasks is that they are algorithm based. That is, each task defines an action to be performed. However, code sometimes needs to be written that is "data based." The main purpose of data-based code is to provide safe concurrent access to shared data. Tasks can implement code that is data based, but the implementation is typically awkward and inefficient. Data-based tasks are usually acceptor tasks that passively wait at the beginning of their selective **accept** statement for entry calls to be made. When an entry call arrives, the task serves the caller, then typically loops back to wait again at the beginning of the selective **accept** statement. Note that the main purpose of these passive acceptor tasks is not to carry out needed processing (an algorithm), but to provide safe concurrent access to shared data. The shared data is safely updated in **accept** statements since **accept** statements have a single thread of execution. (An example of this can be seen by jumping ahead to package P's `Counter` task.)

All of the previous limitations of tasks are overcome by protected objects. Protected objects are much more efficient than tasks and can therefore be used in time-critical applications without incurring an undue performance penalty. Furthermore, protected objects provide an efficient means to communicate asynchronously. Finally, protected objects are data based. They provide mutually exclusive access to data that can be shared among tasks. The data needs to be accessed in a mutually exclusive manner to avoid task interference, which we discussed previously.

Protected objects have the following structure:

```
protected protected object name is          -- specification
    interface to protected operations
private
    shared protected data
end protected object name;


protected body protected object name is      -- body
    implementation of protected operations
end protected object name;
```

Unlike tasks, the specification and body of protected objects can each be separate compilation units. The specification of protected objects begins with the keyword **protected**, followed by the name of the protected object, followed by the keyword **is**. Next comes the specifications of the protected operations. These operations allow tasks to access data that is placed after the keyword **private**. Finally, the keyword **end** appears, optionally followed by the name of the protected object. The body of protected objects begins with the keywords **protected body**, then the name of the protected object, followed by the implementation of the protected operations, then the keyword **end**, optionally followed by the name of the protected object.

In order to better understand the need for protected objects, consider the following code that increments a counter whenever the Increment procedure is called:

```
-- This code does not work for concurrent systems
package Counter is
    procedure Increment (New_Value: out Positive);
end Counter;


package body Counter is
    -- Data cannot safely be updated concurrently
    Data: Integer := 0;

    procedure Increment (New_Value: out Positive) is
    begin
        Data := Data + 1;
        New_Value := Data;
    end Increment;
end Counter;
```

With this code, we have the problem of task interference. If multiple tasks concurrently call Counter.Increment, they may interfere with each other and corrupt the value of the shared variable Data.

In order to avoid the problem of task interference, the code can be written as follows, using tasks:

```
package P is
    task Counter is
        entry Increment (New_Value: out Positive);
```

```
        end Counter;
            ...
    end P;

    package body P is
            ...
        task body Counter is
            Data: Integer := 0;
        begin
            loop
                accept Increment (New_Value: out Positive) do
                    Data := Data + 1;
                    New_Value := Data;
                end Increment;
            end loop;
        end Counter;
    end P;
```

This solution safely allows Data to be concurrently updated. Task interference is avoided by allowing the incrementing of Data to only take place within the **accept** statement.

Notice that in the previous code we had to introduce a task, Counter, just to provide safe concurrent access to Data. This solution seems like overkill. All we need is a passive data structure that is to be protected and only updated through specified subprograms. This need is satisfied by our first approach, which uses the package Counter instead of the task Counter, even though package Counter does not work for concurrent systems. This is where protected objects come into play. A protected object, like our package solution, provides a passive data-oriented construct, but unlike our package solution, avoids the problem of task interference:

```
    -- Clients can increment data by calling Counter.Increment
    protected Counter is
        procedure Increment (New_Value: out Positive);
    private
        -- Users of Counter can only access Data by calling
        -- Increment
        Data: Integer := 0;
    end Counter;

    protected body Counter is -- hidden from users
        procedure Increment (New_Value: out Positive) is
        begin
            Data := Data + 1;
            New_Value := Data;
        end Increment;
    end Counter;
```

The shared data, Data, is protected by being placed in the private part of the protected object. This shared data can only be accessed through calls to the protected operation, Increment. Increment happens to be implemented as a procedure.

(But as we shall see, protected operations can also be implemented as functions or entries.) Procedure `Increment` provides clients with mutually exclusive access to the shared data. A program unit such as a task that wants to increment the counter calls `Increment` as follows:

```
Counter.Increment (New_Value => X);
```

This call results in `Counter` being incremented and the new value being returned to the caller through the integer parameter `X`. Note that if several tasks each call `Counter` once, each task receives a unique returned value.

The reason `Data` can be safely shared among multiple tasks is because calls to `Increment` are mutually exclusive. Only one task can execute the protected procedure, `Increment`, at a time. If several tasks call `Counter.Increment` at the same time, only one of them is allowed to invoke `Increment`. The other tasks must wait their turn. The wait should be minimal because protected operations such as `Increment` are intended to require minimal processing time.

To enforce minimal processing time, protected operations are not allowed to perform potentially blocking operations that may suspend processing. (Potentially blocking operations include an **abort** statement, **accept** statement, **select** statement, **delay** statement, or entry call. Such operations also include the activation of a task or a call to a subprogram that is itself potentially blocking.) In the previous example, minimal processing is achieved since procedure `Increment` merely increments `Data` and assigns the new value of `Data` to `New_Value`. Minimal processing time is desirable because protected objects are intended to be efficiently implemented as "busy waits." This means that waiting tasks are not placed on a queue like tasks waiting on task entries. A task placed on an entry queue is "put to sleep" (its process is suspended) until awakened by the acceptance of its call. In contrast, during a busy wait, the processor keeps actively checking whether the calling task should be allowed to seize the protected object. Suppose task A calls `Counter.Increment` first. It seizes (or locks) the protected object, which momentarily prevents other tasks from calling `Counter.Increment`. As soon as procedure `Increment` is done executing, task A releases the protected object so other tasks may now call `Counter.Increment`. This seizing and releasing is done implicitly, and is not apparent to users of the protected object.

In our example, only one counter object is created. This object belongs to an anonymous protected type, just as individually declared tasks belong to an anonymous task type. If many counter objects are needed, then a protected type can be declared that is analogous to a task type:

```
protected type Counter is
   procedure Increment (New_Value: out Positive);
private
   Data: Integer := 0;
end Counter;
-- protected body is declared as before

C1, C2, C3: Counter; -- Declares 3 counters
Counter_Array: array (1..100) of Counter;
```

```
                -- Declares 100 counters
        type Rec_Type is
           record
              Count_1: Counter;
              Count_2: Counter;
              Int: Integer;
           end record;
        Rec: Rec_Type; -- Rec.Count_1 and Rec.Count_2 are counters
```

These declarations introduce three counters, C1, C2, and C3; an array of 100 counters, Counter_Array; and a record, Rec, with two counters, Rec.Count_1 and Rec.Count_2. These counters can be invoked as follows:

```
        C1.Increment (New_Value => X);
        Counter_Array(N).Increment (New_Value => X);
        Rec.Count_2.Increment (New_Value => X);
```

The data in each of these counters is independent of the data in the other counters.

In the previous example, the protected operation, Increment, is implemented as a procedure. Protected operations can also be implemented as entries or functions. Protected procedures and entries can both read from and write to the protected data. Protected functions, however, can only read the private data. Protected procedures and entries provide mutually exclusive access to the protected data. This is necessary because concurrent writing to data can result in task interference. Protected functions, however, do not need to support mutual exclusion. Since functions can only read the protected data, more than one function can be called at the same time without the problem of task interference.

The following is an example of a "persistent signal" that is implemented with a protected object that declares both a protected entry and a protected procedure:

```
        -- persistent signal
        protected Event is
           entry Wait;          -- waits for an event to occur
           procedure Signal;    -- signals that an event has occurred
        private
           Occurred: Boolean := False;
        end Event;

        protected body Event is
           -- Occurred is an entry barrier that must be True for
           -- the entry to execute
           entry Wait when Occurred is
           begin
              Occurred := False;  -- "consume" the signal
           end Wait;

           procedure Signal is
           begin
              Occurred := True;   -- set Wait's barrier
```

```
        end Signal;
    end Event;
    -- This example is based on the Ada 9X Mapping Rationale,
    -- © 1992 Intermetrics, Inc.
```

Unlike protected procedures (or functions), protected entries such as `Wait` have `Boolean` expressions associated with them that are called barriers. Barriers are somewhat similar to task guards. The barrier must be `True` before the entry body can be executed. If the barrier is `False`, then the entry call is queued, and the calling task waits for the barrier to become `True`. Barriers are needed when the protected operation can only sensibly be executed under certain conditions. In our example, the protected operation `Wait` can only be sensibly executed (thus ending the wait) when a signal has arrived. Whether or not a signal has arrived is determined by the barrier, `Occurred`.

In general, no call on a protected operation may proceed while there is still work for the protected object to perform. Only after the protected object does as much as it can is it able to accept outside calls to its protected operations. In other words, tasks already on the entry queue get preference over tasks just calling the entry. In our example, the entry `Wait` has a guard called `Occurred`. The value of the barrier typically depends on the private data within the protected object. Barriers are allowed to reference global data, but this is discouraged. A barrier is evaluated when its entry is called. All barriers that have queued tasks are re-evaluated whenever the private data they typically access can be expected to change. When a re-evaluated barrier becomes `True`, an entry queued on the previously `False` barrier immediately executes.

In the previous example, tasks wait for an event to occur by calling `Event.Wait`. Another task signals the occurrence of the event by calling `Event.Signal`. Signaling the event causes *one* of the waiting tasks to "consume" the signal and then go its merry way. All of the other waiting tasks continue to wait. The signal is called a "persistent signal" because if no tasks are waiting when the signal occurs, the signal persists until a task eventually invokes `Event.Wait`. Multiple signals occurring when no tasks are waiting are equivalent to just one signal.

After this brief description, let us examine in detail how our example works. Assume that a call to `Event.Wait` occurs first. The calling task places itself on `Wait`'s entry queue and waits for a signal. When a signal eventually occurs, a task whose job it is to notice a signal has occurred calls `Event.Signal`. When `Event.Signal` is called, `Wait`'s barrier is set to `True`. Since procedure `Signal` can (and does) modify the private data `Occurred`, and since a barrier is assumed to depend on the value of the private data, a check is made to determine whether any tasks are waiting on an entry queue. In this case, a task is waiting on the entry queue for `Wait`. Since `Wait`'s barrier is now `True`, the body of wait executes and resets its barrier to `False`. The waiting task that called `Event.Wait` is now released, the signaling task goes on its way, and the process of checking entry queues and barriers is repeated.

Now let us assume that a call to `Event.Signal` occurs first. The barrier, `Occurred`, is set to `True`, and since there is no task waiting on `Wait`'s entry queue, the signaling task goes on its way. The call to signal, however, is not forgotten. It "persists." If a call to `Event.Wait` is made later, the barrier is still `True`, so the body of `Wait` is immediately executed. `Wait` resets its barrier to `False`, and the calling task is allowed to continue on its way.

Although entry barriers are somewhat similar to task guards, they are evaluated at different times. An entry barrier is first evaluated whenever an entry is called. Furthermore, all barriers that have queued tasks are re-evaluated after an entry or procedure body is finished executing. This makes sense, since an entry or procedure body can modify the private data that the barrier's value typically depends upon. Barriers are not re-evaluated after a protected function body is finished executing since functions cannot modify the private data but can only read the data. The following code outline shows when the barrier is evaluated and re-evaluated:

```
protected T is
    entry E;
    procedure P;
private
    Barrier: Boolean := False;
end T;

protected body T is
    entry E when Barrier is -- Barrier evaluated when E called
        -- if Barrier is True, the entry body is executed
        -- if Barrier is False, the entry call is queued
    begin
        . . .
    end E; -- Barrier re-evaluated if
          -- tasks are queued for entry E
    procedure P is
    begin
        . . .
    end P; -- Barrier re-evaluated if
          -- tasks are queued for entry E
end T;
```

The next example is a protected object type that implements a "queued waiting" and has all three kinds of protected operations: an entry, procedure, and function:

```
-- queued waiting
protected type Counting_Semaphores (Initial_Count: Integer := 1)
is
    entry Seize;        -- Seizes a resource
                        -- Suspends caller if none available
    procedure Release;  -- Releases a resource
    function Count return Integer;
        -- returns the current number of resources
private
    Current_Count: Integer := Initial_Count;
```

```
                        -- Count of available resources
         end Counting_Semaphores;

         protected body Counting_Semaphores is
             entry Seize when Current_Count > 0 is
                 -- Seize a resource when available
                 -- Suspend caller if none available
             begin
                 Current_Count := Current_Count - 1;
             end Seize;

             procedure Release is
                 -- Release a resource, making it available to others
             begin
                 Current_Count := Current_Count + 1;
             end Release;

             function Count return Integer is
             begin
                 return Current_Count;
             end Count;
         end Counting_Semaphores;

         Counting_Semaphore: Counting_Semaphores; -- accepts default
                                                  -- disciminant value
```

In this example, Current_Count represents the number of available resources and is initialized to the value of the protected object's discriminant, Initial_Count. (All composite types, except array types, can have discriminants.) Counting_Semaphore does not specify a discriminant value and so accepts the default value of 1.

This protected object type is somewhat similar to the previous example of the task type Resource. A task attempts to seize a resource by calling

```
         Counting_Semaphore.Seize;
```

If a resource is not available, the task will wait in Seize's entry queue until a resource becomes available (Current_Count > 0). A task releases a resource and makes it available for other tasks by calling

```
         Counting_Semaphore.Release;
```

Each time a resource is released, the barrier (Current_Count > 0) is evaluated just once. Tasks determine the number of resources available by calling

```
         Counting_Semaphore.Count
```

The final example of a protected object illustrates the use of a **requeue** statement. An entry can use a **requeue** statement to place its caller back on the same queue or on another compatible entry queue. It is also possible to requeue a caller on a compatible queue of a different protected object or even on a task entry queue. The **requeue** statement is useful when a request requires multiple steps, some of which can be performed immediately, others which need to be requeued for later processing. In particular, the **requeue** statement enables an entry body (of a protected object or task) to requeue a request that cannot be immediately handled and then be free to service new calls. Note that although the calling task continues to wait while its call is requeued, it does not need to be aware that its call was requeued. The following example of a "broadcast signal" illustrates the use of the **requeue**:

```
-- broadcast signal
protected Event is
    entry Wait;
    entry Signal;
private
    entry Reset;
    Occurred: Boolean := False;
end Event;

protected body Event is
    entry Wait when Occurred is
    begin
        null;
    end Wait;
    entry Signal when True is
    begin
        if Wait'Count > 0 then
            Occurred := True;
            requeue Reset;
        end if;
    end Signal;
    entry Reset when Wait'Count = 0 is
    begin
        Occurred := False;
    end Reset;
end Event;
-- This example is based on the Ada 9X Mapping Rationale,
-- © 1992 Intermetrics, Inc.
```

Tasks wait for an event by calling `Event.Wait`. A task looking out for the event notifies the waiting tasks that the event has occurred by calling `Event.Signal`. When an event is signalled, *all* waiting tasks are released, one after the other. After all tasks are released, the wait state is reinstated so that future tasks calling `Event.Wait` will wait. Unlike the previous example of a persistent signal, this signal is not persistent. If no tasks are waiting when a signal arrives, then the signal is "lost."

Let us examine in detail how this code works. Assume that `Event.Wait` was called first. Since the barrier, `Occurred`, is `False`, the calling task is placed on the entry queue. Several tasks may add themselves to the queue. When the entry `Signal` is eventually called, since the barrier is always `True`, its body is immediately executed. Had no tasks been waiting, the task calling `Signal` would exit without updating the barrier. However, since tasks are waiting, the barrier is set to `True`, indicating that an event has occurred. The task is then requeued on the `Reset` entry. The signaling task then checks the queues and sees that the barrier for `Wait` is now `True`. A task is then taken from the `Wait` queue and allowed to proceed. Since the barrier remains `True`, another task is allowed to proceed, then another, and so on, until all the tasks in the queue have been removed. When the `Wait` queue is finally empty (`Wait'Count = 0`), the `Reset` barrier becomes `True` and `Occurred` becomes `False`. Since the queues are now empty, the signalling task can continue on its way. Note that during all of this activity, the protected object is seized (locked), so other tasks that try calling `Wait` or `Signal` must wait for all the queues to clear. (See Exercise 14 at the end of this chapter for a simpler implementation of this code.)

The **requeue** statement is available for tasks as well as for protected objects. The entry that is requeued is typically only for internal use by the task or protected object and should not be available for external clients to call. The requeued entry can be hidden from external users by being placed in a private part of the task specification or protected object specification. In our previous example, entry `Reset` is placed in the private part of a protected object. In the following code, entry `Hidden` is placed in the private part of a task:

```
task T is
   entry Visible;
private
   -- Hidden is not available to external clients but can be
   -- used for requeuing a call from within the body of T
   entry Hidden;
end T;
```

In this case, the task entry, `Hidden`, can only be used for requeuing from within the task body of T.

When discussing the **abort** statement, it was pointed out that tasks are not aborted when waiting on an entry queue. This is true even when the task is waiting on an entry queue that has been requeued. However, one can override this default behavior and allow tasks to be aborted while requeued. To accomplish this, add the keywords **with abort** to the requeue statement:

```
requeue Reset with abort; -- allows requeued task to be aborted
```

Protected objects can have entry families just like tasks. Furthermore, access types can be declared for pointers to protected subprograms. In Chapter 11, we saw how to construct pointers to subprograms. Pointers to protected subprograms are constructed in the same manner, except that the keyword **protected** must be added. The following code, for instance, declares a pointer to the protected procedure `Increment`:

```
protected type Counter is
   procedure Increment;
private
   Data: Integer := 0;
end Counter;

type Ptr_Type is access protected procedure;

Count: Counter;

Ptr: Ptr_Type := Count.Increment'Access;
```

Since the protected procedure Increment is parameterless, it must be invoked (dereferenced) using the keyword **all**:

```
Ptr.all;   -- invokes the protected procedure pointed to by Ptr.
```

## REAL-TIME SYSTEMS ANNEX

**Ada 95 ▶** So far, all the concurrent processing support described in this chapter is provided as part of Ada's core language. This support is adequate for many applications requiring concurrent programming. However, some real-time programming requires extremely efficient code that maximizes execution speed and minimizes code size. The behavior of such programs may need to be finely controlled. The optional Ada Real-Time Systems Annex provides special capacity and performance constraints needed in such applications. In addition, this annex offers more freedom in the choice of priorities. Instead of static priorities that can never change once set, dynamic priorities are provided that can be modified in response to conditions encountered at runtime. This annex also allows more freedom in the selection of scheduling rules. Scheduling rules determine which tasks that are ready to run get assigned available processors. Finally, this annex provides mechanisms to minimize priority inversions. Priority inversion occurs when a high priority task is ready to run but cannot because a lower priority task is running.

Unless your Ada compilation system includes a validated Real-Time Systems Annex, the features described in this section may not be available to you. If a validated Real-Time Systems Annex is provided, then so is the Systems Programming Annex since the latter depends on the former.

The information provided in this section is very brief and is only intended to provide readers with a general notion of what the Real-Time Systems Annex has to offer. For more information, consult the *Ada 95 Reference Manual*.

### Capacity and Performance Constraints

Recall that package Calendar provides a time type, Time, a Clock that returns the time of day, plus a subtype, Day_Duration, for expressing intervals of time in seconds. For real-time systems, Time and Day_Duration are not always accurate enough. (Day_Duration need be no more accurate than 20 milliseconds, although many compilers offer finer accuracy.) In addition, the values of Clock may decrease due to the resetting of the time by a human operator. The Real-Time Systems Annex, therefore, provides package Ada.Real_Time, which overcomes the limitations of package Ada.Calendar. Function Real_Time.Clock represents a real-time clock that has finer granularity than the time-of-day clock in Calendar and is guaranteed to be nondecreasing. The type Real_Time.Time_Span is offered as a more precise version of Day_Duration.

The following code uses package Ada.Real_Time to poll (query) a device every 10 milliseconds:

```
-- assume that Ada.Real_Time is visible and
-- Time_To_Start_Polling is set to a starting time
task body Poll_Device is
    Poll_Time: Real_Time.Time := Time_To_Start_Polling;
    Period: constant Real_Time.Time_Span := Milliseconds(10);
        -- milliseconds defined in Ada.Real_Time
begin
    loop
        delay until Poll_Time;
        Poll_Device; -- Poll the device every 10 milliseconds
        Poll_Time := Poll_Time + Period;
    end loop;
end Poll_Device;
```

## Determining Priorities

Priorities provide the basis for resolving competing demands of tasks for processing resources. Processing resources can either be physical processors or protected objects. A new task is selected for execution on a processor whenever the running task suspends or completes or when a task of higher priority preempts it. A task is preempted when the processor is be taken away from the task by a higher priority task that needs the processor. (Protected objects, on the other hand, are not preemptible.)

The Real-Time Systems Annex defines Priority and Interrupt_Priority as subtypes of Any_Priority, as shown in Figure 15.2.

The base type, Any_Priority, must have at least 31 values, although the specific range of values is implementation defined. Subtype Priority has a range from Any_Priority'First to some implementation-defined upper bound, and must include at least 30 values that are below the interrupt level. Subtype Interrupt_Priority has the range Priority'Last + 1 to Any_Priority'Last. Interrupts typically are given priorities in this interrupt range, since interrupts need to be processed before regular tasks. All of these priority subtypes and types are contained in package System.

There are two basic limitations on priorities in Ada's core language: frequent priority inversion and lack of dynamic priorities. Both these limitations are overcome by features in the Real-Time Systems Annex.

Let us begin by considering the issue of priority inversion. Recall that task

**Figure 15.2**  Priorities.

entry queues are ordered in a first-come, first-served manner. Suppose, for example, that a task entry is first called by task A, then task B, then C, and then D. If the called task is not ready to accept any of these calls, then the calls are placed on the entry queue, as follows:

Calling order: A, B, C, D

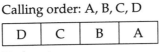

Task entry queue

If the priority of any of these tasks does not match the order in which they are placed on the queue, then priority inversion occurs. Priority inversion means that a high priority task is ready to run but cannot because a lower priority task is using the resources.

The Real-Time Systems Annex defines **pragma** Queuing_Policy that can replace the default first-in, first-out (FIFO)-based entry queues with priority-based entry queues:

```
pragma Queuing_Policy (Policy_Name);
```

Policy_Name can take the values FIFO_Queuing (the default) or Priority_ Queuing. (An implementation may define additional policy names for customized queuing policies.) If Priority_Queuing is chosen, then task entry queues are ordered according to the task's active priority. The task with the highest active priority is placed at the head of the queue. Tasks of equal active priority are placed in the queue in the order of arrival. A task's active priority is evaluated when the entry call is made, and is not re-evaluated. (Active priorities will be explained momentarily.)

Priority inversion can also occur as a result of the arbitrary manner in which different entry queues are chosen. There are two cases to consider: the arbitrary selection among a task's open select alternatives, and the arbitrary selection among a protected object's open queued entries.

Let's consider the first case: Ada's arbitrary selection of open select alternatives. For example, if calls are waiting on both A and B, which call will be accepted is arbitrary:

```
select          -- if calls are waiting on both A and B, one is
    accept A;   -- arbitrarily accepted regardless of the caller's
or              -- priority
    accept B;
end select;
```

The call to A might be accepted even though A's caller might have a lower priority than B's caller. In this case, a task of high priority, B's caller, cannot run because a lower priority task, A's caller, is engaged in the rendezvous.

Such priority inversions can once again be eliminated by choosing `Priorty_Queuing`. When `Priority_Queuing` is chosen, the entry queue is selected with the highest priority task at the head of its queue. If more than one such entry queue exists, then the one listed first in the selective **accept** statement is taken. Thus, in the above example, if the caller at the head of B's queue has a higher priority than the caller at the head of A's queue, then B's caller is accepted. If the callers at the head of A's queue and B's queue have the same priority, then A's caller is accepted since A is listed before B.

Similarly, the arbitrary selection among a protected object's open queued entries may result in priority inversions:

```
protected P is    -- If both entries are called and both barriers
    entry A;      -- are True, one is arbitrarily selected
    entry B;      -- regardless of the caller's priority
end P;
```

The call to A might be accepted, even though this caller might have a lower priority than the caller at the head of B's queue.

Just like the previous case, when `Priority_Queuing` is chosen, the protected entry queue is selected with the highest priority task at its head. If more than one such entry queue exists, then the one listed first is selected.

Priority queuing requires special care since it can lead to task starvation. Assume, for example, that tasks of different priorities call the same entry. A low priority task that calls the entry may never get to the head of the queue because higher priority tasks keep "cutting in line." Such task starvation is not as likely with FIFO queuing, because every caller is placed at the end of the queue and must keep its position in line, regardless of its priority. FIFO queuing, therefore, usually results in fairer scheduling policy than priority queuing.

Besides frequent priority inversion, the other basic limitation on priorities in Ada's core language is the lack of dynamic priorities. As we have seen, **pragma** `Priority` can only be used to set a task's priority statically. The priority is set at compile time and cannot be changed during runtime.

The Real-Time Systems Annex supports dynamic priorities with package `Ada.Dynamic_Priorities`. This package contains procedure `Set_Priority` to enable priorities to change in response to conditions encountered at runtime. This package also contains the function `Get_Priority` to access a task's current priority. If an attempt is made to call these subprograms with a terminated task, then `Tasking_Error` exception is raised.

## Selection of Scheduling Rules

Scheduling rules determine which tasks that are ready to run get assigned available processors. There are two kinds of priorities that allow programmers to control scheduling: base priorities and active priorities. A base priority is the intrinsic priority of a task and acts as a lower bound for active priorities. By default, a base priority is set to the middle value of the subtype `System.Priority`. Pragmas `Priority` and `Interrupt_Priority` can be used to override the default.

An active priority is the priority at which a task competes for processing resources. If `Priority_Queueing` is requested, the active priority of a task is also the priority at which a task competes for entry service. An active priority is initially set to the task's base priority, and is reset by the runtime system (not the user) to any priority the task temporarily inherits.

An activated task inherits the active priority of the activating task. A task accepting an entry call inherits the active priority of the calling task. A task calling a protected operation of a protected object inherits the ceiling priority of the protected object.

The ceiling priority of a protected object places an upper bound on the active priority a task can have when calling a protected operation. If this bound is exceeded, the exception `Program_Error` is raised. In other words, this exception is raised when a task with a higher priority than a protected object attempts to call one of the object's protected operations. The ceiling priority of a protected object is defaulted to `System.Priority'Last`. This default can be overridden with pragmas `Priority` and `Interrupt_Priority`. The advanced reader may wish to explore the following pragma:

```
pragma Locking_Policy(Ceiling_Locking);
```

The pragma can be used with ceiling priorities to avoid priority inversions and deadlocks.

## Interrupts

A hardware interrupt is typically a signal received at a fixed location in memory. This signal instructs the computer to temporarily interrupt current processing and take some special action, such as inputting or outputting certain information or attending to some external piece of equipment. (A software interrupt is similar, except that the interrupt signal is sent from software instead of from hardware.) An interrupt often demands that immediate action be taken in response to an emergency condition such as some hardware failure. The unit of code that responds to an interrupt is called an interrupt handler.

In Ada, interrupt handlers are implemented as parameterless protected procedures associated with a library level protected object. (In Ada 83, interrupt handlers are implemented as task entries. This implementation is still supported but is considered obsolete.) Mapping interrupt handlers to protected procedures makes sense, since both interrupts and protected procedures execute quickly and do not get suspended.

Protected objects containing an interrupt handler must have a ceiling priority in the range of `System.Interrupt_Priority` previously discussed. This is the highest priority range. Interrupts are typically assigned higher priorities than Ada tasks since interrupts often demand that immediate action be taken in response to an emergency condition.

**Pragma** `Interrupt_Handler` enables a protected procedure to be used as an interrupt handler that can be dynamically attached to an interrupt. This pragma provides the compiler with information it might need to generate code enabling a protected procedure to be directly invoked by the hardware when an interrupt occurs.

**Pragma** `Attach_Handler` statically binds a protected procedure used as an interrupt handler to the interrupt. The handler is attached when the protected object is elaborated and is detached when the protected object leaves its scope.

Support for interrupts is provided by the predefined package `Ada.Interrupts`. This package contains an `Interrupt_ID` for identifying interrupts and a `Parameterless_Handler` type for pointing to parameterless protected procedures that implement interrupts. This package also contains procedures such as `Attach_Handler` and `Detach_Handler` for dynamically attaching and detaching interrupts to interrupt handlers, a function `Is_Attached` for determining whether the specified handler is attached to an interrupt, and a function `Current_Handler` that points to an interrupt's current protected procedure handler.

The predefined child package, `Ada.Interrupts.Names`, contains implementation-defined interrupt names needed for the particular hardware.

## Other Features of the Real-Time Systems Annex

A few other features provided by the Real-Time Systems Annex should be briefly mentioned. An optional package, `CPU_Time_Accounting`, enables a processor's time budget to be enforced, and enables the amount of processor time used by a task to be measured.

A pragma, `Simple_Tasking`, allows tasks to be implemented extremely efficiently. This pragma places restrictions on what tasking features are available. Violations of these restrictions are caught at compile time or runtime.

The Systems Programming Annex also provides package `Task_Identification` to obtain a task's identity. This capability is needed for implementing customized task-scheduling algorithms.

Tasks are high-level language constructs. For programmers wishing to build off of low-level tasking constructs, the Real-Time Systems Annex provides two low-level tasking packages: `Ada.Synchronous_Task_Control` and `Ada.Asynchronous_Task_Control`. Package `Ada.Synchronous_Task_Control` provides a "semaphore" for suspending tasks. Package `Ada.Asynchrounous_Task_Control` enables programmers to suspend the execution of a task with a specified task ID or resume its execution. Programmers can also query whether a task with a given ID has been suspended in this manner.

## DISTRIBUTED SYSTEMS ANNEX

**Ada 95 ▶** The optional Distributed Systems Annex is for applications that distribute multiple Ada programs across loosely coupled processors. The following discussion is very brief. Those working with distributed systems should read about this annex in the *Ada 95 Reference Manual*.

Throughout this chapter, we have assumed that a single Ada program is running that contains multiple concurrently executing tasks. Execution of the program consists of elaborating the entire program, running the main subprogram to completion, waiting for all tasks to complete, and then terminating. If the computer system contains multiple processors, then overlapped concurrency is achieved by assigning each task its own processor. This approach works well for "tightly coupled" processors that form an integrated system. For loosely coupled processors that operate independently, however, a distributed approach is often taken. In a distributed system, separate Ada programs (main subprograms) are assigned separate processors instead of tasks within a single Ada program being assigned separate processors.

Support for distributed systems is provided by Ada's optional Distributed Systems Annex. A distributed system consists of multiple partitions. There are two kinds of partitions: active partitions and passive partitions. Each active partition executes an Ada program (main subprogram), typically on a separate processor. In contrast, passive partitions provide data visible to one or more active partitions and usually map to a common address space (region of memory). Type checking is performed between partitions as well as within a partition.

Packages forming distributed systems are categorized as remote call interface packages, shared passive packages, and pure packages. (Packages that do not fit any of these special categories are classified as "normal.") The categorization of a package is established by pragmas `Remote_Call_Interface`, `Shared_Passive`, and `Pure`. These pragmas restrict the kinds of items the packages can contain, thereby allowing the packages to play particular roles in the distributed system.

Remote call interface packages act as remotely callable interfaces to passive partitions. Shared passive packages contain data accessible to one or more partitions. Pure packages cannot contain declarations whose elaboration involves the execution of a program body. In addition, a pure package body cannot contain executable statements. Passive partitions can only contain pure and shared passive packages.

Library units are grouped into partitions at link time (when the linker is invoked to create an executable module). At runtime, the active partitions run Ada programs, each on its own processor.

This chapter has introduced the complex topic of concurrent programming. The next chapter will also introduce an advanced topic: low-level programming.

## EXERCISES

1. What is a task entry? How do task entries relate to the **accept** statement?

2. Give an example of a problem involving a set of independent equations that could be processed concurrently instead of sequentially.

3. Compare the following two versions of package P.

```ada
package P is
    task T is
```

```
            entry E;
      end T;
end P;
package body P is
   task body T is
   begin
      ...
   end T;
end P;


package P is
   procedure Proc;
end P;
package body P is
   task T is
      entry E;
   end T;
   task body T is
   begin
      ...
   end T;
   procedure Proc is
   begin
      T.E;   -- implement this procedure as a task
   end Proc;
end P;
```

What are the advantages of hiding the fact that a task is used?

**4.** Explain the Ada rendezvous. When do the calling task and the acceptor task wait?

**5. a.** Consider the following declarations:

```
type Direction_Type is (Up, Down, Right, Left)
subtype X_Range is Integer range 0..1023;
   -- modify as needed
subtype Y_Range is Integer range 0..1023;
   -- modify as needed
type Coordinate_Type is
   record
      X: X_Range;
      Y: Y_Range;
   end record;
Coordinate: Coordinate_Type;
```

Given the above declarations and the following **accept** statement, write a program that concurrently updates the position of an object and monitors a keyboard for requests to move the object Up, Down, Right, or Left.

```
accept Advance (Direction: in Direction_Type) do
   case Direction is
```

```
            when Up =>
                    Coordinate.Y := Coordinate.Y + 1;
            when Down =>
                    Coordinate.Y := Coordinate.Y - 1;
            when Right =>
                    Coordinate.X := Coordinate.X + 1;
            when Left =>
                    Coordinate.X := Coordinate.X - 1;
        end case;
        Update_Position (Coordinate);
    end Advance;
```

Note: If your computer does not easily support graphics, do not worry about the body of procedure `Update_Position`. Just get your program to compile.

   **b.** Write an exception handler to handle situations where X or Y go out of range. Place this exception handler in the program unit that calls the task entry `Advance`.

6. Explain what the following code within a body of an acceptor task might accomplish:

```
select
    accept Get_Screen_Input (Item: in Character);
or
    delay 900.0;
    Log_Off;
end select;
```

7. How will the preceding **select** statement behave if the second alternative containing the **delay** statement is replaced by an **else** clause?

```
select
    accept Get_Screen_Input (Item: in Character);
else
    delay 900.0;
    Log_Off;
end select;
```

8. What is the problem with each of the following program units?

   **a.**
```
    with P;
    procedure Main is
        task T;
        task body T is
        begin
            Main.A;
        end T;
    begin
        accept A do
            P;
        end A;
    end Main;
```

b.
```
with P;
procedure Main is
    task T2;
    task body T2 is
    begin
        accept E1 do
            P;
        end E1;
    end T2;
    task T1;
    task body T1 is
    begin
        T2.E1;
    end T1;
begin
    null;
end Main;
```

c.
```
with P1, P2;
procedure Main is
    task T3 is
        entry E1;
        entry E2;
    end T3;
    task body T3 is
    begin
        select
            accept E1 do
                P1;
            end E1;
        or
            accept E2 do
                P2;
            end E2;
        end select;
    end T3;
    task T1;
    task body T1 is
    begin
        T3.E1;
    end T1;
    task T2;
    task body T2 is
    begin
        T3.E2;
    end T2;
begin
    null;
end Main;
```

**9.** Classify each of the following **select** statements as either a selective **accept**, timed entry call, conditional entry call, or asynchronous select:

**a.**
```
select
    T.E;
else
    P;
end select;
```

**b.**
```
select
    T.E;
or
    delay 60.0;
    P;
end select;
```

**c.**
```
select
    accept A do
        P1;
    end A;
or
    delay 60.0;
    P2;
end select;
```

**d.**
```
select
    accept A do
        P;
    end A;
or
    terminate;
end select;
```

**e.**
```
select
    delay 1.0;
    P;
then abort
    Q;
end select;
```

**f.**
```
select
    T.E;
    P;
then abort
    Q;
end select;
```

**10.** Find the errors, if any, with each of these selective wait statements.

**a.**

```
select
   accept E1 do
      P1;
   end E1;
or
   accept E2 do
      P2;
   end E2;
or
   delay 10.5;
   P3;
else
   P4;
end select;
```

**b.**

```
select
   terminate;
end select;
```

**c.**

```
select
   accept E1 do
      P1;
   end E1;
or
   accept E2 do
      P2;
   end E2;
or
   delay 3600.0;
   P3;
or
   terminate;
end select;
```

**d.**

```
Update (Day); -- update Day to a value
select          -- from Monday to Sunday
   when Day in Monday .. Wednesday =>
      accept E1 do
         P1;
      end E1;
or
   when Day = Saturday =>
      accept E2 do
         P2;
      end E2;
end select;
```

**e.**

```
select
   accept E1 do
```

```
            P1;
        end E1;
    else
        accept E2 do
            P2;
        end E2;
    end select;
```

11. Which *one* of the following task specifications is illegal?

    a. **task** Cleaning;
    b. **task** Cleaning **is**
          **entry** Vacuum;
          **entry** Mop;
          **entry** Dust;
       **end** Cleaning;
    c. **task** Music **is**
          **entry** Station (1 .. 50) (On: Boolean);
       **end** Music;
    d. **task** Music **is**
          **type** Music_Type **is** (Country, Classical, Jazz,
             Pop);
          **entry** Station (Music: Music_Type);
       **end** Music;

12. How does this code compare in behavior with the persistent signal example in this chapter?

```
task Event is
    entry Wait;
    entry Signal;
end Event;

task body Event is
begin
    loop
        accept Signal;
        for Index in 1 .. Wait'Count loop
            select
                accept Wait;
            else
                null;
            end select;
        end loop;
    end loop;
end Event;
```

13. Implement the body of the following protected object, Counter.

```
protected Counter is
    procedure Increment_Counter;
    procedure Decrement_Counter;
```

```
private
   Counter_Value: Integer := 0;
end Counter;
```

This problem is based on an example in the *Ada 9X Mapping Rationale*, 1992, Intermetrics, Inc.

14. How does the following code compare in behavior with the broadcast signal example presented in the chapter?

```
protected Transient_Signal is
   entry Wait;
   entry Signal;
private
   null;
end Transient_Signal;


protected body Transient_Signal is
   entry Wait when Signal'Count > 0;
   entry Signal when Wait'Count = 0;
end Transient_Signal;
```

15. Write code that uses the **then abort** clause of a **select** statement to abort a complex mathematical operation, if the operation fails to complete within 10 minutes.

16. Assume that a radar on a jet fighter has the following modes: track, search, and track_while_scan. A task called Mode_Manager has an entry, Wait_For_Mode_Change, that returns the value of a new mode whenever the pilot requests a change of radar mode. Use the **then abort** clause within a **select** statement to abort processing within a mode of operation whenever a mode change is requested. After registering the mode change, processing for the new mode is initiated.

17. Compare the task type Resource with the protected type Counting_Semaphore presented in the chapter. What are their advantages and disadvantages? Modify Resource to provide a semaphore count similar to that provided by Counting_Semaphore.

18. **a.** Implement a task body that allows other tasks to read from or write to an integer variable that is protected by being placed in the task body. Use the following task specification:

```
task Protected_Data is
   entry Read (A: out Integer);
   entry Write (A: in Integer);
end Protected_Data;
```

   **b.** Rewrite the preceding task as a protected object. You may use the following specification:

```
protected Protected_Data is
   procedure Write (A: in Integer);
   procedure Read (A: out Integer);
```

```
   private
      Data: Integer := 0;
   end Protected_Data;
```

Which implementation do you prefer and why?

19. Modify the `Resource` task type shown in this chapter so that a time-out is passed to the `Seize` entry as follows:

```
task type Resource is   -- task type declaration
   entry Seize (Time_Out: in Duration);
   entry Release;
end Resource;
```

A calling task can thus seize a resource for a maximum period given by the parameter `Time_Out`. No other tasks can rendezvous with `Seize` until the previous caller calls `Release` or the `Time_Out` expires.

20. Rewrite the following package as a task so that it supports concurrent calls to `Put` and `Get`.

```
package Flag is
   procedure Put (Item: in Boolean);
   procedure Get (Item: out Boolean);
end Flag;

package body Flag is
   Value: Boolean := True;
   procedure Put (Item: in Boolean) is
   begin
      Value := Item;
   end Put;
   procedure Get (Item: out Boolean) is
   begin
      Item := Value;
   end Get;
end Flag;
```

# 16

# Low-Level Programming

**A**s we have seen throughout this book, Ada encourages programmers to think in an abstract, high-level manner. Issues about where data is stored in memory or how the data is physically represented are usually of no concern. However, in systems programming, embedded systems programming, or other applications that require direct interfacing (communication) with the external world, attention to such low-level details may be unavoidable. The "external world" could be the underlying hardware; a device controller for managing such peripherals as a disk drive or printer; or code written in a language other than Ada, such as C, FORTRAN, or Pascal. For example, data that controls a disk (disk control block) may need to be laid out at a particular memory location in a specific format expected by the hardware. Through the disk control block, the Ada program and the hardware give each other commands for controlling the disk and return messages in response to these commands. Programming at this "bit level" is known as low-level programming. Low-level programming also includes machine-specific instructions, addresses, and so on. In general, low-level programming means getting down to the "bare silicon" of the machine.

Low-level programming is often done in assembly code, because many high-level languages provide little support for low-level programming. This is not true, however, with Ada. As mentioned in Chapter 1, Ada was originally designed for embedded systems, that is, systems where the computer or processor running the program is contained within a larger system. The processor within an embedded system, for instance, may control the radar on an aircraft, monitor the fuel injection system of an automobile, or direct a compact disk to play a preprogrammed sequence of recordings. Processors have even been embedded in running shoes to keep track of the number of miles that a runner travels and the number of calories that have been burned. Software for embedded systems requires extensive low-level programming capabilities since it must interface with the larger system in which this processor is embedded.

To perform low-level programming in Ada, the programmer is not obliged to discard Ada's high-level abstractions and think only in terms of bits and bytes. Rather, Ada allows the programmer to describe low-level operations on bits and bytes in terms of high-level abstractions. As a result, not only is code more understandable; it is also more portable. The hardware-dependent portion of the code can be localized and then used by the remaining code to interface with the external world in an abstract, hardware-independent manner.

Much of the information in this chapter is contained in Chapter 13 of the *Ada 95 Reference Manual*, which describes the low-level programming features of Ada. Some of these features are implementation dependent; they can be implemented and handled in different ways. To find out how a feature is handled by your particular compiler, consult Appendix F of your compiler reference manual. Appendix F, which must be included in every reference manual, describes all the implementation-defined characteristics of a given Ada compiler. In addition, Appendix F contains the specification of the packages System and Standard, and lists implementation-defined pragmas and attributes. When possible, we will not assume any particular implementation of Ada, but instead, will provide a general overview of the ways that Ada supports low-level programming.

This chapter begins with a brief introduction to package System. This is followed with representation attributes and attribute definition clauses that deal with data representation. Whereas representation attributes report how data is represented, attribute definition clauses control how data is represented. Next, a pragma that allows composite objects to be packed will be explored, followed by a discussion of unchecked conversion. The chapter concludes with an explanation of how Ada may interface with programs written in other languages.

## PACKAGE SYSTEM

**Ada 95 ▶** Package System, together with packages Ada and Interfaces, is one of the three library units rooted at package Standard that contains every other Ada-defined library unit. Every Ada compiler has its own version of package System. This package contains named numbers, constants, types, and subtypes that specify characteristics of the particular computer that executes the Ada programs. Although the values of these items are system dependent, their names and meaning are not. (If implementors of Ada want to add new functionality to package System, they are encouraged to do so by supplying child packages to System.) When rehosting code to a different computer, therefore, the identifiers for these named numbers and types retain their meaning and do not need to be changed. For example, package System contains the predefined named numbers Min_Int and Max_Int. These numbers hold the smallest and largest integer values that can be represented by a particular system. Thus, on any system, the following declaration will provide the largest range of values allowed in an integer type declaration:

```
type Greatest_Integer is range System.Min_Int..System.Max_Int;
```

The particular values of `Min_Int` and `Max_Int` vary from system to system. However, the meaning of `Min_Int` and `Max_Int` stays the same, and in this sense, the declaration remains portable.

**Ada 95 ▶**    As mentioned in Chapter 11, package `System` declares the address type, `System.Address`, together with relational operators for address values. The child package, `System.Storage_Elements`, defines address arithmetic, which enables programmers to calculate, for instance, address offsets. The address returned by adding an offset depends on one's starting address. Package `System.Storage_Elements` also contains a generic package, `Address_To_Access_Conversions`, which enables access values and addresses to be converted to one another. This type conversion provides "peeking" and "poking" capabilities. That is, it allows one to examine or modify a specific memory location. We will mention other items contained in the package `System` as they are used in this chapter.

## REPRESENTATION ATTRIBUTES

Representation attributes provide information about the low-level characteristics of objects, types, and program units. We will discuss 10 of these attributes: `Address`, `Size`, `Storage_Size`, `Position`, `First_Bit`, `Last_Bit`, `Alignment`, `Component_Size`, `External_Tag`, and `Bit_Order`. Other representation attributes are described in the *Ada 95 Reference Manual*.

### Attribute Address

The `Address` attribute reports where in computer memory an object, program unit, label, or task entry is stored. For example, if `P` is an integer variable or constant, the expression `P'Address` gives the address where `P` is stored. If `P` is a procedure, function, package, or task, then `P'Address` gives the address where the machine code for the body of this program unit begins.

The address value returned by this attribute belongs to type `System.Address`, which is defined in the package `System`. Type `Address` is usually, but not necessarily, some positive integer type. The examples presented in this chapter assume that this is the case.

### Attribute Size

The `Size` attribute applies to an object or type (including a private object or type). When `Size` applies to an object, it yields the number of bits that are allocated to store the object. For example, if `P` is a variable or constant that is stored in a 32-bit word, then `P'Size` yields the value 32. If `Size` is applied to a type, then it yields the minimum number of bits that are needed to hold any possible value of this type or subtype. For instance, on a 16-bit computer, `Integer'Size` often yields 16. This means that at least 16 bits are needed to hold any possible value of type `Integer`. On a different system, of course, `Integer'Size` may yield a different value.

## Attribute Storage_Size

The `Storage_Size` attribute gives information about available storage for pool-specific access types or tasks. If `P` is a pool-specific access type, then `P'Storage_Size` reports the number of storage units that are reserved for storing dynamically allocated variables accessed by pointers of type P. If `P` is a task, then `P'Storage_Size` reports the number of storage units that are reserved for the activation of task P. If `P` is a task type, then `P'Storage_Size` reports the number of storage units that are reserved for the activation of each task belonging to the task type P.

Note that storage size is defined in terms of storage units. A storage unit is the smallest unit of memory that is addressable (that can be referenced by a single address value). The size of storage units may vary, depending on a particular system. A storage unit might be an 8-bit byte, a 16-bit word, a 32-bit word, and so on. To determine the storage size, as measured in numbers of bits, reference the named number `Storage_Unit`, which is contained in the package `System`. For example, on computers where bytes consisting of 8 bits are addressable, the value for `Storage_Unit` is 8. As mentioned in the beginning of this chapter, items such as `Storage_Unit`, provided by the package `System`, allow code to be more portable and general. Even though the value of `Storage_Unit` varies from one system to another, the meaning of `Storage_Unit` stays the same.

## Attributes Position, First_Bit, and Last_Bit

Attributes `Position`, `First_Bit`, and `Last_Bit` apply to record components. These attributes give information about the physical layout of the components within a record. Consider the following declarations:

```
type Record_Type is
   record
      Char: Character;
      Bool: Boolean;
   end record;
R: Record_Type;
```

If we assume that a storage unit is an 8-bit byte, the components of this record might be physically laid out as shown in Figure 16.1. The attribute `Position` yields the number of storage units (in this case, bytes) that a record component is offset from the beginning of the record. Since `Char` begins in byte 1, it is not offset at all from the beginning of the record. Thus, `R.Char'Position` yields the value of 0. Since `Bool` begins in byte 2, it is offset by 1 byte from the beginning of the record. Thus, `R.Bool'Position` yields the value of 1.

The attribute `First_Bit` yields the number of bits that the first bit of a record component is offset from the beginning of the storage unit in which it is contained. Thus, the expression `R.Char'First_Bit` yields 0, and `R.Bool'First_Bit` yields 4.

Finally, the attribute `Last_Bit` yields the number of bits that the last bit of a record component is offset from the beginning of the storage unit that contains the

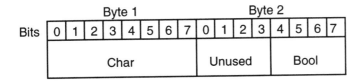

**Figure 16.1**  Record format.

first bit of the record component. Thus, R.Char'Last_Bit yields 7, and R.Bool'Last_Bit also yields 7.

## Attribute Alignment

**Ada 95** ▶ The Alignment attribute applies to an object or type. P'Alignment yields the alignment (in storage units) of P. An alignment of zero indicates that the object is not necessarily aligned on a storage unit boundary.

## Attribute Component_Size

**Ada 95** ▶ The Component_Size attribute applies to an array object, type, or subtype. When Component_Size applies to an array object, it yields the number of bits that are allocated to store components of the object. When Component_Size is applied to an array type or subtype, it yields the number of bits that are allocated to store components of objects of that type or subtype.

## Attribute External_Tag

**Ada 95** ▶ The External_Tag attribute applies a tagged type or tagged subtype T, or to T'Class. This attribute yields a string representation of the tag. The particular string value is implementation defined.

## Attribute Bit_Order

**Ada 95** ▶ The Bit_Order attribute applies to a record type or subtype. This attribute yields values High_Order_First (commonly referred to as "big endian") or Low_Order_First (commonly referred to as "little endian") of type System.Bit_Order. The value High_Order_First means that the first bit of a storage unit (bit 0) is the most significant bit. (The most significant bit has the highest place value.) The value Low_Order_First means that the first bit of a storage unit (bit 0) is the least significant bit. Figure 16.2 illustrates these different orderings for an 8-bit word.

## ATTRIBUTE DEFINITION CLAUSES

**Ada 95** ▶ Whereas representation attributes passively report on the low-level features of items, attribute definition clauses actively control such low-level features. Attribute definition clauses are placed in a package specification or in the declarative

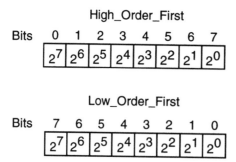

**Figure 16.2** Bit numbering.

part of a program unit. We will discuss four kinds of attribute definition clauses: Size, Address, Alignment, and Bit_Order. Note that an implementation may define additional attribute definition clauses.

All attribute definition clauses have the following form:

```
for T'Some_Attribute use N;
```

Attribute definition clauses begin with the keyword **for**, followed by the name of the item, T, to which it applies, a tick mark (`'`), and the attribute. Next comes the keyword **use**, followed by some value N. Most of the attributes in the previous section of this chapter can be used in an attribute definition clause.

## Size Clauses

Size clauses establish the amount of storage space allocated for objects of a specified type. As shown in the following example, size clauses use the Size attribute previously discussed:

```
type Direction is (Up, Down, Left, Right);
for Direction'Size use 2;
    -- allocates, at most, 2 bits for each object of type
    -- Direction
```

In this example, the size clause forbids more than 2 bits to be used to store an object of type Direction. Two bits are adequate to store the four literals in Direction. For example, the bits 00 could represent Up; 01, Down; 10, Left; and 11, Right. We could allocate more bits for objects of type Direction but not fewer bits. There is no way to store four different objects using only 1 bit. The following size clause is therefore illegal:

```
for Direction'Size use 1;
    -- illegal; 1 bit cannot hold four different literals
```

Furthermore, just because a size clause requests enough space for all the objects of a type, there is no guarantee that a given compiler will be able to honor the request. When a compiler, for whatever reason, cannot honor the request, an error is reported. Thus, a size clause may not be portable; it may be accepted by one compiler and rejected by another compiler.

**Ada 95 ▶**   The size clause may apply to an object instead of a type. When it does, the size specified is the exact size rather than a maximum size.

## Address Clauses

The address clause allows programmers to specify the address of an object, or the starting address of the body of a subprogram, task, or library package.

Suppose that we wish to store an integer variable X at the location 16#ADA#. This may be accomplished as follows:

```
X: Integer;
for X'Address use 16#ADA#; -- places X at this memory location
     -- assumes System.Address in an integer type
```

(This syntax for address clauses replaces the Ada 83 syntax: **for** X **use at** 16#ADA#;. For compatibility, however, Ada 95 supports the obsolete Ada 83 syntax.) Since an address value is being specified, package System must be with'd to get type System.Address.

The starting address of a program unit such as a procedure may likewise be specified:

```
procedure P;
for P'Address use 8#360#; -- starting address of procedure P
```

This address clause instructs the compiler to place the beginning of the machine code for procedure P at the specified location.

## Alignment Clauses

**Ada 95 ▶**   The alignment clause allows programmers to specify how objects are aligned in memory. This clause can apply to either a type or object. The value for the alignment is in terms of storage units:

```
X: Integer;
for X'Alignment use 2; -- aligns X on an even storage unit
```

If the number of storage units specified in an alignment clause is positive, then the address of the object must be a multiple of its alignment. In the previous declaration, X is aligned on an even address, that is, to an address that is a multiple of 2. Other values besides 2 can be used in this clause. For instance, the value 4 places X at an address that is a multiple of 4.

Alignment clauses are most frequently applied to records because a particular alignment may make it easier for the compiler to reference the record's components.

## Bit_Order Clauses

As discussed in the section on the `Bit_Order` attribute, bits can be numbered `Low_Order_First` or `High_Order_First`. This presents a portability problem for code that refers to bit numbers. For example, record representation clauses, to be discussed later in this chapter, describe the location of data through bit positions. Bit positions depend on the order in which bits are numbered. To enhance code portability, one can specify the order of numbering bits by using the `Bit_Order` clause. This clause applies to record types. For example, the following clause forces record type X to number its bits so that the first bit (bit 0) is the least significant bit.

```
for X'Bit_Order use Low_Order_First; -- or High_Order_First
```

Alternatively, one can specify `High_Order_First`.

## ENUMERATION REPRESENTATION CLAUSES

Enumeration representation clauses allow a programmer to specify the underlying internal representation of enumeration literals. With languages such as FORTRAN that do not support enumeration types, programmers often define integer objects in place of enumeration literals. For example, without using enumeration types, six kinds of errors can be represented by declaring six different integer objects: `No_Error`, `Informational`, `Warning`, `Error`, `Fatal_Error`, and `System_Error`. The programmer can then associate each of these objects with a particular integer value. `No_Error` can be assigned the value of 0; `Informational`, the value of 1; and so on.

Unlike FORTRAN, in Ada, the programmer can just declare an enumeration type to represent all six kinds of errors:

```
type Error_Type is (No_Error, Informational, Warning, Error,
    Fatal_Error, System_Error);
```

Unless otherwise directed, the compiler associates the enumeration literals with the values 0, 1, 2, 3, and so on, because these values correspond to the position of the literals within the type declaration. (With type `Boolean`, however, compilers are free to choose any representation scheme.) But what if this default association is not what is desired? In low-level programming, the programmer may need to internally represent enumeration literals with a different set of integer values. This is accomplished with an enumeration representation clause.

Suppose, for example, that a piece of hardware returns, in a 4-bit field, the six kinds of errors listed in `Error_Type`. Each kind of error is represented by a pattern of 4 bits:

| | |
|---|---|
| 0000 | no error |
| 0001 | informational |

| 0011 | warning |
| 0100 | error |
| 1100 | fatal error |
| 1111 | system error |

To associate these bit patterns with the enumeration literals, we can use the following enumeration clause:

```
type Error_Type is (No_Error, Informational, Warning, Error,
    Fatal_Error, System_Error);


-- enumeration clause
for Error_Type use (   No_Error        => 2#0000#,
                       Informational   => 2#0001#,
                       Warning         => 2#0011#,
                       Error           => 2#0100#,
                       Fatal_Error     => 2#1100#,
                       System_Error    => 2#1111# );
```

The enumeration clause consists of the keyword **for**; the name of a previously declared enumeration type; the keyword **use**; and a list of enumeration literals, together with their associated integer representations. These integer representations must be known at compile time. The associations between the enumeration literals and their integer representations are specified as an aggregate. The aggregate in our example uses named notation, but positional notation can also be used:

```
for Error_Type use (0, 1, 3, 4, 12, 15); -- positional notation
```

In addition to using positional notation, this version of Error_Type uses base 10 aggregate values instead of base 2 values. Base 2 is often used, however, so that the bit patterns can easily be discerned. Note that the values in the aggregate are listed in ascending order. This order is required. The order of enumeration literals in their type declaration must match the order of their numeric representations. Note also that the numeric representations are not sequential. In other words, there are gaps between the integer values. This is common.

The enumeration representation clause may apply to a subtype, but all values of the base type must be specified:

```
type Error_Type is (No_Error, Informational, Warning, Error,
    Fatal_Error, System_Error);
subtype Show_Stoppers is Error_Type range Error..System_Error;
for Show_Stoppers use
    (   No_Error        => 2#0000#,   -- required
        Informational   => 2#0001#,   -- required
        Warning         => 2#0011#,   -- required
        Error           => 2#0100#,
        Fatal_Error     => 2#1100#,
        System_Error    => 2#1111# );
```

Before continuing, it is important to understand that the numeric representation specified for each enumeration literal does not affect the value returned by the attribute `Pos`. Thus, `Error_Type'Pos(System_Error)` yields 5 because `System_Error` is the fifth item (counting from 0) listed in the enumeration type. The fact that `System_Error` is internally represented by the integer 15 is irrelevant. (However, the compiler will have to work harder to evaluate `Error_Type'Pos(System_Error)` whenever `System_Error` is not internally represented by this same value, 5.)

So, if `Pos` does not reflect the underlying value of an enumeration value, how do you access the underlying representation? The answer is, you can't. Underlying representations are just that—underlying. Instead of continually thinking in terms of bits and bytes, we can use an enumeration clause to represent bit patterns in terms of enumeration literals. We then use enumeration literals without thinking about their low-level representation. For instance, the bit pattern representing a system error can be referenced by the value `System_Error`. This is yet another example of bit-level details being described in abstract terms. (Actually, if one *must* access the underlying implementation, this can be done using `Unchecked_Conversion`, to be discussed later in this chapter.)

Now let us consider a situation where the preceding error messages `Error_Type` have a second, alternative representation. There is a clever method for giving two different representations to the same set of enumeration literals. This method employs a derived type, which is given a different representation from its parent type:

```
package Alternative_Representations is

    type Form_A is ( No_Error, Informational, Warning, Error,
        Fatal_Error, System_Error );
    type Form_B is new Form_A; -- derived type

private

    for Form_A use
        (  No_Error       => 2#0000#,
           Informational => 2#0001#,
           Warning        => 2#0011#,
           Error          => 2#0100#,
           Fatal_Error    => 2#1100#,
           System_Error   => 2#1111# );

    for Form_B use
        (  No_Error       => 2#0001#,
           Informational => 2#0011#,
           Warning        => 2#0101#,
           Error          => 2#0111#,
           Fatal_Error    => 2#1001#,
           System_Error   => 2#1011# );
end Alternative_Representations;
```

This package specification first defines the enumeration type Form_A. Next, it defines the derived type Form_B, whose parent type is Form_A. These type declarations are followed by the enumeration clauses, which are placed in the private part of the package. These enumeration clauses define the two different representations of the error messages. The derived type is given one representation, and its parent type is given another representation. These two different representations are only allowed if the derived type is declared *before* its parent type is assigned a representation.

It may seem strange that the representation clauses are placed in the private part of the package specification, since this specification does not declare any private types. This placement is not required but is done to remind users of the package not to be concerned with how these enumeration types are internally represented. Information about the internal representation is provided for the compiler's benefit.

Since type Form_B is derived from Form_A, type conversion may be used to convert an object from one type to the other. When an object is converted to a different type, it takes on a different representation, as shown in the following code:

```
with Alternative_Representations;
use Alternative_Representations;
procedure Convert is
    Status_B: Form_B := Error; -- bit representation 0111
    Status_A: Form_A;
begin
    Status_A := Form_A (Status_B);
        -- bit representation 0111 converted to 0100
end Convert;
```

The object Status_B of type Form_B is initialized to the value Error. Status_B is therefore internally represented by the value 2#0111#. When Status_B is converted to type Form_A, the internal representation of its value, Error, is also converted. The internal representation of Error is therefore changed from 2#0111# to 2#0100#.

## RECORD REPRESENTATION CLAUSES

As mentioned in the introduction of this chapter, to interface with the external world, an Ada program often needs to reference fields of bits at specific locations in computer memory. It is through these bit fields that information is exchanged between the Ada program and the external world. To reference these fields, the programmer must format blocks of data into fields of bits containing specific information. Each block of data may be represented by a record, and each field of bits may be represented as a component of this record. A record representation clause can then be used to associate each record component with the specific location of its bit field in the block of data.

Consider, for example, a computer-controlled machine that creates extreme temperatures and pressures inside of a sealed container. Suppose that the designer

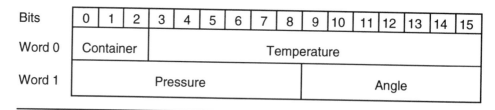

**Figure 16.3**    Format of two-word interface.

of this machine specifies a 32-bit interface consisting of two 16-bit computer words. Each word is divided into fields of bits. The values of the bits that make up a bit field represent specific information about the container. Suppose that there are four bit fields, which, in turn, provide information about the kind of container that is used, the temperature created within the container, the pressure created within the container, and the angle of the container. These four bit fields might be formatted as shown in Figure 16.3.

We are assuming that a storage unit is a 16-bit word and that the bits are numbered from left to right, beginning with 0. The first 16-bit word (word 0) contains information about the container and the temperature within the container. The Container field is located in bits 0 to 2 of word 0. Suppose that the designer of this interface has assigned the following meanings to these bit patterns in the Container field:

```
001    container is a steel pod
010    container is a ceramic chamber
100    container is a carbon cylinder
```

Only the three bit patterns listed have a defined meaning, although five other bit patterns (000, 011, 101, 110, and 111) are possible. As previously mentioned, selecting a subset of possible bit patterns is a common practice.

The next field, Temperature, is located in bits 3 to 15 of word 0. This 13-bit field gives the temperature inside the container. We will assume that Temperature can be represented as an integer number.

The next 16-bit word (word 1) contains information about the pressure and angle of the container. Pressure occupies a 9-bit field, and Angle occupies a 7-bit field. We will assume that Pressure can be represented as an integer number. Angle contains information about the orientation of the container. Let us assume that the following meanings have been assigned to the bit patterns in the Angle field:

```
0000010    container orientation is perpendicular
0001000    container orientation is parallel
0100000    container orientation is skew
```

Again note that only a subset of all possible bit patterns have an assigned meaning.

Let us begin representing the block of data in this 32-bit interface by writing the hardware-independent code, which expresses these bit fields as abstract objects. We will then write the hardware-dependent code, which deals with the actual location of the bit fields within the block of data.

The first step in writing the hardware-independent code is to define the data types associated with each field. The Container field contains information about whether the container is a steel pod, a ceramic chamber, or a carbon cylinder. We can represent this information as an enumeration type:

```
type Container_Type is (Steel_Pod, Ceramic_Chamber,
   Carbon_Cylinder);
```

Note that the enumeration literals follow the same order as their numeric representations: 001, 010, 100. As mentioned in the section on enumeration clauses, this order must be observed.

The Temperature field occupies 13 bits. Assuming that no limits are placed on values of Temperature, we can define an integer type with a range from 0 to the largest number that can fit in 13 bits ($2^{13}-1$):

```
type Temperature_Range is range 0 .. 2 ** 13 - 1;
```

Similarly, for the Pressure field, which occupies 9 bits, we can define an integer type with a range from 0 to the largest number that can fit in 9 bits ($2^9-1$):

```
type Pressure_Range is range 0 .. 2 ** 9 - 1;
```

Finally, we can represent the information about the container's Angle field using an enumeration type:

```
type Orientation is (Perpendicular, Parallel, Skew);
```

Now that we have defined the data types for all the bit fields, the next step is to represent these fields as components of a record type:

```
type Interface_Format is
   record
      Container: Container_Type;
      Temperature: Temperature_Range;
      Pressure: Pressure_Range;
      Angle: Orientation;
   end record;
```

The block of data is thus represented abstractly as a record, and each bit field in the block of data is represented abstractly as a component of the record.

All of the declarations used so far are abstract and hardware independent. We must next write the hardware-dependent code, which associates each record component of Interface_Format with the relative locations of the bit fields:

```
-- hardware-dependent code
-- size clauses
```

```
for Temperature_Range'Size use 9;
for Pressure_Range'Size use 13;


-- enumeration clauses
for Container_Type use (  Steel_Pod         => 2#001#,
                          Ceramic_Chamber   => 2#010#,
                          Carbon_Cylinder   => 2#100# );

for Orientation use (  Perpendicular    => 2#0000010#,
                       Parallel         => 2#0001000#,
                       Skew             => 2#0100000# );

-- record representation clause
for Interface_Format use
   record
       Container at 0 range 0..2;       -- word 0, bits 0 to 2
       Temperature at 0 range 3..15;    -- word 0, bits 3 to 15
       Pressure at 1 range 0..8;        -- word 1, bits 0 to 8
       Angle at 1 range 9..15;          -- word 1, bits 9 to 15
   end record;
```

The first two clauses are size clauses that allocate the appropriate number of bits for objects of types `Temperature_Range` and `Pressure_Range`. The second two clauses are enumeration clauses for the enumeration types `Container_Type` and `Orientation`. These enumeration clauses associate each enumeration literal with its integer representation. Nothing is introduced in these first four clauses that was not covered in the previous sections on size clauses and enumeration clauses. The fifth clause, however, is the first example of a record representation clause. This clause specifies the bit locations of each component of the previously declared record type `Interface_Format`. The clause begins with the keyword **for**, followed by the name of the record type and the keywords **use record**.

Between the keywords **record** and **end record** are specifications for the record components. These specifications establish the physical locations of each component within the record. Consider, for example, the first component specification:

```
Container at 0 range 0..2;
```

The record component `Container` is specified to begin at the first storage unit of the record (word 0) and to span bit positions 0 to 2. `Temperature` is contained in the same storage unit (word 0) and spans the bit positions 3 to 15:

```
Temperature at 0 range 3..15;
```

The other two components, `Pressure` and `Angle`, are contained in the second storage unit of the record (word 1). `Pressure` spans bits 0 to 8 of this second word, and `Angle` spans bits 9 to 15.

Anyone who has worked with hardware knows that the numbering of bit positions varies among manufacturers. Some manufacturers number the bits starting with 0; others, starting with 1. Some manufacturers number bits from left to right (as shown in Figure 16.3); others, from right to left. Ada specifies that for component clauses of record representation clauses, bits must be numbered starting with 0. On the other hand, the Ada standards do not specify how bits must be numbered. To query how bits are numbered by your particular Ada compiler, use the `Bit_Order` attribute. Or for portability, force the bits to be numbered as desired by using the `Bit_Order` definition clause. Both of these features were previously described.

There is another aspect of record representation clauses that is not specified by the Ada standards: whether a record component can span multiple storage units. To find out if this is allowed by your compiler, and if so, how this is accomplished, refer to Appendix F in your compiler's reference manual.

**Ada 95 ▶**     (Ada 83 has a record alignment clause, **at mod**, that can be added after the keyword **record**. In Ada 95, this feature has been made obsolete by the alignment clause, which not only applies to record types, but to other types as well.)

## PRAGMA PACK

The **pragma** `Pack` requests the compiler to represent an array or record type in a packed (compressed) form. Consider, for example, a `Boolean` array type:

```
type Boolean_Array is array (1..16) of Boolean;
```

The amount of storage allocated to store arrays of type `Boolean_Array` varies from compiler to compiler. One compiler might store each `Boolean` array component in a single word. Another compiler might store each `Boolean` array component value in a single byte or in a single bit. The **pragma** `Pack` requests the compiler to store objects of the composite type using as few bits as possible. Some compilers may honor the request and "squeeze" the array components together. Other compilers may choose to ignore this request and issue a warning to that effect.

**Pragma** `Pack` should be used judiciously. Although packed data takes up less memory space, extra object code is typically generated to read and write components of the composite object. This extra code may also result in slower read and write operations.

## UNCHECKED CONVERSION

Unchecked conversion copies a sequence of bits from an object of one type to an object of another type. During this process, the sequence of bits remains unaltered. Only the type of object that this sequence represents is changed. Unchecked conversion thus allows programmers to override Ada's ban against assigning one data type to another. This process is different from the explicit type conversions that we have previously encountered. When, for instance, the integer variable `Int` is explicitly converted to a floating point number, `Float(Int)`, the bit pattern is altered to reflect this new interpretation.

To use unchecked conversion, we must instantiate the predefined generic function `Unchecked_Conversion`. This generic function is a child of package `Ada`. The program unit that references `Unchecked_Conversion` must therefore mention it in a **with** clause. Due to a rename, however, this generic can be accessed without the prefix `Ada`.

The specification of `Unchecked_Conversion` appears as follows:

```
generic
    type Source is limited private;  -- generic parameters
    type Target is limited private;
function Unchecked_Conversion ( S: Source ) return Target;
```

There are two formal generic parameters: `Source` and `Target`. Thus, to instantiate this generic function, two parameters must be provided: one for the source type, the other for the target type. Since the formal parameters are **limited private**, this generic function can be instantiated with any types as generic actual parameters. The function created by instantiating this generic is invoked with a single parameter value of type `Source`. The function returns the same sequence of bits as the parameter value of type `Source` but as a representation of a value of type `Target`.

Let us now consider an example that uses `Unchecked_Conversion`. Suppose that the interface to some piece of hardware requires us to view the same sequence of bits as both a 16-bit integer and also as a bit string (an array of 16 `Boolean` values):

```
with Ada.Unchecked_Conversion; use Ada;
procedure Demo is
    type Boolean_Array is array (1..16) of Boolean;
    pragma Pack (Boolean_Array);
    Bit_String: Boolean_Array; -- assumes 16 bit string
    Int: Integer; -- assumes 16 bit integer

    function To_Bit_String is new Unchecked_Conversion
        ( Source => Integer,
          Target => Boolean_Array );
begin
    Int := 2#0010_1101_1110_1111#;
    Bit_String := To_Bit_String ( Int );
        -- returns as bit string
    ...
end Demo;
```

After the unchecked conversion is performed, each component of `Bit_String` is a `Boolean` variable stored as a single bit. The value of each component of `Bit_String` is `False` or `True`, depending on whether the corresponding bit in `Int` is 0 or 1.

In this example, `Int` and `Bit_String` are assumed to be the same size. When the source object and target object differ in size, some compilers will truncate the longer object, others will report an error, and so on. To find out what your compiler will do, refer to Appendix F in your compiler's reference manual.

Unchecked conversion should only be used when necessary, because it can result in errors. As the word "unchecked" insinuates, the compiler takes no responsibility making sure that the bit pattern of the target object makes sense. This is the responsibility of the programmer. This is in sharp contrast to regular type conversion, which does make sure that the converted value makes sense. Whenever possible, therefore, use regular type conversion instead of Unchecked_Conversion.

**Ada 95 ▶** In cases where Unchecked_Conversion must be used, yet is deemed dangerous, Ada supplies the attribute Valid. This attribute applies to a scalar object and yields True or False, depending on whether the object's value is valid. A value is valid if it lies within range of its type or subtype, otherwise it is invalid. (The attribute Valid can be used whenever one is worried about the validity of a value.)

## INTERLANGUAGE COMMUNICATION

**Ada 95 ▶** Ada recognizes the importance of being able to interface with other languages. Ada, therefore, supports subprogram calls from Ada to a non-Ada language and from a non-Ada language to Ada. Ada also supports interlanguage variable references.

Three pragmas are provided for interfacing to other languages: pragmas Import, Export, and Convention. (**Pragma** Import replaces Ada 83's **pragma** Interface.) **Pragma** Import is primarily used to import subprograms and objects defined in other languages to an Ada program. For example, this pragma allows an Ada program to call subprograms written in other languages. It also allows an Ada program to access variables defined in other languages. These other languages may include other high-level languages such as FORTRAN, Pascal, and C, or low-level assembly languages. The following example shows how the **pragma** Import allows Ada to use three trigonometric functions that are implemented in FORTRAN:

```
package Fortran_Functions is
    function Sin (X: Long_Float) return Long_Float;
    function Cos (X: Long_Float) return Long_Float;
    function Tan (X: Long_Float) return Long_Float;
    pragma Import (FORTRAN, Sin, "DSIN", "Sine");
    pragma Import (FORTRAN, Cos, "DCOS", "Cosine");
    pragma Import (FORTRAN, Tan, "DTAN", "Tangent");
end Fortran_Functions;
```

The first three declarations in this package are FORTRAN function specifications, written using Ada syntax. For each of these function specifications, a **pragma** Import follows. The bodies of these functions consist of the FORTRAN code. Therefore, this package has no body.

**Pragma** Import has four parameters. The first parameter specifies the name of the foreign language with which Ada is to interface. The second parameter specifies the Ada name for the particular subprogram written in this other language. The pragma instructs the compiler to invoke the specified subprogram using the calling conventions (parameter-passing mechanisms) of this other language. The third parameter provides the foreign language's name of the subprogram. The fourth parameter provides the external "link name" known by the system's linker. The third and fourth parameters can be omitted if not needed.

Any Ada program that mentions package Fortran_Functions in its **with** clause may invoke these FORTRAN functions just as if they were implemented in Ada. Many compilers, however, place certain restrictions on how the pragma Import may be used. Once again, refer to Appendix F of your computer's reference manual for details.

**Pragma** Export is the opposite of **pragma** Import. It is primarily used to export subprograms and objects defined in Ada to programs written in other languages. For example, **pragma** Export enables an Ada subprogram to be called from other languages. It also allows variables defined in Ada to be accessed by programs written in other languages.

In the following example, an Ada procedure, For_C, is specified to be callable from a C program:

```
procedure For_C (Item: in Integer);
pragma Export (C, For_C, "forc");
```

**Pragma** Convention instructs the Ada compiler to represent an Ada type using the convention of another language. For example, the following statement might instruct the Ada compiler to represent a two-dimensional array, Matrix, in FORTRAN's column-major order instead of Ada's row-major order:

```
pragma Convention (Fortran, Matrix);
```

Column-major order means that the elements of the array are contiguously stored in memory as one moves down each column. In Ada, array elements are contiguously stored as one moves across each row.

Package Interfaces contains types and operations that are specific to the target machine (the computer running the Ada programs). For example, signed and unsigned integer types such as Integer_16 and Unsigned_32 are provided that correspond to those supported by the target machine. Shift and rotate operations are provided for the unsigned types. Package Interfaces also has optional child packages Interfaces.Fortran, Interfaces.C, and Interfaces.COBOL that provide interfaces to code written in FORTRAN, C, and COBOL. For instance, Interfaces.Fortran provides Ada types such as Integer, Real, Logical, Complex, and Character that have names and internal representations that match those provided in FORTRAN. Package Interfaces.C contains declarations of the standard types in C, including functions that convert between these types and Ada's types. In addition, child packages Interfaces.C.Pointers and Interfaces.C.Strings enable Ada programs to handle pointers and text strings in the same manner as C.

In addition to supporting interfaces to other software languages, Ada supports an interface to the machine language. Machine language is the language of the hardware; it consists of machine code instructions that the computer directly "understands." Machine code instructions may be needed to optimize a small portion of time-critical code when the code generated by the Ada compiler is deemed too inefficient. Machine code may also be needed when a machine instruction is required that the Ada compiler never generates from the Ada source code. For example, a special machine instruction might be needed to control a peripheral device such as a printer.

Ada supports machine code insertions with an optional child package, System.Machine_Code. This package contains records whose components represent fields of machine code instructions. Machine code is inserted into an Ada program by writing a procedure whose body consists entirely of "code statements." Each code statement corresponds to a single machine instruction. A code statement is a qualified aggregate of one of the records defined in Machine_Code. Details concerning this package, if provided at all, vary from compiler to compiler and depend on the nature of the machine code. If you are interested in this capability, refer to Appendix F of your compiler's reference manual. Appendix F contains a listing of package System and all of its child packages.

## EXERCISES

1. Explain the difference between System.Min_Int and Integer'First, and between System.Max_Int and Integer'Last.

2. Explain the differences between System.Address, discussed in this chapter, and access types, discussed in Chapter 11.

3. Write code that stores a character variable Char at address 8#167#.

4. Consider the following record type:

```
type R is
    record
        A: Type_A;
        B: Type_B;
        C: Type_C;
    end record;

X: R;
```

Suppose that this record is stored in a 32-bit word, as follows (where bits are numbered from left to right):

A　　bits 0 to 11
B　　bits 12 to 15
C　　bits 24 to 31

Assuming that the storage unit is an 8-bit byte, what are the values of the following representation attributes?

X.A'Position　　X.A'First_Bit　　X.A'Last_Bit
X.B'Position　　X.B'First_Bit　　X.B'Last_Bit
X.C'Position　　X.C'First_Bit　　X.C'Last_Bit

5. What is the minimum number of bits needed to store the values of the following enumeration type?

```
type B_Flat_Major is (B_Flat, C, D, E_Flat, F, G, A);
```

Write a size clause to establish the amount of storage space allocated for objects of type B_Flat_Major.

6. Use an enumeration clause to associate each of the following bit patterns with the enumeration literals of the following type:

```
type Signal is (Red, Yellow, Green);
```

```
001    red
011    yellow
111    green
```

7. Give the enumeration literals of Signal, in Exercise 6, the following *second* representation:

```
010    red
110    yellow
111    green
```

Once the enumeration literals of Signal are given two different representations, write code to convert an object of type Signal from one representation to the other.

8. Explain why the following enumeration clause cannot be used to associate the specified bit patterns with the enumeration literals of type Status:

```
type Status is (OK, Not_OK, Unknown);
for Status use ( OK        => 2#0101#,
                 Not_OK    => 2#0011#,
                 Unknown   => 2#1000# );
```

9. Reconsider the computer-controlled machine, presented in this chapter, which is capable of creating high temperatures and pressures within a sealed container. Suppose that the 32-bit interface to this machine is changed as follows:

```
Word 0 Container     bits 0 to 2
       unused        bits 3 to 7
       Angle         bits 8 to 14
       unused        bits 15 to 16
Word 1 Temperature   bits 0 to 9
       Pressure      bits 10 to 16
```

Rewrite the machine-dependent code to reflect this change.

10. a. Write a procedure with the following specification:

```
procedure Block_Copy  (From, To: in System.Address;
                       Bytes_To_Move: in Positive );
```

that uses address clauses to copy Bytes_To_Move number of bytes from the From address to the To address.

b. Rewrite procedure Block_Copy using pointers instead of address specifications. Which solution do you prefer?

c. Rewrite Block_Copy using the generic package, Address_To_Access_Conversions in package System.Storage_Elements.

11. Write a program that uses the generic `Unchecked_Conversion` function to represent an integer as a string. How does this differ from the use of the overloaded `Put` statement, discussed in Chapter 14, which outputs an integer value to a string?

12. Since low-level programming features tend to be nonportable and hard to maintain, they should be used only when required. Replace the following code that associates two integer values to each identifier `Alpha`, `Beta`, and `Gamma` with code that avoids low-level programming features. `Alpha` is associated with 10 and 15, `Beta` is associated with 20 and 3. `Gamma` is associated with 30 and 7.

```
declare
    type Values is (Alpha, Beta, Gamma);
    for Values use ( Alpha  => 10,
                     Beta   => 20,
                     Gamma  => 30 );
    function Convert is new Unchecked_Conversion
        (Source => Values, Target => Integer );
    A: constant array (Values) of Integer :=
        (  Alpha  => 15,
           Beta   => 3,
           Gamma  => 7 );
begin
    Put (A (Alpha));          -- Outputs 15
    Put (Convert (Alpha));   -- Outputs 10
    . . .
end;
```

13. Consider the following declaration:

    `Row: array (1..3) of Boolean;`

    Does `Row'Address` necessarily equal `Row(1)'Address`? Explain your answer.

14. Write code that **with**'s the following `Math` package, and uses unchecked conversion to access the underlying implementation of the limited private type, `ID`. [Some, but not all, compilers allow unchecked conversions to or from (limited) private types.]

```
package Math is
    type ID is limited private;
    . . .
private
    type ID is range 1..9;
end Math;
```

# Index